THE WAITE GROUP'S

Windows 98 How-To

Keith A. Powell

SAMS

201 West 103rd Street, Indianapolis, Indiana 46290

The Waite Group's Windows 98 How-To

Copyright © 1998 by Sams Publishing

All rights reserved. No part of this book shall be reproduced, stored in a retrieval system, or transmitted by any means, electronic, mechanical, photocopying, recording, or otherwise, without written permission from the publisher. No patent liability is assumed with respect to the use of the information contained herein. Although every precaution has been taken in the preparation of this book, the publisher and author assume no responsibility for errors or omissions. Neither is any liability assumed for damages resulting from the use of the information contained herein.

International Standard Book Number: 0-672-31436-3

Library of Congress Catalog Card Number: 98-86953

Printed in the United States of America

First Printing: December, 1998

00 99 98   4 3 2 1

Trademarks

All terms mentioned in this book that are known to be trademarks or service marks have been appropriately capitalized. Sams Publishing cannot attest to the accuracy of this information. Use of a term in this book should not be regarded as affecting the validity of any trademark or service mark.

Warning and Disclaimer

Every effort has been made to make this book as complete and as accurate as possible, but no warranty or fitness is implied. The information provided is on an "as is" basis. The authors and the publisher shall have neither liability or responsibility to any person or entity with respect to any loss or damages arising from the information contained in this book or from the use of the CD-ROM or programs accompanying it.

EXECUTIVE EDITOR
Grace Buechlein

ACQUISITIONS EDITOR
Tracy M. Williams

DEVELOPMENT EDITOR
Jeff Perkins

PROJECT EDITOR
Sara Bosin

COPY EDITOR
Pamela Woolf

INDEXER
Heather Goens

PROOFREADERS
Wendy Ott
Elizabeth Deeter-Smith

TECHNICAL EDITOR
John Purdum

SOFTWARE DEVELOPMENT SPECIALIST
Jack Belbot

INTERIOR DESIGN
Gary Adair

COVER DESIGN
Karen Ruggles

LAYOUT TECHNICIANS
Brandon Allen
Tim Osborn
Staci Somers
Mark Walchle

CONTENTS AT A GLANCE

PART I   **HOW TO USE THIS BOOK**

                     INTRODUCTION .3

PART II   **CORE WINDOWS COMPONENTS**

     CHAPTER 1:   **INSTALLATION TIPS** .13

     CHAPTER 2:   **DESKTOP USAGE AND TIPS** 59

     CHAPTER 3:   **THE BOOT PROCESS** 105

     CHAPTER 4:   **THE REGISTRY** 145

     CHAPTER 5:   **QUINTESSENTIAL HARDWARE CONFIGURATIONS** .169

     CHAPTER 6:   **DISK DRIVE MANAGEMENT AND USE** 201

     CHAPTER 7:   **SYSTEM RESOURCE MANAGEMENT** 261

PART III   **NETWORKING ESSENTIALS**

     CHAPTER 8:   **GETTING STARTED FROM THE NETWORK** 317

     CHAPTER 9:   **DIAL-UP NETWORKING** 351

     CHAPTER 10:   **WELCOME TO THE NEIGHBORHOOD; NETWORK, THAT IS...** 393

     CHAPTER 11:   **PRINTER MANAGEMENT** 465

     CHAPTER 12:   **THE INTERNET AND WEB BROWSING** 481

     CHAPTER 13:   **EMAIL AND NEWS** 569

     CHAPTER 14:   **INTERNET PUBLISHING** 633

     CHAPTER 15:   **NETWORK MANAGEMENT** 669

PART IV   THE MULTIMEDIA REVOLUTION

- CHAPTER 16: **MULTIMEDIA BASICS** .... .697
- CHAPTER 17: **WEBTV FOR WINDOWS** .... .729
- CHAPTER 18: **TELECONFERENCING THE MULTIMEDIA WAY** .757
- CHAPTER 19: **GIVING WINDOWS SPECIAL POWERS** .... .787

PART V   HELP!

- CHAPTER 20: **WHERE DID I GO WRONG AND HOW DO I FIX IT?** .... .809
- **INDEX** .... .837

TABLE OF CONTENTS

PART I
HOW-TO USE THIS BOOK
INTRODUCTION 3

PART II
CORE WINDOWS COMPONENTS

CHAPTER 1
INSTALLATION TIPS 13

1.1   Determine the hardware requirements for Windows 98? 17
          Problem 17
          Technique 17
          Steps 17
1.2   Avoid the common installation failure points? 26
          Problem 26
          Technique 26
          Steps 27
1.3   Install Windows 98 on a hardware system that is below standard
      hardware levels? 28
          Problem 28
          Technique 28
          Steps 28
1.4   Install the Windows 98 Resource Kit? 29
          Problem 29
          Technique 29
          Steps 30
1.5   Use the Windows update process? 45
          Problem 45
          Technique 46
          Steps 46

CHAPTER 2
DESKTOP USAGE AND TIPS 59

2.1   Know which desktop to use: the Active Desktop or the Classic Desktop? 63
          Problem 63
          Technique 64
          Steps 65

2.2	Configure the Windows 98 Classic Desktop settings?	66
	Problem	66
	Technique	66
	Steps	66
2.3	Configure the Windows 98 Active Desktop?	69
	Problem	69
	Technique	69
	Steps	69
2.4	Add or remove system icons from my desktop?	75
	Problem	75
	Technique	75
	Steps	76
2.5	Find and remove useless links on my desktop or Start menu?	80
	Problem	80
	Technique	80
	Steps	81
2.6	Change the default view of the My Computer Windows Explorer to explore instead of open?	83
	Problem	83
	Technique	83
	Steps	85
2.7	Place the Recent Documents folder directly on my desktop?	87
	Problem	87
	Technique	87
	Steps	88
2.8	Create a toolbar that shows all my physical drive devices?	90
	Problem	90
	Technique	91
	Steps	91
2.9	Open a DOS window with a quick keystroke?	94
	Problem	94
	Technique	94
	Steps	95
2.10	Hide all of the icons on a Windows 98 desktop?	97
	Problem	97
	Technique	97
	Steps	97
2.11	Change the opening or execution of desktop icons to a Single-Click mode?	101
	Problem	101
	Technique	101
	Steps	101

CHAPTER 3
THE BOOT PROCESS 105

- 3.1 Determine which files load during the Windows 98 boot process? 109
  - Problem 109
  - Technique 109
  - Steps 110
- 3.2 Change the Windows 98 startup process so I can find malfunctioning device drivers? 115
  - Problem 115
  - Technique 115
  - Steps 116
- 3.3 Boot to a DOS prompt? 127
  - Problem 127
  - Technique 127
  - Steps 128
- 3.4 Know what the key system files are? 134
  - Problem 134
  - Technique 134
  - Steps 134
- 3.5 Obtain information on problematic hardware that was encountered during the Windows 98 startup? 136
  - Problem 136
  - Technique 136
  - Steps 137
- 3.6 Force Windows 98 to boot into Safe Mode? 139
  - Problem 139
  - Technique 139
  - Steps 140
- 3.7 Create a Windows 98 Startup disk? 142
  - Problem 142
  - Technique 142
  - Steps 143

CHAPTER 4
THE REGISTRY 145

- 4.1 Restore the Windows 98 Registry to the same state it was in when I last successfully started my PC? 151
  - Problem 151
  - Technique 151
  - Steps 152

4.2	Modify the Registry so that it automatically starts a specific application every time I launch Windows 98?	153
	Problem	153
	Technique	153
	Steps	153
4.3	Recover from incorrect Registry modifications?	160
	Problem	160
	Technique	160
	Steps	160
4.4	Modify the Registry so that a user cannot access the Windows Update feature and fix his own PC?	161
	Problem	161
	Technique	162
	Steps	162

CHAPTER 5
QUINTESSENTIAL HARDWARE CONFIGURATIONS 169

5.1	Choose a keyboard type for Windows 98?	173
	Problem	173
	Technique	173
	Steps	173
5.2	Change the default language for my Windows 98 keyboard?	174
	Problem	174
	Technique	174
	Steps	175
5.3	Change the default character typing speed for my Windows 98 keyboard?	179
	Problem	179
	Technique	179
	Steps	179
5.4	Choose a display monitor?	180
	Problem	180
	Technique	181
	Steps	182
5.5	Select a display configuration within Windows 98?	183
	Problem	183
	Technique	183
	Steps	183
5.6	Configure my system for multiple display monitors?	192
	Problem	192
	Technique	192
	Steps	192

CONTENTS

5.7	Know which mouse or pointer device types to use?	193
	Technique	194
	Steps	194
5.8	Configure my mouse or other pointing device?	195
	Problem	195
	Technique	195
	Steps	195

CHAPTER 6
DISK DRIVE MANAGEMENT AND USE 201

6.1	Know what the differences are between the FAT16 and the FAT32 file systems?	206
	Problem	206
	Technique	206
	Steps	207
6.2	Install the additional disk drive management tools and utilities?	209
	Problem	209
	Technique	209
	Steps	209
6.3	Know whether to use disk compression or FAT32?	211
	Problem	211
	Technique	212
	Steps	213
6.4	Configure and use the Windows 98 Disk Compression tool?	216
	Problem	216
	Technique	216
	Steps	216
6.5	Configure and use the drive converter (FAT32)?	219
	Problem	219
	Technique	220
	Steps	220
6.6	Configure and use the Disk Cleanup utility?	224
	Problem	224
	Technique	224
	Steps	224
6.7	Configure and use the Disk Defragmenter utility?	232
	Problem	232
	Technique	232
	Steps	233
6.8	Configure and use the ScanDisk utility?	236
	Problem	236
	Technique	236
	Steps	236

6.9	Manage my hard disk drive(s)?	.239
	Problem	.239
	Technique	.240
	Steps	.240
6.10	Manage my removable media drive(s)?	.244
	Problem	.244
	Technique	.244
	Steps	.245
6.11	Install a CD-ROM or a DVD-ROM drive?	.246
	Problem	.246
	Technique	.247
	Steps	.247
6.12	Know which additional removable hard drive devices I should install?	.250
	Problem	.250
	Technique	.250
	Steps	.250
6.13	Back up my Windows 98 system?	.251
	Problem	.251
	Technique	.251
	Steps	.252

CHAPTER 7
SYSTEM RESOURCE MANAGEMENT 261

7.1	Determine which components make up the core Windows 98 system resources?	.266
	Problem	.266
	Technique	.266
	Steps	.267
7.2	Know when to use performance monitoring?	.268
	Problem	.268
	Technique	.268
	Steps	.269
7.3	Install the additional System Resource Management tools?	.269
	Problem	.269
	Technique	.270
	Steps	.270
7.4	Use the Resource Meter?	.272
	Problem	.272
	Technique	.272
	Steps	.273
7.5	Use the System Information utility?	.275
	Problem	.275
	Technique	.276
	Steps	.276

7.6	Use Dr. Watson to troubleshoot application faults?	284
	Problem	284
	Technique	284
	Steps	285
7.7	Verify the integrity of my system files?	288
	Problem	288
	Technique	288
	Steps	288
7.8	Track performance changes to my computer system over a period of time?	292
	Problem	292
	Technique	293
	Steps	293
7.9	Use the Maintenance Wizard utility?	297
	Problem	297
	Technique	297
	Steps	298
7.10	Monitor my computer to see if others are attached to it?	302
	Problem	302
	Technique	302
	Steps	302
7.11	Schedule tasks on my computer?	306
	Problem	306
	Technique	306
	Steps	306
7.12	Know if the Windows 98 Resource Kit is good for managing system resources?	312
	Problem	312
	Technique	312
	Steps	312

PART III
NETWORKING ESSENTIALS

CHAPTER 8
GETTING STARTED FROM THE NETWORK 317

8.1	Decide when to install from a network?	320
	Problem	320
	Technique	320
	Steps	321
8.2	Obtain and install the Microsoft Batch utility for Windows 98?	323
	Problem	323
	Technique	323
	Steps	324

8.3	Use the Microsoft Batch utility for Windows 98?	.324
	Problem	.324
	Technique	.324
	Steps	.324
8.4	Use a Cloning tool such as GHOST to deploy Windows 98?	.348
	Problem	.348
	Technique	.348
	Steps	.349

CHAPTER 9
DIAL-UP NETWORKING .... .351

9.1	Access the Internet without a direct connection?	.355
	Problem	.355
	Technique	.355
	Steps	.356
9.2	Use a calling card with the Windows 98 Dial-Up Networking technology?	.362
	Problem	.362
	Technique	.363
	Steps	.363
9.3	Tweak my Windows 98 Dial-Up Networking connection so that it performs better with my digital modem?	.371
	Problem	.371
	Technique	.372
	Steps	.372
9.4	Secure my systems when combining modems and networks?	.377
	Problem	.377
	Technique	.377
	Steps	.378
9.5	Know when to use Virtual Private Networking, and how do I install and configure it?	.379
	Problem	.379
	Technique	.379
	Steps	.380
9.6	Use Virtual Private Networking?	.384
	Problem	.384
	Technique	.384
	Steps	.385
9.7	Use more than one modem at a time with a single Dial-Up Networking connection?	.389
	Problem	.389
	Technique	.389
	Steps	.390

CHAPTER 10
WELCOME TO THE NEIGHBORHOOD: NETWORK, THAT IS... 393

- 10.1 Know what other networks I can connect to? 397
  - Problem 397
  - Technique 397
  - Steps 398
- 10.2 Add and configure additional network clients? 406
  - Problem 406
  - Technique 407
  - Steps 407
- 10.3 Configure my system for multiple users? 415
  - Problem 415
  - Technique 415
  - Steps 416
- 10.4 Add new network adapters? 419
  - Problem 419
  - Technique 420
  - Steps 420
- 10.5 Add new network protocols to my Windows 98 PC? 424
  - Problem 424
  - Technique 424
  - Steps 425
- 10.6 Configure TCP/IP for use on my Windows 98 PC? 431
  - Problem 431
  - Technique 431
  - Steps 432
- 10.7 Know when to add new network services? 444
  - Problem 444
  - Technique 444
  - Steps 444
- 10.8 Configure File Sharing? 451
  - Problem 451
  - Technique 451
  - Steps 451
- 10.9 Automatically log on to my network, using the proper user ID and password? 460
  - Problem 460
  - Technique 460
  - Steps 460
- 10.10 Change either the computer name or workgroup name for my Windows 98 PC? 462
  - Problem 462
  - Technique 462
  - Steps 463

CHAPTER 11
PRINTER MANAGEMENT 465

- 11.1 Add a network-based print device to my computer? 468
  - Problem 468
  - Technique 468
  - Steps 468
- 11.2 Capture a printer port in Windows 98? 474
  - Problem 474
  - Technique 475
  - Steps 475
- 11.3 Share a print device? 476
  - Problem 476
  - Technique 477
  - Steps 477

CHAPTER 12
THE INTERNET AND WEB BROWSING 481

- 12.1 Install any Updates to Internet Explorer? 484
  - Problem 484
  - Technique 485
  - Steps 485
- 12.2 Configure Microsoft Internet Explorer? 495
  - Problem 495
  - Technique 495
  - Steps 496
- 12.3 Obtain the Microsoft Internet Explorer Administration Kit and why would I want to use it? 545
  - Problem 545
  - Technique 546
  - Steps 546
- 12.4 Configure and use Microsoft Wallet and the Microsoft Profile Assistant? 554
  - Problem 554
  - Technique 554
  - Steps 554

CHAPTER 13
EMAIL AND NEWS 569

- 13.1 Install the Internet email and newsgroup components of Windows 98? 573
  - Problem 573
  - Technique 574
  - Steps 574

CONTENTS

13.2	Configure and use the Outlook Express email client?	576
	Problem	576
	Technique	576
	Steps	576
13.3	Configure and use the Outlook Express newsreader component?	600
	Problem	600
	Technique	600
	Steps	601
13.4	Configure Outlook Express when I have multiple users on the same PC?	611
	Problem	611
	Technique	611
	Steps	611
13.5	Perform Outlook Express maintenance tasks?	613
	Problem	613
	Technique	613
	Steps	613
13.6	Use the Outlook Express Address Book?	617
	Problem	617
	Technique	617
	Steps	617
13.7	Configure a digital signature and why would I want to use one?	627
	Problem	627
	Technique	627
	Steps	628

CHAPTER 14
INTERNET PUBLISHING 633

14.1	Install the Internet publishing components, such as FrontPage Express, the Web Publishing Wizard, and the Personal Web Server?	637
	Problem	637
	Technique	637
	Steps	637
14.2	Use FrontPage Express?	646
	Problem	646
	Technique	646
	Steps	646
14.3	Use the Web Publishing Wizard?	653
	Problem	653
	Technique	653
	Steps	653
14.4	Use the Personal Web Server?	659
	Problem	659
	Technique	659
	Steps	659

CHAPTER 15
NETWORK MANAGEMENT 669

- 15.1 Create and configure a Windows 98 peer-to-peer network? 673
  - Problem 673
  - Technique 674
  - Steps 674
- 15.2 Take advantage of the Microsoft Zero Administration Initiative (ZAIW) for Windows? 678
  - Problem 678
  - Technique 678
  - Steps 679
- 15.3 Install and configure the Windows 98 Web-Based Enterprise Management (WBEM)? 681
  - Problem 681
  - Technique 681
  - Steps 682
- 15.4 Install and configure Simple Network Management Protocol (SNMP)? 689
  - Problem 689
  - Technique 689
  - Steps 690
- 15.5 Use system policies? 694
  - Problem 694
  - Technique 694
  - Steps 694

PART IV
THE MULTIMEDIA REVOLUTION

CHAPTER 16
MULTIMEDIA BASICS 697

- 16.1 Install the additional Microsoft multimedia tools? 700
  - Problem 700
  - Technique 700
  - Steps 701
- 16.2 Use the Windows Media Player? 703
  - Problem 703
  - Technique 704
  - Steps 704
- 16.3 Configure Microsoft Comic Chat? 716
  - Problem 716
  - Technique 716
  - Steps 717

CHAPTER 17
WEBTV FOR WINDOWS .... .729

17.1 Install WebTV for Windows and its components? .... .734
    Problem .... .734
    Technique .... .734
    Steps .... .734
17.2 Configure and use WebTV for Windows? .... .736
    Problem .... .736
    Technique .... .736
    Steps .... .737
17.3 Listen to the radio on my Windows 98 PC? .... .748
    Problem .... .748
    Technique .... .748
    Steps .... .748
17.4 Configure WaveTop Data Broadcasting? .... .750
    Problem .... .750
    Technique .... .750
    Steps .... .752

CHAPTER 18
TELECONFERENCING THE MULTIMEDIA WAY .... .757

18.1 Install Microsoft NetMeeting? .... .764
    Problem .... .764
    Technique .... .764
    Steps .... .764
18.2 Configure and use Microsoft NetMeeting? .... .766
    Problem .... .766
    Technique .... .766
    Steps .... .766

CHAPTER 19
GIVING WINDOWS SPECIAL POWERS .... .787

19.1 Use the Make Compatible utility? .... .790
    Problem .... .790
    Technique .... .790
    Steps .... .791
19.2 Use the WinAlign utility? .... .795
    Problem .... .795
    Technique .... .795
    Steps .... .796

19.3	Change or fix file associations?	.799
	Problem	.799
	Technique	.799
	Steps	.799
19.4	Install and use the Microsoft Plus! 98 software add-on for Windows 98?	.803
	Problem	.803
	Technique	.803
	Steps	.804
19.5	Obtain additional security tools for Windows 98?	.805
	Problem	.805
	Technique	.805

PART V
HELP!

CHAPTER 20
WHERE DID I GO WRONG AND HOW DO I FIX IT? 809

20.1	Use the Windows 98 online help?	.813
	Problem	.813
	Technique	.813
	Steps	.813
20.2	Approach a troubleshooting strategy when addressing problems with Windows 98?	.817
	Problem	.817
	Technique	.818
	Steps	.818
20.3	Know who to call for assistance?	.819
	Problem	.819
	Technique	.819
	Steps	.820
20.4	Know where to obtain other means of problem resolution?	.822
	Problem	.822
	Technique	.822
	Steps	.822
20.5	Obtain Microsoft TechNet and why would I want to use it?	.833
	Problem	.833
	Technique	.834
	Steps	.835

INDEX 837

ABOUT THE AUTHOR

Keith A. Powell has over nine years of experience in the technology industry and is presently employed as a senior consultant for KPMG Consulting in Chicago, as part of the e2e Supply Chain Solutions practice. Keith has an MBA from Keller Graduate School, a masters degree in history, bachelors degree in history and political science from Illinois State University, as well as an associates degree from the College of Lake County along with several industry credentials such as the Microsoft MCSE and MCP+Internet certifications.

As a Microsoft Certified Systems Engineer, Keith devotes the majority of his time in the Microsoft Windows and BackOffice arenas for clients, focusing on LAN/WAN assessments, strategies, and technical architectures. He has worked with clients in the planning and implementation of several components of the Microsoft BackOffice suite of products including Windows NT Server and Workstation, Exchange Server, Internet Information Server, Systems Management Server, SQL Server, and Site Server with Commerce Server including the Microsoft Value Chain Initiative. As a 13-year user of the Windows desktop environment, he has extensive experience with all the 16- and 32-bit Microsoft server and client operating systems.

Keith is a coauthor of the *Sams Teach Yourself MCSE Microsoft Exchange Server 5.5 in 14 Days*, and the sole author of the *Windows 98 From A to Z* from Que Publishing. A native of Chicago, Keith spends much of his free time either in Chicago's great museums or inline skating along Lake Shore Drive. Keith can be reached via Internet email at either `kpowell@kpmg.com` or `worldmir@inil.com`.

DEDICATION

To my friends and family, who have each helped me through life thus far:

To Frank and Genevieve Snow, who helped me to believe in myself when it mattered most;

To Kim Feicke, who still makes me think of others;

To Mike Durr, who reminds me of just how far I have traveled;

To Tom Carste, Jerry Blaesing, and Tom Johnson, who all remind me how much further one can travel;

And, finally, to Vannessa Tomlinson, who reminds me that there is still more life to be lived.

ACKNOWLEDGMENTS

Writing this book was a very enjoyable, but hard (at times), experience that I will hold close as a good memory. Luckily, I was fortunate enough to have plenty of assistance from several others.

First, I want to thank Tracy Williams at Macmillan for all her timely guidance, support, patience, and hard work.

I also want to thank Jeff Perkins, the development editor; and John Purdum, the technical editor; and Pamela Woolf of Macmillan, without whose guidance I am sure a few not-so-accurate items would have slipped through.

Thanks to Grace Buechlein and Tracy Williams for giving me the chance to write this book and for having the faith in me to get it finished on time.

Finally, thanks to my family, especially my parents and my friends for all their motivation and support.

TELL US WHAT YOU THINK!

As the reader of this book, *you* are our most important critic and commentator. We value your opinion and want to know what we're doing right, what we could do better, what areas you'd like to see us publish in, and any other words of wisdom you're willing to pass our way.

As an executive editor for the operating systems team at Macmillan Computer Publishing, I welcome your comments. You can fax, email, or write me directly to let me know what you did or didn't like about this book—as well as what we can do to make our books stronger.

Please note that I cannot help you with technical problems related to the topic of this book, and that due to the high volume of mail I receive, I might not be able to reply to every message.

When you write, please be sure to include this book's title and author as well as your name and phone or fax number. I will carefully review your comments and share them with the author and editors who worked on this book.

Fax: 317-581-4663

Email: opsys@mcp.com

Mail: Grace Buechlein
Operating Systems
Macmillan Computer Publishing
201 West 103rd Street
Indianapolis, IN 46290 USA

PART I
HOW TO USE THIS BOOK

INTRODUCTION

WHO SHOULD READ THIS BOOK

The focus of this book is on the intermediate to advanced Windows 98 user. That is, this book is not really meant for someone who just purchased perhaps their first personal computer, that came with the Windows 98 operating system already preinstalled on it. Rather, the focus of this book is for individuals who want to be able to install Windows 98 on a clean system, upgrade an existing version of DOS/Windows to the Windows 98 version, and be able to fine-tune and tweak their installation of Windows 98.

Windows 98 systems professionals such as corporate help desk personnel and desktop system administrators will find this book especially helpful. This book has been arranged into a series of How-To topics, which means that you need to ask yourself "How do I do that?" or "How do I do this?" and you will be able to look up that particular topic somewhere within the confines of this book. For example, say that you want to boot your Windows 98 PC to a DOS prompt. Ask yourself "How do I Boot to a DOS Prompt?" and then look for that type of a question within the outline of the book. You will find this within the Chapter 3, "The Boot Process," under the third topic that is labeled "How do I Boot to a DOS Prompt?" It is that easy.

Power users of the Windows 98 operating system will likewise find this book especially useful, because it is a great troubleshooting resource. Many of the Microsoft-documented and undocumented tips and tricks are detailed throughout this book, including the disabling of the Windows Update utility and the use of cloning tools such as GHOST. Additional details regarding the little-known features of Windows 98 such as Windows Publishing Wizard and the Make Compatible or WinAlign utilities are also discussed. And finally, when you run out of your own knowledge resources, this book provides assistance in obtaining outside resources, such as Microsoft's own TechNet program, to resolve troublesome issues.

Home users who are addicted to the Internet and its immense powers of information serving will definitely enjoy the benefits of this book. There are several chapters with many topics devoted to the various Internet-based aspects of Windows 98, such as the Internet Explorer Web browser (Chapter 12), the Outlook Express email and newsgroup client (Chapter 13), and the various Internet publishing tools (Chapter 14) that are built into the Windows 98 operating system. In fact, there are 25 separate topics within this book that are devoted exclusively to the use of the Internet, and several more that partially cover the use of this powerful new medium.

Finally, this book will aid those home PC users that find it necessary to share a single PC among several family members, without wanting each person to step on someone else's stuff. For example, there are topics that explain the configuration and use of multiple users on the same PC, including the proper sharing of the Outlook Express Internet email and newsgroup system, how to configure the Family Logon process, and so on. Coming from a large family, I can definitely appreciate this latest Microsoft operating system feature, which comes built into Windows 98.

WHAT YOU NEED TO USE THIS BOOK

This book requires the use of the retail release of the Windows 98 operating system, which is also known as build number 4.10.1998 (or version number). At the time of the writing of this book, Microsoft Corporation had a beta version of the OEM release of Windows 98 in development and test, but had not yet released it. It is assumed that after its release, either the retail or the OEM release of Windows 98 will be sufficient for the use of this book. For the majority of the chapters, you need a Windows 98-based PC and perhaps a modem for Internet connectivity. In a few topics within certain chapters, while it would be helpful to have a Windows NT Server available for further testing, it is not necessarily a requirement.

HOW THIS BOOK IS ORGANIZED

This book has been organized into five sections: the Introduction, Core Windows Components, Networking Essentials, The Multimedia Revolution, and Help! Each chapter contains several topics, which are all focused on that chapter's overall topical area. The beginning of each chapter lists a brief description of each topic within each chapter. The book sections, chapters, and their contents are as follows:

Part II: "Core Windows Components"
Chapter 1: "Installation Tips"

- 1.1 How do I determine the hardware requirements for Windows 98?
- 1.2 How do I avoid the common installation failure points?
- 1.3 How do I install Windows 98 on a hardware system that is below standard hardware levels?
- 1.4 How do I install the Windows 98 Resource Kit?
- 1.5 How do I use the Windows update process?

Chapter 2: "Desktop Usage and Tips"

- 2.1 How do I know which desktop to use: the Active Desktop or the Classic Desktop?

INTRODUCTION

2.2   How do I configure the Windows 98 Classic Desktop?

2.3   How do I configure the Windows 98 Active Desktop?

2.4   How do I add or remove system icons?

2.5   How do I find and remove useless links on my desktop or Start menu?

2.6   How do I change the default view of the My Computer Windows Explorer to explore instead of open?

2.7   How do I place the Recent Documents folder directly on my desktop?

2.8   How do I create a toolbar that shows all the physical drive devices?

2.9   How do I open a DOS window with a quick keystroke?

2.10 How do I hide all the icons on a Windows 98 desktop?

2.11 How do I change the opening or execution of desktop icons to a single-click mode?

Chapter 3: "The Boot Process"

3.1   How do I determine which files load during the Windows 98 boot process?

3.2   How do I change the Windows 98 startup process so I can find malfunctioning device drivers?

3.3   How do I boot to a DOS prompt?

3.4   How do I know what the key system files are?

3.5   How do I obtain information on problematic hardware that was encountered during the Windows 98 startup?

3.6   How do I force Windows 98 to boot into Safe Mode?

3.7   How do I create a Windows 98 Startup disk?

Chapter 4: "The Registry"

4.1   How do I restore the Windows 98 Registry to the same state it was in when I last successfully started my PC?

4.2   How do I modify the Registry so that it automatically starts a specific application every time I launch Windows 98?

4.3   How do I recover from incorrect Registry modifications?

4.4   How do I modify the Registry so that a user cannot access the Windows Update feature and fix his own PC?

Chapter 5: "Quintessential Hardware Configurations"

5.1 How do I choose a keyboard type?

5.2 How do I change the default language for my Windows 98 keyboard?

5.3 How do I change the default character typing speed for my Windows 98 keyboard?

5.4 How do I choose a display monitor?

5.5 How do I select a display configuration within Windows 98?

5.6 How do I configure my system for multiple display monitors?

5.7 How do I know which mouse or pointer device types to use?

5.8 How do I configure my mouse or other pointing devices?

Chapter 6: "Disk Drive Management and Use"

6.1 How do I know what the differences are between the FAT16 and the FAT32 file systems?

6.2 How do I install the additional disk drive management tools and utilities?

6.3 How do I know whether to use disk compression or FAT32?

6.4 How do I configure and use the Windows 98 Disk Compression tool?

6.5 How do I configure and use the drive converter (FAT32)?

6.6 How do I configure and use the Disk Cleanup utility?

6.7 How do I configure and use the Disk Defragmenter utility?

6.8 How do I configure and use the ScanDisk utility?

6.9 How do I manage my hard disk drive(s)?

6.10 How do I manage my removable media drive(s)?

6.11 How do I install a CD-ROM or a DVD-ROM drive?

6.12 How do I know which additional, removable hard drive devices I should install?

6.13 How do I back up my Windows 98 system?

Chapter 7: "System Resource Management"

7.1 How do I determine which components make up the core Windows 98 system resources?

7.2 How do I know when to use performance monitoring?

INTRODUCTION

7.3 How do I install the additional System Resource Management tools?

7.4 How do I use the Resource Meter?

7.5 How do I use the System Information utility?

7.6 How do I use Dr. Watson to troubleshoot application faults?

7.7 How do I verify the integrity of my system files?

7.8 How do I track performance changes to my computer system over a period of time?

7.9 How do I use the Maintenance Wizard utility?

7.10 How do I monitor my computer to see if others are attached to it?

7.11 How do I schedule tasks on my computer?

7.12 How do I know if the Windows 98 Resource Kit is good for managing system resources?

Part III: "Networking Essentials"
Chapter 8: "Getting Started from the Network"

8.1 How do I decide when to install from a network?

8.2 How do I obtain and install the Microsoft Batch utility for Windows 98?

8.3 How do I use the Microsoft Batch utility for Windows 98?

8.4 How do I use a cloning tool such as GHOST to deploy Windows 98?

Chapter 9: "Dial-Up Networking"

9.1 How do I access the Internet without a direct connection?

9.2 How do I use a calling card with the Windows 98 Dial-Up Networking technology?

9.3 How do I tweak my Windows 98 Dial-Up Networking connection so that it performs better with my digital modem?

9.4 How do I secure my systems when combining modems and networks?

9.5 How do I know when to use Virtual Private Networking, and how do I install and configure it?

9.6 How do I use Virtual Private Networking?

9.7 How do I use more than one modem at a time with a single Dial-Up Networking connection?

Chapter 10: "Welcome to the Neighborhood; Network, That Is"

10.1 How do I know what other networks I can connect to?

10.2 How do I add and configure additional network clients?

10.3 How do I configure my system for multiple users?

10.4 How do I add new network adapters?

10.5 How do I add new network protocols to my Windows PC?

10.6 How do I configure TCP/IP for use on my Windows 98 PC?

10.7 How do I know when to add new network services?

10.8 How do I configure File Sharing?

10.9 How do I automatically log on to my network using the proper user ID and password?

10.10 How do I change either the computer name or workgroup name for my Windows 98 PC?

Chapter 11: "Printer Management"

11.1 How do I add a network-based print device to my computer?

11.2 How do I capture a printer port in Windows 98?

11.3 How do I share a print device?

Chapter 12: "The Internet and Web Browsing"

12.1 How do I install any updates to Internet Explorer?

12.2 How do I configure Microsoft Internet Explorer?

12.3 How do I obtain the Microsoft Internet Explorer Administration Kit and why would I want to use it?

12.4 How do I configure and use the Microsoft Profile Assistant and Microsoft Wallet?

Chapter 13: "Email and News"

13.1 How do I install the Internet email and newsgroup components of Windows 98?

13.2 How do I configure and use the Outlook Express email client?

13.3 How do I configure and use the Outlook Express newsreader component?

13.4   How do I configure Outlook Express when I have multiple users on the same PC?

13.5   How do I perform Outlook Express maintenance tasks?

13.6   How do I use the Outlook Express address book?

13.7   How do I configure a digital signature and why would I want to use one?

Chapter 14: "Internet Publishing"

14.1   How do I install the Internet Publishing Components, such as FrontPage Express, the Web Publishing Wizard, and the Personal Web Server?

14.2   How do I use FrontPage Express?

14.3   How do I use the Web Publishing Wizard?

14.4   How do I use the Personal Web Server?

Chapter 15: "Network Management"

15.1   How do I create and configure a Windows 98 peer-to-peer network?

15.2   How do I take advantage of the Microsoft Zero Administration Initiative (ZAIW) for Windows?

15.3   How do I install and configure the Windows 98 Web-based Enterprise Management (WBEM)?

15.4   How do I install Simple Network Management Protocol (SNMP)?

15.5   How do I use system policies?

Part IV: "The Multimedia Revolution"
Chapter 16: "Multimedia Basics"

16.1   How do I install the additional Microsoft multimedia tools?

16.2   How do I use the Windows Media Player?

16.3   How do I configure and use Microsoft Comic Chat?

Chapter 17: "WebTV for Windows"

17.1   How do I install WebTV for Windows and its components?

17.2   How do I configure and use WebTV for Windows?

17.3   How do I listen to the radio on my Windows 98 PC?

17.4   How do I configure WaveTop Data Broadcasting?

Chapter 18: "Teleconferencing the Multimedia Way"
- 18.1 How do I install Microsoft NetMeeting?
- 18.2 How do I configure and use Microsoft NetMeeting?

Chapter 19: "Giving Windows 98 Special Powers"
- 19.1 How do I use the Make Compatible utility?
- 19.2 How do I use the WinAlign utility?
- 19.3 How do I change or fix file associations?
- 19.4 How do I install and use the Microsoft Plus! 98 software add-on for Windows 98?
- 19.5 How do I obtain additional security tools for Windows 98?

Part V: "Help!"
Chapter 20: "Where did I Go Wrong and How do I Fix It?"
- 20.1 How do I use the Windows 98 online help?
- 20.2 How do I approach a troubleshooting strategy when addressing problems with Windows 98?
- 20.3 How do I know who to call for assistance?
- 20.4 How do I know where to obtain other means of problem resolution?
- 20.5 How do I obtain Microsoft TechNet and why would I want to use it?

PART II
CORE WINDOWS COMPONENTS

CHAPTER 1
INSTALLATION TIPS

INSTALLATION TIPS

How do I...

1.1 Determine the hardware requirements for Windows 98?

1.2 Avoid the common installation failure points?

1.3 Install Windows 98 on a hardware system that is below standard hardware levels?

1.4 Install the Windows 98 Resource Kit?

1.5 Use the Windows update process?

Microsoft Corporation began work on the next version of its 32-bit Windows operating system less than a month after the August 1995, release of Windows 95. This next release was code-named Memphis and was deemed as the eventual successor to the Windows 95 operating system. Memphis later became known as Windows 98 and was officially released to the computing public on June 25, 1998.

Before diving into the details of the problems associated with installing a new operating system, you will look at the benefits gained from a successful Windows 98 installation. Windows 98 is the consummate end-user operating system. It is capable of acting as a file and print server in a peer-to-peer network. It shines as a personal computer operating system that one can use to

CHAPTER 1
INSTALLATION TIPS

manage finances, perform research on the Internet, play games, write documents and presentations, and in short, do everything that a busy student, professional, homemaker, and the like wants to do as quickly and as easily as possible. Whether you are planning a single version installation of Windows 98 or a mass rollout to thousands of users, the causes for many failed installations are quite simple. This chapter highlights and helps you identify possible pitfalls in your own installation of Microsoft Windows 98.

1.1 Determine the Hardware Requirements for Windows 98

The focus of this How-To is to help you in determining the minimum as well as the recommended hardware components that are necessary for installing the Windows 98 operating system.

1.2 Avoid the Common Installation Failure Points

When you install the Windows 98 operating system, many possible pitfalls are awaiting you at every turn. The goal of this How-To is to assist you in risk avoidance; that is, it should help you avoid many of the common installation errors that many first-time installers of Windows 98 encounter.

1.3 Install Windows 98 on a Hardware System that Is Below Standard Hardware Levels

Sometimes when you have a PC that does not meet the minimum hardware requirements, you are still required (usually by your ever-so-thoughtful and insightful boss) to install Windows 98 on it. This How-To helps you get past these requirements, including the use of a special setup parameter.

1.4 Install the Windows 98 Resource Kit

Well, you have purchased the Windows 98 Resource Kit. Would it not be nice to know the best way to install it? This How-To does exactly that.

1.5 Use the Windows Update Process

Microsoft has a new approach to releasing service patches and packs to its installed Windows 98 customer base through the use of an Internet-based Web site, known as the Microsoft Windows Update site. This How-To walks you through the use of this site.

COMPLEXITY
BEGINNER

1.1 How do I...
Determine the hardware requirements for Windows 98?

Problem

Although the hardware requirements are readily available, many people assume that because an older version of Windows ran on their PC, the newer version (Windows 98) will as well. This simple but deadly assumption might be the problem with your installation. Later in this chapter you will see what the recommended hardware requirements are for installing the Windows 98 operating system.

Technique

The technique for discovering whether your personal computer is compatible with Windows 98 is pretty straightforward. You need to compare hardware components at a high level with the following charts. If your PC comes up short in any of these areas, you should consider upgrading or replacing your computer system. However, should you want to attempt a Windows 98 installation anyway, please review the setup and installation tips at the end of this chapter.

Steps

1. Review the hardware requirements in Table 1.1, and compare it to your computer system.

Table 1.1 Windows 98 Base Hardware System Requirements

COMPONENT	LOW-END REQUIREMENT	RECOMMENDED LEVEL
Available Hard Drive Space	120MB of free hard drive space	A full installation of Windows 98 can command up to 250MB of free space
CPU	Intel or compatible 80486/DX-66MHz CPU	Intel Pentium Processor or better. A high-end AMD processor will also work.

continued on next page

continued from previous page

COMPONENT	LOW-END REQUIREMENT	RECOMMENDED LEVEL
Total System Memory	16MB of RAM	The more you have, the faster your system performs. However, 32MB of memory is considered to be the baseline minimum for Windows 98 to perform effectively.
Display Monitor	16-color VGA	SVGA with at least 16-bit color is preferred. However, in the computing world today base resolutions of 800×600 pixels and 256 colors are not uncommon. This should be your bottom-end video requirement.
Removable Disk Drive	Not required	At least one high-density 3 1/2 inch floppy disk drive is recommended, especially if you plan to install Windows 98 on a new computer system. For more information, you might want to review Chapter 3, "The Boot Process," for details on the Windows 98 Startup disk before deciding not to put a floppy disk drive in your PC.

2. Review the optional hardware components Table 1.2 to see how it compares to your PC as well as your personal requirements for Windows 98 functionality.

Table 1.2 Windows 98 Optional Hardware Components

OPTIONAL PART	LOW-END REQUIREMENT	RECOMMENDED LEVEL
CD- or DVD-ROM Drive (Use to install Windows 98 from a CD-ROM)	Single speed	8x or faster

1.1 DETERMINE THE HARDWARE REQUIREMENTS FOR WINDOWS 98

OPTIONAL PART	LOW-END REQUIREMENT	RECOMMENDED LEVEL
DVD-ROM Drive with Decoder Card (Use to watch full-size motion pictures)	Industry-standard drive and decoder card	One that allows for DVD-video playback with MPEG-2 support
IEEE 1394 bus (Use for high bandwidth digital sound and video transfer; also known as, Firewire)	Optional	PC devices and controller support the IEEE 1394 standards, including the Plug-and-Play and OnNow power management specifications
Modem	14.4 baud internal or external modem	28.8 baud internal or external modem. Given that 57.6 Kbps is the standard today, you might want to make this your minimum requirement for a modem (keep in mind that 57.6Kbps is a one-way speed, the other way operates at 33.6Kbps because of U.S. government regulations).
Mouse	Technically this is an optional hardware device, but in reality at least a Windows 98-compatible pointing device is required	Microsoft IntelliPoint Mouse
Second (or more) video adapter and monitor (Use with the multiple monitor feature)	Optional	A non-ISA bus or PCI or AGP video adapter with a 16-bit color SVGA monitor. See Chapter 5, "Quintessential Hardware and Software Configurations," for more details on using multiple monitors with your PC.
Sound card and speakers	Sound Blaster compatible	Either a full-duplex audio card or an external digital audio card with USB or IEEE 1394 support
TV tuner card (Use with WebTV for Windows)	Optional	ATI All-in-Wonder-Card

CHAPTER 1
INSTALLATION TIPS

3. The key thing to remember when analyzing these tables is that whatever the component you choose, it is recommended that that hardware component be Microsoft-certified as being compatible with Windows 98. If you have access to the Internet, check out the Windows 98 Hardware Compatibility List at the following Web site: `http://www.microsoft.com/hwtest/hcl`. It provides you with the most up-to-date information on which hardware components have been Microsoft-tested for compatibility with the Windows 98 operating system. It is easy to check the compatibility of specific hardware using Microsoft's online Hardware Compatibility List (HCL). This listing is a full reporting of computer systems and other hardware peripherals that have been tested by Microsoft and determined as compatible with the Windows 98 operating system. Therefore, it is wise to ensure all your computer system's major hardware components do indeed appear on the HCL before attempting a Windows 98 installation on that same system.

4. Start your Internet browser and proceed to the URL `http://www.microsoft.com/hwtest/hcl/` as shown in Figure 1.1.

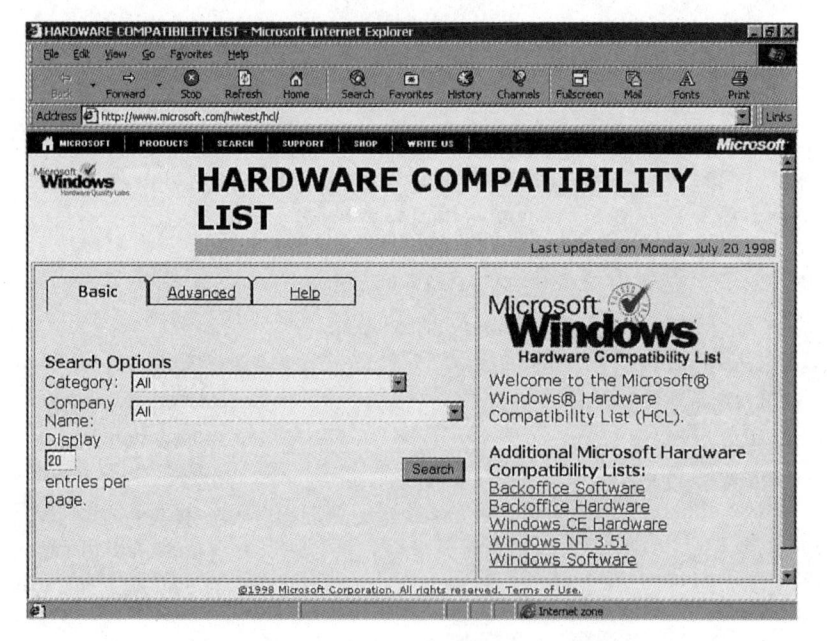

Figure 1.1 Microsoft's Hardware Compatibility List Web site.

1.1
DETERMINE THE HARDWARE REQUIREMENTS FOR WINDOWS 98

> **NOTE**
>
> Access to the Microsoft HCL can be made from any Internet Web browser, not just the Microsoft Internet Explorer browser shown in Figure 1.1 In addition, this HCL Web site provides hardware compatibility information for the other Microsoft operating systems and software application packages.

5. The search options listed on the Basic tab enable you to obtain information by component type, which is known as the Category, as well as by manufacturer (the Company Name drop-down list box) of the component. For example, click on the Category to choose a specific hardware component such as Display Monitor, and then select the hardware manufacturer that produces the monitor that you want to confirm the compatibility of, such as Gateway 2000, as seen in Figure 1.2.

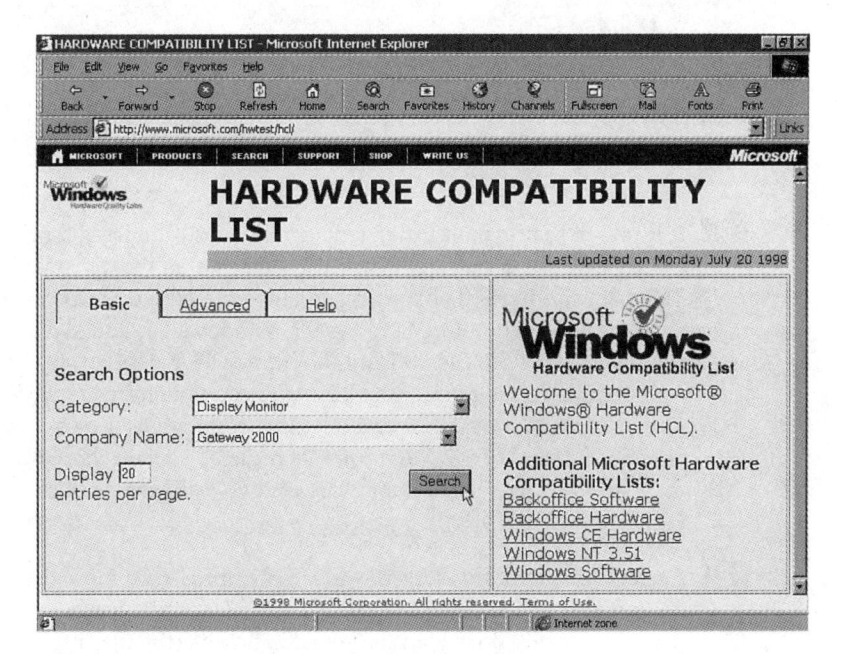

Figure 1.2 Entering search information.

6. Click the Search button to proceed to the next screen, as seen in Figure 1.3.

CHAPTER 1
INSTALLATION TIPS

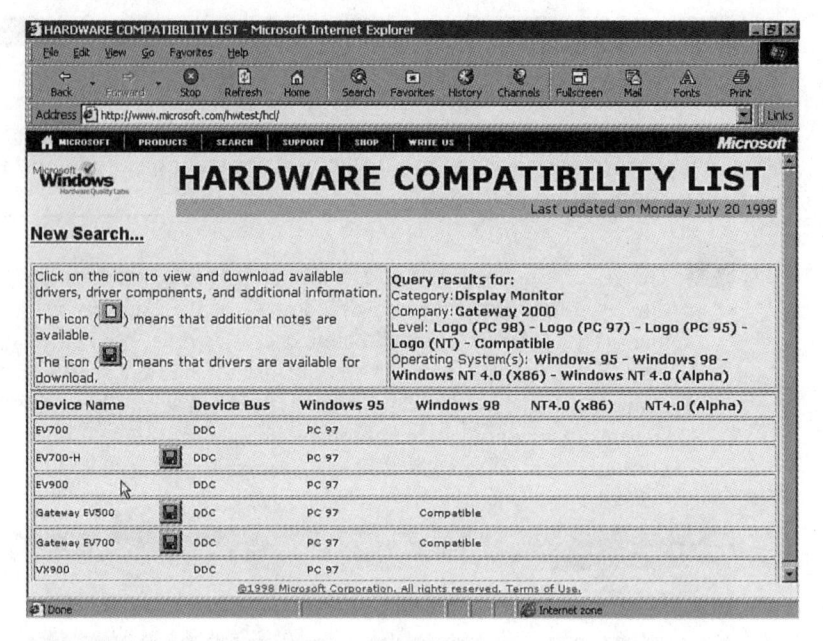

Figure 1.3 The HCL search results screen.

7. A listing of that manufacturer's compatible hardware parts for the specific category, in this case display monitors, appears on the dynamic Web page. There are two items that you should take note of here. First, the listing contains information for Windows 98, Windows 95, and Windows NT version 4.0 for both the x86 and the Alpha CPUs. Second, if an additional icon appears to the right of the hardware component name then either more information or the compatible drivers themselves are available for download directly from Microsoft's Web site. To obtain those drivers, click the icon that looks like a floppy disk and you will see a screen similar to Figure 1.4.

8. After you arrive at this screen, you are presented with more details concerning the file(s) required to update this specific hardware component. To actually download the software drivers (the files listed) for this piece of hardware, click on the Download this driver now button. This takes you to the appropriate Microsoft FTP site where the file transfer your computer commences, as shown in Figure 1.5.

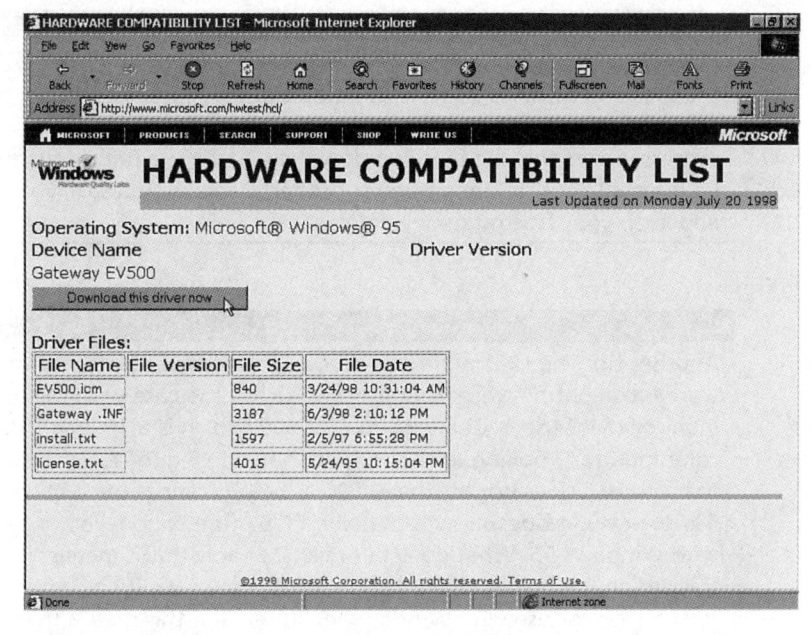

1.1
DETERMINE THE HARDWARE REQUIREMENTS FOR WINDOWS 98

Figure 1.4 Device driver download area for the selected hardware component.

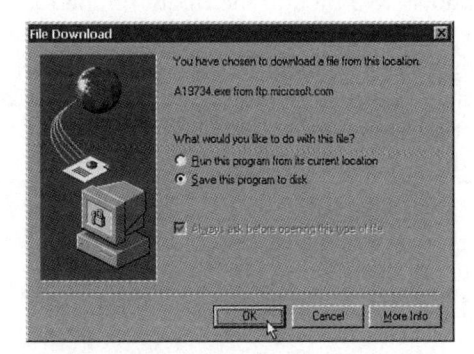

Figure 1.5 The File Download screen.

9. If you select to Run this option from its current location then the file actually downloads itself to a spot on your computer's hard drive. (Probably to C:\Windows\Temp if you are already running some version of Windows, where it will uncompress and automatically begin installing itself onto the existing operating system configuration.) Otherwise, pick a spot on your hard drive to download the file to, and complete the process.

CHAPTER 1
INSTALLATION TIPS

> **NOTE**
>
> I suggested that you select the Save this program to disk option and then install Windows 98 with its default display monitor drivers, probably a 16-color VGA monitor driver. Following the Windows 98 setup process, access this file that you downloaded via the Run command and let it install your system's monitor properly. This should save you time and keep your frustration level down.

> **NOTE**
>
> Another tip: The HCL might not precisely state that your piece of hardware is compatible with Windows 98. Such is the case with the display monitor that I use: a Gateway 2000 EV900, which is a 19-inch SVGA color monitor. Looking at the HCL, as shown in Figure 1.3, you can see that the HCL does not list the EV900 as being compatible with Windows 98. However, it does show it as being PC 97 (the Logo level) compatible with Windows 95. What does this mean? Simply put it means that while this peripheral is fully compatible with Windows 95, it has not yet been fully tested for use with Windows 98. In real life this means that it probably does work, but there are no guarantees. (In my experience it means that it has worked flawlessly for the past 18 months over every beta and release of Windows 98 although this might not be the case for everyone.) Also, display monitor devices are much more forgiving than scanners, digital cameras, and gaming devices. So whereas a monitor might work even though it does not appear on the HCL, it is much more likely that these other types of devices will fail to work at all if they do not appear on the Microsoft HCL.

10. Going back to the first screen of the HCL Web site, (refer to Figure 1.1), you see an Advanced tab. Clicking this tab brings you to the next screen, as shown in Figure 1.6.

11. The same search options found on the Basic tab are also present in the Advanced tab, as well as the capability to limit the HCL search by operating system type. The obvious advantage here is that you are able to confine your hardware component search to those compatible with Windows 98, thereby eliminating much of the rubbish. However, it is suggested that you still select the Windows 95 operating system's check box. This is because it is only the very rare case that a hardware component is compatible with Windows 95, but not Windows 98. The Additional Information section near the bottom of the screen causes the ID and model number of a hardware component to be displayed on the search results screen. Make your selections and click the Search button to continue to the next screen, as shown in Figure 1.7.

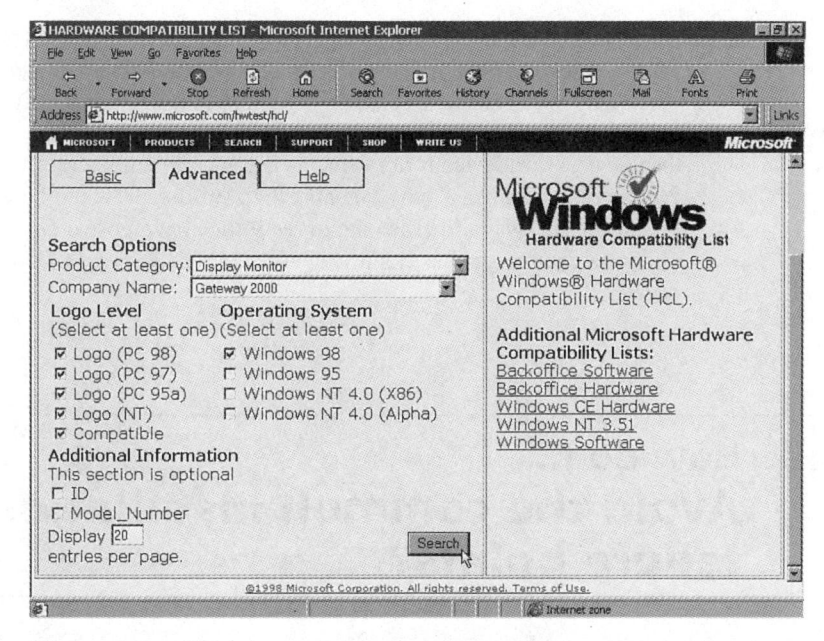

1.1
DETERMINE THE HARDWARE REQUIREMENTS FOR WINDOWS 98

Figure 1.6 HCL Advanced search options screen.

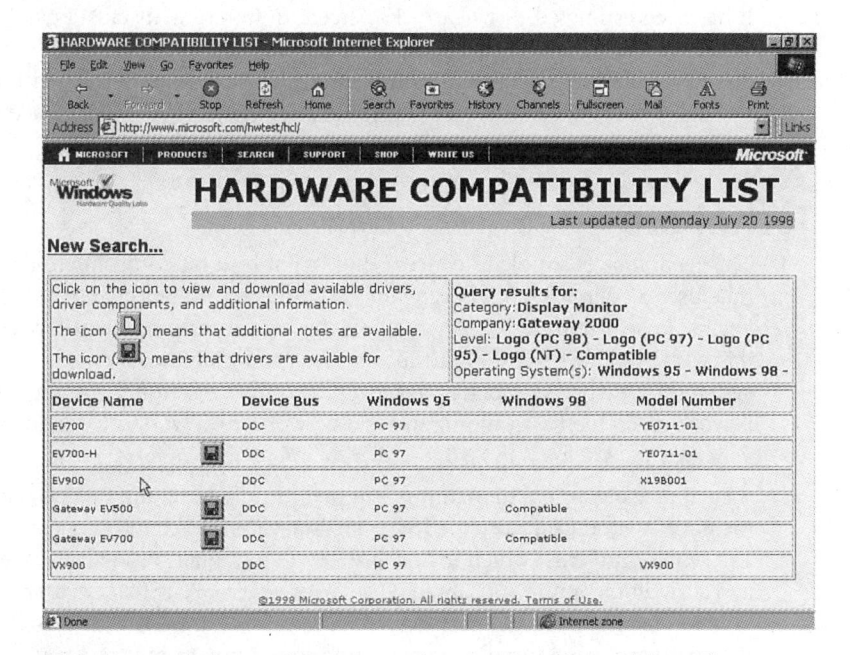

Figure 1.7 Advanced search results screen with model numbers.

12. A screen that looks remarkably similar to Figure 1.3 appears. The main difference is that now you will see the model numbers for each device, when they are available to Microsoft, as well as a listing for only Windows 95 and Windows 98 compatible devices. Again, you see that the EV900 display monitor device is not listed as being compatible, but the Gateway 2000 model number is now available for your use. It would be wise to check out Gateway's Internet site to see if they have posted an updated set of device drivers for this monitor or some other Gateway 2000 computer device.

COMPLEXITY
INTERMEDIATE

1.2 How do I...
Avoid the common installation failure points?

Problem

It has been estimated that nearly 48 percent of first time installations of Windows 98 fail for various reasons. Countless numbers of these failures are due to the lack of basic installation planning and can be avoided by running through a short checklist of tasks prior to running the Windows 98 setup program.

Technique

This technique is simple in concept, but might be a bit confusing to the first time user of Windows 98. Several areas should be covered before installation begins. Ensure that the PC is virus free, the hardware components are compatible with Windows 98, the startup programs and *TSRs* are disabled, the system(s) have been properly backed-up, and the present networking software is working correctly (assuming this is a network installation of Windows 98).

A TSR is a terminate-and-stay-resident software application that starts up but then appears to stop although it is still present in your computer system's memory. A good example of a TSR is an anti-virus protection program, such as Cheyenne AntiVirus, which includes a feature to remain resident in memory and scan all incoming and outgoing email messages. A TSR such as an anti-virus protection package most likely interferes with any software installation, as it sees that software installation as a virus attempting to infiltrate your computer system. This is especially true with the installation of a new operating system, as a new OS will attempt to write information to your computer's boot record.

AVOID THE COMMON INSTALLATION FAILURE POINTS

Steps

1. To ensure that your PC does not contain any computer viruses, install (if you do not have one already) and run a full virus scan on your computer. If any viruses are detected, they should be eliminated before attempting a Windows 98 installation.

2. Check the compatibility of your PC hardware with the Microsoft Hardware Compatibility List found on the Internet, at `http://www.microsoft.com/hwtest/hcl/`.

3. Make sure that all of the auto-start applications have been temporarily disabled. This includes anti-virus software, task schedulers, screen savers, sound system volume controls, and other utilities. On a Windows 95 PC, click the Start button then the Programs menu option, followed by a click on the Startup menu selection. Disable any application shown there by moving it to another temporary folder on your hard drive. On a Windows 3.x PC, look in the Startup folder on your Program Manager desktop. On Windows 95, Windows 3.x, and DOS-based systems, check out the AUTOEXEC.BAT file for TSRs that might be loading there (most antivirus applications have something there). Type in the statement **rem** at the start of any line in this file to temporarily remove it from executing. Remember that all of the programs can be reenabled after Windows 98 installation is complete, so do not delete anything from your hard drive. Also examine your CONFIG.SYS file, making sure that any memory managers, such as EMM386, EMM, and 386MAX, have been properly disabled. Disable a line in this file by typing in the statement **rem** at the start of any line.

4. Catastrophic installation disasters with Windows 98 are rare but can and do occur. It is for this reason that it is strongly suggested that you take the time to fully back up your computer system. This includes not only data files, but also special files such as the Registry (on Windows 95, the USER.DAT and SYSTEM.DAT files); all configuration files such as the .INI, .PWL, .DAT, and *.GRP (in the C:\Windows directory); .BAT and .SYS (in the root directory, usually C:\); and any other special batch files, scripts (such as login or network-attached), or configuration files that you deem critical to your computer system setup.

5. Confirm that your network configuration works properly, assuming that you have a network in place of course. Do this by copying a file to the server, printing a document across the network, checking your email (if you have the capability), and running a network-based application (if there are any). Performing all these tasks helps to ensure that your network configuration is working properly.

6. One final comment: Be sure not to start a Windows 98 installation from a DOS-based PC that has its CD-ROM drive connected through a sound card. This will cause the Windows 98 hardware detection process, and subsequently the Windows 98 install process, to fail. Copy the Windows 98 installation files to your computer's hard drive first, and then run the setup process from there. After Windows 98 has been fully installed, it should recognize your CD-ROM drive and then you can delete the installation files from your PC's hard drive. The best way to do this is to copy the entire Win98 folder from the Windows 98 CD-ROM installation disc onto your hard drive. This folder contains all the files you require for a basic Windows 98 installation. To start the setup process, just open this folder (after you have copied it onto your hard drive) and double-click the Setup.Exe file found within this folder.

COMPLEXITY
BEGINNER

1.3 How do I...
Install Windows 98 on a hardware system that is below standard hardware levels?

Problem
Assuming that a computer is not quite up to Microsoft's baseline hardware specifications, how can one still attempt a Windows 98 installation on that PC?

Technique
While it is strongly recommended that your computer at least meet the minimum hardware requirements for installing Windows 98, it is possible to get around the self-checking for a math co-processor that the Windows 98 setup program will perform.

Steps

1. Boot your computer to DOS prompt. If you already have Windows 95 operating on your computer, exit the Windows 95 GUI by performing a Shutdown and Restart in Microsoft-DOS mode.

2. Place the Windows 98 CD-ROM in the CD-ROM drive (assuming that you are not performing a full floppy disk-only installation).

3. Start the Windows 98 installation process by typing in the `Setup` command followed by the `/NM` (the whole command looks like this: `Setup /NM`). That is all you need to do. The Windows 98 setup process proceeds from here.

COMPLEXITY
INTERMEDIATE

1.4 How do I...
Install the Windows 98 Resource Kit?

Problem

You need to create a deployment strategy for installing Windows 98 on multiple PCs across the company's enterprise infrastructure. What is the best way to do this without turning the process into an installation nightmare? Or perhaps you need to boot multiple language versions of Windows 98 on the same PC. The Windows 98 Resource Kit has all the tools that you need to solve these types of otherwise problematic installations. Even if you are not responsible for performing mass Windows 98 installations, or running a network full of Windows 98 computers, the Windows 98 Resource Kit still comes in handy for the average, non-networked, Windows 98 user. This is because the Resource Kit contains literally thousands of tidbits and system tweaks that are organized in such a way that a reasonably intelligent Windows 98 user will be able to find the information that she needs to fix whatever might be ailing her Windows 98 PC.

Technique

Microsoft created a compact disc chock full of tools and utilities that pertain to the Windows 98 operating system. These tools and utilities make it much easier to deploy, troubleshoot, support, administer, and manage Windows 98. Additionally, the Resource Kit provides specific tools that aid in the Windows 98 scripting process, makes it much more palatable to edit the Registry, and permits you to compare files much quicker and easier. There is a catch, of course; the Windows 98 Resource Kit CD-ROM comes with the nearly 2,000 page Windows 98 Resource Kit book at a cost of $69.99 (USD) and is available from Microsoft Press, Inc.

Networking or desktop systems professionals benefit the most from the Windows 98 Resource Kit because they are required to support large numbers of Windows 98 computers. Help Desk professionals, who support countless numbers of Windows 98 users, will also benefit from the Resource Kit. The book accompanying the Resource Kit does not have pictures, does not have a step-by-step format, and does not express itself well to the entry-level technical person, not to mention non-technical lay person, so its audience is really the technically savvy, power users of Windows 98. The Resource Kit tools on the accompanying CD-ROM are not documented that well, so if you are an entry-level user of Windows 98 (or a newly employed help desk support person) you might find many of the tools on this CD-ROM to be more advanced than you. Many of these tools require you to be able to figure things out on your own, so you should be prepared to do so (or continue reading this book for some more assistance).

The answer for the first problem, creating a deployment strategy for installing Windows 98 on multiple PCs across your organization's enterprise infrastructure, is solved by the various deployment and management tools, whereas actually deploying Windows 98 PCs across the enterprise can be resolved by using the WinBoot utility. So, after you have purchased and installed the Windows 98 Resource Kit from your local bookstore or from an Internet-based store such as `http://www.barnesandnoble.com/` or `http://www.amazon.com` you will be able to use this utility.

Steps

1. Place the Windows 98 Resource Kit disc in your CD-ROM drive and run the Setup.exe file. On most computers the Resource Kit installation screen automatically appears due to the AutoRun capability of Windows 98, as shown in Figure 1.8.

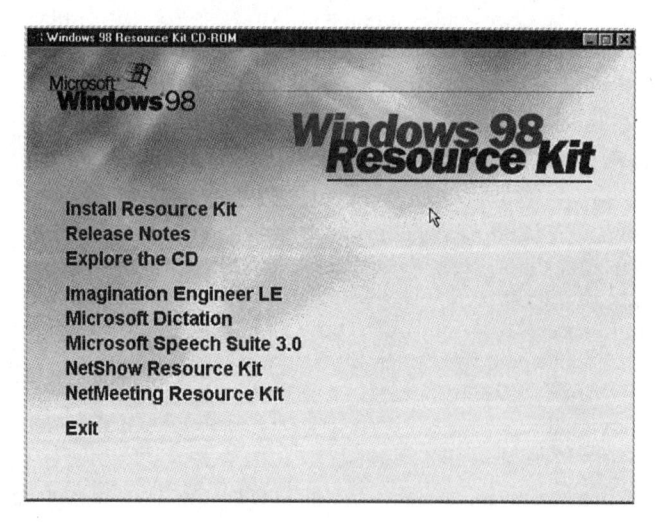

Figure 1.8 Windows 98 Resource Kit welcome screen.

1.4
INSTALL THE WINDOWS 98 RESOURCE KIT

2. Clicking the Install Resource Kit option on the Resource Kit Installation screen causes the Windows 98 Resource Kit licensing agreement to appear. If you executed the Setup.exe file directly then the Software License Agreement dialog box is the first screen you see, as shown in Figure 1.9.

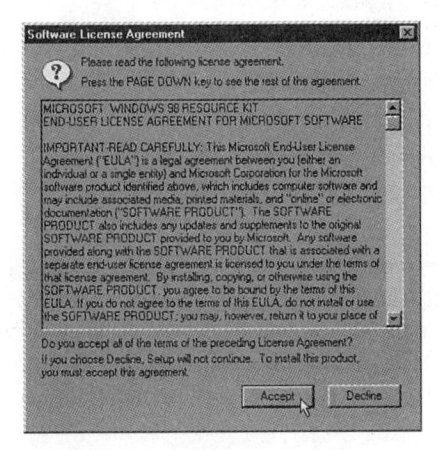

Figure 1.9 Windows 98 Resource Kit Software License Agreement dialog box.

3. Click Accept to continue the installation process. If you click Decline, the installation process prompts you to ensure that you want to terminate the installation process. The Accept button brings you to the screen shown in Figure 1.10.

Figure 1.10 The Windows 98 Resource Kit initial Setup screen.

CHAPTER 1
INSTALLATION TIPS

4. After you have read the Welcome screen, click Continue to proceed. This causes the next screen to appear as shown in Figure 1.11.

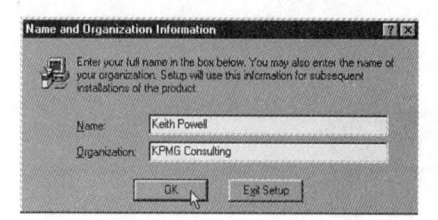

Figure 1.11 The Name and Organization Information entry screen.

5. Enter the name of the person to whom this software is to be registered, as well as the name of the organization or company to which this person belongs. Click OK to continue. You will be prompted to confirm the name of the person and organization. Again click OK to continue. The setup program searches for previously installed components before moving to the Destination Folder screen, as shown in Figure 1.12.

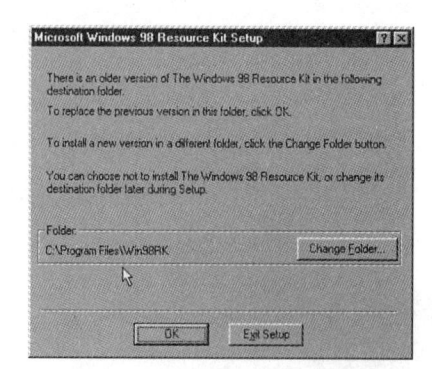

Figure 1.12 The Installation destination folder selection screen.

6. On this screen you are prompted for the destination folder for the Windows 98 Resource Kit's contents. It is suggested that you place the folder inside the C:\Program Files directory; this helps to make your hard disk management that much easier (if you always put application programs there). To change the path of the Resource Kit, click the Change Folder button and make your selection appropriately prior to your return to this same screen. After you have made your selection, click OK to proceed to the next screen as shown in Figure 1.13.

1.4
INSTALL THE WINDOWS 98 RESOURCE KIT

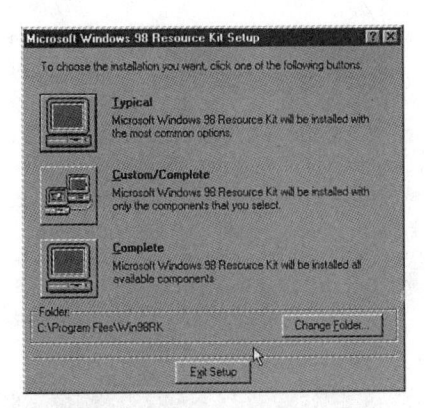

Figure 1.13 The Windows 98 Resource Kit installation method selection screen.

7. One of the first things that you will notice on this screen is that you are again able to select a destination folder for the Resource Kit's contents. Make another selection and move on to choosing the level of installation that you prefer by clicking the button to the left of the installation type. A complete installation is just that: every component is installed. It is suggested that you always choose a Custom/Complete installation whenever you install any software product. This way you only get what you want and need, as opposed to getting whatever someone else thinks you want and need. Clicking the Custom/Complete button takes us to the next screen, as shown in Figure 1.14.

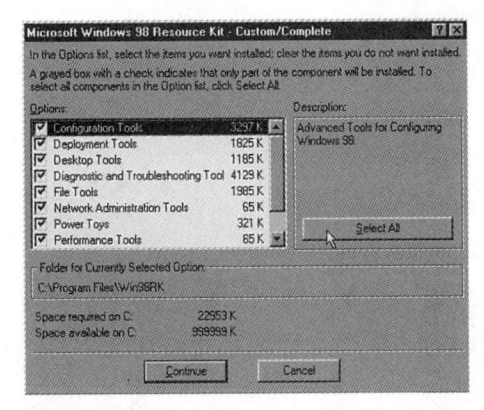

Figure 1.14 The Windows 98 Resource Kit components to install selection screen.

8. Choose the Resource Kit components that interest you by clicking the check box for each item. To mark all items for installation, click Select All. Most of the topics are obvious but Power Toys might not be. This selection will install the infamous TweakUI application, which permits you to more personally customize a Windows 98 installation. The two other options that are not shown on this screen shot are the Scripting Tools and the Windows Logo Requirements options. The Windows Logo Requirements option will install the Windows Logo Requirements Handbook. This book describes the technical requirements necessary for a software application to receive the logo.

> **NOTE**
>
> To actually apply for the logo, software applications developers should refer to the complete application information located on the Microsoft Web site at http://www.microsoft.com/windows/thirdparty/winlogo/.

9. If all 10 options are selected, nearly 23MB of hard drive space is required by the Windows 98 Resource Kit tools and utilities. After you have made all of your selections, click Continue to move to the screen shown in Figure 1.15.

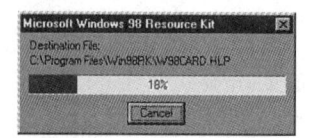

Figure 1.15 The Windows 98 Resource Kit installation in process status message box.

10. The installation process will begin. Do not be alarmed if an error message box should appear during the installation of your Resource Kit, like the one shown in Figure 1.16.

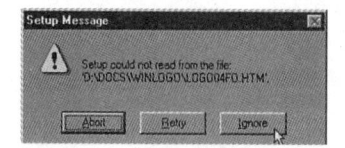

Figure 1.16 Windows 98 Resource Kit error message dialog box.

1.4 INSTALL THE WINDOWS 98 RESOURCE KIT

11. Occasionally CD-ROMs that come with books will bend a little, causing an error or two. CD-ROMs that bend, have some extra book glue on them, or are scratched, might result in installation errors. These types of errors can occur at any point in the installation process, as these are read errors that are occurring on your CD-ROM. If this should happen, it is suggested that you return your Resource Kit to the place you purchased it and request a new one. In the meantime, click the Ignore button to force the installation process to continue, but this definitely slows the installation process.

12. Eventually, the successfully completed message box appears, as shown in Figure 1.17, meaning that the installation is complete. Remove the CD-ROM and you are finished.

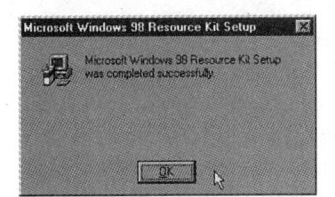

Figure 1.17 The Windows 98 Resource Kit installation process is complete.

There are quite a few tools that come with the Windows 98 Resource Kit. If you want to browse Microsoft's information regarding this kit, you can do so by connecting to the following Internet Web site:
http://mspress.microsoft.com/reslink.

However, this Web site is quite basic in terms of what you get and some of the possible uses for each of the tools. Therefore, following is a complete listing of all the tools that come with the Resource Kit, as well as a brief description of the functionality each tool provides. Microsoft provides a similar listing in its Windows 98 Resource Kit Help files, except those files repeat the same file multiple times with multiple descriptions, which might be a bit confusing for the newer user of a Microsoft Resource Kit. (The reason for this duplication is that several tools can provide multiple uses for you.) A brief description of the tool comes first with the exact filename that executes the tool following in parenthesis. Then on the tools that are not obvious as to what their purpose is, there is a brief description explaining the tool's functionality.

- Animated Cursor Editor (ANIEDIT.EXE)—This tool permits you to edit the various animated cursors that come with the Windows 98 operating system, as well as giving you the capability to create your own from scratch.

- Application Performance Optimizer (WINALIGN.EXE)—This tool is both powerful and dangerous. It allows you to rearrange the manner in which files are executed by the system so that those applications run faster. However, if you use this tool incorrectly or on application packages that are already using this tool internally, you can (and probably will) corrupt or destroy that software package. (The Microsoft Office suite of applications is a good example of a software package that has already been optimized, meaning it can become corrupted through incorrect use of this tool). If you are not a software developer, this tool might not be one for you to play with.

- Associate (ASSOCIATE.EXE)—This command-line tool permits you to either manually or programmatically create or remove the associations between file extensions and Windows 98-compliant program executables.

- Automated .INF Installer (INFINST.EXE)—During the course of creating a custom batch installation file, you might want to add new specialized device drivers for your hardware or more up-to-date network drivers for your NICs. This file gives you the capability to do this without having to manually edit your batch installation script file. This is a useful tool for those desktop administrators who must deploy hundreds or thousands of Windows 98 PCs simultaneously.

- Batch File Wait (SLEEP.EXE)—In a batch file, this utility gives you the opportunity to set a specific wait period. While I have never found a good use for it, I am certain that others have.

- Batch Processing of Files (FORFILES.EXE)—This tool gives you the capability to select a series of files within any folder for use in a batch process. It can be useful in a messaging application that needs to process all the files in a specific in-box and then transmit the accumulation of those files up to a host machine. It is also cheaper than going out and buying a middleware tool, such as IBM's MQSeries, to do the same thing.

- Bulk Configuration Utility (DBSET.EXE)—This utility is absolutely necessary for those network/systems administrators who must deploy hundreds or thousands of Windows 98 PCs simultaneously. It provides you with the capability to customize more than just the computer name and IP address during a mass Windows 98 installation. You are now able to create individualized installation scripts that can merge a template script file (such as the MsBatch.Inf formatted file) with a text-based database that contains the more specific user and computer information for each of the Windows 98 PCs that need to be installed.

- Clip (CLIP.EXE)—This is a command-line output redirector utility. Okay, in English, this means that you can redirect data directly from a DOS prompt command line into the Windows Clipboard. For example, the command Clip <win.ini> will automatically place a copy of all the text within the WIN.INI file directly on to the Windows Clipboard. This can be a useful utility for use with one of your own homegrown applications or batch files.

- Clipboard Buffer Tool (CLIPSTOR.EXE)—This utility permits you to store and organize multiple Windows Clipboards. As you know, Windows 98 presently only permits a single Clipboard in action at a time, so this utility gives you more flexibility when working with the Windows 98 Clipboard.

- Clipboard Organizer (CLIPTRAY.EXE)—This tool gives you the capability to better manage your Windows 98 Clipboard, which includes placing a small icon on the Windows 98 System Tray that gives you a menu-driven capability to access the titles of available ClipTray Entries from its centralized text file.

- Compound File Layout User Tool (DFLAYOUT.EXE)—This utility is also known as the Document File Layout tool, which is used to optimize documents to help lower transmission costs when you want to transmit them over a low bandwidth network or the Internet. This utility does not always work with every compound document but can be a space and time saver.

- Daylight Savings Time (TIMEZONE.EXE)—This utility permits you to update the Daylight Savings Time information inside the Windows 98 Registry.

- Default Printer (DEFPTR.EXE)—This permits you to quickly set the default printer for your Windows 98 installation. You are presented with a drop-down list box that contains all of the printers presently installed on your computer. Select the one you want and click the Commit button.

- Dependency Walker (DEPENDS.EXE)—The Dependency Walker utility is designed for those persons, such as software developers, who need to walk-through the execution process of 32-bit program modules found in an application. This tool also generates a tree-type diagram for all the dependent modules. It is quite a useful tool for debugging situations, as well as troubleshooting systems.

- Duplicate File Finder (DUPFINDER.EXE)—This tools does exactly what you might think it does: it finds all of the duplicate files on your Windows 98 computer. So, if you think you might have 12 copies of an old presentation scattered across your Windows 98 PC, this utility will find all of them and then you will be able to delete those extra copies (thus saving you hard drive space).

- Environment Setting Utility (WINSET.EXE)—This tool can be used at either a command-line prompt or via its scripting tool. It provides you with the capability to add, change, or delete global Windows 98 environment system variables on an as-needed basis.

- Error Message Translation (TRANSLATE.EXE)—This utility is useful for determining the meaning of a specific Windows 98 error message. This tool is run from a command line and will translate a Win32 error code into a more meaningful error message information string for your use.

- Finding the Executable Type (EXETYPE.EXE)—This interesting tool tells you what type of operating environment is required for a specific executable file. For example, if you ran it against the DBSET.EXE file (EXETYPE DBSET.EXE) you would learn that that file is a DOS executable file, which means that it will not run inside a Windows NT window (should you be thinking about using it on your Windows NT system). However, when you point this same tool at the WINSREPS.EXE file, you will learn that this file is actually a 32-bit Windows NT file that was built for the 80386 Intel processor and is capable of running under the Windows GUI subsystem (for example, Windows 98). As a software developer or network administrator, I can think of numerous practical uses for this utility.

- Expand for Windows (EXPAND.EXE)—If you have ever been in the predicament of needing to extract a single file from a Windows 98 .CAB file, this tool is required. With this utility, you can now grab that single file without needing to use one of the more formal Windows 98 means, such as re-running the SETUP.EXE file.

- FAT32 Conversion Information (FAT32WIN.EXE)—Wouldn't it be nice to know approximately how much space you would save by converting your computer over to the 32-bit file allocation table structure? This tool gives you precisely that capability, which now makes it easier for you to make a more intelligent decision on whether to use DriveSpace3 or FAT32 to gain more hard disk drive space on your computer.

- File and Directory Comparison (WINDIFF.EXE)—This utility compares the contents of both files and directories (folders), and then displays a report of the differences.

1.4
INSTALL THE WINDOWS 98 RESOURCE KIT

- File Compress (COMPRESS.EXE)—This utility allows you to compress one or more files at a DOS command-line prompt using a process similar to that of Nico Mak Computing's WinZip product.

- File Locating (WHERE.EXE)—If you cannot find a file you know you left somewhere on your hard drive, this command-line utility is for you. With a simple command and parameter(s), you can quickly discover the location of that long, lost file.

- File Version (FILEVER.EXE)—This command-line utility prints file version information onscreen (or you can capture this same information into either a file or onto a printer device).

- File Wise (FILEWISE.EXE)—This great GUI-based tool lets you know whether one of your files has become corrupted or changed in some way. It uses the CRC (Cyclic Redundancy Checking) key to test for these differences and permits you to report this information to a text file or place it on the Windows 98 Clipboard. This can be a useful tool when you are trying to figure out what files have changed between different versions of the same application, and what the differences might be between two otherwise identical PCs. This data also makes it possible to track different versions of resources that normally do not permit you to store version information on them.

- Free Disk Space (FREEDISK.EXE)—This command-line tool queries a specific hard disk drive to see if it has enough free disk space for you to use. This tool is useful in a batch installation program that first checks to see if there is enough free disk space before the application begins its installation process.

- GRE Protocol Troubleshooting (GREPING.EXE)—This tool does exactly what you might think: it permits you to troubleshoot the GRE protocol should you be having any difficulties in using it with a host computer (probably a UNIX machine). The host computer must have the GRESRVR.EXE tool (listening for GRE packets) running on it or this tool will not work.

- Image Editor (IMAGEDIT.EXE)—This tool is used to edit graphical or cursor image files. It works much in the same way that the Animated Cursor Editor works (see ANIEDIT.EXE).

- Internet Explorer Administration Kit (IEAK) Profile Manager (PROFMGR.EXE)—This tool helps to simplify the creation and ongoing maintenance required with a customized Internet Explorer configuration. You need to have a copy of the IEAK (available at no cost from Microsoft, but you will need to register to obtain a copy) to make use of this tool.

- Link Check Wizard (CHECKLINKS.EXE)—This tool searches for broken links within your desktop area and reports them to you, which then allows you to delete or fix those links (for example, Windows 98 system shortcuts).

- Log Time (LOGTIME.EXE)—This utility permits you to log the start and stop times for a specific command-line program that was started from within a batch file.

- Long Filename Backup Utility (LFNBACK.EXE)—This tool gives you the capability to back up the long filenames on your computer if you need to use it with a cloning tool, such as GHOST. Only the really old version of Clone—a free shareware utility—requires you to do this. If you do not first back up your long filenames then you will no longer have long filenames when you restore this cloned image file in your system.

- Microsoft Copy (MCOPY.EXE)—This tool allows you to copy files and keep a log file with a record of all those copy operations.

- Microsoft Batch 98 Automated Setup (BATCH.EXE)—This GUI-based tool is required for those individuals who are attempting mass installations of the Windows 98 operating system. You will be walked-through the creation process of the MSBATCH.INI file, which otherwise would be a very long and painstaking process.

- Microsoft Remote Procedure Call Print Provider (RPCPP)—This tool permits Windows 98 client PCs to administer print queues on Windows NT networks, provided of course, that the user of this tool has already been assigned the appropriate permissions from the Windows NT server administrator.

- Microsoft Remote Registry Service (REMOTREG)—This tool allows you access to view, modify, or edit the **Registry** of a remote PC that is running Windows 98 on a network. In order to use this tool, both the local and remote PCs must each be running the Remote Registry service, as well as having user-level security enabled on the computer that you are attempting to administer. To actually view or change the remote **Registry**, you must be using either the Windows 98 **Registry Editor** utility or the Windows 98 **System Policy Editor** tool.

- Minitel Emulation Files (MINITEL.TTF)—These are the Minitel font emulation files that are required for use with the Windows 98 HyperTerminal accessory, which emulates the look and feel of a Minitel terminal. It does seem strange that Microsoft did not include these files with the base Windows 98 installation, although it is possible to use the Arial Alternative font as a replacement instead.

1.4 INSTALL THE WINDOWS 98 RESOURCE KIT

- MS-DOS Code Page Changer (CHDOSCP.EXE)—This tool allows you to change the code page for MS-DOS applications so that those programs will match the Windows 98 regional settings. If you do not use multiple languages with your Windows 98 PC, you will probably never need to use this utility.

- Multiple Language Boot (WINBOOT.EXE)—This utility gives you the capability to boot into different language versions of Windows 98 based on those that have already been installed on your computer system. You can also use the tool as a facilitator for installing new language versions of Windows 98 on your computer. Again, if you do not use multiple languages with your Windows 98 PC then you will probably never need to use this utility.

- Network Monitor Agent and Protocol Driver (NMAGENT.EXE)—This is a Windows 98 service that works with the networking protocols to provide access to network traffic information on Windows 98 client computers. It works in conjunction with the NetBIOS networking protocol, which must also be enabled on the client PCs.

- Now (NOW.EXE)—A command-line utility that displays a message with a time and date stamp. You will most likely use this tool from within a batch file, but the options are not limited to just this type of usage.

- OLE/COM Object Viewer (OLEVIEW.EXE)—This is a very useful GUI-based tool that allows you to browse, configure, test, and activate COM classes on your Windows 98 PC. Windows 98 software developers will enjoy this tool the most, but system administrators can definitely find some uses for this tool as well.

- Password List Editor (PWLEDIT.EXE)—This utility gives you the capability to remove existing saved password lists from your Windows 98 password list file (that is, the passwords that were cached by the user at one time or another).

- Power Toys (TweakUI)—This is probably the most used tool within the Windows 98 Resource Kit. It permits anyone to modify their Windows 98 desktop, including the capability to place the Windows 98 version number directly on a Classic Desktop setting. All the Windows 98 Registry areas of the GUI are exposed with this tool, making it very safe and easy for you to change settings without ever having to enter the Windows 98 Registry directly.

- Quick Launch Express (QLE.EXE)—This is a customizable tool that runs from inside the Windows 98 system tray area and permits you to access your commonly-used applications quickly and efficiently. It can quickly access Internet Explorer tools, the Control Panel, and the Windows 98 system tools.

- Regina REXX Scripting Language (REXX.EXE)—This is a full REXX scripting language that includes access to the Windows 98 Registry, various event log functions, and full OLE automation support. This is a great tool, especially for people who are comfortable with the OS/2 operating system scripting environment.

- ScanReg.Ini Editing (SREDIT.EXE)—This tool permits you to override certain configuration settings within the Windows 98 ScanReg system tool.

- Server Time Synchronization (NETTIME.EXE)—This is a command-line, time-zone independent tool that gives you the capability to set the time on multiple servers simultaneously (that is, you can now synchronize the time stamps on multiple servers from a Windows 98 batch file).

- String Search (FINDSTR.EXE)—This utility allows you to search and find strings within files. This can be a very useful tool when attempting to debug batch files.

- System File Information (FILEINFO.EXE)—This is version 5.0 of this utility, which gives you far more information than the System File Information capability found within the base Windows 98 operating system. Through tabbed screens you are able to quickly discover detailed information about files on your computer system, including what .CAB file it was installed from (if applicable), its local destination, the file date and uncompressed size, and so on. I find this to be a very useful tool when attempting to determine the origin of unknown files on my computer system.

- System Policy Editor (POLEDIT.EXE)—This utility is used to create specific administrative policies for your Windows 98 computer and its users. It works just like the one provided with Windows NT, in case you are familiar with that operating system's policy editor.

- System Stress Testing (CREATEFILE.EXE)—This tool permits you to create an empty file of any size for the purpose of stress testing your computer system. In the hands of the wrong kind of user it can be used to easily crash your computer system, server(s), and network, so do not leave a copy of this utility out for anyone to readily access.

- System Tray (QUIKTRAY.EXE)—This utility permits you to organize the application icons that presently appear in the Windows 98 system tray. This includes the capability to add new applications as well as delete old ones.

1.4 INSTALL THE WINDOWS 98 RESOURCE KIT

- System Troubleshooting (MSCONFIG.EXE)—This tool works like the one provided within the base Windows 98 operating system, and it gives you the capability to automate routine troubleshooting steps when you need to diagnose problems with your Windows 98 PC.

- Task Killing (KILL.EXE)—This utility allows you to end or *kill* any active task by specifying the Process ID (PID) number for that specific Windows 98 task. To figure out the proper task or PID number, you will use the Task List Viewer (TLIST.EXE) Resource Kit tool. This tool is useful for halting those programs that do not appear in the standard Windows 98 Close Program utility screen.

- Task List Viewer (TLIST.EXE)—This tool is usually used as a predecessor to the KILL.EXE utility because it gives you a complete listing of the active tasks and processes on your Windows 98 computer system. This is a command-line utility that shows a list comprised of three columns: the PID number, the active filename of the task or process, and a descriptive name of that task or process (where available).

- Text Editor (LIST.EXE)—This is a DOS-based utility that is useful for editing text files. It is comparable to the EDIT.COM utility that is built into the Windows 98 operating system.

- Text Viewer (TEXTVIEW.EXE)—This GUI tool provides you with the capability to quickly scan text files using a Windows Explorer-like interface.

- Time This (TIMETHIS.EXE)—This is a command-line utility that you can use to determine how long your system takes to completely execute a single, specific command.

- Time Zone Utility (TZEDIT.EXE)—This GUI-based utility permits you to create or edit time zone entries that appear in the Date/Time option of the Windows 98 Control Panel.

- USB Device Troubleshooter (USBVIEW.EXE)—A GUI-based utility that gives you the capability to display configuration information for USB (Universal Serial Bus) devices that are already installed on your Windows 98 PC.

- User Input for Batch Files (CHOICE.EXE)—This utility gives you the capability to prompt users for input from inside a Windows 98 batch file.

- UUdecode and UUencode Utility, 32-bit (UUCODE.EXE)—This GUI-based utility permits you to encode and decode files according to the UUencoding standard. If you are using a fairly powerful email application, such as Microsoft Exchange or the Microsoft Outlook client software, you will not need to perform manual UUencoding or UUdecoding. However, if you are attempting to send files back and forth between a non-Windows system (such as UNIX, for example) via an FTP process, you might want to use this type of utility.

- Wait For (WAITFOR.EXE)—This command-line scripting utility gives you the capability to force your Windows 98 computer to wait for a signal to be sent over your organization's network. However, each Windows 98 PC is limited to just a single `WaitFor` command at any one time.

- Windows 98 Adapter Card Help (W98CARD.HLP)—This help file is an excellent way to supplement your network, SCSI, and sound card adapters' documentation. It provides very detailed technical information for these types of hardware devices including interrupt numbers (IRQ), I/O base, RAM base addresses, and the like, as well as providing you with some very good illustrations that show the location for jumper settings on each of the cards.

- Windows 98 Hardware Compatibility List (HCL.EXE)—This copy of the Windows 98 Hardware Compatibility List is obviously not as up-to-date as the one on Microsoft's Internet Web site, but then again it is more easily accessible by you. This file does not automatically install with the rest of the Windows 98 Resource Kit; instead you must manually access it by going to the \Diagnose\HCL subfolder on the CD-ROM and then double-click the HCL.EXE file to begin using the listing. You can always copy it over to your hard drive, but it does require more than 10MB of hard disk drive space.

- Windows 98 SNMP Service (SNMP Agent)—This utility enables your Windows 98 PC to communicate on SNMP (Simple Network Management Protocol) networks. If you do not have an SNMP network established, installing this agent is a waste of your time and system resources.

- Windows Boot Editor (BOOTEDIT.EXE)—This GUI-based tool provides you with an excellent way in which to modify the Windows 98 boot process. It walks you through the various means to modify the boot process, without having to make you directly modify either your system's `Registry` or the MSDOC.SYS file. If you were to make any mistakes in the direct editing of either of those two areas, you could easily disable or destroy your implementation of Windows 98.

- Windows Report Tool (WINREP)—This is one of my favorite GUI tools because it gives you the capability to report problems with Windows 98 via the Internet to Microsoft. If you happen to see a repeatable bug in the Windows 98 operating system, you now have a means in which to effectively report this bug to Microsoft (which appears to fix things that are reported).

- Windows Report Tool Software Development Kit (WINREP SDK)—This tool provides you with the documentation and the capability to extend the functionality of the Windows Report tool so that you can use it within your own organization. For example, you would be able to create a system so that your Windows 98 users could have a quick and easy way of submitting requests for technical support (from either a third party or your corporate Help Desk). Because this tool does not automatically install with the standard Windows 98 Resource Kit, you will need to access the \Diagnose\WinRep subfolder on the CD-ROM in order to actually install this SDK.

- Windows Scripting Host—Documentation and sample scripts, along with a Programmer's Reference Guide can also be found on the Windows 98 Resource Kit CD-ROM. These tools are made for those individuals who want to extend the functionality and flexibility of the Windows Scripting Host tool that comes built into the base Windows 98 operating system.

One thing you might notice right away is that Microsoft has duplicated some of the tools you find in the Resource Kit with those that are now available directly inside the base Windows 98 operating system. This is a good thing for most everyone because you might now have better support mechanisms for these tools (since Microsoft does typically not support Resource Kit utilities). If you are the user of a single Windows 98 PC, you no longer need to purchase the Resource Kit now that you see many of the standalone-type utilities are being provided directly in the Windows 98 operating system itself (such as the MSConfig and Msinfo32 utilities).

COMPLEXITY
BEGINNER

1.5 How do I...
Use the Windows update process?

Problem

Quite frequently, Microsoft will post updates to its Windows 98 operating system to its Internet Web site. Individual Windows 98 users, as well as corporate system administrators responsible for thousands of computers will want at least some of these updates. The problem is how do you access them? Also, if you have either physically moved or changed your email address, how do you update your information with Microsoft so that you continue to get updated information regarding your Windows 98 software purchase?

Technique

The process is easy, after you have done it the first time. It requires a connection to the Internet, either dial-up or a direct connection (the high-speed connection is preferred, obviously) and the use of an Internet Web browser (the version of Microsoft's Internet Explorer that is integrated into the Windows 98 OS is preferred, but Netscape works as well). Then, follow the steps as outlined here.

Steps

1. Connect to the Internet via a Dial-Up Networking connection or a LAN/WAN direct connection.

2. To access the initial Microsoft Windows 98 Update Web site, either click the Windows Update menu option installed on your initial Start menu, as shown in Figure 1.18, or click the Windows Update menu option that Windows 98 installed in the \Start \Settings menu, as shown in Figure 1.19.

Figure 1.18 The Windows Update menu selection on the main Windows 98 Start menu bar.

1.5
USE THE WINDOWS UPDATE PROCESS

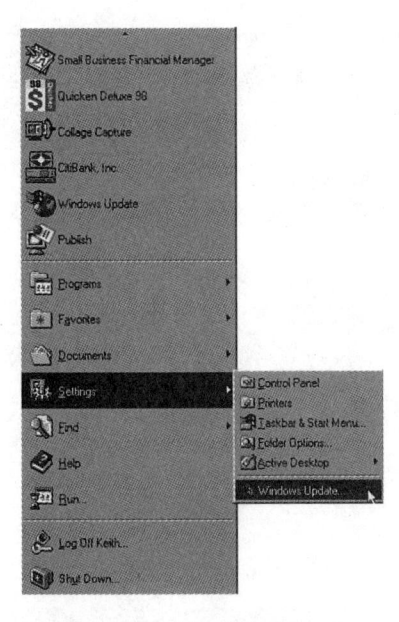

Figure 1.19 The Windows Update menu selection from the Settings menu selection.

3. The third way to access the site is the old-fashioned way: type in the correct URL (uniform resource locator) Web address of `http://windowsupdate.microsoft.com/` as shown in Figure 1.20.

4. After you have arrived at the Web site, you will notice a series of tabs along the left-hand side (Windows Update Home Page, Product Updates, and Member Services). These tabs control access to the entire site and can be used as a place to quickly jump to another location on the Web site. For example, if you have moved and need to update your physical (your home) or logical (email) address with Microsoft, then you would click the Member Services tab; this causes the tab to expand with other selections. Next, you click the Update Your Information selection, as shown in Figure 1.21.

5. The Update Your Information frame appears where you click the Update My Registration arrow-shaped button at the bottom of the screen, and the Microsoft Windows 98 Registration wizard appears, as shown in Figure 1.22.

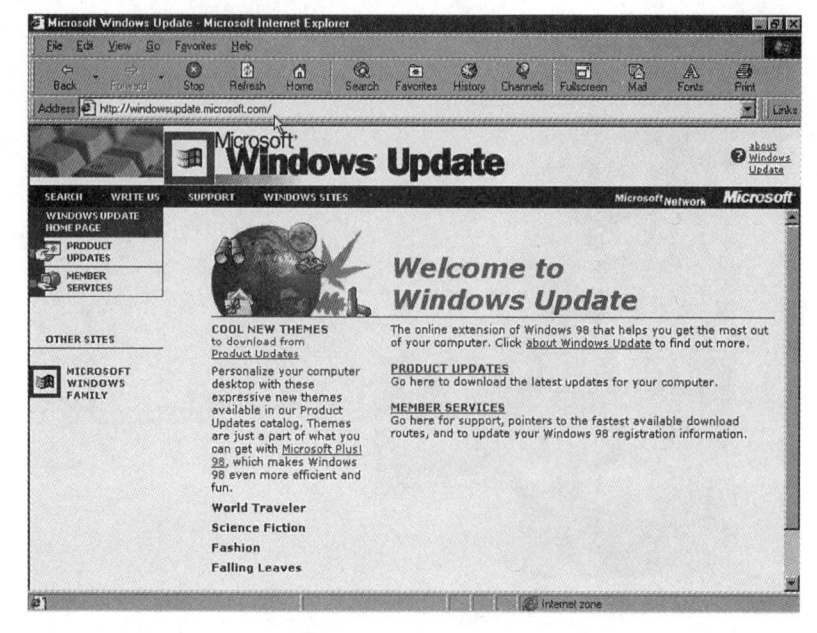

Figure 1.20 The Microsoft Windows Update home page.

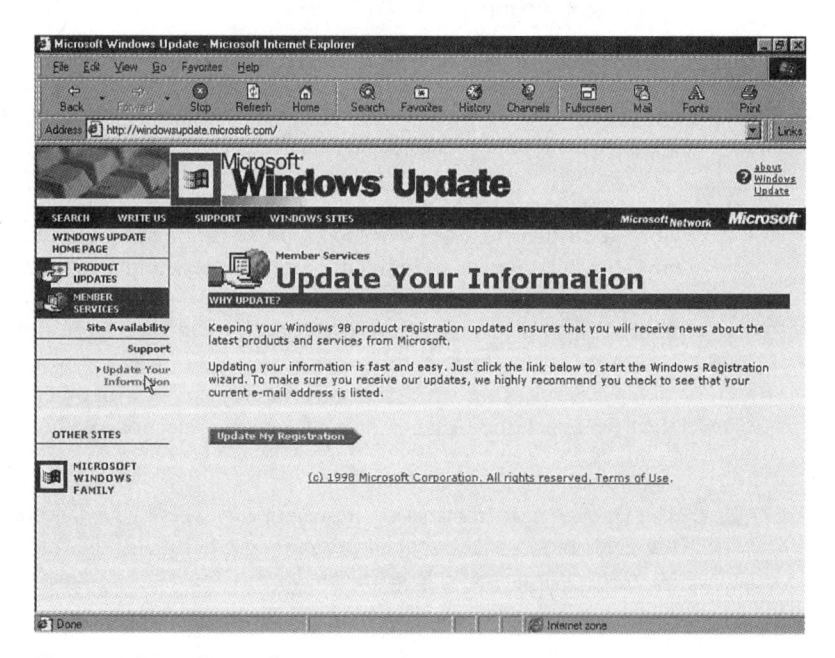

Figure 1.21 The Update Your Information Web page.

1.5
USE THE WINDOWS UPDATE PROCESS

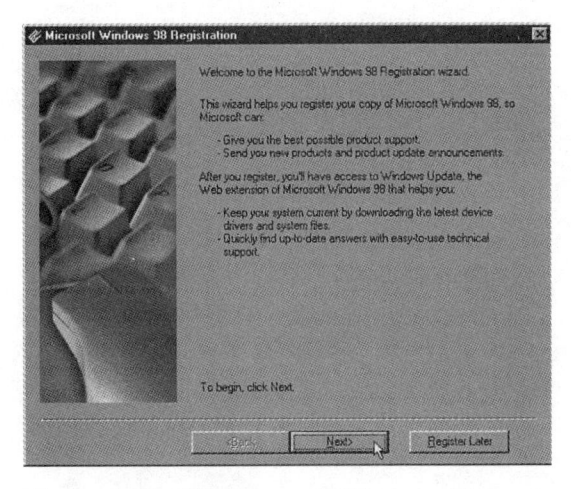

Figure 1.22 The Microsoft Windows 98 Registration wizard.

6. This first screen contains basic information, so read it and then click the Next> button to continue the update process, as shown in Figure 1.23.

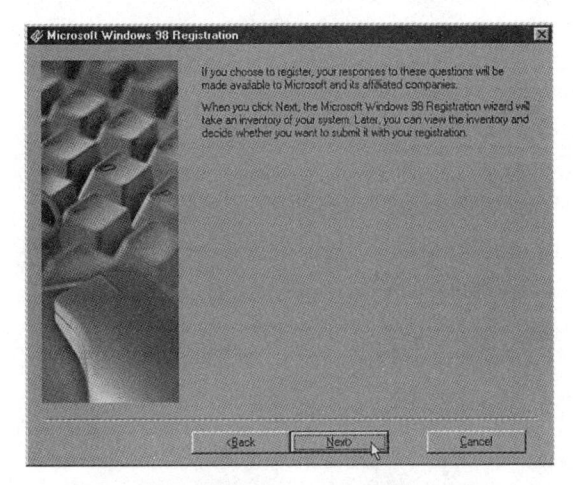

Figure 1.23 The Microsoft Windows 98 Registration wizard information screen.

7. This screen acts as if you have not registered your copy of Windows 98 yet, but you probably have. Click the Next> button to continue the update process, as shown in Figure 1.24.

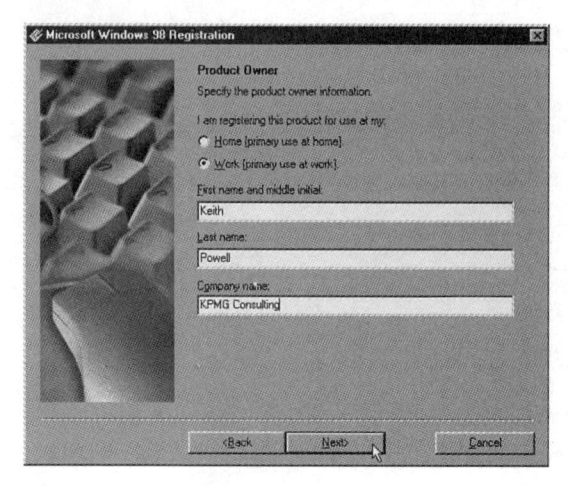

Figure 1.24 The Microsoft Windows 98 Registration wizard product owner information screen.

8. If you have already registered your copy, this screen already contains all your information. Change the pertinent information, if any, and click the Next> button to continue the update process as shown in Figure 1.25.

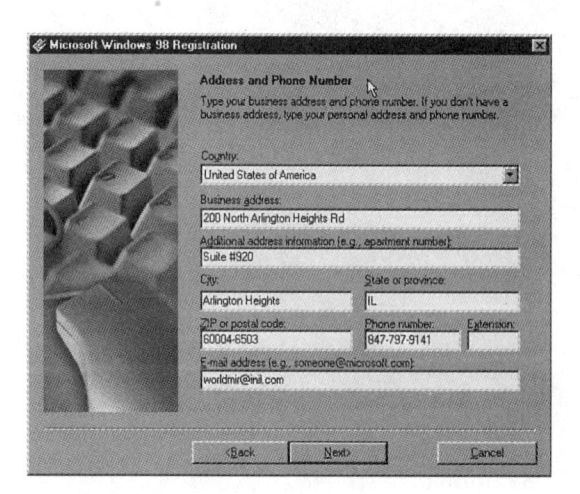

Figure 1.25 The Microsoft Windows 98 Registration Wizard product owner's address update screen.

1.5 USE THE WINDOWS UPDATE PROCESS

9. Again, this screen should already contain your information. Examine your physical address and the email address to ensure these fields contain the correct data. Change any appurtenant information, and then click Next> to continue the update process as shown in Figure 1.26.

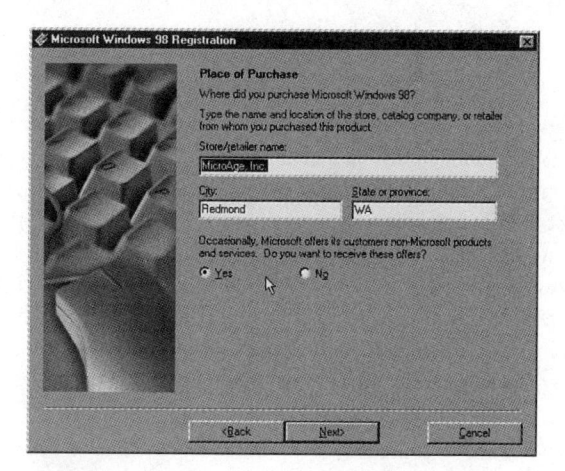

Figure 1.26 The Microsoft Windows 98 Registration Place of Purchase information screen.

10. Again, this screen should contain your purchasing information. Change any data you feel necessary, including whether you still want to receive the additional snail mail and email updates from Microsoft. When you have completed this screen, click Next> to move to the next screen in the update process as shown in Figure 1.27.

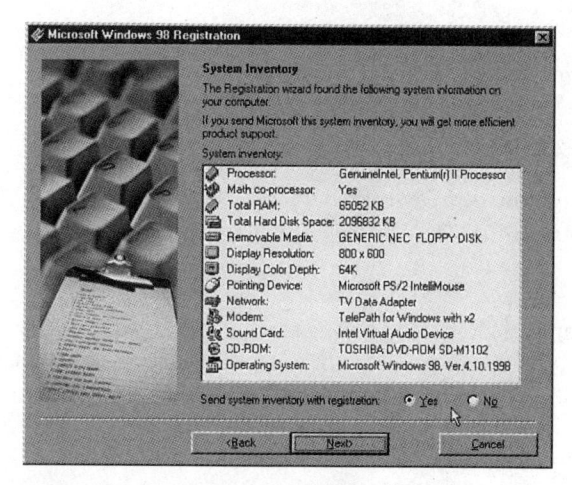

Figure 1.27 The Microsoft Windows 98 Registration Wizard System Inventory screen.

CHAPTER 1
INSTALLATION TIPS

11. The System Inventory screen appears. This screen presents a nice accounting of the physical structure of your computer, with the exception of the Total Hard Drive Space (this function does not work correctly, as it appears unable to recognize FAT32 drives over 2GB in size). For further details on FAT32, refer to the FAT32 topics in Chapter 6, "Disk Drive Management and Use." The only choice you have here is whether you want to send a copy to Microsoft. I always say yes, as it helps, should you ever need to call Microsoft's Windows 98-product support. However, for users who purchased Windows 98 from an OEM manufacturer (for example, if Windows 98 came preinstalled on your Gateway, Dell, or Compaq, computer), you are ineligible for direct Windows 98 support from Microsoft. It is recommended that you keep your own copy of this screen and not share it with Microsoft. This does not mean that you cannot download updated files from Microsoft or use the Windows Update screens. It means that you cannot call Microsoft's 800 number for technical Windows 98 support and expect to be given it at no cost; you should be calling your OEM dealer for this type of advanced support. Change your selection, if you want, and then click Next> to proceed to the next screen in the update process as shown in Figure 1.28.

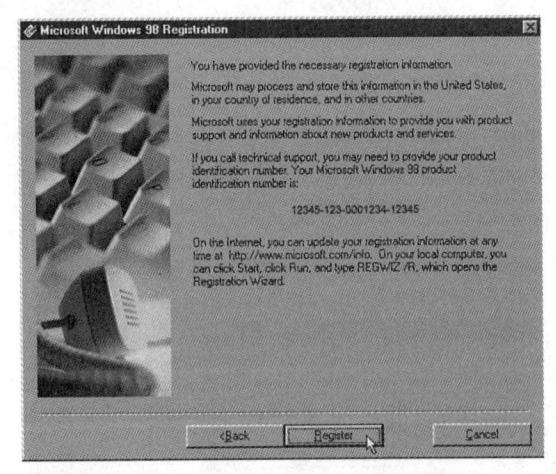

Figure 1.28 The Microsoft Windows 98 Registration wizard product ID information screen.

12. It is recommended that you print a copy of this screen or write down your Windows 98 product identification number somewhere handy, because this is the number you will need should you ever need to contact Microsoft's product support lines. After you have documented your number, click the Register button to continue update process as shown in Figure 1.29.

1.5
USE THE WINDOWS UPDATE PROCESS

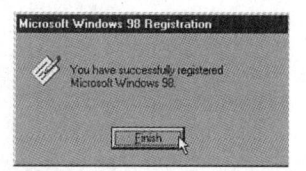

Figure 1.29 The Microsoft Windows 98 Registration wizard is complete.

13. That's it! The registration update process is complete. Now it is time to proceed to the real core of the Windows Update Web site: the actual Windows 98 application software update area. To get there, first click the Finish button to get rid of the Microsoft Windows 98 Registration complete message box. Next click the Product Updates tab, located on the main Windows Update Web site as shown in Figure 1.30.

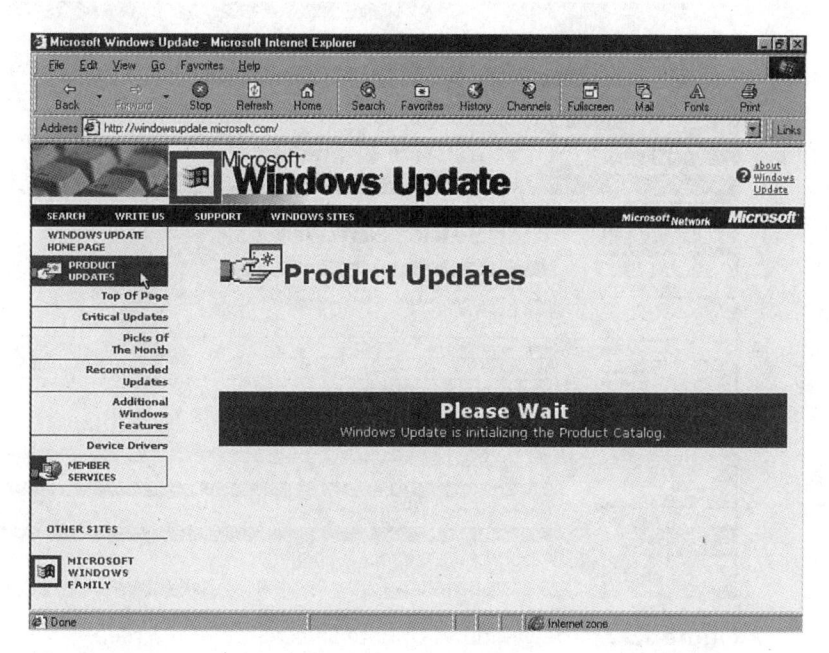

Figure 1.30 The Windows 98 Product Updates catalog screen.

14. It takes a few seconds for the Product Catalog page to initialize, and it might take longer if this is your first visit to the Web site. Be patient and eventually the Windows Update message box appears, as shown in Figure 1.31.

CHAPTER 1
INSTALLATION TIPS

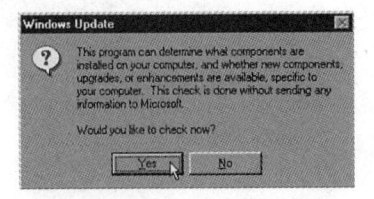

Figure 1.31 The Windows Update dialog box.

15. It is strongly recommended that you reply Yes to the question asked, "Would you like to check now?" as this will permit a more accurate updating of your installation of Windows 98. Obviously, if you are hoping to access an update for use with many computers, you might want to click No and skip this step. In the example presented, I have clicked Yes, which reveals the screen shown in Figure 1.32.

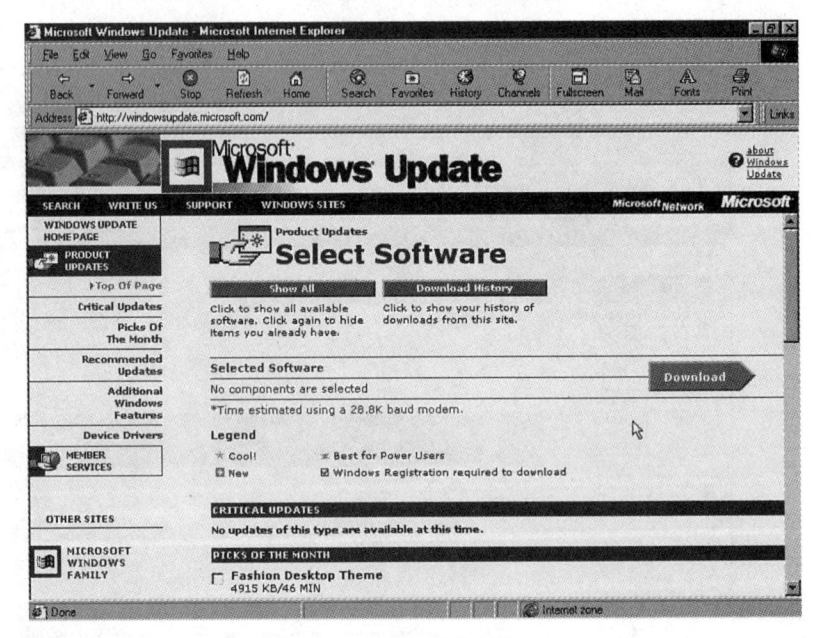

Figure 1.32 The Windows Update Select Software screen.

16. Actually, the screen that appears will be similar in both appearance and content even if you had responded negatively to the question in step 15. Scroll down the screen and select the components that you want to add to your Windows 98 installation, by clicking the check box located to the left of each selection. The Microsoft Web site automatically presents an

1.5
USE THE WINDOWS UPDATE PROCESS

estimated download time for you, so you can judge how long these selections will take. When you have finished making all of your choices, scroll down to the bottom of the screen to review the totals (both size and time) as shown in Figure 1.33.

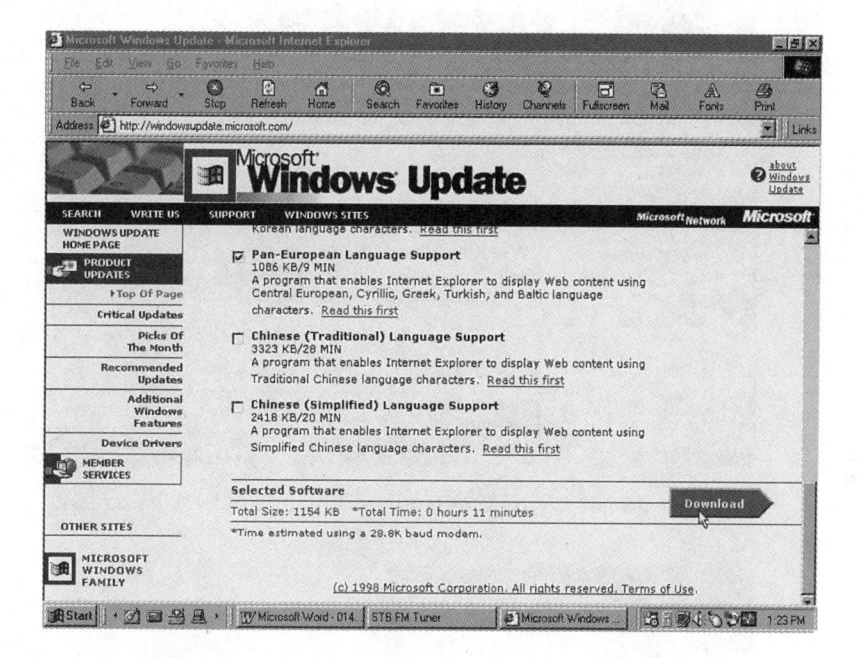

Figure 1.33 The bottom half of the Windows Update Select Software screen.

17. I have made three selections: the Microsoft Active Accessibility Update (61KB/1 minute); the Internet Connection Wizard Phone Book Update (7KB/1 minute); and the Pan-European Language Support (1,086KB/9 minutes). If these are acceptable to you, click the Download button (refer to Figure 1.33) to initiate the download process shown in Figure 1.34.

18. Again, Microsoft attempts to confirm your choices. If they are correct, click the Start Download button (see Figure 1.34) to initiate the download process shown in Figure 1.35.

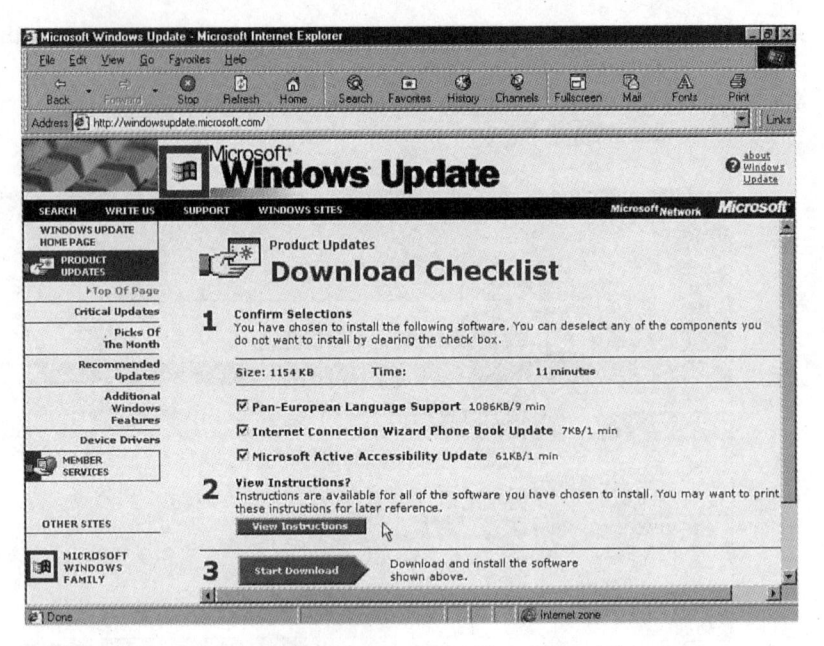

Figure 1.34 The Windows Update Download Checklist screen.

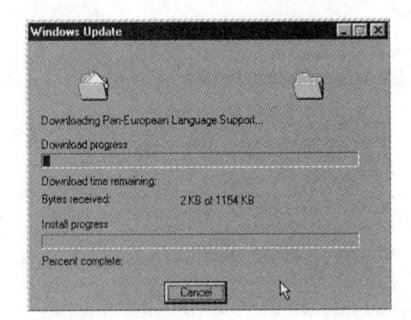

Figure 1.35 The Windows Updates software download progress bar message box.

19. Be patient. This process goes very slow at times, much slower than the actual possible speed of your Internet connection. If the process is more painful than you imagined, click Cancel to terminate the download. This will permit you to try a smaller download instead or nothing at all. After the download and installation process has completed and Microsoft Update has automatically applied the patches to your system, a confirmation message box appears as shown in Figure 1.36. Click OK to finish the download process.

USE THE WINDOWS UPDATE PROCESS

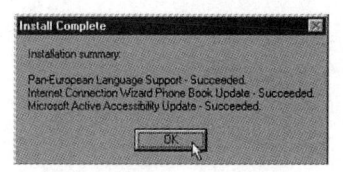

Figure 1.36 The Windows Updates Software Install Complete message box.

20. Of course the greatest Microsoft operating system "bug" will probably appear: the request to reboot your computer in order to finish the process, as shown in Figure 1.37. This request is normally done to facilitate the installation of new files that have older versions currently running, but in the case of nearly all Windows 98 Windows Updates, you will be forced to restart your computer even if no older versions were running or even installed on your computer.

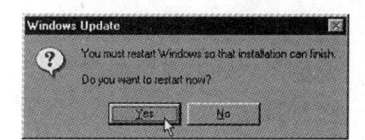

Figure 1.37 The Windows Update restart message box.

21. What choice do you really have here? None. It is strongly recommended that you close down everything else you are working on and allow the operating system to reboot. Failure to do so might result in a patch being applied incorrectly. After the system has restarted itself, the Windows Update process is considered complete. That is all you need to do each time!

CHAPTER 2
DESKTOP USAGE AND TIPS

2

DESKTOP USAGE AND TIPS

How do I...

- **2.1 Know which desktop to use: the Active Desktop or the Classic Desktop ?**
- **2.2 Configure the Windows 98 Classic Desktop?**
- **2.3 Configure the Windows 98 Active Desktop?**
- **2.4 Add or remove system icons from my Desktop?**
- **2.5 Find and remove useless links on my desktop or Start menu?**
- **2.6 Change the default view of the My Computer Windows Explorer to explore instead of open?**
- **2.7 Place the Recent Documents folder directly on My desktop?**
- **2.8 Create a toolbar that shows all the physical drive devices?**
- **2.9 Open a DOS window with a quick keystroke?**
- **2.10 Hide all the icons on a Windows 98 desktop?**
- **2.11 Change the opening or execution of desktop icons to a Single-Click mode?**

CHAPTER 2
DESKTOP USAGE AND TIPS

This chapter covers the Windows 98 desktop environment, including both the Classic and Active Desktop modes. The Classic mode is the version of the desktop that was first introduced with Windows 95, whereas the Active Desktop mode is the Internet-ized version of the desktop that came with the integration of the Microsoft Internet Explorer browser directly into the features of the Classic Windows desktop. Also included in this chapter are additional tips on how to customize one's desktop areas, how to hide icons on a Windows 98 desktop, and a quick entry mode into a DOS window.

2.1 Know Which Desktop to Use: the Active Desktop or the Classic Desktop
The purpose of this How-To is to help you figure out which version of the Windows 98 is best in your environment.

2.2 Configure the Windows 98 Classic Desktop
This How-To shows you exactly how to configure the Windows 98 Classic desktop, which most closely resembles the original Windows 95 desktop environment.

2.3 Configure the Windows 98 Active Desktop
This How-To shows you exactly how to configure the Windows 98 Active desktop, which most closely resembles the Internet Explorer 4.x Add-on to the Windows 95 desktop environment.

2.4 Add or Remove System Icons from My Desktop
There will be times when you do not want system icons shown on your Windows 98 desktop. This topic demonstrates how to add or remove these types of icons from your Windows 98 desktop.

2.5 Find and Remove Useless Links on My Desktop or Start Menu
When you start installing and subsequently removing software products on to and from your Windows 98 PC, you will inevitably create orphaned or dead links. This How-To walks you through the available options for finding and removing useless links (Windows 98 shortcuts).

2.6 Change the Default View of the My Computer Windows Explorer to Explore Instead of Open
This How-To explains the intricacies involved when you want to change your Windows Explorer views by altering the state of file types on your Windows 98 PC.

2.7 Place the Recent Documents Folder Directly on My Desktop

This How-To explains how to move your Recent Documents folder to another location on your Windows 98 PC.

2.8 Create a Toolbar that Shows All the Physical Drive Devices

This How-To explains the toolbar creation process.

2.9 Open a DOS Window with a Quick Keystroke

This How-To shows you how to create a special quick-stroke for opening a DOS window. For the non-developers in the crowd you might want to skip this section, because if you are not always using a DOS prompt within Windows 98 then creating this is definitely overkill for your system.

2.10 Hide All the Icons on a Windows 98 Desktop

There will be times when you do not want any icons to be shown on your Windows 98 desktop. This topic demonstrates how to hide all types of icons from your Windows 98 desktop.

2.11 Change the Opening or Execution of Desktop Icons to a Single-Click Mode

The focus of this How-To is to change the execution process of icons on your Windows 98 desktop.

COMPLEXITY
INTERMEDIATE

2.1 How do I...
Know which desktop to use: the Active Desktop or the Classic Desktop?

Problem

Windows 98 offers the end user or the network system administrator two primary methods in which to present the Windows 98 desktop display. General users can easily manipulate the many settings and switches to personalize his or her work or play environments, to the extent of actually creating multiple configurations. The LAN administrator is able to control the Windows 98 desktop using system and group policies that are set from a Windows NT

Server (running at least at version 4.0). Either way, the basic questions of which base desktop to use still needs to be decided on. Should you use the old-fashioned, Windows 95 look and feel of the Classic Desktop or should you jump into the Internet-focused Windows 98 Active Desktop?

Technique

Foremost you need to understand the differences between the Active and Classic Desktop modes. We'll examine the Active Desktop first. The reason that this desktop mode is called *active* is that it permits you to place active content directly on top of it. This active content might originate from an Internet Web page or channel or it might consist of an HTML file that you created yourself. A popular idea for active content is a stock ticker, perhaps from your companyís intranet site, which keeps your business users informed of the status of the companyís stock price. Active Desktops tend to be very graphical in nature, which in turn leads to an increased need for system resources. This last item should put a red flag in your mind: The more system resources that are required for maintaining an Active Desktop, the more financial resources you will probably have to pour into your usersí desktop computer systems.

The Classic Desktop mode is the one that exactly resembles the original Windows 95 desktop. When it was introduced in August 1995, it was quite a revolutionary spin from the old Windows Program Manager interface. However, as time drags on, this interface is the same as it was when it was introduced four years ago. Now, most users probably don't care because they view their PCs as tools for getting their jobs done and not as a personal statement of their creativity. If there is little or no Internet or intranet connectivity required, then the need for a Classic-styled desktop becomes obvious: You do not require the Active Desktop, so the Classic Desktop fits your needs.

This does not mean that users of the Classic Desktop cannot customize their desktops in creative ways, it simply means that they cannot channel Internet-based information directly through their desktop schemes. You can still set a funky background color and picture with various sound events and colors. That is not limited by either Desktop mode: Active or Classic.

Next, you will need to breakdown the user community into segments by work function, and then analyze each one to determine their PC working requirements. Then determine the amount (if any) of Internet and intranet activity for each group, because the Windows 98 Active Desktop features are focused on these two areas. Finally, analyze the hardware capabilities of the PC that is running Windows 98, being sure to take into consideration the network across which the Active Desktop features will be accessing its data. Having done all that, you then need to compare the needs of each user group with the features and benefits that the Active Desktop offers to determine whether its use will be beneficial for each group of users.

Steps

1. Make a listing of all the users within your working environment. If this decision is being made for a single PC, you will probably finish quickly. If you are a home PC user then you are the only one on the list. Therefore, you should use these steps to walk yourself through the decision process on which desktop mode to choose.

2. On the list created in the preceding step, create a column where you will check-off whether this PC requires some type of Internet or intranet connectivity.

3. If no Internet or intranet connectivity is necessary or desired, the Classic Desktop is most likely the choice for that PC. Type No next to each of these users.

4. If the user identified as a No in step 3 wants flashy graphics that move, shake, and make sounds then make that person a Yes because only Active Desktop permits the use of those types of things.

5. Otherwise, leave your list as is and you will have a complete listing of those computers that will be utilizing the features offered by the Windows 98 Active Desktop. Additionally, computers that require the Windows 98 Classic Desktop operating environment will also be noted.

6. If your version of Windows 98 was installed with the Active Desktop, follow the steps in section 2.2, "How do I Configure the Windows 98 Classic Desktop?" for returning to the Classic Desktop configuration. Otherwise, use the steps in section 2.3, "How do I Configure the Windows 98 Active Desktop?" to configure the Windows 98 Active Desktop.

7. To get a better idea on how to automate this desktop selection process during the Windows 98 installation process, you might want to review Chapter 1, "Installation Tips." Also, you should examine the Windows 98 Resource Kit, paying particular attention to the Batch 98 and the Profile Manager utilities that come with the kit (available from Microsoft Press).

COMPLEXITY
BEGINNER

2.2 How do I...
Configure the Windows 98 Classic Desktop settings?

Problem
I want to configure my Windows 98 desktop environment with the old Windows 95 look and feel. Can I do this without getting rid of Windows 98 and going back to Windows 95?

Technique
Windows 98 provides a simple manner to avoid using the new Active Desktop feature that installs with the Windows 98 operating system. This How To section guides you from start to finish.

Steps

1. Start Windows 98 by booting all the way in to the GUI. The desktop environment you see is the one that you selected (or had selected for you by your organizationís Desktop Support personnel) during the Windows 98 installation process. You will probably see the standard Windows 98 Active Desktop environment, as shown in Figure 2.1.

> **NOTE**
> For 99 percent of the people who use Windows 98, they will always want to go directly into the Windows 98 graphical user interface. However, for the other one percent, you should know that it is possible to boot to a Windows 98 DOS Prompt, just like in the old Windows 286/3.x/DOS worlds of long ago. This means that you will be required to type in the command `win` to actually enter the Windows 98 GUI working environment. Please review Chapter 3, "The Boot Process," for more details.

2. Click once with the alternative mouse button on an open area of the screen (for example, not on any of the icons, HTML pages, shortcuts, and so on) to reveal the desktop options pop-up menu, as shown in Figure 2.2.

2.2 CONFIGURE THE WINDOWS 98 CLASSIC DESKTOP SETTINGS

Figure 2.1 The Windows 98 Active Desktop.

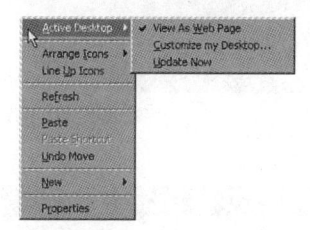

Figure 2.2 Desktop options pop-up menu.

> **NOTE**
>
> The *primary* mouse button is the left button for right-handed users, and the right button for left-handed users. Whereas the *secondary* mouse button is the right button for right-handed users, and the left button for left-handed users. The terms primary and secondary are used throughout this book, because this is the proper terminology for mouse buttons instead of assuming that everyone in the world is right-handed.

3. The top-most option is the Active Desktop. Placing the mouse pointer on this option reveals a side menu that has the View As Web Page menu selection. If there is a check mark to the left of this selection, you know that your PC has the Active Desktop feature enabled. If there is no check mark then obviously the opposite is true.

CHAPTER 2
DESKTOP USAGE AND TIPS

4. To disable the Active Desktop shown previously, click the View As Web Page menu selection to remove the existing check mark. This causes Windows 98 to revert to its Windows 95 look and feel, as seen in Figure 2.3.

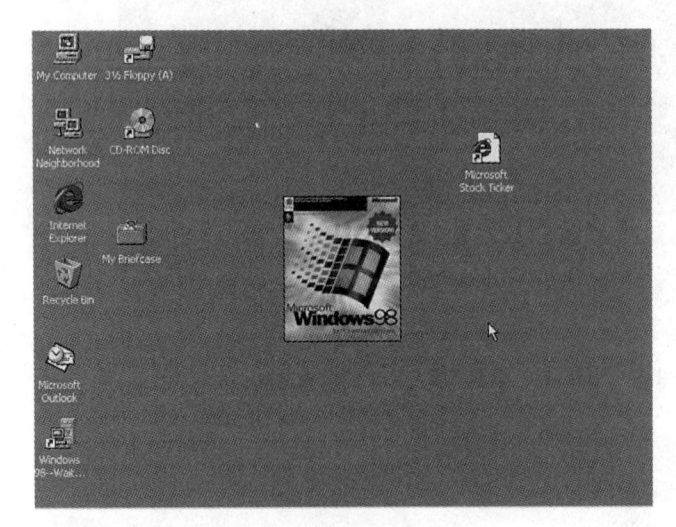

Figure 2.3 The Windows 98 Classic Desktop.

> **NOTE**
>
> Notice that not only has the revolving globe with the Windows 98 logo been removed, the Channels Bar is missing as well. If you want the Channels Bar to remain, you must maintain the Active Desktop environment. Likewise, note that the Microsoft Stock Ticker shortcut is still visible, meaning that you can continue to have shortcuts that can take a user directly to a Web site without incurring the extra hardware overhead (increased hard disk space and system memory resources) that the Active Desktop requires.

2.3 How do I...
Configure the Windows 98 Active Desktop?

COMPLEXITY: **BEGINNER**

Problem

My version of Windows 98 was installed with the old Windows 95 look and feel of the Classic Desktop. How do I do convert this to the Active Desktop?

Technique

Windows 98 allows for a quick changeover to the Active Desktop feature. This How To section demonstrates the steps required to utilize the Windows 98 Active Desktop.

Steps

1. Start Windows 98 by booting all the way in to the GUI so that the Classic Desktop environment appears.

2. Click once with the secondary mouse button on any open part of the desktop, this causes a small pop-up menu to appear as shown in Figure 2.4.

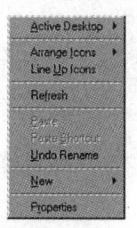

Figure 2.4 The Windows 98 pop-up desktop menu.

3. At the top of the menu is an option for the Active Desktop. Click on this option once for another submenu to appear as shown in Figure 2.5.

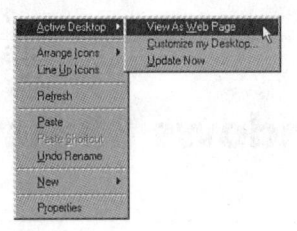

Figure 2.5 The Active Desktop submenu.

4. By again selecting View As Web Page, you effectively change your desktop from the Classic view to the Active view, as shown in Figure 2.6.

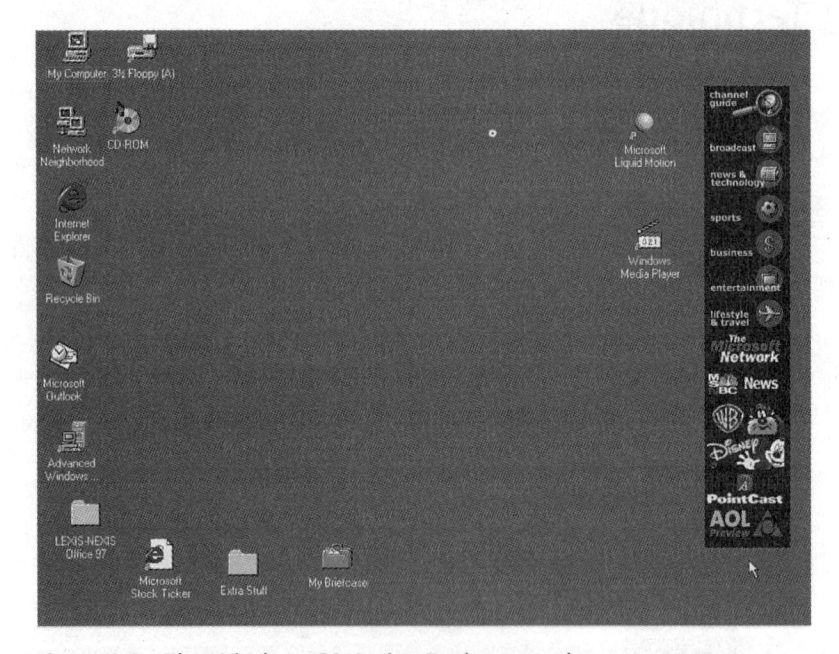

Figure 2.6 The Windows 98 Active Desktop mode.

> **NOTE**
>
> There are two things to note here. First, in the lower-right corner of the Classic Desktop screen you can see the current version of your Windows 98 installation. Obviously, in today's world most everyone has the same version, so this might not be anything exciting. However, as updates are produced, either in the form of OEM releases or actual service packs, these tidbits of information might prove useful to system and network administrators. Second, the Classic Desktop view appears to be flat compared to the multidimensional Active Desktop format. This is partly due to a lack of flashy, animated GIF picture files on the desktop.

2.3
CONFIGURE THE WINDOWS 98 ACTIVE DESKTOP

5. After making the switch to an Active Desktop, you will notice a few differences. First, the background logo that you might have had on your Classic Desktop is gone. Next, you will notice that the Windows 98 version number has disappeared. Finally, you will see that the Windows 98 Channel Bar has automatically placed itself on your Active Desktop. To activate your Active Desktop you need to configure it by again using that same menu found in step 1 of this procedure. Click once with the secondary mouse button on any open part of the desktop, which causes a small pop-up menu to appear. Move your mouse pointer up to the Active Desktop menu option and then over to the Customize My Desktop menu selection as seen in Figure 2.7.

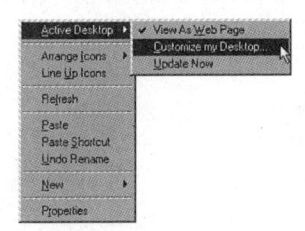

Figure 2.7 The Active Desktop submenu.

6. Doing this causes the Display Properties window to appear with the Web tab selected, as shown in Figure 2.8.

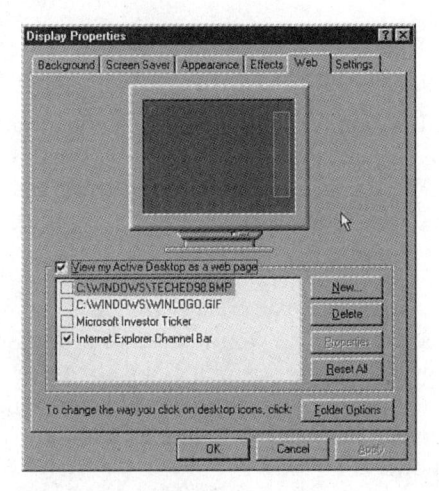

Figure 2.8 The Windows 98 Display Properties screen.

CHAPTER 2
DESKTOP USAGE AND TIPS

7. The top picture is supposed to represent your display monitor, which contains one or more blocks on the monitor. Each one of these blocks represents the Internet Explorer Channel Bar, a graphical file, or an HTML file (Web page). The tall rectangular shape shown in Figure 2.8 represents the Internet Explorer Channel Bar, which you notice has a check mark in the box next to it on the bottom-half of this screen. Clicking the Reset All button returns your Active Desktop settings back to their preordained Windows 98 defaults. The Delete button deletes whatever is currently selected (HTML files, pictures, and so on). The remaining option is the New... button, which adds more content to your Active Desktop, and is what you will do next. Click once on the New... button to go to the New Active Desktop Item window as seen in Figure 2.9.

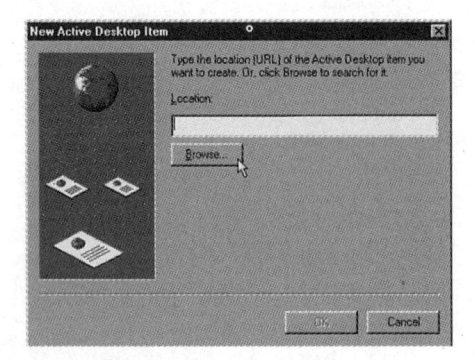

Figure 2.9 The New Active Desktop Item Location entry screen.

8. Enter the path into the Location box for the object that you want to add, or use the Browse button to search for that object via a Windows Explorer-type window. You do not need to be connected to the Internet to do this. After you have selected an object, click OK to continue, as seen in Figure 2.10.

9. The wizard process ends and places you back at the Display Properties window, still on the Web tab selection. You will see your new Active Desktop object placed on the monitor, as well as a path to that object on the selections below the monitor. Click OK to accept your changes to the Active Desktop configuration, which then returns you to the general Windows 98 view as shown in Figure 2.11.

2.3
CONFIGURE THE WINDOWS 98 ACTIVE DESKTOP

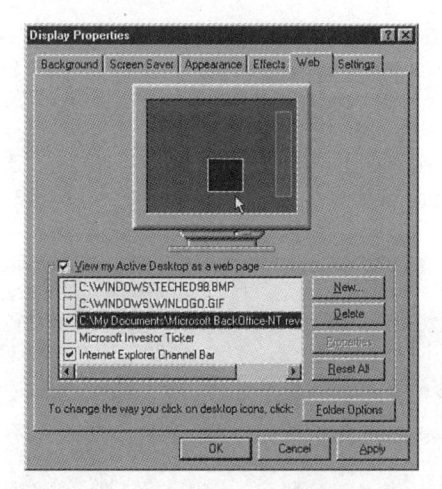

Figure 2.10 The Web tab of the Windows 98 Display Properties screen.

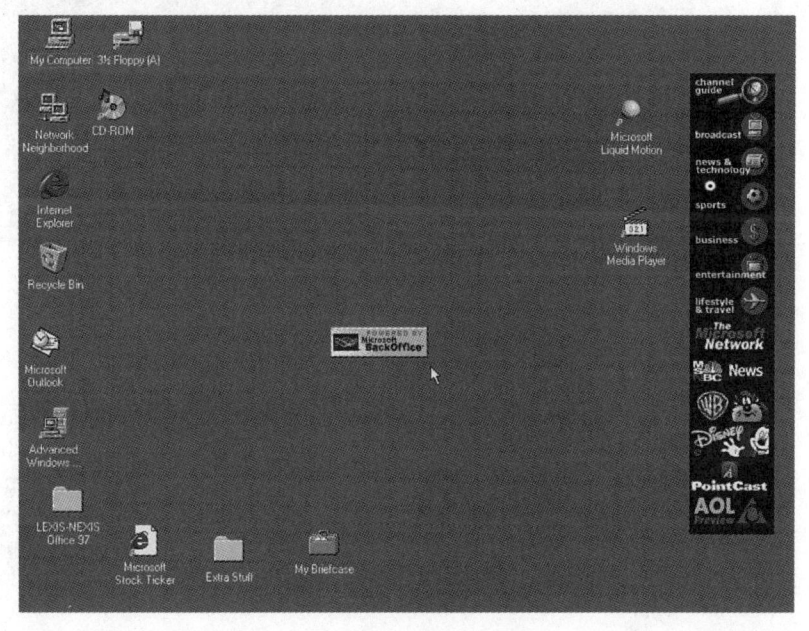

Figure 2.11 The Windows 98 Active Desktop with an animated GIF file.

CHAPTER 2
DESKTOP USAGE AND TIPS

10. To change the placement of any Active Desktop components, you must actually be viewing the desktop outside of the normal Display Properties window where all of the other configuration-type changes are made. Position your mouse pointer above the Active Desktop component that you want to relocate and a small frame with a down arrow on the left side and an X on the right side will appear, as shown in Figure 2.12.

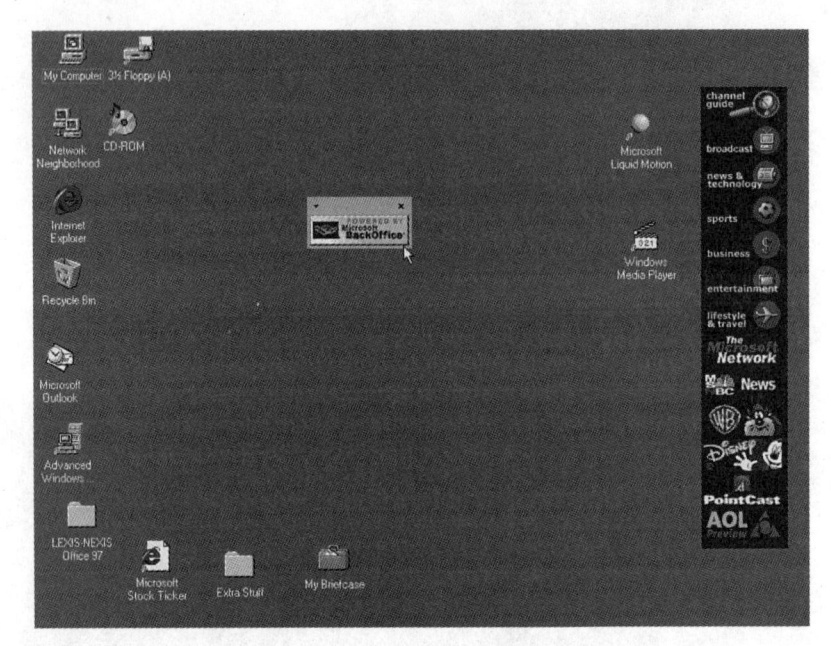

Figure 2.12 Accessing an Active Desktop graphics file.

11. Click and hold any corner of the Active Desktop component, and you will be able to resize that component at will. Be careful though, if the component contains any textual information it can quickly become distorted and difficult to read. It is equally as difficult to reset that component back to its original shape and size. Click and hold the center of any side of the frame around the Active Desktop component and you will be able to freely move it around your Active Desktop monitor. You might want to play with your Internet Explorer Channel Bar to get a feel for this.

COMPLEXITY
INTERMEDIATE

2.4 How do I...
Add or remove system icons from my desktop?

Problem

I am creating a simple desktop environment for my child to use for school, but I do not want any system-related icons (My Computer, Recycle Bin, or Network Neighborhood) to appear just in case she decides to play instead. How do I accomplish this task?

Technique

The quickest and safest method is to use a Windows 98 utility known as Tweak UI. Tweak UI comes as part of the Windows 98 Resource Kit and is also expected to be released on to the Microsoft Corporation Web site at some point in the future. Tweak UI for Windows 95 is already available on Microsoft's Internet Web site (`http://www.microsoft.com/windows98`). Purchasing the Windows 98 Resource Kit is the current way to obtain a copy of Tweak UI, and it can be found on the CD-ROM that comes as a part of the Resource Kit. Follow the steps outlined in Chapter 1 of this book for Resource Kit installation assistance. Next, complete the following steps for details on how to use the Tweak UI utility.

Keep in mind that Tweak UI is doing nothing more than providing a graphical interface for editing the Windows 98 Registry, which is something that you could actually do directly via the Windows 98 utility tool known as REGEDIT.EXE (see Chapter 4, "The Registry," for details on using this tool). The greatest advantage Tweak UI has over direct registry editing is that Tweak UI won't let you do anything to destroy your system (from a software perspective).

> **NOTE**
>
> The REGEDIT.EXE application permits direct editing of the Windows 98 system and user Registry. It is possible that you might make a minor change that actually prevents you from loading the Windows 98 operating system, which means that you could not recover from a supposedly simple fix to your PC. (Not a good thing.) So if you only remember a single thing, it should be this: *The Windows 98 Registry is a very fragile and delicate. Make a mistake and you could be history. Do not make guesses when you are altering your Registry directly through the REGEDIT.EXE tool! One false move and you can destroy your own Windows 98 system!*

CHAPTER 2
DESKTOP USAGE AND TIPS

Steps

1. Start the Tweak UI utility by double-clicking the Tweak UI icon in the Windows 98 Control Panel, as shown in Figure 2.13.

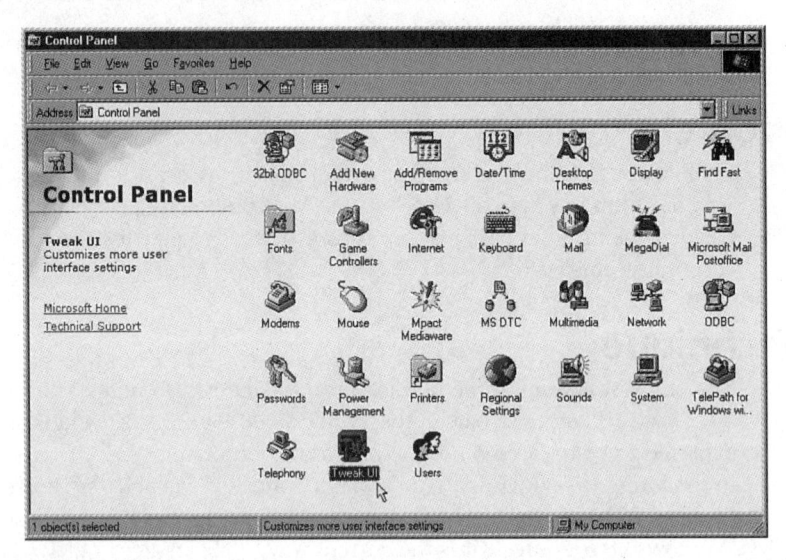

Figure 2.13 Accessing the Tweak UI icon in the Windows 98 Control Panel.

2. This takes you directly into the first tab (for your mouse or pointing device) of the Tweak UI utility. Click the Desktop tab to switch to that section's topics, as shown in Figure 2.14.

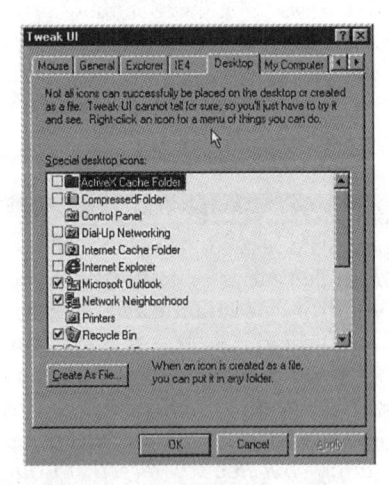

Figure 2.14 The Tweak UI Desktop tab.

2.4
ADD OR REMOVE SYSTEM ICONS FROM MY DESKTOP

3. Click the box located next to each desktop icon to either select it or deselect it. If a box has a check mark in it, it is considered selected, meaning that it appears on the Windows 98 desktop. Remove the check mark and the icon disappears. It is recommended that you remove (at least) the Network Neighborhood, Dial-Up Networking, and Scheduled Tasks icons, if they are presently enabled on your child's desktop (or on anyone else's desktop that you do not believe as technically sound enough to be altering the manner in which the system operates).

4. The other option on this tab gives you the capability to create any of these special desktop icons as a file (basically, this is creating a shortcut to one of these icons). After an icon has been created as a file, you are able to move that file into any folder anywhere on your Windows 98 computer. This effectively means that you are able to launch the Scheduled Tasks accessory directly from the Start menu, which is found inside the Start menu chain. To do this, click the Scheduled Tasks line inside the Special desktop icons selection box, as seen in Figure 2.15.

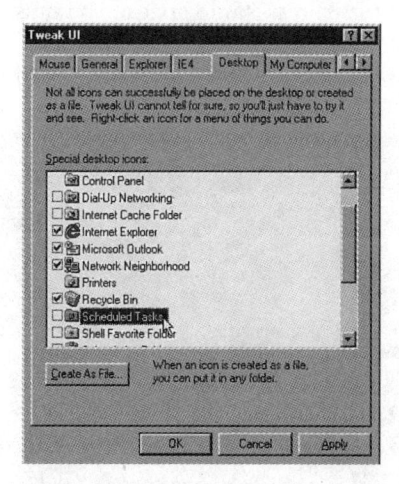

Figure 2.15 Changing access to the Scheduled Tasks icon on the Desktop Configuration tab.

5. To actually create the file, you can click the Create As File... button found near the bottom of the screen. Otherwise, you might click once with the secondary mouse button when the mouse pointer is located directly on top of the Scheduled Tasks icon selection, and then click again on the Create As File... menu selection. Either way, you will be brought to the Save As window, probably with the C:\Windows path as the default, as shown in Figure 2.16. It is recommended that you save the file directly on the Windows 98 desktop because you will be dragging and dropping it elsewhere in the next step. For purposes of demonstration, this is where it was saved during the production of the example.

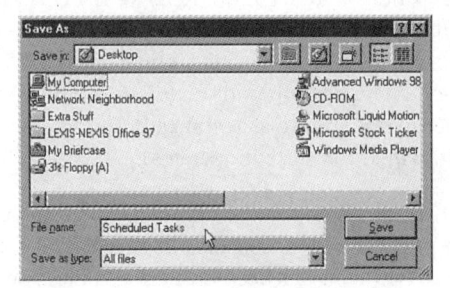

Figure 2.16 The Save As file window.

6. Now the fun begins. Click and hold on the Scheduled Tasks icon that you just created, and then drag it over to the Start Button then up to the location on the Start menu bar that you want, as shown in Figure 2.17. Keep in mind that in order to get the Start menu to appear, you must drag your icon on top of the Start button first, which causes the menu to appear, and then you drag the icon upward to into the spot you would like.

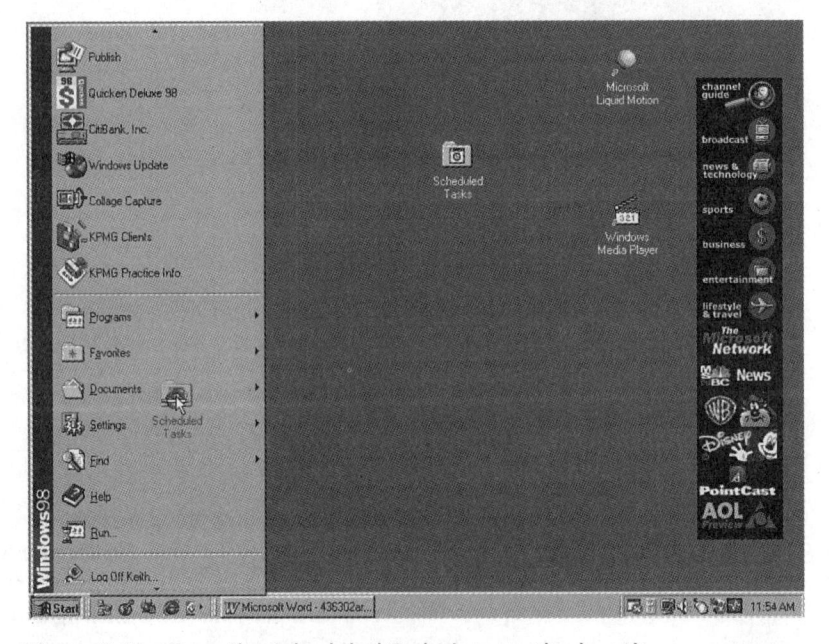

Figure 2.17 Drag the Scheduled Tasks icon to the location you want.

2.4
ADD OR REMOVE SYSTEM ICONS FROM MY DESKTOP

7. When you get to the area that you want to put the icon in let go of the mouse button and the Scheduled Tasks icon will be placed there, as seen in Figure 2.18.

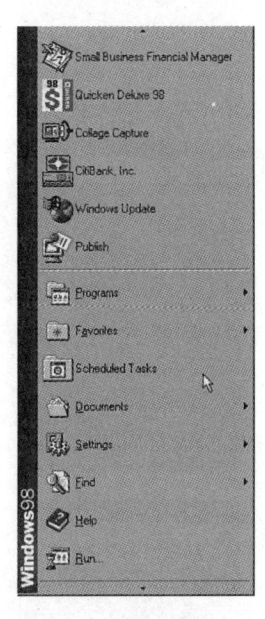

Figure 2.18 The Scheduled Tasks icon as shown on the Start menu bar.

> **NOTE**
>
> Remember that you should place the icon either inside the Programs or Favorites menu options, or above the line that breaks the Start menu bar in half. Although in this example, for purposes of demonstration, the Scheduled Tasks icon was dropped onto the bottom half of the menu (below the Favorites menu option), that icon will not remain on the bottom half of the menu, just below the Favorites menu. Windows 98 will automatically adjust that icon up to the bottom of the top half of the Start menu bar, as shown in Figure 2.19.

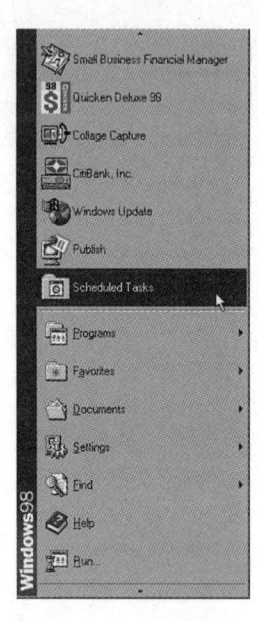

Figure 2.19 The Scheduled Task icon in its final location on the Start menu.

COMPLEXITY
INTERMEDIATE

2.5 How do I...
Find and remove useless links on my desktop or Start menu?

Problem

Over time, through the installation of new software and the deletion of old programs and data files, you will probably be left with an assortment of useless links (shortcuts) on both your Windows 98 desktop as well as the Start menu. Hunting down and killing off these already dead links is a time-consuming and painful process.

Technique

There is a solution to this problem, though, and it comes in the form of the Windows 98 Resource Kit. The tool required is known as Checklinks and is one of the many utilities that come on the Resource Kit's CD-ROM. Unfortunately, this is not a free utility, you must first purchase the Windows 98 Resource Kit. Another way to find these dead links is to manually click on every icon on your

FIND AND REMOVE USELESS LINKS ON MY DESKTOP OR START MENU

desktop and in each of the subfolders inside the \Start\Programs menu option, which is not a fun task. Or, you could always use Windows Explorer and browse each link's shortcut file, using that link's Properties option to determine whether it is a valid link or not.

Steps

1. The Checklinks application is launched either from inside the Microsoft Management Console (MMC) or via the Run command box using the file CHECKLINKS.EXE. Using either of these two methods starts the Link Check Wizard, as shown in Figure 2.20.

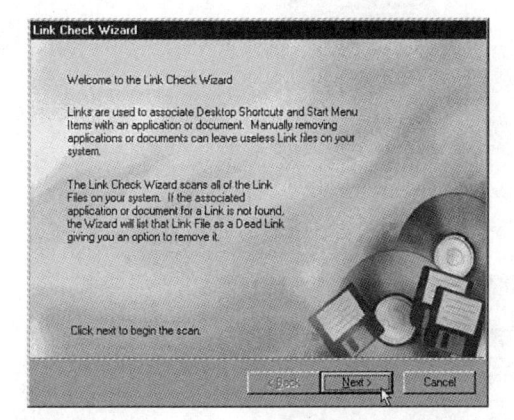

Figure 2.20 The first screen of the Link Check Wizard.

2. This screen contains background information related to precisely what the wizard is and does. Read it over and then click the Next> button to continue, as shown in Figure 2.21.

3. The wizard might run for quite some time, depending on how many links you have created as well as how much activity (adding and deleting software applications) your PC has endured. If your system is configured for multiple users, you will probably see duplicates of links that are considered dead. Don't worry, as this is considered normal, because each time a new user is created, the old folder structure was probably duplicated for that user and thus the dead links were also duplicated. Clicking the Select All button places a check mark into each of the check boxes located just to the left of each dead link. A check mark means that you want the wizard to remove that specific link. If you want more details on a particular link, first highlight that link with a single-click from the mouse pointer. Next, click once with the secondary mouse button and a

Properties window automatically appears (yes, I'm sure Microsoft meant to document this feature from within the utility), as shown in Figure 2.22.

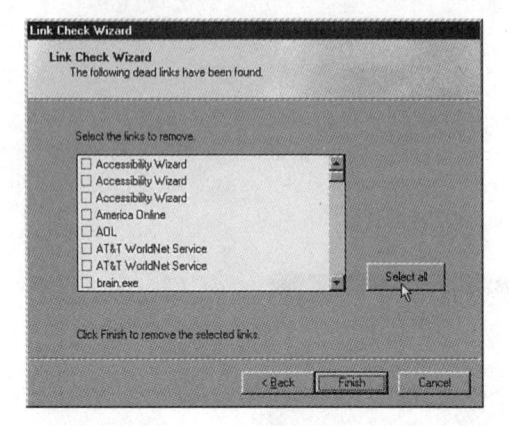

Figure 2.21 The check box listing of all located dead links.

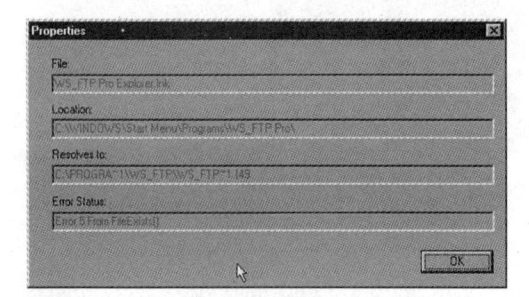

Figure 2.22 The Properties screen for one of the dead links.

4. The File field contains the precise name of the link (or .LNK) file. The Location field is where the link file is stored on your computer. The Resolves to field is the path with the executable/document file that Windows 98 believes the link is attempting to use. The Error Status field presents the status information regarding this link. For instance, an error value of 5 means that the destination file for the link does not exist (or the link cannot find that destination file). After you have finished examining these properties, click OK to return to the screen previously shown in Figure 2.21.

5. When you are certain of your choices for removal, click the Finish button to start the removal process. This process moves pretty fast and when it's complete, a status box appears, as shown in Figure 2.23.

CHANGE THE DEFAULT VIEW TO EXPLORE INSTEAD OF OPEN

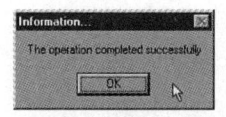

Figure 2.23 The Check Link Wizard complete message box.

6. Click OK and the status box, along with the Link Check Wizard, closes.

7. Examine your link structure to make sure that you removed all the links that you wanted to and then you're finished. The Link Check Wizard can be run as many times as is necessary, so repeat these steps as needed.

COMPLEXITY
ADVANCED

2.6 How do I...
Change the default view of the My Computer Windows Explorer to explore instead of open?

Problem

When you double-click the My Computer icon found on the desktop, you are presented with the standard Open format instead of the Explore format, as shown in Figure 2.24.

For most Windows 98 users this probably will not be an issue, but for many power users it may well be, as maneuvering within an open-style window is slower than an Explore-style window (see Figure 2.25).

Technique

Changing the default view requires you to manipulate the File Types section within the Folder Options of Windows 98. This is not a difficult task, but care should be taken when modifying a file type. A file type in Windows 3.x was known as an *association* and as you know, if a file type becomes corrupted or associated with the wrong type then it essentially becomes useless. This is why care should be taken during the modification process. If you would like to learn more about file types and their associated extensions, refer to Chapter 19, "Giving Windows Special Powers."

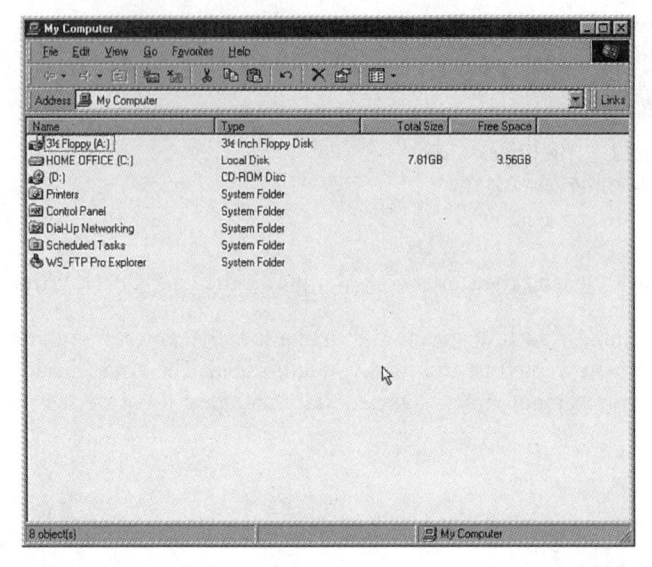

Figure 2.24 The Windows Explorer in open-formatted view.

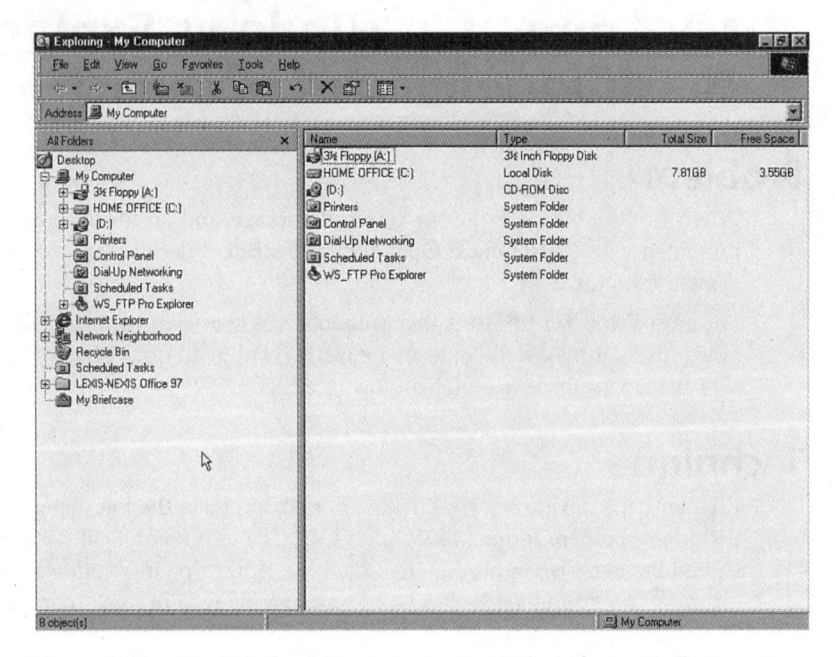

Figure 2.25 The Windows Explorer in its explore-formatted view.

2.6 CHANGE THE DEFAULT VIEW TO EXPLORE INSTEAD OF OPEN

Steps

1. Open the My Computer icon on your desktop by double-clicking it. This will take you into the Windows Explorer screen as shown in Figure 2.26.

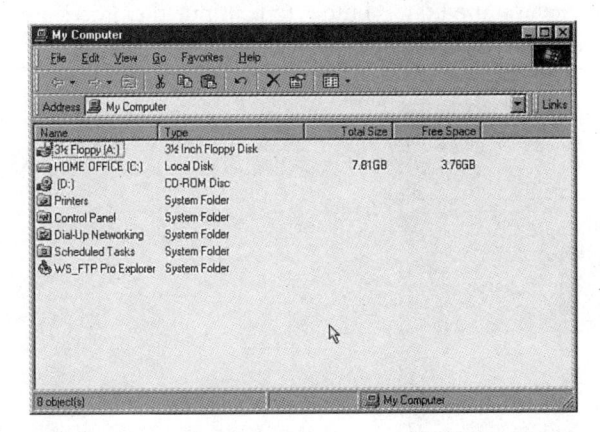

Figure 2.26 Windows Explorer in open-formatted view.

2. Click the View menu option and then click the mouse pointer on the Folder Options... menu selection. This will take you into the Folder Options window where you need to click the File Types tab, as shown in Figure 2.27.

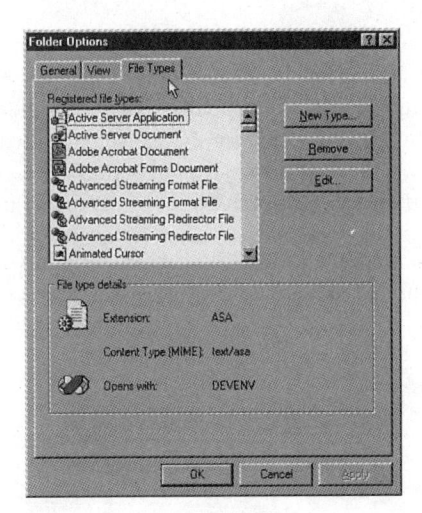

Figure 2.27 The File Types tab of the Folder Options window.

CHAPTER 2
DESKTOP USAGE AND TIPS

3. Scroll down to the Folder file type by using the scrollbar or do a quick jump to the start of that area by pressing the letter F. (You might still need to go down a few more file types inside the letter F, but this saves you some use of the slower scrollbar.) Select the Folder file type by clicking it, and then click on the Edit... button to continue the process, as shown in Figure 2.28.

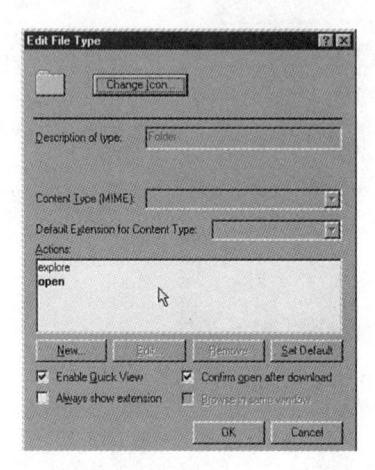

Figure 2.28 Editing a file type.

4. Highlight the action word Explore, which can be found inside the Actions area (it is the big box-shaped area on the bottom-half of the screen), and then click Set Default key.

5. This changes the default setting for the My Computer icon to be a Windows Explorer type mode instead of the old Open view mode. Click Close (the OK button that you see in Figure 2.28 automatically changes to a Close button whenever you edit or change an action) to confirm your changes, and then close the My Computer window that is still in use.

6. After reopening the My Computer icon by double-clicking it, you will now be presented with the Windows Explorer view mode as seen in Figure 2.29.

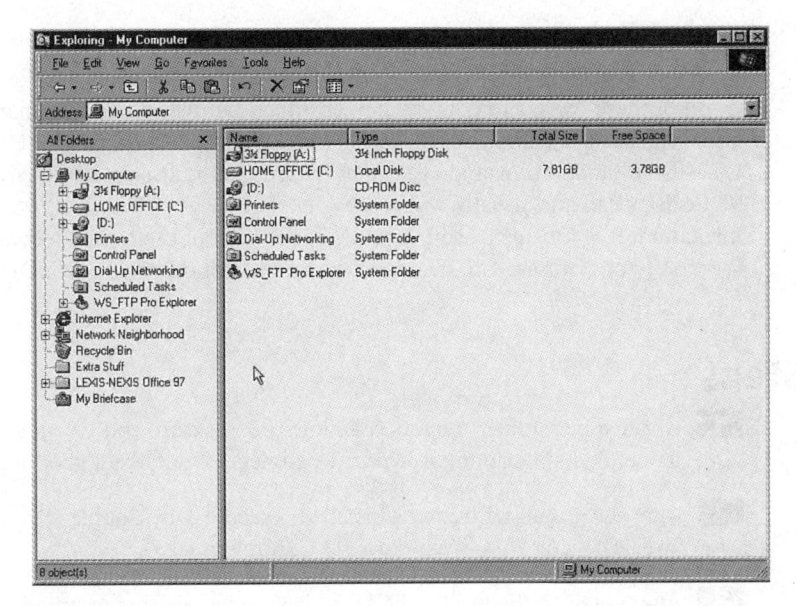

Figure 2.29 The Windows Explorer in explore-formatted view.

COMPLEXITY
INTERMEDIATE

2.7 How do I...
Place the Recent Documents folder directly on my desktop?

Problem

Sometimes you might find yourself editing documents on a frequent basis. The current method of clicking the Start button then the Documents menu option, and then the name of the recently used document that you want to edit might seem a bit tedious to do over and over again. Would it not be much faster if your Recent Documents folder existed directly on your Windows 98 desktop? The question then becomes, exactly how does one move the Recent Documents folder so that it exists directly on the desktop?

Technique

Use of the Windows 98 Resource Kit is required to solve this problem. One of the Resource Kit utilities is known as Tweak UI, which permits you to tweak the user interface. By now you have probably realized just how powerful the Tweak UI tool can be in the Windows 98 operating environment. You might want to experiment with this utility, especially when it comes to placing Windows 98 system folders in locations other than their originally intended locale.

All of these tweaks that are being performed by this tool can be manually achieved through a direct modification of the Windows 98 Registry. However, it is has been proven time and again that incorrect modifications to the Windows 98 Registry can and usually will damage or destroy your Windows 98 implementation. It is for this reason that the Tweak UI tool is strongly recommended for modifying your system, instead of using the Windows 98 REGEDIT.EXE file.

Steps

1. Create a new folder on your Windows 98 desktop, and give it a good name. Perhaps naming it Recent Documents would be a good idea.

2. After the Tweak UI utility is installed, execute it by double-clicking the Tweak UI icon in the Windows 98 Control Panel.

3. After entering the utility, click the General tab, as shown in Figure 2.30.

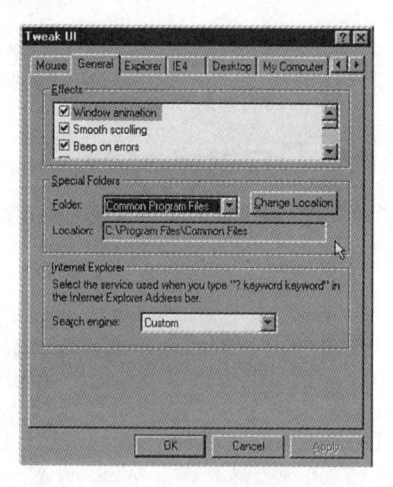

Figure 2.30 The General tab of the Tweak UI editing screen.

4. The General tab is split into three parts: Effects, Special Folders, and Internet Explorer. The section you are concerned with is Special Folders. The purpose of this section is to modify the location of Windows 98 system folders. The Folder field is used for displaying the folder type, whereas the Location field tells you the exact physical path on your hard drive for that folder. Using the drop-down list box, click once on the folder that you want to change. In this case, you will go all the way down to the Recent Documents selection, as shown in Figure 2.31.

2.7
PLACE THE RECENT DOCUMENTS FOLDER DIRECTLY ON MY DESKTOP

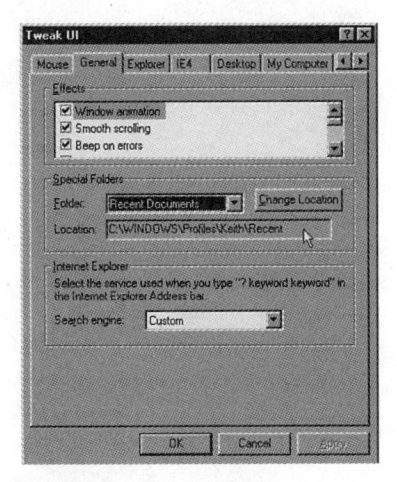

Figure 2.31 Changing the Recent Documents (a Special folder) Location.

5. Once you have the Recent Documents folder highlighted in the drop-down list box, click the Change Location button to select another place to store your Recent Documents folder. Doing this causes the Browse for Folder window to appear as seen in Figure 2.32.

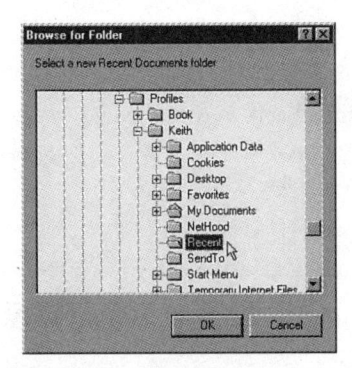

Figure 2.32 Browsing for a New Location for the Recent Documents folder.

6. Now for the important part: Scroll up to the location for your new Recent Documents folder (the one you created in step 1 of these instructions). Assuming you created the folder directly on your Windows 98 desktop, this folder will be found in the multi-user configuration path of C:\Windows\Profiles*username*\Desktop\Recent Documents, as shown in Figure 2.33. If you have a single user setting to your Windows 98 environment, the path will be C:\Windows\Desktop\Recent Documents.

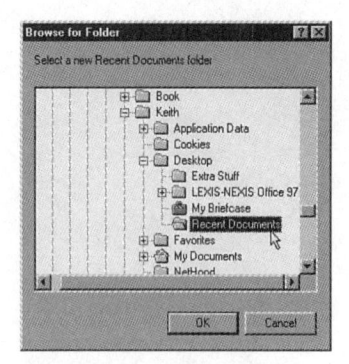

Figure 2.33 Selecting the New Location for the Recent Documents folder.

7. Click once on this new folder and then click OK to confirm your selection. A message box appears telling you to log off and then back on before this setting can take effect, as shown in Figure 2.34.

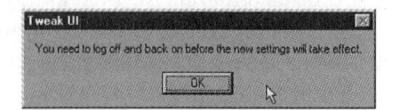

Figure 2.34 Confirming the completion of the process.

8. After you have logged off and then back on (or rebooted your system), the change will take effect. You can change back to the original setting at any time by following these same steps.

COMPLEXITY
INTERMEDIATE

2.8 How do I...
Create a toolbar that shows all my physical drive devices?

Problem
There are times when having direct access from the taskbar to any of the specific drives on your computer would be very helpful. Especially if you have multiple other screens open all over the place, such as when you are developing

Visual InterDev or Visual Basic applications. The desktop area can get messy, and being able to find your Jaz, SyQuest, or A:\ drive would be easier if they were on a toolbar window.

Technique

Toolbar creation under Windows 98 is both easy and complex. That is, the operating system provides you with the means to easily create as many new toolbars as you like, but this can quickly lead to a very complex taskbar where it becomes difficult to maneuver. There is no additional software to install, as this task is part of the standard Windows 98 operating system.

Steps

1. First, you need to create a storage location where the drive shortcuts or links are to be placed. This should be someplace on your hard drive where you are unlikely to accidentally delete things, such as the C:\Windows\Config directory. Create an empty folder and give it a good name, such as System Drives (catchy, huh?), as shown in Figure 2.35.

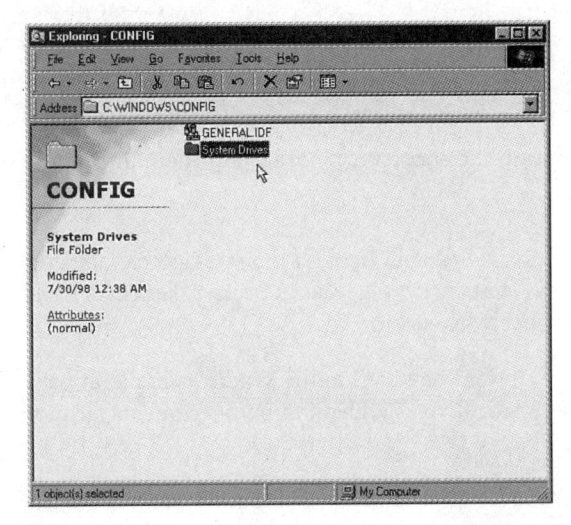

Figure 2.35 Creating a new folder inside the C:\Windows\Config folder.

2. Next, you need to populate this folder with shortcut links to each of the physical drive devices that you want to appear in your new toolbar. To do this, open your My Computer icon by double-clicking it, while keeping your new folder's location open as well (if you closed it, then re-open it).

CHAPTER 2
DESKTOP USAGE AND TIPS

3. In the Exploring My Computer window, highlight each drive letter that you want included and then drag those drives over to the new folder (in the example, this is the System Drives folder) as shown in Figure 2.36.

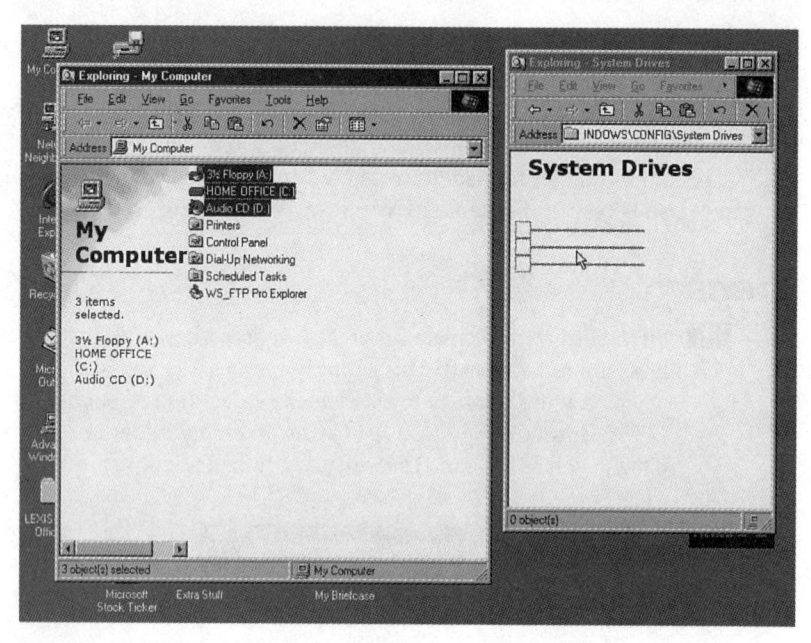

Figure 2.36 Creating the shortcuts by dragging them into the new location.

4. A pop-up message box appears with the message *You cannot move or copy this item to this location. Do you want to create a shortcut to the item instead?* Reply affirmatively by clicking Yes.

5. Now migrate upward one level in the Windows Explorer path so that you only see the System Drives folder and not its contents anymore, as shown in Figure 2.37.

6. Now comes the fun part. Click and drag the System Drives folder and drop it onto an open part of the Windows 98 taskbar. A good spot to do this is just to the left of the SysTray area (the place where Windows 98 puts the clock, the Task Scheduler, and any TSRs that you might have loaded).

7. A new toolbar is automatically created, as shown in Figure 2.38.

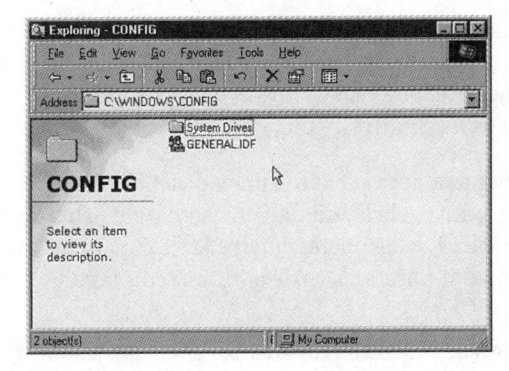

2.8
CREATE A TOOLBAR THAT SHOWS ALL MY PHYSICAL DRIVE DEVICES

Figure 2.37 Browsing one level higher in the folder structure.

Figure 2.38 Your New System Drives toolbar.

8. I know what you are thinking. Though the toolbar is created, it is too big for my taskbar as it has scrunched everything else on the bar. No problem, you just need to change the default properties for this toolbar. To do that, click once with the secondary mouse button on the System Drives (or whatever you named your toolbar) title for this toolbar, to display the pop-up menu shown in Figure 2.39.

9. Clicking once on the Show Title menu selection removes the folder's title of System Drives from the toolbar.

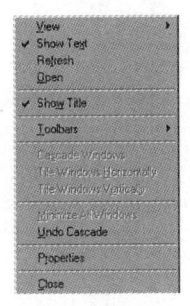

Figure 2.39 The pop-up menu for the System Drives toolbar.

CHAPTER 2
DESKTOP USAGE AND TIPS

10. Repeat step 8 (except click on a corner of the new toolbar, as the title is no longer displayed on the System Drives toolbar) to redisplay the pop-up menu, and then click the Show Text menu selection to eliminate the text descriptions for each drive's icon.

11. On the vertical bar that appears to the immediate left of your first drive, in this case the A:\ drive, click and drag it to the right. This decreases the size of the new toolbar, while increasing the size of main taskbar that contains your active applications as demonstrated in Figure 2.40.

Figure 2.40 The System Drives toolbar without any text descriptions.

12. If you place the mouse pointer on top of any of these drives, a ToolTip will appear giving you the full text for each drive. Because of this, it is recommended that you do not waste precious taskbar space with needless text descriptions for each icon.

COMPLEXITY
INTERMEDIATE

2.9 How do I...
Open a DOS window with a quick keystroke?

Problem

Despite all the technology advances by Microsoft over the past 17 years, DOS (disk operating systems) still exists. Yes, the Microsoft marketing machine will argue that DOS is gone and everything is GUI, but you and I both know better. Having said that, wouldn't it be nice to be able to quickly jump to a DOS window with a one-handed keystroke? This would greatly aid those system administrators and home power users who still want to perform a quick edit on one of their Windows 98 configuration files such as AUTOEXEC.BAT, CONFIG.SYS, or MSDOS.SYS.

Technique

One fast way to perform this task is to jump to a DOS window by typing in the word **command** in the **Run** command's window. However, this still requires you to click Start, followed by a click on the Run... button, and finally, type in the

2.9 OPEN A DOS WINDOW WITH A QUICK KEYSTROKE

word **command**. (Not really an efficient process if you stop to think about it.) For this problem, you will need a Microsoft or Microsoft-compliant keyboard that supports the use of the Windows key. After you have this, it is a matter of either creating a new link file or moving and copying the one that Windows 98 installed during its initial installation process.

Steps

1. First, check to make sure that you have not deleted the MS-DOS Prompt icon that Windows 98 created on the Programs menu structure during its installation process. It should be near the bottom of the menu screen, as shown in Figure 2.41.

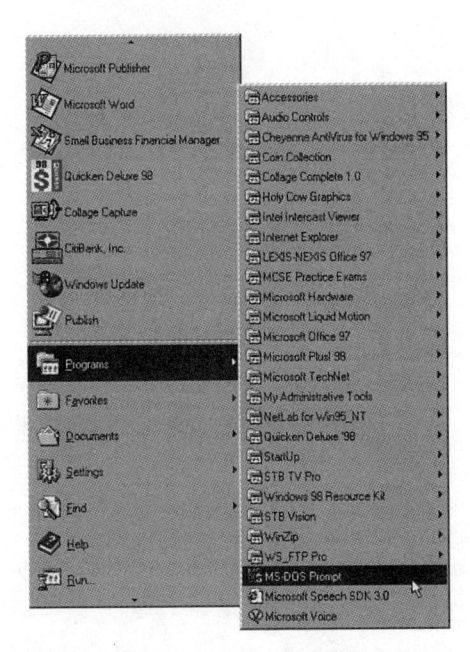

Figure 2.41 Finding the MS-DOS Prompt icon on the Programs menu bar.

2. If the icon exists, the process becomes even easier. Simply click and drag the icon to the top of the Start menu bar while holding down the Control key. This will actually copy the icon, instead of a straight move action. If you want to move it, that is okay too.

3. The MS-DOS Prompt icon should now reside at the top of the Start menu bar, as seen in Figure 2.42.

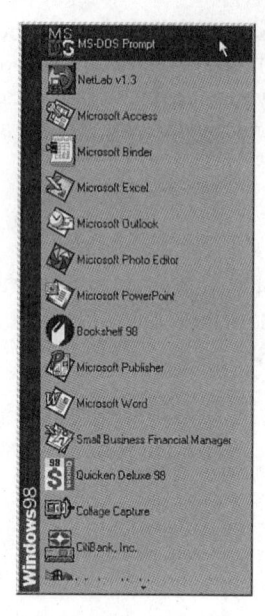

Figure 2.42 Copying the MS-DOS Prompt icon to the Start menu bar.

4. You are finished with the tough part, now it is time to use the newly created/moved icon. Use the following keystroke sequence to activate your icon: Windows, M, Enter, (these keys should be pressed individually, and can be used very quickly).

5. If you did not have an MS-DOS Prompt icon to move or copy, that is okay and does not present a problem. Just create a new shortcut directly on the Start menu bar by clicking once with the secondary mouse button on an open part of your primary taskbar.

6. When the Taskbar Properties window appears, click the Start Menu Programs tab.

7. Next, click Add under the Customize Start menu section of this screen.

8. This takes you to the Create Shortcut Wizard. Type in the word **command**, (this is not case sensitive), and then click the Next> button.

9. On the Select Program Folder screen, click the Start Menu to choose that location.

10. Click the Next> button to continue.

2.10 HIDE ALL OF THE ICONS ON A WINDOWS 98 DESKTOP

11. When the Select a Title for the Program window appears, you need to name your shortcut. It is suggested that you call it MS-DOS Prompt, but you can name it anything you want. Type in your descriptive name and click OK to accept the name.

12. When you are returned to the Taskbar Properties window, click OK to close the window and you are finished.

13. Make sure that your newly created icon resides at the top of the Start menu structure. To move any icon, click and drag it to the location that you want.

14. Use the following keystroke sequence to activate your icon: Windows, M, Enter, (these keys should be pressed individually, and can be used very quickly). If you did not name your shortcut as MS-DOS Prompt, then instead of pressing the M key you need to press the key that represents the first letter of your description (for example, use the D key if you named your shortcut DOS).

COMPLEXITY
INTERMEDIATE

2.10 How do I...
Hide all of the icons on a Windows 98 desktop?

Problem
My company does not want temporary workers to be able to see any icons on the Active Desktop. How do I accomplish this task?

Technique
The Windows 98 Active Desktop must be used in order to perform this task. No additional software is required, as this feature is built into the Windows 98 operating system.

Steps

1. Activate the Active Desktop feature of Windows 98 by clicking any open space on the desktop with the secondary mouse button.

2. When the popup menu appears, click the Active Desktop menu option, and then click the View As Web Page menu selection.

CHAPTER 2
DESKTOP USAGE AND TIPS

3. When the Display Properties window appears, click once on the Effects tab as shown in Figure 2.43.

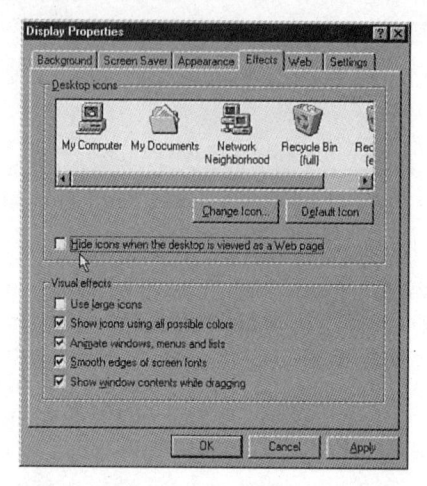

Figure 2.43 The Effects tab of the Display Properties window.

4. Click the check box next to the option Hide Icons When the Desktop is Viewed as a Web Page to select it. By placing a check mark in this box, all of the desktop icons are automatically hidden from view.

5. Insert the check mark and click Apply then watch all the icons on your desktop disappear from view, as shown in Figure 2.44.

6. The desktop is nearly empty. The Windows 98 Internet Explorer Channel Bar might still be on your desktop. No problem, eliminating the Channel Bar requires just a few more steps. Click on any empty spot on your desktop (this should not be too hard to find) with the secondary mouse button.

7. When the pop-up menu appears, click on the Active Desktop menu option at the top of the menu first, and then click on the Customize my Desktop menu selection.

8. When the Display Properties window appears, it will automatically open on the Web tab, as shown in Figure 2.45.

2.10
HIDE ALL OF THE ICONS ON A WINDOWS 98 DESKTOP

Figure 2.44 A Windows 98 Desktop without icons.

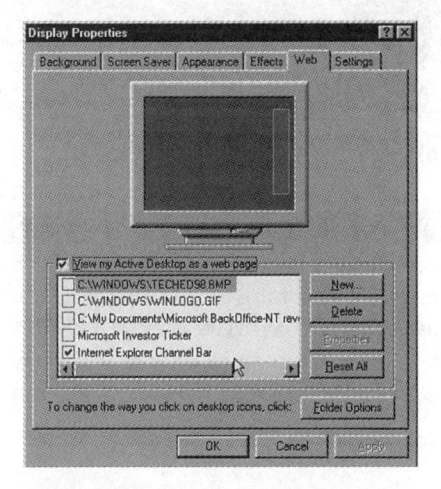

Figure 2.45 Removing the Internet Explorer Channel Bar from the Windows 98 Desktop.

9. Within the View my Active Desktop as a Web Page section, uncheck any boxes that might be checked. In this case, there is only one, the Internet Explorer Channel Bar. As soon as you uncheck it and then click OK to confirm your decision, your desktop becomes empty in appearance, as shown in Figure 2.46.

Figure 2.46 A completely blank Windows 98 Desktop area.

> **NOTE**
> The fact that you were successful in eliminating all icons from the Windows 98 desktop might give you a false sense of security. Without a proper Policy setting that is enforced via a Windows NT Server 4.0 (or higher) logon configuration, anyone can easily defeat an empty desktop. Please review Chapter 15, "Network Management," for more ideas on this topic.

COMPLEXITY
INTERMEDIATE

2.11 How do I...
Change the opening or execution of desktop icons to a Single-Click mode?

Problem
I want to be able to single-click any icon on my desktop, instead of double-clicking as I have to now. How do I configure this setting?

Technique
Either of the Windows 98 desktop configurations (Active or Classic) can be used with this feature. No additional software is required, as this feature is built into the Windows 98 operating system.

Steps

1. Open the My Computer icon by double-clicking it.

2. Click the View menu option and then click the Folder Options menu selection.

3. This causes the Folder Options window to appear. Make sure that the General tab is displayed, and then click the bottom radio button selection named Custom, based on settings you choose has been selected, as demonstrated in Figure 2.47.

4. Next, click the Settings button to display the Custom Settings window, as shown in Figure 2.48.

5. In the bottom section, Click Items as Follows, is where you want to focus your concentration. The first radio button is the one necessary to switch your double-clicking days over to an easier, single-click for icon execution.

6. The two sub-radio buttons are used to determine when an icon is underlined. The first selection will do it all the time, whereas the second option will cause an icon or item to be underlined only when it comes into focus (for example, the mouse pointer is pointed at the item in question). After you have made your selection, click OK to confirm your choices.

CHAPTER 2
DESKTOP USAGE AND TIPS

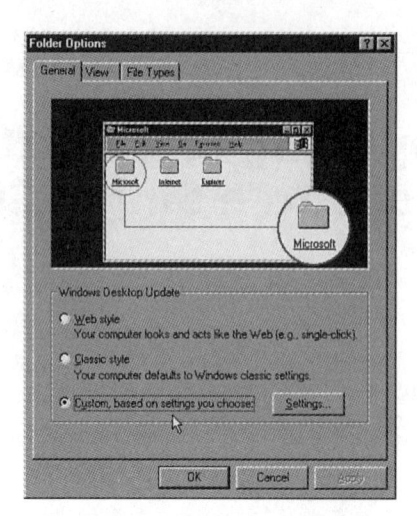

Figure 2.47 Changing the settings on the Folder Options window.

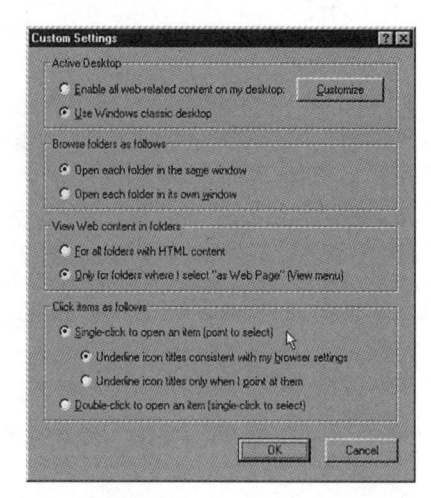

Figure 2.48 Making your selections on the Custom Settings screen.

7. This returns you to the Folder Options window where you need to click Close to end the modification process of your Windows 98 folder options.

8. When you look at your Windows 98 desktop you will see that everything is either underlined all the time, as shown in Figure 2.49, or only when you point at an individual icon.

2.11
CHANGE DESKTOP ICONS TO SINGLE-CLICK MODE

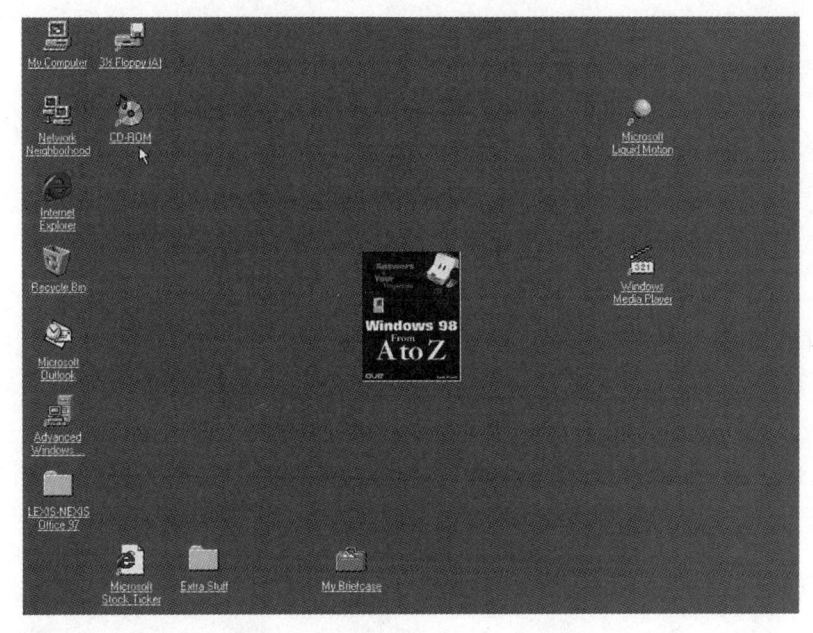

Figure 2.49 Sampling a desktop icon.

9. That's all you need to do. You might want to play with the custom settings that appear on this screen, as most of these options are really geared to an individual's taste.

CHAPTER 3
THE BOOT PROCESS

3

THE BOOT PROCESS

How do I...

3.1 Determine which files load during the Windows 98 boot process?

3.2 Change the Windows 98 startup process so I can find malfunctioning device drivers?

3.3 Boot to a DOS prompt?

3.4 Know what the key system files are?

3.5 Obtain information on problematic hardware that was encountered during the Windows 98 startup?

3.6 Force Windows 98 to boot into Safe Mode?

3.7 Create a Windows 98 Startup disk?

The startup or boot process to Windows 98 is important, and is the focal point of this chapter. It is the procedure that the operating system takes each time you turn your computer on or restart it, and yet most people have no idea what is going on in the background. The ability to modify the startup mode of Windows 98 can be a powerful tool in diagnosing problems such as bad device drivers, erratic TSR (terminate-and-stay resident) software applications, and other startup configurations.

This chapter is broken into topical areas. The first covers the Windows 98 boot process, followed by a topic on the Windows 98 system files, and then a coverage of the additional tools that can be used for making changes to the various system components that comprise the boot process. Additionally, you will discover how to access several system tools built into the Windows 98 operating system, which are not exactly readily accessible to the everyday user. These tools include the following Windows 98 utilities:

- Automatic Skip Driver Agent
- Dr. Watson
- Registry Checker
- ScanDisk
- Signature Verification tool
- System Configuration Utility
- System File Checker
- Update Wizard Uninstall
- Version Conflict Manager
- Windows Report tool

One final item you need to be aware of: This chapter is meant for intermediate users of Windows 9x. If you are a relatively new user of one of Microsoftís 32-bit operating systems, such as Windows 98, then you might want to skip over this chapter for now. There are many instances in this chapter that if done incorrectly, the operating system does not notify you of your mistake until you restart your computer. At which time it will fail to boot, which is how you know you made a mistake in the first place. Like Chapter 4, "The Registry," this chapter can inflict quite a bit of pain on you and your computer system if used improperly. It is because of this that you will want to take extra care when trying things out in this chapter.

3.1 Determine Which Files Load During the Windows 98 Boot Process

This How-To walks you through the files that are loaded during the Windows 98 startup process.

3.2 Change the Windows 98 Startup Process so I Can Find Malfunctioning Device Drivers

This How-To shows you how to modify the Windows 98 boot process, which helps you to locate software drivers that might be failing.

3.3 Boot to a DOS Prompt

Sometimes it is nice to be able to boot directly into DOS instead of the Windows 98 GUI. This How-To shows you how to do just that.

3.4 Know What the Key System Files Are

This How-To explains what the important system files are and what they can do for you.

3.5 Obtain Information on Problematic Hardware that Was Encountered During the Windows 98 Startup

This How-To explains how to find more detailed information on hardware that might not have been configured properly during the Windows 98 installation and startup process.

3.6 Force Windows 98 to Boot into Safe Mode

Sometimes it is necessary to access the Windows 98 Safe Mode, even if nothing is wrong with your PC. This How-To tells you how to do it.

3.7 Create a Windows 98 Startup Disk

This How-To walks you through the creation of a Windows 98 Startup disk and also explains the need for such a disk.

COMPLEXITY
ADVANCED

3.1 How do I...
Determine which files load during the Windows 98 boot process?

Problem

Sometimes it becomes necessary to determine exactly which files were loaded by the Windows 98 operating system during its boot process. This might be because your system hangs during startup or maybe you have a hardware device that is not working so you think its software driver is not loading properly. Whatever the reason, the question remains, how do you figure out what those files are?

Technique

There is a little known system utility called Dr. Watson for Windows 98. Dr. Watson has been around since the early days of Windows, but only in the 32-bit world has it become useful to more people than the hard-core systems application developer. This is not to mention that in its current revision, it is much more powerful and easier to use. Probably the biggest reason that few people know about Dr. Watson is because Microsoft buried its execution deep inside the System Information tool (as it has with many other great utilities) for some unknown reason.

Steps

1. There are two ways to launch the Dr. Watson utility. The first is by typing in the command **drwatson** in the Run command box; the other way is by accessing the System Information tool. After inside the System Information utility, click the Tools menu option, and then click again on the Dr. Watson menu option. This will start the Dr. Watson for Windows 98 System tool, as shown in Figure 3.1.

Figure 3.1 Finding the Dr. Watson icon on the Windows 98 taskbar.

2. Do you see it yet? Probably not, as Windows does not take you directly into the application GUI. Instead, it loads the application into memory and places a tiny icon on your system tray. If you place your mouse pointer on top of it, a ToolTip pops up identifying the Dr. Watson system utility. To actually view the Dr. Watson utility GUI, as shown in Figure 3.2, you must first double-click that tiny icon.

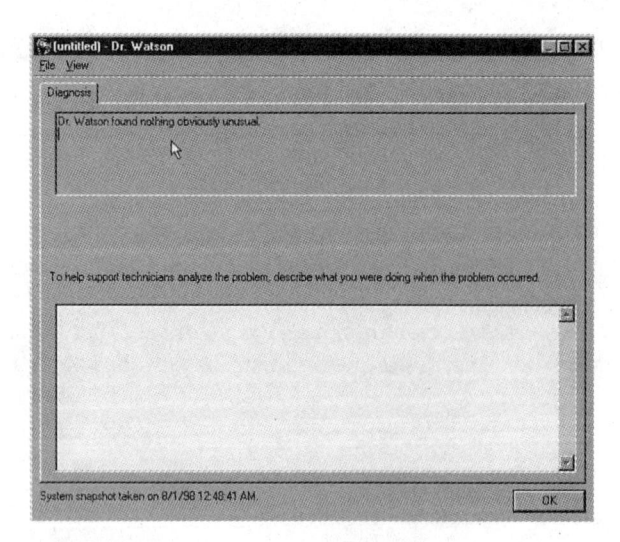

Figure 3.2 Reviewing the Diagnosis of the Dr. Watson utility.

3.1 DETERMINE WHICH FILES LOAD DURING THE BOOT PROCESS

> **NOTE**
>
> Just before you actually enter the GUI for the Dr. Watson utility, a quick series of pop-up message boxes appear and disappear automatically, as shown in Figure 3.3. These boxes tell you that the Dr. Watson utility is generating a *snapshot* of your system, as it is that very moment when you double-click its System tray icon.

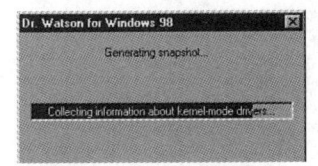

Figure 3.3 Generating a new Dr. Watson System Information snapshot.

3. Upon entering the utility, Dr. Watson will probably blithely note that there is nothing obviously unusual with your system. This is its way of telling you that everything with your system is operating properly. What this also means, is that Dr. Watson could not detect any standard problems with your system. That is, if a device does not fail outright, Dr. Watson will usually not be capable of telling you that the device is not working correctly because it knows that the same device is not inoperable either. To get to the details, click the View menu option and then click again on the Advanced View menu selection. This will change what you see in a very radical fashion, as shown in Figure 3.4.

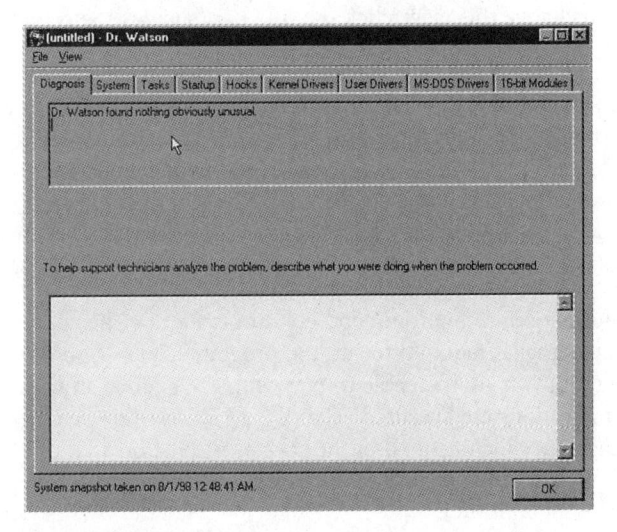

Figure 3.4 Deciding where to go next on the Advanced Dr. Watson tabs.

4. An additional eight tabs appear inside the Dr. Watson application window, other than the initial Diagnosis tab. This is where the good doctor earns his pay. Click the Startup tab to view a listing of the applications that start when your computer boots up, as shown in Figure 3.5.

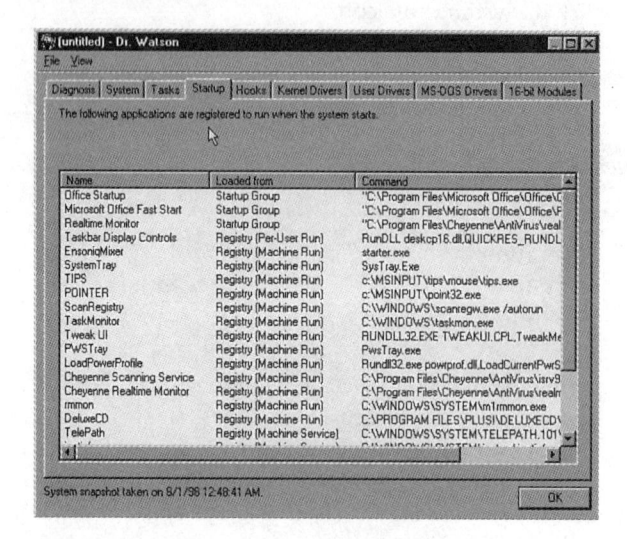

Figure 3.5 Reviewing the files that start whenever Windows 98 begins.

5. One of the nicest things about this tab's information is that the utility automatically sorts the listing by the location from where each application starts. To change this view, click the title bar (such as the Name) for the column by which the list should be sorted.

6. Knowing where the application loaded from tells you where to go in order to make modifications to that startup application's configuration. In the example shown, you see that only a few applications loaded from the Windows 98 Startup group, while a dozen or so loaded by the system Registry. This is important when trying to track down an errant file or application.

7. The information in the Command column is the specific command with parameters that is required to run the program. Thus, with this information, you are then able to play with the manner in which some of your applications are executed. That is, not all software vendors "remember" to document all of the special parameters that can be used with their applications (such as doing a `dir.log` command in a DOS-prompt window).

3.1
DETERMINE WHICH FILES LOAD DURING THE BOOT PROCESS

8. Another section of the Dr. Watson utility that helps you determine what files have been started by Windows 98 during the boot process is found on the Tasks tab. To show these files, click the Tasks tab as shown in Figure 3.6.

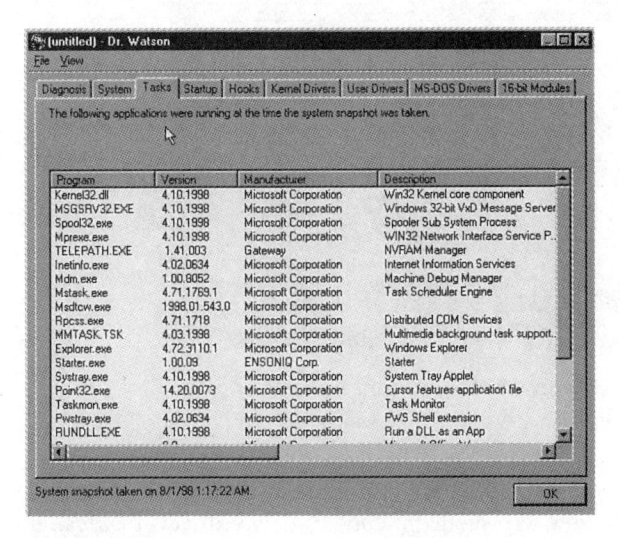

Figure 3.6 Reviewing the tasks that were activated when Dr. Watson took its system information snapshot.

9. If you run the Dr. Watson utility as soon as your system has completed its boot process and before you open any other applications, the Tasks tab will contain some useful information for you. Not only does this tab list the precise filenames, their location, version number, description, and manufacturer's name of the file, but it also informs you as to whether the file in question is actually part of the Windows 98 operating system. To see this last bit of information, click the horizontal scrollbar to scroll the window to the right, as shown in Figure 3.7.

10. Being able to determine whether a device driver is part of the Windows 98 OS is critical when you are attempting to obtain direct technical support from a software vendor. For example, you might have assumed that the INETINFO.EXE file was part of Windows 98 directly, but in reality it is part of the Internet Information Server (IIS). This is important data because it usually helps to provide the vendor's technical support staff with as much data as possible when they are attempting to solve your problem over the telephone (in person, this is not big deal). Additionally, sometimes another application's program file might have overwritten a file of the same name by a different vendor. This listing helps you clarify who belongs with what, and vice-versa.

CHAPTER 3
THE BOOT PROCESS

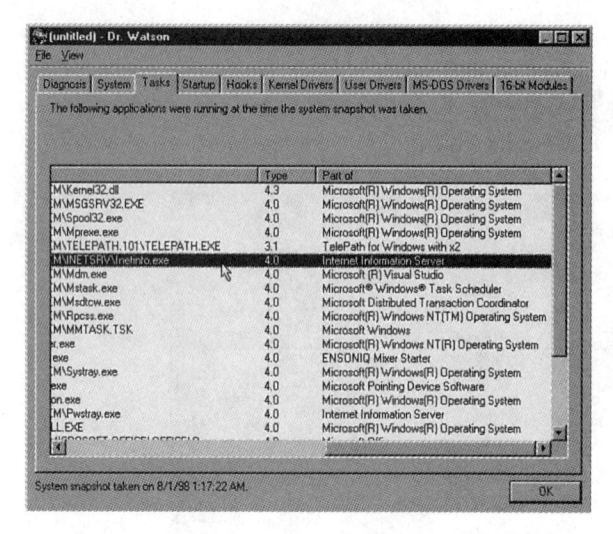

Figure 3.7 Reviewing the information for one of the active files.

11. The User Drivers section of this utility is great for helping you identify the names of the user-mode multimedia device drivers that load during the initial Windows 98 startup. To access this list, click the User Drivers tab as shown in Figure 3.8.

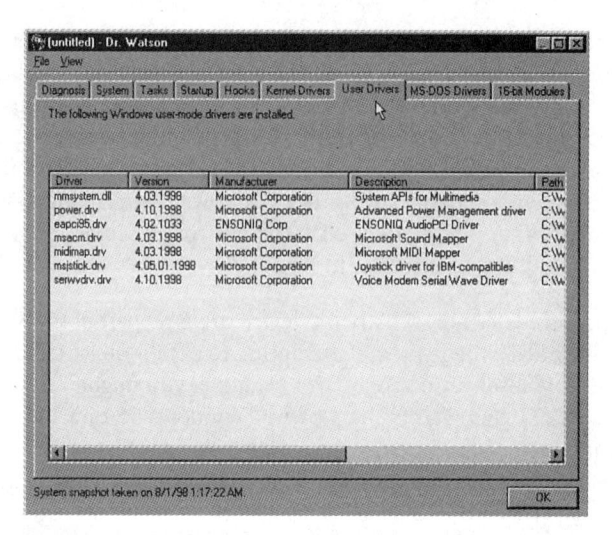

Figure 3.8 Checking out the installed user-mode drivers.

12. Exact version information as well as the precise location of the drivers is found on this screen. Additionally, a description of each device driver and its manufacturer are listed here also.

COMPLEXITY
ADVANCED

3.2 How do I...
Change the Windows 98 startup process so I can find malfunctioning device drivers?

Problem

The computer does not appear to be loading software device drivers correctly during the Windows 98 boot process. How do I perform a diagnostic startup of my Windows 98 PC, so that I can interactively load device drivers and other boot process software as well as tweak the system configuration files?

Technique

To modify the Windows 98 startup or boot process, use the Windows 98 System Configuration utility (Microsoft Config tool). This utility allows you to modify essential system file components including the CONFIG.SYS, AUTOEXEC.BAT, WIN.INI, and the SYSTEM.INI files. Additionally, you are able to modify the Windows 98 Startup group by choosing a specific startup mode.

The System Configuration utility can either be started from a Run command box or the System Information tool. It is imperative that someone who is not familiar with the more detailed aspects of these system configuration files (CONFIG.SYS, AUTOEXEC.BAT, WIN.INI, and SYSTEM.INI), does not attempt to make these changes on a production machine. Even though the changes to these four files are made via a GUI-based configuration tool, it does not mean that you will be safe from doing dumb things that can potentially crash the operating system.

If you are not that familiar with the previously mentioned configuration files, perhaps a quick refresher course on the use of Microsoft DOS and Windows 3.x might be in order. To quickly get up to speed on the Windows initialization files (*.INI files), I suggest you pick up a copy of one of the Microsoft Windows Resource Kits (any version from WFW 3.1 through Windows 98 cover these files pretty well, with the best information coming in the Windows 3.x kits), which are available from Microsoft Press. Your Microsoft DOS manual is probably a good starting place for learning more about the CONFIG.SYS and AUTOEXEC.BAT files, but there are many good books still available on this topic in the larger chain bookstores.

If you have trouble visualizing where DOS commands might come into play in real life, you should pick up a copy of the book *Upgrading and Repairing Networks* (by Craig Zacker and Paul Doyle, Que Corporation, 1996), which concisely shows where DOS fits into the larger picture. Pay close attention to the introductory section and Chapter 11, "Network Client Software," and you will suddenly see the light.

Steps

1. Start the System Information tool by clicking Start then click the Programs menu option, followed by a click on the Accessories menu option, down to the System Tools menu option, and finally on the System Information menu selection. This takes you directly into the System Information tool, as shown in Figure 3.9.

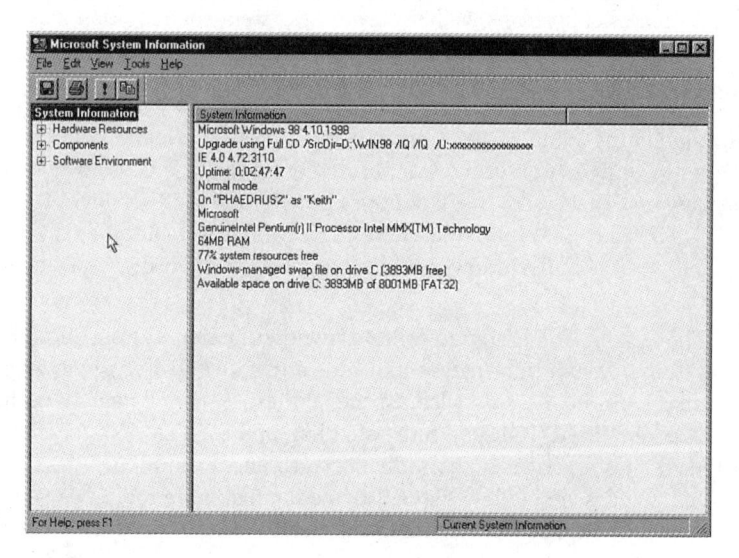

Figure 3.9 Reviewing the primary Microsoft System Information screen.

3.2
CHANGE THE STARTUP PROCESS TO FIND MALFUNCTIONING DRIVERS

2. After the utility starts, click the Tools menu option. This drops down a menu bar where you find ten additional system tools, which are great for helping you track down problems and inconsistencies in your installation as well as providing a few more GUI-based tools for manipulating the Windows 98 Registry. Click the System Configuration utility menu option to startup that utility, as shown in Figure 3.10.

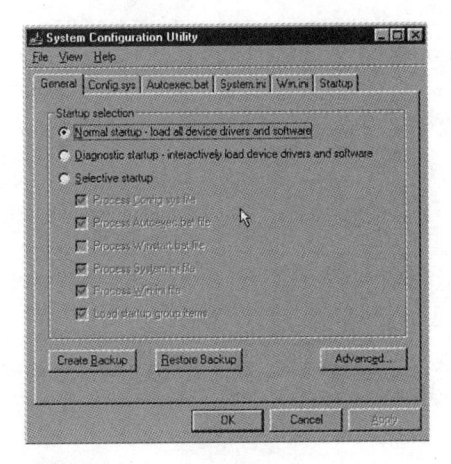

Figure 3.10 Choosing a startup method for your PC.

3. On this first screen you can select a startup mode. The default setting is Normal startup, which means that Windows 98 starts up like it usually does. If you are not experiencing any difficulties with your system, it is recommended that you do not alter the startup mode.

4. However, because you are having trouble with a possible faulty device driver, you should click the middle radio button once. This button places your system into what is known as a Diagnostic startup mode, meaning that Windows 98 will interactively load device drivers and software during the boot process. Click OK to accept this change.

5. A pop-up message box appears prompting you to restart your system. Click Yes to perform the reboot process.

6. Upon reboot, Windows 98 displays its Startup menu while still in a DOS mode. Use the step-by-step confirmation option, which allows you to carefully walk through the boot process.

7. This is where it gets a little tricky. Because you believe the problem is a faulty software device driver, it would be wise not to enable any of the device drivers found in either the CONFIG.SYS or the AUTOEXEC.BAT files. Do this by replying No (the letter N) to each driver as it appears onscreen.

8. Of course, with any troubleshooting technique it is possible to make a bad situation worse. In the event that your PC stops working, press the Reset key on your computer or turn it off and then back on. Then, repeat step 7, but this time try to include any disk-specific drivers, such as references to the files DBLSPACE.BIN or DRVSPACE.BIN.

9. After the full Windows 98 GUI has initialized, check to see whether the problem still exists. If it does not, then you know that the bad driver is starting from within either the CONFIG.SYS or the AUTOEXEC.BAT files. From here it is a process of elimination. That is, you need to skip only one driver at a time until you the find the culprit. To fix the bad driver usually means that you re-install the software for that driver or utilize the Windows Update utility(see Chapter 1,"Installation Tips," of this book for more details on using this tool) to search for any updates directly from Microsoft.

> **NOTE**
> Using Diagnostic Startup mode changes your display monitor settings from its current state to the industry VGA standard resolution mode of 640¥480 and 16 colors. Obviously, if you had been running a much higher resolution on your system, it might no longer be possible for you to even see the OK button in the System Configuration utility much less click on it. If this is the case, you need to click the File menu option. On the drop-down menu that appears, click the Close menu selection, which saves your settings and safely shutdowns the System Configuration utility.

10. If the problem still exists, you know that neither the CONFIG.SYS nor the AUTOEXEC.BAT files are to blame. However, you now need to select another mode to help track down the problem. That mode is known as the Selective startup process. Go back into the System Configuration utility and make sure the General tab is shown as in Figure 3.11. A much faster way to get there is enter the command `msconfig` in the Run command box from the Windows 98 Start menu.

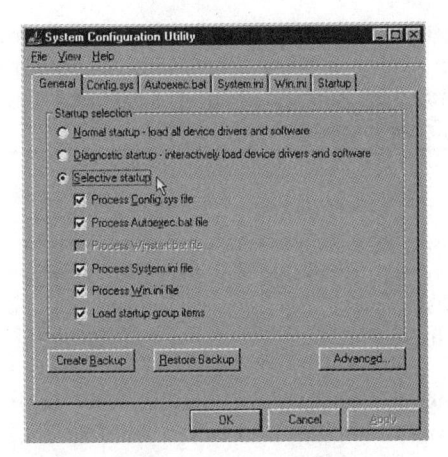

3.2
CHANGE THE STARTUP PROCESS TO FIND MALFUNCTIONING DRIVERS

Figure 3.11 Deciding on the Selective startup options.

11. The Selective startup mode is very similar to that of the Diagnostic startup mode, with the exception of the video display. The Selective startup process does not reset your display monitor to a standard VGA 16-color palette. Of the six options present, the Process WINSTART.BAT file, will only apply during the Windows 98 installation operation. Therefore, the option box for this item might be grayed-out on your screen. From the previous steps you discovered that the CONFIG.SYS and the AUTOEXEC.BAT files work properly, so you should drop down to the Load startup group items option and uncheck that option box.

12. Click OK to save this selection, and then respond Yes to the pop-up box that appears asking you to reboot your system.

13. When restarting the system, check to see if there are any problems with your device drivers. If not, you now know where the problem lies: one of the entries within the Windows 98 Startup group. If the problem still exists, return to the System Configuration utility and re-enable the Load startup group items check box.

> **NOTE**
> Before making a modification to any system file, it is strongly suggested that you make a backup copy of that file (or files). When you are working from within the System Configuration utility, backing up your files is a lot easier than you might think. All you need to do is go back
> *continued on next page*

continued from previous page

to the General tab and click the Create Backup button. Should you later change your mind about making whatever alterations you might have made, simply click the Restore Backup button and all of your files will quickly be restored to their original format.

14. From this point on, you will require a more innovative approach to troubleshooting your system. In the System Configuration utility there are five tabs other than General: Config.Sys, Autoexec.Bat, System.ini, Win.ini, and Startup. Each one of these tabs can be used individually to narrow-down your faulty driver using a trial-and-error methodology. However, the steps we took previously should have ruled out the first two and the last tabs (Config.Sys, Autoexec.Bat, and Startup). But, in case they did not, click once on the Config.Sys tab as shown in Figure 3.12.

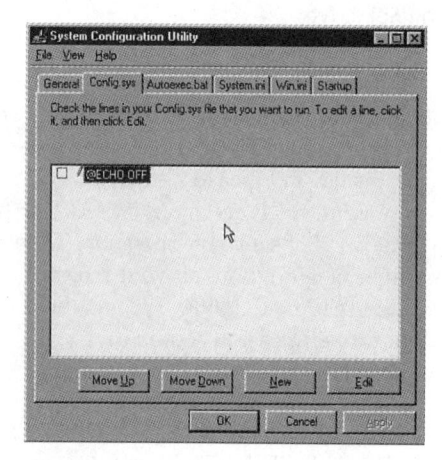

Figure 3.12 Editing the CONFIG.SYS file.

15. This screen shows all of the lines used within your CONFIG.SYS file. If a line has a check mark in the box located on the left side of each line, that means the line is being used by your system. That is, if there is no check mark, then Windows 98 automatically skips the information in that line item; sort of like a REM statement. To change any line, click the Edit button to enter the Edit mode for this screen. If you need to add another line to the CONFIG.SYS file, you would use the New button.

NOTE

If all you want to do is include or exclude lines, then you do not need to use the Edit mode. Just click once on the check box for a line to place a check mark in it or to remove it. Clicking the Edit button permits you to modify the line-item statement directly. For example, you might have

3.2 CHANGE THE STARTUP PROCESS TO FIND MALFUNCTIONING DRIVERS

a statement such as Device=C:\Windows\EMM386.EXE (remember that Windows 98 configuration files are not case-sensitive). Perhaps, in order to get a non–plug-and-play PCMCIA/PC-card device to work on your laptop you need to enter a reserved memory address of D200-DFFF and no expanded memory. Clicking the Edit button allows you to modify the original statement without having to retype the entire line. This way you can add the parameters at the end so the line statement now looks similar to this: Device=C:\Windows\EMM386.EXE NOEMS X=D200-DFFF.

16. As you can see in the example shown, there is only one line in the CONFIG.SYS file and that one is not even in use. It is effectively re-marked out, so that it is not recognized by the Windows 98 operating system. It is recommended that your CONFIG.SYS file also be empty or not used at all, if you have a fully compatible plug-and-play PC. The exception to this recommendation would be if you use older hardware with your computer, such as non–plug-and-play equipment such as some 8-bit sound cards, early to market joysticks, and CD-ROM devices, and so on.

17. The next file you should examine is the AUTOEXEC.BAT file, which can be found by clicking the Autoexec.Bat tab as shown in Figure 3.13.

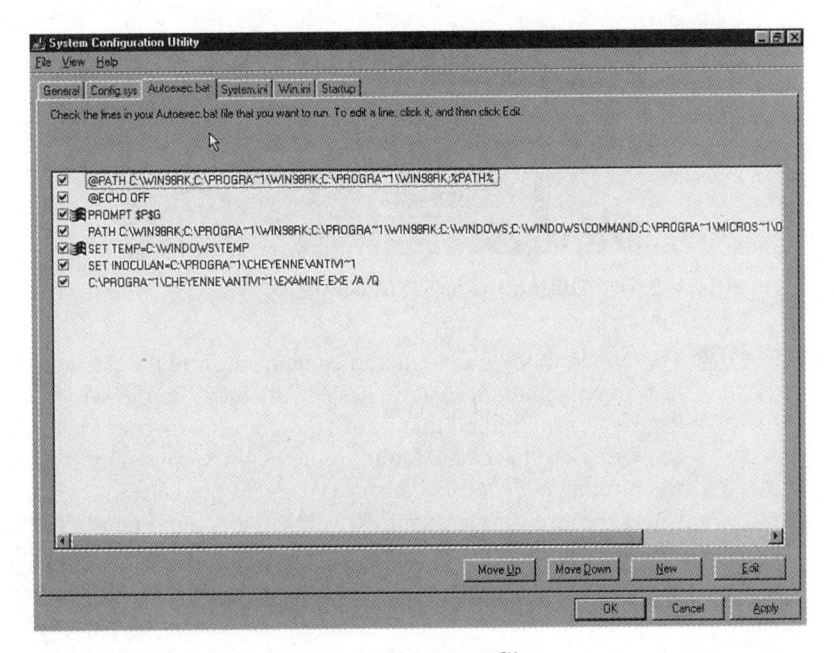

Figure 3.13 Editing the AUTOEXEC.BAT file.

18. Talk about a coincidence. The buttons used to modify this file are exactly the same as the Config.Sys tab. This should make things a bit easier. The important lines to examine in this file are the Path statement and any line that is executing a program or another batch file. Typically, the device driver software is not loaded via the AUTOEXEC.BAT file, because device drivers are most likely started in the CONFIG.SYS or the SYSTEM.INI files (or in the Windows 98 Registry). However, as the old saying goes, anything is possible through DOS, so do not rule out this file via an assumption. You should actually verify each line statement to be sure.

19. Click once on the System.ini tab to reveal that next file's contents in our search, as shown in Figure 3.14.

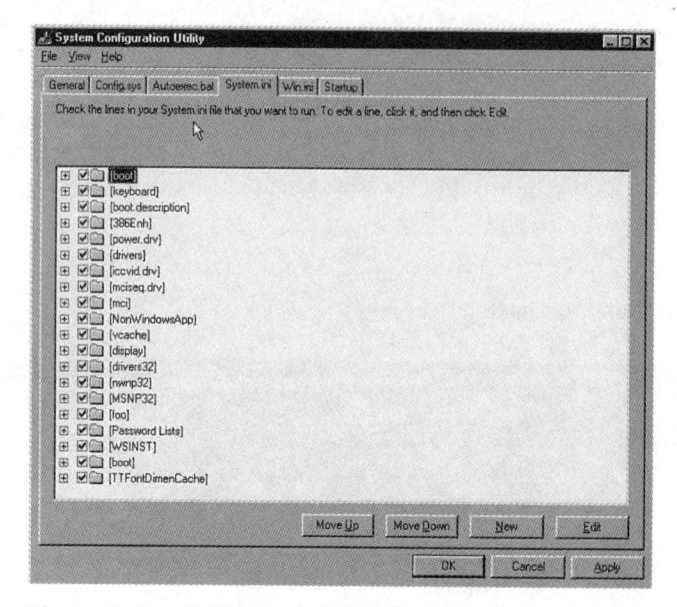

Figure 3.14 Editing the SYSTEM.INI file.

20. The Windows 98 System.ini tab contains most of the operating system's driver configurations that are not usually found in the Windows 98 Registry. Keep in mind that this file might actually contain duplications of configuration statements found in the Registry, so you must be careful when ruling out potential errors as it might not be readily clear as to where the error-prone driver exists. Also, it is important to make a backup copy of both the Registry as well as this file prior to making changes, just in case you make any editing mistakes. The plus signs inside

3.2
CHANGE THE STARTUP PROCESS TO FIND MALFUNCTIONING DRIVERS

the little boxes on the far left of the screen mean that the line item contains more data within it. Click on any of those plus (+) symbols and the plus changes to a minus symbol (-) as it opens the subsections below that main section.

21. Each bracketed section refers to a section heading within this file. The section names ending in .DRV are actually individual driver files (hint, hint: look at these first). In most cases, even if you click the plus symbol on these types of lines, there will not be anything more than an empty space line below them. However, as they say, it never hurts to look. The second place you should look for faulty drivers is the section entitled [drivers]. Click once on the plus sign to the left of the [drivers] check box to reveal its contents, as seen in Figure 3.15.

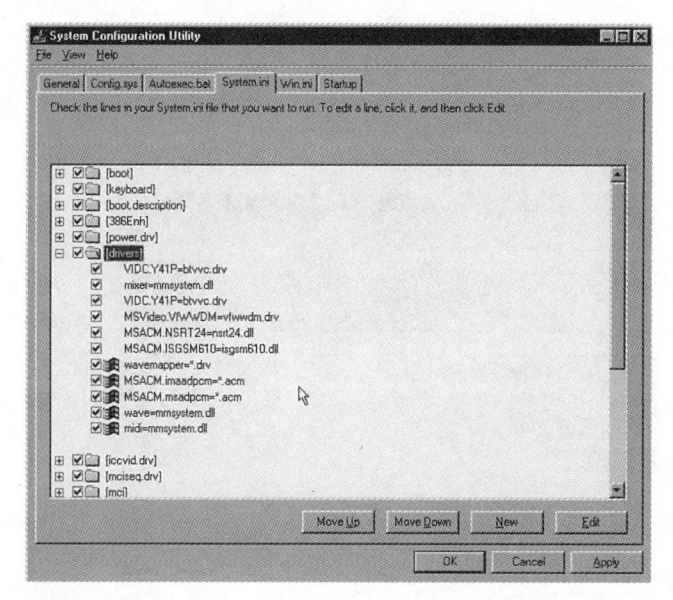

Figure 3.15 Changing the drivers section of the SYSTEM.INI file.

22. At this point the guessing game begins. You can either use the more scientific trial-and-error method of unchecking one line item box at a time, rebooting, and then checking to see if the problem has been corrected, or use more of a guesswork approach. In the latter case, you look at each device line item to narrow-down the number of times you have to restart your computer. That is, if you are suffering from a multimedia device error (your sound system does not work), then you might want to focus only on those drivers that use the MMSYSTEM.DLL file(a multimedia dynamic link library file) or the WAVEMAPPER file.

CHAPTER 3
THE BOOT PROCESS

> **NOTE**
>
> You might have noticed that some of the lines have a small Microsoft Windows logo between the check box and the device statement, whereas others do not. The reason for the logo is that it marks which lines will be used by the system when the Selective startup mode has been disabled for that particular file. This means these are the lines that will be executed even if you have told Windows 98 not to use the SYSTEM.INI file during the boot process, provided that this file was excluded through the use of the Selective startup mode on the General tab of the System Configuration utility. You might still disable the use of these lines, but more than likely you will cripple some aspect of your computer system in doing so.

23. If the problem still exists even after you have tried all the device drivers in this section, then the next section you should examine is the [boot] area. Click the plus sign to the left of the [boot] check box to reveal its contents, as seen in Figure 3.16.

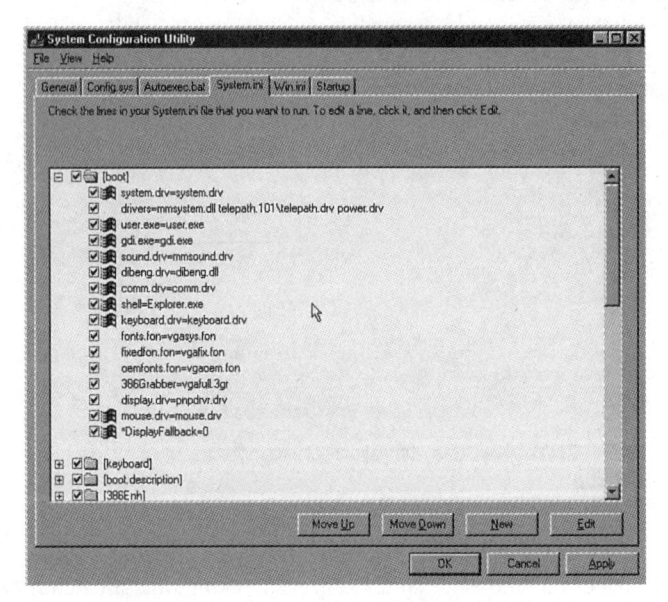

Figure 3.16 Changing the boot section of the SYSTEM.INI file.

3.2 CHANGE THE STARTUP PROCESS TO FIND MALFUNCTIONING DRIVERS

24. One of the most likely culprits in this section can be found in the statement **drivers=** (most likely there is more text following the equal sign). In the example presented, the TelePath driver is the modem driver for the example system's internal modem, which caused grief in tracking it down during an installation of an early Windows 98 beta. You should remember that a large percentage of proprietary hardware vendor device drivers will still dump its configuration into an .INI file instead of the Windows 98 Registry; an important fact when you are trying to troubleshoot faulty drivers.

25. Click once on the Win.ini tab to access the primary Windows 98 configuration initialization file, as shown in Figure 3.17.

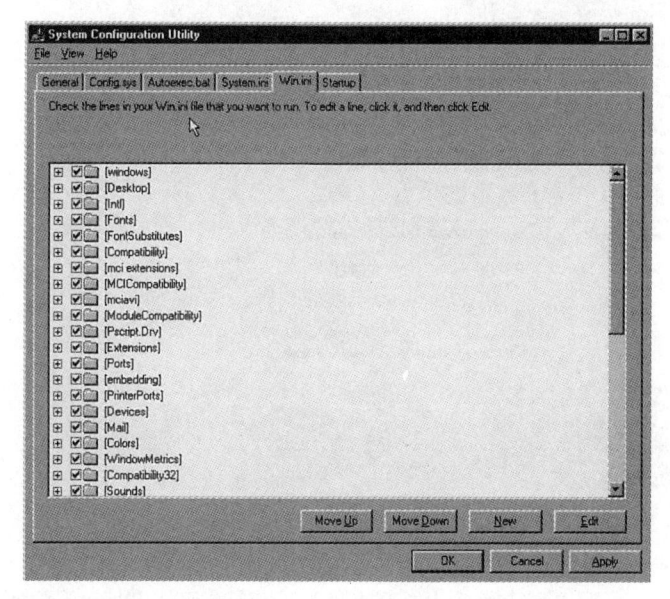

Figure 3.17 Reviewing the various sections of the WIN.INI file.

26. Assuming that your trial-and-error efforts have not yet been successful, you should now examine the WIN.INI file's [windows] area. Click the plus sign to the left of the [windows] check box to reveal its contents.

27. Two important statements are in this section: the **load=** and the **run=** lines. The **load** statement attempts to load an application of some sort into memory, whereas the run statement is usually used for executing an application as soon as the Windows 98 GUI starts. Unfortunately, some smaller hardware vendors still do not get it and use these two lines interchangeably, even when their device driver really could be managed better by Windows 98 than their own proprietary software drivers (some printer vendors like to do this). You should try commenting out both of these lines individually (assuming your system has something in either or both of these statements), in an attempt to further troubleshoot your system. If this does not work, it is time to move on. Click the Startup tab to reveal the next screen, as shown in Figure 3.18.

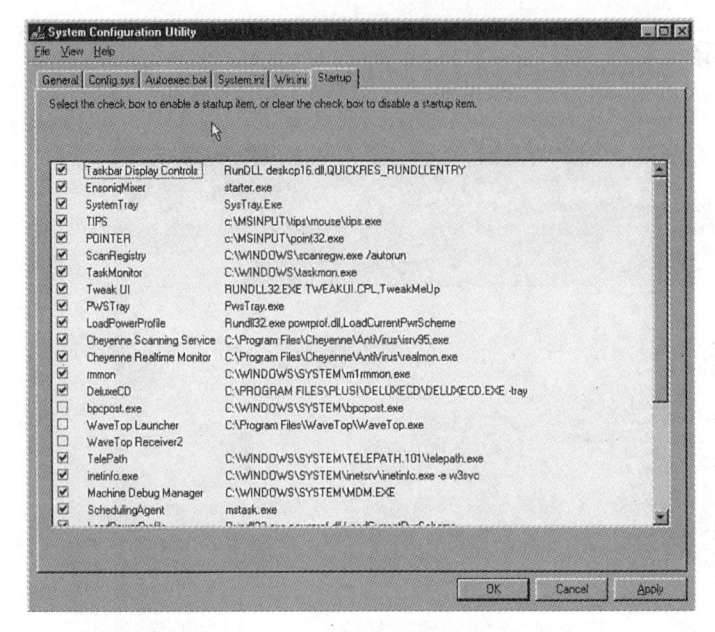

Figure 3.18 Changing selections within the Startup file.

28. The Startup section of the System Configuration utility is a handy place to visit, even if there is nothing wrong with your PC. This is because it will present you with a listing of the various system components that load during the boot process of your computer, as well as letting you see what the actual files are for those applications that reside in the System Tray area of the Windows 98 taskbar.

29. However, you are still trying to track down a software device error. Now in all likelihood, you will know the name of the driver that is failing: either the specific filename or the hardware component it is failing on. For example, the first time I installed WebTV for Windows, a message box kept appearing saying that the ANNCLIST.EXE file was not working properly. Through a quick examination of the Startup tab, I was able to determine that the file was associated with the Announcements portion of the WebTV for Windows application. Further analysis showed that by disabling this file via the Startup portion of the System Configuration utility, the rest of the WebTV for Windows application would continue to work until I could obtain an updated driver from the vendor. That is exactly what I did, and I was able to work around this error message until an updated file was available for download and reinstallation.

30. You can follow the same sort of methodology for tracking down your own computer errors and repairing them as necessary. Like all the other sections of the System Configuration utility, the Startup line items can be commented-out by unchecking each individual box as needed until you find the problematic driver. If after using all the areas of this utility you still cannot track down your problem, there is one place left to check: the Windows 98 Registry. For more details on how the Registry works, how to edit it, and how to maneuver through it, refer to Chapter 4 of this book.

COMPLEXITY
INTERMEDIATE

3.3 How do I... Boot to a DOS prompt?

Problem

Maybe you are one of those old-fashioned types who want their Windows 98 PC to boot to a plain, old MS-DOS prompt. Alternatively, perhaps you have a real business need because you must run an old DOS program as part of your job and no matter what you do to configure it, the application will not run under the Windows 98 GUI. Despite the efforts of the Microsoft marketing machine, it is very possible to boot to a C:\ prompt just like the days of yesteryear.

Technique

There are three ways to configure your system to do this. The easiest and most basic way is to use the System Configuration utility, which is built into Windows 98. The best way to perform this feat of magic is to use a Windows 98 Resource Kit utility known as Tweak UI. A combination of both these ways can be accomplished using a DOS window and manually editing the MSDOS.SYS file yourself. The third way does not require the Tweak UI utility, but it still provides you with the same end results that Tweak UI can give you.

This is by far the most dangerous approach because it is possible to mess up your system to the point that it will not boot if you edit this file incorrectly.

There is one other manual way to view the Windows 98 Boot menu: hold down the Ctrl key while your system is rebooting. This method is kludgy at best, because some older computer systems will detect the key being held down and then lock up the keyboard or fail to boot due to a keyboard system error. However, on the newest computers shipped today, this is hardly ever a problem.

Steps

1. First, the easy, but very basic and inflexible way. Start the System Configuration utility either from the System Information tool or via the `MSConfig` command from the Run box, as shown in Figure 3.19.

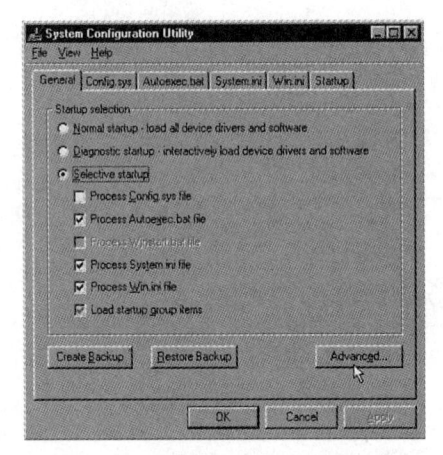

Figure 3.19 Selecting the Advanced options for the System Configuration utility.

2. Next, after the General screen of the utility appears, click the Advanced tab that is located near the bottom right corner of the screen.

3. Doing this will take you into the Advanced Troubleshooting Settings window, as shown in Figure 3.20.

4. Click the check box located to the left of the Enable Startup Menu option. This will cause the system to display the Windows 98 Startup menu when your system reboots.

3.3 BOOT TO A DOS PROMPT

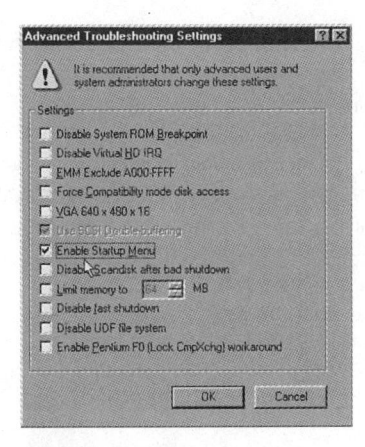

Figure 3.20 Changing an Advanced Troubleshooting Setting option.

5. Click OK to accept this change. When you are prompted for a system reboot, click Yes to allow the system to restart itself.

6. As the system reboots, but prior to it loading the Windows 98 GUI, you will see the Boot menu as shown in Figure 3.21.

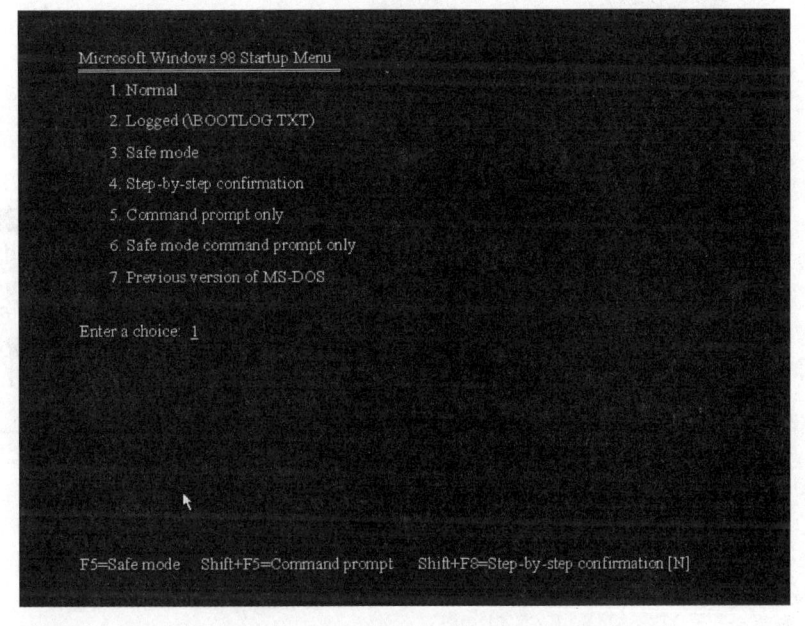

Figure 3.21 The Microsoft Windows 98 Boot menu.

7. Use the arrow keys on your keyboard to move up and down amongst the selections, and choose the one that best fits your needs (such as the Command Prompt Only option).

8. Now you will do the same thing, but via a very powerful and flexible utility known as Tweak UI. If you recall from Chapter 1, you learned how to obtain and install the Tweak UI utility. To help prod your memory go to the Windows 98 Control Panel and double-click the Tweak UI icon.

9. After the utility starts, click the Boot tab as shown in Figure 3.22.

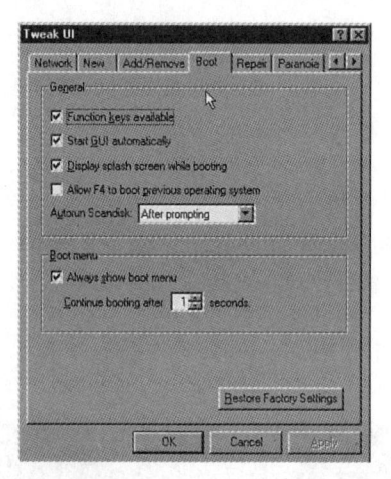

Figure 3.22 Revising Windows 98 Boot options with the Tweak UI utility.

> **NOTE**
> The Tweak UI utility provides you with a very clean way to modify the MSDOS.SYS file with most of its booting possibilities, but without any of the danger that is present when you modify the file yourself directly. It is for this reason alone that it is strongly recommended that you acquire a copy of this utility for configuring the manner in which your PC boots the Windows 98 operating system.

10. The fastest method for making your system boot to a DOS prompt is to uncheck the box next to the Start GUI automatically option, as this will keep Windows 98 from going directly into its graphical user interface. Thus, by default, you will be dropped into a DOS prompt whenever you reboot your computer.

BOOT TO A DOS PROMPT

11. To make the Boot Menu appear onscreen even if you have unchecked the Start GUI automatically option, place a check mark in the Always show boot menu option box located at the bottom of the screen in Figure 3.22. If this option is selected, you should think about setting a reasonable length number of seconds (such as 10) as the default for the menu's display time. The time should be long enough to let you pick a boot option, but short enough so that your system will boot up in a reasonable amount of time in case you have to step away from your computer momentarily.

12. Clicking the Restore Factory Settings button will automatically restore the Windows 98 boot system options to the same as they were when Windows 98 was first installed.

13. As stated previously, the final method for configuring your system to boot to a DOS prompt is by manually modifying the MSDOS.SYS file. This file is stored in your Windows 98 root directory (usually the C:\ drive), and has the attributes of SHR (a system file that is hidden and read-only by default).

14. To begin the modification process, open a DOS window and change the directory to the system root. It is wise move to create a backup copy of this file in case you accidentally mess it up.

> **NOTE**
> For those of you who might not recall your DOS command structure as well as you used to, you might be interested to know that you cannot make a backup copy of a hidden system file using the DOS Copy command. In order to successfully make the backup copy using this command you must first remove the hidden system attributes. Of course, you could make the backup copy from inside the Windows Explorer application by using the Cut and Paste functionality.

15. Next, you need to change the attributes of this file so that it is no longer a hidden, read-only file (you can leave the system attribute on, but it is easier to remove them all for now). To do this, type in the command `attrib MsDos.Sys -r -s -h` (this is not a case-sensitive command, but I used the different case to help make the filename more readable) and then press Enter, as shown in Figure 3.23.

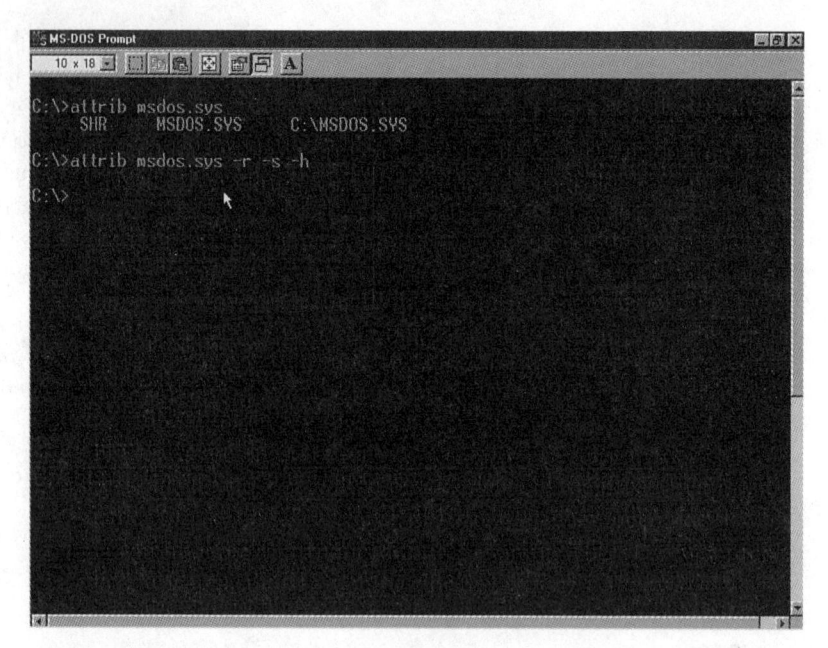

Figure 3.23 Changing file attributes from inside a DOS Prompt window.

16. Perform another attribute directory listing for this file be certain that you changed the attributes correctly. Now start the edit of this file using the DOS **Edit.com** command file or whatever DOS editor you feel comfortable using, as shown in Figure 3.24. For this example, use the DOS **Edit.com** command file.

> **NOTE**
>
> If you remember nothing else about editing this file, remember this: *Do not, for any reason whatsoever, delete all those lines of XXXs that are found inside this file.* If you do this, it is very likely that the file will fall below its mandatory 1K size limit (for example, 1,024 bytes). If this does happen and you attempt to reboot your computer system, then your PC will fail to boot into the Windows 98 operating system. It will then take the use of an Emergency Repair disk or Windows 98 Startup disk to fix this problem; definitely not a recommended procedure to try.

17. The MSDOS.SYS file is broken into two distinct sections: the [Paths] section and the [Options] section. Place path-specific information in the [Paths] section (obviously), such as the defined name of the Windows 98

3.3
BOOT TO A DOS PROMPT

directory and the location of the boot drive's root directory. All of the specific boot options, such as use of the Windows 98 logo, Novell NetWare network information, the boot menu functionality, and AutoScan settings are to be placed into the [Options] section. Failure to follow these guidelines can, at best result, in a feature not working and, at worst, your system might fail to boot properly.

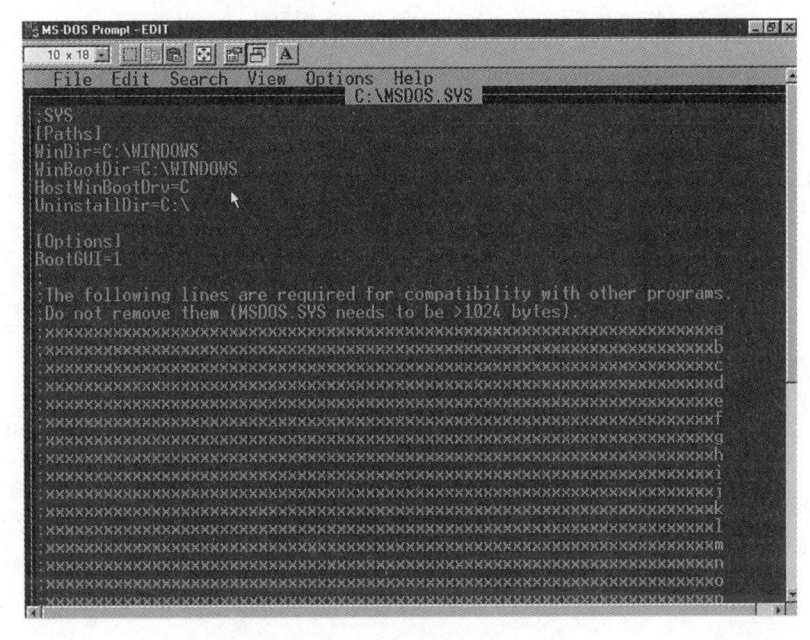

Figure 3.24 Editing the MSDOS.SYS file.

18. So, in the [Options] section, change the command `BootGUI=1` to `BootGUI=0` (the number **1** represents a Yes, whereas the number **0** equates to a No). Leaving this statement as being equal to **1** is just like having a `win` statement in an AUTOEXEC.BAT file under Windows 3.x (ah, the good old days).

19. After you have made this change, as well as any others that you might be interested in trying out, save your changes and exit the DOS editor program.

20. On a side note, one additional change that you might be interested in is the Logo= option. If you set this option to the number **0** causes Windows 98 to not display the animated Windows 98 logo upon the starting of the operating system. This capability is very beneficial because it permits the

Windows 98 OS to not hook various other interrupts as it starts, and these interrupts are the same ones that often cause third-party memory managers to fail.

21. One final comment, Windows 98 does not support the Safe Mode with Networking feature that Windows 95 had incorporated into its settings. Therefore, attempting to load a Network=1 statement into the MSDOS.SYS file does nothing in a Windows 98 world.

COMPLEXITY
INTERMEDIATE

3.4 How do I...
Know what the key system files are?

Problem

When troubleshooting a boot issue, it is helpful to know the names of the system configuration files that affect the boot process. Additionally, if your home-grown application page faults on a regular basis, or if it brings down the entire Windows 98 operating system, then perhaps it would behoove you to consider the other Windows 98 system files that your application might be affecting.

Technique

The first part of the technique is to read the following list of important Windows 98 system files. Beyond that, you should make note of the various other Windows 98 system tools and utilities that can be used to modify these system files in a manner that benefits you the most.

Steps

1. Examine the listing of Windows 98 system files, making sure to note where each of these files can be found on your own computer. The path in the brackets next to each file's name in the following list is the most probable location for the file so you should look there first.

3.4
KNOW WHAT THE KEY SYSTEM FILES ARE

- AUTOEXEC.BAT [C:\]
- CONFIG.SYS [C:\]
- MSDOS.SYS [C:\]
- SYSTEM.DAT [C:\Windows]
- SYSTEM.INI [C:\Windows]
- WIN.INI [C:\Windows]
- WIN.DAT [C:\Windows]

2. Note that all these files, with the exception of those with a .DAT extension, can be modified using the standard DOS text editor. The other two files, SYSTEM.DAT and WIN.DAT, are the Registry files created and stored by the Windows 98 operating system. To modify these files, refer to Chapter 4 of this book.

3. As discussed previously in this chapter, the Windows 98 System Configuration utility is a great starting point for checking and modifying the other configuration files listed here. Other tools built into the Windows 98 operating system that you should consider using include the Windows Registry Checker, Dr. Watson for Windows 98, the Version Conflict Manager, and the Automatic Skip Driver Agent.

> **NOTE**
>
> These four additional tools are all discussed in detail in this book. Information on the Windows Registry Checker can be found in Chapter 4, "The Registry." Dr. Watson for Windows 98, the Version Conflict Manager, and the Automatic Skip Driver agent can all be found in Chapter 7, "System Resource Management." All these tools can be found and launched from within the System Information tool, which should be one of the first places you go when encountering difficulties with Windows 98 installation.

COMPLEXITY
ADVANCED

3.5 How do I...
Obtain information on problematic hardware that was encountered during the Windows 98 startup?

Problem

When I installed the Windows 98 operating system on my machine, the process stalled at least one time, requiring an extra reboot of my PC. How can I figure out what caused the system to stall and what can I do to resolve any residual issues that might still be around?

Technique

The Windows 98 setup program uses an automatic hardware detection mode during the setup process to facilitate a smoother installation of itself. It records the start of each detection test and its results in a hidden file known as the DETLOG.TXT file, while placing information regarding installation crashes in the DETCRASH.LOG hidden file (both files can be found in the root directory of your boot disk). During the installation process Windows 98 uses this method, but now that Windows 98 has finally been installed you might need extra assistance if you change your hardware configuration.

After the operating system has been installed, Windows 98 uses a special software agent known as the *internal Automatic Skip Driver agent (ASD)* to detect and disable those hardware devices that cause problems. These difficulties are the ones that would otherwise cause your system to crash during the boot process, and so the ASD provides assistance in order for the startup process to continue.

ASD works by recognizing and recording those hardware devices that were not capable of *enumerating* when Windows 98 starts up. Think of enumeration as the process by which Plug and Play devices that Windows 98 sees in your PC are assigned system resources to make sure that the hardware component works properly. If a device fails to enumerate properly twice, the ADA agent jumps to disable that device.

Because the ASD agent works in the background, performing its work first and then telling what it did (well, sort of anyway), you might want to know the details. In order for you to know the basics of what might have happened, you can check the Windows 98 Device Manager. Anything that has been disabled by

OBTAIN INFO ON PROBLEMATIC HARDWARE FOUND DURING STARTUP

ASD now appears in the Device Manager with a yellow exclamation point next to it. However, there are no real details as to when, where, or how the ASD marked that particular device. Further, unless you are a very proactive systems person who checks their Device Manager on a regular basis, you might not notice these problems until something has gone massively wrong with your computer. The way you figure out what the ASD is doing is to run it yourself.

Steps

1. Start the System Information tool by clicking the Start button then click the Programs menu option, click on the Accessories menu option then click on the System Tools menu option, and finally on the System Information menu option. Alternatively, you could always launch this tool much faster by typing the `Msinfo32` command into the Windows 98 Run command box, and then either pressing Enter or clicking OK.

2. After the System Information tool initiates, click the Tools menu option. Then click the Automatic Skip Driver Agent menu option. Again, if this startup process seems a bit lengthy, you can always type the **ASD** command into the Windows 98 Run command box, and then either press Enter or click OK, as shown in Figure 3.25.

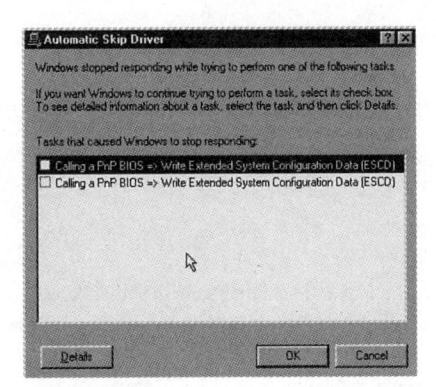

Figure 3.25 Using the ASD agent.

3. Any problem that the Automatic Skip Driver agent tool has detected with your computer will appear inside this box.

> **NOTE**
>
> If you believe that you have a sporadic problem with a hardware device, you might want to review the ASD.LOG file. This file contains every problem that the ASD application has ever found in conjunction with your computer, whereas the box in Figure 3.25 will only show files that failed the last time you started your system.

4. To obtain more information behind the failure of one of the tasks listed in the box, click the check box next to the task you want to analyze.

5. Doing this places a check mark in the box to show you it has been marked for further information. Next, click the Details button (shown in Figure 3.25) to bring up the Function Details dialog box in Figure 3.26.

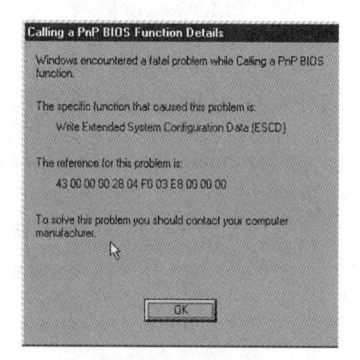

Figure 3.26 Obtaining details on a failed Plug and Play BIOS function.

6. As you have probably noticed in this example, the ADA Agent tool does not always exactly clarify things for the average Windows 98 user. The first indented section describes the specific function or task that caused the problem in the first place.

7. The second indented section contains the reference data for the problem. This data is in a hexadecimal format (Base-16), and can be converted to decimal format using the Windows 98 calculator (use in Scientific mode) if need be. However, unless the internal bits of your computer system truly concern you, you might want to instead take a message such as this and forward it to the technical support engineers for the company that made your computer system. The final section gives you an idea of what you should do to correct the problem. In this case, you should contact the manufacturer the PC (Gateway 2000).

3.6 FORCE WINDOWS 98 TO BOOT INTO SAFE MODE

> **NOTE**
>
> Sometimes the detailed view of the ASD presents you with very cryptic information that might appear too vague for you to use. However, it is useful to someone, usually the manufacturer of the computer. In the example, the helpful engineers of the computer manufacturer were able to trace the problem back to a corrupted VXD for the video card. While it was not crashing the system, it did limit some functionality that would otherwise have been useful. Therefore, it is important for you to use the ADA agent tool, at least on a periodic basis.

COMPLEXITY
INTERMEDIATE

3.6 How do I... Force Windows 98 to boot into Safe Mode?

Problem

Your computer appears to stall for an extended period of time during the boot process. You want to try to fix this, but to do so you must boot into the Windows 98 Safe Mode. How do you accomplish this? Alternatively, your video display either stops working or it appears a bit crazed after you boot the Windows 98 GUI. Again, to fix this, you must boot into Safe Mode, but how?

Technique

The Windows 98 Safe Mode process is a very controlled use of the Microsoft Windows 98 operating system. It limits the resolution of the display monitor by loading only the standard VGA device drivers, it does not process either the CONFIG.SYS or AUTOEXEC.BAT files, and it loads only the mouse and keyboard drivers. Other hardware devices such as network interface cards (NICs), removable media drives, and telecommunications devices will probably not function in a Safe Mode setting.

> **NOTE**
>
> Windows 98 differs from Windows 95 in that there is no longer any support for the Safe Mode with networking configuration in Windows 98. This means that should your system go into Safe Mode, you will be completely disconnected from your network(s).

Safe Mode can be forced through a series of keystrokes, or it can be a regular option for you. Changing your access to the Windows 98 Boot menu is what can make Safe Mode a regular option for your system. Please review the previous sections in this chapter for more details on how to modify the boot process using the Tweak UI utility.

Steps

1. To enter Safe Mode, restart your Windows 98 computer or turn it on if it is off. Hold down the Ctrl key on the keyboard during the reboot or starting process. This causes Windows 98 Startup menu to appear. If it does appear, this means that the Ctrl key on your keyboard has been mapped for other purposes. Therefore, you must enable the Startup menu through another means.

> **NOTE**
> Windows 98 automatically boots into Safe Mode when your computer is incapable of booting properly. Moreover, because it does this, some of these first steps are not required unless you want to boot to a Safe Mode with a DOS prompt.

2. The other way to get to the Windows 98 Startup menu is through the Windows 98 System Configuration utility. To get to this utility, start the System Information tool by clicking Start button, then click on the Programs menu option, click the Accessories menu option, then click on the System Tools menu option, and finally click on the System Information menu option.

3. After the System Information tool initiates, click its Tools menu option. Then click the System Configuration utility menu option to display the tool as shown in Figure 3.27. Alternatively, you can always launch this tool much faster by typing in the `MsConfig` command into the Windows 98 Run command box, and then either pressing Enter or clicking OK.

4. After the System Configuration utility opens, click Advanced button (see Figure 3.27) to access the Advanced Troubleshooting Settings screen shown in Figure 3.28.

5. When the Advanced Troubleshooting Settings window appears, click the check box next to the Enable Startup Menu option. This will enable the option and display the Startup menu the next time you reboot your computer.

FORCE WINDOWS 98 TO BOOT INTO SAFE MODE

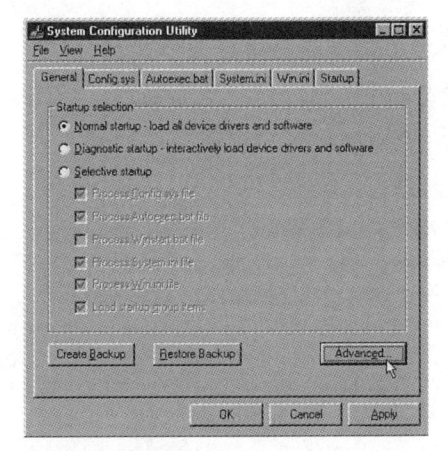

Figure 3.27 Reviewing the primary System Configuration utility screen.

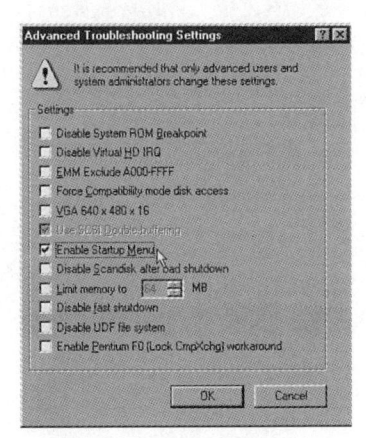

Figure 3.28 Enabling the Windows 98 Startup menu using the Advanced Troubleshooting Settings screen.

6. The Startup menu can list many options, including the following:

- Normal
- Logged (BOOTLOG.TXT)
- Safe Mode
- Step-by-Step Confirmation

- Command Prompt Only
- Safe Mode with Command Prompt Only
- Previous version of MS-DOS

7. The third and sixth options are the ones you should be most interested in. The standard Safe Mode (option three) is started with only the most minimal of software drivers and bypasses your normal startup files. The Safe Mode with Command Prompt Only option is recommended when you cannot get all the way into the Windows 98 GUI (even with regular Safe Mode), when you need to use any command-line utilities, or when you want to avoid loading the HIMEM.SYS or IFSHLP.SYS files into memory while booting Windows 98.

8. Once you have made it into Safe Mode, either at a DOS prompt or in the Windows 98 GUI, the actual troubleshooting process begins. You might want to use the ASD agent, the Registry Checker, the System File Checker, or the System Configuration utility to help in the troubleshooting process. All of these tools are discussed in detail in this book.

COMPLEXITY
BEGINNER

3.7 How do I... Create a Windows 98 Startup disk?

Problem

There will be times when you need to perform a clean boot of your computer directly from a floppy disk. This might be because you want to eliminate a virus from your computer (the virus detection packages usually cannot be installed on to an infected PC, so a clean boot keeps the virus from loading itself into memory), or it might be because your Windows 98 installation is failing and you want to troubleshoot its failures.

Technique

A Windows 98 Startup disk permits you to perform a clean boot of your computer system. Creating the Startup disk requires a single high-density 3 1/2-inch disk and about five minutes of your time. The facility to create this

3.7
CREATE A WINDOWS 98 STARTUP DISK

disk is built into the operating system, so there is nothing extra you have to go buy or download from the Internet. You will also need to have your Windows 98 CD-ROM handy during the creation process.

Steps

1. The easiest way to create a Startup disk is to have done so during the installation of Windows 98. If you recall, during the installation process you were prompted to insert a floppy disk into your A:\ drive for precisely this reason. However, if you are following these steps, you probably skipped on making a Startup disk at that time.

2. The other way to create a Startup disk is by using the Add/Remove Programs feature of Windows 98. If you recall, you can start the Add/Remove Programs icon by double-clicking it in the Windows 98 Control Panel.

3. After the Add/Remove Programs screen appears, click the Startup Disk tab to access its screen, as shown in Figure 3.29.

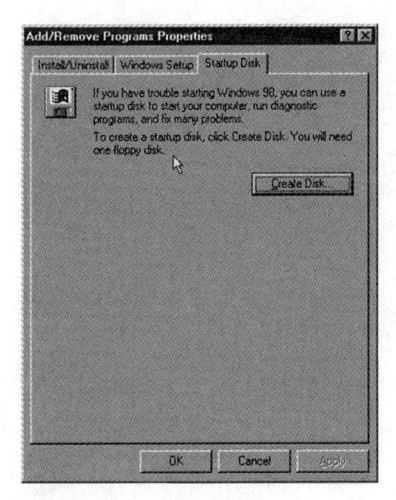

Figure 3.29 Creating a Windows 98 Startup disk.

4. To create the Startup disk, insert your blank (formatted) floppy disk into your computerís A:\ drive. Click the Create Disk button as shown in Figure 3.29.

CHAPTER 3
THE BOOT PROCESS

5. A pop-up message box appears asking you to insert your Windows 98 CD-ROM before clicking OK to continue. Do this and then click OK.

6. A status bar appears showing how the creation operation has progressed. Somewhere around the 20 percent complete mark it prompts you to place a formatted floppy disk into your computerís A:\ drive. Because you have already done this (step 4), click on OK to continue.

7. The disk creation process continues automatically and when it is complete the following screen appears, as seen in Figure 3.30.

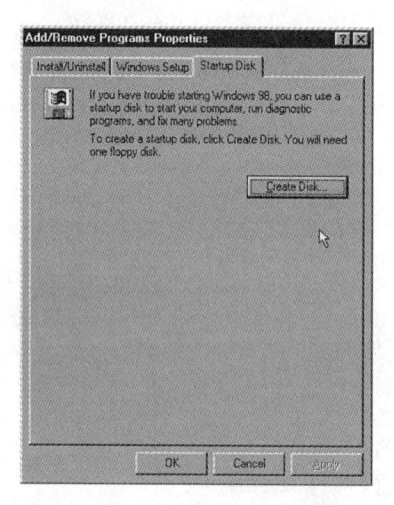

Figure 3.30 The completion screen following a Windows 98 Startup disk creation process.

8. This screen looks a bit familiar. Yes, thatís correct, it is the exact same screen that you started with. Windows 98 does not give you any indication that the Startup disk creation process finished, much less whether it did so successfully. When the progress bar disappears, you are just supposed to know intuitively that the process is complete.

9. You should test out the Startup disk that you made by rebooting your computer with the disk still in the floppy drive. If your system boots, it works! If it does not, you need to repeat the Startup disk creation process (now wouldnít a Startup disk Complete message be a better idea…are you listening Microsoft?).

CHAPTER 4
THE REGISTRY

4

THE REGISTRY

How do I...

4.1 Restore the Windows 98 Registry to the same state it was in when I last successfully started my PC?

4.2 Modify the Registry so that it automatically starts a specific application every time I launch Windows 98?

4.3 Recover from incorrect Registry modifications?

4.4 Modify the Registry so that a user cannot access the Windows Update feature and fix his own PC?

This chapter covers the Windows 98 Registry. The *Windows 98 Registry* is the logical database that contains all the critical, and sometimes dynamic, information regarding your Windows 98 operating system implementation. For a subject that most people know very little about, the Windows 98 Resource Kit is capable of concisely describing it in a mere 63 pages of very technical jargon without even touching upon how the Registry affects application developers (that takes whole books). Think of the Registry as the center of the Windows 98 universe, much like the sun is to the earth. Without the sun, everything on Earth dies...without the Registry, Windows 98 is dead in the water. Other than the Windows 98 Resource Kit (Microsoft Press), you might want to review Jerry Honeycutt's book *Using the Windows 98 Registry* (Que Corporation, 1998).

> **NOTE**
>
> The Windows 98 Registry is a dangerous place for beginners or relatively inexperienced Windows 98 users! This cannot be stressed enough! One mistake, and you might cause your computer to stop working, without any chance for a do-over or a mulligan. Keep this in mind whenever you make a modification to the Windows 98 Registry.

Although the Registry is almost always referred to as single data store, you should really understand that the Registry consists of three files. These software components are known as the USER.DAT, the SYSTEM.DAT, and the POLICY.POL files. The first two of files are initially stored in the primary Windows folder (usually C:\Windows), whereas the latter one can be found in the same place or one of the Windows sub-folders.

The USER.DAT file contains the user-specific information for your Windows 98 installation. It holds the information that a typical user would change on her computer, such as the desktop configuration colors; logon profiles, including the username; and the changeable Windows 98 folder structure that exists on the Start menu. Although on a single user environment this file is important, once you start putting several users on the same Windows 98 workstation (such as in a call-center operation or on a corporate-controlled network), it becomes a vital file to managing user information. If there are multiple users on the same PC, this file will be stored in the %windir%\Profiles\%username% folder (where %windir% equates to the location of the Windows 98 installation; and %username% will equal the logon profile name for each individual user). If you are connected to a network, then this file might well be stored on your local file server and not on your Windows 98 PC.

The SYSTEM.DAT file stores the computer-specific hardware information for your Windows 98 computer. It contains information such as IRQ settings, the Plug and Play enumerations, application-specific data, and network configurations. This file is always found in the Windows root folder (typically C:\Windows), and is stored as a hidden, read-only file. This is by far the single, most critical Windows 98 system file. Lose it, delete it, or corrupt it, and your system will most certainly be in a world of hurt.

The POLICY.POL Registry file is actually an optional one. It does not have to exist for Windows 98 to function properly, nor will its accidental corruption or deletion crash your Windows 98 implementation. What the POLICY.POL file does for you, is to store Windows-specific information that automatically overrides any information stored in either the USER.DAT or SYSTEM.DAT Registry files. Thus, in a sense, the POLICY.POL file is a Windows 98 security file. It contains specific information that your network administrator uses to better manage the multitude of computers across the company's networks, while providing some sense of security to the local Windows 98 user. Now, in reality, you know that Windows 98 will probably never be viewed as a "secure" operating system, you also know that altering the POLICY.POL file is beyond the average user. For added security, it is recommended that this file be stored on a Windows NT 4.0 Server (or newer), which is forced down to each user (in background, of course) whenever they log on to the network. This way, even if someone alters their local version of this file, a new one would override the changed version the next time they logged on to the corporate network systems.

In many ways the Windows 98 Registry resembles a collection of *.INI initialization files. This is due to the fact that many 16-bit and almost all 32-bit applications store their configuration data in the Registry instead of the old Windows 3.x-style ASCII initialization files that possess the .INI file extension. In addition, the Registry keys can be imported and exported at will, which means you can edit those keys with a common text editor such as the Windows Notepad the same way you edit an .INI file.

The Windows 98 Registry architecture has not really changed much from its Windows 95 counterpart. It has a few more keys for items that did not exist in Windows 95, such as those for WebTV for Windows, WBEM, the Version Conflict Manager, and so on. However, for the most part you will find the Registry organized much the same way in Windows 98. It has the same key structure, with the same six Registry hives:

- HKEY_CLASSES_ROOT
- HKEY_CURRENT_USER
- HKEY_LOCAL_MACHINE
- HKEY_USERS
- HKEY_CURRENT_CONFIG
- HKEY_DYN_DATA

Additionally, these hives are all edited directly with the Windows Registry Editor tool known as REGEDIT.EXE (found in the local Windows root folder).

NOTE

Windows 98 is different from Windows 95 in two primary ways. First, you are no longer limited by the 65,536-byte limit for a single Registry key. What this means, is that now for the first time it becomes realistic to store and use more applications that use shared dynamic link library (DLL) files (a DDL file contains programming information that is vital to the execution of a particular Windows 98 application). Look in the \Windows\System sub-folder and to find most of the DLL files on your computer in this folder. This should be a very good change for Windows

continued on next page

continued from previous page

98 users because permits applications to share more files between them and hopefully cuts down on the useless redundancy of too many files on your PC. The other difference is in the way that the Windows 98 operating system handles the Registry, including its self-healing aspects (for example, the Registry can automatically find its own problems and fix them without human intervention).

The HKEY_CLASSES_ROOT Registry section is used to store important object linking and embedding (OLE) information, which tells the operating system how to handle its drag-and-drop operations as well as system links. This section is actually a pointer to the Registry key setting of the HKEY_LOCAL_MACHINE\Software\Classes section of the Windows 98 Registry. The HKEY_CURRENT_USER portion of the Registry holds user-specific configuration data for the user that is presently logged on to the Windows 98 PC, and is actually a pointer to the specific branch in the HKEY_USERS for that user. The HKEY_LOCAL_MACHINE Registry hive contains the hardware details for your computer. This is a very important hive, and is the one that you will find yourself in 80 percent of the time, changing and tweaking tiny aspects of your system to make it work better. The HKEY_USERS Registry hive is similar to the HKEY_CURRENT_USER section, except that the HKEY_USERS hive holds the data for all registered users of this installation of Windows 98. The HKEY_CURRENT_CONFIG key is similar to the HKEY_LOCAL_MACHINE hive, except that it only contains information regarding the hardware configuration of your PC at this very moment in time. The last hive, HKEY_DYN_DATA, holds all the dynamic data for various system devices such as your modem, tape drive, or monitor. The current status of each hardware device is tracked in this section of the Windows 98 Registry and contains subkeys for every additional user that might log on to your PC at some time.

Now that you have sufficient background to work in your Registry, it is time to get started. Remember, though, that the Registry is a very fragile item that is very unforgiving should you make a mistake or delete something you should not have. While the direct editing of the Registry is a very powerful aspect of using Windows 98, any error here, no matter how small, can spell disaster for your computer system!

4.1 Restore the Windows 98 Registry to the Same State It Was In When I Last Successfully Started My PC

This topic takes you back to the future so that your computer once again works. That is, let's say you "fix" your Registry and now your PC will not boot. This How-To helps you restore the working version of the Windows 98 Registry.

4.2 Modify the Registry so that It Automatically Starts a Specific Application Every Time I Launch Windows 98

The purpose of this How-To is to create a Startup-like folder entry, but not place it in the Windows 98 Startup folder or in the WIN.INI file (as you would have done in the Windows 3.x and Windows 95 world).

4.3 Recover from Incorrect Registry Modifications

The focus of this How-To is to recover from bad Registry modifications, meaning, correcting your previous Registry "fixes."

4.4 Modify the Registry so that a User Cannot Access the Windows Update Feature and Fix His Own PC

This How-To allows a system administrator to block users from accessing the Windows Update Web site in order to fix her own Windows 98 PC.

COMPLEXITY
ADVANCED

4.1 How do I...
Restore the Windows 98 Registry to the same state it was in when I last successfully started my PC?

Problem

My computer will not boot into the Windows 98 GUI, no matter how many times I turn it off and then turn it back on again. How do I restore the Windows 98 Registry so it works like it used to the last time it booted successfully?

Technique

Windows 98 uses a backup copy of the Registry that it makes on a periodic basis to perform this feat of magic. There are no additional tools required to make this happen, just the Windows 98 Startup disk or the ability to boot to a Windows 98 DOS-command prompt.

Steps

1. Start your Windows 98 PC so that you boot to a DOS-command prompt. If you do not know how to do this, please refer to Chapter 3, "The Boot Process," for further details.

2. If, by chance, you are able to boot into the Windows 98 GUI in Safe Mode, you can restart your system in MS-DOS mode from the Shutdown menu (\Start, \Shut Down..., Restart in MS-DOS mode).

3. After you have arrived at the DOS-command prompt, change directories so that you are in the Windows root folder (probably the C:\Windows folder).

4. Type the command `scanreg /restore` and press Enter, as shown in Figure 4.1.

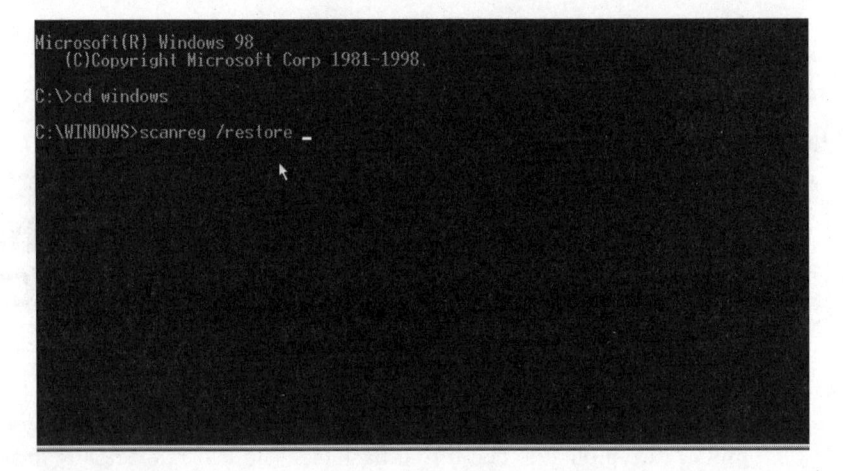

```
Microsoft(R) Windows 98
   (C)Copyright Microsoft Corp 1981-1998.

C:\>cd windows

C:\WINDOWS>scanreg /restore _
```

Figure 4.1 Using the ScanReg command from a DOS prompt.

> **NOTE**
> For the true techies in the audience, the SCANREG.EXE file can be found in the \Windows\Command folder, whereas the SCANREG.INI and SCANREGW.EXE files are located in the \Windows root folder. The SCANREG.INI contains additional information on creating more than the five default backup copies of your Registry, as well as the details in case you want to tweak the backup file destinations.

5. Once the backup copy has been restored (you will have control of the DOS prompt again), the restoration process is complete, as you have now restored your Registry back to the same state it was in last time you booted successfully.

6. Reboot your computer by turning it off and back on again or by pressing the Ctrl+Alt+Del keys simultaneously, and you are finished.

COMPLEXITY
ADVANCED

4.2 How do I...
Modify the Registry so that it automatically starts a specific application every time I launch Windows 98?

Problem

My users all use Windows 98 mostly for word processing, and I want the application to start automatically when they boot their PCs. This setting needs to be Registry-based, as these users tend to "accidentally" delete items from the Startup group that they do not understand. How do I modify the Windows 98 Registry to accommodate this need?

Technique

Windows 98 provides a simple tool known as the Registry editor (REGEDIT.EXE file), or RegEdit as it is more commonly referred to. This tool is built into the operating system and is found in the Windows root directory. As with any Registry operation, care should be taken when making any alterations or even when you are just surfing the Windows 98 Registry. Accidental deletions cannot be undone, nor can mistakes be easily found or rectified.

Steps

1. From inside Windows 98 (when you are not in Safe Mode) you need to launch the Registry Editor tool. To do this, enter the command `RegEdit` (not case sensitive) in the Run command box and press Enter or click OK.

2. This command starts the Registry Editor application, as shown in Figure 4.2.

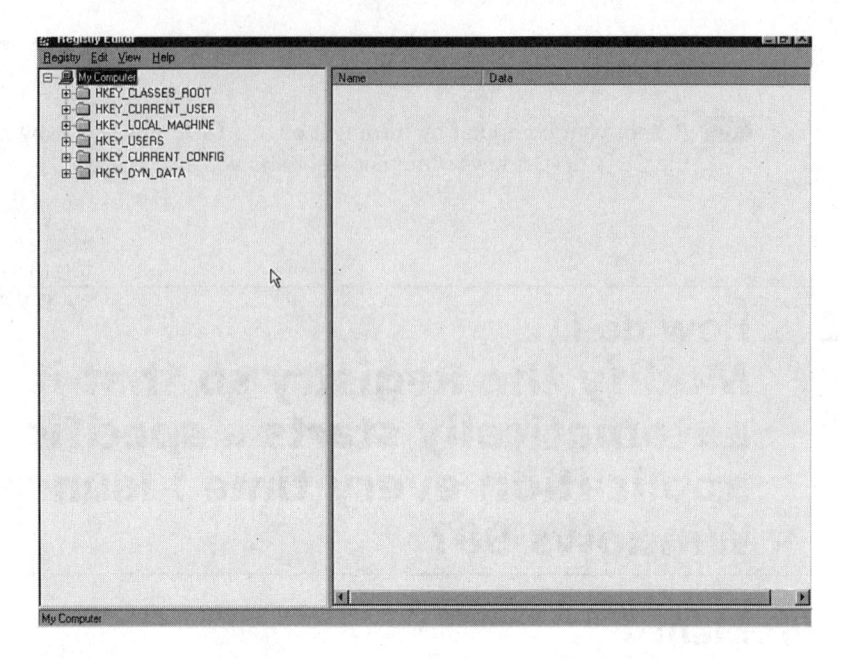

Figure 4.2 Viewing the primary screen of the Windows 98 Registry Editor.

3. Clicking once on the plus symbol next to any line causes that line to open and reveal any subkeys below it. This also works for the My Computer line, which will then hide or display the six hives that comprise the Windows 98 Registry. Practice clicking around the Registry to get a feel for moving around. When you feel comfortable, click the plus symbol next to the HKEY_LOCAL_MACHINE hive to continue.

4. The hive will open to reveal about 10 top-level keys, the one labeled SOFTWARE is the one you want to use. Within this section of the hive, you will see a folder entry for each manufacturer of the software products installed on your Windows 98 computer. While no software vendor should be listed more than once, this sometimes does occur due to that vendor's inability to properly upgrade its software when you are installing upgrades from that vendor, as shown in Figure 4.3 (look at the entries from STB Systems).

5. Continuing on, you need to select the key labeled Microsoft, by clicking on it once.

6. Next, click the plus symbol next to the Microsoft key once to reveal its contents.

7. From here, you need to maneuver inside the Microsoft key going down to the subkey labeled Windows. Click the plus symbol next to the Windows key once to reveal its contents.

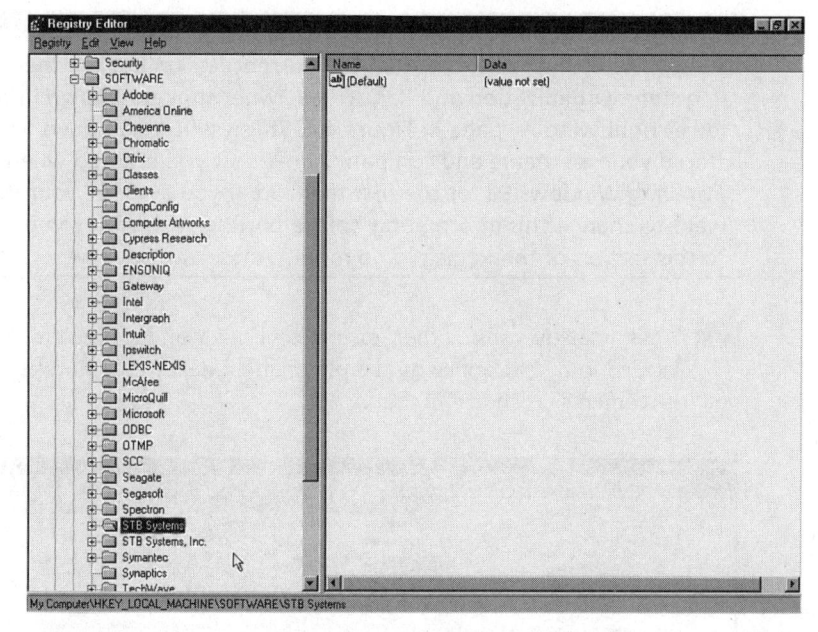

4.2 MODIFY THE REGISTRY SO IT STARTS A SPECIFIC APPLICATION

Figure 4.3 Scrolling through the Registry to find a specific subkey entry.

8. Next, maneuver inside the Windows key and proceed to the subkey labeled CurrentVersion. Click once the plus symbol next to the CurrentVersion key to reveal its contents, as shown in Figure 4.4.

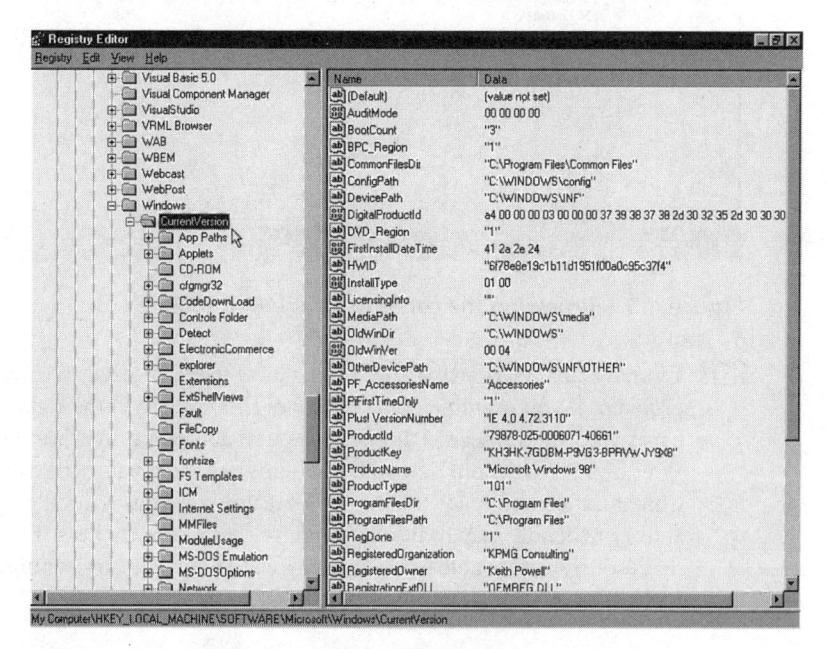

Figure 4.4 Opening a subkey and examining its contents.

CHAPTER 4
THE REGISTRY

> **NOTE**
>
> A few interesting subkeys within the CurrentVersion key are the RegisteredOrganization and RegisteredOwner subkeys, shown in the lower-right window pane in Figure 4.4. This is where Windows 98 stored your username and company name that you entered when installing Windows 98 for the first time. So, if you ever sell your PC and want to change this information before parting with your computer, go to this section of the Registry and modify these two subkeys.

9. Next, maneuver inside the CurrentVersion key and proceed to the subkey labeled Run. Click once on the plus symbol next to the Run key to reveal its contents, as shown in Figure 4.5.

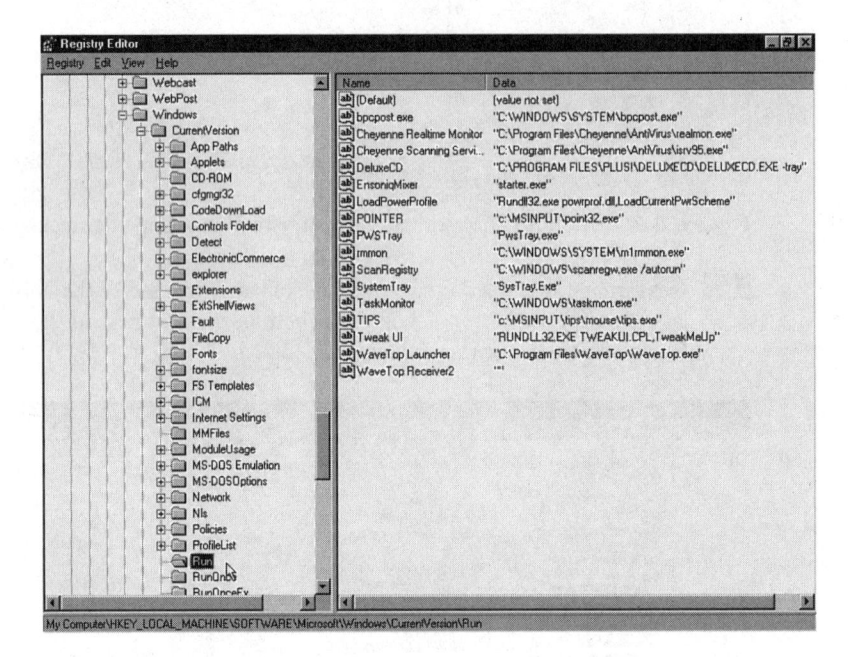

Figure 4.5 Reviewing the contents of the Run subkey.

10. You have finally arrived at the subkey level that you need to solve your problem. If you examine the contents of this subkey in the right window pane, you will see several applications that automatically start when Windows 98 kicks off. Remember when you where using the System Configuration utility in Chapter 3? That utility acts as a more graphical and user-friendly way to modify some of these Registry keys. By using that tool, you were able to make changes to your Registry settings directly without as much risk as you are exposed to now.

4.2
MODIFY THE REGISTRY SO IT STARTS A SPECIFIC APPLICATION

11. To add a new entry to this subkey, click once on the Edit menu option then click once on the New menu option, finally clicking again on the String Value menu selection, as shown in Figure 4.6.

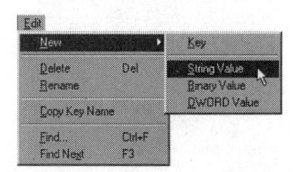

Figure 4.6 Creating a new string value.

> **NOTE**
>
> Some more background information and a few definitions are necessary here before proceeding. It is from this part of the Registry Editor menu that you create all new keys and registry data information, regardless of where you are at in the Windows 98 Registry. If you choose to create a new Key, you will be creating a new folder in the left window pane. The other three options (String Value, Binary Value, and DWORD Value) will all add information to the right window pane. A string value consists of a text-based set of null-terminated characters of a varying length. A binary value consists of hexadecimal digits also of a varied length. A DWORD (double-word) value consists of a sole 32-bit value, which appears to you as a hexadecimal number that is fixed at eight digits.

12. Because the present entries in the right window pane are in red and start with an **ab**, you know that these are string values. If they were blue with tiny 1s and 0s (the binary digits), with a value that resembled a hexadecimal number (two digits separated by a space, then two more digits, then two more digits, and so on), you would realize that they were binary values. Likewise, if they were blue with tiny 1s and 0s (the binary digits) with a value that resembled a zero immediately followed by an X, immediately followed by eight more zero-filled digits (such as 0x00005678) and a number in brackets after that, you would recognize this as a DWORD value.

13. Because all the other entries consist of string values and because of what you know from step 12, your new entry must also be a string value entry. Thus, you need to create a new string value, as shown in Figure 4.6.

14. When this new entry appears, it is highlighted in such a way that you are able to rename it from its default value name of New Value #1, as shown in Figure 4.7.

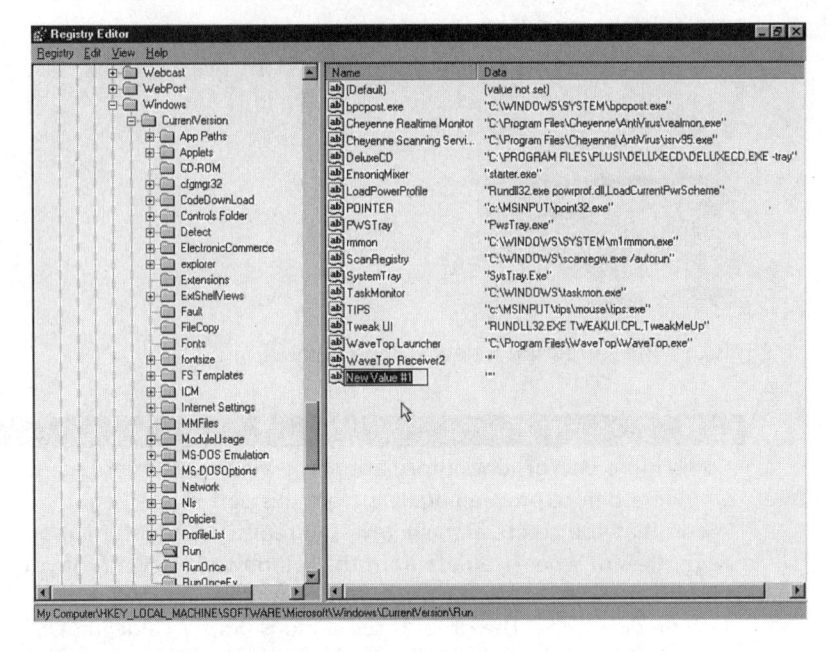

Figure 4.7 Renaming the new subkey value.

15. Because we are a progressive company, we have chosen the descriptive name Microsoft Word 2000 (the next version name of Microsoft Word). The name for each value is just a descriptive name. You can name it anything you want. This is the easy part. Next comes the more difficult task, creating the actual value's value.

16. By clicking once with the secondary mouse button on the item we just created, a small menu will appear as shown in Figure 4.8.

Figure 4.8 Accessing the String Edit function via the Modify menu.

17. At the top of the menu is the option to Modify the value's entry. The two menu selections on the bottom half of this menu permit you to either Delete the entire subkey entry entirely or to rename the descriptive Name for this entry. To continue, click once on the Modify menu selection shown in Figure 4.8, which takes you into the Edit String window shown in Figure 4.9.

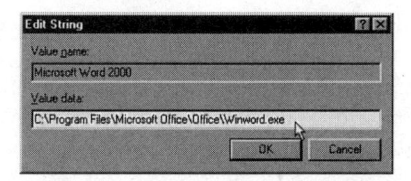

4.2
MODIFY THE REGISTRY SO IT STARTS A SPECIFIC APPLICATION

Figure 4.9 Editing a subkey's value string.

18. Upon entering the Edit String window (brought up by the Modify menu selection), you are presented with a two-section box. The top part contains the Value's name, which you cannot modify here (you must use the Rename feature from the previous menu). The bottom part contains the Value's data, which you are supposed to modify on this window. Enter the path, the executable, and any parameters that are necessary to start the application you want to run automatically each time Windows 98 is started.

19. After you have entered the proper information for the path, the executable, and any parameters, click OK to accept your entries. Doing this returns you back to the main Registry Editor screen as shown in Figure 4.10.

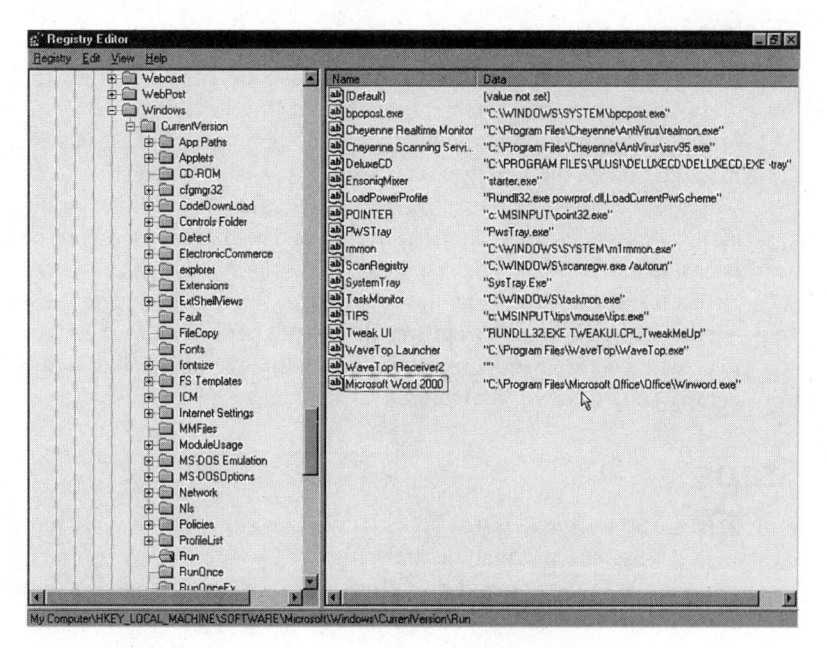

Figure 4.10 Reviewing your subkey modifications.

20. Examine this screen closely and you will notice that you have successfully entered the information for your new subkey entry. That is all you need to do. Close the Registry Editor window and reboot your system to test out your new key's information setting. If it works then Microsoft Word will start up (or whatever software application you wanted to start). Otherwise, you will need to go back to that Registry subkey and make the appropriate modifications.

COMPLEXITY
ADVANCED

4.3 How do I... Recover from incorrect Registry modifications?

Problem

What do I do if I incorrectly modified my Windows 98 Registry? Is there anyway to undo my mistakes, perhaps by re-creating that part of the Registry?

Technique

Fixing or recovering a corrupted Windows 98 Registry is part luck, part skill, and part black magic. You can use a mix of Windows 98 provided tools, bit of intuition, and plain-old common sense to figure out most aspects of the Registry. One of the more popular tools to use is known as the *Registry Checker*, which comes with the operating system. The Registry Checker performs a variety of tasks. It scans your Registry on a daily basis seeking out corruption; it backs up configuration files on a daily basis; and it checks the Registry for excess free space, removing it as required and then compacting the Registry as necessary, which in turn improves the overall performance of your system. This free space checking and compacting procedure works just like it does when you compact a database or an Outlook Express email .PST file.

Steps

1. To access the Registry Checker, you can either get to it via the Windows 98 System Information application or by entering the command `ScanRegW` in the Run command box. If you decide to go through the System Information utility, you can select the Registry Checker application from the Tools menu option.

2. Once the Registry Checker utility begins, it automatically performs a scan of the entire Windows 98 Registry. A status message box appears with the results, as shown in Figure 4.11.

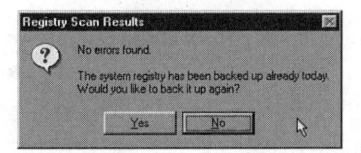

Figure 4.11 The Registry Scan Results dialog box.

3. If any errors had been found the Registry Scan Results message box will inform you of that event. In any case, the Windows Registry Checker asks you if you would like to back up your system Registry, even if it has already been backed up today or not. If no errors were found during the scan of your Registry, reply yes to this message box by clicking the Yes button. If any errors were found, do not reply affirmatively and click the No button to exit the Registry Checker utility.

4. So, assuming at least one error had been discovered by the Registry Checker utility, you will need to perform a restoration of a copy of your Registry. To do this, follow the exact steps that are presented in the section, "How do I restore Windows 98 Registry to the same state it was in when I last successfully started my PC?" earlier in this chapter. However, since you are already inside the Windows 98 GUI, use the Restart in MS-DOS mode feature, as you must be at a Windows 98 DOS prompt to safely use the restoration feature of the Registry Checker.

COMPLEXITY
ADVANCED

4.4 How do I...
Modify the Registry so that a user cannot access the Windows Update feature and fix his own PC?

Problem

The Windows Update feature built into the Windows 98 operating system is a very powerful and useful tool indeed. Unfortunately, in the hands of a beginner, especially in a corporate network environment, this feature of Windows 98 can prove deadly to many a users' PCs. Luckily, there is a way to "fix" this potential problem for those special users in your business environment.

Technique

There are the obvious steps of deleting the Windows Update icons from the Start menu locations, and anywhere it might appear in your corporate desktop environment. However, eventually somebody is going to figure out that the file WUPDMGR.EXE in the C:\Windows folder runs the process from the Windows 98 side. Moreover, the prospect of having to lock out only some user groups from this feature while permitting others to have it by modifying your corporate proxy server will probably drive the network administrators to drinking much earlier in their careers than normal. That really only leaves a Registry fix to effectively lockout 90 percent of the computing public (those who know how to workaround a Registry fix, are probably on the IT side of the house anyway).

There are two ways to enforce this fix: Implement system policies and maintain and enforce them via a Microsoft Windows NT Server network (not a feasible aspect if you are in a Novell or Banyan Vines shop); or try your hand at a little Windows 98 Registry trickery. If the first way is how you want to do it, refer to Chapter 15, "Network Management," for the details. Otherwise, all you need to perform this modification is the Registry Editor tool, (REGEDIT.EXE) found in the Windows root folder and approximately 10–15 minutes of your valuable time.

Steps

1. Start the Registry Editor application by entering the `RegEdit` command in the Run command box and pressing Enter or by clicking OK. This will take you directly into the main Registry Editor screen, as shown in Figure 4.12.

2. As you probably expected, you are going to jump into the HKEY_LOCAL_MACHINE Registry hive first, and then maneuver your way down to the SOFTWARE key then into the Microsoft key. These steps are the obvious ones. The next ones start to get a little tricky.

3. While still inside the Microsoft key, you need to continue deeper inside the key structure and click the Windows key first then the CurrentVersion key, followed by a click on the Policies key, as shown in Figure 4.13.

4. In Figure 4.13, you only see two subkeys: Network and Ratings. It is what you do not see that makes all the difference: a subkey first for Explorer, and then a subkey of Explorer known as NoWindowsUpdate. That is, if the subkey NoWindowsUpdate is missing, the Windows Update process is still enabled.

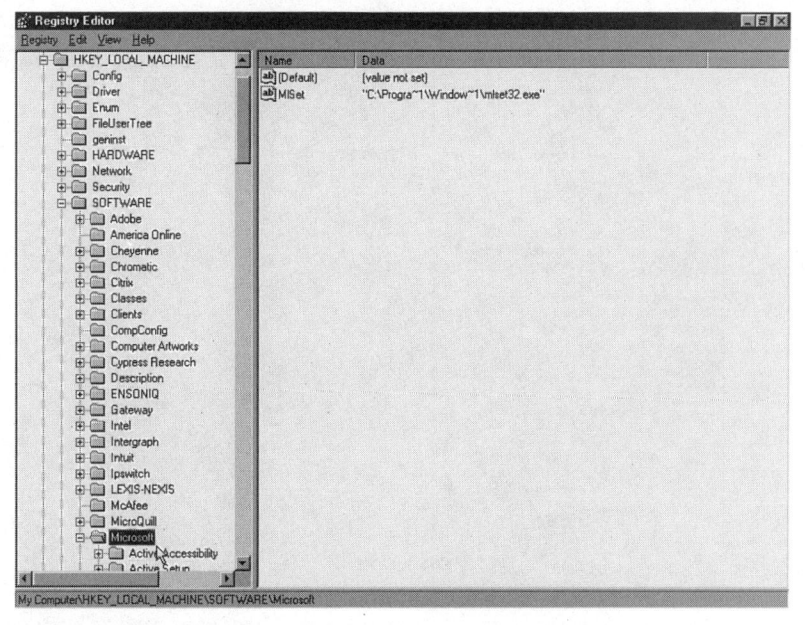

4.4
MODIFY THE REGISTRY SO A USER CANNOT ACCESS WINDOWS UPDATE 163

Figure 4.12 The main Registry Editor screen.

5. To disable Windows Update, first create a subkey of the Policies key known as Explorer.

6. Next, create a subkey of the Policies key known as NoWindowsUpdate.

7. Modify the NoWindowsUpdate subkey's value so that it contains a binary value of 1 (remember that this value is in a hexadecimal format).

8. The first part of this process is now complete. Jump over to the RunOnce Registry key found inside the same CurrentVersion subkey as the Policies key was located.

9. Inside this subkey you are going to create a new string value, this one known as WUCheckShortcut.

10. Give this subkey a string value of "WupdMgr.exe -shortcut"(on your Registry Editor screen, this key's value should look just like this, quote marks and all), as shown in Figure 4.14.

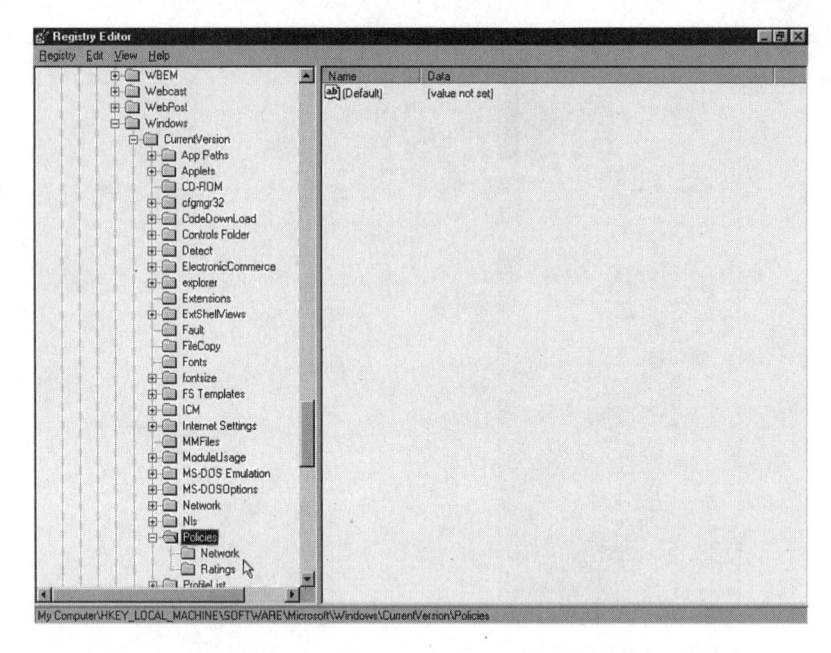

Figure 4.13 Accessing the Policies subkey.

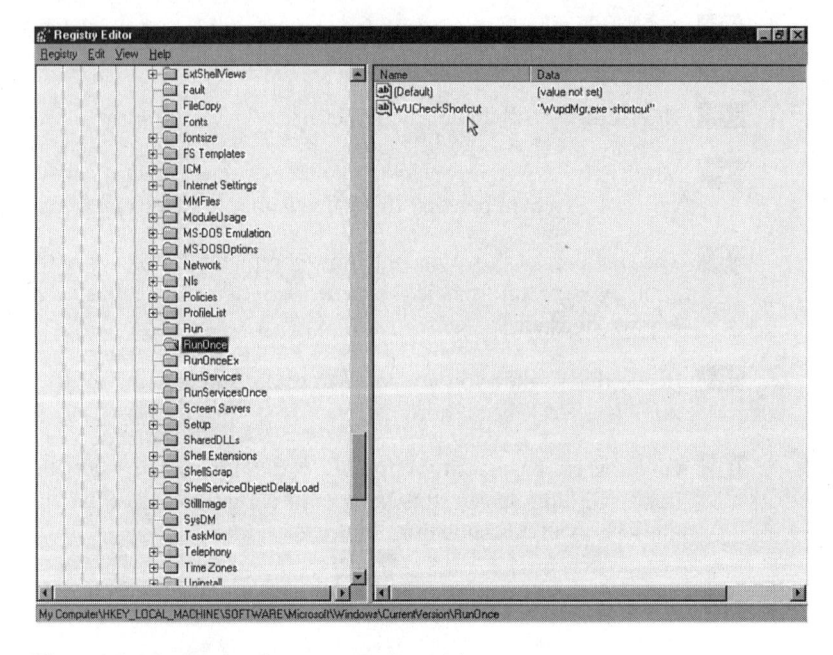

Figure 4.14 Reviewing your String Value entry.

4.4
MODIFY THE REGISTRY SO A USER CANNOT ACCESS WINDOWS UPDATE

11. Doing this last step will cause Windows 98 to automatically delete the shortcut (the link file) to the Windows Update process from the user's PC.

12. Next, you need to hop over to the Windows Update subkey under the HKEY_LOCAL_MACHINE\SOFTWARE\Policies\Microsoft Registry structure, as shown in Figure 4.15.

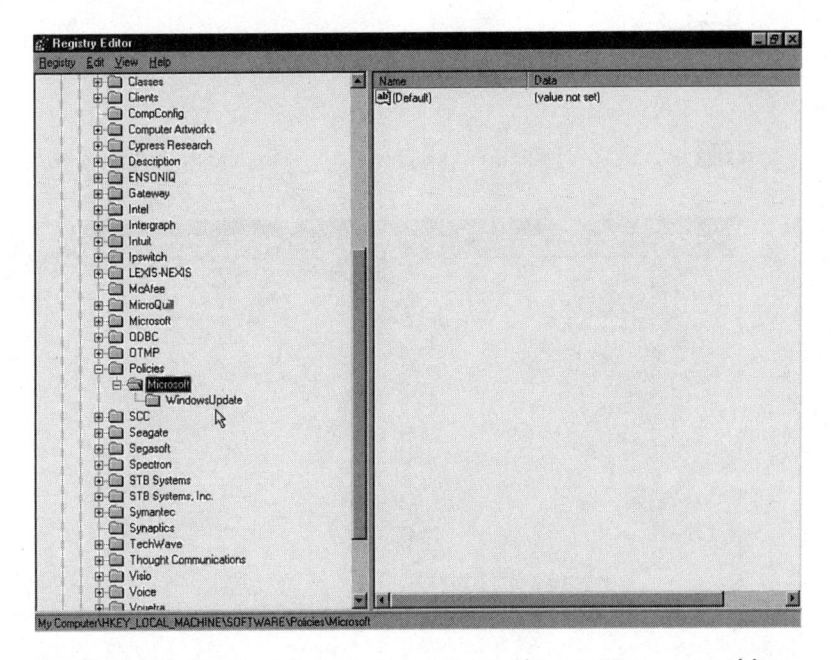

Figure 4.15 Determining whether you need to create a new subkey tree structure.

13. More than likely, you will need to create most of this Registry tree, as it is very doubtful that any of it exists on your computer already. Consider yourself lucky if you have even the Policies subkey under the Software Registry key. Once you have made it to the Microsoft Registry key, add one more. This new subkey should be named WindowsUpdate (how's that for a good name?).

14. After you have found and built the entire base structure, you will need to add a local and remote URL to complete the final piece of the puzzle. Click once on the WindowsUpdate subkey (the bottom one in this long chain of Registry keys) to select it.

15. Next, you need to add two new string values to this subkey: Local URL and Remote URL.

16. The actual data values you add are entirely up to you. The local URL value redirects the Windows 98 user to that location the first time the Windows Update process is executed. (Suppose the user copied the file from a friend and put it on their company PC because you had already deleted the original Windows Update executable file from that person's computer).

17. The remote URL value redirects the user to this URL anytime the user types in an URL on a Web browser pointed at the Windows Update Web site.

18. Examples of the final possible settings are shown in Figure 4.16.

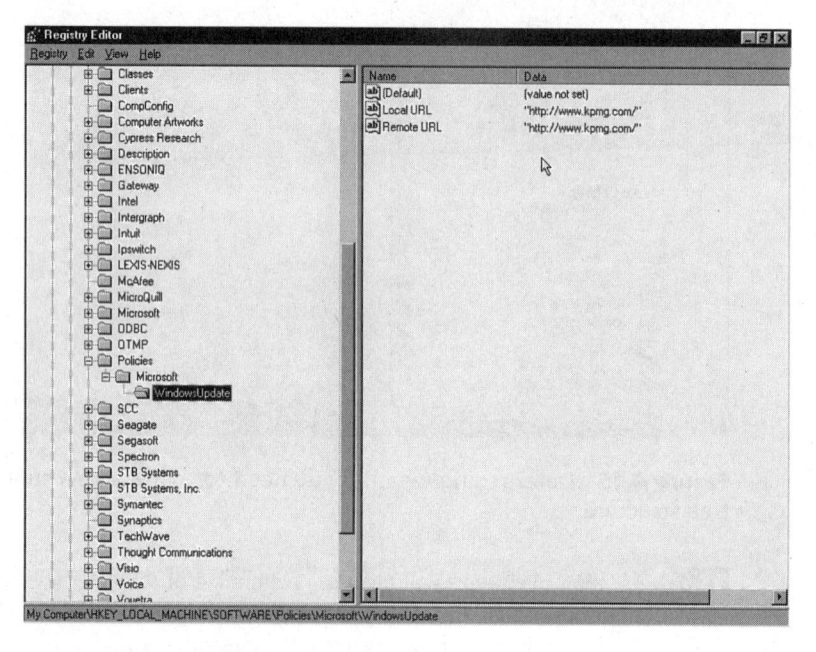

Figure 4.16 Reviewing possible Windows Update subkey values.

> **NOTE**
> The Web addresses shown in Figure 4.16 are only examples of what you can put in either of these two string values. You should consider making one of the values your company's Internet site and the other the corporate intranet site. Which one is which is really up to you, whatever makes sense for your organization. Remember: This is Windows 98, it is not Windows NT Workstation 4.0 (or newer). This means that because you cannot truly secure the user desktop, you have to resort to these types of trickery and chicanery to fool your user community into believing what they can and cannot do.

19. Close the Registry Editor window and you are finished!

> **NOTE**
>
> An even easier way to disable the Windows Update process is to simply rollout an Internet browser that is incapable of supporting the ActiveX controls that Windows Update requires, such as an older version of one of Netscape's browser clients or perhaps an antiquated version of Mosaic. Of course, the obvious downside to doing something as devious as this, is that you are limiting all other aspects of your corporate Internet/intranet/extranet strategy.

CHAPTER 5
QUINTESSENTIAL HARDWARE CONFIGURATIONS

5

QUINTESSENTIAL HARDWARE CONFIGURATIONS

How do I...

- 5.1 Choose a keyboard type?
- 5.2 Change the default language for my Windows 98 keyboard?
- 5.3 Change the default character typing speed for my Windows 98 keyboard?
- 5.4 Choose a display monitor?
- 5.5 Select a display configuration within Windows 98?
- 5.6 Configure my system for multiple display monitors?
- 5.7 Know which mouse or pointer device types to use?
- 5.8 Configure my mouse or other pointing device?

This chapter covers topics near and dear to everyone's hearts: the keyboard, the display monitor, and the pointing device (mouse) configurations. Okay, so maybe these are not the topics on your mind every day, but these certainly are items that you use most every day. The essential system components of the display monitor, the pointing device, and the keyboard are usually overlooked. This is especially the case with many people, because most folks consider these items to be the "easy stuff." When you select each of these hardware components, certain aspects of each item should be considered carefully in order to minimize the impact on the rest of your system.

5.1 Choose a Keyboard Type

This How-To assists you in the selection of a keyboard that fits your needs and comfort levels.

5.2 Change the Default Language for My Windows 98 Keyboard

In many cases, especially for those road warriors that travel incessantly, the capability to change the default language of a Windows 98 keyboard is more than a nicety—it can actually become a necessity. This How-To shows you how to do just that.

5.3 Change the Default Character Typing Speed for My Windows 98 Keyboard

Everyone should know how to do this, which will make your keyboard appear more compatible with you for your Windows 98 PC. This How-To walks you through these simple steps.

5.4 Choose a Display Monitor

This How-To assists you in the selection of a display monitor that fits your needs and comfort level.

5.5 Select a Display Configuration Within Windows 98

Everyone should know how to do this, which will make your display monitor work better in accordance with your visual tastes. This How-To walks you through the steps.

5.6 Configure My System for Multiple Display Monitors

In many cases, especially for those of you who are constantly giving presentations, such as in a classroom environment, the capability to use more than one display monitor becomes more than a nicety—it can actually become a necessity. This How-To shows you how to do just that.

5.7 Know Which Mouse or Pointer Device Types to Use

This How-To assists you in the selection of a pointing device or mouse that fits your needs and comfort level.

5.8 Configure My Mouse or Other Pointing Device

Everyone should know how to do this, which will make your mouse or other pointing device easier to use with your Windows 98 PC. This How-To walks you through these simple steps.

COMPLEXITY
BEGINNER

5.1 How do I...
Choose a keyboard type for Windows 98?

Problem

There are so many different brands of keyboards on the market today. Which one works best, and how do I tweak its configuration under Windows 98?

Technique

Start by making a list of your preferences and needs, and then balance that against what type of computer system you have. Obviously, if your PC is a laptop, you might want to consider an external keyboard small enough to take with you or a normal-sized one to stay at home or the office along with your docking station. Next, you need to determine any extra features that are required, such as a built-in mouse pad, a USB port, and so forth. Finally, you need to decide how ergonomically fashionable you want or need to be, which will either steer you toward or away from the Microsoft Natural Keyboard. Once you have decided on the keyboard of your dreams (or if you keep the one you have), then the next process is to configure it through the Windows 98 interface. These steps are covered in the following sections.

You might want to consider the ergonomics of all your hardware purchasing decisions. Heavy keyboard users might find that one of the "natural models" really does help their body, especially those developers who have had their hands go numb while coding. People who have switched to one of these "natural" keyboards find that their numbness goes away and they do not seem to experience any more problems in this area. Also, wrist pads for those folks who like their "conventional" keyboards are a good investment as well. Anything to keep the pressure off your wrists is usually a good idea.

Steps

1. Purchase your keyboard if it did not already come with your personal computer. Two quick tips: (1) If you are not an adept typist, the Microsoft

Natural Keyboard might not be for you because it makes it harder for the "hunt and peck" approach to typing. If you can type, though, I find it much easier on the wrists and hands while actually improving the accuracy of my typing skills. (2) The Microsoft Natural Keyboard provides two of the Windows Logo keys (on both sides of the Spacebar key), which function to make use of the Windows 95/98 GUIs that much easier.

2. Turn your PC off so that you can attach your new keyboard.

3. Once you have your keyboard, plug it into the small, round spot on the back of your computer. Be careful where you insert the keyboard plug, as it might fit the mouse port as well (although it will not work, it can cause you to waste extra time while you hunt down a keyboard failure error upon rebooting your computer). If you have one on the newest keyboards that act as a USB hub, you will want to keep your keyboard in a more accessible place on your computer desk (to make it easier to plug the additional USB devices into). Visit Cherry Corp.'s home page for details on this feature; they can be found at http://www.cherrycorp.com/ on the Internet.

4. Turn your computer back on and wait for it to complete the boot sequence.

5. That's it, you're finished.

COMPLEXITY
INTERMEDIATE

5.2 How do I...
Change the default language for my Windows 98 keyboard?

Problem

When Windows 98 installs, it does so with whatever language that you purchased it in as the default language. This is fine as long as you have no multilingual needs. However, suppose you purchased your copy of Windows 98 in the United States (an English version only), but you like to practice your Russian language skills for school. How would you be able to install this language set for your keyboard?

Technique

There are two ways to approach this problem. The first is to purchase the Russian version of Windows 98 from Microsoft directly (contact the Microsoft

CHANGE THE DEFAULT LANGUAGE FOR MY WINDOWS 98 KEYBOARD

Sales Information Center in Redmond, Washington, USA from 6:30 a.m. till 5:30 p.m. Pacific time), and then re-install Windows 98 using this new version. The other way is to install an alternative language for the keyboard and then make it the default keyboard setting or use a hotkey to switch to it as necessary.

Steps

1. First, figure out which language you want to install. For this example, Russian language was selected.

2. Start Windows 98.

> **NOTE**
> Anytime you are adding any new or additional software choices or utilities to your base installation of Windows 98, you need to have your Windows 98 CD-ROM available. This is because Windows 98 only installs the software drivers it requires for use at a particular moment in time for the hardware that you have already installed. Additional software drivers are necessary for changing a language keyboard set, so you will be prompted to insert your Windows 98 CD-ROM during this installation process.

3. After entering the Windows 98 GUI, proceed to the Control Panel. Inside the Control Panel, double-click the Keyboard icon to reveal the Keyboard Properties screen as shown in Figure 5.1.

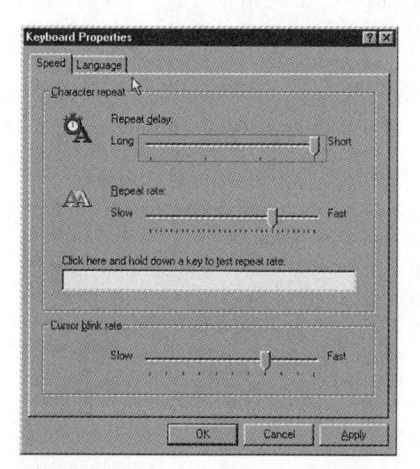

Figure 5.1 The Windows 98 Keyboard Properties screen.

CHAPTER 5
QUINTESSENTIAL HARDWARE CONFIGURATIONS

4. This first screen allows you to make changes to the keyboard click rates, as well as your cursor blink rate. If you want to make any changes, you might as well do it before you move on. Once you have made any changes (or none at all), click once on the Language tab to reveal the next screen as shown in Figure 5.2.

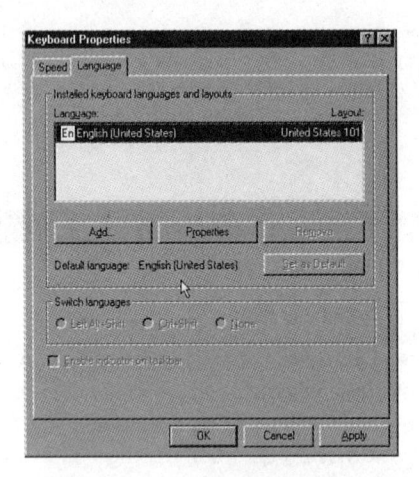

Figure 5.2 Determining the language type on the Language Properties tab.

5. As you can see, English (the United States version) is the default operating system language for this PC. Believe it or not, there are actually eight other versions of the English language besides the U.S. version. Anyway, to add the Russian language (or whichever one that you want) click the Add... button that appears in the middle of the screen. This causes the Add Language screen to appear as shown in Figure 5.3.

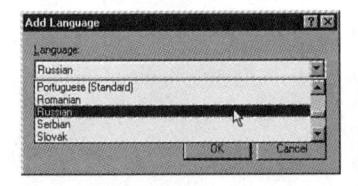

Figure 5.3 Adding a new language type for use with your PC keyboard.

5.2
CHANGE THE DEFAULT LANGUAGE FOR MY WINDOWS 98 KEYBOARD

6. Choose the language you want to add by clicking it once; in the example Russian is selected. Next, click OK to accept your selection and return to the Keyboard Properties screen as shown in Figure 5.4.

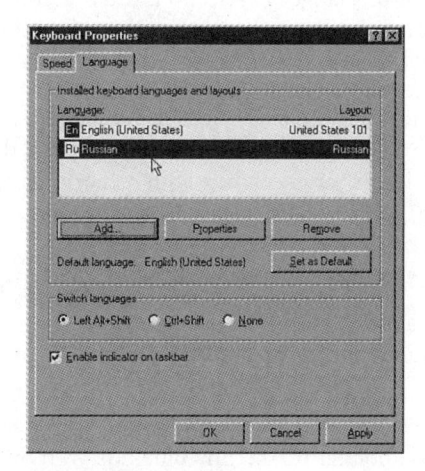

Figure 5.4 Viewing the available language types on the Language properties tab.

7. You now see your new language selection, as it appears on this screen just below the English Language choice. To make any keyboard the default, select it by clicking that language type first, and then click the Set as Default button once. This changes the Default language name as it appears just to the left of the Set as Default button.

8. The Switch Languages box is now available for your use (before adding a second language, it was grayed-out). The purpose of this option box is to permit you set a hotkey option for switching back and forth between any language choices that you have installed. (The only complaint I have with this section is that you must use one of the two methods that Windows 98 has defined; you are not able to define one of your own.) Choose the method that you want to use by clicking the radio button to the left of either of the two options or click next to the None option to disable the switching feature.

9. The Enable indicator on taskbar check box will put a small icon on the System tray section of the Windows 98 taskbar that helps you change your keyboard language selections more quickly and easily. To enable this feature, click the check box once so that it contains a check mark. To disable this feature, click once to remove the check mark. By default, this feature is enabled by Windows 98.

10. Once you have made your selections, click OK to confirm your choices. Windows 98 prompts you to put your Windows 98 CD-ROM in the CD drive, because it needs to install a few software drivers that are required by the operating system for this language selection. After it has completed the software driver installation process, the Keyboard Properties screen disappears automatically.

11. The easiest way to determine a successful language configuration is to look on the taskbar in the System tray area, provided of course that you left the Enable indicator on taskbar check box with a check mark in it (this is the default setting), as shown in Figure 5.5.

Figure 5.5 Finding the language indicator on the Windows 98 taskbar.

12. By positioning your mouse pointer on the tiny blue box with two letters inside, you see a small ToolTip box appear that displays the entire text that describes the default language. If you click this language box, a small menu appears that displays all of the possible languages that you can quickly and easily switchover to, as shown in Figure 5.6.

Figure 5.6
Accessing the pop-up menu on the taskbar language indicator.

13. Switch to a different language by clicking that language once. The default keyboard language is denoted by the tiny triangle located to the left of the language's descriptive title. In the example shown, this is the one labeled English (United States).

14. That's all you need to do to enable more than one language on your computer. One word of caution: If you do not know a particular language, you might not want to play around and pick one that looks funny to you. You might find it very difficult to reverse your steps should you select something that is so foreign to you that you cannot figure out how to switch back.

> **NOTE**
>
> Keep in mind that if you are changing between languages that are based on a completely different Character Code Page set, you might have to first modify your AUTOEXEC.BAT file to first reflect this different Character Code Page set and then reboot your system to effect the change. For example, if you did not already have the proper Code Page setting loaded into memory for the Russian language, it would not have taken effect when you attempted to switch back and forth between it and the English language.

COMPLEXITY
BEGINNER

5.3 How do I...
Change the default character typing speed for my Windows 98 keyboard?

Problem

When Windows 98 installs, it sets a predetermined character repeat rate for your computer's keyboard. If I think that this rate for my PC is too slow, how do I make this change manually?

Technique

The process, by which you make alterations to either the character repeat rate or the repeat delay, is a simple one. You can find everything you need on the Keyboard Properties screen, which is accessed via the Windows 98 Control Panel. The catch here is that you will probably need to play with the settings in order to determine exactly which one is right for you. Use these steps to help you in making the adjustments you need for your computing environment.

Steps

1. After entering the Windows 98 GUI, proceed to the Control Panel. Inside the Control Panel, double-click the Keyboard icon to reveal the Keyboard Properties screen, as shown in Figure 5.7.

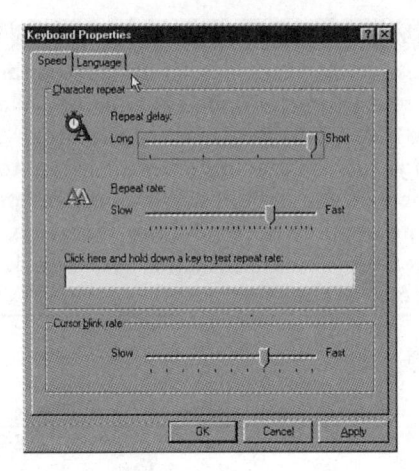

Figure 5.7 The Windows 98 Keyboard Properties screen.

2. This screen allows you to make changes to the keyboard click rates, as well as your cursor blink rate. If you want to make any changes, click once with the primary mouse button and hold it down on the slider bar for any of these options then drag the slider bar to the setting that you desire.

3. The box that appears in the middle of the screen is a test area that you can use to determine the repeat rate of any of the keyboard characters. It is much easier for you to test this rate inside this box, as opposed to trying to make a change and test it from inside another application (such as your word-processing program). Once you have made your selections, click OK to accept your changes and exit this screen.

COMPLEXITY
BEGINNER

5.4 How do I...
Choose a display monitor?

Problem

There are hundreds of different types of display monitors available on the personal computer market today. You can find everything from the old 13-inch VGA monochrome monitors to the 31-inch SVGA destination monitors that support millions of colors, which are offered by Gateway 2000, Inc. The trick is to figure out which one is right for you, whether you are a home PC user or a corporate customer.

Technique

The choice, for the most part, comes down to personal taste, coupled with a few basic business requirements. If you have trouble seeing multiple applications simultaneously and need to be able to see them all at the same time, then a 17-inch (or larger) monitor is for you. Conversely, if you are a mobile computing user, you are probably going to be looking in the 11–13 inch range of notebook computer LCD panel display monitors. Regardless of the need, if you are using a personal computer then you probably want a color monitor that is capable of displaying at least 256 colors in a super VGA (SVGA) or better resolution (640×480 pixels or greater).

A secondary consideration when choosing a display monitor is to make sure that you select the appropriate video card (also known as a display adapter or a video graphics adapter) to go along with that monitor. The quickest path to failure in purchasing a display monitor is to buy an under-powered video display adapter, which might prevent you from seeing all the possible screen colors that your display monitor is capable of showing in the resolution that you want to see them in.

The final consideration when purchasing a display monitor is the *dot pitch*. The dot pitch of a monitor can best be described as the size of the smallest dot or pixel that your display monitor can present. Dot pitch sizing is usually presented as a fraction of a millimeter, such as a 0.26mm or 0.34mm. Remember that the smaller the dot pitch, the crisper the images appear onscreen. However, a smaller dot pitch directly relates to a higher price for the display monitor. To put it more succinctly, the lower the dot pitch, the higher the price.

NOTE

When purchasing a display monitor, the salesperson might want to impress you with his limited knowledge of display monitor technology. One common approach is to refer to the number of bits per pixel when referencing the sheer number of colors a display monitor is capable of displaying. The best thing to remember is that more is better. That is, a single bit per pixel means that the monitor is not capable of color at all, it is a monochrome monitor. An 8-bit per pixel monitor can handle up to 256 colors. Sixteen bits per pixel translates into 65,536 (64K) colors, whereas 24-bits equates to 16.7 million colors. If anyone tries to sell you a 32-bit monitor and you are not a high-resolution graphic designer, quickly walk away. The difference between 24 and 32 bits is not so much in the sheer number of colors (that remains the same at 16.7 million possible) but rather in the clarity of the true colors possible, based on the degree of translucency that you attempt to use on your monitor and eventually your end presentation graphics work.

continued on next page

continued from previous page

Also, remember that as you increase the number of colors that you are attempting to display on your monitor, the more of an impact it will have on your computer. That is, if your video graphics adapter card does not have enough video RAM, your system will struggle to display all the colors that you want. There is a fine balance here between the sheer number of colors to be displayed and the amount of system resources you are willing to throw at the display monitor and its resolutions.

Steps

1. Just as you did when deciding on the correct keyboard for your computer, start the display monitor selection process by making a list of your preferences and needs, and then balance that against what type of computer system you have. If your PC is a laptop, you probably want a monitor that is small enough so that it keeps the total weight of the notebook computer to a minimum. Likewise, if you have a home or office docking station to plug into, you might want to consider an additional normal-sized display monitor that is larger than the one provided with the notebook computer.

2. Next, you should determine the depth of the monitor resolution that is necessary for your computing needs. If you are a general home user that likes to surf the Internet, play an occasional game or two, and use educational-type CD-ROM applications then a standard 15- or 17-inch SVGA color monitor that displays up to 800×600 pixels of resolution is probably right for you. Likewise, if you are a computer software application developer, the minimum sized monitor that you would want is probably at least a 17-inch SVGA color monitor that can display 800×600 or even 1,024×768 pixels of resolution. (Remember, this is a starting point; many software developers I know love their 19-inch monitors, which easily handle the 1,600×1,400 pixel resolution). Again, the wants and needs of the end user have to be carefully balanced against the home or corporate budget, in order to find that perfect balance between cost and functionality.

3. Now that you have figured out which display monitor best meets your requirements, you still need to select a video display adapter card (video card, display adapter, or video adapter). One of these adapter cards will contain a certain amount of memory (video RAM) on them and as with everything else with Windows 98, more is definitely better. Typically, a standard desktop PC has 2MB of video RAM whereas a basic notebook computer has a single megabyte or even just 512KB of video RAM. High-end desktop computers, especially those considered as multimedia workstations, should have a minimum of 4MB video RAM. If you happen to be a graphics designer, you might want to consider investing in a top of the line video card (such as a Matrix) that can handle up to 8MB of video RAM. You should try to set your minimum at 4MB of video RAM for each desktop computer system and at least 2MB for each mobile computer (laptop or notebook PC), because the need for video RAM is going to keep increasing over time. Whatever card you do wind up choosing, make sure that it appears on the Windows 98 Hardware Compatibility List before you actually buy it. Because if it is not on this Microsoft-approved listing then it will probably not work, at least not correctly.

4. Finally, to maintain ergonomic standards as well as your eyesight, you might want to consider a guard for your display monitor that reduces the amount of the glare that is produced and might physically damage your eyesight (such as increased astigmatism, damaged pupils, and so on). A standard glare screen can easily cost $50 (USD) for a 15–17 inch monitor, and more if you have a 19- or 21-inch monitor or larger.

COMPLEXITY
BEGINNER

5.5 How do I... Select a display configuration within Windows 98?

Problem

My computer system came preinstalled with Windows 98, which already had the display monitor configuration set. How can I change this display configuration without messing up my Windows 98 installation?

Technique

The route to solving this problem is pretty straightforward. Start with the Windows 98 Display Properties screen and try to make all your changes from within this screen and its various tabs. This will ensure that your changes are somewhat consistent, while making it easier for you to better configure your display monitor.

Steps

1. Now that you have selected the monitor that is right for you, it would be helpful to be able to configure it properly. To do so, double-click the Display icon in the Windows 98 Control Panel to access the Display

Properties screen, where you then need to click once on the Settings tab as shown in Figure 5.8. Another way to access this same screen is to first right-click an open part of your Windows 98 desktop to bring up the small Display menu then click once on the Properties menu selection, and then click once on the Settings tab. Both ways work, so just pick the one that you are most comfortable with.

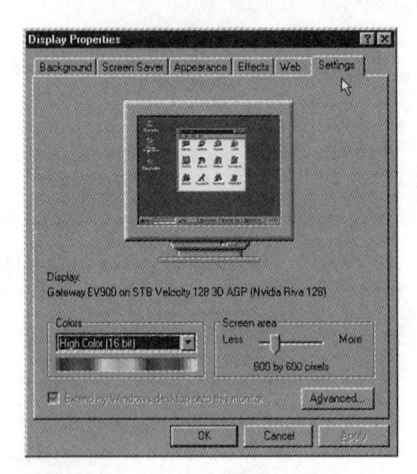

Figure 5.8 The Settings tab of the Windows 98 Display Properties screen.

2. The Settings tab of the Display Properties window is split into three parts: the display; the number of colors to be displayed; and the screen area resolution size. The display area shows a smaller version of your display monitor, which is supposed to represent precisely what you see if you modify either the number of colors or the resolution of your display monitor. Additionally, underneath the label Display, you see a descriptive name of both your display monitor as well as your video adapter card. If you examine the example presented in Figure 5.8, you will see the following: Gateway EV900 on STB Velocity 128 3D AGP (Nvidia Riva 128). What this means in English is that I have a Gateway 2000 display monitor, model number EV900. My video adapter card is technically known as a STB Velocity 128 3D AGP (Nvidia Riva 128) card, and is Nvidia compatible. The manufacturer of the STB card is Entropy Engineering, Inc. (something you probably would not have guessed by looking at the technical name), and works hand-in-hand with my STB TV Tuner card. It contains 4MB of video RAM (an amount that unfortunately cannot be readily determined from either the base Windows 98 software or the Windows 98 Resource Kit tools), which is perfect for a home use multimedia system.

SELECT A DISPLAY CONFIGURATION WITHIN WINDOWS 98

> **NOTE**
>
> If you use a computer that includes MMX technology, such as an Intel Pentium CPU that supports it or an Intel Pentium II CPU, you must use at least version 3.0a of Microsoft's DirectX technology. Now, with Windows 98 that is not a problem because it ships with version 5.0. However, the Windows 98 Multimedia Enhancement Pack that shipped in fall 1998, includes DirectX version 6.0. It is strongly recommended that you upgrade to at least this version, as it provides several performance-enhancing features that are sure to make your computer appear to run much faster whenever the graphics and some sound or gaming technologies are utilized on your computer system.

3. The two configurable portions of the Settings tab are the Colors and Screen area sections. Click once on the drop-down list box within the Colors section to reveal the various color settings your present display monitor and adapter can handle, as shown in Figure 5.9.

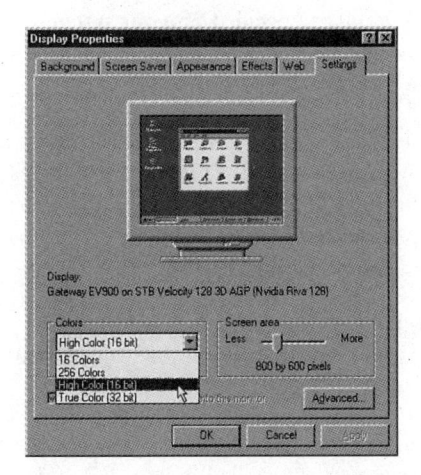

Figure 5.9 Changing the number of colors shown by your display monitor.

4. All the possible color configurations for your computer should be listed within this drop-down list box. If you believe that a higher color mode is possible, but not shown, then you will want to reconfirm that both your display monitor and adapter are configured correctly. The best way to do this is to check out the System Properties screen within the Control Panel and make sure that there are no immediate problems with either of these devices. In addition, you might want to look on the Internet FTP and Web sites for the manufacturers of both devices to see if they have posted any updated software drivers for Windows 98. If they have, download those drivers and install as suggested by the manufacturer of the device. Again, keep in mind that you will probably never see either a 1- or 4-bit color capability listed for a monitor that is attached to a computer that runs Windows 98. Those types of color capabilities are typically reserved for network servers and ancient computing devices that cannot technically support the Windows 98 operating system.

5. Click once on the color quality of your choice to select it. Click once on the Apply button to make the change permanent, but still leave you inside the Display Properties screen so that you can make other display alterations prior to clicking OK.

6. The other configurable area of the Display Properties screen is the Screen area. This section permits you to alter the overall resolution of the display monitor by changing the pixel content. That is, you can change the number of horizontal and vertical pixels that are displayed on your display monitor. Remember, though, that this setting is directly related to the amount of video RAM you have installed on your system. So if you have a minimal amount of video memory, your choices will be severely curtailed.

7. Use the sliding bar to make your selection, if you choose one other than what is already present on your system. Just like the Colors area, you can click once on the Apply button to make the change permanent and remain inside the Display Properties screen. If you choose to make the change permanent and exit immediately, click OK.

8. The final item on this tab is the Advanced... button. Clicking once on this button opens the specific properties screen for your particular video card, as shown in Figure 5.10.

9. The number of tabs that appear on this screen has a direct correlation to the type of video card that you have installed in your PC. If you have an older, non–plug-and-play video adapter, you probably only see the first three or four tabs. With some other video cards with proprietary software drivers installed, you might actually see all these tabs plus another one for that specific card.

10. The only thing of much interest on this screen is the Display section on top. From here, you can change the default screen font size (do not alter this if you do not understand what a screen font does), as well as permit Windows 98 to show a display settings icon on the taskbar in the System tray area. The default setting for the Font Size area is a normal font size of 96 dots per inch (DPI), which in the case of my display monitor means a Small Fonts selection from the drop-down list box. The Show Settings

5.5 SELECT A DISPLAY CONFIGURATION WITHIN WINDOWS 98

Icon on Task Bar is one of my favorite enhancements of Windows 98. This icon (which looks like a tiny display monitor with a ruler next to it), when clicked with a mouse button, pops up a menu of all the available monitor resolutions for your display monitor, as shown in Figure 5.11.

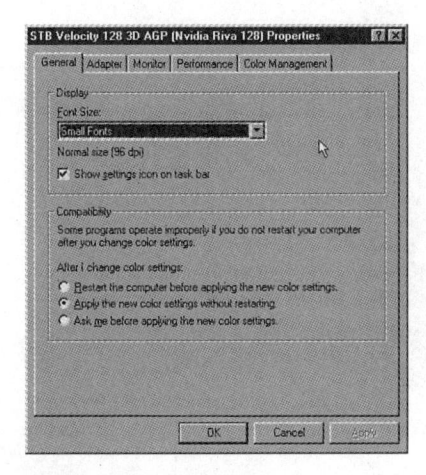

Figure 5.10 Reviewing general information regarding the PC video card.

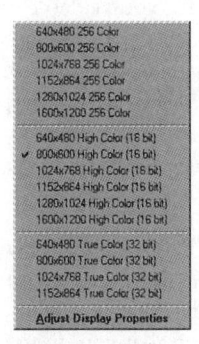

Figure 5.11 Adjusting the resolution of the display monitor.

11. To automatically resize your display monitor, click once with the primary mouse button on any of the display monitor resolutions shown in the listing. This causes the new resolution to instantly take effect (this is similar to the video test button in Windows NT).

CHAPTER 5
QUINTESSENTIAL HARDWARE CONFIGURATIONS

12. Click the Adapter tab to display the contents of that screen, as shown in Figure 5.12.

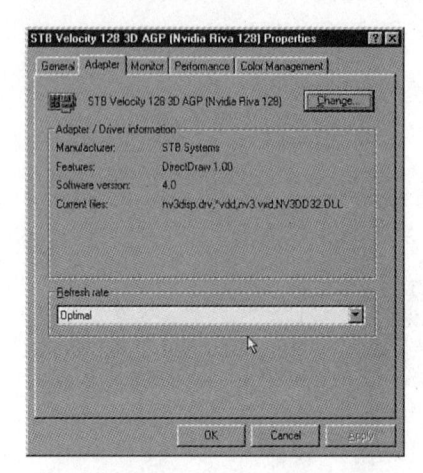

Figure 5.12 Setting the Refresh rate of the display monitor.

13. The purpose of the Adapter tab is to provide you with specific technical information regarding your video display adapter card, as well as act as a starting point to change the software drivers for your video card. Clicking the Change button will initiate the Windows 98 Update Device Driver Wizard, which walks you through the screens necessary to install an updated software device driver for your video card. If you are planning to install a new video card, perform the actual software driver installation for that card through the Add New Hardware icon found in the Control Panel.

The other important area on this tab is the Refresh Rate section. It is in this area that you can select a specific refresh rate for your display monitor or use the default setting of Optimal. Again, if you do not understand all the implications of changing the refresh rate then it is strongly advised that you do not change it.

> **NOTE**
>
> A computer monitor's refresh rate is the speed at which the display monitor is refreshed each second. A refresh rate for a monitor is measured in hertz (Hz), with the current industry standard set at the VESA rate of 75Hz when displaying SVGA resolutions of 640×480 or greater. What this means is that the monitor redraws the display at a rate of 75 times per second. The faster the display monitor's refresh

5.5
SELECT A DISPLAY CONFIGURATION WITHIN WINDOWS 98

rate, the less the monitor flickers. Take great care in setting the refresh rate because to do so at a level higher than what your monitor is capable of might harm your computer monitor.

14. Moving on, you should click once on the Monitor tab to reveal the screen shown in Figure 5.13.

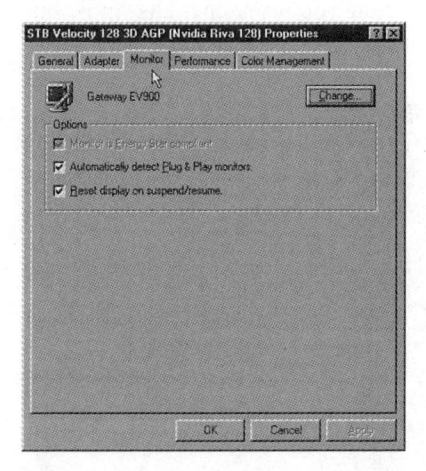

Figure 5.13 Reviewing monitor settings options.

15. The Options section is self-explanatory and will appear as grayed-out if you do not possess a plug-and-play monitor that is capable of these features. At the top of the screen is a descriptive label for your display monitor. The Change button on this screen does exactly what it did on the Adapter page but with a monitor focus: it initiates the Windows 98 Update Device Driver Wizard, which walks you through the screens necessary to install an updated software device driver for your display monitor. Again, if you are planning to install a new display monitor, perform the actual software driver installation for that monitor through the Add New Hardware icon found in the Control Panel.

16. To set the graphics acceleration speed of your display monitor you need to click the Performance tab, as shown in Figure 5.14.

17. The Performance screen is used for setting the graphics acceleration of your display monitor hardware. It is recommended that you leave this setting on Full if you are not presently experiencing any problems. However, if you continue to see the error message Invalid Page Fault in

CHAPTER 5
QUINTESSENTIAL HARDWARE CONFIGURATIONS

Kernel32.dll or if you are seeing garbled or corrupted text on your display monitor, this setting is likely the cause of your problem. Reducing the acceleration rate is done by clicking the slider bar and moving it to the left (toward None) until you have reached the setting you want. Try moving the slider bar one click at a time and then testing your selection in order to achieve the optimal hardware acceleration rate while still fixing any garbled or corrupted text problems you might be experiencing. After you have selected the rate you want, click the Apply button for the change to take effect immediately.

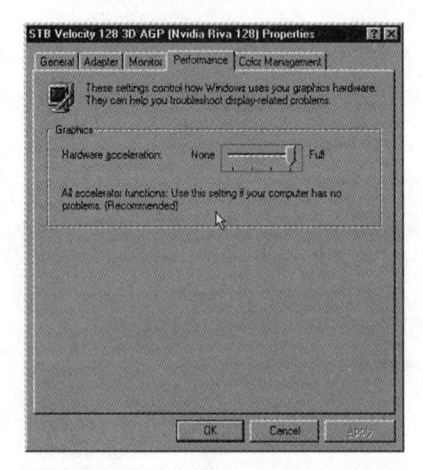

Figure 5.14 Changing the hardware acceleration from the Performance tab.

18. The next tab you should examine deals with the color management of your computer system's display, but this tab might not be present for those of you with the older display equipment (for example, the non–plug-and-play crowd). Click once on the Color Management tab to continue, as shown in Figure 5.15.

19. The contents of the Color Management tab permit you to set a default monitor profile for your display monitor. By default, Windows 98 does not set one up for you, instead leaving this more difficult task for you. It is important that you select the proper one (that is, if you want one at all), because making a bad choice here can lead to utter confusion for you when you print your color presentation and it doesn't match what you see on the display screen. To add a monitor profile, click once on the Add... button located near the bottom of the screen. This causes the Add Profile Association window to appear as seen in Figure 5.16.

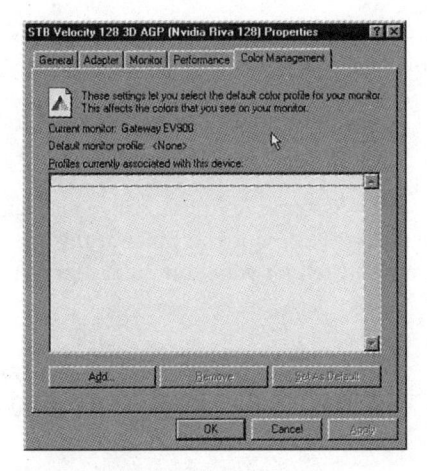

SELECT A DISPLAY CONFIGURATION WITHIN WINDOWS 98

Figure 5.15 Setting the Color Management options for the display monitor.

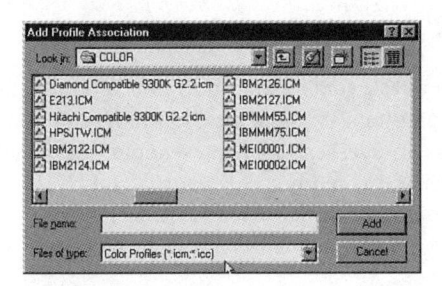

Figure 5.16 Adding a new profile association to the monitor.

20. This window takes you to the %WinRoot%\System\Color (usually C:\Windows\System\Color) path where it is necessary for you to select a Color Profile. If you do not understand the concept of a color profile, you should probably either leave this setting to your graphics designer or not select one at all. In any event, should you want to continue, do so by clicking the profile of your choice, and then clicking the Add button.

21. This will return you to the Color Management tab where you now see your choice in the Profiles Currently Associated with This Device box. You should also take note that the color profile you selected is now set as the default monitor profile for your computer. If you have more than one color profile in the Profiles Currently Associated with This Device box, you might select a different default monitor profile by first clicking the color profile of your choice, and then clicking once the Set As Default button.

22. Click OK to confirm your changes, which then returns you to the original Display Properties screen.

23. Click Close to close the Display Properties screen and return you to the Windows 98 desktop area.

24. You might be prompted with a Systems Settings Change message box that asks you whether you want to restart your computer at this time. Click Yes to respond affirmatively and reboot your computer accordingly.

COMPLEXITY
INTERMEDIATE

5.6 How do I...
Configure my system for multiple display monitors?

Problem

You find yourself as a presenter at a trade show and want to be able to better represent a computer-based presentation on several monitors simultaneously, as there is too much glare to use an overhead LCD presentation device. However, you do not know what equipment is required for your PC much less how to configure it.

Technique

Windows 98 theoretically supports up to nine individual display monitors simultaneously, but for all practical purposes you should probably try to limit yourself to just three or four monitors at once. You will need a desktop computer to configure your PC for multiple display monitors, as each monitor (PCI or AGP only) must be attached via a separate video card. Due to the practical limits of today's personal computer technology, it is highly doubtful that you will find a PC with more than four or five open PCI slots. However, Microsoft has successfully tested this feature with nine monitors simultaneously, so if you can duplicate their resources then you are set.

Steps

1. After you have acquired the equipment and assembled it inside your computer, you need to turn your computer on and let it boot all the way inside the Windows 98 GUI. Along the way, you might encounter the Add New Hardware Wizard, because your PC will probably detect the monitors and video adapter cards that you have just installed. The

KNOW WHICH MOUSE OR POINTER DEVICE TYPES TO USE

Windows 98 CD-ROM is required during the installation process, so you might as well already have it inside your CD-ROM drive. You might or might not have to reboot during this process, but eventually you should return to the Windows 98 desktop GUI.

2. Once you get there, open up the Display Properties screen by double-clicking the Display icon inside the Control Panel or by clicking once with the secondary mouse button on any open spot on the desktop and then clicking once on the Properties menu selection.

3. When the Display Properties screen appears, click the Monitors tab. It is on this screen that you are able to configure your multiple monitor experience.

4. Next, click on the check box next to the Extend my Windows Desktop onto this Monitor label. This enables the multiple monitor support under Windows 98. If there is no check in the box then the support is disabled. If no box appears on your screen (it should be at the bottom, just below the Colors and Screen area sections of the Monitors tab, your computer system is not recognizing more than one display adapter and monitor.

5. The number in the enclosed area represents a separate monitor for each display device available. The number 1 is the primary display device for your computer, whereas numbers 2 through 9 are used for the secondary devices. Double-click any of these displays to select them. Remember that you must have marked the Extend my Windows Desktop onto this Monitor check box in order to use each display monitor.

6. For simplicity's sake, you want to physically arrange your display monitors in the same order as they are numbered on this screen. Otherwise, it becomes a nightmare trying to figure out which computer is which, whenever you want to change screen resolutions and so forth.

7. Click OK to accept your configuration and any changes you might have made and you will return to the Windows 98 desktop area.

COMPLEXITY
BEGINNER

5.7 How do I...
Know which mouse or pointer device types to use?

There are dozens of different mouse and pointer devices available on the market today for general computer users. Which one is right for me, and can I have more than one?

Technique

Start by making a list of your preferences and needs and then balance that against what type of computer system you have. Obviously, if your PC is a laptop, then you might want to consider a centralized trackball, a mouse pad small enough to take with you, or a normal-sized mouse or pointing device to stay at home or the office along with your docking station. Next you need to determine if any extra features are required, such as a Puff and Sip pointer, for those of you unable to physically use a keyboard or a mouse; an eye-gaze system, for the physically disadvantaged; a rolling device in addition to the normal mouse, such as the one you find on a Microsoft IntelliPoint Mouse. Finally, you need to decide how ergonomically fashionable you want or need to be. After you have decided on the mouse/pointing device you want (or keep the one you have), the next process is to install it through the Windows 98 interface. These steps are covered in the following section.

Steps

1. Purchase the mouse/pointing device you want if it did not already come with your personal computer. A quick tip: If you would like to be able to scroll a screen without actually moving the mouse then the Microsoft IntelliPoint Mouse is right up your alley. It makes life so much easier to move about in Microsoft-centric software (it does not work in Quicken or in a Netscape browser), without having to constantly move your hand up and down to scroll around or zoom in on stuff.

2. Turn your PC off so that you can attach your new mouse/pointing device.

3. Once you have your mouse/pointing device, plug it in to the small, round spot on the back of your computer. Be careful where you insert the mouse/pointing device plug, as it might also fit into the keyboard port (although it will not work, it can cause you to waste extra time while you hunt down a keyboard failure error upon rebooting your computer. If the mouse is plugged into the keyboard port then your keyboard is probably plugged into the mouse port). If you are connecting an alternative pointing device ,such as one of the two previously mentioned, you might need to plug it in to a serial or USB port instead of the mouse port. Consult the manuals for your new hardware mouse/pointing device as necessary.

4. Turn your computer back on and wait for it to complete the boot sequence.

5. That's all you need to do to install the mouse/pointing device. However, if this device is an alternative pointing device then you will need to install and configure the Accessibility options for your Windows 98 PC. If the Accessibility options are already installed, you configure them via the

Control Panel. If they are not present then you need to add them via the Add/Remove Programs icon that is also found in the Control Panel.

COMPLEXITY
BEGINNER

5.8 How do I... Configure my mouse or other pointing device?

Problem

I purchased a Microsoft IntelliPoint Mouse. How do configure all the bells and whistles for this new pointing device (or any other device for that matter)?

Technique

Whenever you purchase a mouse or any other pointing device, it should come with its own set of software device drivers. You should install these drivers according to the manufacturer's directives, and then startup the Windows 98–driven configuration options that are present in your system.

Steps

1. Double-click the Mouse icon found in the Windows 98 Control Panel, which reveals the Mouse Properties screen as shown in Figure 5.17.

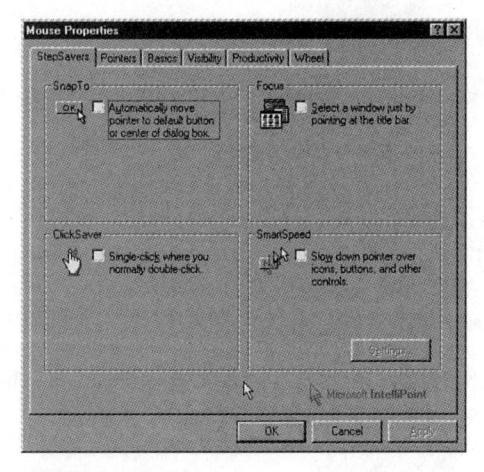

Figure 5.17 Setting the StepSavers options on the Mouse Properties screen.

2. The six tabs that appear on this screen might or might not be present on yours, as some of these options are vendor-specific for the pointing device that I have installed (Microsoft IntelliPoint Mouse). Whereas the screens might be named differently, you will notice that the features are more or less the same.

3. On the first screen you see, the StepSavers tab, you are able to accelerate your access to various Windows 98 activities. For instance, enabling the SnapTo section automatically moves your mouse pointer to the OK/Yes/Close button (whichever happens to be the default answer) following another entry within a configuration area. It does not matter whether you are in a Microsoft application or not, it appears to work this way every time. (The other three options are just as self-explanatory, so I will not waste any more trees explaining them.)

4. Next, click the Pointers tab to move to that section of the Mouse Properties configuration, as shown in Figure 5.18.

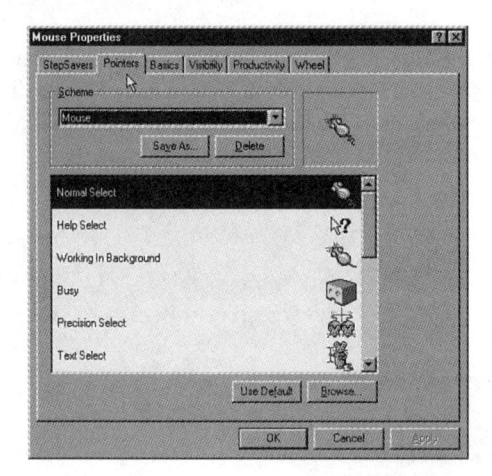

Figure 5.18 Picking a mouse pointer visibility scheme.

5. This tab should appear on nearly everyone's system, as this is a Windows 98–default area that is present as part of the operating system. However, it is possible for some proprietary mouse/pointer device software drivers to override and disable this screen, so you might not see it after all. The purpose of this screen is to enable you to select a graphical scheme for your mouse pointer device. As you can see in the example given, I have selected the one labeled Mouse, which can be changed by clicking the drop-down list box under the Scheme section of this tab.

5.8
CONFIGURE MY MOUSE OR OTHER POINTING DEVICE

6. Click once on the Basics tab to move to that screen, as shown in Figure 5.19.

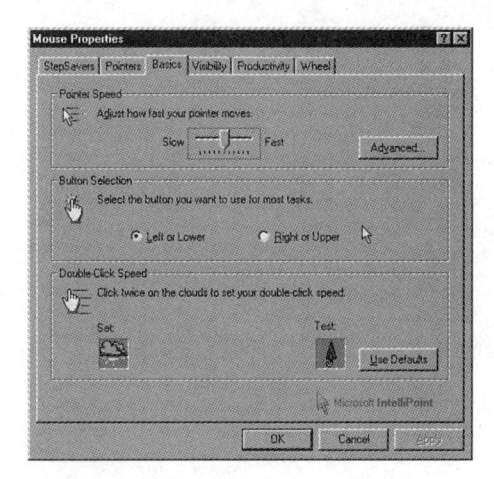

Figure 5.19 Adjusting the basics for the mouse or pointing device.

7. Mouse pointer speed, button selection, and double-click speed are all set via this screen. The section you should be most interested in, assuming you are a network/system administrator, is the Button Selection area. This is where you determine the configuration of the primary mouse button (this is the one on the left for you right-handed folks, but the one on the right for those lefties out there). Because the majority of your users are probably right-handed, it is suggested that you please the majority and apologize to the minority user community when you select the left mouse button as the primary mouse button. The other two settings are simple enough to use, so follow the screen prompts for these.

8. Click once the Visibility tab to move to that screen, as shown in Figure 5.20.

9. The contents of the Visibility tab perform the very functions you would probably guess: They allow you to modify the ways in which you can easily spot your mouse pointer on the display monitor. There is nothing amazing or earth-shattering on this screen so examine it, make any changes you might want, and then click the Apply button to make those alterations take effect. After you are finished, click the Productivity tab to go to that screen, as shown in Figure 5.21.

CHAPTER 5
QUINTESSENTIAL HARDWARE CONFIGURATIONS

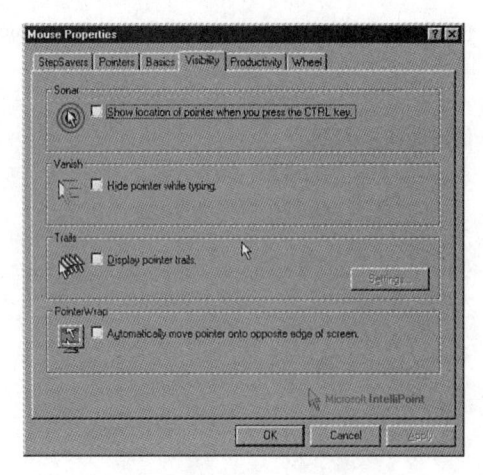

Figure 5.20 Assigning the Visibility options for the pointing device.

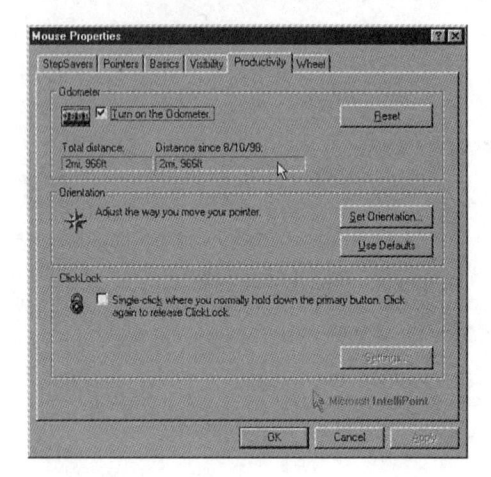

Figure 5.21 Setting the Productivity options for the pointing device.

10. None of the settings on this screen really improve your productivity, rather, they are designed to permit you ease of movement in the use of your mouse. The Odometer section is completely worthless from a productivity standpoint, but it is helpful to see just how much you have moved your mouse pointer since you first enabled this option. The date function in this section has a "bug" in it, in that the date shown is always today's date, regardless of when you actually activated this feature (which is when the total distance odometer started counting). That is why the Total distance and the Distance since 9/9/99 are always the same amount.

5.8
CONFIGURE MY MOUSE OR OTHER POINTING DEVICE

11. Moving on, click the Wheel tab to reveal the final screen in the Mouse Properties window, as shown in Figure 5.22.

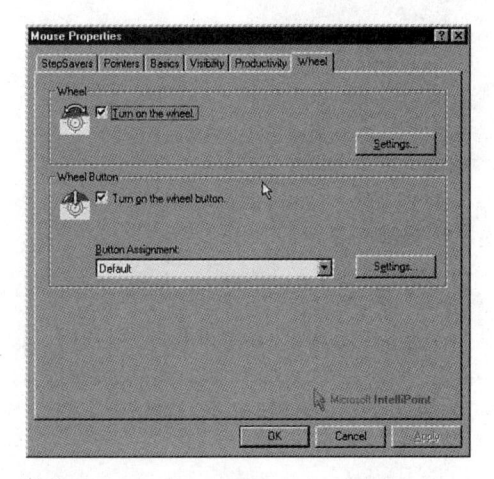

Figure 5.22 Adjusting the Wheel features of the Microsoft IntelliPoint Mouse pointing device.

12. The Wheel tab refers to the small wheel that is present between the two mouse buttons on a Microsoft IntelliPoint Mouse. Click the check box inside the Wheel section to enable the wheel for use in its rolling capabilities. Click the check box inside the Wheel Button section to enable the wheel for use as an alternative button (press it down and you can feel it clicking very softly).

13. By default, the wheel as a button does nothing. However, if you click the drop-down list box below the Button Assignment label, you will see four possible choices: Double-Click; Help (F1); Windows Explorer; and the Start Menu. Highlight any of these selections and then click the Apply button to confirm your choice. If you do make a button assignment selection, then the Settings... button next to this section will be grayed-out.

14. If you click the Settings*f* button inside the Wheel section then the Settings for Wheel screen shown in Figure 5.23 will appear.

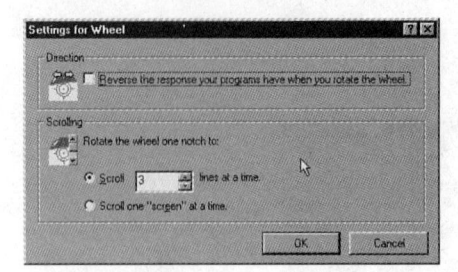

Figure 5.23 Setting the Direction and Scrolling options for the Microsoft IntelliPoint Mouse.

15. This screen allows you to reverse the normal top to bottom use of the wheel, and gives you the capability to set the scrolling speed that the mouse wheel generates. These options are the true productivity options, and they should be tested to make sure that you are setting them properly to meet your own usage patterns.

16. Click OK to accept your changes, if any, and return to the previous screen.

17. Click OK to accept your changes, if any, and the Mouse Properties screen closes completely.

> **NOTE**
>
> For those of you who are using old, non–plug-and-play mouse or pointing devices, be sure to look at any statements that might exist in either your CONFIG.SYS or AUTOEXEC.BAT configuration files. With the older equipment, these two files sometimes played a much larger role in the configuration aspect than one might normally suspect in a 32-bit Windows world. So, the key concept to remember is that if you do use older pointing device equipment, you might be limited to operating just a single device at a time; an important factor if you require the use of the Windows 98 Accessibility options with multiple devices.

CHAPTER 6
DISK DRIVE MANAGEMENT AND USE

6

DISK DRIVE MANAGEMENT AND USE

How do I...
- 6.1 Know what the differences are between the FAT16 and the FAT32 file systems?
- 6.2 Install the additional disk drive management tools and utilities?
- 6.3 Know whether to use disk compression or FAT32?
- 6.4 Configure and use the Windows 98 Disk Compression tool?
- 6.5 Configure and use the drive converter (FAT32)?
- 6.6 Configure and use the Disk Cleanup utility?
- 6.7 Configure and use the Disk Defragmenter utility?
- 6.8 Configure and use the ScanDisk utility?
- 6.9 Manage my hard disk drive(s)?

CHAPTER 6
DISK DRIVE MANAGEMENT AND USE

6.10 Manage my removable media drive(s)?

6.11 Install a CD-ROM or a DVD-ROM drive?

6.12 Know which additional removable hard drive devices I should install?

6.13 Back Up my Windows 98 system?

This chapter covers hard disk drive usage in detail, with specific information on how to care for your drives, removable or not. Although your hard drive is probably the most important piece of your computer system, most people hardly recognize that it exists, "other than some computer memory thing where stuff is stored." Proper maintenance and care can easily extend the life of your disk drives. A walk-through of adding new hardware to your computer, such as a CD- or DVD-ROM, is included toward the end of this chapter. Additional coverage is given to the Microsoft Windows 98 Backup utility, including a few strategies on how to create and maintain a backup schedule for your computer system.

6.1 Know What the Differences Are Between the FAT16 and the FAT32 File Systems

Most people never pay attention to the file allocation table sizes (12, 16, and 32), much less try to thoughtfully decide which one is best for their system. This How-To helps you determine which file system is best for your PC and provides some insight as to how one file system can save you space and performance over the other.

6.2 Install the Additional Disk Drive Management Tools and Utilities

Many very useful tools and utilities are built into the Windows 98 operating system. This How-To provides a quick mechanism for learning how to install all of them at once.

6.3 Know Whether to Use Disk Compression or FAT32

The decision to use FAT32 or a Disk Compression tool such as DriveSpace 3 can be a difficult one, fraught with peril at many intervals. The wrong decision now cannot necessarily be fixed later on, so it is very important to get it right the first time.

CHAPTER 6
DISK DRIVE MANAGEMENT AND USE

6.4 Configure and Use the Windows 98 Disk Compression Tool
This How-To focuses on the configuration and use of the Disk Compression tool that is included with the Windows 98 operating system.

6.5 Configure and Use the Drive Converter (FAT32)?
This How-To focuses on the configuration and use of the Disk Drive Converter tool known as FAT32, which is included with the Windows 98 operating system.

6.6 Configure and Use the Disk Cleanup Utility
This How-To focuses on the configuration and use of the Disk Cleanup tool that is included with the Windows 98 operating system.

6.7 Configure and Use the Disk Defragmenter Utility
This How-To focuses on the configuration and use of the Disk Defragmenter utility that is included with the Windows 98 operating system.

6.8 Configure and Use the ScanDisk Utility
This How-To focuses on the configuration and use of the ScanDisk tool that is included with the Windows 98 operating system.

6.9 Manage My Hard Disk Drive(s)
Many people give little, if any, thought to the organization and management of their computer's hard drive. This can lead to a waste of drive space as well as a waste of time (which is lost trying to find "missing" files). This How-To focuses on providing several suggestions and tips on how to best manage.

6.10 Manage My Removable Media Drive(s)
Like hard disk management, it is very important to manage the organization of your removable media drives or they will become a disorganized disaster waiting to happen. This How-To helps you manage your removable media drives.

6.11 Install a CD-ROM or a DVD-ROM Drive
Many people mistakenly believe that all you need to do is install the hardware device and Windows 98 will handle everything automatically. This How-To gets you started on the software side of a Windows 98 hardware implementation.

6.12 Know Which Additional Removable Hard Drive Devices I Should Install

A veritable blizzard of removable hard drive devices are available on the consumer market, some of which do not work well with Windows 98 (despite their advertisements). This How-To addresses the more popular (and compatible) devices, and provides insight into the differences between these very similar-looking devices.

6.13 Back Up My Windows 98 System

The vast majority of computer users never back up their computer's hard disk drive, no matter how many times they have previously lost data. This How-To demonstrates how easy it is to quickly back up your PC and to restore one or more files if necessary.

COMPLEXITY

INTERMEDIATE

6.1 How do I...
Know what the differences are between the FAT16 and the FAT32 file systems?

Problem

Windows 98 comes with something called FAT32. Is this a useful technology or more smoke and mirrors being presented by the Microsoft marketing hype machine? Also, if I choose to convert over to it, will I lose any data or access to my system?

Technique

File allocation table structures have come a long way since the original 12-bit FAT that was introduced with Microsoft DOS 1.0 in the early 1980s. FAT12 was useful on hard drives of less than 16MBs in total, a gigantic number considering that it was not until 1985 that the general public began to purchase PCs with hard drives , which were still only in the 5–10MB range. With the introduction of Microsoft-DOS version 3.0, the 16-bit file allocation table structure (or FAT16 as it is more commonly known as) was born. With FAT16 came fairly

KNOW WHAT THE DIFFERECES ARE BETWEEN FAT 16 AND FAT 32

extensive support for hard drives all the way up to that space-age futuristic, fantastic amount of 512MBs (not too bad, considering that most IBM-compatible personal computers still only had 640K of memory and a 30MB hard drive).

The 32-bit file allocation table (FAT32) structure that is offered within Windows 98 is the same as what was first offered to the public via the OSR2 release of Windows 95 (this was the OEM release that appeared in 1996). You can think of a file allocation table structure as a series of filing cabinets. You have countless numbers of drawers that equate to the number of cylinders on your hard drive. These drawers all contain an equal amount of folders (or clusters), which is where you store information.

On an FAT16-formatted system, these folders are probably 32KB in size each. If all of your data files are exactly 32,768 bytes each (32K), life is wonderful. Now, let's assume you have a mixture of files, some of which are tiny configuration files (such as the CONFIG.SYS or AUTOEXEC.BAT files), whereas others are huge database files each consuming multiple megabytes of drive space. Each one of your 1,500-byte configuration files takes an entire folder, thus leaving each folder about 90 percent empty but unable to take on another file. Next, multiply this by the number of small files on your system and you are looking at a lot of wasted space. On a FAT32-formatted system, your folder (cluster) size is 4,096 bytes each (4K); you can do the math and figure out the savings (quite significant, don't you agree?).

Anyway, FAT32 is not for everyone. If your hard disk drive is 512MB in size or smaller, attempting a conversion is a waste of your time and drive space; you will gain nothing and lose time in the process. Because other operating systems that run FAT16 (such as DOS-based or the original Windows 95–based system) or another 32-bit file structure (such as NTFS under Windows NT) cannot see a FAT32-formatted drive, you might want to rethink your FAT32 strategy. This is especially the case if you must communicate with other devices like these. In addition, if your PC is on a corporate network full of Windows NT Servers (other than the latest Windows NT version, version 5.0), then FAT32 definitely should be avoided unless you are willing to take on the ire of an irate systems or network administrator.

Complete the following steps to help determine whether this latest file allocation table structure from Microsoft is right for you.

Steps

1. Check the size of your hard disk drive. Is it smaller than 512MB? If the answer is yes, stop the decision making process because FAT32 is not an option for you. If no, then continue on to the next step.

2. Is the hard drive greater than 2GBs in size? If so then you really should take a hard look at FAT32, because the FAT16 structure does not support partitions larger than 2GB in size. Of course, you can always partition the hard drive so it is possible to use FAT16 on an 8GB drive by making at least four DOS partitions. However, FAT32 will manage this drive's total disk space much more efficiently than FAT16 ever could.

3. If your current hard drive is compressed with a hard drive compression tool such as DriveSpace or DoubleSpace, you might not want to make the switch to FAT32. Because FAT32 will not coexist with any drive compression tool, you will need to back up all of your files, remove the compression tool, restore what files you can (remember, your drive has now shrunk by as much as 60 percent), and then convert over to the FAT32 structure. Is this much work worth the hassle? Only you can determine this.

4. Is there a need to dual-boot the computer that you want to use the FAT32 file structure on, with either an older version of DOS/Windows or Windows NT 4.0? If the answer is yes, stop the decision-making process because FAT32 is not an option for you. If no, then continue on to the next step.

5. Does this computer need to communicate directly with other non-FAT32 systems, in that other systemsv users would be attempting to access a shared drive on the FAT32 structured PC? If the answer is yes, stop the decision making process as FAT32 is not an option for you. If no, then continue on to the next step.

6. Is this computer one that hibernates? For instance, IBM ThinkPad laptops have long had this feature, and if your version of hibernation is not compatible with FAT32 then your computer might fail to hibernate or might not boot at all. If the answer is yes, you will need to carefully test and verify that FAT32 is right for you (or your organization). If you do not use or require a hibernation feature then move on to the final test.

7. When making the switch to FAT32 you will replace the Master Boot Record (MBR), which can tend to throw antivirus protection programs off, as well as boot programs, such as System Commander. Additionally, there are some PC BIOS manufacturers' software that will not function correctly with FAT32. You will need to specifically test each BIOS version with FAT32 to ensure that your organization's FAT32 rollout goes smoothly, especially with computers that utilize a Suspend (similar to hibernation) feature.

6.2 How do I...
Install the additional disk drive management tools and utilities?

COMPLEXITY
BEGINNER

Problem

Windows 98 provides several additional disk drive management tools and utilities, not to mention some of those that are available from the Windows 98 Resource Kit. How do I identify and then install all these additional tools and utilities?

Technique

One of the nicest features of Windows 98 is its capability to provide access to its various tools and utilities via the Add/Remove Programs icon in the Control Panel. Through this Control Panel option you can install these tools in just about any combination you want, without having to hunt and peck through a variety of other methods. However, should you require more technical information that cannot be retrieved via the basic Windows 98 methods, there is always the Windows 98 Resource Kit. This kit contains 73 additional tools that can help you further manage your Windows 98 installation. For information on obtaining and installing the Windows 98 Resource Kit, please refer to Chapter 1, "Installation Tips," for details on how to install the base set of Windows 98 tools and utilities.

Steps

1. Start Windows 98, go all the way into its GUI desktop, and then pull up the Control Panel. Once inside the Control Panel, double-click the Add/Remove Programs icon, and then click the Windows Setup tab to reveal the screen shown in Figure 6.1.

2. This screen is the access point for nearly all of the add-on tools and utilities for Windows 98. To select an item, click on its check box to place a check mark inside the box. If a box has a check mark with shading in it as well, then that means not all of the subcomponents for that topic have been chosen. Scrolling down toward the bottom of this listing, you will see the topic labeled System Tools. Click this selection to highlight, and then click the Details... button to view the individual components as shown in Figure 6.2.

CHAPTER 6
DISK DRIVE MANAGEMENT AND USE

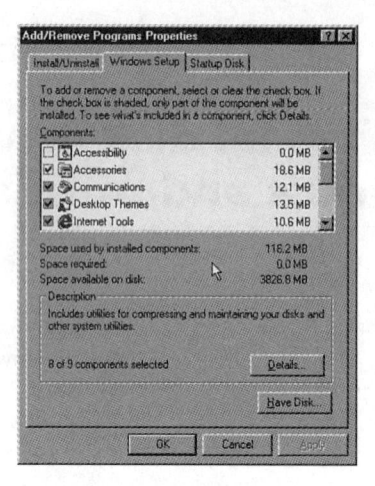

Figure 6.1 The Windows Setup tab of the Add/Remove Programs Properties screen.

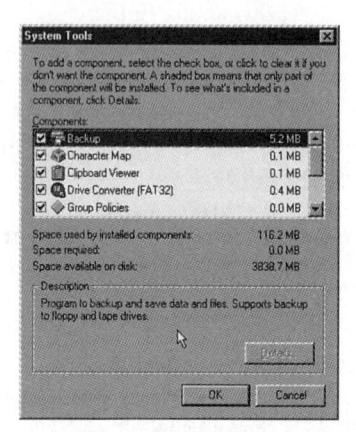

Figure 6.2 The System Tools selection screen found within the Windows Setup tab.

3. Within this listing, the items you should be most interested in are the Backup and Drive Converter (FAT32) tools, as these two will aid you in the management of your disk drive(s). Select both of these, if they are not already installed on your PC, and then click OK.

4. After returning to the higher-level System Tools screen, click OK to begin the installation process for the tools that you want to add to your existing Windows 98 installation.

5. You will be prompted to put your Windows 98 CD-ROM into your CD drive, and then the copying will commence. If you are prompted to overwrite any files, such as the one seen in Figure 6.3, it is usually best to keep your existing file because it is the most recent version.

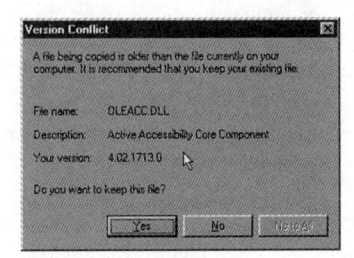

Figure 6.3 The Version Conflict message box.

6. The installation process continues for some time, depending on how many other tools and utilities you have chosen from the other component categories. When the process is complete, click Yes when asked if you want to restart your computer. It is usually best to reboot each time after you have installed new system components, especially ones from the System Tools section.

7. After rebooting, you are finished. Any time you want to add or remove a Windows 98 system component, this is the place to perform that task.

COMPLEXITY
INTERMEDIATE

6.3 How do I...
Know whether to use disk compression or FAT32?

Problem

I have very little hard drive space remaining but I cannot afford to add a second hard drive to my computer. What can I do to otherwise alleviate the problem? A secondary issue to this is that I have a laptop computer with the same problem, but there is no spot for a second drive. What alternatives do I have in the case of a portable computer?

Technique

Within the Windows 98 operating system there are a few different ways in which you can approach this problem. The first is deciding whether you want to use a disk compression program or change the file allocation table structure of your computer system. Another way is to invoke a self-cleaning program where you go through your computer and discard all the junk you have probably accumulated since you purchased it way back when. A practical way is to back up the older information and applications that you have not used in quite some time, and then delete the originals of those files and applications from your existing hard drive. The final way is to purchase a removable piece of hardware storage, such as a Jaz, Zip, SyQuest, SparQ, or a PC-card hard drive system.

All four ways should get you to the same result: more space to accumulate even more data and programs than you had in the first place. The old rule of thumb with personal computers is that no matter how big the hard drive, you will always be able to eventually fill it up and run out of available space. It has been like this since the early days of personal computing when people were constantly switching between cassette tapes, and it will probably be like this long into the future even with DVD, optical drives, and the next new technology on the horizon.

The first step is to decide whether to use a disk compression program such as DriveSpace (which comes with the Windows 98 operating system) or a third-party utility (such as Stacker). Or you need to decide if you should change your file allocation table (FAT) structure to a 32-bit FAT using the built-in Windows 98 utility known as the Drive Converter (FAT32). Use the steps in this section to help determine which of these technologies you want to use. After you have decided, you can use the information contained later in this chapter to help you in the configuration and usage of both of these technologies.

The second method, cleaning up your hard drive(s), is performed via two Windows 98 utilities known as the Disk Cleanup utility and the Defragmenter utility. The Disk Cleanup utility helps you identify and delete the garbage or little-used applications on your system, while the Defragmenter utility reorganizes and reclaims the misused space on your disk drives. There are detailed discussions later in this chapter on how you can configure and use both of these technologies.

The third method—backing up the older information and applications that you have not used in quite some time and then deleting the originals of those files and applications from your existing hard drives—is one of my favorites. It is also usually the most practical way in which to find extra hard drive space without either impacting system performance or running the danger of deleting something you should not have. The final discussion in this chapter explains how you can configure and use this technology.

6.3
KNOW WHETHER TO USE DISK COMPRESSION OR FAT32

The final method is also discussed toward the end of this chapter. You can always go out and buy external removable hard drive disk storage, but this obviously comes at both a financial cost and a performance cost. These types of drives are usually, but not always, slower than the real thing, and are usually more expensive per megabyte than internal system hard drives.

So, go back to the first method—deciding whether to use a disk compression program or perhaps change your file allocation table structure to FAT32. You might want to review the section that appeared at the start of this chapter, which discussed the finer details of 16- and 32-bit FAT structures, for more intricate details. However, complete the following steps and you will become better prepared to answer your own question of "Do I use disk compression or FAT32?"

Steps

1. If you are using a relatively small hard drive (less than 512MB total), the answer is easy: you must use disk compression, because FAT32 is not available on small hard drives.

2. Likewise, if the hard drive is large (greater than 2GB total) and you insist on using a single partition then the answer is just about as easy: most disk compression programs do not support partitions greater than 2GB in size, DriveSpace 3 included.

3. Basically, if you cannot use FAT32 for whatever reason (dual booting, required compatibility with other operating systems, drive sharing for others, and so on), your only choice becomes drive compression or to add additional hardware to your system. Both imply a cost to you: one real and the other in performance. You need to take this into consideration should these items be a factor.

4. Disk compression in the form of the DriveSpace (version 3) utility built into Windows 98 can be an excellent solution to your problem. It is free, can act as a long-term solution, and on Pentium systems it does not impact performance too much.

5. Perhaps the best way to decide is to compare how much free space each utility will provide you with if you use it. Using the Windows 98 Resource Kit (see Chapter 1 for information on obtaining and installing this kit), double-click the FAT32 Conversion Information tool inside the Microsoft Management Console to display an estimate of how much space you will gain using the FAT32 utility, as shown in Figure 6.4.

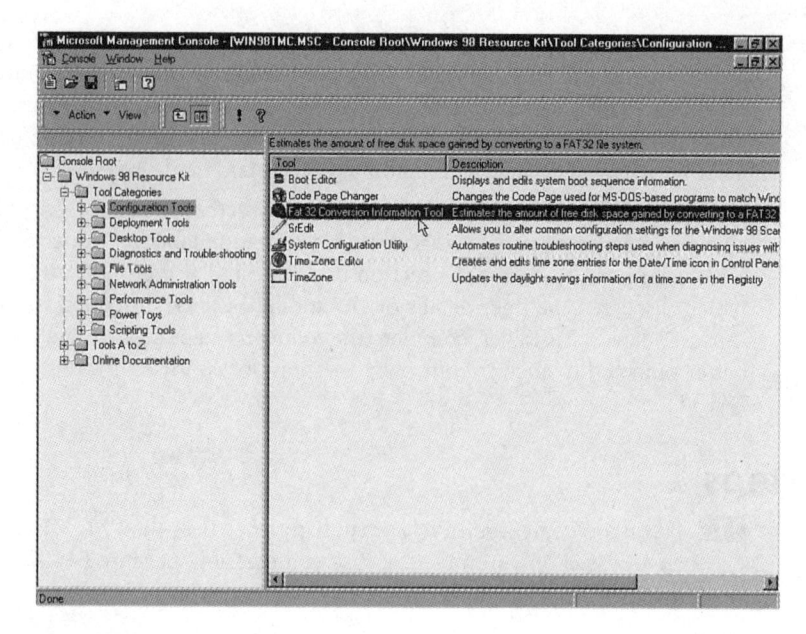

Figure 6.4 The primary screen of the Microsoft Management Console.

6. Doing this causes the FAT32 Conversion Information window to appear, as shown in Figure 6.5.

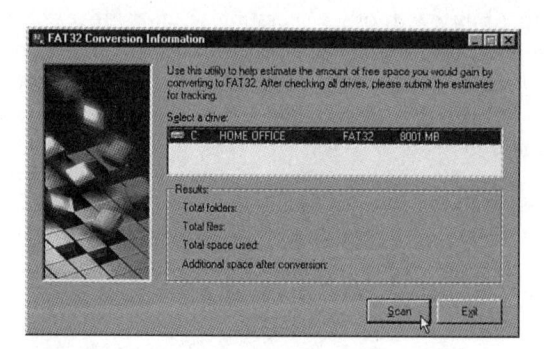

Figure 6.5 The FAT32 Conversion Information screen.

7. This screen shows you the drives that are available for conversion, and provides you with a breakdown of how much disk space is presently being used and how much additional space will become available

6.3
KNOW WHETHER TO USE DISK COMPRESSION OR FAT32

following a conversion over to a FAT32 structure. Click the Scan button to initiate the FAT32 Conversion Information process.

8. To check for how much new space can be made available using the Windows 98 disk compression program DriveSpace, start that application from the System Tools menu.

9. Follow the prompts through this tool until you reach the Compress a Drive screen as shown in Figure 6.6. This screen appears before you actually start the compression process.

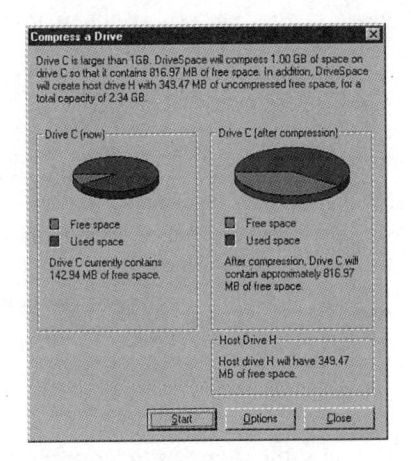

Figure 6.6 The Windows 98 DriveSpace 3 Compress a Drive screen.

10. After this screen appears, print it out or write down the information that appears. After you have copied the information, click the Close button to cancel out of this process without actually performing any kind of compression whatsoever.

11. Compare the data from the DriveSpace screen to that of the FAT32 Conversion Information screen, and voilà! You will have your answer as to which utility gives you the most new free space. From here the decision becomes even easier.

CHAPTER 6
DISK DRIVE MANAGEMENT AND USE

COMPLEXITY
INTERMEDIATE

6.4 How do I...
Configure and use the Windows 98 Disk Compression tool?

Problem

Okay, I have decided to use the Windows 98 Disk Compression tool. What do I do now? Where does this tool come from and how do I configure it for use with my computer?

Technique

Windows 98 provides a utility known as DriveSpace 3. To install it, if it does not already exist on your \Programs \Accessories \System Tools \DriveSpace menu path, use the Windows Setup procedure that was discussed in the section, "How do I Install the additional disk drive management tools and utilities?" earlier in this chapter. After you see it on your menu structure, follow the steps listed here to configure it for use with your computer system.

Steps

1. After entering the DriveSpace utility, the Compress a Drive screen appears as shown in Figure 6.7.

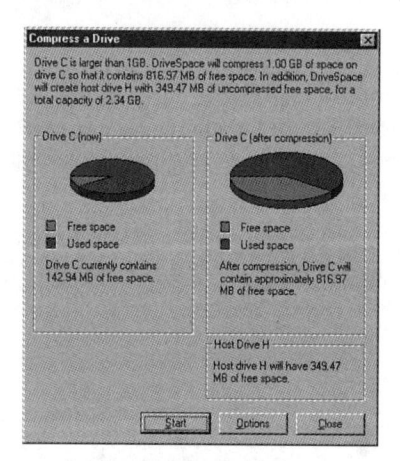

Figure 6.7 Starting to compress a drive using the DriveSpace utility.

6.4 CONFIGURE AND USE THE WINDOWS 98 DISK COMPRESSION TOOL

2. This portion of the DriveSpace utility is very useful, as it predicts fairly accurately the final results of your drive compression activities. It does this through a before and after graphic shown on the left (the now state) and right (the after compression state) sides of the screen. It also notifies you of the amount of space that will exist on the host drive, as well as what the drive letter assignment will be for that host drive.

> **NOTE**
>
> Think of the host drive as the physical drive where the compressed volume file is stored (this is the file that actually contains all your compressed data), and think of the "new" C:\ drive as your logical drive. That is, the C:\ drive is not real, rather, it is a slightly more solid figment of your imagination. The information that you see as the new C:\ drive is actually stored in a file with a .000 file extension that has a name such as DRVSPACE.000 or DBLSPACE.000 (these are not case-sensitive files). If you notice files such as these on your system, do not delete them or try to alter them in any way because doing so can cause you to lose all the information contained within that compressed drive's volume.

3. If you will be connecting this computer to a Novell network then you might want to avoid assigning the letter F as the host drive letter. You do this by clicking the Options... button to reveal the screen shown in Figure 6.8.

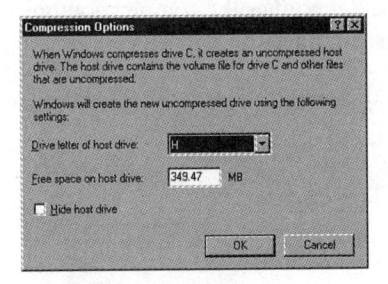

Figure 6.8 Deciding on the Compression options.

4. The Compression Options window appears with a drop-down list box containing the available drive letters for the new host drive. Pick a drive letter that is suitable to you, if the default letter assignment (usually H) is not palatable. Also found on this window is a setting for the amount of free space to be left on the host drive. Windows 98 attempts to set this number for you, but you can change it to almost any amount you like (provided, of course, that you really have that much space available at your discretion). If you require a chunk of uncompressed hard drive space for use with another application then this is where you make that setting. Click OK to return to the previous screen.

5. Click the Start button to begin compressing your hard drive.

6. As soon as you start the compression process, DriveSpace prompts you to create a Windows 98 Startup disk (just in case difficulties are encountered) as shown in Figure 6.9.

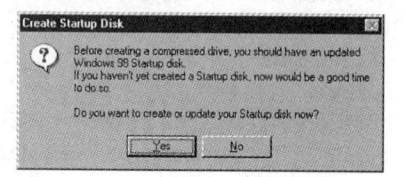

Figure 6.9 Deciding whether to create a Windows 98 Startup disk.

7. When the Create Startup Disk window appears, you need to decide whether you want to make a disk or not. It is strongly suggested that you do make this disk, because there is always an outside chance that something will go wrong and you might not have any way back into your computer system other than a Windows 98 Startup disk. To make the disk, place a blank, formatted disk into your A:\ drive, and then click Yes. This creates the disk and then continues the compression process. Otherwise, click No, and the compression process continues immediately.

8. The Create New Compressed Drive window appears, as shown in Figure 6.10.

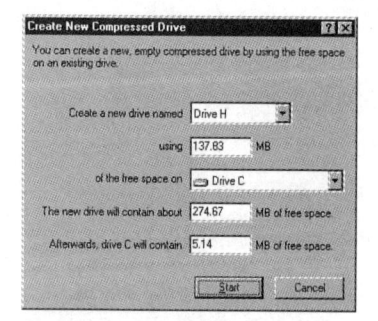

Figure 6.10 Finalizing the compressed drive options and starting the compression process.

6.5 CONFIGURE AND USE THE DRIVE CONVERTER (FAT32)

9. This screen contains all of the settings that are used in the creation of your new compressed drive. Look it over very carefully, and then click Start to continue the process.

10. The Are you sure? window appears next, as shown in Figure 6.11.

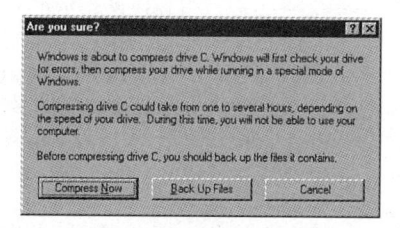

Figure 6.11 Confirming your choice to compress the hard drive.

11. This window prompts you to back up all your data files that exist on your computer. It would be wise to at least make copies of your most critical data files, as once again there is a chance that you will be compressing your computer drive into oblivion. After you click on the Compress Now button, the DriveSpace disk compression program begins. You cannot stop the process from this point on until it has completed. Disruption of the disk compression process most certainly destroys the data on your hard drive, so it is very unwise to attempt any interruptions.

12. After the process is complete, you need to reboot your computer, and then you are finished.

COMPLEXITY
INTERMEDIATE

6.5 How do I...
Configure and use the drive converter (FAT32)?

Problem

After careful deliberations, I have decided to implement the FAT32 on my PC. My hard drive fits all the requirements, but I am unsure as to how to actually implement the FAT32 structure. How do I accomplish this task?

Technique

Windows 98 provides a tool literally known as the Drive Converter (FAT32). The purpose of this utility program is to convert a hard drive from the 16-bit file structure over to the 32-bit file structure that is better known as FAT32. Remember that this is a one-way process: Windows 98 does *not* provide any means from undoing a FAT32 conversion process, so this is a final step. After you convert to FAT32, the only way back to a 16-bit file allocation table structure is to FDisk your hard drive, re-create the partition table(s), and then reformat your hard drive. This is a very long, involved process that definitely is not for the weak of heart. To use the Drive Converter, carefully follow these steps, taking care not to accidentally skip any of them.

Steps

1. Install the Drive Converter (FAT32) utility if it does not already exist on your \Programs \Accessories \System Tools \DriveSpace menu path. To install it, use the Windows Setup procedure that was discussed earlier in this chapter. When you see it on your menu structure, double-click that menu option to start the process.

2. After you enter the Drive Converter (FAT32) utility, a screen appears prompting you to select the drive you want to convert, as shown in Figure 6.12.

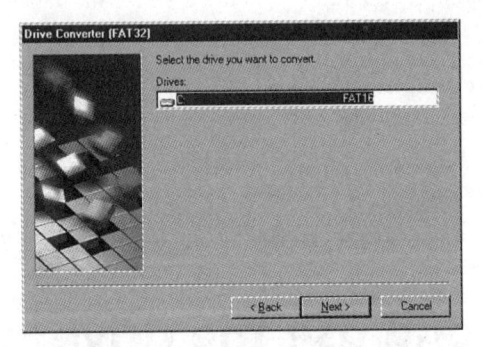

Figure 6.12 Deciding which hard disk drive to convert to FAT32.

3. If there is more than one available drive then it would automatically be shown on this screen. When you are certain of the drive letter that you want to convert, click Next> to continue, as shown in Figure 6.13.

6.5 CONFIGURE AND USE THE DRIVE CONVERTER (FAT32)

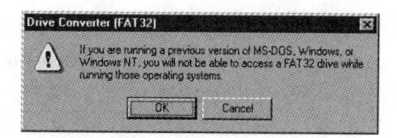

Figure 6.13 FAT32 conversion process caution message box.

4. Windows 98 quickly prompts you with a message box that warns you of FAT32's inefficiencies when it comes to interoperability with other operating systems. If this does not scare you, and you want to continue, click OK to continue, as shown in Figure 6.14.

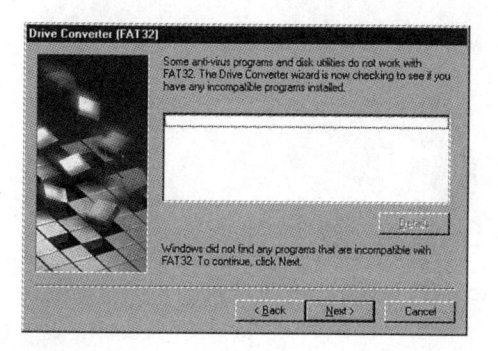

Figure 6.14 Checking for incompatible FAT32 programs and utilities.

5. Any *TSRs* that might be running, especially those for antivirus applications, appear in the box within this window.

> **NOTE**
>
> A *TSR* (terminate-and-stay-resident) is a software application that starts up, but then appears to stop although it is still be present in your computer system's memory. A good example of a TSR is an antivirus protection program, such as Cheyenne AntiVirus, which includes a feature to remain resident in memory and scan all incoming and outgoing e-mail messages. A TSR such as an antivirus protection package will most likely interfere with any software installation, as it views that software installation as a virus attempting to infiltrate your computer system. This is especially true with the installation of a new operating system, as a new OS will attempt to write information to your computer's boot record.

CHAPTER 6
DISK DRIVE MANAGEMENT AND USE

5. The focus here is on applications and BIOS programs that monitor the master boot record (MBR) and any attempts to modify the MBR. The Drive Converter (FAT32) utility does exactly that—it modifies the MBR in such a way that most antivirus utilities will detect it and believe that the Drive Converter (FAT32) application is actually a computer virus. It is for this reason that you will want to deactivate any virus applications that you might have running, as well as any other TSRs that might be active. After you have taken care of these items, click the Next> button to continue, as shown in Figure 6.15.

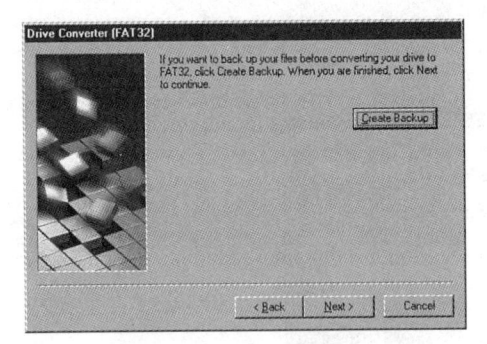

Figure 6.15 Prompt to back up your files one last time before converting.

6. This next window prompts you to back up all of your data and files that exist on your system. It is wise to at least make copies of your most critical data files, as there is a real chance that the FAT32 converter might obliterate your hard drive. It is not likely to do so, but it has been known to happen. When you have backed up your PC to your satisfaction, click the Next> button to continue, as shown in Figure 6.16.

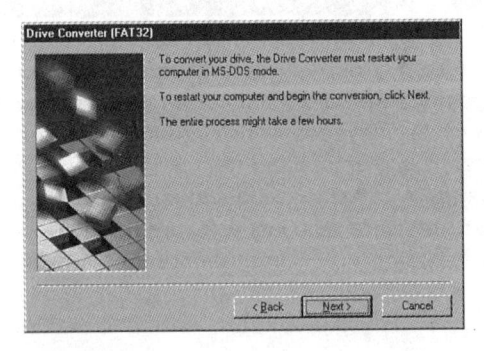

Figure 6.16 Starting the actual FAT32 conversion procedure.

6.5 CONFIGURE AND USE THE DRIVE CONVERTER (FAT32)

7. This is your last chance to stop the FAT32 conversion process. Your system will start to convert over to the 32-bit file allocation table structure as soon as you click the Next> button.

8. Once you start this process you cannot stop it until it is complete. Disruption of the FAT conversion process will destroy the data on your hard drive. This includes power failures to your computer, hibernation modes, suspend operations, and so on. Therefore, it is strongly suggested that you have an 8–12 hour block of time that you can perform this conversion process, such as overnight. Make sure that you leave your computer plugged in so it does not attempt to run this process on battery power alone.

9. One last tip: When the FAT32 conversion process is complete, it automatically starts the Disk Defragmenter utility. You need to permit this second utility to run completely, because your new FAT32 file structure will seem sluggish until you run the Disk Defragmenter application at least once all the way through. Unfortunately, if you have a heavily used drive that is very large (greater than 4GB), the Disk Defragmenter utility might take another 6–8 hours to run. Therefore, you might want to consider running this entire procedure on a weekend when you do not really need full use of your computer system.

> **NOTE**
>
> The Disk Defragmenter utility program is used to rearrange the files on your hard drive so that they are in order and together near the start of the hard drive, with all of the free space (disk drive clusters) arranged consecutively at the end of the hard drive. (Of course, they meet somewhere in the middle.) This makes it easier for your computer system to find files faster because the files are now in a logical order (logical to your computer, that is). Also, when your computer needs to copy a large chunk of data to the hard drive, it does not need to search around for the free space because it is in a single area. This too makes it seem as if your computer system is running faster.
>
> Although you can use your PC while the defragmentation process is running, it will slow down the Disk Defragmenter utility and take more time to finish. During the defragmentation process, the utility has to restart every time other applications make any changes to your hard disk drive, which is why it takes longer to run. Thus, it is recommended that you do not use your PC at all during a disk defragmentation processing time, ensuring that your computer has ample time to complete this very important disk maintenance process.

COMPLEXITY
INTERMEDIATE

6.6 How do I...
Configure and use the Disk Cleanup utility?

Problem

I want to clean up my hard drive, but I don't know how to find and delete the garbage or little-used applications that I am sure exists on my PC. How do I find these items, and then what is the safest way to remove them after they have been identified?

Technique

Windows 98 has a new tool known as the Disk Cleanup utility. This utility in its base form comes as part of the Windows 98 operating system and can be installed with all the other system tools via the Add/Remove Programs icon found in the Control Panel. An enhanced version of this tool is available via the Windows 98 Plus! package, which anyone can purchase for Windows 98 from Microsoft Corporation. For more details on the Windows 98 Plus! package, refer to Chapter 19, "Giving Windows Special Powers." When you have installed the utility, comply with the following steps for details on how to best utilize the Disk Cleanup utility on your computer system.

Steps

1. After starting the Disk Cleanup utility from the System Tools menu, you are prompted to select a drive to clean up, as shown in Figure 6.17.

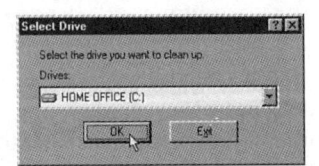

Figure 6.17 Selecting the drive you want to clean up.

2. Pick a drive from the drop-down list box, such as the C: drive, and then click OK to continue.

3. The utility displays a message box telling you that it is in the process of calculating how much space can be saved on the drive you selected. After

6.6
CONFIGURE AND USE THE DISK CLEANUP UTILITY

the calculation is complete, the main Disk Cleanup screen appears as shown in Figure 6.18.

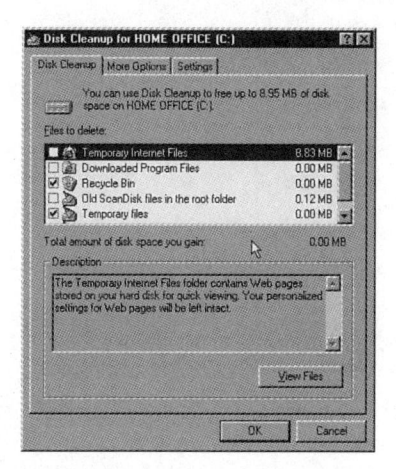

Figure 6.18 Windows 98 Disk Cleanup Selection tab.

4. You will arrive at the Disk Cleanup tab first. It is from here that the utility gives you a chance to delete everything it found all at once, or you can selectively delete some files by group but not others. For example, in the screen shown back in Figure 6.18, you can see that not all of the items have been marked for deletion (the ones with check marks have been marked for deletion). To delete everything, place a check mark in each of the boxes listed, and then click OK.

5. On three of the items: Temporary Internet Files, Downloaded Program Files, and the Recycle Bin, you have an additional option of viewing the individual files within each of those areas. The Temporary Internet Files and the Recycle Bin are normally the safest ones to delete, because neither of these should impact your computer's operation in any way. The deletion of the Downloaded Program Files normally will not do any harm either, unless you have some application open and in use that you just got from the Internet (or your organization's intranet). To view these files, click any of these three topical areas to highlight it, and then click the View Files button. This takes you to a window where you can individually delete the files you want, as seen in Figure 6.19. You might also use this button to confirm that you really do want to remove all of these files via the Mass Delete option (place a check mark in its box) on the main Disk Cleanup screen.

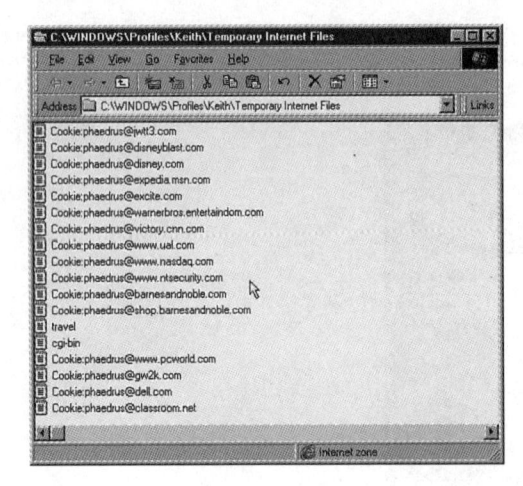

Figure 6.19 Deciding which of the temporary Internet files you want to keep and which ones to delete.

> **NOTE**
>
> As soon as you click OK, the Disk Cleanup utility prompts you with a small message box asking you if you are sure that you want to go through with the deletion process. If you are not, click No once. Otherwise, click Yes to continue the mass deletion process.

6. To delete any single file, click it once to highlight it. Then click once with your secondary mouse button to reveal a small menu. Go to the third option from the top, Delete, and click that menu selection. The file that you had highlighted will automatically disappear. After you have deleted the individual files that you want or after you have reviewed the screen(s) of information, close this window and you will see the Disk Cleanup window behind it.

7. The final item that you should know about on this first tab is the bottom one in the list labeled Non-Critical Files. If you place a check mark in this box and click OK, you will go to the Disk Cleanup utility that was created by a third-party vendor (CyberMedia). This will not happen though until the automatic cleanup of the files from any of the other sections is complete.

8. Microsoft describes the functionality of the CyberMedia portion this way: "Non-critical files are files commonly found on your system but are seldom used. Many of these files can be safely deleted. Unlike other cleaners, this cleaner is not automatic, but will instead bring up an Explorer-like interface allowing you to remove the non-critical files." After

6.6
CONFIGURE AND USE THE DISK CLEANUP UTILITY

this piece has started, a SmartLinks database will be built first, and then you will be presented with a screen similar to the one shown in Figure 6.20.

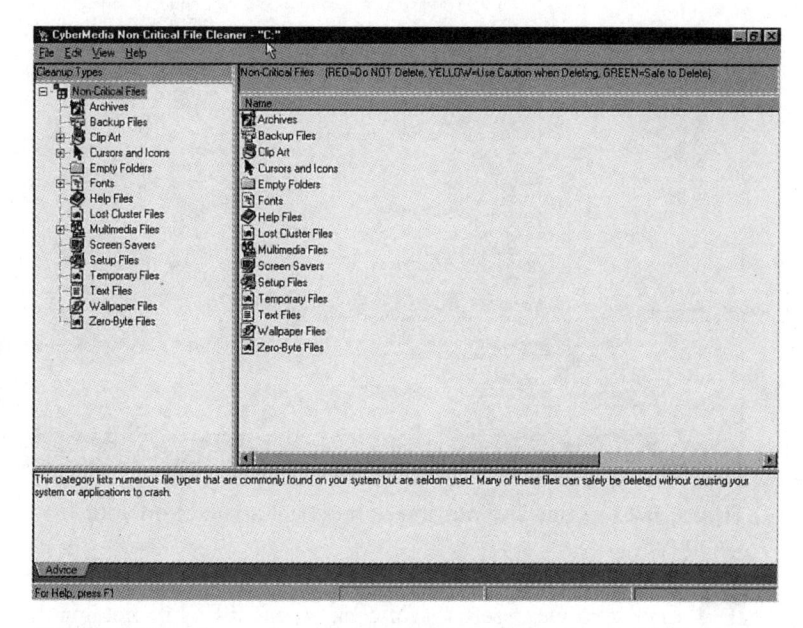

Figure 6.20 The main screen of CyberMedia's Non-Critical File Cleaner.

9. The CyberMedia program window closely resembles that of a Windows Explorer screen and works much the same way. Click once on any of the Cleanup Types found in the left column, and the right-side column window will fill-up with all the files and folders found in that section, as seen in Figure 6.21.

10. By clicking on the label on top any of the columns inside the right-hand window (such as Name, Type, Size, Date, or Location), the CyberMedia application automatically re-sorts the window based on that column's data contents.

11. Before you actually delete any of these files, be sure to check their relevancy to your computer system. There is a series of colored shapes, a red circle, a yellow square, and a green triangle. Red means stop, you probably do not want to delete this file. Yellow warns of caution, as you might or might not want to pursue the deletion process. Green means that you should probably go ahead and delete this file, as it has not been modified (for example, used, read, altered, and so on) in the past six months. Think of this warning system as a traffic light, and you will be able to maneuver through it much faster and easier.

CHAPTER 6
DISK DRIVE MANAGEMENT AND USE

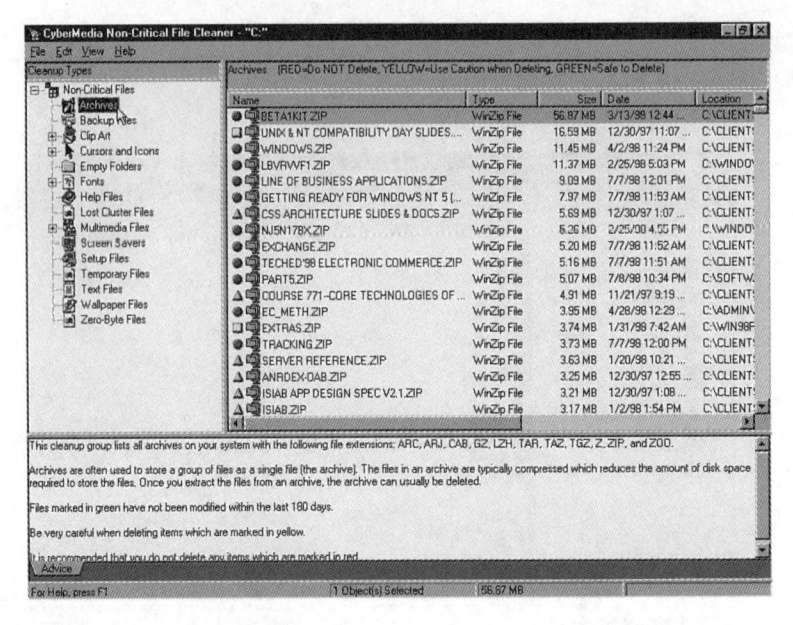

Figure 6.21 Checking out the non-critical archives on your computer.

12. Click on a file to select it, or click on one file while holding the Shift key down and then click on another file above or below it in the list and you will be able to select a whole series of files at the same time.

13. If you are still unsure what you want to do with any of these files in any of the categories, you can print out a listing of them. To do this, click on the File menu option and then click again on the Print List menu selection. When the Print message box appears, click OK to print the listing for the subtype that you have highlighted. One more thing: make sure that your print device is connected and turned on.

14. A few more tips: If you are really desperate for drive space, try deleting Help files, extra fonts, Setup files, Wallpaper files, and clip art. I have found that these areas tend to consume the most space, while at the same time usually being the most worthless files on one's computer system. Ninety-nine percent of these files can be safely deleted without affecting the operation of your PC, while at the same time freeing up hundreds of megabytes of disk space. Try it, you'll like it.

15. When you are finished deleting whichever file(s) you want to remove, exit the CyberMedia Non-Critical File Cleaner application and you will be completely out of the Disk Cleanup utility. To finish cleaning your system though, you will need to restart the Windows 98 Disk Cleanup utility, as you did at the beginning of these steps.

6.6
CONFIGURE AND USE THE DISK CLEANUP UTILITY

16. After the utility has reopened, click once on the More Options tab to access that screen, as seen in Figure 6.22.

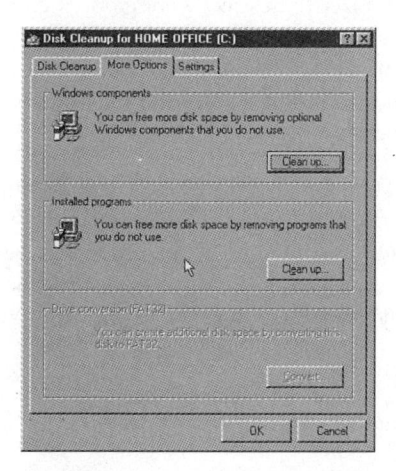

Figure 6.22 The More Options tab for the Disk Cleanup utility.

17. The three components of this tab relate to the Windows 98 utilities and options that you have installed and also to the additional software packages you have installed on your Windows 98 computer. The top section, Windows Components, takes you to the Windows Setup area of the Add/Remove Programs properties screen, as shown in Figure 6.23. To go there, click the Clean up... button in that section.

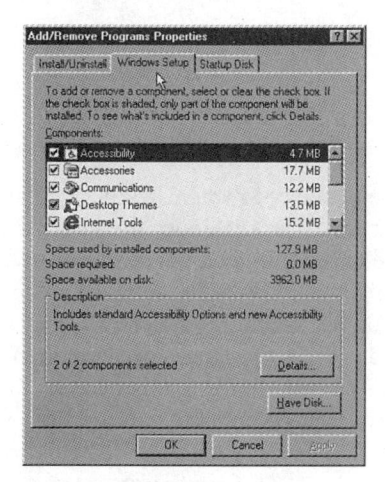

Figure 6.23 The Windows Setup tab of the Add/Remove Programs Properties screen.

CHAPTER 6
DISK DRIVE MANAGEMENT AND USE

18. This screen should look very familiar to you (if it doesn't, go buy the *Windows 98 From A to Z* book and study before continuing on with this one). Uncheck any of these boxes to deselect a component group or click the Details... button to deselect a sub-item within a component group. After you have made all your changes (selections/deselections), click OK for your changes to take effect. This exits you from this screen, leaving the Disk Cleanup utility open.

19. The middle section of the More Options tab of the Disk Cleanup program is known as the Installed Programs section. This section helps you remove the programs that you do not use anymore or no longer will want to use in the near future. To initiate a cleanup in this section, click the Clean up... button and the Install/Unistall tab appears, as shown in Figure 6.24.

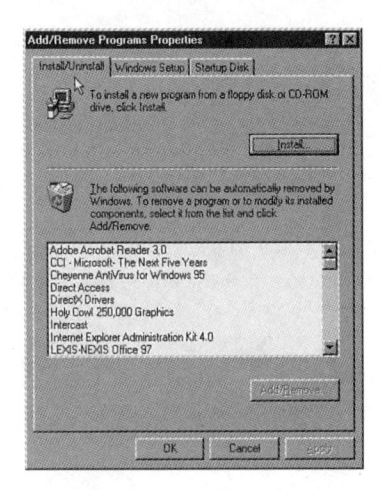

Figure 6.24 Deciding which Windows 98 applications to uninstall.

20. Again, this screen should look familiar to you. Click once on an application in this listing to select it, and then click once the Add/Remove... button. This might have one of two effects: it might start the removal process immediately, or it might take you to the setup program for that particular application that you are attempting to remove from your computer. Follow the prompts for that program, until the uninstall process is complete. You might be prompted to reboot your computer. Do so if prompted, otherwise, click OK to leave the Add/Remove

6.6
CONFIGURE AND USE THE DISK CLEANUP UTILITY

Programs Properties screen. This will exit you from the Install/Uninstall section, so you can return to the Disk Cleanup utility.

21. The third option on this tab of the Disk Cleanup utility is for a conversion to a 32-bit FAT structure for your computer. If you already have a FAT32 configuration, this section will be grayed out. If not, you can start a FAT32 conversion by clicking the Convert... button. Review the FAT32 topic found earlier in this chapter for detailed instructions on how to perform the 32-bit FAT conversion process.

22. The final tab of the Disk Cleanup utility is the Settings tab, as shown in Figure 6.25.

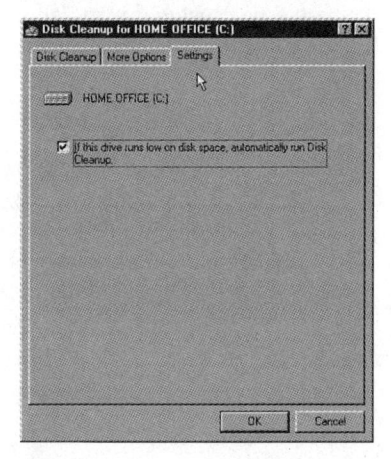

Figure 6.25 The Disk Cleanup Settings tab.

23. The option on this page could not be any easier to configure. To invoke it, click the check box to place a check mark in the box. If the box is empty, the Disk Cleanup utility will not automatically execute when you start to run low on free disk space. Unfortunately, Windows 98 does not really define what the concept of low free disk space is, so it is possible that this utility will start even if you do not believe you are almost out of space. Personally, I would leave the option enabled, because a few false alarms might just be worth it when it comes to you really running out of space while you have an important document open (and cannot save it because there is nowhere to save it to).

COMPLEXITY
INTERMEDIATE

6.7 How do I...
Configure and use the Disk Defragmenter utility?

Problem

My Windows 98 system appears to be sluggish, and takes much longer to load applications than it ever used to. I have not made any changes to my system other than maybe installing one or two new applications, and perhaps deleting a couple of files here and there. What could be causing this to happen and can it be fixed without having to purchase any third-party utilities or having to reformat and reload my entire system?

Technique

Windows 98 provides a tool known as the Disk Defragmenter utility. This tool is built into the operating system and is automatically installed when you first install Windows 98. The easiest way to understand the concept of the Disk Defragmenter tool is to think of your hard drive as a filing cabinet with lots of drawers and folders within those drawers. The Defragmenter tool examines the filing cabinet and begins to put things in the correct drawers, and then arranges the items in such a way that you can find them faster once you have found the right drawer.

The Disk Defragmenter utility keeps track of applications on your hard drive so that it can rearrange the executable files in such a way that your applications start more quickly. It does this through the use of another application known as the *Windows 98 Task Monitor*. This program logs your applications in a Windows sub-folder known as AppLog (usually, C:\Windows\AppLog), and also places a text file labeled OPTLOG.TXT in that folder. This text file contains a listing of those applications that are being tracked and arranged. It is a useful file for making sure that all your best applications are being ordered correctly.

When you run the Disk Defragmenter utility, you are actually starting the Defrag.Exe program. This program in turn executes the CvtApLog.Exe application, which in turn builds the APPLOG.* text files (there can be a lot of these files, all of which are found in the AppLog sub-folder within the Windows root directory). The execution of these files can be important because if you go to the AppLog directory and delete all the files (maybe because you did not know what they were there for), the Disk Defragmenter utility might not be as effective as it could have otherwise been. To use the Disk Defragmenter utility, follow the steps listed here.

6.7 CONFIGURE AND USE THE DISK DEFRAGMENTER UTILITY

Keep in mind that use of the Disk Defragmenter utility can take awhile to run completely, especially if it has been awhile (or ever) since the last time you used this utility. This usually translates into an hour or so for every gigabyte of hard disk drive space that you have (that is a total amount, not just the amount of free drive space). You should schedule this utility to run overnight, because the best time for doing this is probably when you are sleeping. (See Chapter 7, "System Resource Management," for more details on using the System Scheduler tool.)

Steps

1. Start the Disk Defragmenter utility by selecting it from the System Tools menu option found within the Accessories menu folder. This will start the application, as shown in Figure 6.26.

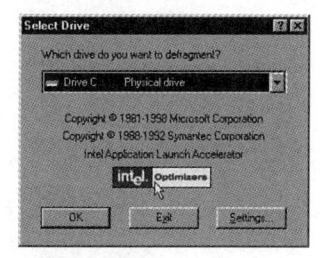

Figure 6.26 Selecting the hard disk drive you want to defragment.

2. The first box that appears prompts you to select a drive to be defragmented. If you click the Settings... button, the Disk Defragmenter Settings dialog box appears as shown in Figure 6.27.

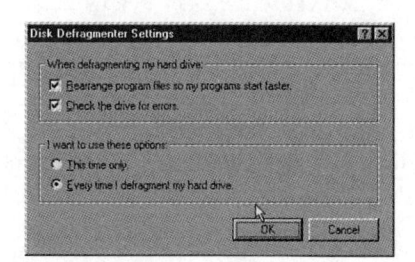

Figure 6.27 Choosing the Disk Defragmenter settings.

3. Although there are a few options on this screen, the important one is the Rearrange program files so my programs start faster option at the top of the screen. If you select this option by clicking the check box next to it, your applications will seem to open faster due to their rearrangement on your system's hard drive. When you have finished making your selections, click OK to return to the original starting window.

4. Select the drive you want from the drop-down list, and then click OK to start the defragmentation process, as shown in Figure 6.28.

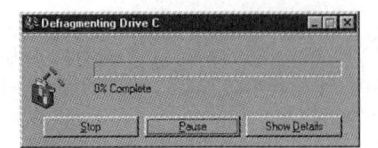

Figure 6.28 The Disk Defragmenter status bar.

5. When the Disk Defragmenter utility actually starts running, it might take several hours to complete. You can click the Show Details button but it does not really give much information. It fills your screen with some color but serves no real purpose.

6. Clicking once on the Pause button stalls the process until you want to start it back up.

7. Click Stop to halt the utility. You will be prompted with a message box that says "Windows has not finished defragmenting Drive x," at which point you click Exit to finish stopping the process.

8. Any other active application, including something as simple as a screen saver or a music CD playing, will cause the Disk Defragmenter utility to thrash about and take an incredibly long time to get partially through its process. To avoid this, you might want to have this tool start up automatically the next time you boot Windows 98. To do this, you need to place a simple command directly into your computer's Windows 98 Registry. First, start the Registry Editor tool, REGEDIT.EXE, and then open up HKEY_LOCAL_MACHINE Registry hive as shown in Figure 6.29.

9. Continue surfing your way through this Registry hive until you reach the final subkey and Registry hive path:\Software\Microsoft\Windows\CurrentVersion\RunServicesOnce, or you could put it into the final

6.7
CONFIGURE AND USE THE DISK DEFRAGMENTER UTILITY

subkey: \Run if you want the Defragmenter utility to run every single time you restart your Windows 98 computer. After arriving at this key, you need to add a new value.

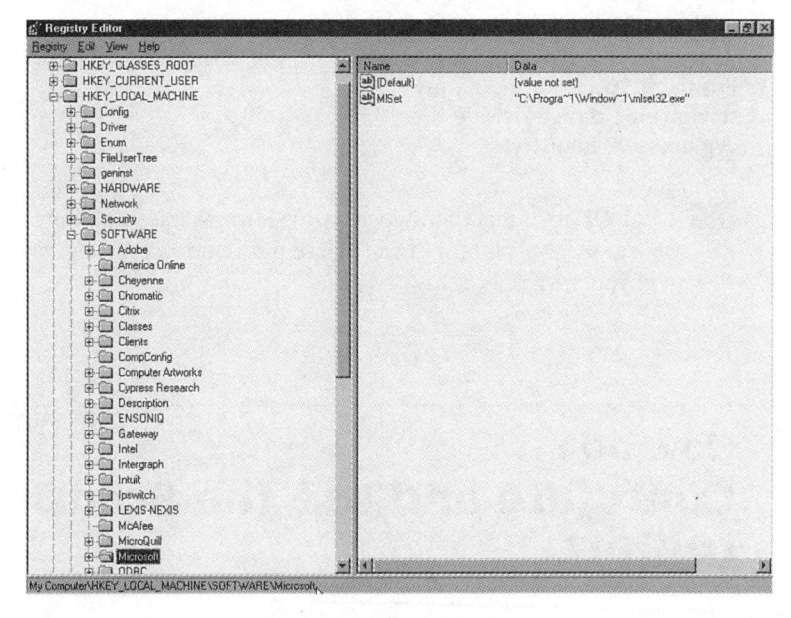

Figure 6.29 Using the Registry Editor to set boot options.

10. So, while you have either the \Run or \RunServicesOnce subkey highlighted, click the Edit menu selection then click on the New menu selection, and then finally on the String Value menu option. This creates a String Value entry, which requires a name. It is suggested that you call it something meaningful such as Disk Defragmenter Program.

11. Once this has been done, click the secondary mouse button to reveal a small menu where you can click the Modify menu option.

12. When the Edit String window appears, as shown in Figure 6.30, type in the command `Defrag.exe /all /noprompt` (these last two statements are command switches that tells the Disk Defragmenter utility to defragment all the drives and to do so without any intervention from you). It is suggested that you use both of these switches, which keeps you from having to baby-sit your computer during this painfully long and boring process.

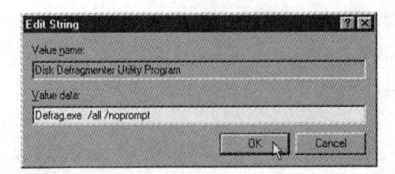

Figure 6.30 Creating a new string value directly inside the Windows 98 Registry.

13. Click OK to accept the change to this String Value and return to the general Registry Editor screen. Close the Windows 98 Registry Editor tool and you are finished.

COMPLEXITY
INTERMEDIATE

6.8 How do I...
Configure and use the ScanDisk utility?

Problem

I think that my hard drive has some sort of an error on it. Occasionally, one of my word processing files will get scrambled with another. Is there a way to figure out what is going on with my system and fix any problems that might exist?

Technique

Windows 98 provides a tool known as the ScanDisk utility. This tool is built into the operating system and is automatically installed when you first install Windows 98. The purpose of this utility is to assist you with the scanning of your disk drives (hence, its name), repairing errors as they are located. It is recommended that you run this utility at least once a week on your system so that you can detect occasional errors before they build up into a real problem for your computer.

Steps

1. Start the ScanDisk utility by selecting it from the System Tools menu option found within the Accessories menu folder. This starts the application, as shown in Figure 6.31.

6.8 CONFIGURE AND USE THE SCAN DISK UTILITY

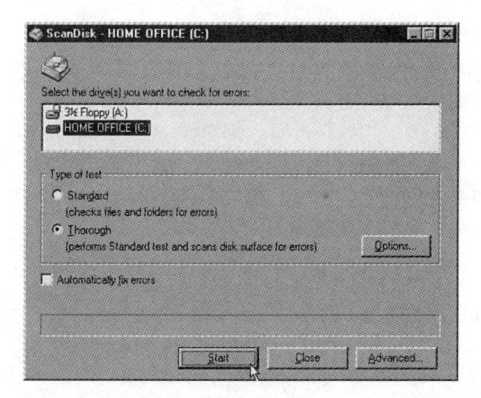

Figure 6.31 The Primary Options screen for the Windows 98 ScanDisk utility.

2. The screen that appears is the primary one from where you will start the Windows-based version of the ScanDisk utility. If you want to use any of the command-line parameters for executing this utility, you should start ScanDisk from a DOS-command prompt prior to entering the Windows 98 GUI. You can do this by using a function key to interrupt the Windows 98 boot process, or by making the appropriate selection from the Windows 98 Startup menu. Please review Chapter 3, "The Boot Process," for more details on stopping at a DOS-command prompt. However, there are a few ways to change the settings from within the Windows-based version.

3. One way is to click the Options... button to alter any of the additional settings, as shown in Figure 6.32.

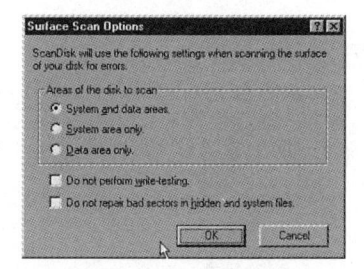

Figure 6.32 The ScanDisk Surface Scan Options window.

4. The top section, labeled Areas of the disk to scan, allows you to change the portions of the hard drive that you want to examine. For example, if you believe that your problem lies with a database or a series of data files, you might want to only look at the data area of your system. In this case, you would click the radio button next to the Data area only label. The system will default to the top setting of System and data areas, a setting that you should not change for your periodic disk scanning process.

5. The advantage of not performing write-testing is that it speeds up the disk scan and repair process. The primary advantage of not repairing bad sectors found in your hidden or system files is that it is likely these files are the ones that control your system's boot process and operations. Repairing these types of files might also damage them to the point that they no longer function correctly. Of course, if you never repair them when they are fixable, eventually your system will crash inexplicably; sort of a catch-22. To disable the use of these options, click in the appropriate check box to place a check mark in that box. This prevents that box's action from occurring. After you have made all of your selections, click the OK button to return to the main screen.

6. There is an additional set of advanced ScanDisk options that you can also choose from. To activate any of these items, click the Advanced... button to reveal the screen shown in Figure 6.33.

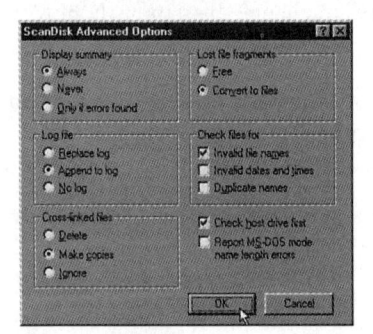

Figure 6.33 Advanced options for the Windows 98 ScanDisk utility.

7. Most of these options are self-explanatory, but there are a few you should take a closer look at, such as the Check files for section. At a cursory view, these appear to be pretty straightforward, but the boxes labeled Check Host Drive First and Report MS-DOS mode name length errors can be misleading. The first one only applies if you are using a disk compression tool such as DriveSpace on your system. Otherwise, you do not have a host drive, and looking for one is a waste of time. The search for name length errors can be damaging because MS-DOS only recognizes name lengths up to 66 characters. However, the full Windows 98 character name path can be up to 255 characters, so an error under DOS is not necessarily an error under a pure Windows 98 system. Using this setting coupled with the Automatically fix errors setting (found on the main ScanDisk screen) can be a formula for disaster if you like to use a lot of long filenames on your PC, so be careful when using this option.

8. Make all your selections, and then click OK to return to the primary ScanDisk screen.

9. Click Start and the Windows 98 ScanDisk utility will run using all of the options and settings you have chosen. If you do not want to run it at this time, click once on the Close button to exit this utility.

10. If you want to test the ScanDisk utility, it is possible to run it in a preview testing mode. To do this, reboot your system so that it is at a DOS prompt (prior to entering the Windows 98 GUI). Then use the command `ScanDisk /All / p` (leave a space between the command itself, and each of the parameters) at the command-line prompt. The utility is run by the use of the SCANDISK.EXE executable program, the `/all` parameter tells it to check all your system's drives, and the `/p` parameter means to do all of this in a Preview mode only. Preview mode is a simulated mode that, although it looks like things are being fixed and changed, nothing is really being written to your hard drive. This can be useful for those of you who have never run the ScanDisk utility before and want to see how it looks in action prior to actually using it on your own computer.

COMPLEXITY
INTERMEDIATE

6.9 How do I...
Manage my hard disk drive(s)?

Problem

Windows 98 has the capability to see a single hard drive that is up to 2 terabytes (TBs) in size, which equals 2,000GB when you are using the 32-bit FAT structure. As the trend toward larger and larger hard drives continues on its merry way, you need the capability to better manage your hard disk drive(s). The problem then becomes how to best manage your hard disk drive(s)? What are some of the best practices when it comes to organizing applications, folders, and files on desktop Windows computer?

Technique

Windows 98 gives you the groundwork to make your computer very usable and manageable, but at the same time allows you to be a slob who mismanages your computer in countless ways. This freedom and flexibility is great for organized system administrators and pure chaos for those computer-challenged folks out there. Of the several built-in Windows 98 tools and utilities, one of the best is the Disk Cleanup utility. However, the one tool that everyone has, but a lot of people fail to use, is pure common sense.

To discover more about the Disk Cleanup utility and how to use it, you should refer to section 6.6, "How do I configure and use the Disk Cleanup utility?" earlier in this chapter. If you have the ability to plan ahead for managing your system's drives, you might want to consider using the FDisk utility that is found in the \Windows\Command folder on your system's hard drive or on the Windows 98 Startup disk. The advantage to this utility is that you can create multiple partitions on your hard drive(s). The downside is that in order to create more than one partition you will destroy any existing ones. The final disk management tool is you. Following the discussion on how to use the FDisk utility, pay attention for a few suggestions on how to use yourself to better manage your computer's hard disk drives.

Steps

1. Use of the FDisk utility should be performed from either a floppy disk that you booted from or directly from your hard drive at a DOS prompt before you ever boot into the Windows 98 GUI. (Refer to Chapter 3 for more details on the Windows 98 boot process, if you are unsure as to how to do this.) Although it is possible to run FDisk from within the GUI to set up a second or third hard drive, it is still not recommended because any problems can cause massive difficulties for you and your system. It is always safer to do this from a DOS prompt.

> **NOTE**
> Using the FDisk utility to either create or delete existing disk partitions requires you to completely remove all the files and data from that drive. Whatever you do not back up will be lost.

2. If your hard drive is larger than 512MB, you will be prompted to use the Large Disk Support feature with it. This is a sneaky way to say FAT32. Do not use FAT32 now if you do not understand all of the implications, because you can always convert to it later (unless of course you want to create partitions that are greater than 2GB in size). If you want to create 2+GB partitions then you must enable the Large Disk Support. However,

6.9 MANAGE MY HARD DISK DRIVES(S)

you should review the discussions earlier in this chapter regarding FAT32 because there are many intricacies to this Windows 98 feature.

3. When you have decided whether you want Large Disk Support or not, you will have these four options presented to you as shown in Figure 6.34:

  1. Create DOS partition or Logical DOS Drive

  2. Set active partition

  3. Delete partition or Logical DOS Drive

  4. Display partition information

```
                    Microsoft Windows 98
                   Fixed Disk Setup Program
               (C)Copyright Microsoft Corp. 1983 - 1998

                         FDISK Options

Current fixed disk drive: 1

Choose one of the following:

1. Create DOS partition or Logical DOS Drive
2. Set active partition
3. Delete partition or Logical DOS Drive
4. Display partition information

Enter choice: [1]




Press Esc to exit FDISK
```

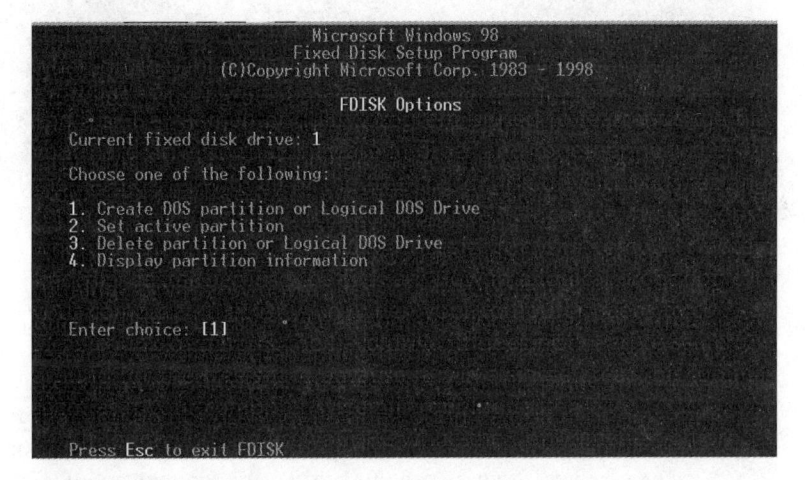

Figure 6.34 The main screen of the Windows 98 fixed disk setup program.

4. If you have more than one disk drive installed on your computer, you will be prompted with a fifth option labeled Change Current Fixed Disk Drive. This option permits you to create or delete partitions that exist on other physical disk drives.

5. Each menu option does exactly what it implies. Number 1 is used to create a partition or a logical drive within that partition. Number 2 is used to mark a partition as Active, which means this is the partition from which your Windows 98 system attempts to boot (be careful with this one, as marking the wrong partition active will prevent your system from booting correctly the next time you try). Number 3 is used to delete a partition or a logical drive within a partition, whereas Number 4 presents the layout of the partitions on that particular hard drive device.

6. To select any of these options, enter the number of the option in the brackets next to the label Enter Choice. For example, put the 1 in the brackets and press Enter . This automatically takes you to the screen shown in Figure 6.35.

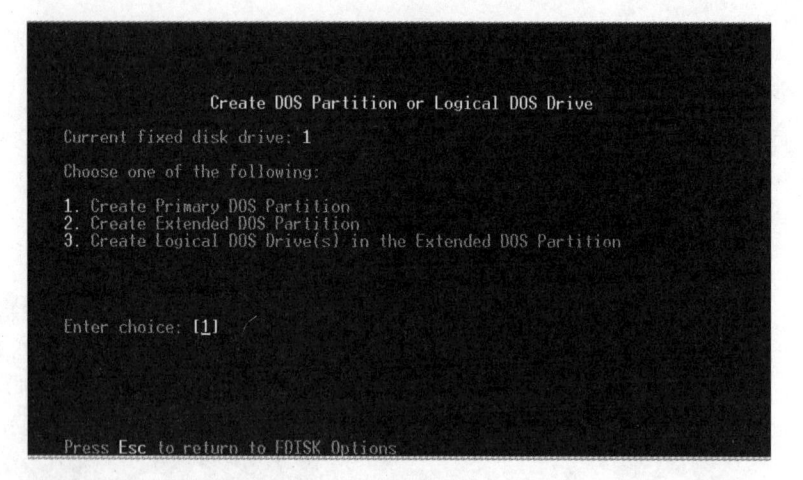

Figure 6.35 Using the Create DOS Partition or Logical DOS Drive entry screen of the FDisk utility program.

7. Pressing the Esc key takes you backward to the previous screen, just in case you choose the wrong option.

8. The FDisk feature is one that has been around for over a decade, and is just as useful today as it was way back in the early days of computing. Learn how to use it by examining the menu options and understanding what each option means. A good way to do this is to enter option 4 (Display partition information), and review the base information for your own system the way it is configured today, as shown in Figure 6.36.

9. All the logical drives within the partitions for this physical drive are listed on this screen. If the usage percentages for all these partitions do not total 100 percent, it means that you still have some free, unpartitioned space available for use. If this is the case, create a new partition and use the remaining amount of space for this new drive. Once you have done that, create a logical drive within that new partition then reboot for the changes to take effect. After rebooting and returning to Windows 98, format the new drive and you will have more space.

6.9 MANAGE MY HARD DISK DRIVE(S)

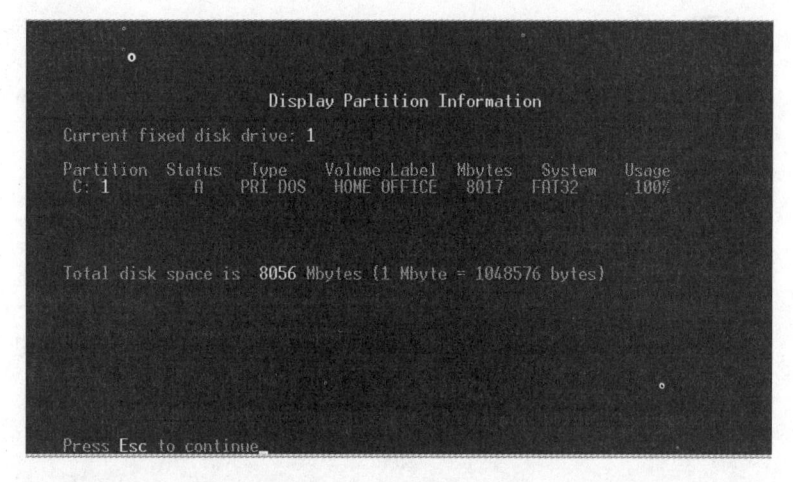

Figure 6.36 Using the Display Partition Information screen of the FDisk utility program.

> **NOTE**
>
> If you have any drives that show a Type of non-DOS then do not remove them without thinking about it first. A non-DOS partition might contain EISA utilities, a Windows NT configuration, your Red Hat Linux system, and so forth. Deleting one of these types of partitions might be disastrous, so be careful and make sure that what you are deleting belongs to you specifically and is not required by your computer to function properly.

10. So, what can you do to better manage your drive with wits alone? It's easier than you might think. Try to make the art of disk management as easy as possible. That is, when you arrange programs and folders on your hard disk drive, you should try to follow consistent practices. For example, most applications sold by commercial companies (such as Microsoft) will attempt to install their programs in the \Program Files folder (on the Windows root drive). This is a good idea, because it leaves you with a common starting point for most of the applications on your hard drive.

11. The general rule of thumb is that you want to minimize the number of files that you copy and install in to your root drive's (C:\) directory. This makes troubleshooting the Windows 98 operating system errors easier, and limits some potential harm that you could self-inflict by copying too many similarly named files to the same directory, which has a lot to do with how your computer system actually works anyway.

12. Another good idea is to leave the long filenames structure enabled during a Windows 98 installation. Trying to force everything into the 8.3 naming convention format so your Windows 98 users are more compatible with your other older Windows 3.x/DOS/legacy systems is not only a poor choice, but it can have potentially disastrous results (from real 32-bit applications refusing to work correctly, to actually corrupting data when other front-end applications attempt to access back-end databases).

13. The preceding steps are generally considered to be the best practices and are in no way the only means to perform disk drive management. These suggestions can make your life easier, but if you know of another way to do it, by all means do so.

COMPLEXITY
INTERMEDIATE

6.10 How do I... Manage my removable media drive(s)?

Problem

Windows 98 management for removable media drives is quite a bit easier than it is for fixed disk drives. However, as the trend toward using increasing numbers of removable drives continues, you need the capability to better manage removable disk drive(s). The problem then becomes how to best manage these drive(s).

Technique

Just as with fixed disk drives (for example, hard disk drives), Windows 98 gives you the groundwork to make your computer usable and manageable or make it a sort of organized, chaotic atmosphere. With these types of drives, though, common sense is probably the most valuable tool in your war chest. One of the better techniques is to physically arrange the devices in and around your computer in the same logical order as Windows 98 views them. For instance, if you have a Zip drive, an external CD-ROM drive, and a SyQuest drive in this order from left to right, assign them a drive letter in order (from left to right). Doing this might mean the Zip drive has the assignment of G:\, the external CD-ROM drive is H:\, and the SyQuest drive is I:\. This make your life a little easier when trying to figure out which drive letter does what.

Another tip is to always have your 3 1/2-inch floppy disk drive set as drive letter A:\, and your system boot partition set to C:\. When you install some

6.10 MANAGE MY REMOVABLE MEDIA DRIVES(S)

software applications, they will make this assumption anyway, and it might make your life easier to just have your computer setup in this manner. The next set of steps helps you put the rest of your removable media devices into a more orderly fashion.

Steps

1. To set a specific drive letter for a removable media device, you need to go to the Device Manager tab of the System Properties screen (inside the Control Panel), as shown in Figure 6.37.

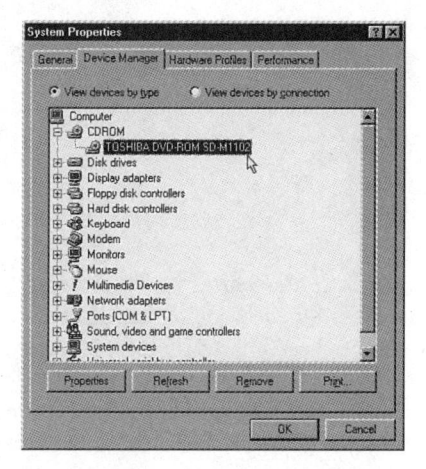

Figure 6.37 Checking the Device Manager of the System Properties screen.

2. Click the plus symbol next to a topical area, such as CDROM, to reveal its contents. Then highlight a removable system device drive such as your CD- or DVD-ROM drive, and then click the Properties button (or double-click that drive's entry).

3. This takes you directly into the Properties screen for that specific device. Once there, click the Settings tab, as shown in Figure 6.38.

4. The Settings tab contains the specific drive letter information for this specific removable device, which is also a modifiable item. Near the bottom of this screen is the Current drive letter assignment area, which contains a small grayed-out box with the actual drive letter for this removable media device. If you look a little bit farther down toward the bottom of this screen, you notice the Reserved drive letters section. This is where you set the new drive letter.

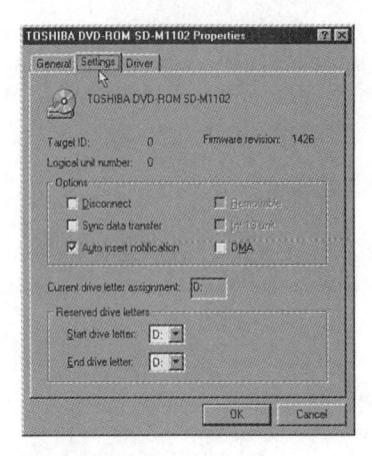

Figure 6.38 Checking options on the Settings tab of the DVD-ROM device selected.

5. Using the drop-down list boxes for the Start drive letter and the End drive letter, select the same letter for each one of these boxes. By placing the same letter in both boxes, you can effectively force Windows 98 to recognize this device as the letter Q, (assuming you chose the letter Q in each of the drop-down list boxes). A couple of key points: Do not select a letter that is already in use by your system. Avoid using the letters F or Z if you have to work in conjunction with an older Novell NetWare network system; and don't use the letter C, because this is just asking for trouble (Windows 98 hates it when you do this, although it might work temporarily in some instances).

COMPLEXITY
BEGINNER

6.11 How do I...
Install a CD-ROM or a DVD-ROM drive?

Problem

I just purchased a new CD-ROM or DVD-ROM device, but now what do I do? What are the steps I should follow in order to best install this new hardware device on my Windows 98 PC?

6.11 INSTALL A CD-ROM OR DVD-ROM DRIVE

Technique

Windows 98 has a software wizard that can help walk you through the installation of a new hardware device, such as a CD- or DVD-ROM drive. Carefully follow these steps and you will be watching DVD movies or listening to music CDs on your computer system in no time.

Steps

1. Shut your computer system down and physically power it off.

2. If this is an internal device, open up your computer's casing and install the CD- or DVD-ROM drive device, paying strict attention to the manufacturer's own set of installation instructions. Screw (or snap) the drive into place and attach the power cable, the drive cable, and any sound system wires that might be necessary.

3. If this is an external device then plug it in to the appropriate port on your computer, as mandated by the manufacturer's installation instructions. Power the device on.

4. Plug your computer system back in and turn the power back on. When Windows 98 boots back up, it should take you into the Add New Hardware Wizard automatically because it sees this new hardware device.

5. If this wizard does not automatically start itself up then manually start it by double-clicking the Add New Hardware icon found in the Windows 98 Control Panel. This takes you into the first screen of the wizard, as shown in Figure 6.39.

Figure 6.39 Starting the Add New Hardware Wizard.

6. When the wizard begins this way it prompts you to close all active programs. If it starts when you first startup the computer then you will

skip right past this screen because nothing else should be running anyway.

7. To continue, click Next>.

8. Another informational screen quickly appears telling you that the hardware wizard is going to search for a new plug-and-play device. Click the Next> button so that the search begins. For those of you who have systems which started the Add New Hardware Wizard automatically, this is the point where you started.

9. Following the search for plug-and-play devices, the wizard tells you it is going to search for non–plug-and-play compatible devices, as shown in Figure 6.40.

Figure 6.40 Telling the Add New Hardware Wizard to search for the newly installed hardware component.

10. Unless this is your first time ever installing hardware on your own or if you like to wait around, it is strongly suggested that you do not take the default setting of letting the wizard search for these non–plug-and-play compatible devices. Instead, you should click the bottom radio button that tells the wizard you want to select your new equipment from a listing. After you have selected this radio button, click the Next> button to continue, as shown in Figure 6.41.

11. A listing appears with the different kinds of hardware that you could install into a Windows 98 computer. Click the hardware type of CD-ROM controllers (even if you are really installing a DVD-ROM device), and then click the Next> button to continue, as shown in Figure 6.42.

6.11
INSTALL A CD-ROM OR DVD-ROM DRIVE

Figure 6.41 Manually selecting a new CD-ROM controller component.

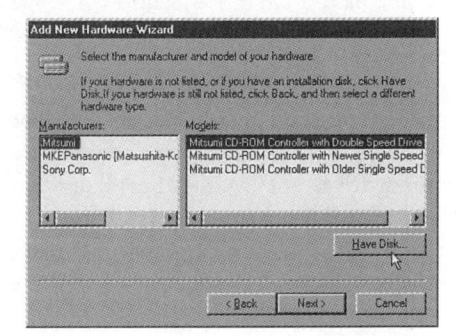

Figure 6.42 Finding the correct manufacturer and model of the new hardware device.

12. At this point in the wizard you have one of two choices: pick one of the manufacturers listed and the appropriate hardware device model, or click the Have Disk… button to use the hardware device drivers disk that probably came with your CD- or DVD-ROM device. The best thing is to first try the disk that came with the drivers from the folks who manufactured your new drive. If these do not work then use the ones that come with Windows 98.

13. When the software device drivers are installed, click Yes to permit Windows 98 to reboot, at which time the installation process is complete.

NOTE
This installation process works fine for any other hardware devices that you might want to install in your computer. Whether you are installing additional hard drives, global positioning devices, PC-card sockets, or other devices you can use the Add New Hardware Wizard.

COMPLEXITY
BEGINNER

6.12 How do I...
Know which additional removable hard drive devices I should install?

Problem

I am out of hard drive space but my computer system has no more slots for additional hard drives. Are there other removable hard drive devices or hardware that can be used in place of a hard drive disk system?

Technique

Windows 98 supports a number of removable hard drive devices that you can use in place of a second drive. These types of devices include, but are not limited to, the Iomega Zip and Jaz drives, the SyQuest SparQ and SyJet drives, as well as other PCMCIA/PC-card hard drives made by vendors such as Fujitsu. You can use the following steps as guidelines in your attempt to determine which types of removable hard drive devices you might want to use with your computer system.

Steps

1. The first thing you need to decide is how much space you think you need. This is both the easiest and the toughest part of the process. Do not only take into account your needs today, but try to anticipate your future disk drive space demands over the next few years (if possible).

2. The next step is to decide what you will use this space for. That is, are you going to just back up extraneous files and programs for future use, or are you going to attempt to actually run applications directly from this removable drive media? If it is the latter, you are probably looking at a SCSI-type connection for this device. The removable devices that connect via a serial or parallel port usually do not have the throughput to actually sustain an application in a real-time mode.

3. After you have determined both the size and the usage, you can begin to narrow the field of likely candidates. If the size you have decided on is in the hundreds of megabytes then you have effectively ruled out the Zip drive because it cannot handle any quantity over 100MB. Similarly, if you discover that you need this device to run applications from, you have cut the field to one of the SyQuest devices, the Iomega Jaz, or a PC-card drive.

4. However, if you do not have an available PCMCIA slot on your computer, or are not willing to install this type of a device in a desktop computer, the PC-card drive device is also ruled out.

5. Next comes cost. If you cannot afford more than $150 for the drive unit then you are back to a Zip drive. Something else to keep in mind is that while the average access time for a Jaz drive is just a little bit faster than the SparQ or SyJet drives, the price of a single removable drive cartridge is more than double the cost of the SyQuest devices.

6. Confused yet? You should be. There are a lot of options for each of these devices, so you might want to consider creating a pros and cons matrix. This not only makes feature tracking easier to document, but it also makes the final selection process easier. Another hint for your matrix is to rank each item (access rate, cost, size, market acceptance, and so on) with a weighting system so the device that has the most points wins. In any event, good luck.

COMPLEXITY
INTERMEDIATE

6.13 How do I...
Back up my Windows 98 system?

Problem

I store a lot of very valuable information on my computer, and I am worried that one day I might lose it all due to a computer hardware failure, a power outage/surge, or my own mistakes. How can I best back up the data on my computer using the utilities that come with Windows 98?

Technique

Within Windows 98 is a scaled-down version of Seagate Software's backup software utility known as *Microsoft Windows 98 Backup*. This software works great for the general home user, but if you are a corporate user that wants to schedule your backup times quickly and easily there is a $49 upgrade offered by Seagate at their Web site (http://www.seagatesoftware.com/). However, for most users of standalone computers, the one built into Windows 98 works great all by itself. Use the following steps to walk through the backup process, which can be used to save data on another part of your hard drive, on a floppy or removable disk drive, or on a tape device (the best place to back up).

Steps

1. This utility can be found within the System Tools menu folder that is part of the Accessories menu option, off the Start menu. Start the utility, which takes you to the first screen, as shown in Figure 6.43.

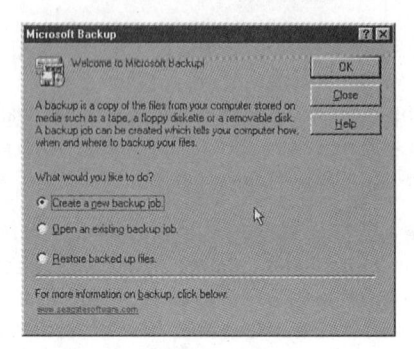

Figure 6.43 Backing up your system for the first time.

2. On this first screen you need to decide whether you want to create a new backup job, to open one that you have created, or to restore files from a previous backup session. I will assume that this is the first time the backup software is being run, so the default choice of creating a new backup job will remain as the selection. To accept this choice and continue, click the OK button, as shown in Figure 6.44.

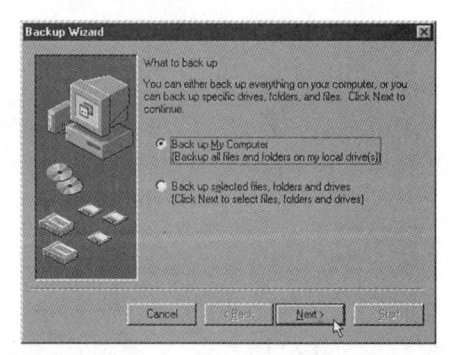

Figure 6.44 Deciding what to back up on your computer.

> **NOTE**
>
> If you want to upgrade your Microsoft Backup Software to the full-blown version offered by Seagate Software, Inc., you can do this by

clicking the Seagate Software Internet URL found at the bottom of Figure 6.43 (assuming that you have already connected your PC to the Internet). When you click the URL, your default Web browser opens and takes you directly to that part of the Seagate site where you are offered the chance to purchase the upgrade there. For $49 (USD) this upgrade is not a bad value, but for a home user on a single desktop computer it still might be considered overkill (unless you truly are a *power* user).

3. The Backup Wizard screen appears and prompts you for the type of backup process you want to perform. That is, do you want to back up your entire computer (even if it has multiple hard drives) with all its programs and data, or do you want to preserve specific data and files? It is recommended that if you have a large enough backup device connected to your PC, you should use the default setting of backing up everything (do this at least once with your computer). After you have made your selection, click the Next> button to continue.

4. If this is not the first time you have backed up your entire hard drive, you might see a screen that asks you whether you want to back up all of the selected files or just all the new ones plus those that have changed since the last backup procedure. Decide which radio button to select, and then click Next> to continue as shown in Figure 6.45.

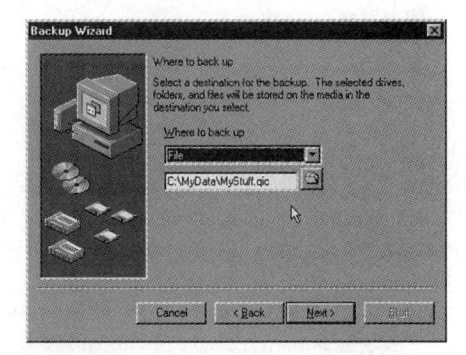

Figure 6.45 Deciding where to back up your PC files.

5. At this point in the wizard you must choose where you will back up your files. Clicking the drop-down list box reveals all the possible locations. For this example, the Where to back up location of File will be used (this means that you will copy your files to a local hard drive). It is strongly recommended that you back up data to a removable media device or a tape backup unit. The cartridges for these types of devices can be removed from your computer and stored in a safe off-site location, such as your office, a safe-deposit box, or even a friend's house.

6. When saving to a local drive device, the default is to save all of the backup files to the root directory of C:\. This is a poor idea because you will be messing up your disk drive management routines by using the root directory for nonessential files. Instead you should put your backup files into a specially created directory such as C:\MyData. The name of the backup job is MyBackup.Qic (this is automatically assigned by the backup software, but can be changed). To continue with the backup process, click Next> to decide how to back up your files, as shown in Figure 6.46.

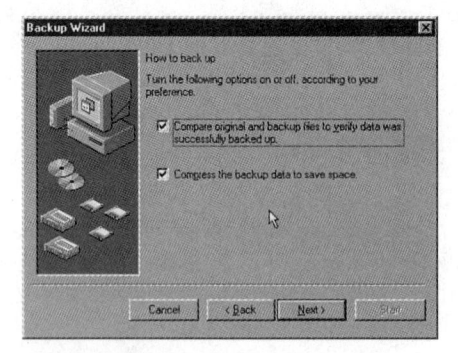

Figure 6.46 Deciding how to back up your computer's files.

7. This screen prompts you to set a few backup options. Do you want to compare the original files to those that are backed up to ensure that the backup process ran correctly? And should the backup software compress the backup data in order to save on hard drive space? The first option is actually just a verification of the data backup process, and is a good idea to use if the data is important to you. The second option alters the manner in which the data is stored on the backup device so that a file takes up less space than it might otherwise have. Keep in mind that either of these options will slow the entire backup process, so if you are in a hurry you might want to skip them.

8. Click the Next> button to continue the process by naming the backup job, as shown in Figure 6.47.

9. On this screen you should provide a descriptive name to this newly created backup job. Once you have typed in a name that makes sense to you, click Start to begin the backup process, as shown in Figure 6.48.

6.13
BACK UP MY WINDOWS 98 SYSTEM

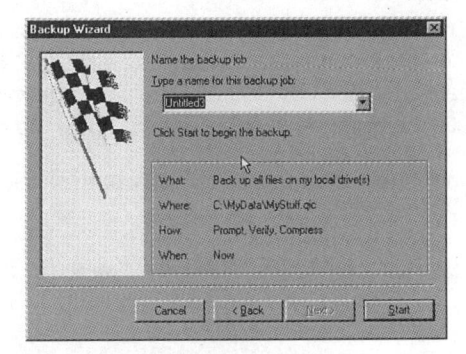

Figure 6.47 Picking a name for your backup job.

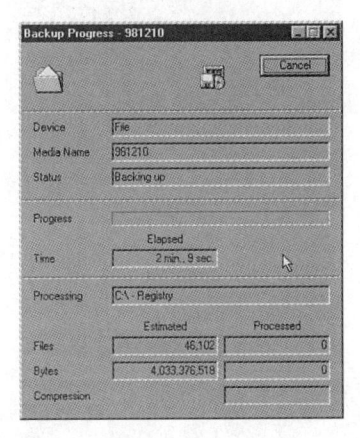

Figure 6.48 The Windows 98 Backup Progress status screen.

> **NOTE**
>
> To make sorting through multiple backup jobs easier, you might want to consider using a date naming scheme. That is, put the today's date in a YYMMDD format, (where YY is the last two digits of the current year, MM is the two digits for the current month, and DD is the two digits for the current day). For example, today's date is December 10, 1998, so in this format the name of the backup becomes 981210.

10. A Selection Information screen appears that informs you of a file and byte estimate for the actual backup job. You might be prompted with a message box that says "This media contains one or more backup sets. Do you want to overwrite?". It is recommended that you click the Overwrite button and continue the process.

11. As files are copied, a running total is kept of the number and size of files being copied. When the backup process is complete, a message box pops up telling that it is finished. Click OK, and then the Backup Progress window appears (it has the backup job name written on its top edge).

12. Click the Report... button to view a quick summary of the backup job that you just completed.

13. Click OK to end the backup job process. This takes you to the main Microsoft Backup screen, as shown in Figure 6.49.

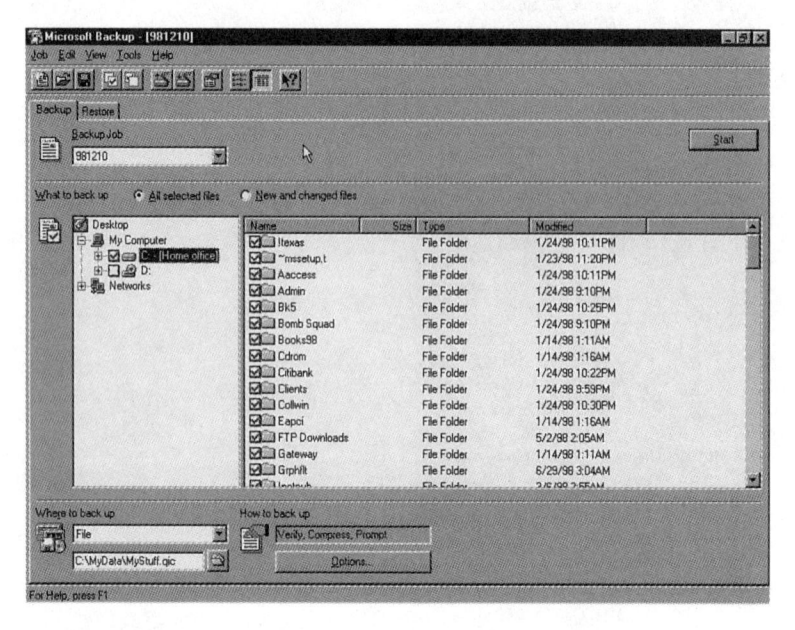

Figure 6.49 Examining the contents of the C:\ drive that is going to be backed up.

14. All the boxes with check marks in them mean that those drives and folders are set to be backed up the next time the backup job is executed. Any combination of hard drives, folders, and files can be selected. Click once on the Options... button to reveal the screen shown in Figure 6.50.

15. The General tab contains the same options that you set when you first configured the Microsoft Backup software. This is an easy location to update those choices. Click on the Password tab to reveal that screen, as shown in Figure 6.51.

6.13
BACK UP MY WINDOWS 98 SYSTEM

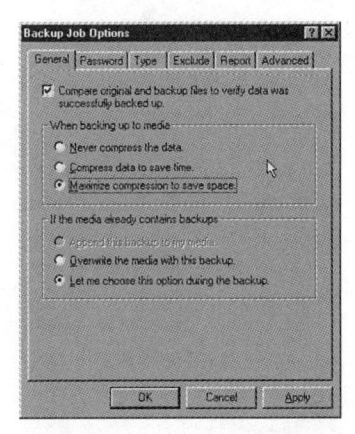

Figure 6.50 Modifying the General Backup Job options.

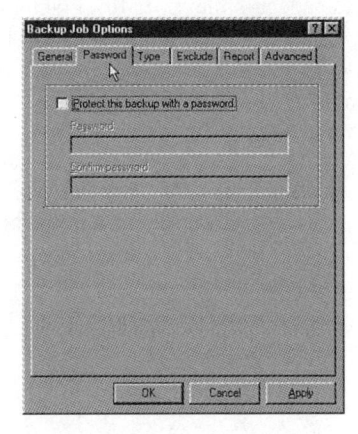

Figure 6.51 Modifying the password options for this backup job.

16. If you check the only box on this screen, you will be able to password protect your backup job(s). Once you mark the check box, enter a password that you will remember. It is suggested that it not too easy that anyone can guess, but also not too hard for you to remember. After making your selection, click the Type tab to continue to the screen shown in Figure 6.52.

17. Again, this is where you are able to set the backup type, which you chose during the Backup Wizard. After making your selection, click the Exclude tab to continue to that page, as shown in Figure 6.53.

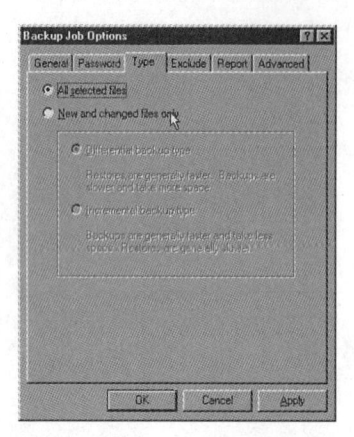

Figure 6.52 Modifying the backup job type.

18. This screen allows you to exclude specific file types from being backed up. A good candidate for this section is the Windows 98 swap file type of *.SWP. After making your selection(s), click the Report tab to continue to that page, as shown in Figure 6.54.

19. The boxes on this screen permit you to add additional information into the text file report that can be generated following any backup procedure. It is always recommended that you select all of these options, because this will make your recovery process easier should you need to restore your system in times of duress. Click the Advanced tab to reveal the final Backup Job Options screen, which is shown in Figure 6.55.

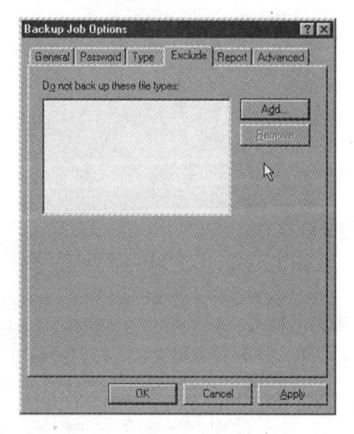

Figure 6.53 Modifying which file types are to be excluded during processing of this backup job.

6.13
BACK UP MY WINDOWS 98 SYSTEM

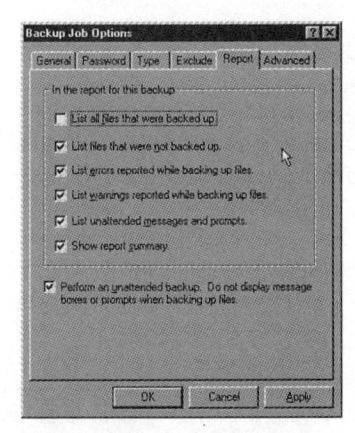

Figure 6.54 Modifying the Report options for this backup job.

20. The only option on this screen is to back up the Windows 98 Registry for your computer. Although this is a rather large file unless you are very short on space on your backup device, it is always a great idea to back up the Windows Registry. Without the Registry, you will not be able to perform a full restoration of your computer system, should you ever have a fatal drive crash. Click OK to accept all your Backup Job Options changes and to return to the primary Microsoft Backup screen.

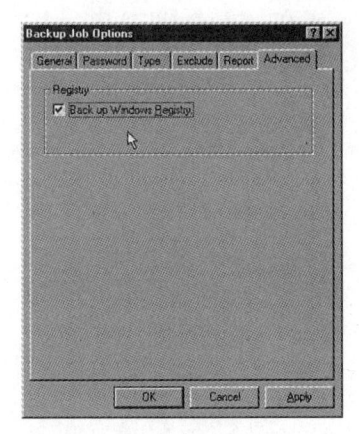

Figure 6.55 Deciding whether to back up the Windows 98 Registry.

21. A few additional pieces of advice regarding the backup process for your computer:

- The Windows 98 Backup utility is capable of restoring backup jobs that you might have originally created with your Windows 95 Backup utility.

- To modify an existing Backup Job, you are not able to use the Backup Wizard. Instead, you must manually select the options, files, folders, and drives that you want to back up.

- The restoration process for a backup created by the Windows 98 Backup utility is very easy to do. It is simply a reversal of efforts; you tell the system where to put the restored files, instead of telling it where to back up the files from.

- You cannot restore backup jobs that you might have originally created with an MS-DOS 6.x version Backup utility.

- The Windows 98 Backup utility now provides support of SCSI tape drives, a significant improvement over previous versions of Microsoft's Backup Software.

- Advanced backup support, such as scheduling of jobs and remote access of backups, is not possible through the Backup Software that ships with Windows 98. You must purchase the upgraded version from Seagate Software, Inc. in order to perform these types of functions.

CHAPTER 7
SYSTEM RESOURCE MANAGEMENT

7

SYSTEM RESOURCE MANAGEMENT

How do I...

- **7.1 Determine which components make up the core Windows 98 system resources?**
- **7.2 Know when to use performance monitoring?**
- **7.3 Install the additional System Resource Management tools?**
- **7.4 Use the Resource Meter?**
- **7.5 Use the System Information utility?**
- **7.6 Use Dr. Watson to troubleshoot application faults?**
- **7.7 Verify the integrity of my system files?**
- **7.8 Track performance changes to my computer system over a period of time?**
- **7.9 Use the Maintenance Wizard utility?**
- **7.10 Monitor my computer to see if others are attached to it?**
- **7.11 Schedule tasks on my computer?**
- **7.12 Know if the Windows 98 Resource Kit is good for managing system resources?**

CHAPTER 7
SYSTEM RESOURCE MANAGEMENT

The purpose of this chapter is to introduce you to the various aspects of system resource management including performance monitoring, performance tuning, and the general management of your computer system resources. This is not meant to be an all-encompassing guide, rather, it acts as a starting point to guide you in the correct direction for better determining how to monitor and tune your installation of Windows 98. There are entire books written on this subject, with many theories and techniques widely available. This chapter provides you with the foundation of knowledge that helps you determine which of these theories and techniques are best-suited for your Windows 98 environment.

7.1 Determine Which Components Make Up the Core Windows 98 System Resources

The purpose of this How-To is to assist you in figuring out what the core Windows 98 components consist of.

7.2 Know When to Use Performance Monitoring

There is a fine line between monitoring system performance to analyze possible performance problems and having the system performance monitoring actually impact system performance so that it causes those performance problems. This How-To helps you step through that minefield of what to do and how to do it.

7.3 Install the Additional System Resource Management Tools

This How-To teaches you how to install all the additional Windows 98 System Resource Management tools, which is a relatively easy process.

7.4 Use the Resource Meter

This Windows 98 tool helps you to track the usage of your primary system resources. Through the use of this How-To, you will be able to quickly get up to speed on the use of this utility.

7.5 Use the System Information Utility

This Windows 98 tool helps you to quickly view the details of your computer system. This section teaches you how to use this utility.

7.6 Use Dr. Watson to Troubleshoot Application Faults

Dr. Watson is a Windows tool with origins dating back to the early days of Windows. It is a very detailed-oriented troubleshooting tool that you can use to figure out the inner workings of your Windows 98 PC. This How-To takes you through the steps necessary to aid in troubleshooting efforts, especially in the area of application faults.

CHAPTER 7
SYSTEM RESOURCE MANAGEMENT

7.7 Verify the Integrity of My System Files

There are going to be times when you may question the stability of your Windows 98 PC, which is something that ties directly back to the integrity of your Windows 98 system files. This How-To speaks to the use of a Windows 98 tool that will help you to verify the integrity of your system files.

7.8 Track Performance Changes to My Computer System over a Period of Time

System monitoring is very useful for first establishing a benchmark of your Windows 98 PC, and then tracking the changes to that PC over time. This How-To addresses this topic, including a few tidbits on why this type of information is useful.

7.9 Use the Maintenance Wizard Utility

Windows 98 disk utilities can take several hours each to run, which is partly why the Maintenance Wizard appears in Windows 98. The purpose of this How-To is to assist you in automating the use of these many tasks.

7.10 Monitor My Computer to See if Others Are Attached to It

It would be nice to know when others are logged on to your Windows 98 PC, especially for when you did not want anyone to connect to you. This How-To helps you discover which persons are connected to your PC, as well as what files and folders they might be accessing.

7.11 Schedule Tasks on My Computer

The focus of this How-To is to assist you in automating tasks for use with your Windows 98 computer system.

7.12 Know if the Windows 98 Resource Kit Is Good for Managing System Resources

The Windows 98 Resource Kit provides dozens of utilities, tools, and help files, but do they really help the average user or are they meant for the techno-geeks in the audience? This How-To focuses on determining if this kit is helpful in managing system resources and why.

COMPLEXITY
INTERMEDIATE

7.1 How do I...
Determine which components make up the core Windows 98 system resources?

Problem
In order to better track the system resources within my Windows 98 system, I need to know what to track and what components make up the primary Windows 98 system resources. How do I determine what these components are?

Technique
In terms of which system resources one should track within the Windows 98 operating system, the Windows 98 components are very similar to Windows NT. You need to track memory, CPU, file system, network, and disk resources on a regular basis. This helps you maintain a better working knowledge of what is considered normal behavior by your computer, because when the problems start you need to know the when and where in order to better handle them. Without a baseline of your system resources, you might never know of your impending doom until it is too late.

Microsoft provides several tools within the Windows 98 operating system to help you carry out system resource management including performance monitoring and tuning. These tools involve the use of these Windows 98 features:

- File System Profiles
- Maintenance Wizard
- Net Watcher
- Resource Meter
- Scheduled Tasks Manager
- System File Checker
- System Information utility
- System Monitor
- Windows 98 Swap File Optimization

7.1 DETERMINE WHICH COMPONENTS MAKE UP THE CORE SYSTEM RESOURCES

Of the preceding Windows 98 features, some have utilities of the same name that perform those same tasks. Otherwise, there are specific locations within other objects that you use to tune your Windows 98 PC, as is the case for optimization of the Windows 98 swap file.

It is important that you do not overload your computer with ongoing, real-time monitoring operations so much so that in your efforts to monitor your system, you actually cause it to fail. One final note: Although Windows 98 permits its users to tune the performance settings of their CD-ROM drive(s), it is impossible for anyone to further tweak performance settings for DVD-ROM drives.

Follow the steps listed here to locate all the tools mentioned in this section. For detailed instructions on how to use a specific tool, please refer to that topic's specific section found within this chapter.

Steps

1. The System Resource Management tools (of the Maintenance Wizard), the Net Watcher utility, the Resource Meter, the Scheduled Tasks Manager application, the System File Checker, the System Information utility, and the System Monitor are within the System Tools menu option, which is part of the Windows 98 Accessories menu folder.

2. To locate the Windows 98 Swap File Optimization location, you need to use the System icon in the Control Panel. From there you select the Performance tab of the System Properties screen, and then move down to the Virtual Memory button to access this area.

3. File System Performance Profiles are also maintained within the Performance tab of the System Properties screen. However, you need to click the File System button to access these profiles.

4. The Windows 98 Resource Kit provides an additional tool known as WinAlign, which can be used to optimize the performance of program executables by rearranging sections of these files into specific boundaries that are more efficient for x86 CPUs and memory pages. A more detailed discussion of this tool is found in Chapter 19, "Giving Windows Special Powers."

COMPLEXITY
INTERMEDIATE

7.2 How do I...
Know when to use performance monitoring?

Problem

I hear so much about performance monitoring and why it is a good idea to do it on a periodic basis. Other than the first time, which is when I obtain the baseline performance for my computer, when should I be monitoring the performance of my PC?

Technique

Performance monitoring and any subsequent tuning should be performed on a periodic basis, such as a monthly event. However, if you are a very heavy user of your computer, installing and deleting several applications, files, folders, and so on, you might want to make this a bimonthly event. Also, if you have installed any additional hard disk drives, CPUs, or memory, you should run another baseline monitoring on your computer at that time, ensuring that your system is as tuned as possible.

The use of all the Windows 98-provided tools should be utilized during your monthly examination, with the possible exception of the System File Checker. Use of the System File Checker tool should be limited to specific times, usually based on error messages received by the user. For example, assume that you have just rebooted your computer and received an error message saying that a particular Windows 98 system file could not be found or did not execute properly. In order to figure out which file(s) were affected, you would use the System File Checker tool that is built into the Windows 98 operating system.

The performance monitoring tool known as WinAlign, provided by the Windows 98 Resource Kit, is not necessary for the majority of Windows 98 computer users. Besides, this is not a free utility because you must purchase the Resource kit in order to obtain it. The WinAlign tool can be used whenever you install a new application, provided of course that the application is compatible with this Windows 98 tool. Be careful when using the WinAlign tool because improper use of this utility can create havoc on your system in regards to how specific applications execute. For example, do not attempt to use this tool with the Microsoft Office suite of applications, because Microsoft has already optimized this software suite for Windows 9x and use of the WinAlign tool would actually harm your system configuration instead of making it work better.

Use the following steps to help you better determine the frequency of your performance monitoring activities, as well as for determining the regularity of your Windows 98 tuning sessions.

Steps

1. Make sure that you document all your answers to the questions found in each step, as this makes it easier for you to eventually tune your Windows 98 computer.

2. What is the role of your computer? Is it a mobile PC, a desktop computer, or will it function as a server for other computers on your peer-to-peer network? This is very important, as it tells you what your setting should be for optimizing your File System performance.

3. Itemize your hardware: Compile a complete listing of your hardware specifications down to the amount and type of memory/DRAM chips, CPUs, hard disk drives, removable drives, motherboard, NICs, other accessory cards, and video card including the amount of VRAM. All this helps you out at one time or another during the performance monitoring and tuning sessions.

4. Make a separate itemized listing of your network protocols, specialized software applications, such as Stacker or memory-performance enhancers, and all of the terminate-and-stay resident (TSR) applications that you use on your computer. These types of software programs greatly impact any monitoring or tuning practices, so it helps to stay abreast of these type of activities at all times.

5. Keep these listings handy while you begin your system resource management and monitoring activities because they will come in handy.

COMPLEXITY
BEGINNER

7.3 How do I... Install the additional System Resource Management tools?

Problem

Windows 98 provides several System Resource Management tools and utilities, not to mention those that might be available in the Windows 98 Resource Kit. How do I identify and install all these additional tools and utilities, such as the Resource Meter, System Information, System Monitor, Maintenance Wizard, Net Watcher, Scheduled Tasks Manager, and the System File Checker?

CHAPTER 7
SYSTEM RESOURCE MANAGEMENT

Technique

One of the nicest features of Windows 98 is its capability to provide access to its various tools and utilities via a common installation method: Add/Remove Programs icon in the Control Panel. Through this Control Panel option you can install these tools in just about any combination you want, without having to hunt and peck through a variety of other methods.

However, if you require the WinAlign tool as well, then you must acquire the Windows 98 Resource Kit separately. For information on obtaining and installing the Windows 98 Resource Kit, please refer to Chapter 1, "Installation Tips." For details on how to install the built-in Windows 98 System Management tools and utilities, please comply with the following steps.

Steps

1. Start Windows 98, enter the GUI desktop, and then pull up the Control Panel. Once inside the Control Panel, double-click the Add/Remove Programs icon, and then click the Windows Setup tab to reveal the screen shown in Figure 7.1.

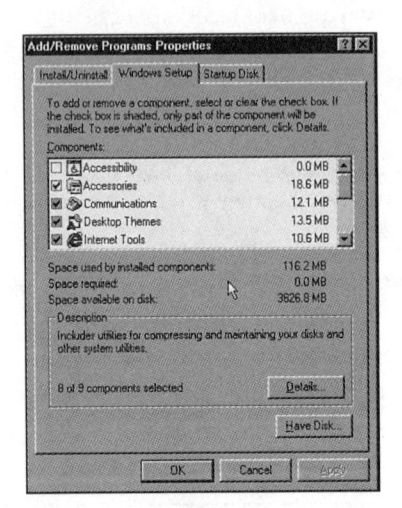

Figure 7.1 Reviewing the Windows Setup tab within the Add/Remove Programs Properties screen.

2. This screen is the access point for nearly all the add-on tools and utilities for Windows 98. To select an item, click on its check box to place a check mark inside it. If a box has a check mark with shading in it as well then that means not all the sub-components for that topic have been

7.3 INSTALL THE ADDITIONAL SYSTEM RESOURCE MANAGEMENT TOOLS

selected. Scrolling down toward the bottom of this listing, you see the topic labeled System Tools. Click once on this selection to highlight it, and then click the Details... button to view the individual components as shown in Figure 7.2.

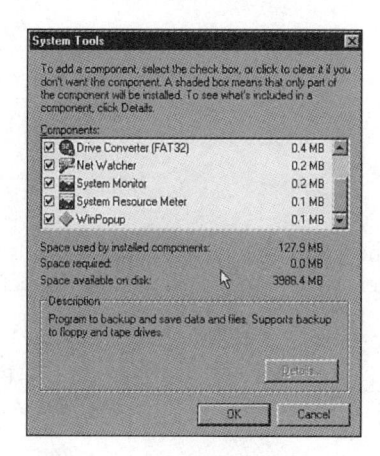

Figure 7.2 Reviewing the available Windows 98 System tools.

3. Within this listing, the ones you should be most interested in are the Net Watcher, System Monitor, and the System Resource Meter tools. These are the ones that will aid in the management of system resources. All the others that you need (other than WinAlign) are already installed on your system by default. Select all these if they are not already installed on your PC, and then click OK.

4. After returning to the higher level System Tools screen, click OK to begin the installation process for the tools that you want to add to your existing Windows 98 installation.

5. You will be prompted to put your Windows 98 CD-ROM into your CD drive, and then the copying commences. If you are prompted to overwrite any files, such as the one seen in Figure 7.3, it is usually best to keep your existing file (because it is the most recent version).

6. The installation process continues for some time, depending on how many other tools and utilities you have chosen from the other component categories. When the process has completed, click Yes to respond affirmatively to the question regarding whether you want to restart your computer or not. It is usually best to reboot each time after you have installed new system components, especially ones from the System Tools section.

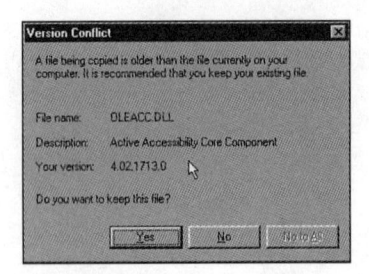

Figure 7.3 Deciding whether to keep the old or new file.

7. After rebooting, you are finished. Any time you want to add or remove a Windows 98 system component, this is the place to perform that task.

COMPLEXITY
INTERMEDIATE

7.4 How do I...
Use the Resource Meter?

Problem

I want to figure out if I am running low on my system resources. For example, my system appears to be thrashing about quite often. I think that it might be due to a lack of memory. Is there a quick and easy way to check the availability of my system resources?

Technique

The Windows 98 Resource Meter is probably the easiest monitoring tool to master. It consists of a single screen and three picturesque bar graphs. It provides you with a quick glance at the status of your overall System, User, and GDI resources. These three areas comprise the Windows 98 core, which lies at the heart of the operating system. Therefore, if you monitor and track these three components, you will always have your hand on the heartbeat of your Windows 98 computer system.

A little more background information might help you at this point. *GDI* is an acronym for *graphical device interface* and is the piece of Windows 98 that manages the information you see displayed onscreen. What many people do not realize is that the GDI also manages all graphical support for other output devices, including printers.

The User portion of the core consists of the input from devices such as your keyboard, mouse, pen device, trackball, and so on. It also covers the output of

7.4
USE THE RESOURCE METER

messages to the user interface (screens, menus, message boxes, icons, windows, and so on). The 32-bit threads might each have its own message queue, but all of the 16-bit threads share the same queue. This is something to keep in mind if you run a lot of 16-bit applications and the percentage of User resources suddenly dips.

The System portion of the Windows 98 core consists of the operating system's *kernel*. The kernel is king so to speak. If it runs out of resources, everything else will die right along with it, so you might want to pay close attention to it. The kernel is the part of Windows 98 that loads applications into memory (the .EXE and .DLL files), manages all the file input/output (I/O) operations, task scheduling, virtual memory management, exception handling, and provides the *thunking* services for mapping a 16-bit value to a 32-bit value.

NOTE
Windows 98 automatically provides a service for you known as thunking. Thunking is a programming term, which is the process by which a 16-bit program is capable of "talking" to its 32-bit program interface. To put it a much simpler way, thunking is what allows you to run 16-bit applications on a 32-bit operating system.

To use the Resource Meter, follow the steps listed here. The Resource Meter is easy to access and makes a good benchmarking tool for your system when you are trying to establish a baseline for your system.

Steps

1. Using the menu tree from the Start button, click once on the Accessories menu selection then on the System Tools menu option, and then click once more on the Resource Meter menu selection. After you click on the Resource Meter menu selection, it may seem like something started but you will not see a screen popup or any similar action. However, to confirm that the meter started properly, look on the Windows 98 taskbar in the System Tray area, as shown in Figure 7.4.

Figure 7.4 Reviewing the system resources from the Windows 98 taskbar.

2. The very first time you run the Windows 98 Resource Meter utility, you might see a popup message that informs you that the utility might cause a strain on your system. Therefore, you might not want to run it when you have many critical applications open and operating on your system.

CHAPTER 7
SYSTEM RESOURCE MANAGEMENT

3. In the corner of the System Tray you will see a tiny rectangle that looks like it is standing on end; it should have three small green bars inside of it. If you place your mouse pointer on top of this icon, a percentage for the available System, User, and GDI resources appears. For the typical computer system, readings in the low eightieth percentile (80–83 percent) is an acceptable level. If you are using a laptop or notebook computer or a standard desktop configuration without much running (except maybe Microsoft Word or Lotus 123), these are normal levels. You do not really need to be concerned unless any one of these numbers slips into the 40s, or if all three of them slip into the low sixtieth percentile. This means that your system is in danger of failing and you might want to avert this by preemptively shutting down all of your applications and rebooting your PC.

4. If this is too small for you to see, you can expand the icon in two ways. If you click the icon with your secondary mouse button, a menu appears. Click the Details menu selection and the larger Resource Meter screen appears. The other option permits you to exit this utility. Double-click the icon and that same larger Resource Meter screen appears, as shown in Figure 7.5.

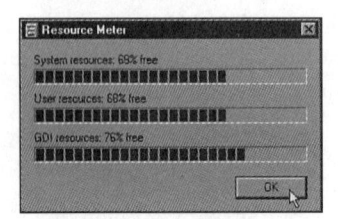

Figure 7.5 Examining the Windows 98 Resource Meter screen.

5. Click OK to close this screen. You must use the menu option from the Resource Meter icon on the System Tray to actually exit this utility, though.

6. If you are in a hurry to obtain a check on your System resources, there is a way to quickly do it other than using the Resource Meter. While holding down the Alt key on your keyboard, double-click the My Computer icon found on the Windows 98 desktop. This takes you directly into the System Properties screen, as shown in Figure 7.6.

7.5 USE THE SYSTEM INFORMATION UTILITY

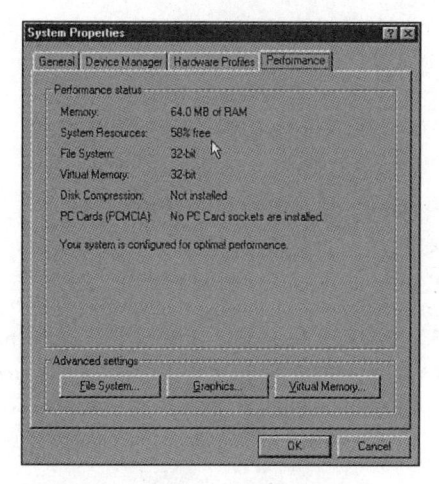

Figure 7.6 Finding the status of the System Resources on the Performance tab of the System Properties screen.

7. Click the Performance tab and look at second item from the top labeled System Resources; it has a percentage free number located next to it. This is the one that appears in the more formal Resource Meter. I find it much easier and faster to use this one to check my System Resources, rather than drilling through the Start menu maze, and then still needing to double-click the System Tray icon. Perhaps you will too.

COMPLEXITY
INTERMEDIATE

7.5 How do I...
Use the System Information utility?

Problem

I really do not know much about the nitty-gritty details of my PC, other than what was written on the invoice from the vendor I purchased it from. I want to know more about the specifics, such as what versions of Windows 98 and Internet Explorer I am running, what kind of CPU I have, and how much memory and hard drive space I have. I also want to know if there is anything wrong with my system that Windows 98 might have already automatically detected for me. How do I find out all of this stuff, as well as what types of software applications are running on my computer? Can someone who wants to become more technical, but is not quite there yet do this?

Technique

Windows 98 has a System Information tool that is perfect for a task such as this. It provides enough of the high-level information so anyone can quickly gain a better idea of the capabilities of their PC, but definitely provides enough of the details to aid in the monitoring of your computer system. This tool, coincidentally enough, is called the System Information utility. It is built into Windows 98 and is automatically installed when you install the Windows 98 operating system, even on a minimal installation.

Steps

1. Using the menu tree from the Start menu, you can find the System Information utility inside the System Tools menu option, which is part of the Accessories menu selection. When you click the System Information menu selection, its main screen appears as shown in Figure 7.7.

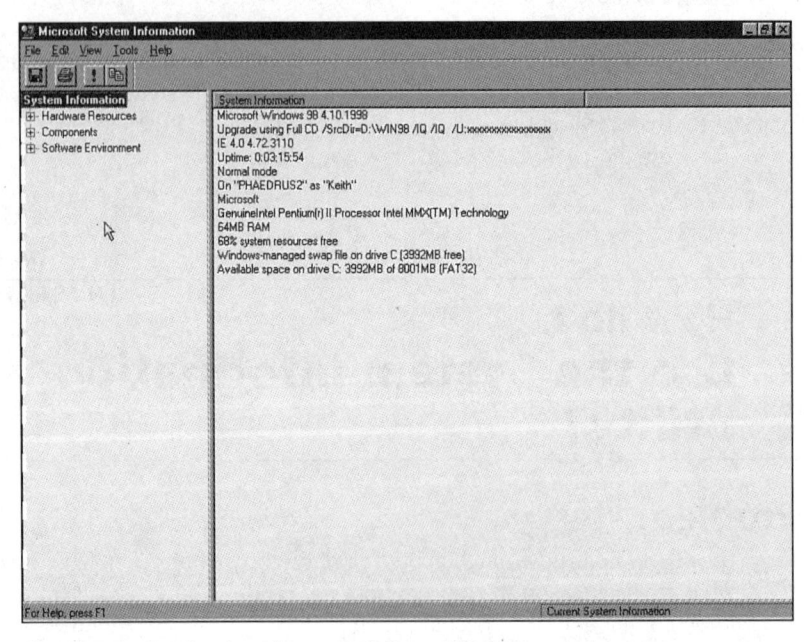

Figure 7.7 Reviewing the main Microsoft System Information screen.

7.5 USE THE SYSTEM INFORMATION UTILITY

2. There are three essential areas of the Microsoft System Information screen: the Tools menu option, the System Information data (left column), and the actual data area (right windowpane). If you click the Tools menu option you will see a listing of ten very important Windows 98 troubleshooting utilities:

- Update Wizard uninstall
- Signature Verification tool
- Windows Report tool
- System File Checker
- Registry Checker
- Automatic Skip Driver agent
- Dr. Watson
- System Configuration utility
- ScanDisk
- Version Conflict Manager

3. All these utilities can be executed by clicking any of these specific menu selections. These tools are discussed in detail throughout the various chapters of this book, so I will not go into any detail here, other than to mention the two that will help you in the management of your computer system's resources: Dr. Watson and the System File Checker. Dr. Watson takes a snapshot of your computer, which is very useful for setting a baseline of performance for your computer. The System File Checker helps you to monitor the life of specific files on your computer. That is, this tool can tell you if a system-critical file is of the correct version or not, a very important issue if something goes wrong with your PC.

4. The data area of the screen (the windowpane on the right side) is where all the information appears whenever you click an item found in the left windowpane.

5. The System Information area of the screen is where you need to focus, especially when you attempt to determine system activity or which applications are active, and when you need to secure more details about your hardware devices. If you look in this area, you will see that this part of the utility has three sub-areas, each with its own header:

- Hardware Resources

- Components

- Software Environment

6. If you click once on any of the headers in this area, the specifics for that section will appear in the windowpane to the right, as shown in Figure 7.8.

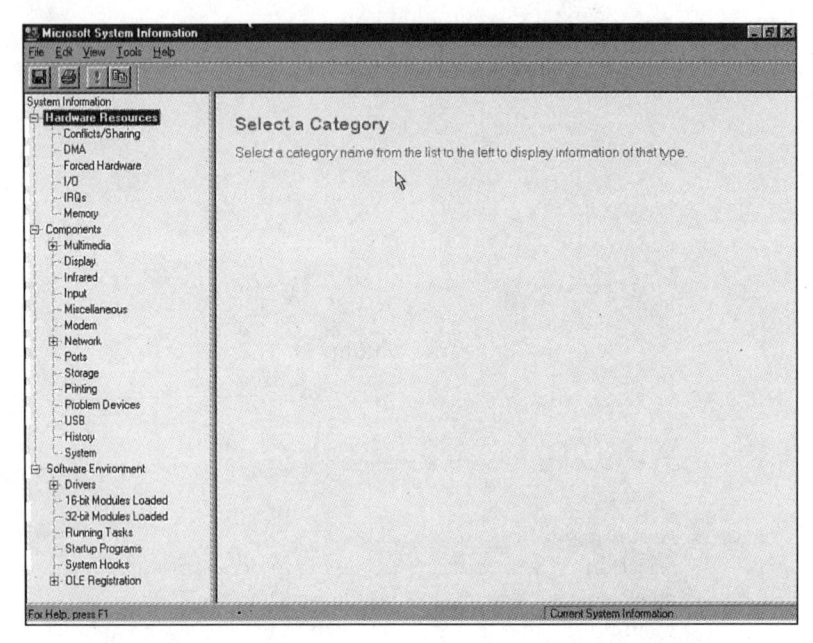

Figure 7.8 Reviewing the hardware resources within the Microsoft System Information tool.

7. To expand any of these topics, click the plus symbol next to the descriptive name and that topic's sub-areas automatically appear.

8. The quintessential points of interest in the Hardware Resources header are Conflicts/Sharing, Forced Hardware, and IRQs. The Conflicts/Sharing area highlights conflicts between ISA devices and those PCI devices with shared resources. As you can see in Figure 7.9, this can be a very informative bit of information.

7.5
USE THE SYSTEM INFORMATION UTILITY

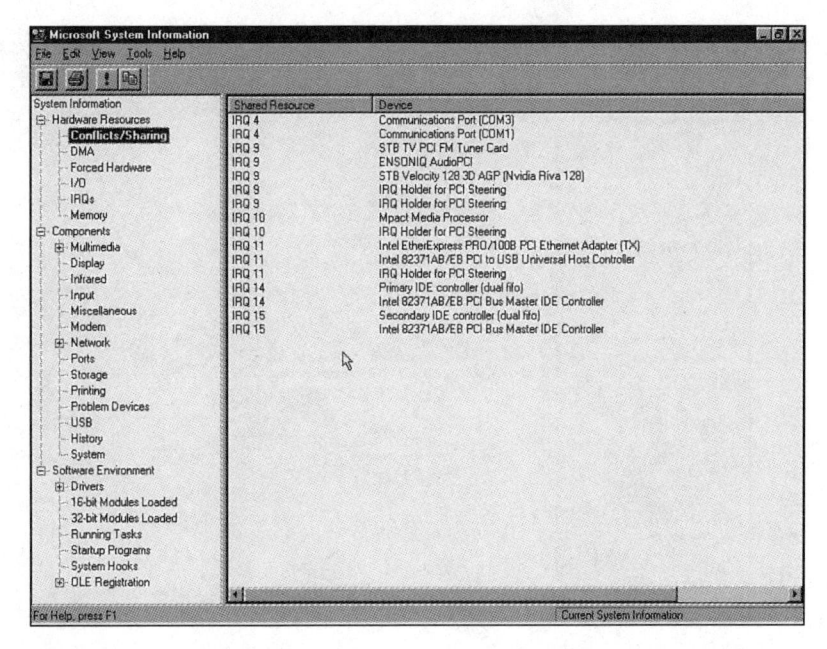

Figure 7.9 Discovering which devices share or have conflicts with interrupts.

9. By knowing which devices share resources, you can proactively head-off any potential conflicts when upgrading any of your hardware devices. It is useful if you print out a copy of this screen for your future reference, especially if you are planning an upgrade of some type, such as a new TV tuner card. Remember that you should be using PCI devices wherever possible, because they work and play well with other cards, unlike most ISA devices.

10. If there were any conflicts, this screen (refer to Figure 7.9) tells you about them. However, in the example given, there were none.

11. The beauty of the Forced Hardware section is that is reminds you of all the hardware devices that have pre-set resources (that the user specified) instead of using the settings prescribed by the Windows 98 operating system. If you ever have the displeasure of troubleshooting a plug-and-play device, especially token-ring network cards, this section quickly becomes a lifesaver for you.

12. The IRQs (interrupt settings) section, as shown in Figure 7.10, is another great source of information. Print out a copy of this section once you have your system set, and then use it as a baseline to return to if you encounter any difficulties.

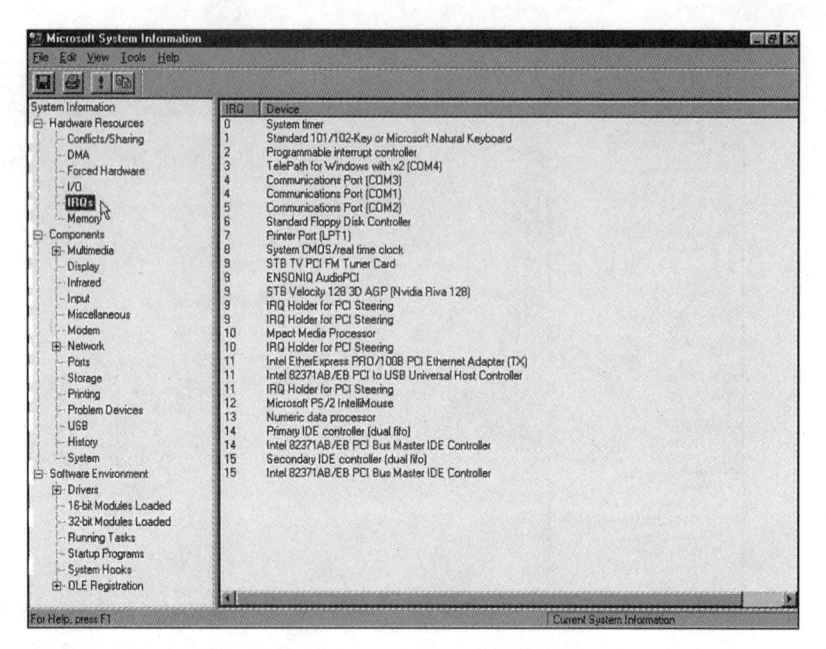

Figure 7.10 Reviewing the current use of the computer's interrupt settings.

13. A comprehensive listing of a system's IRQs is easily worth its weight in gold. This especially becomes a truism when dealing with the many devices that share interrupts, such as communication ports (serial ports), peripheral devices (TV tuner cards, sound cards, and network interface cards), and drive controller devices. All computers that are capable of running Windows 98 have a total of 16 interrupts. These interrupts are numbered zero (0) through fifteen (15). After closer examination of the computer system in the example, you will notice that all 16 interrupts are already in use.

14. Now let us assume that you need to add another device to this computer, such as a SCSI controller interface card. What will you do? How are you going to add it, especially since you know that you will probably need a dedicated IRQ port for this type of controller card? Without a screen such as this to lay out all your options for you (they are there, you just need to examine these IRQs closer), you would probably be back to a best guesstimate while installing a card such as this.

15. The answer: Remove your COM2 port, because there is no physical device presently attached to it, and assign this interrupt to the SCSI controller card. Having a list to work from makes this sort of hardware configuration pretty easy to do. The Windows 98's Add New Hardware

7.5
USE THE SYSTEM INFORMATION UTILITY

Wizard could not have made this happen, as it programmatically seeks out open interrupts first, and then tries to share second (it usually fails on things such as this).

16. The Components header contains many sections, including two with sub-areas: Multimedia and Network. The best section for you to periodically take a look at is Problem Devices. This section informs you of any devices in your system that might not be working up to par. After closer examination of this section you will notice a series of radio buttons along the top of the data area in the right column, as shown in Figure 7.11.

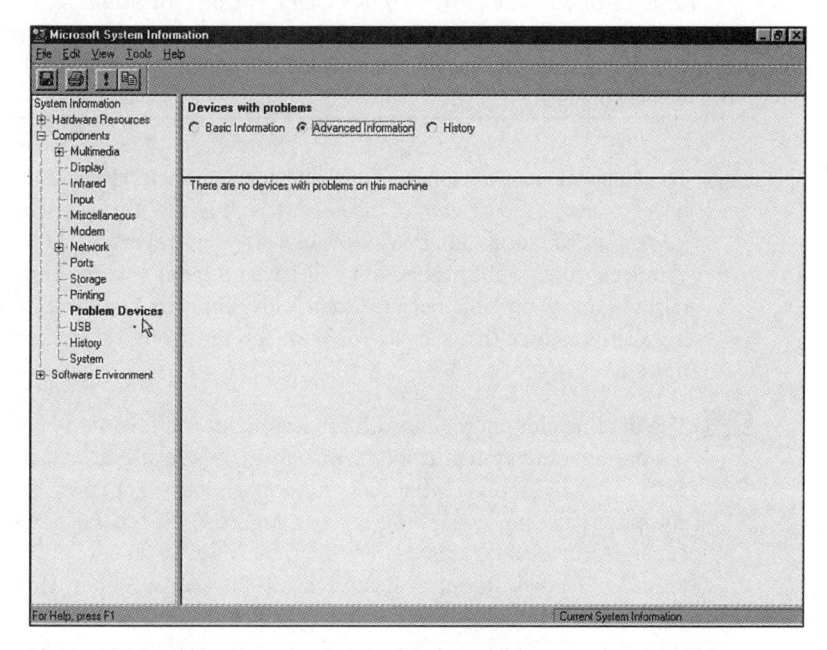

Figure 7.11 Selecting the level of information you want to see.

17. There are three radio buttons to choose from: Basic Information, Advanced Information, and History. These options appear only in those areas where the device(s) have software drivers. Of the three, the History radio button is the most interesting. This one gives you a timeline, or history, of the software drivers that you have had installed for this particular device at one time or another. The typical difference in data presented between the Basic and Advanced Information buttons is minimal. Occasionally you will see more data for the Advanced portion, but a lot of the time it will be the same within the Components heading. Click each of the different choices at least once in order to get a feel for the types of data that are displayed for each of them.

18. If you want to see the additional sections within either the Multimedia or Network sections, click the plus symbol next to each of the labels. The Multimedia section contains information about each of the audio and video CODECs that your computer has installed, as well as more detailed information about your CD-ROM device (it says CD-ROM even if you have a DVD-ROM device).

> **NOTE**
>
> The Windows 98 term CODEC means COmpression/DECompression (see how this acronym was derived?). A CODEC is used for audio and video files in such a manner that it permits your computer to more effectively manage its multimedia functions. One of the more popular CODECs is the MPEG format.

19. The Network section contains an entry for WinSock. However, if you have WinSock 2.0 or greater installed, it will ignore this entry and contain no real information. Since Windows 98 ships with version 2.0 of WinSock, it is doubtful that you will have an older version present (although it is possible because some older Internet Web browser software installations force their version of WinSock into your Windows 98 configuration).

20. The final header entry, Software Environment, is a favorite for troubleshooting and system resource management because it presents you with a detailed look at what files and applications are present in your computer's memory. As you can see in Figure 7.12, this header area expands into several areas: Drivers, 16-bit Modules Loaded, 32-bit Modules Loaded, Running Tasks, Startup Programs, System Hooks, and OLE Registration. The Drivers and OLE Registration sections each contain sub-areas.

21. Within the Drivers section you can find the data broken apart by some of the Windows 98 core areas: Kernel Drivers, MS-DOS Drivers, and User-Mode Drivers. The Kernel area shows you which ring 0 drivers are loaded. The MS-DOS Drivers area presents a listing of which real-mode device drivers exist in memory, and the User-Mode Drivers area shows you the three device drivers that currently exist in memory.

22. It is very important that you print a copy of this so that you have a hard copy of your baseline configuration. If you do not make a copy now, you might be unable to view specific settings during a time of trouble as the Microsoft System Information tool is unable to present any data regarding any hardware you have during a Safe Mode boot.

7.5
USE THE SYSTEM INFORMATION UTILITY

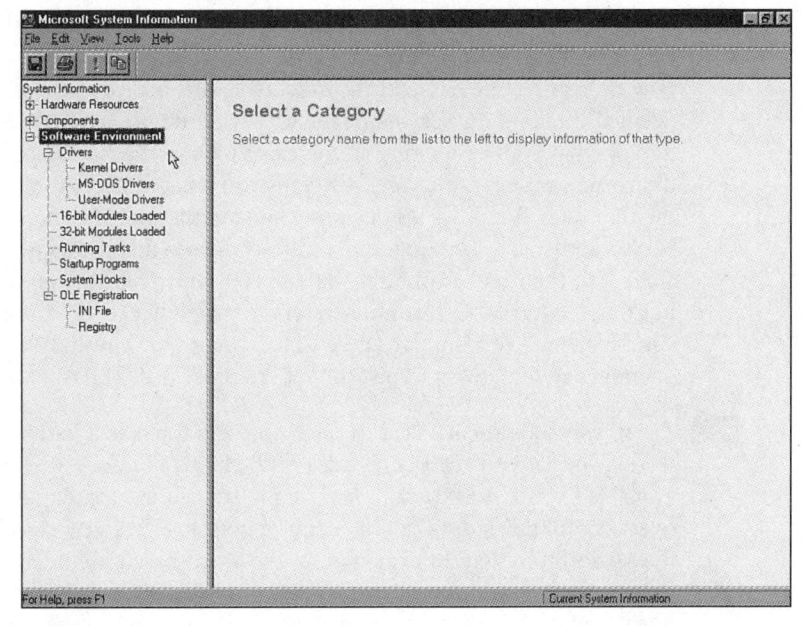

Figure 7.12 Reviewing the system's Software Environment file.

23. One of the more useful sections within this header topic is the Running Tasks area, as shown in Figure 7.13.

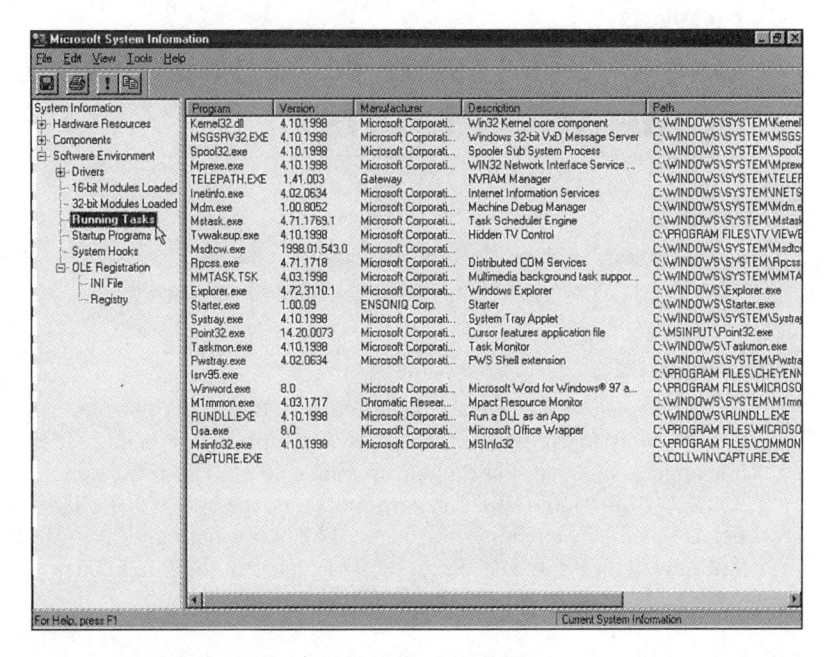

Figure 7.13 Finding out what tasks are presently running on your PC.

24. By clicking this area once, a complete listing of the program tasks that exist in your computer's memory areas is displayed in the Data area. Not only do you see the name of the executable file, but you also see a detailed version number, the manufacturer of the program file, a description of what you are looking at, the exact path to the executable file, and the version number. This area also tells you what file is part of, such as the Microsoft Windows 98 operating system, the Internet Information Server, and so on. The first time most people see this listing, they are amazed at the number of tasks that are constantly running on their PC. For those Windows NT administrators in the audience, the information you see here is very similar to the Task Manager within the Windows NT operating system, except you will not see process ID (PID) information.

25. Again, you should click at least once on every topic area within this section so that you get a better idea of the kinds of information that are available to you. Additionally, you might want to use the Export menu selection, found under the File menu option, to selectively copy data from the Microsoft System Information tool to a text-based file. If you do this for your entire system, you can keep this data electronically for inventory purposes for each PC that you manage.

COMPLEXITY
ADVANCED

7.6 How do I...
Use Dr. Watson to troubleshoot application faults?

Problem

My computer keeps producing application faults, but I am unable to figure out what is going wrong. Is there a way to capture what is going on?

Technique

Dr. Watson is a tool built into the Windows 98 operating system; it gives you the capability to capture all the details of an application fault; that is, problematic applications that you can consistently cause to fail in the same manner. If you suffer from intermittent system problems, the only way for Dr. Watson to detect them is by already being active. The best way to do this to drop a String Value entry for it into the Windows 98 Registry in the Run subkey.

USE DR. WATSON TO TROUBLESHOOT APPLICATION FAULTS

Steps

1. Start the Dr. Watson utility by starting up the Microsoft System Information tool, clicking the Tools menu option, and then clicking the Dr. Watson menu selection. The Dr. Watson utility will start, but is present only as an icon on your Windows 98 taskbar in the System Tray, as shown in Figure 7.14.

Figure 7.14 Locating the Dr. Watson icon on the Windows 98 taskbar.

2. If you place your pointing device on top of the Dr. Watson icon, you will also be able to see the ToolTip for that icon. To force Dr. Watson to stop and generate a snapshot of your computer, double-click this icon. This produces the snapshot and opens the main Dr. Watson window, as shown in Figure 7.15.

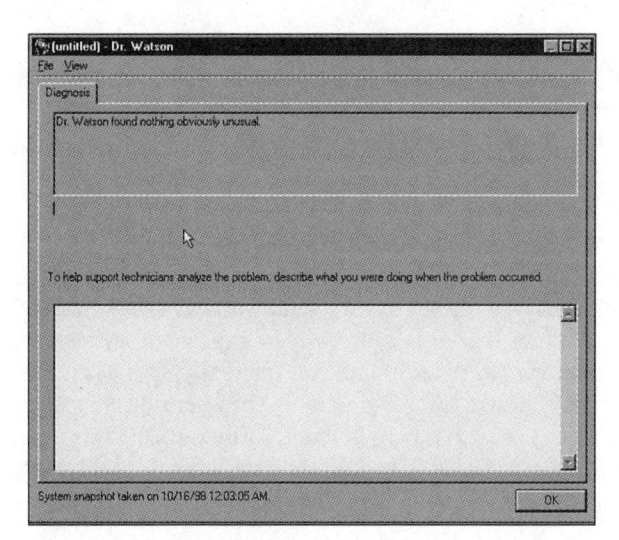

Figure 7.15 Reviewing the diagnosis of the good doctor (Watson, that is).

3. You will see a read-only window on the top half of the screen that gives you its diagnosis of the existing problem(s), if any. The purpose of the bottom half of the screen is to give you a Notepad-like area to jot down notes about what you see onscreen. You would type any comments here and save the log file first then email it to a technical support person, such as someone at Microsoft. Obviously, if you are the only one who works on this particular PC then writing yourself notes might or might not be beneficial.

4. You might want to consider expanding the view for this screen from Standard to Advanced. To do this, click the View menu option, and then click again on the Advanced View menu selection, as shown in Figure 7.16.

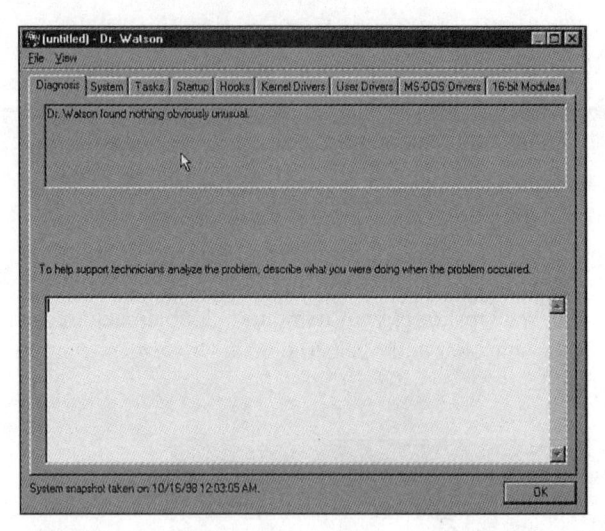

Figure 7.16 Reviewing Dr. Watson's advanced system information.

5. As soon as you select the Advanced View menu option, an additional eight tabs appear on the Dr. Watson screen. As you examine these tabs, you will notice that they cover the same areas as the Microsoft System Information tool. This is because you are capable of saving the data into a log file from the Dr. Watson tool, and then viewing it again from inside the Microsoft System Information tool. The Microsoft System Information tool provides you with the capability to print out data from specific sections, whereas the Dr. Watson utility can only print the entire informational file in a lump sum: a total that can easily exceed 20 pages in length.

6. A general rule of thumb is that you should use the Dr. Watson utility only for diagnosing application faults, and use the Microsoft System Information tool for determining the baseline for your computer system's hardware and software resource management. Attempts to use Dr. Watson as a general information gathering tool, while possible, do not really constitute sound business practices.

7. Another useful feature of Dr. Watson is its capability to set certain levels for log files and disassembly options, and to change the default view to

7.6
USE DR. WATSON TO TROUBLESHOOT APPLICATION FAULTS

the Advanced view. To do this click the View menu option, and then click again on the Options... menu selection and the Dr. Watson options dialog box appears, as shown in Figure 7.17.

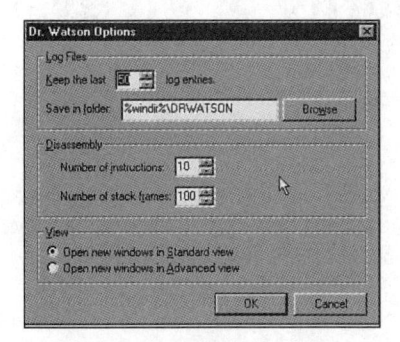

Figure 7.17 Setting the options for the Dr. Watson utility.

8. You can set the parameter for the number of different log entries that you keep in the Dr. Watson log file, as well as choose the specific location for the log file.

9. The Disassembly section of the Dr. Watson Options window allows you to set limits for the number of instructions and the number of stack frames. These two settings are specifically for use by Microsoft Technical Support personnel and should never be changed unless you are instructed to do so by someone at Microsoft. However, if the application that is blowing up is one that someone in your organization developed, you should set these two parameters based on input from your internal development staff.

10. The View area of this screen is where you can set the default view for the Dr. Watson utility. It is suggested that you click the Advanced View radio button to make this view your default selection. When you have made all your selections, click OK to close this window.

11. If you want to keep a copy of this, you should use the Save or Save As... menu option from the File menu selection. If you have finished examining the Dr. Watson screens, click OK to close this particular snapshot.

12. To exit Dr. Watson completely, click once with your secondary mouse button on the System Tray icon, and then click the Exit Dr. Watson... menu selection. This closes down the utility and removes it from your computer's memory.

COMPLEXITY
BEGINNER

7.7 How do I... Verify the integrity of my system files?

Problem

I believe that one or more of my system files might have become corrupted or changed from its original state. Is there an easy way to determine which of the system files might be different or broken, and how can I remedy this situation?

Technique

Windows 98 provides a utility known as the System File Checker. It is also one of the tools started from inside the Microsoft System Information tool, or it can be started directly from the Windows 98 Run command box. The purpose of the System File Checker is to scan your important system files and figure out which ones have been altered since you installed Windows 98. It also determines whether any files have been corrupted, and then offers to restore any of these corrupted files from backup copies that Windows 98 automatically preserves for you elsewhere on your PC.

Steps

1. Open the System File Checker utility by starting the Microsoft System Information tool then clicking the Tools menu option, and then clicking the System File Checker menu selection. Otherwise, open up the Run command box from the Start button, type in the command **SFC.exe**, and then click OK (or press Enter).

2. Performing either of these methods takes you into the primary screen of the System File Checker utility, as shown in Figure 7.18.

3. You can take two directions within the System File Checker utility. The top radio button option gives you the ability to perform a scan on your computer for altered system files. If this option discovers a corrupted system file, it prompts you to repair that file by restoring a copy of the original file. The bottom radio button gives you the ability to restore a specific file from the Windows 98 CD-ROM installation disc, provided of course that you known the exact name of the file you want to restore.

7.7
VERIFY THE INTEGRITY OF MY SYSTEM FILES

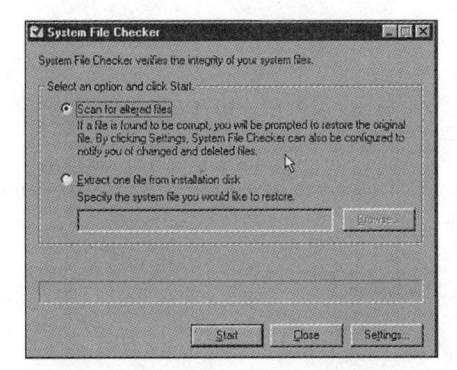

Figure 7.18 Setting the base type for the System File Checker.

4. Before you do anything, however, you might want to better configure the options of the System File Checker utility to your liking. To do this, click the Settings… button, which brings you to the System File Checker Settings screen shown in Figure 7.19.

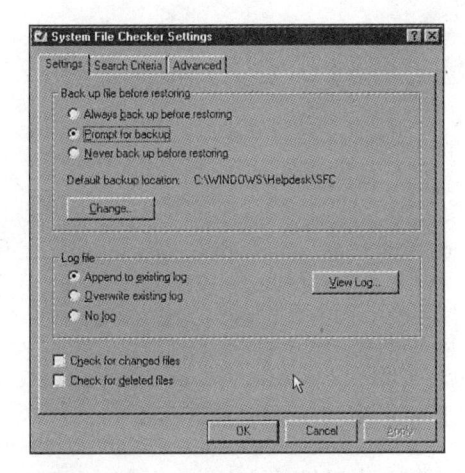

Figure 7.19 Selecting your System File Checker settings.

5. The Settings tab gives you the ability to set the location for file backups, restore file prompt settings, append or overwrite log file options, and check for changed or deleted system files. These last two options are probably the most powerful ones on this screen. If you enable either or both of these options, the System File Checker utility will look not only at corrupted system files but also at files that have been deleted or changed (its CRC has been altered) in any way.

CHAPTER 7
SYSTEM RESOURCE MANAGEMENT

6. If you want to change the location of the backup files, you may do so by clicking the Change... button and selecting a new locale. To view an existing log file (for example, a log from a previous use of the System File Checker utility), click the View Log... button.

7. Click once on the Search Criteria tab, to reveal that screen's contents as seen in Figure 7.20.

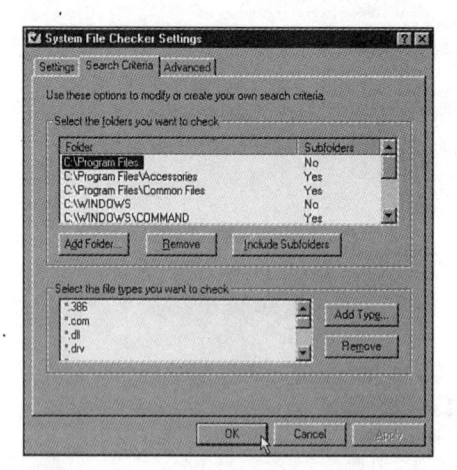

Figure 7.20 Modifying the search criteria for System File Checker usage.

8. The Search Criteria screen provides you with the ability to modify the manner in which the System File Checker utility scans your PC. The default set of system folders to be scanned is provided for you, but you may modify these folders as you deem necessary. In addition, you may add or remove system file types. For example, assume you have created a custom application in which files must never change. If you were to add that file type to this listing then the System File Checker utility would automatically search for any alterations to your custom application's files.

9. Click once on the Advanced tab, to reveal its contents, as shown in Figure 7.21.

10. The purpose of the DEFAULT.SFC file is to provide a default configuration of your computer's system files. You can use this screen to create a new default file, if the old one is somehow deleted. It is possible to restore the default system information settings by restoring the original DEFAULT.SFC file since it comes on the Windows 98 installation CD-ROM. To perform this restoration process, click the Restore Defaults button.

7.7
VERIFY THE INTEGRITY OF MY SYSTEM FILES

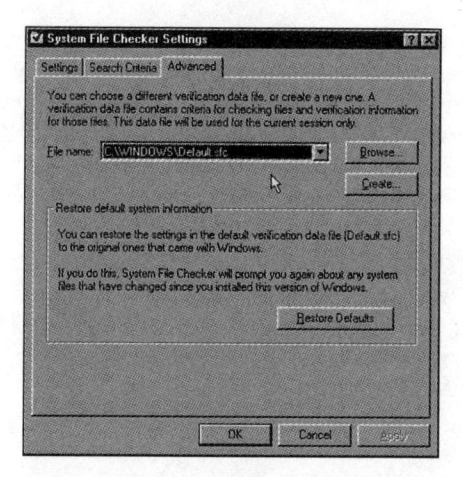

Figure 7.21 Selecting the Advanced options for the System File Checker.

11. When you have finished making any alterations to the System File Checker Settings screens, click OK to accept these changes. This returns you to the primary screen of the System File Checker utility.

12. To begin the scanning process, click the Start button, as shown in Figure 7.22.

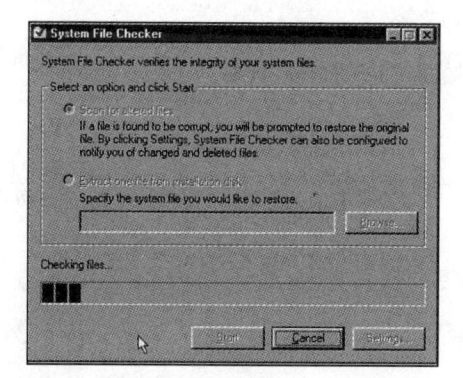

Figure 7.22 Initiating use of the Windows 98 System File Checker.

13. The two radio button options are immediately grayed-out and the System File Checker utility commences its examination of your computer's system files. During the processing of this utility, your system becomes very sluggish if you are attempting to use any other applications at the same time as the System File Checker tool.

14. After the scanning process is complete, the System File Checker utility displays a Finished message window that informs you it has finished examining your system files. Click OK to accept this information and close the utility. Otherwise, click the Details… button to discover more about exactly what the utility did to and for your system over the past several minutes, as shown in Figure 7.23.

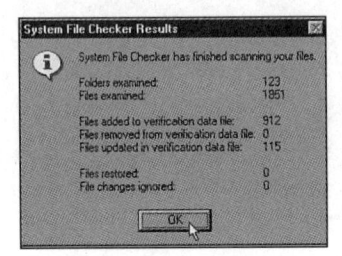

Figure 7.23 Examining the System File Checker results.

15. The System File Checker Results window is strictly an informational message box that provides you with the details about what was checked on your computer. Once you have examined the data to your satisfaction, click OK to close this window. You will be returned to the Finished message window where you should click OK again to close this window, and then return to the original System File Checker screen.

16. Click Close to completely exit out of the System File Checker utility.

COMPLEXITY
INTERMEDIATE

7.8 How do I…
Track performance changes to my computer system over a period of time?

Problem

I do not believe that my system is performing at the level it could if it only had more memory. How can I track performance changes to my computer over a specified time period, in order to help justify a memory hardware upgrade to my computer?

7.8
TRACK PREFORMANCE CHANGES TO MY COMPUTER SYSTEM

Technique

Built into the Windows 98 operating system is a little-known tool called the System Monitor. Refer to the first part of this chapter for details on how to install this utility from the Windows 98 CD-ROM. When the utility has been installed, you can use it as an aid in monitoring and evaluating the performance of your computer. Through the use of this tool it should become apparent as to which hardware component might be hindering the faster processing of data, including pointing out those hardware devices that might be bottlenecks to the entire process.

Steps

1. Using the menu tree from the Start button, you can find the System Monitor utility inside the System Tools menu option, which is part of the Accessories menu selection. Once you click on the System Monitor menu selection, its main screen appears, as shown in Figure 7.24.

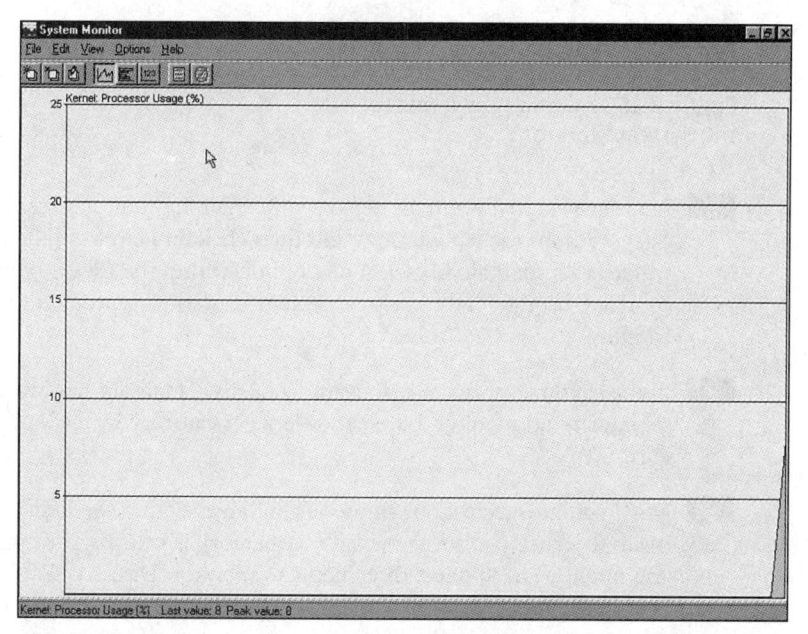

Figure 7.24 Viewing the primary System Monitor screen.

2. The Windows 98 System Monitor tool gives you the capability to closely track how specific resources are being used within your computer.

3. Click the File menu option, and then click the Start Logging menu selection to begin using this utility. You are prompted for a location to place the SYSMON.LOG text-based log file, which can be put anywhere on your computer's hard disk drive system.

4. When the logging process has started, click the Edit menu option, and then click the Add Item... menu selection to add a system process to be monitored.

5. This causes the Add Item window to appear, as shown in Figure 7.25.

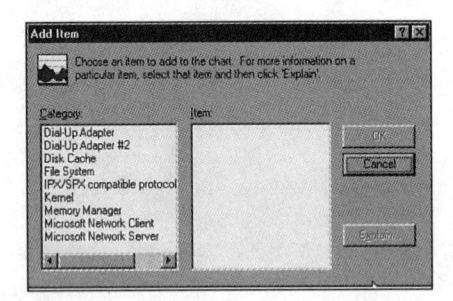

Figure 7.25 Adding new items to the System Monitor.

6. In order to actually add an item to your System Monitor screen, click a category from the left window, and then click an item from the right window. As soon as you select any option within the Category window, a complete listing of all the available items instantly appears in the Item window.

7. In the example problem, you want to justify a memory hardware upgrade, so you should monitor a Memory Manager category by clicking that category.

8. Next, you must select one of the topical areas within the Item window. Again, because you suspect a lack of memory is causing your problems, you might want to select three items to monitor: Discards, Page-Outs, and Unused Physical Memory. The last one is pretty obvious, but the first two might not be. If both the Discards and Page-Outs counters appear high consistently, you might have a memory problem. Likewise, if the Unused Physical Memory graph shows that you never have any free physical memory then this is also a very good indication of a shortage. To select more than one item at a time, click the first one once, and then while holding the Ctrl key down click each of the other items you are interested in seeing on your monitor's chart.

7.8
TRACK PREFORMANCE CHANGES TO MY COMPUTER SYSTEM

> **NOTE**
>
> The Windows 98 System Monitor works much like its counterpart in Windows NT. It has the same look and feel, as well as many of the same settings as the Windows NT version. The biggest difference between these two operating systems (other than the sheer number of settings possible in Windows NT) is in the contents of the Explain button. In Windows 98, this button contains vague references to the System Monitor's data points, whereas in Windows NT this button provides much more detail about the use of the topic as well as the definition of what you are using.

9. Once you have made all of your selections, click OK to accept these changes to your monitor, and they will open inside the main System Monitor screen, as shown in Figure 7.26.

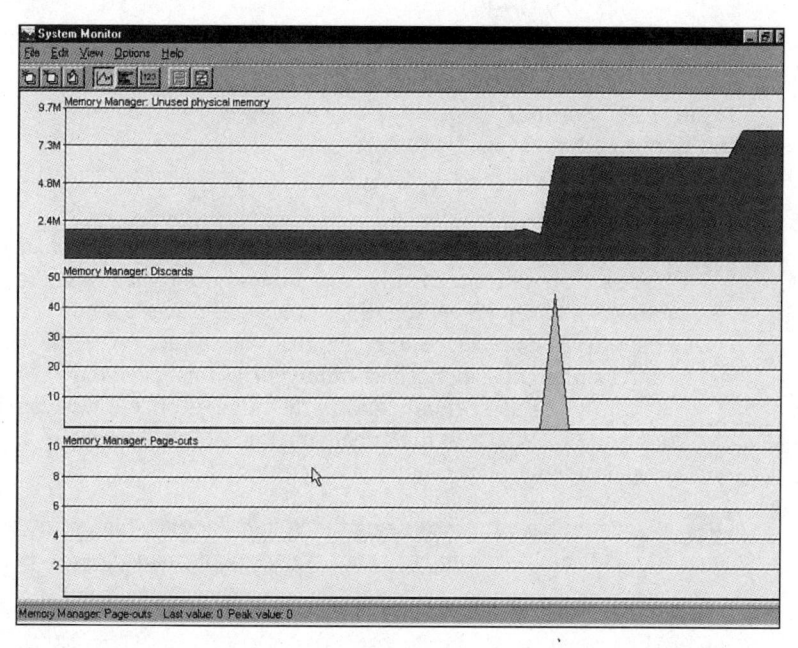

Figure 7.26 Watching the Windows 98 System Monitor at work.

10. Chances are that you might occasionally have several hundred discards and very little physical memory (4–8MB) left unused on your system at any one time, but this can be from processing normal activities. These numbers are in the normal range, as long as you are not experiencing many Page-Outs (less than 10–12).

11. When you view your chart, you see the three values laid-out in a horizontal fashion. This is the default view for your system monitor, but it can be changed if you want.

12. Click the View menu option, and then the Bar or Numeric Charts menu selections and you will change the manner in which the monitor is graphically presented. To add more items, remove any that you have, or edit an existing item, click the Edit menu option. Then click once on the appropriate menu selection.

13. If you click once on the Options menu option and then on the Chart... menu selection, you will see the Options window appear, as shown in Figure 7.27.

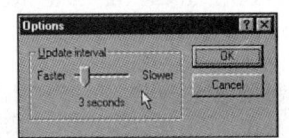

Figure 7.27 Setting the Update interval for the System Monitor.

14. Click and hold the slider bar with your mouse pointer to change the Update Interval for the entire System Monitor application. It is very important to remember that this application places a strain on your computer system, so the numbers that you see appear in the various charts and graphs are not just from your normal everyday operations. You are impacting those numbers with the number of counters you are operating and the speed of the update intervals. (The shorter the interval, the more burden it places on your system.)

15. When you have finished using the System Monitor make sure to close it so that it no longer impacts your system performance.

7.9 How do I... Use the Maintenance Wizard utility?

COMPLEXITY
INTERMEDIATE

Problem

I want to be able to schedule the use of some of the more time-intensive maintenance utilities, such as Disk Defragmenter, ScanDisk, Compression Agent, and so on, as to when these utilities should automatically start. Is this even possible, and if so, how do I do it?

Technique

Windows 98 provides the Maintenance Wizard utility for you to perform this task. The executable file for this is the TUNEUP.EXE, which is available for use directly from the Windows 98 Run command box or can be found as a menu item. This wizard contains several of the more powerful disk performance-improving applications:

- Compression Agent (for use only with DriveSpace3 Drives)
- Delete Unnecessary Files
- Disk CleanUp
- Disk Defragmenter (Speed-Up Programs)
- ScanDisk

If you have installed the Plus! package for Windows 98, you will have an additional component inside your version of the Maintenance Wizard:

- Clean-Up Your Start Menu (this includes finding broken links)

These tools can be scheduled individually by you without the use of the Maintenance Wizard utility, but this wizard definitely makes things much easier. To use the wizard, complete the following steps.

CHAPTER 7
SYSTEM RESOURCE MANAGEMENT

Steps

1. Using the menu tree from the Start button, you can find the Maintenance Wizard utility inside the System Tools menu option, which is part of the Accessories menu selection. When you click the Maintenance Wizard menu selection, its initial setup screen appears, as shown in Figure 7.28.

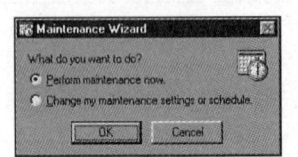

Figure 7.28 Setting the schedule for the Maintenance Wizard.

2. You can also gain quick access to this utility by accessing the Windows 98 Run command box and entering the command `TuneUp.exe`. (This is not case-sensitive, and you do not necessarily need the `.exe` portion of the command.)

3. If you have already configured the Maintenance Wizard utility at least once, you can quickly execute all the tasks within this wizard in order by using the following command: `TuneUp /AutoRun`. (Again, this is not case-sensitive.)

4. When the Maintenance Wizard window appears, you can either click the top radio button to perform your maintenance configuration immediately, or click the bottom radio button to change the settings to your wizard configurations. The default setting is to perform the maintenance now, so click the radio button next to the Change my maintenance settings or schedule option. Then click OK to start the process, (regardless of the option you chose), as shown in Figure 7.29.

5. If you selected the Perform maintenance now radio button in the previous step, the Maintenance Wizard utility would begin processing the various tasks instead of going to the screen shown in Figure 7.29.

6. After arriving at this next screen in the wizard process, you can select an Express setup configuration (this is the default) or use the Custom option. For the purposes of this example select the Custom—Select each maintenance setting myself radio button option by clicking on it. When you have made your selection, click Next> to continue, as shown in Figure 7.30.

7.9
USE THE MAINTENANCE WIZARD UTILITY

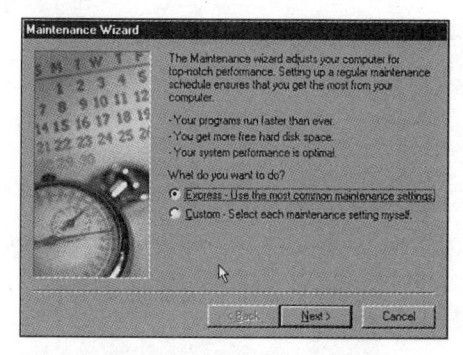

Figure 7.29 Choosing between the Express or Custom Maintenance Wizard setup process.

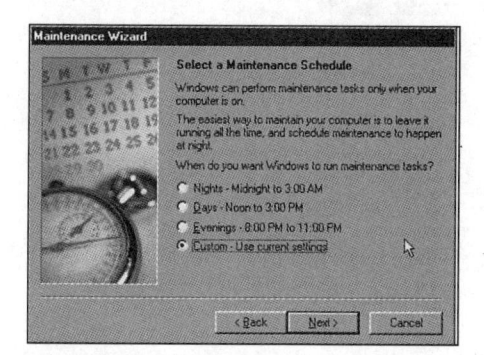

Figure 7.30 Selecting a maintenance schedule.

7. Choose a region of time to run these disk maintenance tasks, or if you have been inside this screen at least once previously, you might keep your timing by clicking the Custom œ Use current settings radio button option. Make your selection, and then click Next> to continue, as shown in Figure 7.31.

8. The next screen that appears in the example only shows up if you have the Microsoft Windows 98 Plus! package installed on your computer. Otherwise, this screen does not appear as an option for you.

9. The purpose of the Start Menu Cleanup utility is to remove any dead links (or shortcuts) that might exist on any of your menus, as well as on your Windows 98 desktop. This is a very useful utility, one that almost justifies the $49 cost of the Microsoft Windows 98 Plus! package. Make your selections and any changes to the scheduling of this tool by using the Reschedule... or Settings... buttons, and then click the Next> button to continue, as shown in Figure 7.32.

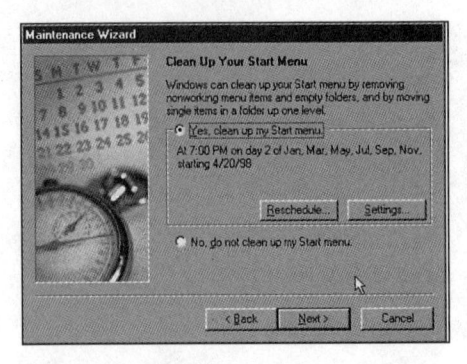

Figure 7.31 Deciding whether to clean up your Windows 98 Start menu.

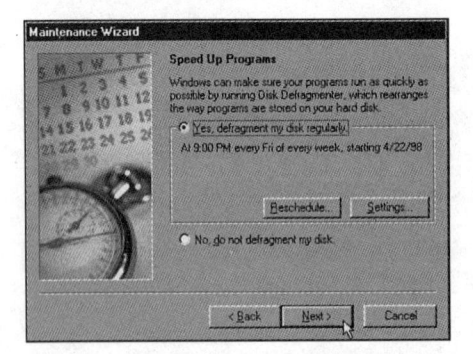

Figure 7.32 Deciding whether to speed up your Windows 98 programs.

10. The Speed Up Programs section appears. This is where you define the settings for the Disk Defragmenter application. Make your selections and any changes to the scheduling of this tool by using either the Reschedule… or Settings… buttons, and then click once the Next> button to continue, as shown in Figure 7.33.

11. The ScanDisk section appears. This is where you define the settings for the ScanDisk application. Make your selections and any changes to the scheduling of this tool by using the Reschedule… or Settings… buttons, and then click once Next> to continue, as shown in Figure 7.34.

7.9
USE THE MAINTENANCE WIZARD UTILITY

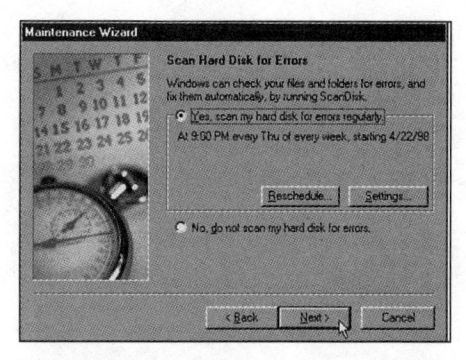

Figure 7.33 Deciding whether to scan your hard disk drive for errors.

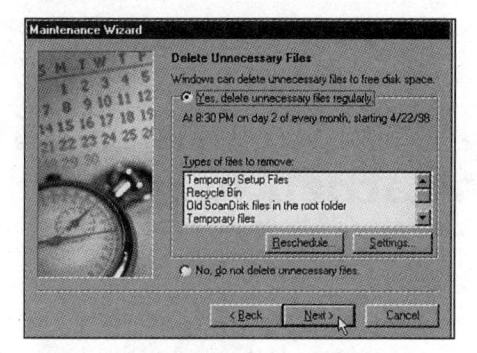

Figure 7.34 Deciding whether to delete unnecessary files on your hard drive.

12. The Delete Unnecessary Files section appears. This is where you define the settings for the Disk CleanUp application. Make your selections and any changes to the scheduling of this tool by using the Reschedule... or Settings... buttons, and then click Next> to continue, as shown in Figure 7.35.

13. The final screen of the Maintenance Wizard appears. This is where you review your previous settings, and then end the wizard. If you place a check mark in the box at the bottom of this screen, all of the scheduled tasks run for the first time as soon as you click the Finish button. Decide whether you want to run these selections then click Finish to complete the Maintenance Wizard process.

14. The Maintenance Wizard utility closes completely if you do not tell it to run your scheduled tasks. Otherwise, it begins executing all the scheduled tasks in order; a process that could easily take several hours to complete.

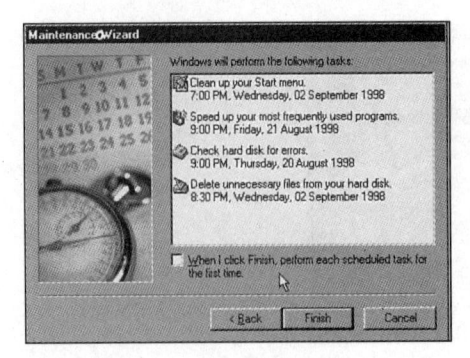

Figure 7.35 Reviewing the Maintenance Wizard settings.

COMPLEXITY
INTERMEDIATE

7.10 How do I...
Monitor my computer to see if others are attached to it?

Problem

I have shared my hard drive with others in my workgroup, and I want to know who is attached to my PC at various times. Is there a way that I can monitor the other computers that might be signed on to my PC?

Technique

The Net Watcher utility does not install automatically with the typical Windows 98 installation, so you must use the steps outlined earlier in this chapter to install it. The Net Watcher utility is also very useful for creating, adding, or deleting shared resources on remote computers. It also manages your own computer's resources in a networked environment. To use this utility you must have the File and Printer Sharing option enabled on your computer and have at least the Microsoft Networking Client installed. Follow the next set of steps carefully to determine how you can use this tool for monitoring networking activity on and with your PC.

Steps

1. Using the menu tree from the Start button, find the Net Watcher utility inside the System Tools menu option, which is part of the Accessories menu selection (provided, of course, that you have already installed it).

2. You can also gain quick access to this utility by accessing the Windows 98 Run command box and entering the command `NetWatch.exe` (this is not case-sensitive, and you do not necessarily need the `.exe` portion of the command).

3. After you click the Net Watcher menu selection or use its `Run` command, the initial setup screen appears, as shown in Figure 7.36.

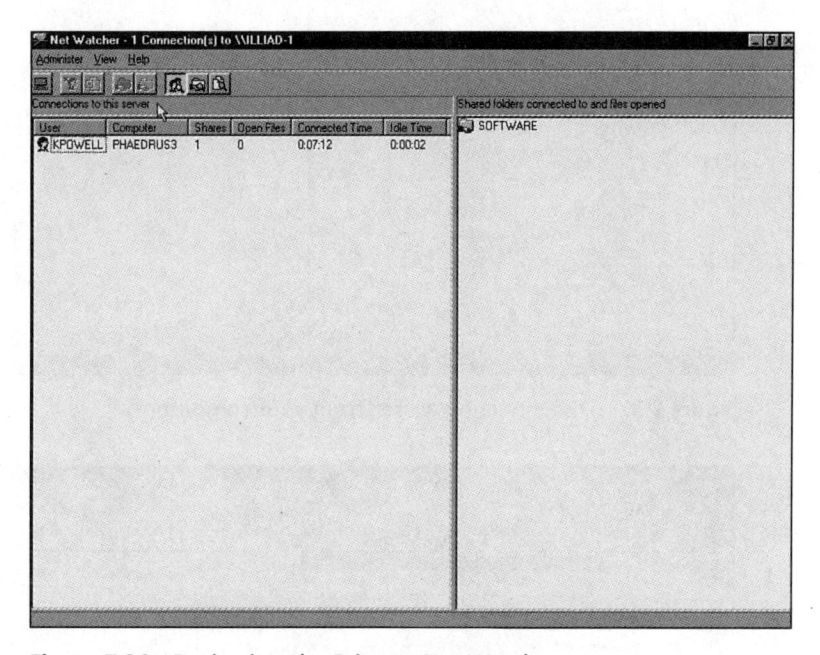

Figure 7.36 Reviewing the Primary Net Watcher screen.

4. You are shown a complete listing of all the computers and users presently connected to your PC. If you want to force someone off your system, click once on that person's computer User name, and then click the Disconnect User icon, as shown in Figure 7.37.

5. Through the use of the Administer menu option, coupled with the Select Server... menu selection, you can remotely administer other computers on your network. Of course, you must already possess the administrative rights to do this and the PC you want to administer must also be configured to accept remote administration.

6. If you click the View menu option, you can quickly get a listing of all the shares that are created on your computer, as shown in Figure 7.38.

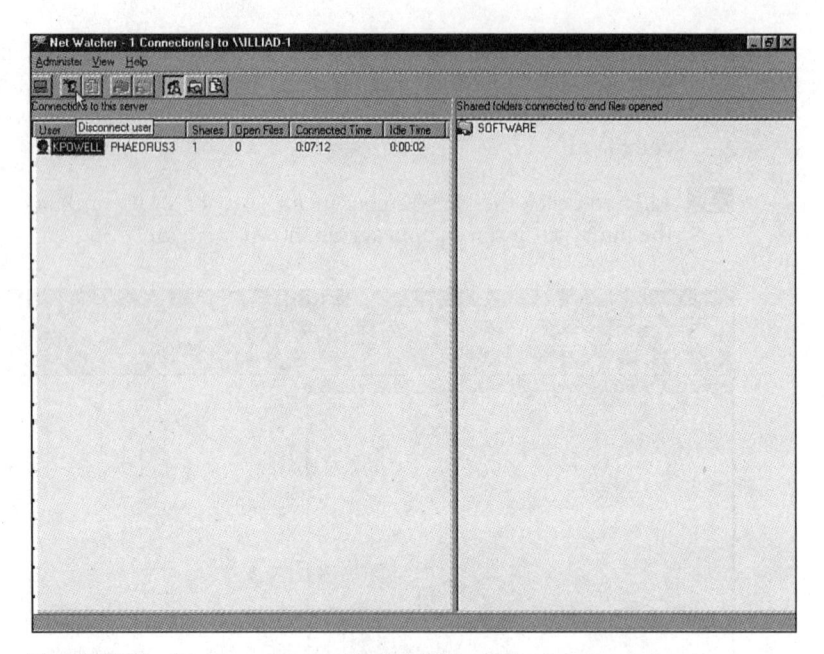

Figure 7.37 Disconnecting a user from your computer.

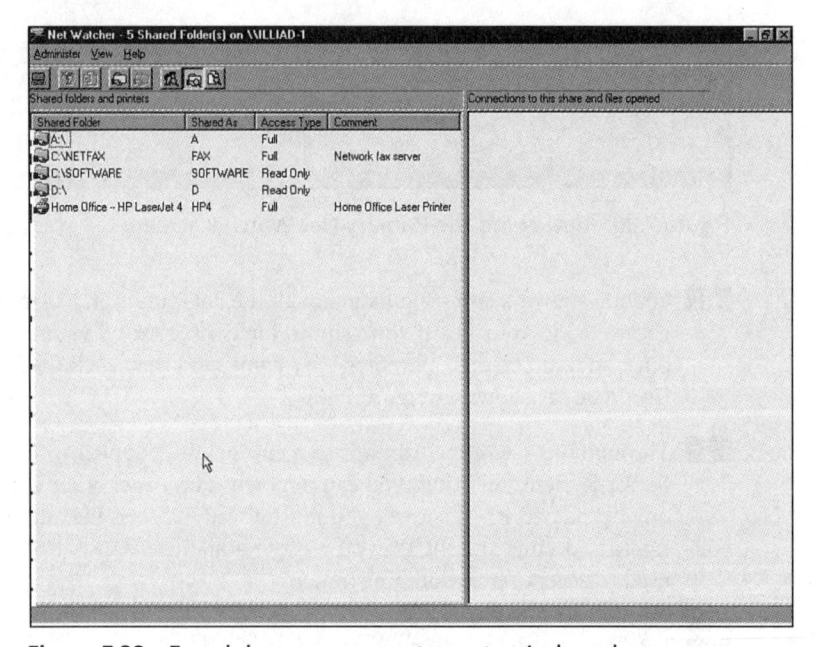

Figure 7.38 Examining your computer system's shared resources.

MONITOR MY COMPUTER TO SEE IF OTHERS ARE ATTACHED TO IT

7. To stop sharing any of these areas, highlight the one you want to stop by clicking it, and then click the Stop Sharing button on the menu bar (or use the Administer menu option and click the Stop Sharing Folder menu selection). This causes a Net Watcher message box to appear, which prompts you to click Yes, which stops the sharing process for that particular share, or click to No, which cancels this process.

8. If you click the Yes button, the share will stop and disappear instantly from this screen.

9. If you click the View menu option, and then click the by Open Files menu selection, you can quickly get a listing of all the files that are in use on your computer, as shown in Figure 7.39.

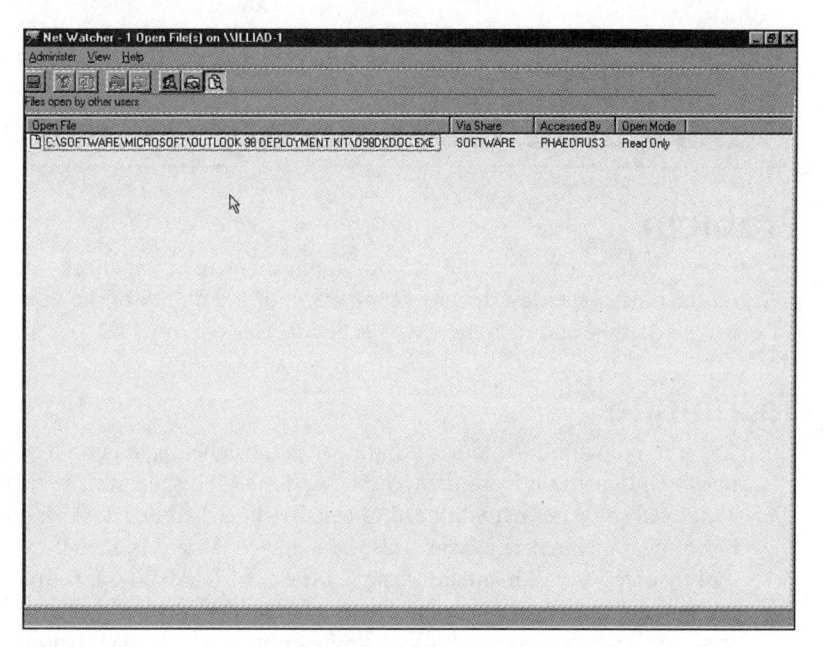

Figure 7.39 Reviewing the files in use by others.

10. To quickly close any file, highlight the file you want to stop the use of by clicking it once. Then click the Close File button on the menu bar (or use the Administer menu option and click the Close File menu selection). This causes a Net Watcher message box to appear, which prompts you to click Yes, which closes the file in question, or to click No, which cancels this process.

11. If you click Yes, the file closes and disappears instantly from the screen.

> **NOTE**
>
> If you close a file in this manner, it is very possible that you might slightly corrupt or even destroy the file you are attempting to limit access to. It is wiser to secure your files through Windows 98 sharing security, rather than precariously halting file usage in this manner.

12. When you have finished using this utility you should close it rather than leave it running in the background. Like all Windows 98 system tools, the Net Watcher consumes precious system resources and unnecessarily bogs down your system if left open in an unmonitored mode.

COMPLEXITY
BEGINNER

7.11 How do I... Schedule tasks on my computer?

Problem

I want to be able to schedule various applications to automatically run, based on the time of the day, the day of the week, or the month of the year. Is there a way to do this, and if so, how do I schedule tasks on my PC?

Technique

The is a tool within Windows 98 known as the Scheduled Tasks tool. This tool installs automatically with the typical Windows 98 installation, so there is no additional software that you need to install. The Scheduled Tasks is useful for performing maintenance tasks (the Maintenance Wizard is actually a scheduling tool that creates and maintains tasks for the Scheduled Tasks), running a custom applications that perhaps polls a home office legacy database, and so forth. Its possible uses are endless, limited only by your imagination. Follow the next set of steps carefully to determine how you can use this tool for the scheduling of jobs on and for your computer.

Steps

1. If you look closely at the Windows 98 taskbar in the System Tray area, you will see the icon for the Scheduled Tasks, as shown in Figure 7.40.

7.11
SCHEDULE TASKS ON MY COMPUTER

Figure 7.40
Finding the Scheduled Tasks icon on the Windows 98 taskbar.

2. The Scheduled Tasks icon closely resembles the old Windows 3.x Program Manager window with a time clock in front of it and a small number 98 in the upper-left corner. Double-click this icon to open the full Scheduled Tasks screen, as shown in Figure 7.41.

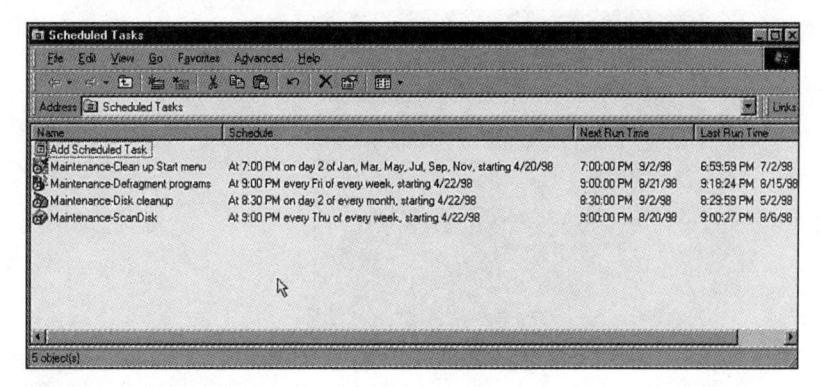

Figure 7.41 Examining the newly opened Scheduled Tasks window.

3. If you have ever run the Windows 98 Maintenance Wizard utility, your Scheduled Tasks screen probably contains four tasks in it already. These tasks are the ones that the Maintenance Wizard utility creates and maintains automatically for you. However, you can change any of these within this screen and the Maintenance Wizard utility will recognize those changes.

4. Assume that you want to create a new task to be run every Monday morning. To do this, double-click the Add Schedule Task icon, found in at the top of the list, as shown in Figure 7.42.

5. The first screen of the Scheduled Task Wizard appears. This first screen is informational only, and after you have read it, you should click the Next> button to continue the wizard process, as shown in Figure 7.43.

CHAPTER 7
SYSTEM RESOURCE MANAGEMENT

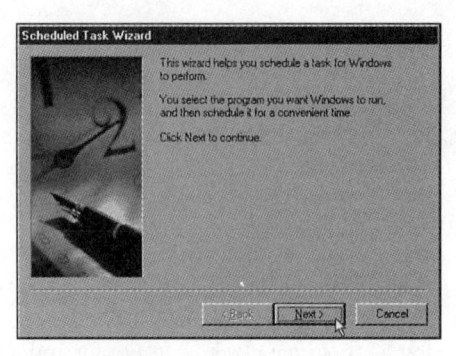

Figure 7.42 Starting the Scheduled Tasks Wizard.

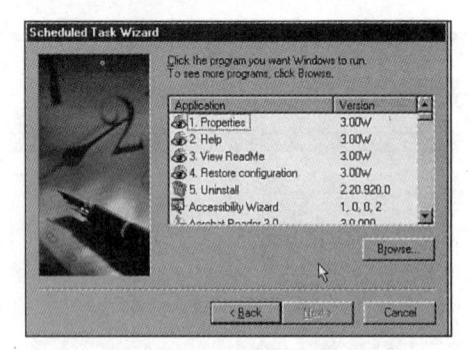

Figure 7.43 Picking a Windows 98 task to schedule.

> **NOTE**
> It will probably take a few minutes to generate this next screen because the computer is quickly determining what all the possible applications are that you might want to add to the Scheduled Tasks area. Be patient and the window eventually appears.

6. Select any program in this listing by clicking it once to highlight it. If the application you want to use is not present in this listing, you may add one by clicking the Browse... button and following the standard Windows Explorer-type prompts. (after selecting one, you return to this point in the wizard). When you have made your selection, click Next> to continue the wizard process, as shown in Figure 7.44.

7. If it is Monday, then it must be time to start the week playing a game of Spider Solitaire (part of the Windows 98 Plus! package). Click the radio button next to the runtime option for this task (in this case, the Weekly option is selected), and then click the Next> button once to continue the wizard process, as shown in Figure 7.45.

7.11
SCHEDULE TASKS ON MY COMPUTER

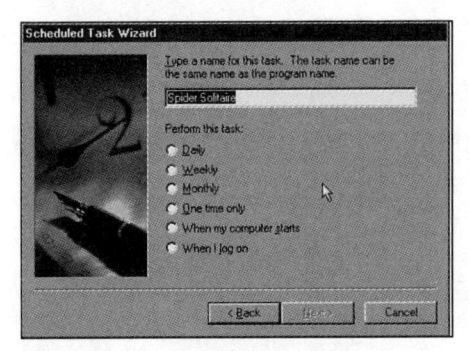

Figure 7.44 Naming the new task and picking the task's runtime.

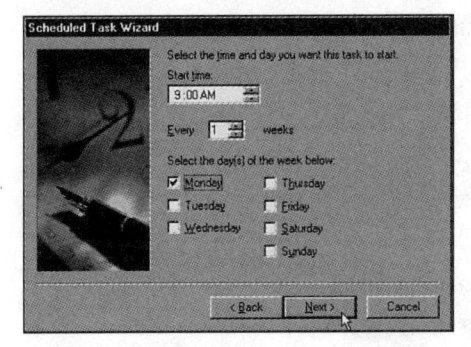

Figure 7.45 Choosing the detailed runtime options.

8. The screen that appears is the one that you use to detail the time and date frequency for your program's execution. The Start Time and Day of the Week are obvious settings, but the Every *xx* Weeks setting can be confusing. What this option means is that if you put a 1 in the box, this program will run every week. However, if you place a 3 in the box, this application will execute only every third week (quite an ingenious parameter setting capability). When you have made your selections, click Next> to continue the wizard process as shown in Figure 7.46.

9. Your new program task is configured. By default, the option for opening the Advanced Properties settings screen is disabled (for example, there is no x in the box). If you click Finish with this box blank, the wizard ends and you see your newly created task in the Scheduled Tasks window. However, if you click the Open advanced properties for this task when I click Finish option box, and then click Finish, you are taken directly to the Task tab of the Spider Solitaire properties window (or whatever program you set up), as shown in Figure 7.47.

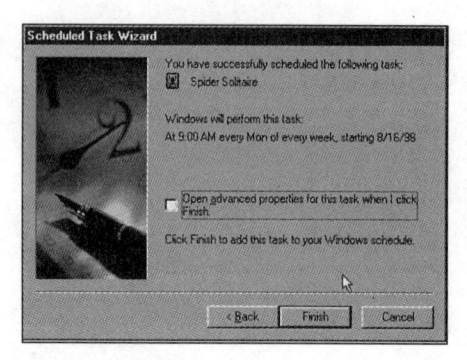

Figure 7.46 The Scheduled Task Wizard completion screen.

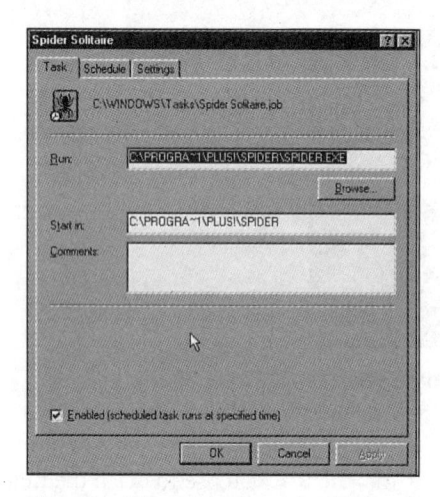

Figure 7.47 Reviewing the Task tab of the Advanced Properties screen.

10. The Task tab will be the first screen you see when you enter the Advanced Properties section. The only real option on this screen is at the bottom named Enabled. If you uncheck this box then this scheduled task will be disabled and will not operate as you originally planned. After you have made your selections, if any, click the Schedule tab to continue as shown in Figure 7.48.

11. This screen looks like the one you originally completed with two exceptions: an option box for showing multiple schedules for this task, and an Advanced... button that permits you to create those multiple schedules. The Advanced... button is easy to configure because you are simply selecting times and dates to run your scheduled task. After you make your selections or changes, if any, click once the Settings tab to continue as shown in Figure 7.49.

7.11
SCHEDULE TASKS ON MY COMPUTER

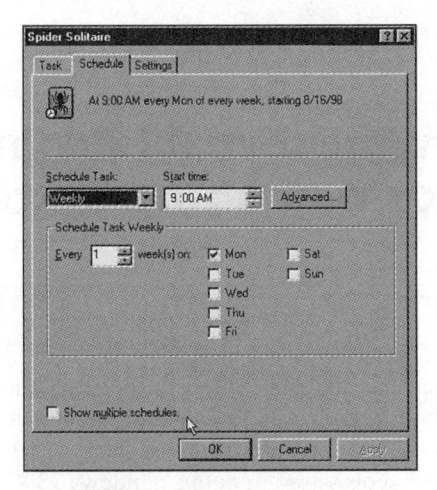

Figure 7.48 Deciding which options to change on the Schedule tab.

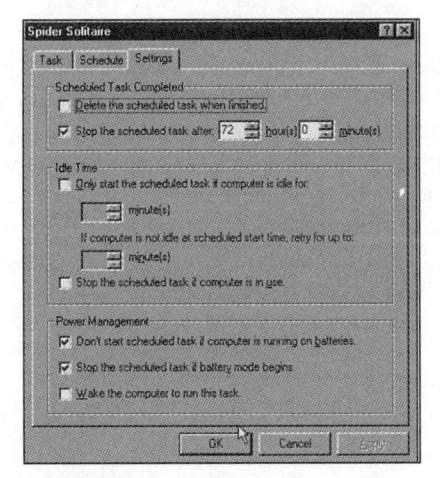

Figure 7.49 Deciding which options to change on the Settings tab.

12. The only new feature on this screen, compared to its Windows 95 counterpart, is the capability to "wake" your computer (automatically start it up or release it from suspend mode) in order to run this scheduled task. After you make your selections or changes, if any, click OK once to close the advanced options section of the wizard.

13. You now see your newly created scheduled task in the main Scheduled Tasks screen.

COMPLEXITY
INTERMEDIATE

7.12 How do I...
Know if the Windows 98 Resource Kit is good for managing system resources?

Problem

I keep seeing ads, both electronically and via snail mail, telling me that I should purchase a copy of the Microsoft Windows 98 Resource Kit because it adds a great deal to my capability to manage a Windows 98 installation. Is this true, and if so, how do I know which tools to use from the Windows 98 Resource Kit to manage my computer system resources?

Technique

The Windows 98 Resource Kit does provide a number of Microsoft Management console-based tools to assist you in the management of your Windows 98 PC. Although the focus of these tools is from a network or system administrator's perspective and not from an individual user's vantage point. This means that if you have Windows 98 installed on your home PC you will probably gain little benefit from the Windows 98 Resource Kit, as it is meant more for network installations, at least when it comes to managing system resources. However, if you purchase it, there are a few things you can do to make the management of your Windows 98 system resources a little bit easier.

Steps

1. Install and Start the Windows 98 Resource Kit, and enter its main console area as shown in Figure 7.50.

2. As you can see, the kit is arranged in three ways: Tool Categories, Tools A to Z, and Online Documentation. The kit is laid-out in such a way that you will be able to quickly jump to the tool that you need to perform your tasks.

3. The better system resource management tools are found in the Configuration Tools section, the Diagnostics and Troubleshooting folder, and the Scripting Tools area. These tools include (but are not limited to) the credit, the System Configuration utility, the Dependency Walker scanner, the Kill utility, the USB Viewer, the Copy tool, the waiter tool, and the Wines tool.

7.12
KNOW IF THE RESOURCE KIT CAN MANAGE SYSTEM RESOURCES

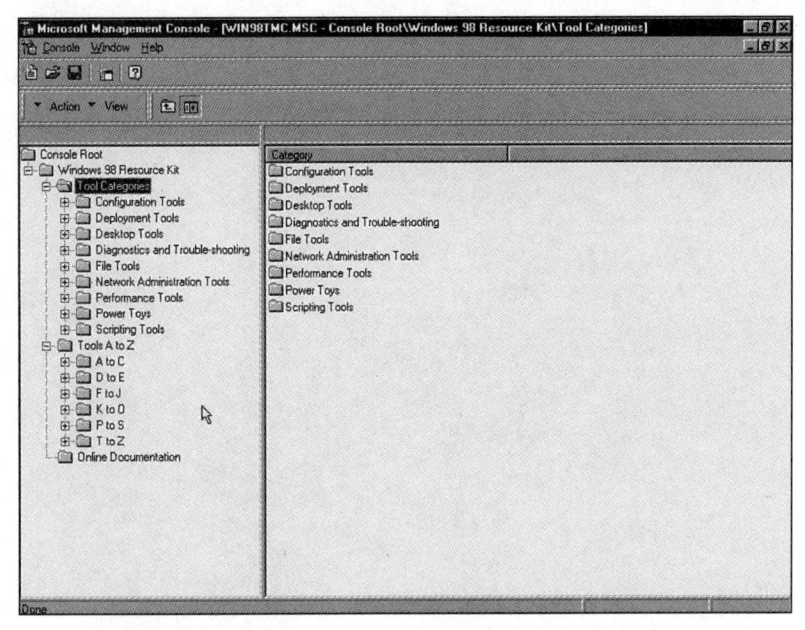

Figure 7.50 Reviewing the primary screen of the Microsoft Management Console.

4. While the previously listed tools are the ones I find most useful, you might not necessarily agree. Which list is the best remains to be seen. If you are a system administrator who must manage dozens, if not hundreds or thousands, of Windows 98 computer installations, the Windows 98 Resource Kit is a must because of the tools it contains. The book that accompanies the Resource Kit is not a bad reference source, but the CD-ROM is by far the best part.

PART III
NETWORKING ESSENTIALS

CHAPTER 8
GETTING STARTED FROM THE NETWORK

8

GETTING STARTED FROM THE NETWORK

How do I...

8.1 **Decide when to install from a network?**

8.2 **Obtain and install the Microsoft Batch utility for Windows 98?**

8.3 **Use the Microsoft Batch utility for Windows 98?**

8.4 **Use a cloning tool such as GHOST to deploy Windows 98?**

The purpose of this chapter is to assist network administrators, help desk support personnel, and others in the deployment of large numbers of Windows 98 computers simultaneously. The decision to do individual installations or use additional support tools to assist with such a deployment must first be decided. After this decision is made, the people in charge must decide what tool(s) to use to assist with mass deployments as well as to at least gain a better understanding of how to configure a mass deployment. This is something that can be started with the help of a book such as this one, but will take a lot of experimenting and a pilot installation before you truly have the correct implementation techniques defined. This chapter aids you in the initial definition of those techniques.

CHAPTER 8
GETTING STARTED FROM THE NETWORK

8.1 Decide When to Install from a Network

The focus of this How-To is to inform a system administrator what types of criteria should be considered before deciding that a network-based installation of Windows 98 is the appropriate path for their organization.

8.2 Obtain and Install the Microsoft Batch Utility for Windows 98

This section discusses how to obtain and install the Microsoft Batch utility for Windows 98, which allows you to do mass installations of Windows 98 in a more organized fashion.

8.3 Use the Microsoft Batch Utility for Windows 98?

This How-To assumes that you have already obtained and installed the Microsoft Batch utility for Windows 98, but now you need to know how to use it.

8.4 Use a Cloning Tool such as GHOST to Deploy Windows 98?

The focus of this How-To is the various operating system cloning tools available, with an in-depth look at the most popular one known as GHOST.

COMPLEXITY

INTERMEDIATE

8.1 How do I...
Decide when to install from a network?

Problem

I am the desktop manager for my organization. At what point should I have my staff stop deploying Windows 98 on an individual basis and instead use a network-based point of installation for Windows 98?

Technique

There are a few issues at stake here. Obviously, if you are going to be implementing 2,000 or 8,000 or 50,000 Windows 98 workstations, you will be performing a mass network installation (or you will go crazy attempting to do individual installs). When you get over that magic number of 1,000 desktops computers, you will need to use a complex and comprehensive deployment tool such as Microsoft's System Management Server (SMS) or XcelleNet's RemoteWare product. However, if you are a small to midsize group, with

8.1
DECIDE WHEN TO INSTALL FROM A NETWORK

50–500 PCs that need to have Windows 98 installed on them, the question of how to do this becomes very muddled. To help you through the confusion, follow these steps to determine the best method for your organization.

Steps

1. The first thing you need to do is determine the exact number of computers that you want to install the Windows 98 operating system on. This listing should contain all computers, including those that might not yet be directly connected to the company's network(s).

2. Once you have this list, you need to compile some details regarding the hardware involved. More specifically, you should compile all the following details for all computers in your organization, including

    - CPU (including vendor and chip speed)

    - Total memory (DRAM)

    - Total hard drive space

    - Available hard drive space

    - Current operating system (include both if a dual-boot PC)

    - Connected to the network? (yes or no)

    - Display monitor type, including adapter card (vendor and model)

    - Listing of other installed cards (such as sound, TV tuner, and so on)

3. Now that you know how many computers you want to install Windows 98 on, as well as a general hardware description, it is time to get a bit more detailed in the process. You must now compare this listing to Windows 98 Hardware Compatibility List to determine whether your existing PC hardware can even support a Windows 98 installation. For more details about the minimum hardware requirements for Windows 98, review Chapter 1, "Installation Tips."

4. Along with this process, you must decide whether your computers are similar enough to support a mass installation. You will find it very difficult to perform a mass installation with a cloning tool (such as GHOST) or the Windows 98 Resource Kit tool Batch for Windows 98, if all (or most) of your computers are home-grown PCs that your IS organization built from clone parts. That is, if you did not outfit your organization with brand name PCs, you might find it difficult to establish a baseline for rolling-out a mass installation of Windows 98. Not to say that a mass

installation is impossible, only that it becomes much more difficult to plan and execute.

5. Next, you must decide whether this is a Push or Pull type of installation process.

6. With Push installation, the Windows 98 install process is configured and initiated by the network system administrator(s) using a series of batch files and an automated systems tool such as Microsoft's Systems Management Server (SMS). A Pull install process means that the end user initiates the process using tools and guidelines set forth by the network system administrator(s) in your organization.

7. In real life, Pull installations work best if the end users are already using Windows 95, whereas Push deployments are better for users who have either the DOS, Windows 3.1, or Windows for Workgroups 3.11-based operating systems. Either type of installation works from either a Windows NT or a Novell NetWare server. In addition, Push deployments can be used on Windows 95 clients, and vice versa.

> **NOTE**
> Exercise extreme care when using a Push deployment of Windows 98, as too many simultaneous deployments can actually bring down your entire network. In addition, because Push deployments are initiated via a login script to some network server, you might want to limit Windows 98 installations by user group to ensure that you do not bring down the entire network inadvertently. Finally, employ some sort of version-checking in your Push scripts so that you do not override a user who has already gone through the Windows 98 installation process.

8. When you have decided on a Push versus a Pull installation process, you need to define what components of Windows 98 you want to install, along with a timetable on how long you want to take for the entire deployment process. Keep in mind that you should attempt various pilot phases of both types of deployments, just in case you discover that the process model you chose does not really work well in your organization's computing environment.

9. Next, map out a strategy for upgrading the hardware for all of the computers that do not meet at least the recommended minimum hardware requirements for a Windows 98 installation. This should include an estimation of the cost per PC, what is required, how long it will take to upgrade each PC, and what impact this will have on the end user of that computer.

10. Finally, you need to determine a strategy for upgrading those users whose computers are not yet attached to the corporate network. Should you attach them just for the sake of the Windows 98 deployment? And if so, do you then leave them attached after the deployment is complete? These types of questions must be addressed for every computer within your organization. If you decide not to put all of your group's computers on the network, how will you upgrade them (or if you upgrade them) becomes a secondary issue that should be answered as part of this project.

11. At some point during this process you might want to perform a software product evaluation of the various systems software tools that can be used for either a Push or a Pull type of Windows 98 deployment. You might want to examine tools such as XcelleNet RemoteWare, Microsoft Systems Management Server, GHOST, Batch for Windows 98, and so on. Some of these tools and their associated infrastructure hardware and software can be quite expensive. Be sure you are seeing the entire picture, not just what the tool itself costs, but also a financial and a network-impact perspective as well.

COMPLEXITY
ADVANCED

8.2 How do I...
Obtain and install the Microsoft Batch utility for Windows 98?

Problem

My organization has decided that it wants to deploy Windows 98 using the Microsoft tool known as Batch for Windows 98. Where do I get a copy of this tool, how expensive is it, and how do I install it?

Technique

The Microsoft tool known as Batch for Windows 98 comes as a part of the Windows 98 Resource Kit. This kit is published by Microsoft Press, Inc., and can be obtained from most popular bookstores as well as directly from Microsoft Corporation. The cost of the kit is $69.99 (USD), £64.99 (including V.A.T. in the U.K.), or $100.99 (Canadian suggested retail price). The tool itself is found on the CD-ROM that is included on the back cover of the Resource Kit book.

Steps

1. After you have purchased the book, place the Windows 98 Resource Kit in your CD-ROM drive and run the SETUP.EXE file. For detailed systematic instructions on installing the Resource Kit, please refer to Chapter 1 of this book.

2. Now that the kit is installed, reboot your computer to ensure that all of the new Registry settings are firmly in place. This completes the installation phase of the process.

COMPLEXITY
ADVANCED

8.3 How do I...
Use the Microsoft Batch utility for Windows 98?

Problem

I have purchased a licensed copy of the Microsoft Batch for Windows 98 tool and installed it properly. Having done all this, how do I use this utility in conjunction with my need to perform a mass deployment of Windows 98?

Technique

The Windows 98 Resource Kit tool known as the Microsoft Batch for Windows 98 tool is accessed from within the Microsoft Management Console (MMC) that is the primary access point for most of the Resource Kit's tools. You will start this utility from this point, and then all the rest of the process is performed from directly inside the Batch for Windows 98 tool itself. Keep in mind that you should be running this utility from a PC that is very similar (if not exactly the same) as the computers onto which you are going to be attempting this mass implementation of Windows 98.

Use these steps to walk through this detailed and complicated process, as you might need to redo or tweak the final result file after you have finished using this tool. It is this final .INF file that is used in the actual deployment of Windows 98, and is called directly by the Microsoft Windows 98 SETUP.EXE file. This file will be named MSBATCH.INF by the Batch for Windows 98 utility.

Steps

1. Access the Batch for Windows 98 from within the Microsoft Management Console. To access this management console, either execute the command

8.3
USE THE MICROSOFT BATCH UTILITY FOR WINDOWS 98

`C:\Win98RK\TMC\WIN98TMC.MSC` from inside the Windows 98 Run command box (assuming of course, that you installed the Resource Kit into its default directories), or access it via the Start menu structure (\Start\Programs\Windows 98 Resource Kit).

2. When you start the Microsoft Management Console, you will first see the Tip of the Day screen with a tip on how to best use the MMC. Click the Close button to continue into the Microsoft Management Console GUI, as shown in Figure 8.1.

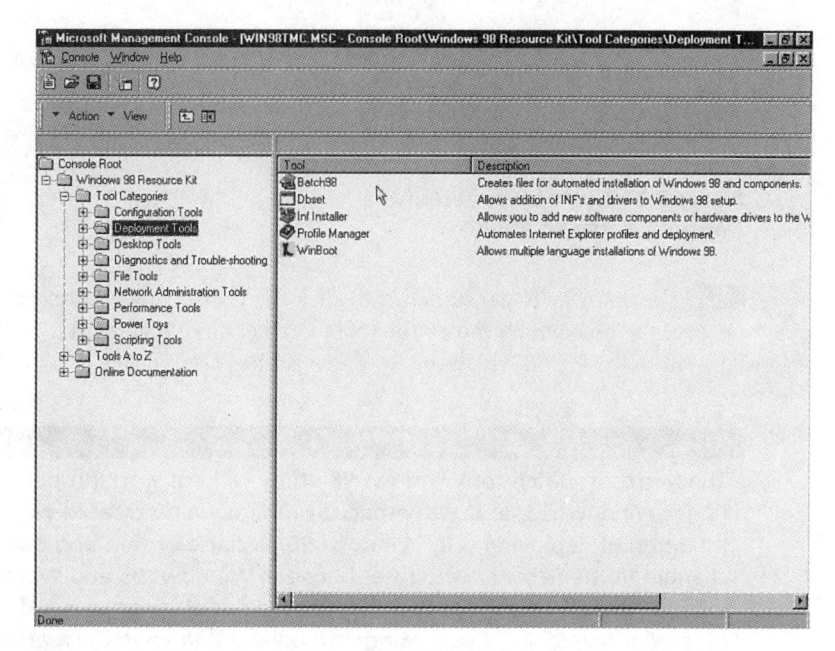

Figure 8.1 Using the Microsoft Management Console.

3. The kit is laid out by category and is in alphabetical order, making it very easy to locate the tool you are planning to use here. Click the Tool Categories folder, and then click the Deployment Tools folder to locate the tool labeled as Batch98 (the short name for the Microsoft Batch for Windows 98 utility). Double-click the Batch98 icon to reveal the next screen, as shown in Figure 8.2.

4. The Microsoft Batch 98 window is the access point to all the options within this powerful Windows 98 setup configuration tool. It is from here that you will be able to create the automated installation script(s) that are required when you want to configure either a Push or Pull deployment of the Windows 98 operating system.

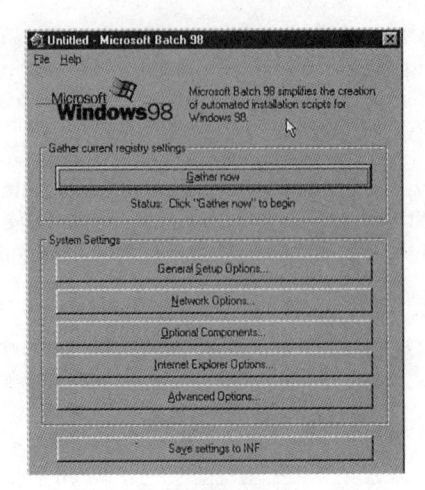

Figure 8.2 The main screen of the Microsoft Batch 98 utility.

5. The best way to get started is to click the Gather now button (at the top of the list), which causes the tool to gather all of the Registry settings from the PC on which the Resource Kit has been installed.

> **NOTE**
>
> The Microsoft Batch for Windows 98 utility will not work properly under Windows 95, as it was especially designed and created with the intention of deploying only Windows 98. Because of this, and due to changes in the Registry structures between Windows 95 and Windows 98, it is strongly recommended that you do not attempt to run this tool on a Windows 95 PC. Attempting to modify a Windows 95-created MSBATCH.INF file instead of creating the correct Windows 98 MSBATCH.INF file, in order to fake the process, is a bad idea. You will be inviting disaster if you take this approach.

6. The gathering process takes only seconds, with the result being noted on this same screen. The Status area changes from Gather Now to Complete.

7. When this process is finished, it is time to start using the next section. However, just before you start each section, it is useful to save often as you move throughout this process (just in case you experience a power outage: a frequent event if you happen to be in the Chicago area and suffer through the electrical service known as ComEd).

8. Click once on the File menu option, and then on the Save menu selection. Use the default name of MSBATCH.INF for now, anyway. Click Save to complete the save process and to close the Save window.

8.3
USE THE MICROSOFT BATCH UTILITY FOR WINDOWS 98

9. Moving out of the Gather current Registry settings and into the System Settings area, the first button you see is the General Setup Options... button. Click once on this button to reveal the next screen, as shown in Figure 8.3.

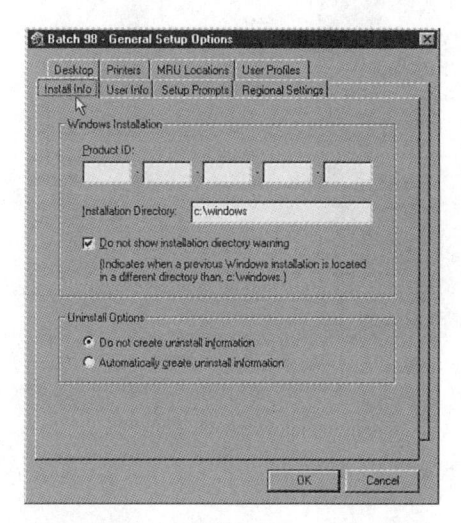

Figure 8.3 Inputting the installation information required.

10. The Batch 98 - General Setup Options screen appears, with the Install Info tab showing first. It is on this screen that you input the product ID number (this is the license number) for this Microsoft product, define the installation directory, and decide whether to use the possible Windows 98 uninstall process.

11. In the case of a mass deployment of Windows 98, you will have a product ID or license number that was provided to you by your local Microsoft sales representative. Use this number or the one that came with your Windows 98 CD-ROM. The other two options are rather self-explanatory, so make your selections as necessary. After you are finished, click once on the User Info tab to proceed as shown in Figure 8.4.

12. The user and network information content are input on this screen. Do not attempt to create variables such as %UserName% or %ComputerName%, as the Windows 98 MSBATCH.INF interprets the percent signs as being part of the real name. This results in a username: of %UserName% and a computer name: of %ComputerName%. Put in some default information now, and you will use another tool later to change this data. Fill in all the fields and click the Setup Prompts tab to continue, as shown in Figure 8.5.

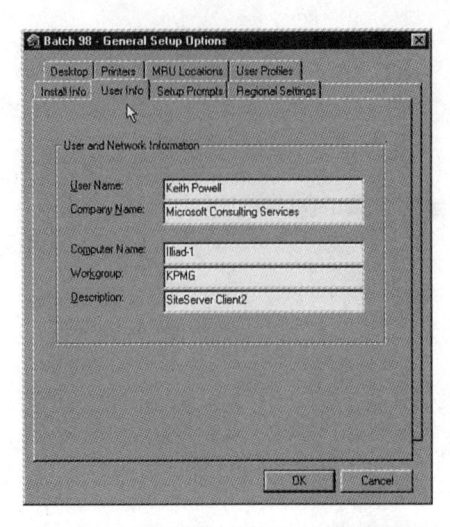

Figure 8.4 Adding the user information for your installation(s).

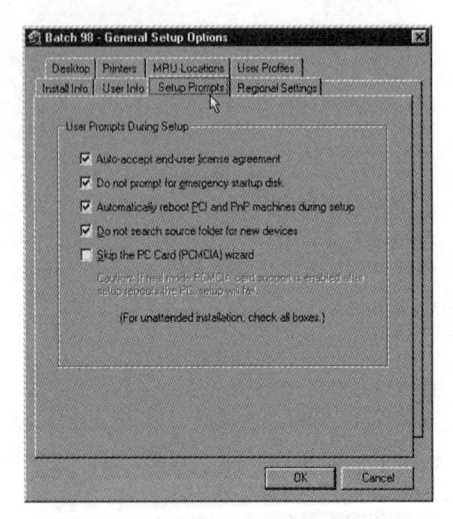

Figure 8.5 Deciding on the setup prompts.

13. On the Setup Prompts tab, place a check mark in every box so that the installation process is fully automated. To select all these boxes, click once on each box until it has a check mark present. You might want to include some sort of batch file that checks for, and disables if necessary, the presence of any real-mode PCMCIA (or PC-card) drivers in either the CONFIG.SYS or the AUTOEXEC.BAT system configuration files. Once you have made all the selections your organization requires, click the Regional Settings tab to continue, as shown in Figure 8.6.

USE THE MICROSOFT BATCH UTILITY FOR WINDOWS 98

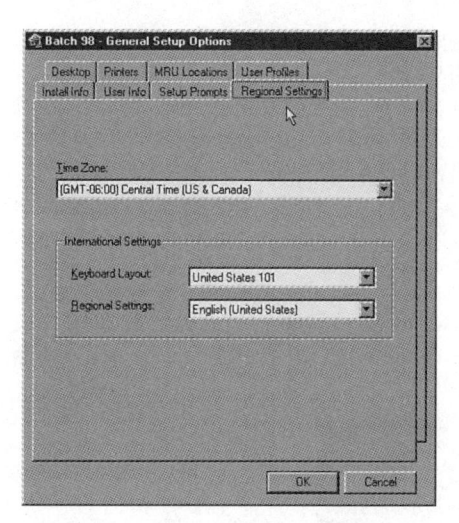

Figure 8.6 Selecting the regional settings.

14. On the Regional Settings tab, select the appropriate time zone as well as the precise language formats for the keyboard and regional settings configuration areas. If you are using a tool such as the Microsoft Systems Management Server, the automation of these settings across a multiple time-zone deployment becomes much easier. After you have made the selections your organization requires, click the Desktop tab to continue, as shown in Figure 8.7.

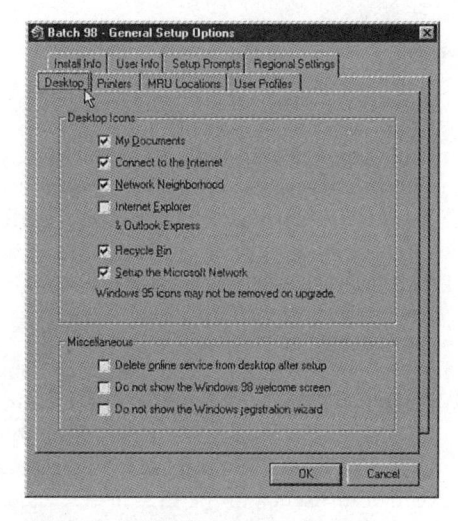

Figure 8.7 Picking your desktop icons and miscellaneous information.

15. On the Desktop tab, decide which icons you want to see deployed on every user's Windows 98 desktop environment. Additionally, you need to decide what your stance is for the online services, as well as whether you want the user community to see the Windows 98 Welcome screen and Registration Wizard. Although the MSBATCH.INF upgrade file is incapable of removing Windows 95 icons, this can be achieved using additional batch files that run elsewhere in your upgrade process; make the appropriate deletions via Windows 98 Registry hacks.

16. Make your selections according to your Windows 98 deployment plan, and then click on the Printers tab to continue, as shown in Figure 8.8.

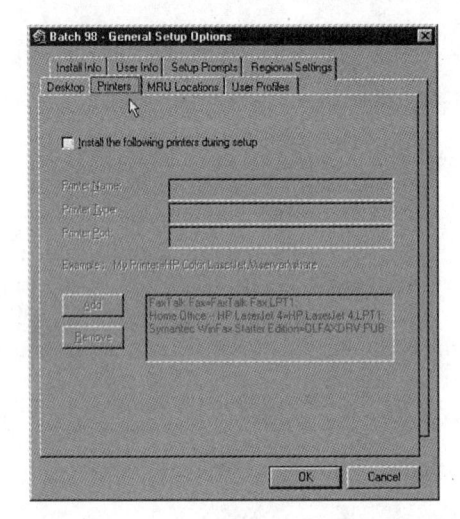

Figure 8.8 Making the printer selections.

17. On the Printers tab you are provided with the opportunity to create a default printer configuration for each new Windows 98 user. It is suggested that you pick at least one printer for every user, but this is up to you. Make your choices according to your organization's Windows 98 deployment plan, and then click the MRU Locations tab to continue as shown in Figure 8.9.

18. MRU literally means *most recently used path*, and refers to the physical path location to the Windows 98 setup configuration files. On this tab it is recommended that you pick one central MRU location for your user community to easily find the Windows 98 CAB files. This generally improves relations between your users and the IS staff and lessens the number of Windows 98-related calls to the local help desk. After you have configured the MRUs for your organization, click the User Profiles tab to continue, as shown in Figure 8.10.

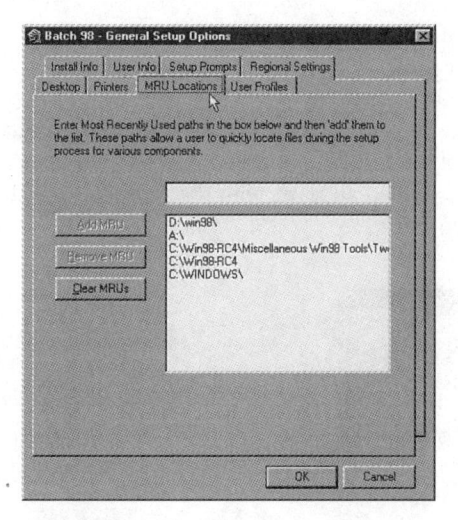

8.3
USE THE MICROSOFT BATCH UTILITY FOR WINDOWS 98

Figure 8.9 Setting the most recently used path(s).

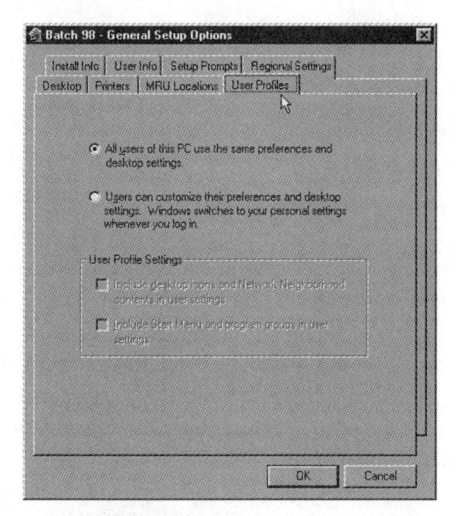

Figure 8.10 Customizing user profile settings.

19. On the User Profiles tab you are prompted to choose the base settings for each user. What this means is that from this screen you can decide to have each Windows 98 PC automatically support different profiles for each user who logs on to that particular computer. The use of user profiles makes it much easier to support multiple users who all share the same computer. Review the section on configuring multiple users in Chapter 5, "Quintessential Hardware Configurations," for further details.

20. Click OK to accept all the changes that you have made and to return to the primary Batch 98 screen.

21. From this screen, you need to click the Network Options... button to enter the next stage of the building of the MSBATCH.INF file. The Batch 98 - Network Options screen appears, with the Protocols tab showing first, as shown in Figure 8.11.

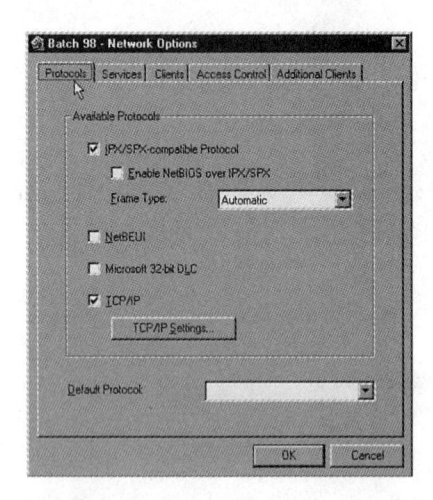

Figure 8.11 Determining network options.

22. On this screen you are able to configure the networking protocols for your new Windows 98 installations. Three well-known choices are listed (IPX/SPX-compatible Protocol, Microsoft NetBEUI, and the Microsoft TCP/IP stack) as well as one that most people might not recognize, the Microsoft 32-bit DLC protocol, which is typically used for mainframe connectivity. Make your choices as required by your organization's network, paying close attention to the IPX/SPX Frame Type (examine that drop-down list box closely) and the TCP/IP Settings... button. Click the TCP/IP Settings... button to reveal the Batch 98 – TCP/IP Options screen shown in Figure 8.12.

23. The purpose of the DNS Configuration tab is to identify the domain name server information for your Windows 98 deployment. If you use DNS then the host and domain names are required fields. The DNS server and domain suffix search orders are optional, but probably desired in your networking environment.

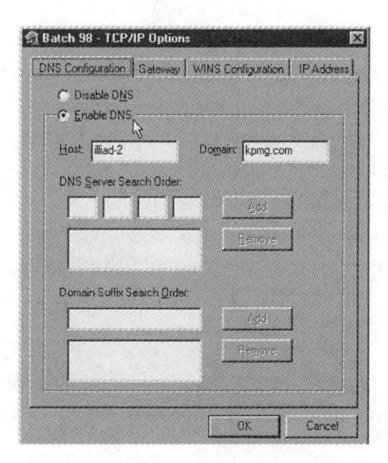

8.3
USE THE MICROSOFT BATCH UTILITY FOR WINDOWS 98

Figure 8.12 Configuring the TCP/IP settings.

> **NOTE**
>
> A DNS server is different from a Windows NT Server's domain name; if you do not understand the difference, please refer to one of the many books on this subject. A favorite of mine is the Sams Publishing, Inc.'s TCP/IP Unleashed, which was published in 1996, and authored by Timothy Parker, et al. The chapter that you will probably want to spend some time with is Chapter 33, "Implementing DNS," (by Salim Douba).

24. After you have made your selections here, click once on the Gateway tab to continue as shown in Figure 8.13.

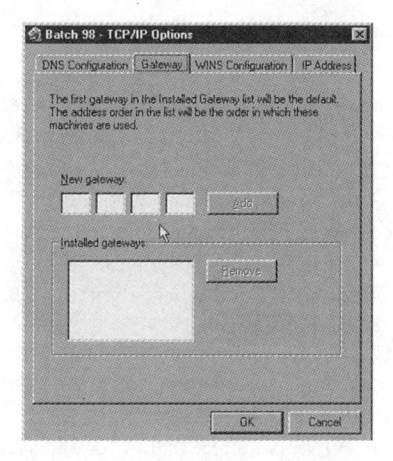

Figure 8.13 Adding a TCP/IP gateway.

25. The TCP/IP Gateway screen appears where you need to enter the default gateway. You might not use a gateway, or you might enter several. The choice is yours, but you might want to consider chatting with your organization's network administrators in order to determine the real need for a gateway address. The address is entered in typical TCP/IP address formatting, just without the dots (that is, the address 130.130.5.1 would be shown here as 130 130 5 1). In layman's terms, a *gateway address* is usually the address to a physical hardware router (although it can be a software-based router, and can be done through Windows NT Server 4.0+).

26. After you make your selections and input any data, click the WINS Configuration tab to continue, as shown in Figure 8.14.

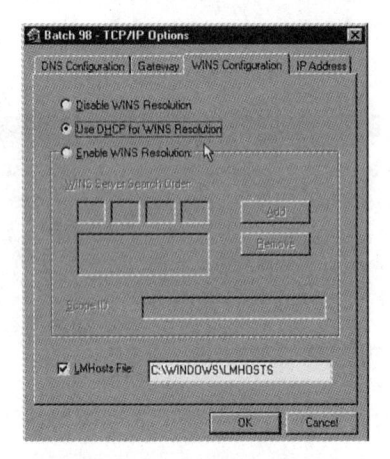

Figure 8.14 Deciding on a WINS configuration.

27. The term *WINS* literally means *Windows Internet Naming Service*, and is a Microsoft-specific technology (read: a new Microsoft Standard). WINS was supposed to be Microsoft's answer to DNS, but DNS has prevailed in the world of TCP/IP networking standards. The purpose of WINS is to resolve NetBIOS names to dynamic TCP/IP addresses; remember that DNS is a static technology, whereas WINS is a dynamic technology (of course, this all changes in Windows NT 5.0 where dynamic DNS is introduced, but that is a topic for another day).

28. If your Windows 98 PCs are going to be rolled-out into a network that involves the use of many Windows NT Servers and very little, if any Novell NetWare servers, then WINS is a great technology for you. Otherwise, you might want to carefully consider your options; perhaps by reading a bit on both WINS and DNS in the book mentioned previously, *TCP/IP Unleashed*.

8.3
USE THE MICROSOFT BATCH UTILITY FOR WINDOWS 98

29. After you make your selections and input any data, click the IP Address tab to continue to the screen shown in Figure 8.15.

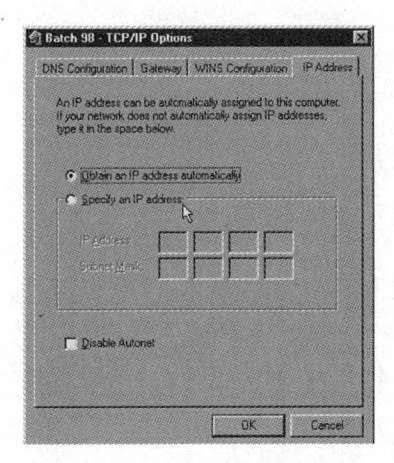

Figure 8.15 The IP Address tab for TCP/IP Options.

30. This screen works just like the WINS and Gateway tabs in that you need to decide what you want to do, and then type in an IP address (and the subnet mask) in the standard addressing format, excluding the dots, of course.

31. The check box at the bottom of this screen allows you to disable the use of Autonet. This option is only available when using DHCP to obtain an IP address automatically, because when you manually assign IP addresses this box is grayed out. Click this box to place a check mark in it and disable the Autonet feature.

32. If your network uses routers or if the network is connected to the Internet without the use of a proxy server, you will probably want to disable the Autonet feature (which gives the Windows 98 PC the capability to automatically assign itself a private IP address). Keep in mind that computers using private IP addressing are not capable of communicating with computers on other subnets, as well as those PCs that do not have private IP addressing enabled.

33. Click OK to return to the general Batch 98 – Network Options screen. Click the Services tab to reveal that screen, as shown in Figure 8.16.

34. The Services tab is used to configure those networking services that you have deemed necessary for your Windows 98 computing environment. If you do not plan to use any of the peer-to-peer networking features of

Windows 98, it is strongly encouraged that you disable the File and Printer Sharing services by clicking the top radio button (of the same name).

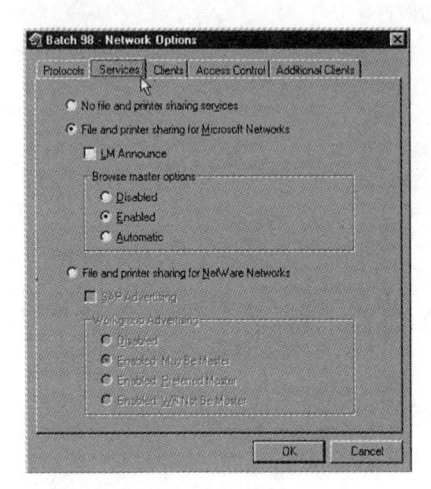

Figure 8.16 Deciding which network services to use.

35. However, if you do decide to enable the File and printer sharing services by clicking once on the second radio button (from the top), then several additional options are made available to you. The box labeled LM Announce means that if enabled, it broadcasts LAN Manager announcements to the network (this is for backward compatibility with older non–32-bit Windows operating systems). The Browse master options are straightforward. Select the one you want by clicking the radio button next to your choice.

36. Note that you cannot enable the File and printer sharing services for both Microsoft networks and Novell networks simultaneously. This is an either-or option. Make your selection by clicking the radio button next to the appropriate network type. When you have made your selections on this screen, click the Clients tab to reveal that screen, as shown in Figure 8.17.

37. The options found on the Clients tab might go hand-in-hand with those found on the Services tab. That is, you will want to invoke the client for Microsoft networks if you enable File and printer sharing services, because having the file and print sharing services enabled without the client enabled does not really work.

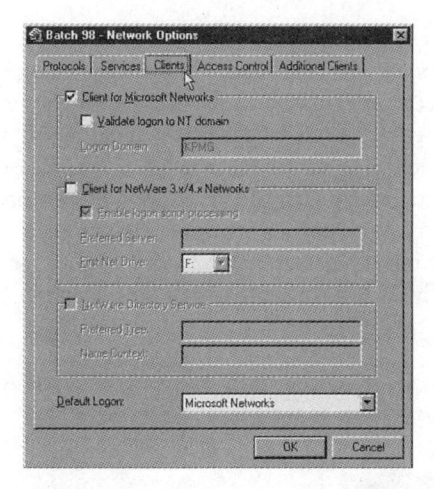

8.3
USE THE MICROSOFT BATCH UTILITY FOR WINDOWS 98

Figure 8.17 Sharing printers and files for your PC.

38. You are able to install the networking client software for both Novell and Microsoft clients simultaneously. Also, using the drop-down list box at the bottom of the screen, you can automatically define which network type the Windows 98 user will authenticate to first.

39. Make your selections by clicking the check boxes next to the appropriate network client type, and then typing in the necessary information. After you make your selections onscreen, click the Access Control tab to reveal that screen, as shown in Figure 8.18.

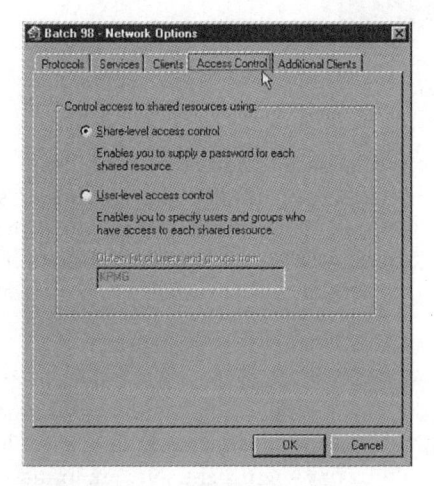

Figure 8.18 Picking an access control method.

40. The purpose of the Access Control tab is to define precisely how access can be made to the Windows 98 computers that you are going to be deploying. The two selections cannot both be chosen, so you need to select one of them. *Share-level access* means that a Windows 98 user assigns a password to each share that he or she creates on his or her computer. *User-level access* means that the Windows 98 users are using predefined groups (from a Windows NT computer), who then have access to each shared resource on that person's Windows 98 PC. If file sharing is not enabled then it really does not matter which type is chosen, as it becomes a meaningless option.

41. When you have made your selections on this screen, click the Additional Clients tab to reveal that screen, as shown in Figure 8.19.

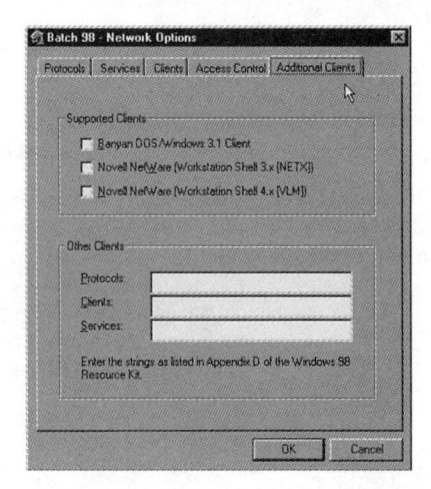

Figure 8.19 Deciding whether to add additional client software.

42. The Additional Clients screen is used to add additional client software (other than the standard Microsoft or Novell client networking software) to this Windows 98 deployment. These clients include the Banyan Vines DOS/Windows 3.1 clients and the Novell NetWare Workstation Shell clients version 3.x and 4.x (NetX and VLM connectivity; these are the real mode clients).

43. You are able to specify other clients using the string values in the three boxes at the bottom of the screen (refer to the Windows 98 Resource Kit's Appendix D for the complicated string value string formats). Clients such as a UNIX NFS client could be one such client software format that your Windows 98 rollout supports.

8.3
USE THE MICROSOFT BATCH UTILITY FOR WINDOWS 98

44. After you have made your selections onscreen, click OK to save all your selections and return to the primary msbatch.inf – Microsoft Batch 98 screen.

45. From this screen, click once on the Optional Components... button to continue the MSBATCH.INF configuration process, as shown in Figure 8.20.

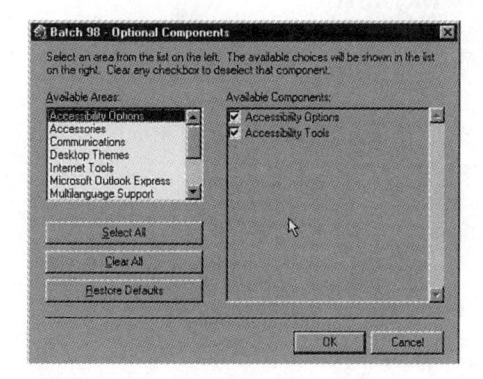

Figure 8.20 Picking additional Windows 98 components.

46. When the Batch 98 – Optional Components screen appears, you see a layout similar to the one found in the Windows 98 Add/Remove Programs Setup tab. That is, by checking (selecting) or unchecking (disabling) a series of boxes, you are defining which Windows 98 components will be installed when you perform your automated installation program. The end user is not prompted for this information; rather, you are making all the choices for them so that the installation process goes as smoothly as possible.

47. If you want a complete installation of all the possible Windows 98 features and components, click once on the Select All button. Otherwise, if you want a Typical installation of Windows 98, click once on the Restore Defaults button. The Clear All button enables you to start with a clean slate of options; you will need to click once on every single Windows 98 component that you want to have installed during your mass-deployment process.

48. As you click on a component area from the left window's scrollable listing, those options that are available for installation will automatically appear in the window to the right. Mark the components that you want by clicking once on that option's check box (which signifies that that component is to be installed during the deployment process).

49. When you have made your selections onscreen, click OK to save all your selections and return to the primary msbatch.inf – Microsoft Batch 98 screen.

50. From this screen, click the Internet Explorer Options... button to continue the msbatch.inf configuration process, as shown in Figure 8.21.

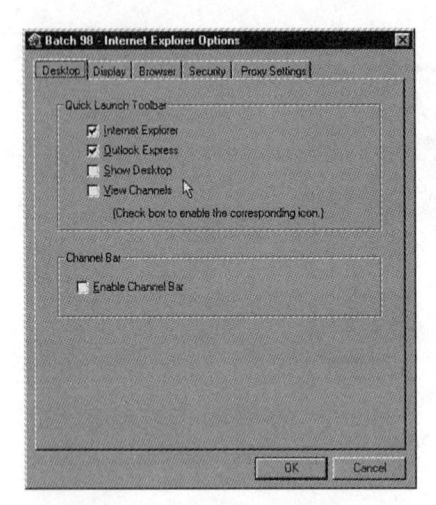

Figure 8.21 Choosing the Internet Explorer options for your Windows 98 installation.

51. The Batch 98 - Internet Explorer Options screen appears with the Desktop tab displayed. It is on this tab that you configure those items that will be placed on the Quick Launch toolbar. Additionally, you must decide whether to permit the channel bar to be shown on the Windows 98 users' desktops.

52. If you use an intranet within your organization, it is strongly encouraged that you enable the channel bar to be shown on the Windows 98 desktop. However, using another tool such as Systems Management Server or your own series of batch files, you should modify the default Windows 98 Channel Bar to reflect only your own organization's intranet locations.

53. After you have made your selections onscreen, click once the Display tab to reveal that screen, as shown in Figure 8.22.

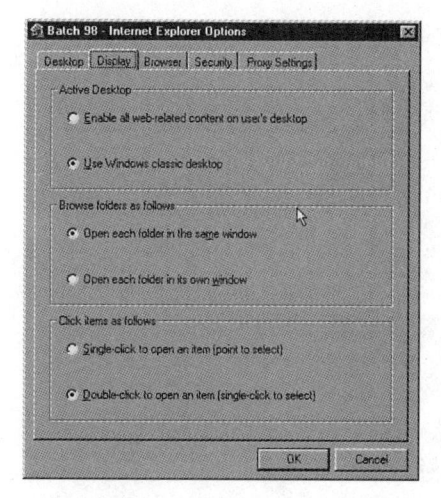

8.3 USE THE MICROSOFT BATCH UTILITY FOR WINDOWS 98

Figure 8.22 Selecting a display configuration.

54. To truly enjoy the power of Windows 98, it is recommended that you enable the Active Desktop feature. However, if you do not have a powerful network infrastructure (such as Fast Ethernet, FDDI, ATM, or Gigabit Ethernet backbones, and so on) and reliable high-end computers (90MHz Pentium PCs with 24MB of memory and sizable hard drives) for your user community, then the Active desktop could be one feature presently out of your reach for a stable networking and desktop-computing environment.

55. Make your choices as you deem necessary for your organization, and then click the Browser tab to reveal the screen shown in Figure 8.23.

56. The purpose of the Browser tab is to define precisely how access to the Windows 98 Internet Explorer browser will be made. Obviously, if your network does not support Internet connectivity, you must make the appropriate changes to this screen's settings. Perhaps you could change the home page URL to reflect your company's default intranet site, with the post setup page and the online support page URL being set to locations inside the help desk's intranet site. If you don't have an intranet or a help desk then leave these boxes blank.

57. Make your choices as are necessary and click the Security tab to reveal the screen shown in Figure 8.24.

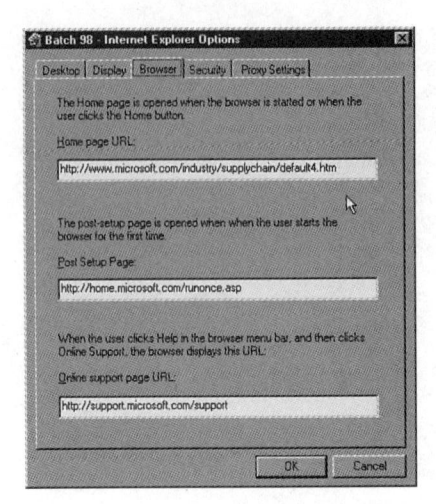

Figure 8.23 Setting organizational URLs.

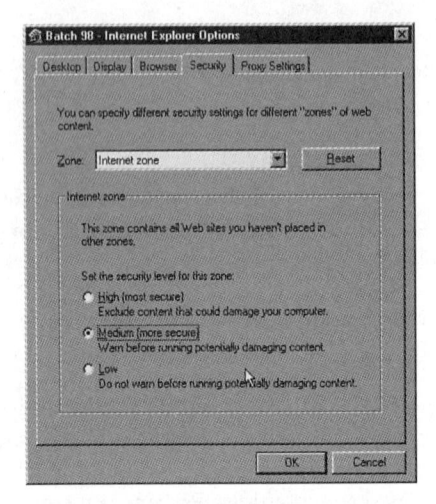

Figure 8.24 Establishing a security level for your Windows 98 PCs.

58. The purpose of the Security tab is for you to be able to establish a baseline level of security for your new Windows 98 users. These settings can be changed later by the users themselves or by your administrative support staffs through the use of the Internet Explorer Administration Kit (IEAK). The IEAK is available free of charge from Microsoft Corporation after you have filled out a small questionnaire for them.

8.3
USE THE MICROSOFT BATCH UTILITY FOR WINDOWS 98

59. There are multiple security zones that can be set, so pay close attention to this section of the screen (it is the top drop-down list box shown). Once you have made your selections, click the Proxy Settings tab to reveal the screen shown in Figure 8.25.

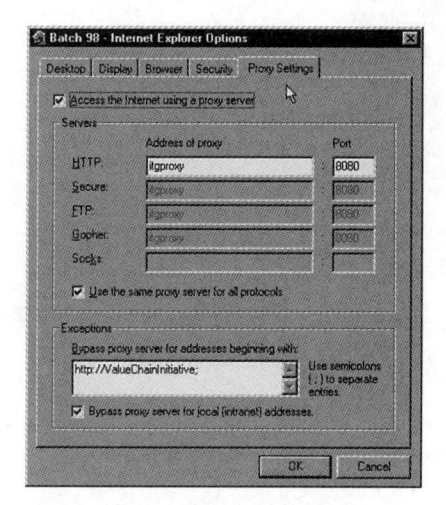

Figure 8.25 Configuring the Internet Explorer proxy settings.

60. The Proxy Settings tab reveals the connection methods your Windows 98 users use to connect to the Internet, as well as to any intranet servers you might have in place. If you use different port settings for the various Internet options (HTTP, FTP, Socks, and so on), then uncheck the Use the same proxy server for all protocols check box by clicking it once and change the port number for each item as needed. You might also select different proxy servers for each of the various Internet options.

61. Because most intranet servers do not require the use of a proxy server, you might want to check the bottom box labeled as Bypass proxy server for local (intranet) addresses. This enables this feature and the proxy server(s) specified previously will not be used when navigating to and from your organization's intranet servers.

62. After you make your selections on this screen, click OK to save your selections and return to the primary msbatch.inf – Microsoft Batch 98 screen.

63. From this screen, click the Advanced Options... button to continue the MSBATCH.INF configuration process, as shown in Figure 8.26.

CHAPTER 8
GETTING STARTED FROM THE NETWORK

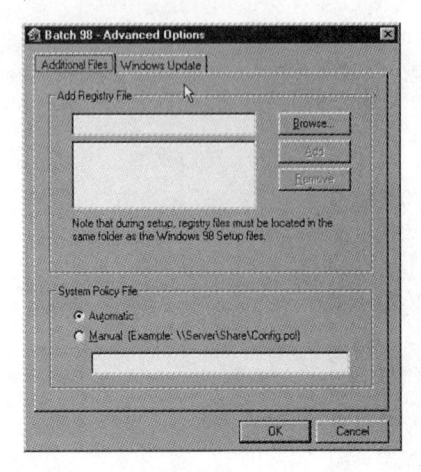

Figure 8.26 Adding additional Registry settings to your Windows 98 installation configuration.

64. When the Batch 98 – Advanced Options screen appears, you will start on the Additional Files tab.

65. This first screen is crucial if you are planning to distribute the same Registry file, or groups of Registry update files, to your general Windows 98 deployment users. Use the Browse... button to locate the precise file or set of files that you want to utilize here.

66. Additionally, if you use the services of a Windows NT Server to manage system policies on the network, you will probably want to make a Manual System Policy File selection at the bottom of this screen. Review Chapter 15, "Network Management," for more details on how to use system policies.

67. When you have made your selections click the Windows Update tab to reveal that screen, as shown in Figure 8.27.

68. The Windows Update tab reveals the default locations of the whereabouts of the administrator-defined update Web sites. This is a nice feature because it enables you as the Windows 98 network administrator to better control the user population as to where those folks can actually go to update their Windows 98 installation. Although it is always possible for your Windows 98 users to go to the actual Microsoft Windows 98 Update Web site (unless you have disabled this possibility; review the last section in Chapter 4, "The Registry," for details), you can divert those users by sending them to these sites instead.

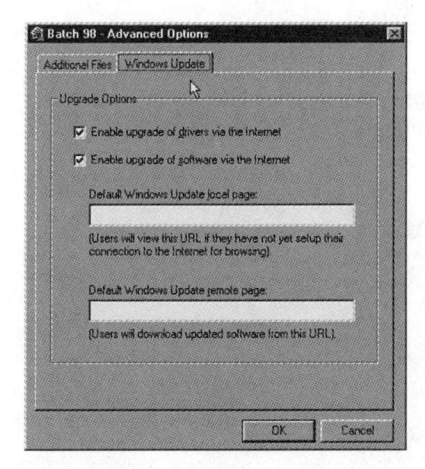

8.3
USE THE MICROSOFT BATCH UTILITY FOR WINDOWS 98

Figure 8.27 Choosing a Windows update methodology.

69. After you make your selections onscreen, click OK to save your selections and return to the primary msbatch.inf – Microsoft Batch 98 screen as shown in Figure 8.28.

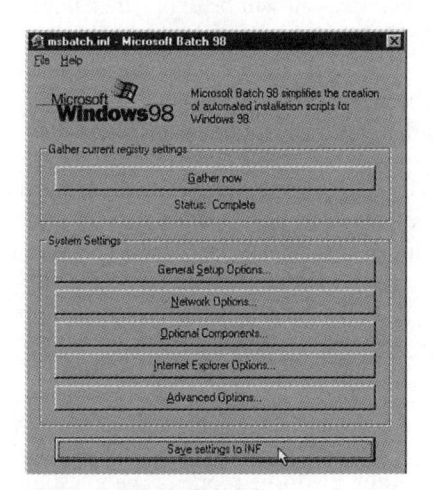

Figure 8.28 The Primary Microsoft Batch 98 screen.

70. Return to the msbatch.inf – Microsoft Batch 98 screen, click the Save settings to INF file button at the bottom of the screen. This causes all your configured settings thus far to be saved to this ASCII installation file.

71. Next, assuming that this file is going to be used with many different PC names, you need to define that file to the MSBATCH.INF file. To do this, click the File menu option, and then click again on the Multiple Machine-Name Save... menu selection. This reveals the screen shown in Figure 8.29.

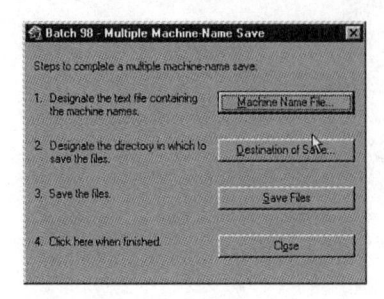

Figure 8.29 Determining Multiple Machine-Name Saves.

72. The purpose of the Batch 98 - Multiple Machine-Name Save screen is to define the name and location of the text file that contains all the names of the Windows 98 computers that you will be deploying. Typically, the name of this file is MACHINE.TXT, and it is located in the same folder as your MSBATCH.INF file. Of course, please remember that you are the creator (or going to be the creator) of this file, so if it does not yet exist on your PC, this means that you still need to define it.

73. The format of the MACHINE.TXT file is simple enough. It is a text file that contains each computer's name, and IP address if you want, so that you can create setup scripts for multiple computers. The format looks like this:

```
Illiad-2, 130.130.5.234
ExchUser1, 130.130.5.235
Phaedrus
Dante
Machiavelli
```

74. When reviewing the preceding file format, one of the first things you should note is that some computers might have predefined IP addresses while others will not. Also, make sure that you have input a carriage return or line feed following each row in this file.

75. When you have the MACHINE.TXT file in place, click the Destination of Save... button to create the *SAVEHERE*.TXT (or whatever filename you prefer) text file.

8.3
USE THE MICROSOFT BATCH UTILITY FOR WINDOWS 98

76. After this file is created, click the Save Files button to continue the process and save all the files involved. The Windows 98 Batch 98 process saves each computer name into a file with an INF file type, and beginning with the letters BSTP. For example, the files BSTP0001.INF, BSTP0002.INF, BSTP0003.INF, BSTP0004.INF, and BSTP0005.INF are created, as shown in Figure 8.30.

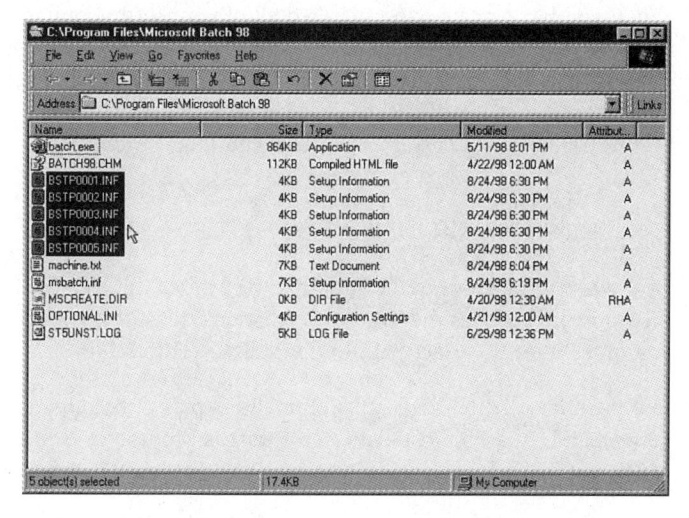

Figure 8.30 Reviewing the INF files that were created.

77. Click the Close button on the Batch 98 – Multiple Machine-Name Save window to close this application.

78. Because you are now done with the Windows 98 Batch 98 tool, you should close any remaining screens as well.

79. Once you have your MSBATCH.INF file created in the manner that you find best-suited to your organization's Windows 98 deployment plans, you are well on you way to performing the rollout itself.

80. If you need to update any of the Windows 98 INF files to reflect new hardware devices that you want to include in your deployment, use the Windows 98 Resource Kit tool known as the INF Installer to perform this function.

81. If you want to dynamically add INF files into your already-defined MSBATCH.INF file or elsewhere in the Windows 98 deployment process, you will want to examine the Windows 98 Resource Kit tool known as DbSet. This is very powerful but extremely complex tool. It permits you to dynamically set the usernames, machine names, IP addresses, server names, and so on. The best aspect of this tool is its inherent power, the worst is that it is DOS-based tool (yep, that's right, there is no GUI for this tool). If you do not have at least the basics down for writing applications and DOS-batch files, you probably won't want to mess with this tool.

82. When you have created and tweaked all of your setup configuration files, you will want to use them in action. To do this as part of your setup process, you will want the Windows 98 SETUP.EXE file to be executed in a manner so that it will use your newly-created customized MSBATCH.INF file. This is easier than you might think; follow this format:

- Setup MSBATCH.INF

83. Now, wasn't that easy? Make sure that the MSBATCH.INF file is located in the same directory as the Windows 98 source files. If it is elsewhere, then you must enter the exact path to the MSBATCH.INF file.

84. In a Push installation the setup command is part of the logon script that you created. In a Pull installation, the user is prompted to either enter this command or click on an icon that executes this same command.

COMPLEXITY
INTERMEDIATE

8.4 How do I...
Use a Cloning tool such as GHOST to deploy Windows 98?

Problem

I want to deploy several hundred Windows 98 computers, all with the exact same hardware and software configuration. Is there an easier way to manually create all these logon scripts, setup scripts, and scripts to manage even more setup scripts?

Technique

The best way to deploy brand-new PCs with the Windows 98 operating system is through a cloning method. This way you will be ensured that everyone has the exact same environment, both hardware and software. A cloning deployment can be handled from a network, a removable media device (such as a SyQuest, Jaz, or other removable hard disk device), or a CD-ROM server.

8.4 USE A CLONING TOOL SUCH AS GHOST TO DEPLOY WINDOWS 98

Many cloning products are available on the market today, but the clear leader is still one of the oldest: *GHOST* by Binary Research Limited. GHOST is essentially a disk copying program that takes an original master copy of a disk drive and duplicates it as needed onto as many other systems as you want. The term GHOST is an acronym for General Hardware-Oriented Software Transfer. The Internet address is http://www.ghostsoft.com/main.htm (there is a free, sample period download available for test and evaluation purposes).

There is a caveat to using cloning tools such as GHOST, mostly in the naming areas: You will be creating exact duplicates of each computer you deploy, so you will still want to use a script file or two to update this type of information during the final deployment phase.

To gain a better understanding of what is involved, follow these steps in the ghosting process.

Steps

1. Create the "perfect" Windows 98 installation.

2. Install the cloning product such as GHOST on any device.

3. Run the GHOST cloning product against the perfect installation of Windows 98 to create the master image file.

4. Copy the master image file up to a centralized source, such as a network server or burn it on to a CD-ROM for distribution purposes.

5. Start the GHOST dump (restore) process whereby the master image is duplicated on to the target machine(s).

6. After completing the dump process, run a batch file with the system reboot that automatically changes the computer (machine) and server name.

7. Repeat steps 5 and 6 as necessary, until all your Windows 98 computers have been deployed.

8. You are finished!

CHAPTER 9
DIAL-UP NETWORKING

9

DIAL-UP NETWORKING

How do I...

- **9.1** Access the Internet without a direct connection?
- **9.2** Use a calling card with the Windows 98 Dial-Up Networking technology?
- **9.3** Tweak my Windows 98 Dial-Up Networking connection so that it performs better with my digital modem?
- **9.4** Secure my systems when combining modems and networks?
- **9.5** Know when to use Virtual Private Networking, and how do I install and configure it?
- **9.6** Use Virtual Private Networking?
- **9.7** Use more than one modem at a time with a single Dial-Up Networking connection?

CHAPTER 9
DIAL-UP NETWORKING

This chapter focuses specifically on connectivity for the mobile person using the Windows 98 technology known as Dial-Up Networking. It also provides some insights into using this technology with desktop computers, especially those that are directly connected to your organization's networks. Further support is given to the topic of security, with an examination of Virtual Private Networking (VPN) using the point-to-point tunneling protocol (PPTP).

9.1 Access the Internet Without a Direct Connection

This How-To addresses the common prospect of having to use a modem for dial-up connectivity to the Internet.

9.2 Use a Calling Card with the Windows 98 Dial-Up Networking Technology

Many people, especially those in business, need to use a calling card in conjunction with the Windows 98 Dial-Up Networking technology. This How-To addresses the ins and outs of using calling cards with the Windows 98 Dial-Up Networking communications accessory.

9.3 Tweak My Windows 98 Dial-Up Networking Connection so that It Performs Better with My Digital Modem

Many people are unaware that Windows 98 is set up to function best with analog Dial-Up Networking modems, and it does not necessarily automatically re-tune itself when a digital modem connection is made. This How-To specifically addresses this topic.

9.4 Secure My Systems when Combining Modems and Networks

This How-To walks you through a series of steps that helps you create a certain level of security for your organization.

9.5 Know when to Use Virtual Private Networking, and How do I Install and Configure It

A definition of Virtual Private Networking (VPN) is given, along with specific instructions on how to install and configure it.

9.6 Use Virtual Private Networking

After VPN is installed you need to know how to use it. This How-To helps you understand how to use this newest technology from Microsoft.

9.7 Use More than One Modem at a Time with a Single Dial-Up Networking Connection

This How-To concentrates on the concept of Multilink, which permits you to bind modems together (similar to the way ISDN works) to increase your bandwidth during a Dial-Up Networking session.

COMPLEXITY
INTERMEDIATE

9.1 How do I...
Access the Internet without a direct connection?

Problem

I want to connect to the Internet without using an expensive online service provider such as America Online or Prodigy. I do not have a direct connection from my company's network, so how do I access the Internet through a regular telephone line?

Technique

Windows 95 created a new remote access services (RAS) client known as *Dial-Up Networking*, and Windows 98 has fine-tuned this remote client connectivity software. Dial-Up Networking is usually installed with most default installations of Windows 98 on laptop and notebook computers but not desktop computers. If you do not see the menu option for Dial-Up Networking in the Communications folder of the Accessories menu option, you will need to install this Windows 98 component from the Add/Remove Programs icon in the Control Panel.

A modem is necessary to permit the Dial-Up Networking software to work correctly. With a modem (modulator/demodulator) device, you are able to connect your computer via a POTS (Plain Old Telephone System) telephone network directly to another Windows 98 PC or your organization's networks (assuming of course that they support remote connectivity and you possess the proper permissions). Without a modem, you will not have the middle piece of technology required to physically connect your computer to that remote host. To get started with using the Windows 98 Dial-Up Networking software, follow these steps.

Steps

1. Access the Dial-Up Networking software from the Communications folder that is found inside the Accessories menu option from the Windows 98 Start button. Although it is possible to start this software from a Run command prompt, it is not a good idea because you need to precisely enter the entire startup string including the Registry key entry. The entire command string looks like this: `C:\WINDOWS\EXPLORER.EXE ::{20D04FE0-3AEA-1069-A2D8-08002B30309D}\::{992CFFA0-F557-101A-88EC-00DD010CCC48}`.

2. When you start Dial-Up Networking you are taken directly to its primary screen, as shown in Figure 9.1.

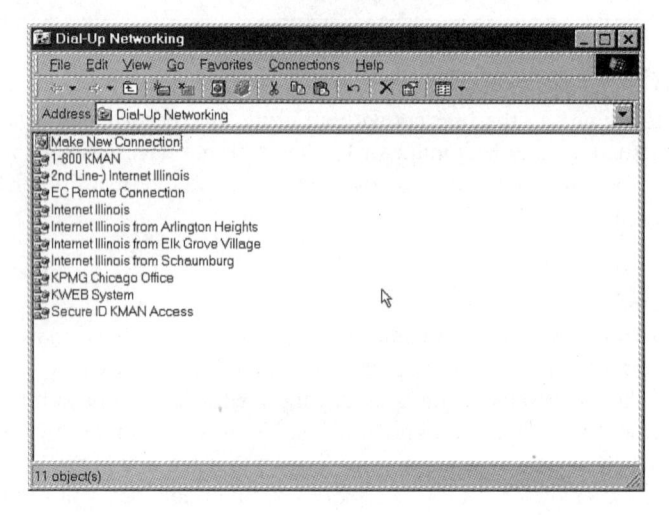

Figure 9.1 The Primary Dial-Up Networking screen.

3. This screen contains all the connections that you have created thus far, and provides the means to create other connections. General Dial-Up Networking preferences and configurations are set via this screen as well. To add a new connection, double-click the Add New Connection icon to start the Make New Connection Wizard, as shown in Figure 9.2.

4. The Make New Connection Wizard appears. On this first screen you are prompted to give your new connection a more descriptive name and select the modem device that you will use to make contact with the remote computer host system. After you have made all your selections, click the Next> button to continue to the next screen of the wizard, as shown in Figure 9.3.

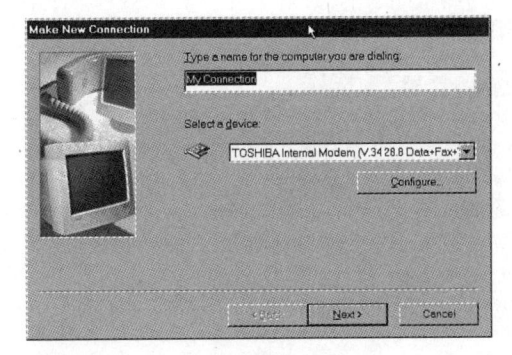

9.1 ACCESS THE INTERNET WITHOUT A DIRECT CONNECTION

Figure 9.2 Starting the Dial-Up Networking Make New Connection Wizard.

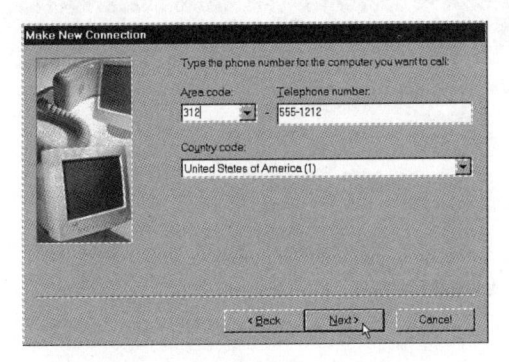

Figure 9.3 Entering the telephone number information details. (Note that the phone number for Information is used here only as an example.)

5. Here you need to enter the telephone number of the destination computer (the remote system that you are calling). Dial-Up Networking splits up the telephone number first by area code then the core number, and then by the country code (in the United States this is the number 1 because a U.S. citizen invented the telephone, as you might recall). After you have entered a complete and valid number, click the Next> button to continue on to the final wizard screen, as shown in Figure 9.4.

6. This is strictly an informational screen that reminds you what you named your new connection, as well as informing you of what you need to do to change any properties of this connection at some later date. Read the information on this screen, and then click the Finish button to complete the wizard. Figure 9.5 reviews your new Dial-Up Networking connection.

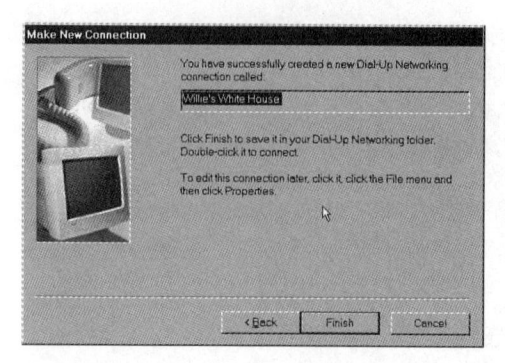

Figure 9.4 Finishing the Make New Connection Wizard.

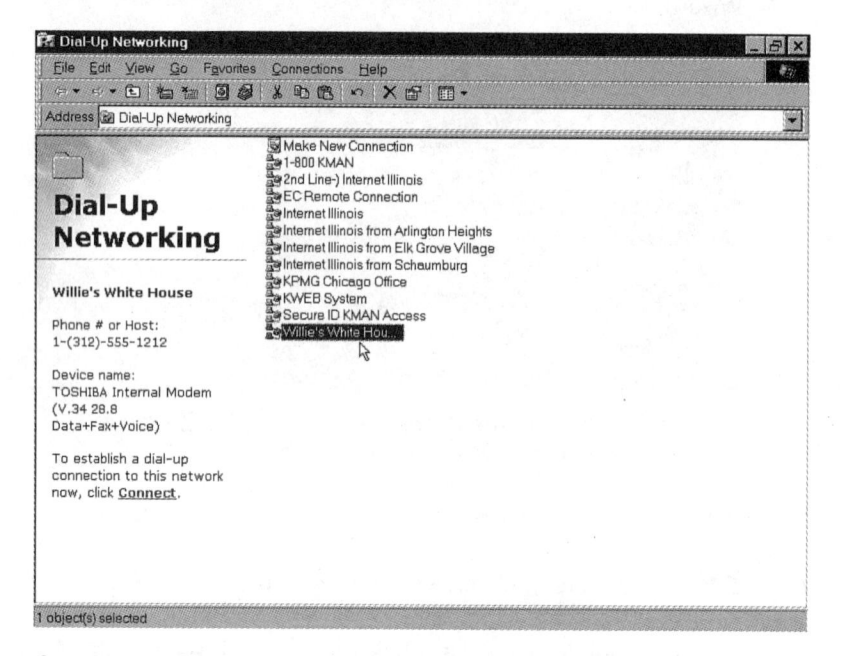

Figure 9.5 Reviewing your newly created Dial-Up Networking connection.

7. Notice that your connection is now present somewhere in the listing, usually at the bottom. If you want to use your new connection right away, you need to double-click the icon that represents your newly created connection. This takes you into the sign-on screen for that Dial-Up Networking connection, as shown in Figure 9.6.

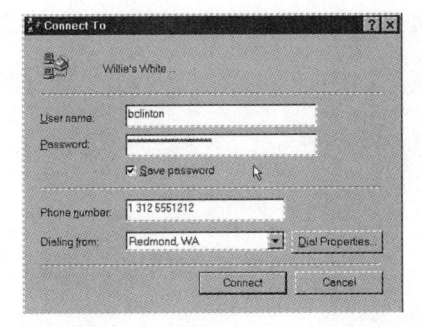

9.1
ACCESS THE INTERNET WITHOUT A DIRECT CONNECTION

Figure 9.6 Starting the connection process.

8. On this screen, you should enter your username and password that is required for you to be properly authenticated by the host computer system. This is information that is routinely provided by your organization's help desk or other information services department support personnel. If you do not want to type in your password each time, click once on the Save password check box to place a check mark in that box.

9. The dial properties are underneath the user sign-on information. Here you should modify the telephone number connection, if needed, as well as the other connectivity options such as a calling card, an outside number access code, or if you want to disable call waiting. To modify the number, you can actually change it in the top box. However, any changes you make here are not permanent, they are just for this one-time connection. To further modify these options, you should click the Dial Properties... button to go to the Dialing Properties dialog box, as shown in Figure 9.7.

10. The sole tab on this screen is labeled as My Locations. This screen allows you to create multiple dialing locations from which you might have to use different access codes for gaining access to outside telephone lines (such as dialing a 9 then a comma--which causes the dialing sequence to pause for a 2 1/2 second period). Also, by setting up different cities and area codes, the Windows 98 Dial-Up Networking software is smart enough to realize that you probably do not want to dial a 1 plus the area code if you are already inside that area code. To set up more detailed rules on when you want Dial-Up Networking to use area code information, click the Area Code Rules... button. This takes you to the Area Code Rules dialog box, as shown in Figure 9.8.

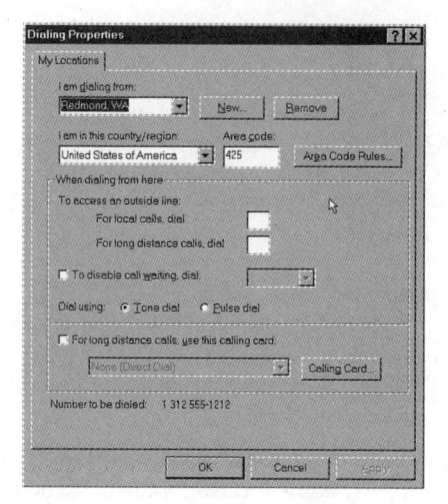

Figure 9.7 Accessing the Dialing Properties screen.

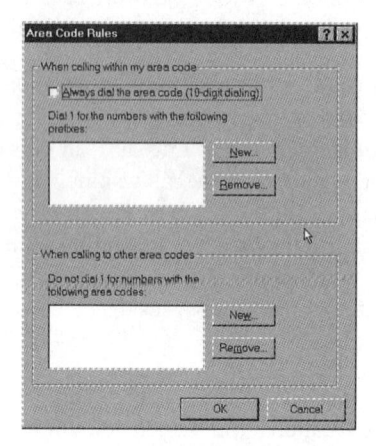

Figure 9.8 Defining area code rules.

11. The Area Code Rules screen provides you with the flexibility to always dial the area code with a telephone number, regardless of where you are calling from, as well as the capability to specify when Dial-Up Networking should not dial a 1 prior to making a long-distance telephone call. (This is especially useful when making international telephone calls.) Click the New button in either area to create new rules, or click the Remove button to delete existing rules in either area.

12. After you have finished making your modifications to this screen, click OK to return to the original My Locations screen.

9.1
ACCESS THE INTERNET WITHOUT A DIRECT CONNECTION

13. In the middle section of this screen, you are able to specify whether you are using Tone dial (touch-tone) or Pulse dial (rotary) service. To pick one, click the appropriate radio button.

14. Also in this section is the option to disable call waiting. You no longer have to remember to type in a *70 to disable call waiting on a touch-tone line or an 1170 on a rotary type of connection.

15. The third topic covered within the When dialing from here section deals with what numeric code you need to dial in order to access an outside line. For those of you who spend lots of time living in hotel rooms across the country, this is a great feature. Sometimes you need to dial the number 8 to obtain an outside line, other times it is a 9, and in one real wacky place in Iowa I had to dial a 75 to obtain a free line. There are two boxes, one for local calls and the other is for long distance. For example, in many Hilton hotels you need to dial a 9 for local calls, but an 8 for long distance numbers. Without separate boxes, this would quickly become a hassle because you would forever be jumping back and forth between the configuration screens within Dial-Up Networking and your various client sessions. Another wacky thing that you might have to do at times is force the dialing to begin (if you are not able to wait for a pulse tone). In this case, you would use a capital letter P in place of the capital letter T that you would use in a tone-dialing world.

16. The final section on this screen refers to the use of credit cards or calling cards when performing a Dial-Up Networking connection. If you want to use a calling card, click once on the check box in this section to enable it. Then click the drop-down list box to select the credit or calling card that you want to use when calling from this location. Please refer to the next section in this chapter, "How do I use a calling card with the Windows 98 Dial-Up Network technology," if you require additional assistance in configuring a calling card or credit card with one of your Dial-Up Networking locations.

17. At the very bottom of this screen, you see an example of the telephone number exactly in the format that it will be dialed by the Windows 98 Dial-Up Networking software. For example, if you used a calling card, an area code, the number 9 to access an outside line, and disabled your call waiting, the number shown looks similar to the one shown in Figure 9.9.

18. This feature is very nice because it shows you that what you see is exactly what you get. Click OK and you are returned to the Connect To screen.

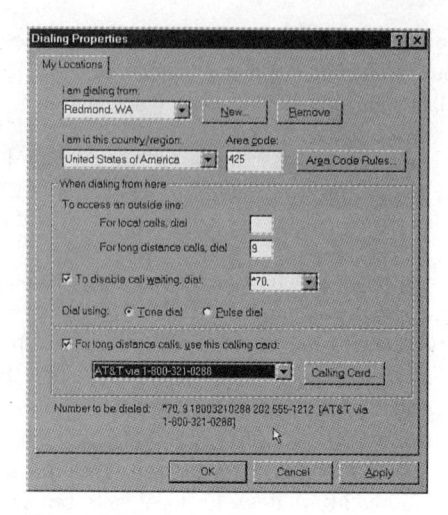

Figure 9.9 Reviewing your entries.

19. Click the Connect button and the Windows 98 Dial-Up Networking software starts your connection to the Internet, using the configurations that you have just set.

20. After successfully completing the connection, Windows 98 informs you via a message box that you are able to minimize down to your task bar into the System Tray area. That is all you need to do to connect your computer to the Internet without having a direct Internet connection.

COMPLEXITY
INTERMEDIATE

9.2 How do I...
Use a calling card with the Windows 98 Dial-Up Networking technology?

Problem

I want to pay for my Dial-Up Networking telephone calls with a calling card instead of having these calls charged to my telephone or the hotel bill. Is there a way to do this for my Dial-Up Networking connections without being a technical guru who can write my own scripts?

9.2 USE A CALLING CARD WITH WINDOWS 98 DIAL-UP NETWORKING

Technique

The Windows 98 Dial-Up Networking software provides an easy-to-use method for configuring and storing your credit and calling card information for use with a Dial-Up Networking connection. This feature is built-in, does not require any additional software to use, and takes less than five minutes to configure (less, if you are a fast typist). Carefully follow the steps provided, and you will soon be charging your Dial-Up Networking telephone charges to your corporate calling card.

Steps

1. To configure a payment card, you must double-click the Dial Properties... button of the Connect To screen, as shown in Figure 9.10. To get to this screen. open your Dial-Up Networking window first (the easiest way to do this, is to double click the My Computer icon on your Windows 98 desktop and then double-click the Dial-Up Networking icon that appears inside the My Computer Explorer screen). Here you will double-click the Dial-Up Networking session that you want to initially use the payment card with, and then hit the Dial Properties... button.

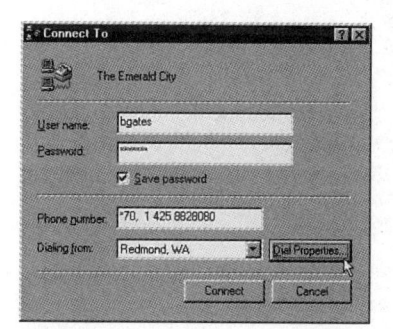

Figure 9.10 Accessing the Dial Properties screen from the Connect To screen.

2. The Dialing Properties screen appears, as shown in Figure 9.11.

3. In the bottom section you see a check box with the label For Long Distance Calls, Use this Calling Card. Select this option by clicking on it once with your primary mouse button. Next, click the Calling Card... button to reveal the Calling Card dialog box, as shown in Figure 9.12.

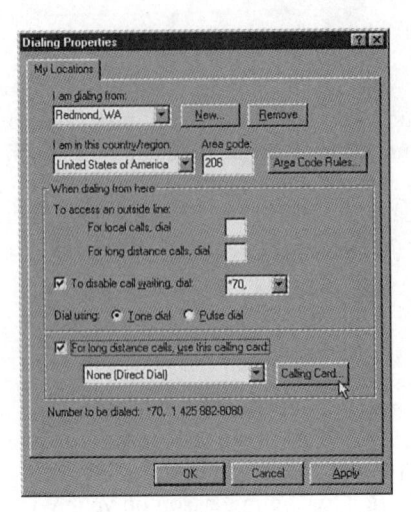

Figure 9.11 Reviewing your calling card selections on the Dialing Properties screen.

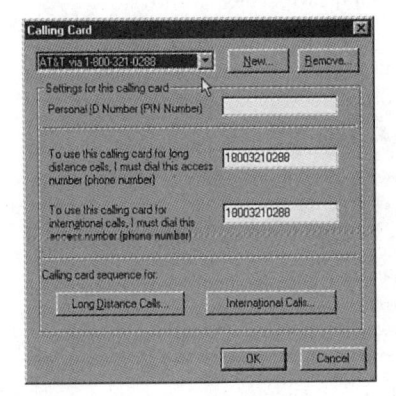

Figure 9.12 Choosing the calling card type to use.

4. The purpose of this screen is to provide a single point of configuration for all electronic payment cards (calling cards, credit cards, and so on), in conjunction with the Windows 98 Dial-Up Networking service. The screen is split into two areas, with the second area having three sections. The top area contains the drop-down list box that holds all the access methods, along with two buttons (New and Remove) that are used to add or delete any of the various access methods. The second area deals with creating or modifying the settings for the calling card, including the PIN number, access telephone numbers, and additional card sequencing configurations.

5. To start, click the drop-down list box and select one of the predefined calling cards, such as MCI, AT&T, Sprint, and so on. For the purposes of this example, I used one that I had defined for a previous Dial-Up Networking session, which is labeled AT&T via 1-800-321-0288 (1-800-321-0ATT).

6. The top box within the Settings area is where you type in your real calling card or other payment card number. This is the number for the card that will be charged when the local telephone company (regardless of where you are at) processes this telephone call. In the case of an AT&T calling card, this is the exact same number that you see on your card, without any of the dashes.

7. Many cards require you to enter a special access telephone number for local and international calls. Very few locations permit you to just dial 0, and then enter your calling card number anymore (...the good, old days).

8. After you have filled in these boxes in the manner you want, click the calling card sequence button that you want to configure first. In this example, this means you will click the Long Distance Calls... button to go to the Calling Card Sequence dialog box, as shown in Figure 9.13.

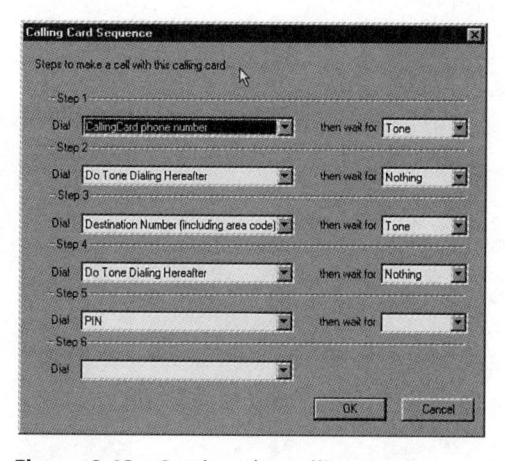

Figure 9.13 Setting the calling card sequence.

9. The Calling Card Sequence screen is where you configure the timing arrangement of your Dial-Up Networking session's telephone call. More than likely, the first thing that you need to do is dial the CallingCard phone number, so click this item from the drop-down list box that appears under step 1. Your choices from this list box include:

- CallingCard phone number
- Destination Number (without area code)
- Destination Number (including area code)
- Destination Country/Region
- PIN
- Specified Digits
- Done
- Do Tone Dialing Hereafter

10. Most of these choices are self-explanatory, with the possible exception of the Specified Digits and Do Tone Dialing Hereafter selections. The option for Specified Digits provides you with the capability to define your own dialing string in the first step, instead of using this pseudo-wizard and placing something in each step. Although you will not see any reference for help here, you can press the F1 function key to retrieve the help screen shown in Figure 9.14.

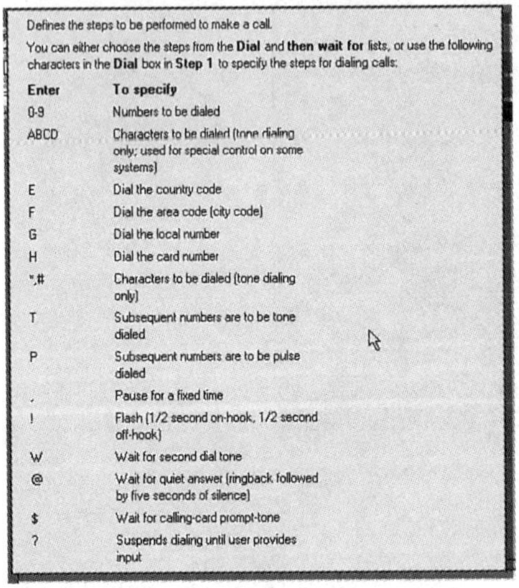

Defines the steps to be performed to make a call.
You can either choose the steps from the **Dial** and **then wait for** lists, or use the following characters in the **Dial** box in **Step 1** to specify the steps for dialing calls:

Enter	To specify
0-9	Numbers to be dialed
ABCD	Characters to be dialed (tone dialing only; used for special control on some systems)
E	Dial the country code
F	Dial the area code (city code)
G	Dial the local number
H	Dial the card number
*,#	Characters to be dialed (tone dialing only)
T	Subsequent numbers are to be tone dialed
P	Subsequent numbers are to be pulse dialed
,	Pause for a fixed time
!	Flash (1/2 second on-hook, 1/2 second off-hook)
W	Wait for second dial tone
@	Wait for quiet answer (ringback followed by five seconds of silence)
$	Wait for calling-card prompt-tone
?	Suspends dialing until user provides input

Figure 9.14 Reviewing the Dialing Codes Help screen.

USE A CALLING CARD WITH WINDOWS 98 DIAL-UP NETWORKING

11. Personally, I would use the individual steps for defining your calling card sequencing process instead of attempting to do it through the use of a series of specified digits. Because this is exactly how you had to do it with Windows 95, you might want to copy over any dialing strings that you had in the older version(s) of Dial-Up Networking. In any event, if you specify the use of the Specified Digits selection from the drop-down list box, a small box labeled Digits to Dial appears. It is in this box that you enter any dialing string you want.

12. If you choose to use the Do Tone Dialing Hereafter on any of the next few steps, Windows 98 interprets this as meaning that you want to actually dial whatever combination appears in the following step (such as the Destination Number or the PIN).

13. Therefore, once you have made the appropriate selection in the first drop-down list box (next to the option labeled Dial), you need to decide what to wait for. To do this, review the then wait for label next to the drop-down list box on the right side of the screen. Many options are available in this drop-down list box:

- Nothing
- Tone
- Done
- 2 seconds
- 4 seconds
- 6 seconds
- 8 seconds
- 10 seconds
- 14 seconds
- 18 seconds
- 22 seconds
- 28 seconds
- 36 seconds
- 46 seconds

14. The first one, Nothing, means that you do not want to wait at all and should immediately proceed on to the next step. The Tone option tells the computer to wait for a dial tone before continuing. The Done option is exactly that; you are finished with the dialing sequence for this Dial-Up Networking session. All the other options are time-related. These all tell the Dial-Up Networking operation how long to wait prior to attempting the next step. Typically, you will never want to wait more than 4–8 seconds before trying the next step (I found this to be accurate in Europe and Asia, as well as most of the Americas).

15. I realize that these last few explanations might be confusing to the first-time user, but let us re-examine the Calling Card Sequence screen shown again here in Figure 9.15.

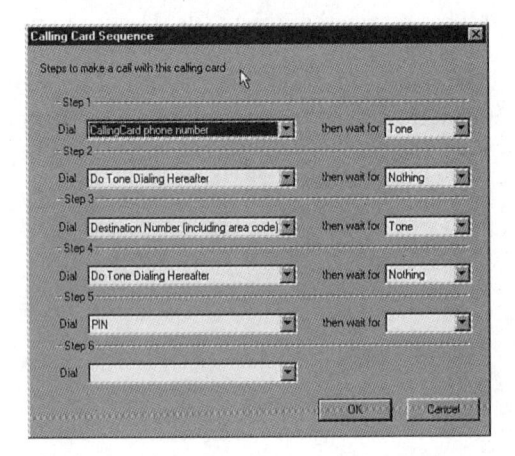

Figure 9.15 Reviewing the Calling Card Sequence selections.

16. As you can see, in Step 1 you decided to Dial the CallingCard phone number, and then wait for Tone. This is the access number for your calling card (1-800-321-0288), which was dialed according to your rules that were defined previously (such as to dial a 9 to get an outside number, or dialing *70 to disable call waiting).

17. Next, in Step 2, Dial-Up Networking performs only Tone Dialing Hereafter while waiting for nothing.

> **NOTE**
> On some telephones, Step 2 is not necessary as it is considered redundant by the telephone system you are trying to connect through.

9.2
USE A CALLING CARD WITH WINDOWS 98 DIAL-UP NETWORKING

However, on my home telephone (Ameritech is the local carrier and AT&T is the long-distance provider), this step is necessary. You might have to experiment with these settings in order to find the one that works best in your environment.

18. The PC immediately dials the destination telephone number (425-882-8080), and then waits for Tone (Step 3).

19. After another respite of performing only Tone Dialing Hereafter while waiting for nothing (Step 4), Dial-Up Networking enters your calling card's PIN number as you had entered it earlier (Step 5).

20. Some people need to have the then wait for option of Done specified following the dialing of the PIN number, while others (like me) do not need anything for the dialing sequence to work perfectly. Again, this is going to vary by telephone system and carrier, so you might have to play with it. I found that outside of the United States, you almost always need to specify the Done option.

21. After you have completed your options on the Calling Card Sequence screen, click OK to return to the Calling Card screen, as shown in Figure 9.16.

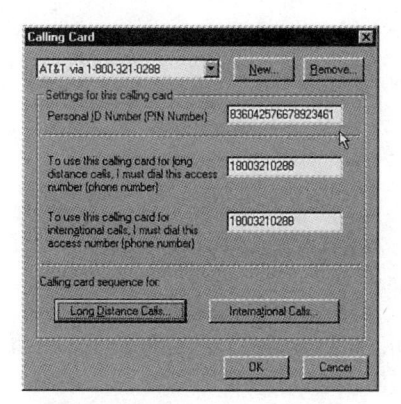

Figure 9.16 Entering your calling card's PIN number.

22. When you return to this primary Calling Card screen, make sure you have correctly entered your payment card's number sequence into the box next to the Personal ID Number (PIN Number) box. Without a valid calling card number, this feature of the Windows 98 Dial-Up Networking will not work correctly.

CHAPTER 9
DIAL-UP NETWORKING

> **NOTE**
>
> A quick note to all the hackers, phone phreakers, and so on in the audience: The PIN number shown is not valid, much less even being of the correct length for an AT&T calling card, so don't bother trying it on your own systems. The telephone number shown for this example is bogus as well.

23. After you have entered a valid PIN number, click OK to return to the My Locations tab of the Dialing Properties screen, as shown in Figure 9.17.

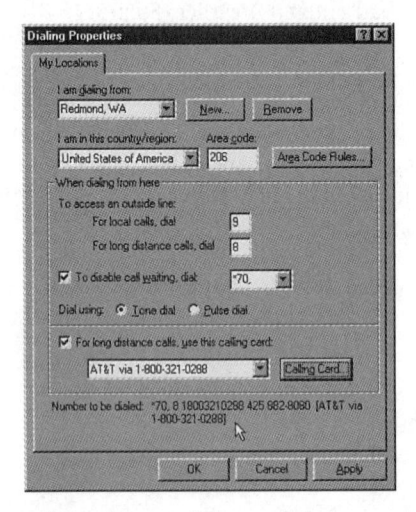

Figure 9.17 Reviewing the telephone number to be dialed.

24. Along the bottom of this screen you see a representation of the dialing string that you have configured. If this is correct, click OK to continue. If not, make the appropriate corrections before clicking OK to continue. Keep in mind that this string next to the label Number to be dialed will not show the calling card's payment number, so do not be surprised when you do not see it.

25. After clicking the OK button in the previous step, you return to the Connect To screen, as shown in Figure 9.18.

26. If you move your pointer inside the Phone number box, you see the entire dialing sequence string as you defined it. Use the arrow keys to move left and right throughout this box. Note that Windows 98 automatically figured out that you needed a $T option in various places, and placed a comma after the *70 (to disable call waiting) option to provide the necessary pause. The dollar sign provides the necessary wait for the calling card prompt (a tone), whereas the capital letter T provides for the notation that the next set of numbers are to be tone dialed (sure beats having to remember these intrinsic codes yourself, doesn't it?).

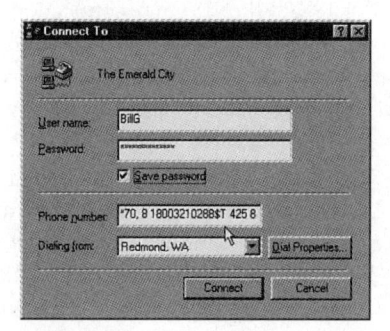

Figure 9.18 Reviewing the dialing sequence string on the Connect To screen.

27. At this point, you can either click the Connect button to test out your calling card sequence and attempt a connection to your host computer system, or click the Cancel button to end the use of this Dial-Up Networking session.

COMPLEXITY
ADVANCED

9.3 How do I...
Tweak my Windows 98 Dial-Up Networking connection so that it performs better with my digital modem?

Problem

I have heard rumors that the Windows 98 Dial-Up Networking software can be tweaked so that it works better with all high-speed digital modems, as well as some of the faster analog modems (such as cable modems). Is this true, and if so, how can I tune my version of Dial-Up Networking so that it works better?

Technique

Although Dial-Up Networking is automatically configured to work in the best manner possible for the majority of users and modems, it is possible to gain a little bit more productivity out of some modems. This is, of course, assuming that the connection is made via the TCP/IP protocol, as this tweak becomes irrelevant when making a NetBEUI or IPX/SPX (NWLink) connection. With a cable modem, for example, it is possible to quicken download times by as much as 65 percent. However, this is the extreme, and in most cases you will probably only see a 15–20 percent improvement in download times with ISDN, cable, or leased-line connections.

To achieve these faster times, Windows 98 provides two options: a direct Registry hack (which I will show, but do not recommend unless you are very, very familiar with editing your Registry, as the wrong move can be fatal), and by making a slight change using the Windows 98 GUI. So, without further ado, carefully follow these steps (the GUI change will be presented first) and begin enjoying a faster download of items from remote host systems.

> **NOTE**
> If you have an analog modem that is of the 57.6Kbps variety or slower, then you really should skip this section. With an incredible amount of testing on multiple modem types and bandwidth speeds, I have never seen an improved download time on anything slower than an ISDN line. This is not to say that it is impossible, only that it is very unlikely and I do not see the point for you to waste your time trying.

Steps

1. Open the Network properties for your Dial-Up Adapter. You can do this by either holding down the Alt key and double-clicking the Network Neighborhood icon on the Windows 98 desktop, or by double-clicking the Network icon in the Windows 98 Control Panel.

2. Either way, the Network screen appears. First you need to select the Dial-Up Adapter, and then click once the Properties button.

3. Next, click the Advanced tab, on the Dial-Up Adapter Properties screen, to reveal the window shown in Figure 9.19.

4. The option that you want to manipulate under the Property: window is the IP Packet Size. This option allows you to set the actual size of the Internet Protocol Packet that you are sending when making a Dial-Up Networking connection.

9.3 TWEAK MY WINDOWS 98 DIAL-UP NETWORKING CONNECTION

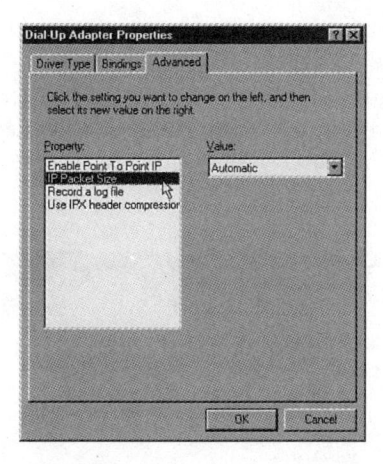

Figure 9.19 Setting an IP Packet Size.

5. The default setting is a value of Automatic (which appears in your Windows 98 Registry as 0). The choices that you have are to change the packet size to small, medium, or large. Of course, Windows 98 does not tell you what small, medium, or large means numerically, much less inform you through the help screens.

6. If you check in your Registry, following a change here and a reboot, you will see that a setting of small equates to a size of 576, medium equates to a size of 1,000, and large equates to a size of 1,500.

7. For best performance, change your setting to large (1,500), and then click OK to return to the original Network screen.

8. Click OK, which causes Windows 98 to prompt you to restart your computer.

9. Click the Yes button to answer affirmatively, and allow Windows 98 to automatically restart your computer system. After rebooting you are set up for improved download times. On a Motorola cable modem, this makes for a faster download time from the Microsoft Internet FTP site of 6MB of data every 45 seconds instead of every minute. On a large download, such as a 229MB download of Windows NT Server version 5.0, this means that instead of having to wait nearly 39 minutes for a complete download, it only takes just over 28 minutes—a savings of over 10 minutes or roughly 28 percent.

10. Okay, now that you have experienced the GUI way to better performing modems, it is time to use the Registry modification approach. In some ways this approach is nicer, because you can precisely set the IP Packet Size to any number that you want (from zero to 9,999 or more). On my computer the GUI worked just fine, but perhaps on your PC a more finely-tuned number will work better. In any event, start the Registry Editor that comes with the Windows 98 operating system (REGEDIT.EXE), as shown in Figure 9.20.

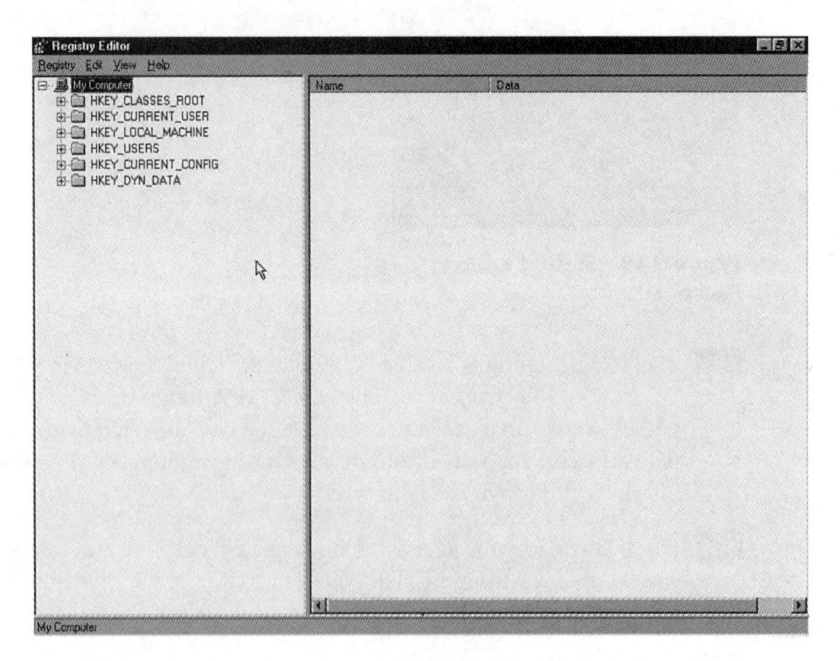

Figure 9.20 Viewing the primary Registry Editor screen.

11. Click the Start button then click the Run... menu option, and then type in the command **RegEdit** (this is not a case-sensitive command) in the Run command box and either click OK or press Enter.

12. After seeing the primary Registry Editor screen, maneuver down to the HKEY_LOCAL_MACHINE Registry hive and open the appropriate keys and subkeys, all the way down to first the IPMTU subkey, and then the enum subkey as shown in Figure 9.21.

13. The full path is as follows: `HKEY_LOCAL_MACHINE\System\CurrentControlSet\Services\Class\Net\0000\Ndi\params\IPMTU\enum`.

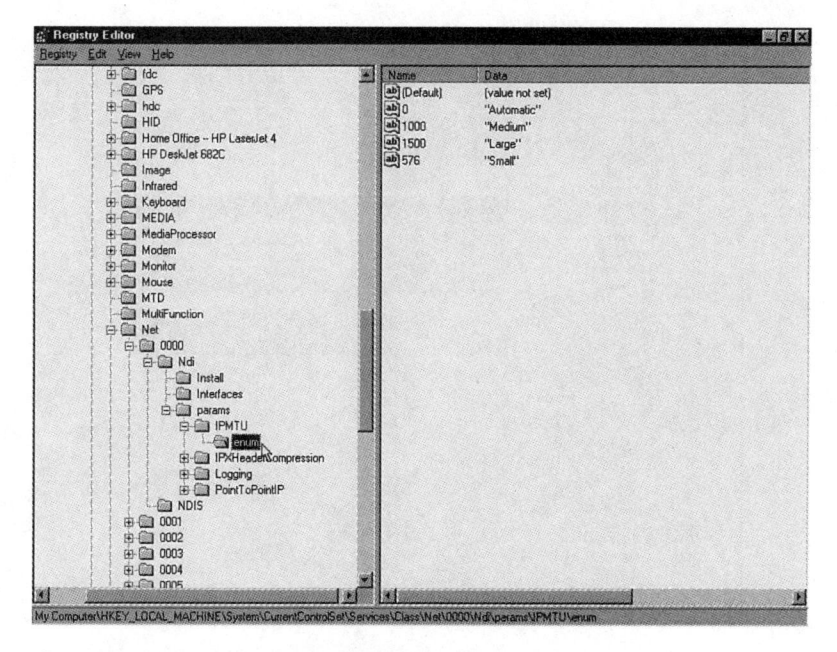

9.3
TWEAK MY WINDOWS 98 DIAL-UP NETWORKING CONNECTION

Figure 9.21 Reviewing Windows 98 Registry subkeys.

14. This is a long path, so be careful to make sure that you are in the correct location. Each of the numbered sets you see under the Net subkey refers to the various versions of your Registry that exist. If any of this does not make sense to you, you should refer to Chapter 4, "The Registry," of this book or the Windows 98 Resource Kit by Microsoft Press, Inc.

15. As you can see, all four of the settings are present within this Registry setting: Automatic, Medium, Large, and Small (they appear in alphabetical order, not size order).

16. If you want to modify the default IP Packet Size, click once on the IPMTU subkey. Next, select the Default value by clicking it once, and then click again with your secondary mouse button to reveal a tiny menu.

17. Click the Modify option to open the Edit String window, as shown in Figure 9.22.

18. Enter the default IP Packet Size that you want in the Value data box, and then click OK to accept this new IP Packet Size value.

19. You see that the new default setting for the IP Packet Size appears instantly. Exit the Windows 98 Registry Editor and restart your computer manually. This forces the new default size to take effect, and you are finished.

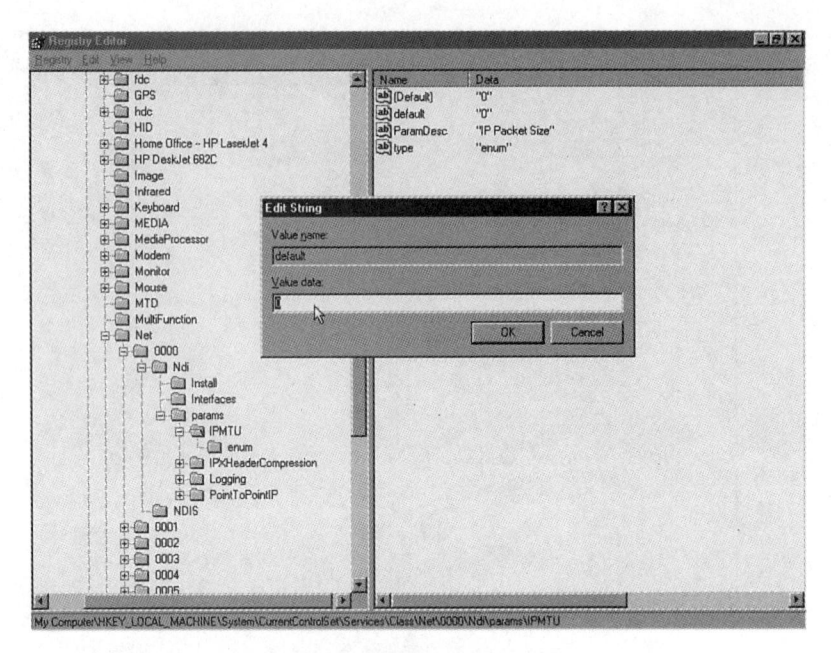

Figure 9.22 Entering a subkey's data string value.

> **CAUTION**
>
> If you make a mistake while editing the Windows 98 Registry, there is no Undo option. This means that once you make a change, it is made. All sales are final here...there are no returns. Therefore, obviously, it is in your best interest to make sure that your Windows 98 Startup disk is up to date and that you have a disk-based version of your Windows 98 Registry prior to making any changes directly to the Registry. Failure to perform these steps correctly can cause your PC to be inoperable, even to the extent that you can no longer boot your computer.

COMPLEXITY
INTERMEDIATE

9.4 How do I...
Secure my systems when combining modems and networks?

Problem

The obstinate people in the information systems (IS) department at work will not provide me with a modem to dial up to my ISP directly because they claim this makes their network less secure. Is this a true statement, and if so, are there any ways to make this type of connection secure enough to let me directly connect a modem to my computer at work?

Technique

One of the easiest ways to gain access to a corporate network today is through dial-up access to someone's computer who is already authenticated to their organization's network. This can be accomplished in a variety of ways:

- Surf a user's PC and connected network, when that person is both dialed in to the Internet and connected to their network (or vice versa) and they have File and Print Sharing enabled on their PC.

- A PC is turned on with its modem connected, authenticated to the corporate network, and has a modem and telephone line that permits inbound calls.

- A PC is turned on with its modem connected, and has a modem and telephone line that permits incoming calls.

While there are other methods, they get a bit complicated and are not meant for a book like this. For more information, check out one of the many hacker sites on the Internet, such as http://www.l0pht.com or http://www.dark-secrets.com; or check out a book on network security, such as *Firewalls and Internet Security: Repelling the Wily Hacker*, by William Cheswick and Steven Bellovin, published by Addison-Wesley Publishing. To use both a modem and a network connection at work, you might want to try one or more of the following steps to help make your local and remote host connectivity a little bit more secure.

Steps

1. Use a telephone line that does not permit inbound calling. This way, even if you do forget to turn your computer off at night, no one from outside your organization can communicate with your PC from that open telephone line.

2. Try to always remember to disconnect from your corporate network when you are not using your computer. That is, sign-off and sign back on frequently! I cannot think of an instance where an IS professional would mind increased network traffic through frequent computer authentications, as opposed to users of the corporate network leaving their computers signed-in constantly (even though those persons are at lunch, gone for the day, and so on).

3. Perhaps you might even want to contact your organization's help desk to see if they can set your system to log off automatically, when you have stopped using it for some predefined period of time. Mainframe-based systems, as well as Novell NetWare and Windows NT network-based computer systems, are more than capable of this feature, so do not be too shy to ask. You might be surprised by the answer you receive.

4. Turn off the File and Print Sharing feature of Windows 98, especially if you are using the Client for Microsoft Networks client software feature, from within the Networks properties panel by clicking the File and Print Sharing... button. The File and Print Sharing dialog box appears, as shown in Figure 9.23.

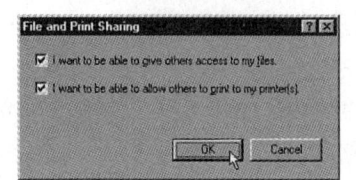

Figure 9.23 Reviewing your current File and Print Sharing options.

5. This does a few things for you. First, it limits your exposure to the outside world, in that it becomes much more probable that someone unbeknownst to you will no longer be able to access your computer without your knowledge or consent.

6. Second, it prevents your Windows 98 computer from broadcasting itself to the various Windows NT Master Browsers that might be present on

your network, and keeps other Windows 98 computers from "seeing" your PC inside their Network Neighborhood icon.

7. Third, it lessens network traffic, especially if you have ISDN (or some other periodic) connectivity to the Internet. It does this by not prompting your ISDN connection to want to open every time it receives an automatic broadcast message packet from your File and Print Sharing process.

8. The easiest way to prevent unauthorized access to your network while you are using a modem is to physically unplug your network cable from the NIC (network interface card) in your PC. This way, no matter how hard anyone tries it is impossible for anyone coming in through the modem connection to access your company's private data on the corporate network.

COMPLEXITY
INTERMEDIATE

9.5 How do I...
Know when to use Virtual Private Networking, and how do I install and configure it?

Problem

I work for a company that wants to start sending customer orders over the Internet from the salespersons' Windows 98 notebook computers. As the IS manager I need to know how to do this without having to go out and buy expensive and difficult to maintain, much less deploy, encryption devices. Is there a way to do this with Windows 98?

Technique

Microsoft offers a more secure Dial-Up Networking communications method known as *Virtual Private Networking (VPN)*. This communications technique is based on the industry standard technology known as the Point-to-Point Tunneling Protocol (PPTP), which forms the underpinnings of Microsoft's networking communications technology. PPTP is a relatively new technology that provides support for multiprotocol VPNs. PPTP is used whenever you want to send secure, private transactions or communiqués across a public network such as the Internet.

By incorporating the Microsoft VPN/PPTP technology with your Dial-Up Networking client, you can send important documents or financial transactions without fearing that some unscrupulous person might intercept your private or corporate information. For example, assume you are employed as a salesperson for a major manufacturing company and your corporate IS department has implemented a sales force automation solution. With the Microsoft implementation of VPN into the Windows 98 Dial-Up Networking technology, you are able to submit those customer orders directly into your back-end order entry system via the Internet without fear of a competitor (or anyone else) intercepting your orders. This means that your IS staff no longer needs to build that massive modem bank, and incur the expensive long-distance charges that they once did, to allow you to submit your orders electronically and faster for your customers.

In other words, you are now able to dial in to a local ISP, connect to the Internet, and transmit your messages in a secure and encrypted fashion across this very public medium. To be able to use this technology, you will need to install a special network adapter known as the VPN Adapter that works with your Windows 98-compatible modem. To install and configure this adapter, follow the accompanying steps, which take you quickly through the process.

Steps

1. Open the Network properties screen for your computer. You can do this by either holding down the Alt key and double-clicking the Network Neighborhood icon on the Windows 98 desktop, or by double-clicking the Network icon in the Windows 98 Control Panel.

2. This causes the Network screen to appear, where you need to click once on the Add button to reveal the Select Network Component Type screen shown in Figure 9.24.

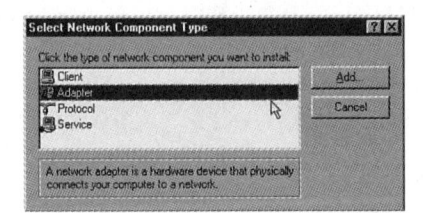

Figure 9.24 Selecting a new network component.

3. Click once on the Adapter selection to highlight it, and then click once on the OK button to continue to the Select Network Adapters dialog box shown in Figure 9.25.

9.5
KNOW WHEN TO USE VPN, AND HOW DO I INSTALL AND CONFIGURE IT

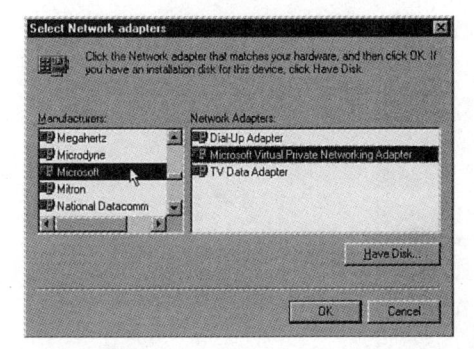

Figure 9.25 Selecting a new network adapter.

4. Click once on the Microsoft selection in the Manufacturers window to highlight that choice. This causes a few adapters to be displayed in the Network Adapters window.

5. Click once on the Microsoft Virtual Private Networking Adapter selection to highlight it. Then click OK to continue.

6. Windows 98 prompts you to insert your Windows 98 CD-ROM (or asks you for the disk location of the Windows 98 CAB files). Insert the disk or tell it the precise location of the necessary CAB files and click the Yes button when you have finished, which causes your system to restart as need be.

7. After your computer has restarted itself, reenter the Network Properties screen, where you can now see that the Dial-Up Adapter #2 (VPN Support) is present, as shown in Figure 9.26.

8. This adapter is labeled as #2 because it is the second Dial-Up Adapter that is present in your computer (your modem's Dial-Up Adapter is actually the first one, although it is not labeled that way).

9. To configure this adapter, click it once to highlight it, and then click the Properties button to go to the Driver Type tab shown in Figure 9.27.

10. The Dial-Up Adapter #2 (VPN Support) Properties screen will appear. On the Driver Type tab there is probably no choice to be made. You might be prompted to make a selection on what type of network driver to use, but more than likely all but the top choice will be grayed-out. If you had a real-mode device driver installed for your networking option(s) in either the CONFIG.SYS or AUTOEXEC.BAT system configuration files, there might be other selections to be made here.

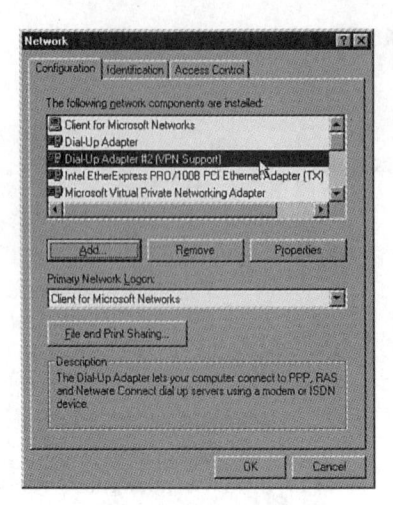

Figure 9.26 Reviewing your Dial-Up Networking with VPN support.

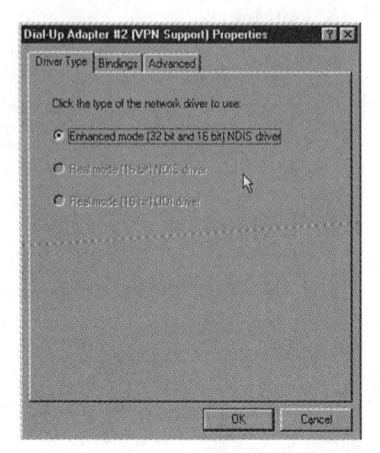

Figure 9.27 Setting the driver type(s) on the VPN Support Properties screen.

11. Click once on the Bindings tab to reveal that screen, as shown in Figure 9.28.

12. One of the best things about VPN under Windows 98 is that it supports more than just the TCP/IP protocol, whereas many other implementations of the Point-to-Point Tunneling protocol (PPTP) only support TCP/IP. In Windows 98 you can use the Microsoft TCP/IP stack, the IPX/SPX-compatible Protocol, and the NetBEUI protocol with the VPN Adapter.

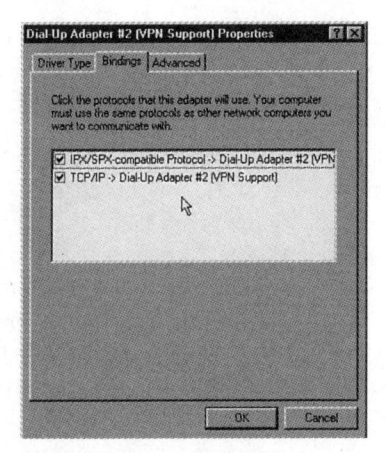

9.5
KNOW WHEN TO USE VPN, AND HOW DO I INSTALL AND CONFIGURE IT

Figure 9.28 Setting the binding(s) on the VPN Support Properties screen.

13. By default, the Dial-Up Adapter #2 (VPN Support) in Windows 98 attempts to use every networking protocol that has been installed on your computer. Deselect those you do not want to use by clicking on that protocol's check box to remove the check mark. After you have made all your deselections, click the Advanced tab to reveal its screen, as shown in Figure 9.29.

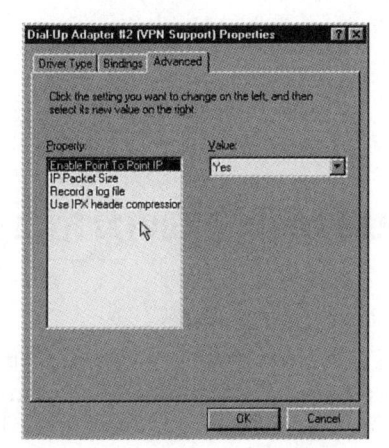

Figure 9.29 Setting Advanced options on the VPN Support Properties screen.

14. If you have different networking protocols installed on your computer system, some of the options you see under the Property window might not be on your screen. So, if they are different, try not to panic.

15. Make changes to the IP Packet Size option only if you have a high-speed modem installed (review the preceding section in this chapter, "How do I secure my system when combining modems and networks?" if you have any qualms about altering the option). The Record a Log File option defaults to No (in the Value drop-down list box), but it is recommended that you change this to Yes. You should record a log file at least a few times so you can see the effects of using VPN on your computer. I use it all the time for troubleshooting failed connections with my corporate network, and you might find it very useful as well.

16. Once you have made all your changes, click OK to complete the reconfiguration process to your VPN Adapter and return to the Network properties screen.

17. Click OK on the Network properties screen to save all your changes and exit this screen. You are prompted to restart your PC. Reply affirmatively to the message box that appears by clicking Yes on the System Settings Change message box.

18. After your computer restarts, you are ready to begin using your VPN Adapter in conjunction with your existing modem and its Dial-Up Adapter.

COMPLEXITY
INTERMEDIATE

9.6 How do I...
Use Virtual Private Networking?

Problem

I have installed and configured my Dial-Up Adapter #2 (VPN Support) within the Windows 98 Network Properties screen. Now what do I do to invoke its use, so that my Dial-Up Networking sessions invoke the usage of the PPTP within VPN?

Technique

Use of the VPN Adapter within a Dial-Up Networking session is a lot easier than you might think. All you need to do is create a new Dial-Up Networking session specifically for the VPN server that you want to communicate with.

9.6 USE VIRTUAL PRIVATE NETWORKING

Next, you need to make your normal Dial-Up Networking session between you and your ISP. Then you will perform the creation of the VPN connection to expose the "tunnel" between you and your remote host's VPN server.

All communications from your computer now use the ISP's server for automatic routing to your remote host's VPN server, using the Internet as the virtual trail. Of course, when you invoke VPN, you will no longer "see" any other hosts on the Internet except the VPN host that you are communicating with, because you are inside an encrypted tunnel (hence, the name: Virtual Private Networking).

Carefully follow these steps to first create the Dial-Up Networking session for the VPN server, and then to walk through a VPN connection.

Steps

1. Open the Dial-Up Networking screen, as shown in Figure 9.30. The easiest way to get to this screen is by double-clicking the My Computer icon on the Windows 98 desktop.

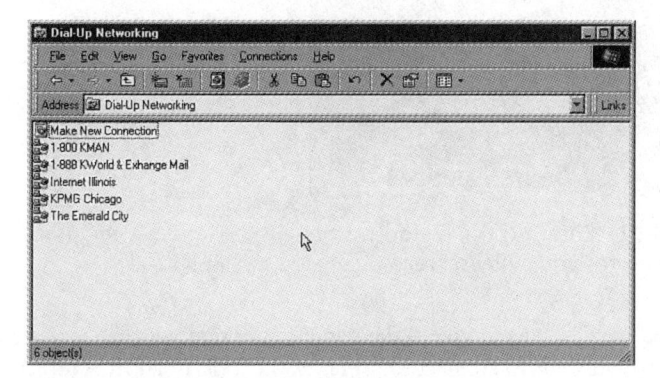

Figure 9.30 Reviewing the primary Dial-Up Networking screen.

2. Start the Make New Connection Wizard by double-clicking on the icon of the same name, as shown in Figure 9.31.

3. Select an appropriate and descriptive name for the connection you are about to create.

4. Then select the Microsoft VPN Adapter from the drop-down list box under the Select a Device label.

5. After you have performed both of these steps, click the Next> button to continue to the next screen of the wizard, as shown in Figure 9.32.

CHAPTER 9
DIAL-UP NETWORKING

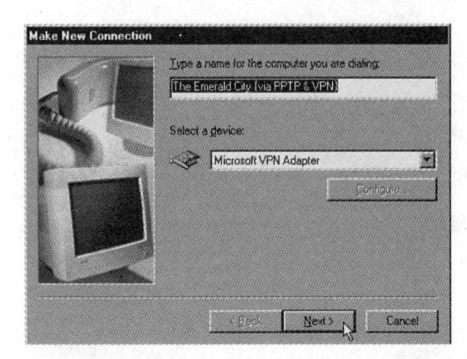

Figure 9.31 Starting the Make New Connection screen.

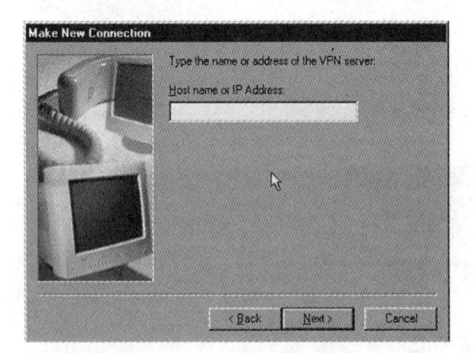

Figure 9.32 Entering the IP address or host name for your VPN server.

6. You need to either type in the name of the remote VPN server computer that you want to connect to, or enter the TCP/IP address for that same computer. If you are actually trying to create a VPN connection within your own corporate network, it might be easier to use a host name rather than an IP address.

NOTE
When making a VPN connection inside your own corporate WAN, you do not need to use another Dial-Up Networking connection along with the Dial-Up Networking session that you are creating in these steps. Instead, after this VPN connection is created, you will secure a connection to the VPN server, and then use your own, other means for transporting the data back and forth along your new encrypted tunnel.

9.6
USE VIRTUAL PRIVATE NETWORKING

7. Type in the necessary information, and then click the Next> button to continue. The final screen in the Make New Connection Wizard appears, as shown in Figure 9.33.

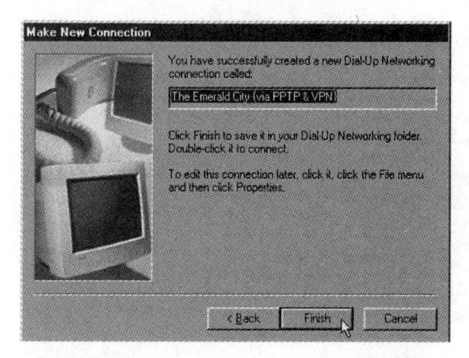

Figure 9.33 Finishing the Make New Connection Wizard.

8. This is an informational screen only. Read the information and click Finish to continue, as shown in Figure 9.34.

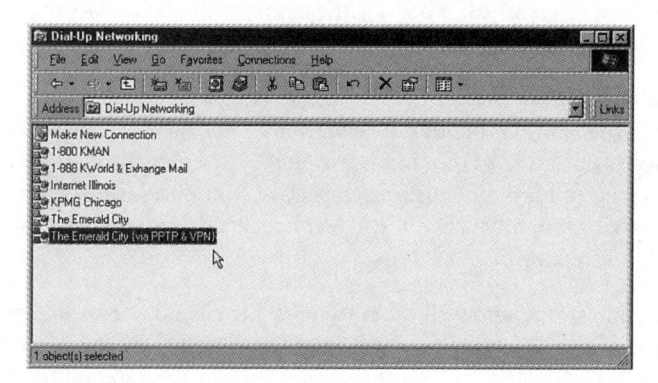

Figure 9.34 Reviewing your newly created VPN/PPTP Dial-Up Networking connection.

9. You now see the Dial-Up Networking screen, with your newly created connection at the bottom of the list. To start using PPTP through a VPN session, you first need to make your connection to the Internet. You do this by double-clicking the Dial-Up Networking session icon for your ISP, and then clicking once on the Connect button on the Connect To screen that appears for that ISP.

10. Once this connection has been established, then you will need to start your VPN session by double-clicking on the new VPN icon that you just created as shown in Figure 9.35.

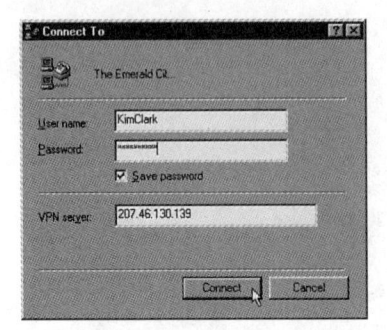

Figure 9.35 Entering your username and password on the Connect To screen.

11. The Connect To screen for your new VPN connection appears. If you look closely, you will notice that there is no box with a telephone number. Instead, there is just a box for the name or IP address of your VPN server. Click once on the Connect button to start this connection as well.

12. After you have been authenticated by your VPN server, as well as your ISP, your ISP's computers automatically route all of the network traffic from your PC over the Internet to the VPN server that you have connected to. From a user's perspective, you now have an encrypted tunnel through which you can send packets of information without fear of interception.

13. If you want to know all the nitty-gritty details on Microsoft's implementation of the PPTP protocol, you might want to review the Microsoft technical white paper on the same subject. It can be found on the Internet at http://www.microsoft.com/communications/ and is named "Installing, Configuring, and Using PPTP with Microsoft Clients and Servers."

14. To end a PPTP session with a VPN server, just click once on the Disconnect button that you see on the connection screen to your ISP and the connection screen to the VPN server.

9.7 How do I...
Use more than one modem at a time with a single Dial-Up Networking connection?

COMPLEXITY
INTERMEDIATE

Problem

I find that with a penchant for more multimedia content on the Internet, I no longer am able to surf the Web as fast as I used to. I cannot afford a high-speed digital connection to the Internet such as ISDN, xDSL, or T1, and the analog cable modem technology has not made it to my neighborhood yet. Is there any way that I can combine existing home analog telephone lines together to make one faster connection?

Technique

With the advent of Windows NT Server 4.0, came a new technology known as *Multilink*. Multilink provides you with the capability to combine multiple physical modems and communications lines together to form a single higher-speed connection to a host computer system. Microsoft embedded this technology into the Windows 9x platforms starting with an upgrade to the Windows 95 Dial-Up Networking client and as the Dial-Up Networking method under Windows 98.

The requirements for sustaining a Multilink connection to the Internet are simple. You must have two or more modems that can be of varying speeds, 33.6Kbps modems are perfect for this (for example, one modem could be a 57.6Kbps, one 28.8Kbps, and another one a 33.6 fax/voice modem); you must have a single physical telephone line connection for each modem that you use; your ISP must support the point-to-point communications protocol (PPP) and Multilink connectivity; and you must be able to sign on multiple times from your Internet account simultaneously. You will find that if all the modems used are all of the same speed, the Windows 98 Multilink process works that much better. Additionally, the use of Multilink is only possible through the Windows 98 Dial-Up Networking clients and not the server versions.

There are, of course, some caveats to using Multilink with a Windows 98 Dial-Up Networking connection. Because Multilink was originally designed for use with ISDN, it does not always work perfectly with analog communications lines. You might experience a problem known as a *serial overrun*, which means that data being transmitted to and from your PC via a Multilink connection might essentially step on itself. In addition, you might quite frequently find yourself using two 57.6Kbps modems, but only connecting at 96.6Kbps. This could be a problem with your ISP's incapability to properly configure and use Multilink, or it could be an issue with your local telephone company. Regardless of who is to blame, it never really makes you feel any better knowing you are losing those extra 18.6Kbps of bandwidth to unnecessary overhead.

To install and configure Multilink with one of your Windows 98 Dial-Up Networking sessions, carefully follow these steps and you will soon be on your way to a faster surfing experience.

Steps

1. Open the Dial-Up Networking screen. The easiest way to get to this screen is by double-clicking the My Computer icon on the Windows 98 desktop.

2. Highlight the Dial-Up Networking session that you want to use Multilink with by clicking it.

3. Then click once with the secondary mouse button to reveal a small menu. At the bottom of this menu, click once on the Properties menu selection to open that Dial-Up Networking session's properties screen.

4. Next, click the Multilink tab (farthest to the right), in order to reveal the screen shown in Figure 9.36.

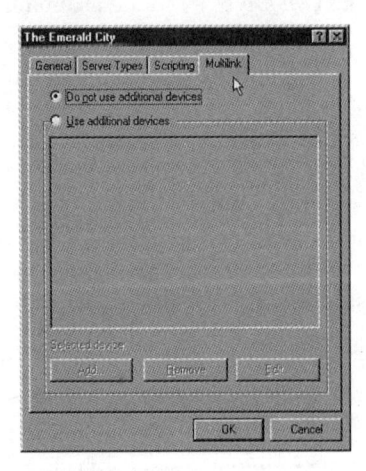

Figure 9.36 Deciding whether to use Multilink on your PC.

9.7
USE MORE THAN ONE MODEM WITH A SINGLE CONNECTION

5. The screen that you see is labeled whatever you named your Dial-Up Networking session. In the example, you see that it is called *The Emerald City*. There are two radio button options here. The top one marks the Multilink capability as disabled while the second one enables it.

6. Click the radio button next to the label Use Additional Devices, and then click once on the Add... button at the bottom of the screen. The Edit Extra Device window appears, as shown in Figure 9.37.

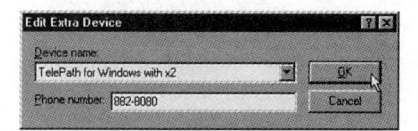

Figure 9.37 Selecting the second modem device to be used.

7. Use the drop-down list box to select the secondary modem that you want to use with this Dial-Up Networking session. Be careful to choose a modem that is not the same physical device that you used when configuring the original Dial-Up Networking session (for example, they cannot be the same physical device; you must have at least two physical modem devices installed in your computer). Next, type in the telephone number for the ISP (or host computer) that this additional modem will dial, and then click OK. The Multilink tab appears, as shown in Figure 9.38.

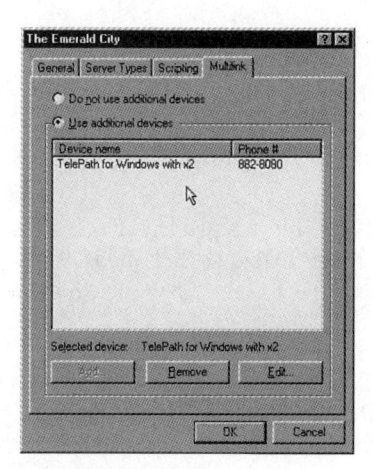

Figure 9.38 Reviewing your Mulitlink device list.

8. Although you can define multiple modems to use with a Multilink connection, it is probably not practical to have more than two or three modems configured for any one Multilink session. The reasoning for this is that you must have a physical modem and telephone line for each device configured for use with a Multilink session. This becomes rather tough with a home PC, especially because many homes do not have more than one or two telephone lines. But, assuming that they do, it is still very difficult to configure more than two serial modems on a home computer, unless you have taken the trouble to install an additional serial card or a multiport device, such as a DigiBoard (this is a SCSI-based device that adds 8, 16, or 24 additional serial ports to your computer). A DigiBoard is not that cheap (about $600) when compared to the cost of the hardware required for an ISDN connection, so you might want to carefully compare costs prior to procuring this type of a device for your PC.

9. After you have added all the devices you want, click OK to return to the Dial-Up Networking screen as shown in Figure 9.39.

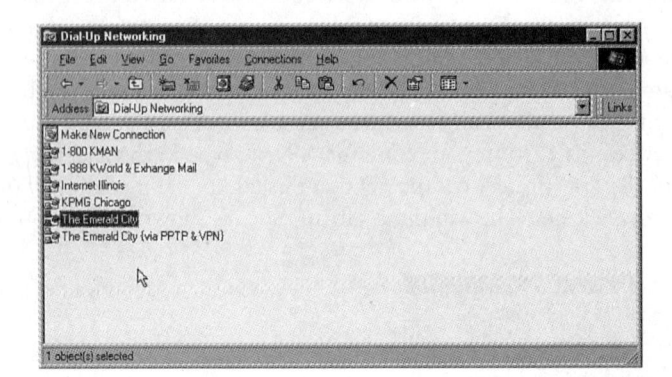

Figure 9.39 Accessing your Multilink connection.

10. Your Dial-Up Networking session appears just as it has before. To use it with Multilink, all you need to do is double-click the Dial-Up Networking icon. After the Connect To window appears, click the Connect button to initiate the Multilink connection.

11. Both modems dial (in a synchronous fashion) and make your authenticated connection to your ISP or other remote host computer. When both connections have been made, you can start to surf the Internet or that remote computer at a much greater rate that you have been able to previously.

12. To end the Dial-Up Networking session, you simply click the Disconnect button as you always have in the past. That is all you need to do to configure and use the Windows 98 Multilink feature.

CHAPTER 10
WELCOME TO THE NEIGHBORHOOD: NETWORK, THAT IS...

10

WELCOME TO THE NEIGHBORHOOD: NETWORK, THAT IS...

How do I...

- 10.1 Know what other networks to which I can connect?
- 10.2 Add and configure additional network clients?
- 10.3 Configure my system for multiple users?
- 10.4 Add new network adapters?
- 10.5 Add new network protocols to my Windows PC?
- 10.6 Configure TCP/IP for use on my Windows 98 PC?
- 10.7 Know when to add new network services?
- 10.8 Configure File Sharing?
- 10.9 Automatically log on to my network using the proper user ID and password?
- 10.10 Change either the computer name or workgroup name for my Windows 98 PC?

CHAPTER 10
WELCOME TO THE NEIGHBORHOOD: NETWORK, THAT IS...

The focus of this chapter is networking, establishing network connections as a client PC to a host server, and networking in a peer-to-peer type of connectivity. This includes network client software, networking protocols, and networking services. The various types of networks that Windows 98 can act as a client in are covered, as well as how to make some of the more popular network connections. Strategies for configuring and performing File Sharing are also discussed. Additional items include advanced network topics such as browser configuration, Novell NetWare connectivity, and how to troubleshoot browsing problems with your Windows 98 PCs.

10.1 Know What Other Networks to Which I Can Connect

This How-To assists you in familiarizing yourself with the other network operating systems (OS) to which a Windows 98 PC can connect.

10.2 Add and Configure Additional Network Clients

Now that you know what types of network systems Windows 98 is capable of connecting to, you need to be able to install the proper networking client software for accessing those other networks as well as to perform the basic configuring for that new networking client software.

10.3 Configure My System for Multiple Users

The focus here is to be able to configure a Windows 98 PC for use with multiple users, where each person's information is kept distinctly separate from anyone else's data. This How-To explains the steps involved for setting up your Windows 98 PC in such a way.

10.4 Add New Network Adapters

Now that you know what types of network systems Windows 98 is capable of connecting to, you need to be able to install the proper network adapter software for accessing those other networks.

10.5 Add New Network Protocols to My Windows PC

Now that you know what types of network systems Windows 98 is capable of connecting to, you will now need to be able to install the proper network protocols for accessing those other networks.

10.6 Configure TCP/IP for Use on My Windows 98 PC

The process of configuring the Transmission Control Protocol/Internet Protocol (TCP/IP) on a Windows 98 PC can get complicated. Therefore, the focus of this How-To is to help you walk through this maze of complexity.

10.7 Know When to Add New Network Services

Now that you know what types of network systems Windows 98 is capable of connecting to, you need to be able to install the proper network services software for accessing those other networks.

10.8 Configure File Sharing
The focus here is to help you configure your Windows 98 PC so that you can share files across a network, regardless of whether it is public or private.

10.9 Automatically Log On to My Network, Using the Proper User ID and Password
This How-To shows you how helpful it would be if you could make that Windows 98 server-type system automatically re-log on to your network in case of an unattended reboot of that computer.

10.10 Change Either the Computer Name or Workgroup Name for My Windows 98 PC
This How-To explains how to change your computer and workgroup name for your Windows 98 PC in case you change your mind about the original names you set up.

COMPLEXITY
INTERMEDIATE

10.1 How do I...
Know what other networks I can connect to?

Problem
I know that I can use a Windows 98 client PC with both Windows NT and Novell NetWare Servers, but my company has UNIX servers on corporate network as well. Can I use Windows 98 as a client on those types of networks? How do I know what other networks I can connect to?

Technique
Windows 98 is capable of acting as a client machine on a multitude of networks such as:

- Windows NT (any version)
- Novell NetWare (version 3.x or later)
- Windows 95/98 Peer-to-Peer Workgroups
- Artisoft LANtastic (version 7.0 or later)

- Banyan Vines (version 7.1 or later)
- Sun Solaris UNIX (using an NFS add-on)
- Hewlett-Packard HP-UX UNIX (using an NFS add-on)
- IBM mainframe and AS/400 host computer systems

The most important concept to remember is the networking protocol that is being used for connectivity across your organization's networks. It is the networking communications protocol that actually defines the type(s) of PCs and servers that your Windows 98 computer is capable of connecting with. For example, if IPX/SPX is the only available protocol, you know right away that you will be connecting with either a Windows NT or a Novell NetWare system because UNIX and IBM host systems are not capable of "speaking" the language of IPX/SPX.

Many other networking operating systems can use Windows 98 computers as client due to the extensive protocol support that Microsoft has built into its latest 32-bit operating system. For example, you can use the Microsoft TCP/IP protocol stack to connect across your organization's networks in order to communicate with all kinds of non-Microsoft operating systems. These non-Microsoft systems include Apple's Macintosh systems, IBM mainframes and AS/400s, countless types of UNIX systems (such as HP-UX, Sun Solaris, Red Hat Linux, IBM AIX, SCO UNIX, and so on), Open VMS systems, or other Internet host computers. Connectivity via TCP/IP to a Novell NetWare Server running NetWare/IP is made possible by using the Novell Client for Windows 98.

The process for determining the types of networks that you are able to connect your Windows 98 PC is a pretty straightforward effort. Follow these instructions to learn what networks you can or cannot connect to.

Steps

1. First, you need to determine whether you have a bridged or routed network (or neither, if it is a peer-to-peer network). This becomes important because some network protocols are not routable (such as Microsoft's NetBEUI), which means that its data packets cannot be passed across a router (a networking component that is used to connect various networks or subnets together). A bridged network uses either a hardware or software bridge to connect two or more same protocol LANs together, whereas a router can do the same thing but also for different protocols as well as different TCP/IP subnets.

2. Determine the types of servers that exist on your organization's network; this can be accomplished in many ways. Most Information Services (IS) departments do (and should) have a network schematic of their existing networks, including the types of network operating systems and networking protocols in use. With this data, you can start to make intelligent decisions regarding the types of networks that your Windows 98 computer(s) are capable of interfacing with.

3. Create a report, with columns, by using the following list as your guide:

- Server OS vendor name
- Server OS
- Protocol vendor name
- Type of protocol
- Want ✔

4. The columns with the labels Vendor name contain the names of the vendors that supply that particular server OS or networking protocol. The Server OS column is where you keep track of the various operating systems that exist on your organization's networks. The Type of protocol column is where you keep track of the networking protocols that are within your organization's networks. The Want ✔ column is obviously where you place a check mark that denotes whether you want to use either this server OS or networking protocol with your Windows 98 computers.

> **NOTE**
>
> Keep in mind that it is important to track the vendor for both the OS and the networking protocols. Although at first glance this might appear to be extra work, it does pay off in the long run. For example, everyone knows who makes NetWare or Windows NT, as well as NetBEUI, but it can be tough to figure out who the vendor is for Linux (a UNIX operating system). In addition, when you get your TCP/IP protocol stack it can be almost anyone: IBM, Microsoft, Novell, Sun, and so on. Take the time up front so that the analysis portion of this project takes less time and is of more benefit to you and your organization.

5. After you have a complete list of all the server operating systems and networking protocols, the hard work begins. You need to determine whether you want to connect your Windows 98 PC to each of these network servers using the protocols available. You can, of course, add new networking protocols at any time, but you should evaluate each new protocol's impact on your networks before actually implementing them (a whole new project).

6. To help you figure out which network systems can be accessed by which protocol(s), you should carefully examine the following list:

- Microsoft Windows NT servers can be accessed by Windows 98 computers via the Microsoft TCP/IP stack, the Microsoft IPX/SPX-compatible protocol (which works fine with Novell NetWare servers as well), and Microsoft NetBEUI.

- Novell NetWare servers can be accessed using the Microsoft IPX/SPX-compatible protocol with either the Microsoft Client for NetWare Networks or the Novell Client for Windows 95/98. It is important to remember that the Microsoft TCP/IP stack does not work as a replacement to the NetWare/IP stack, which means that you cannot use the Microsoft IP stack for accessing the Novell NetWare servers via TCP/IP.

- The 32-bit DLC (Data Link Control) protocol that comes with Windows 98 can be used to connect to IBM mainframe and AS/400 computer systems. The DLC protocol is commonly found in implementations that require the use of a host terminal-emulation software package (such as a 3270 emulator).

- IBM Mainframe systems can also be accessed via the Microsoft TCP/IP protocol if the mainframe supports the TCP/IP protocol stack or with the assistance of an SNA gateway such as Microsoft's SNA Gateway product.

- UNIX systems also support the Microsoft TCP/IP protocol, but usually require the use of an NFS client to permit a Windows 98 user full access to that UNIX system. There are different NFS clients on the market for the most popular UNIX systems, such as Sun Solaris, Hewlett-Packard HP-UX, and IBM AIX. If you are only using a particular UNIX box for database connectivity, the use of an NFS client software package is probably not necessary. That is, if your network application runs off of a Windows NT Server and interacts with your Windows 98 PC clients using the UNIX machine only as its database server, it is most likely that you only require the use of a TCP/IP protocol stack (such as the Microsoft-provided one that comes with Windows 98) to access that UNIX host. The additional expense that comes with an NFS client is probably not required here.

7. So much for the Windows 98-supplied networking protocols. A Windows 98 client PC is capable of accessing many other network types via third-party protocols and their associated client networking software for

10.1
KNOW WHAT OTHER NETWORKS I CAN CONNECT TO

Windows 98. The following list is a sampling of the network types available to you, for use with the Windows 98 PC clients:

- Using the Artisoft LANtastic protected-mode client software, you are able to use Windows 98 with an Artisoft LANtastic server. There are a few catches though: Any version prior to version 7.0 is not only unsupported, it is strongly recommended that you avoid anything earlier. Also, you will want to install the Windows 98 operating system first. Then, you install the client software for your LANtastic network because trying to do both simultaneously is a recipe for disaster and a failed Windows 98 installation process. You might want to check out Artisoft's Internet Web site (http://www.artisoft.com) for more up-to-date details.

- With software provided by Banyan Systems, Inc., you are able to install either a 16- or 32-bit version of the client software for connectivity to its fading VINES server environments. This includes support for the Banyan Enterprise Clients for Windows 95, protected-mode clients, and real-mode clients with the Banyan VINES version 7.1 or later. It is strongly recommended that you stick with the 32-bit protected-mode client software under Windows 98, as well as with Banyan VINES servers of version 7.1 or newer. Keep in mind that you need version 7.32 of the Banyan Enterprise Client software if you want to use system policies, whereas version 8.02 or newer of this same software is required for user policies. You might want to check out Banyan's Internet Web site at http://www.artisoft.com for more up-to-date details on using Windows 98 client computers to connect to Banyan VINES servers.

- Remember that world-famous server software by DEC (now Compaq, Inc.) known as DIGITAL PATHWORKS 32? Yeah, well me neither. However, Microsoft Windows 98 can use the DECnet protocol along with the DIGITAL PATHWORKS 32 client software (available from Compaq) to connect to nodes on networks that are running the DECnet protocol. The only downside with Windows 98 is that it is probably impossible to make any earlier versions of PATHWORKS work on a Windows 98 PC. However, on the bright side, neither DEC nor Compaq support the earlier versions either. Contact Compaq on the Internet at http://www.compaq.com for further support details.

- Some more history: Remember Microsoft's first attempt at a 32-bit operating system? You guessed it. OS/2 (a joint venture between IBM and Microsoft). If all you need to do is access non-secure shares on either an IBM OS/2 LAN server or an IBM OS/2 Warp server, you can use the Client for Microsoft Networks that comes with the Windows 98 OS. However, if you need to be authenticated by either of these two IBM server types or if you need to access secured areas as well as execute scripts, you must install an IBM-supplied software client for use with Windows 98. That client software is known as the IBM Networks Client for Windows 95. The installation of this client software is very easy; follow the prompts and click OK a few times. Keep in mind that you must use either the Microsoft NetBEUI or TCP/IP networking protocols with this software. Additionally, you must already have installed the Client for Microsoft Networks client software that comes with the Windows 98 OS, before you will be able to successfully install the IBM Networks Client for Windows 95. If you have questions, seek out the IBM Web site on the Internet at http://www.ibm.com (this is a well-developed site, so you should not have any difficulties finding what you need).

- To connect a Windows 98 PC to an IBM AS/400 midrange computer, you can use the IBM PC Support application software that usually comes with an AS/400 computer when you buy/lease it. Make sure that you are using the Basic Mode and not the Extended Mode configuration because Windows 98 does not support it. Also, you might want to check to see which networking protocol is in use with the AS/400 (such as DLC, IPX/SPX, and so on) before you attempt to configure your Windows 98 computer(s) because you must install these same protocols on your Windows 98 computer(s) first.

8. A few more thoughts you might want to consider, and then you are finished. First, the Windows 98 Client for NetWare Networks does not always support lowercase extended characters (found on your keyboard) with Novell NetWare 4.1, so you might need to change to all uppercase characters. Consider a visit to Novell's Internet Web site at http://www.novell.com for further details.

9. During a mass rollout of Windows 98, using the MSBATCH.INF scripting file, you will not be able to install the 16-bit Banyan VINES client software. In order to install this version of the Banyan software, you need to first deploy Windows 98, and then go back and install the 16-bit Banyan VINES client software.

10. Many of the third-party TCP/IP protocol stacks do not work with Windows 98, such as FTP Software's OnNet32 TCP/IP protocol stack. If you must use this protocol stack, it would be a very wise decision to install it prior to deploying Windows 98 on that same PC. This is due to a

10.1
KNOW WHAT OTHER NETWORKS I CAN CONNECT TO

problem within Windows 98 that sometimes prevents these third-party TCP/IP stacks from installing correctly after the Windows 98 OS has been installed.

11. If you must connect to a Samba server, you first must cripple the password encryption that Windows 98 automatically sets for all its passwords. That is, Windows 98 prohibits the use of clear text (plain text) passwords in its base implementation unless you intentionally disable the encrypted password setting in the Registry. To do this, you need to start the Windows 98 Registry Editor tool known as RegEdit.exe (use the Run command box from the Start menu).

12. Type in the command `RegEdit.exe` (not case-sensitive), and then either click OK or press Enter.

13. This takes you into the Windows 98 Registry, where you need to maneuver your way down to the HKEY_LOCAL_MACHINE\System\CurrentControlSet\Services\VxD subkeys, as shown in Figure 10.1.

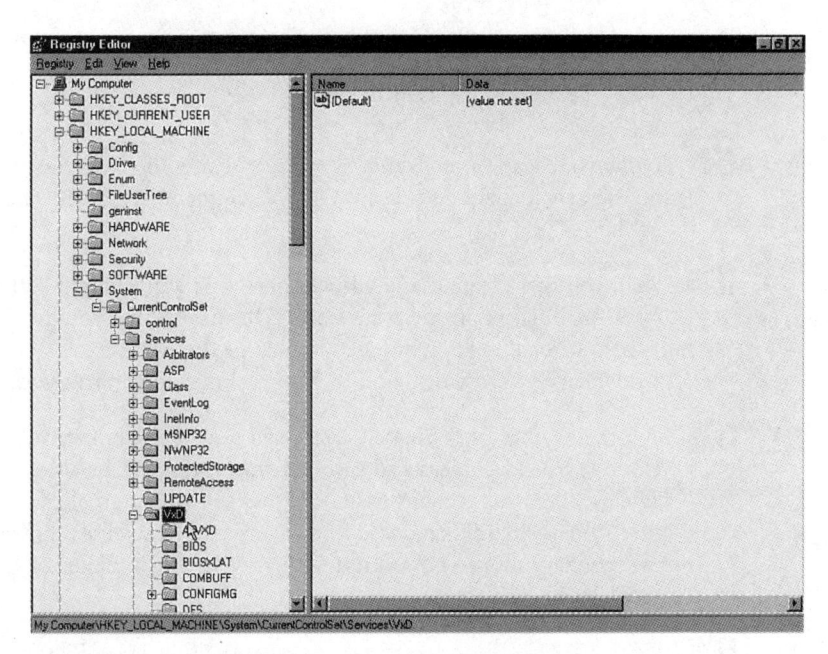

Figure 10.1 Disabling the Encrypted Password feature of Windows 98.

14. This is where the fun begins. Now you need to add a new Registry subkey to your Windows 98 system. Click once on the Vnetsup subkey folder (found under the Vxd subkey). From this subkey click the secondary mouse button (the right mouse button for all you right-handed folks out there) to reveal the small menu shown in Figure 10.2.

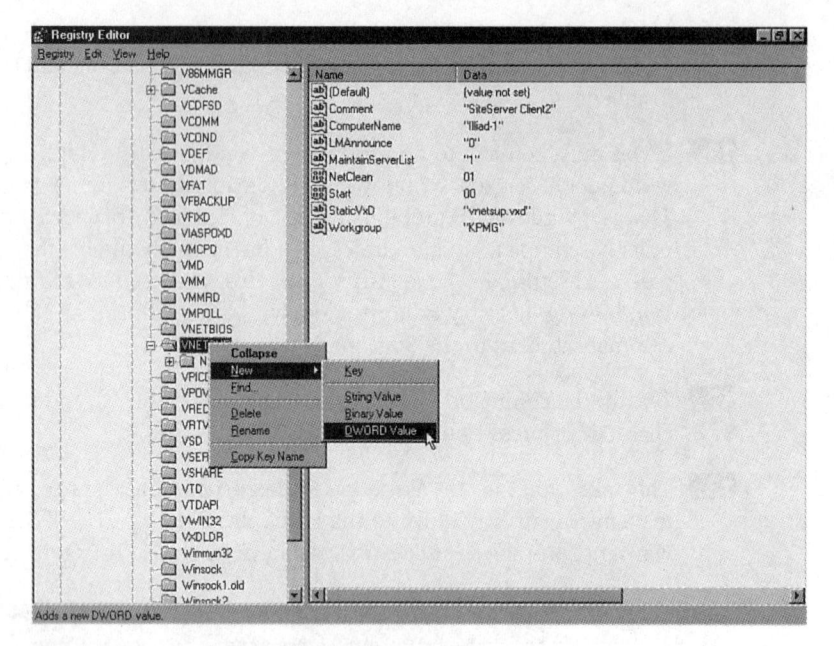

CHAPTER 10
WELCOME TO THE NEIGHBORHOOD: NETWORK, THAT IS...

Figure 10.2 Revealing the Registry.

15. Follow your way through this menu by clicking the New menu option, and then click again on the DWORD Value menu selection. This creates a new key.

16. When you first create the key it will have a default dummy name and appear highlighted inside a faint box. This means that you are able to edit the name. For this key, you need to change the name to EnablePlainTextPassword, and then press Enter to confirm your choice.

17. After the key has been created, you need to give it a binary value so that Windows 98 can understand it (don't worry, you will be able to enter this value as a decimal number that Windows 98 will automatically convert into its own machine-readable format). To add this value, click once with the secondary mouse button to reveal another small menu, as shown in Figure 10.3.

18. Click once on the Modify menu to reveal the Edit DWORD Value screen, as shown in Figure 10.4.

10.1 KNOW WHAT OTHER NETWORKS I CAN CONNECT TO

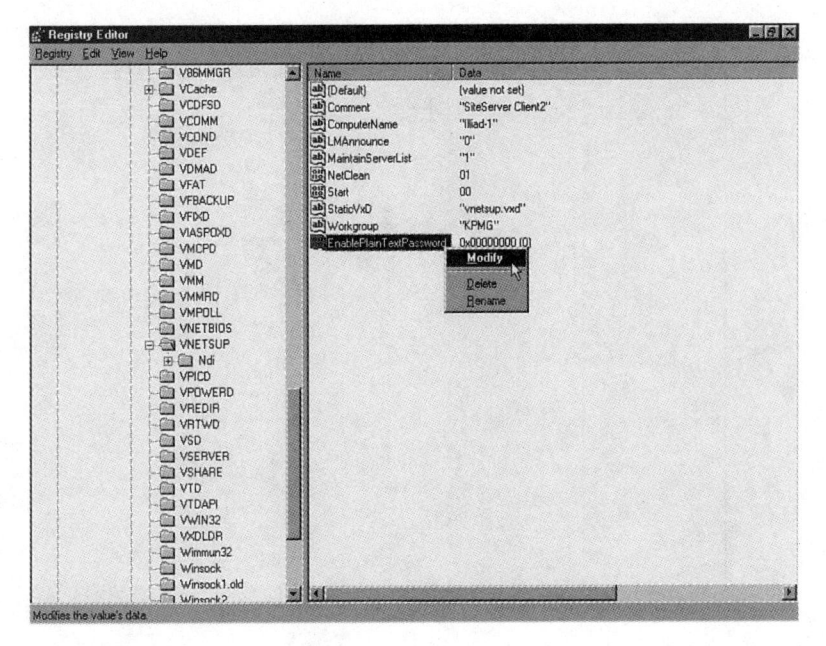

Figure 10.3 Naming a Registry key then accessing the Modify menu.

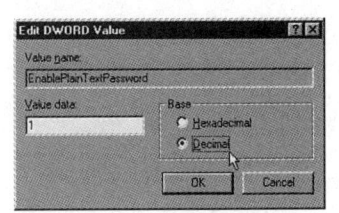

Figure 10.4 Adding a new Registry key's value.

19. The value's name appears in the top box (so you know that you are editing the correct Registry key). Click the Decimal radio button to select that format of the Base numbering system. Then, type in the number 1 in the Value Data box that appears just to the left of the Base area. This sets the value's meaning to Yes, as in "Yes, I want to enable plain text passwords on my Windows 98 PC." Click OK to review your settings, as shown in Figure 10.5.

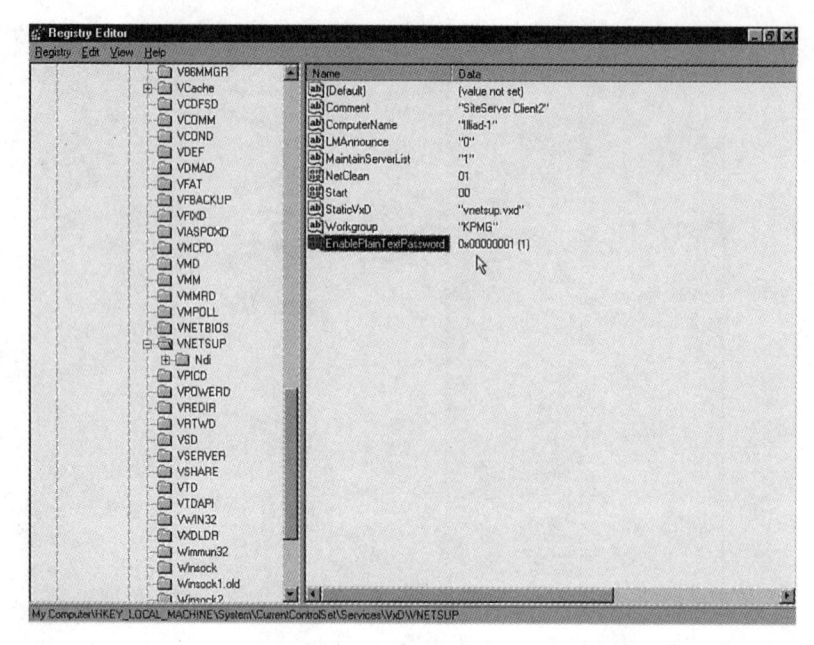

Figure 10.5 You can now review your settings in the Registry Editor.

20. If at any time you want to disable clear text passwords on your Windows 98 PC, either change the value to a zero or delete the entire key value. To delete a value, highlight it with a single-click of your mouse pointer on the specific key, and then press the Del key on your keyboard to complete the deletion process.

COMPLEXITY
INTERMEDIATE

10.2 How do I...
Add and configure additional network clients?

Problem

I used to only connect to a Windows NT Server, but now there is a Novell NetWare Server on the network that contains important files I must connect to. How do I configure an additional network client for use with my Windows 98 PC? Also, how would I configure my Windows 98 PC for a networking logon-type system for a home family use?

ADD AND CONFIGURE ADDITIONAL NETWORK CLIENTS

Technique

The Windows 98 OS makes it straightforward to add new client software to it, including both the built-in clients as well as any third-party networking client software. The only place where this might get a little confusing is for the home or family user of Windows 98, who might be trying to configure the Microsoft Family Logon client software. To do this, you must first configure your PC for use with multiple users (review the next topic in this chapter if you are unsure as to how to do this), *before* you install the Microsoft Family Logon client software.

For demonstration purposes only, you will install the client software for both a Novell NetWare LAN and the Microsoft Family Logon. To get started, follow the next set of instructions and you will be on your way to connecting your Windows 98 PC with all types of server and network operating systems, as well as your local peer-to-peer network.

Steps

1. Access the Windows 98 Control Panel by clicking the Start button, and then click the Settings menu option, followed by a click on the Control Panel menu selection.

2. This takes you into the Control Panel screen where you need to double-click the Network icon to reveal the next screen, as shown in Figure 10.6. Alternatively, you can quickly go to this same screen by holding down the Alt key on your keyboard and double-clicking the Network Neighborhood icon on the Windows 98 desktop (assuming, of course, that you have at least one networking software client already installed; otherwise, there will not be a Network Neighborhood icon on your desktop).

3. After the Network window appears, you should take a closer look at it because it possesses a wealth of useful information. In the top boxed area you see a listing of all the networking components that are already installed on your computer. Use the scrollbar along the right side of the box if there are more items listed than appear in the window area. At the top of the listing is all the networking client software (in the example you see only the Client for Microsoft Networks), as denoted by a small computer icon to the left of the client software product's name.

The next set of objects is the various network adapters (NICs) that you have installed on your computer. These are denoted by the icon that looks like a small network card with a fuzzy letter P on the right side of it. Keep in mind that these network adapters can be real, physical cards that are physically installed inside your PC or they might be virtual (for example, logical devices) that are software-created cards that exist only in your computer's memory systems.

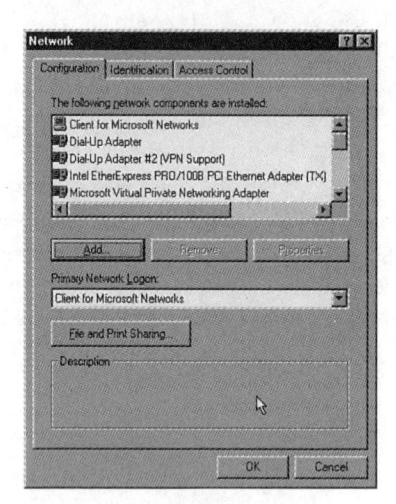

Figure 10.6 Accessing the Windows 98 Network Configuration tab.

Below the NICs are the networking protocols that are already installed on your computer. These are marked with a small cable-looking icon that has a plug in the middle of it (just as the cable slopes downward). Windows 98 comes with several network protocols: the ATM Call Manager; the ATM Emulated LAN, the ATM Emulation Client, the Fast Infrared, the IPX/SPX-compatible, the Microsoft 32-bit DLC, the Microsoft DLC, NetBEUI, and TCP/IP protocols. Additionally, you have the ability to install many other third-party networking protocols as well.

The final item(s) in the box are the networking services that are already installed on your Windows 98 PC. The icon that resembles a PC with an outstretched hand underneath it denotes these services. Windows 98 has three networking services built into it: File and Printer Sharing for Microsoft Networks, File and Printer Sharing for NetWare Networks, and the Service for NetWare Directory Services. However, there are literally hundreds of third-party services available for the Windows 95/98 OS, most of which are installed via this networking screen you see.

In the middle of this screen you can see what the primary network client logon has been set as the default for your computer. Using the drop-down list box, you are able to alter this logon choice however you see fit. Below

10.2
ADD AND CONFIGURE ADDITIONAL NETWORK CLIENTS

this drop-down list box you can use the File and Printer Sharing... button to select and install this feature for whichever client software is set as your system's primary network logon means.

4. So, to continue on, click once on the Add... button just above the Primary Network Logon text label, near the middle of this screen. This takes you to the next screen, as shown in Figure 10.7.

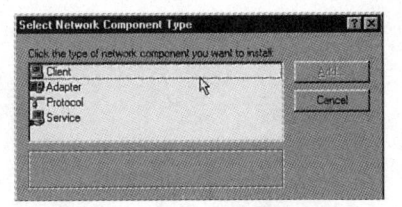

Figure 10.7 The Select Network Component Type screen.

5. Click once on the Client network component option, and then click on the Add... button to continue. This brings up the Select Network Client screen, as shown in Figure 10.8, which is used to add the appropriate networking component to your Windows 98 PC.

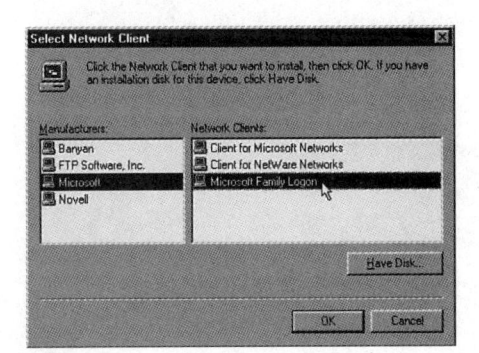

Figure 10.8 Adding a new client network component.

6. Choose the manufacturer of the networking component in the left windowpane by clicking that vendor's name, such as Microsoft. Then, all the available network clients for that particular vendor appear in the right windowpane (under the text label of the same name). So, click the Microsoft name under the Manufacturers windowpane (on the left), and then click the Microsoft Family Logon selection under the Network Clients windowpane (on the right) to select it. Click OK to continue, which take you back to the Network screen, as shown in Figure 10.9.

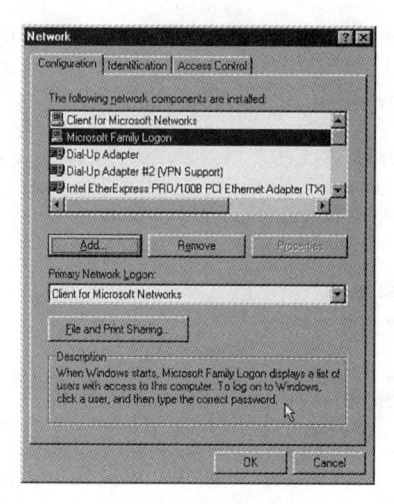

Figure 10.9 Viewing your newly added client network component.

7. Because you want to also add the client software for a Novell NetWare LAN, you need to click once more on the Add... button. What you are doing is essentially redoing step 5. Only this time, instead of selecting the Microsoft Family Logon selection under the Network Clients windowpane, you need to choose the Client for NetWare Networks, as shown in Figure 10.10.

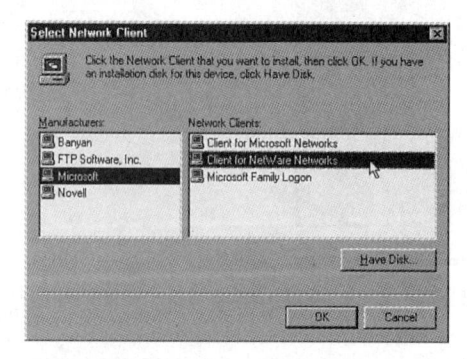

Figure 10.10 Adding a second client network component, the client for NetWare networks.

8. After you have highlighted this client software component, click OK to return to the Network screen, as shown in Figure 10.11.

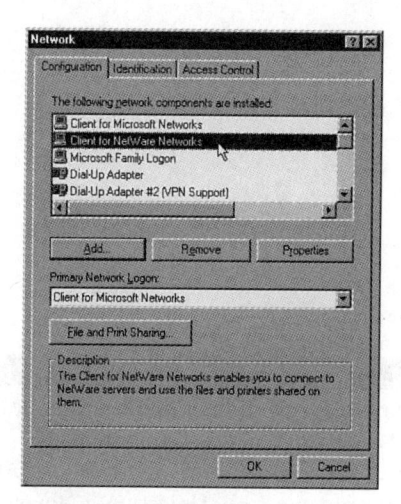

10.2 ADD AND CONFIGURE ADDITIONAL NETWORK CLIENTS

Figure 10.11 Viewing both of the newly added client network components.

9. On the Network screen you can see all three of the client network software components. However, there is a bit more work to be done before you get to the actual installation of the software bits. With the Client for NetWare Networks highlighted, click the Properties button to reveal the next screen, shown in Figure 10.12.

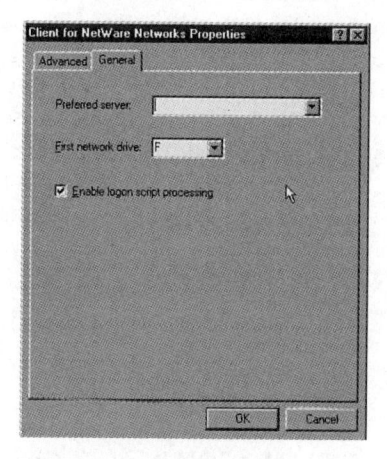

Figure 10.12 Viewing the Client for NetWare Networks Properties General tab.

10. The Novell NetWare network operating software likes to have a Preferred Server named on the client side so that the client PC is better capable of locating the proper server on the Novell LAN for authentication purposes. The NetBIOS name of that server is what you type into the Preferred server drop-down list box area.

11. You also need to select the First Network Drive for the NetWare network. Type in the alpha letter for the network drive that you want to be the first for your connection.

> **NOTE**
> The setting of the first network drive can be misleading to a lot of people. It is a commonly held assumption since the early days of Novell networking that the first network drive for a Novell NetWare LAN must be the letter F, but in fact this is not the case. Unless your Novell NetWare system administrator has hard-coded this letter as part of your logon scripts, either on the server side or the client side, you can use any available letter in the alphabet as the first network drive letter.

12. The last area to configure on this tab is the Logon Script Processing option. This too, can be very misleading to many users of NetWare. It is generally assumed that if your system administrators have created long, complex logon scripts for everyone in the organization, you must enable the processing of those scripts in order to do your work each day. For the most part, this is a false statement. With Windows 98, if all you use the NetWare servers for is File Sharing and print services, enabling this option is a waste of time and your computer's system resources. As long as you authenticate to the Novell LAN and manually map any drives that you use (instead of the 10 or more that Novell LAN administrators love to assign for whatever reason), there is really no reason to enable the logon script processing feature of the Client for NetWare Networks in Windows 98. However, if you want or need to enable it, click the Enable Logon Script processing check box to place a check mark in the box (which enables this feature).

13. After you have made all the entries you need or want, click the Advanced tab to move to that screen, shown in Figure 10.13.

14. The default setting on this screen's only option is to enable the Preserve Case property function. Unless your NetWare administrator advises otherwise, you probably want to leave this enabled so that case settings are preserved when copying/moving/creating files around on your NetWare servers. After you have made your selection, click OK to return to the Network screen.

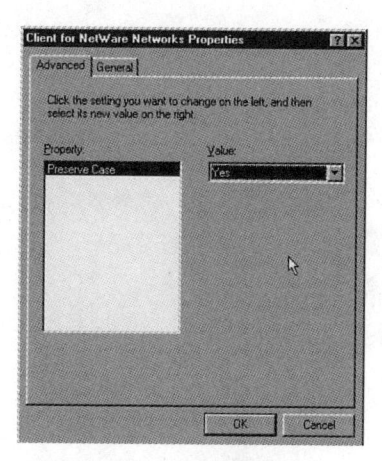

10.2
ADD AND CONFIGURE ADDITIONAL NETWORK CLIENTS

Figure 10.13 Viewing the Client for NetWare Networks Advanced options tab.

15. After you have arrived at the Network screen, you need to set the default network logon type. To do this, click the drop-down list box that appears below the Primary Network Logon label, as shown in Figure 10.14.

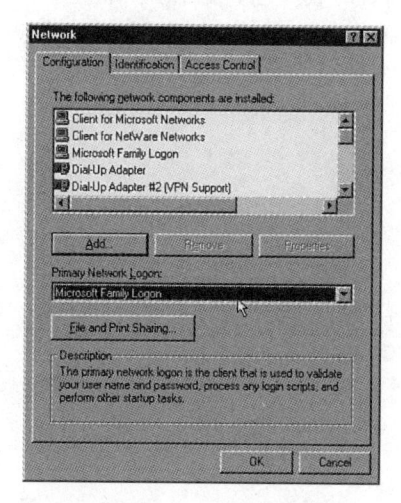

Figure 10.14 Changing the Primary Network Logon selection.

16. When you have made your choice, in this case Microsoft Family Logon client is selected, click OK to confirm all your choices and begin the installation of the actual networking software from the Windows 98 CD-ROM.

CHAPTER 10
WELCOME TO THE NEIGHBORHOOD: NETWORK, THAT IS...

17. You are prompted to insert your Windows 98 CD-ROM into your CD-ROM (or DVD-ROM) drive, at which point several new networking-related files are installed onto your computer. When the file installations are complete, the System Settings Change message box appears, as seen in Figure 10.15.

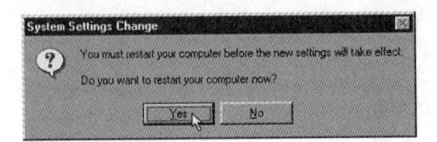

Figure 10.15 Deciding whether to reboot your Windows 98 PC.

18. Click Yes to permit Windows 98 to restart so that the changes you have made take effect. You might want to close any other active applications you have prior to restarting your system (just in case you had some other active programs).

19. After restarting your system, you are presented with the Microsoft Family Logon screen where you need to select the name of the user that you want to log on as. All the registered users (set up in the Users section of the Windows 98 Control Panel) of this Windows 98 PC automatically appear in the listing shown in this logon box, as shown in Figure 10.16.

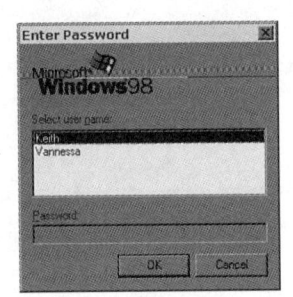

Figure 10.16 The Windows 98 Logon screen for the Microsoft Family Logon Networking Client software.

20. The Microsoft Family Logon screen is a very basic and non-secure way in which to manage a Windows 98 PC, which is perfect for the home PC where many people have to share the same computer. Now, if your primary logon method had been set to the Client for Microsoft Networks (or Novell, which was the other networking client that you installed) instead of the Microsoft Family Logon selection, the first screen you saw would be quite different, as you can see in Figure 10.17.

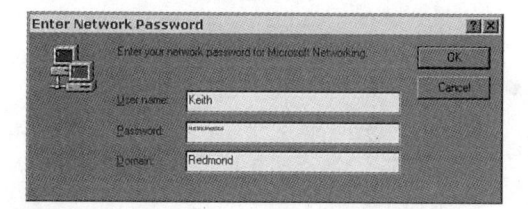

Figure 10.17 The Windows 98 Logon screen used to log on to a Microsoft Windows NT Server.

21. Most of the other networking client software that you install, be it for a Novell NetWare or a Microsoft Windows NT Server, will look pretty similar to this logon screen. There will be a spot for your user name, another box for the password, and probably a third box for your primary logon server's name (or directory service tree name). The gist is, is that with the exception of the Microsoft Family Logon screen, nearly all of the other networking clients have a similar look-and-feel to their logon screens.

COMPLEXITY
BEGINNER

10.3 How do I... Configure my system for multiple users?

Problem

I work in a call center group and we have several people all sharing the same computer. Is it possible to configure the PC so that it automatically recognizes new users to the PC, while at the same time giving the appearance of some level of security on the computer, possibly through a user ID logon with a password?

Technique

Windows 98 covers both of these requirements via a technology it refers to as a User Profiles. You need to first activate this multiple user technology, and then configure it for your computer. All these settings are part of the base Windows 98 OS and do not require any additional third-party software.

Steps

1. The User Profiles technology within Windows 98 is enabled from within the Control Panel. Open the Control Panel and double-click the User icon. This takes you into User Settings screen, as shown in Figure 10.18.

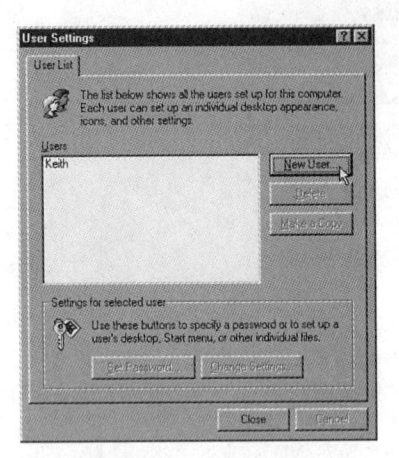

Figure 10.18 Creating a new user account for a multiuser Windows 98 PC.

2. On this screen is a listing of all the users that have already been created for this particular computer. If none had been created thus far, you would have been taken directly into the Add New User Wizard process to add the first user. For the example, assume that a single user already exists, but you want to add a second person to this computer via the wizard (which is the same wizard you would have seen when creating the first user). To start the wizard, click once on the New User... button to go to the Add User screen, as shown in Figure 10.19.

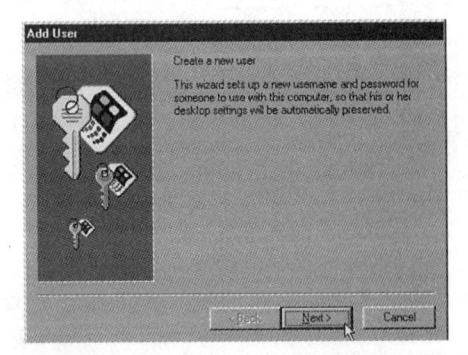

Figure 10.19 Starting the Create New User Wizard.

10.3
CONFIGURE MY SYSTEM FOR MULTIPLE USERS

3. This first screen contains some basic background information. Read it so that you understand it, and then click once on the Next> button to continue to the next screen, as shown in Figure 10.20.

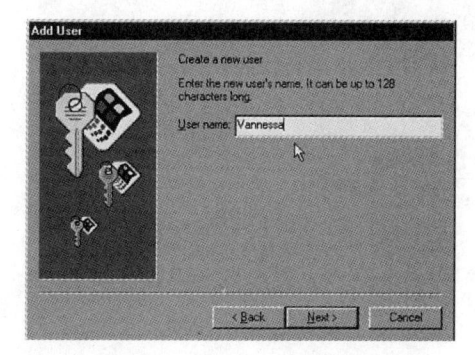

Figure 10.20 Entering the new user's name.

4. On this screen, type in a descriptive name for the user that you want to add. Once you have completed this task, click the Next> button to continue to the Password screen, as shown in Figure 10.21.

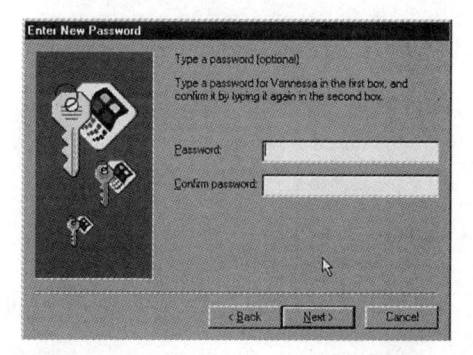

Figure 10.21 Creating a password for the new user.

5. Type a password in the top box, and then repeat that same password in the bottom box to confirm it. If you want this user to be created without a password, leave these two boxes blank. A Windows 98 user can change their password once they sign onto their computer. After you have completed this task, click the Next> button to continue to the Items Settings screen, as shown in Figure 10.22.

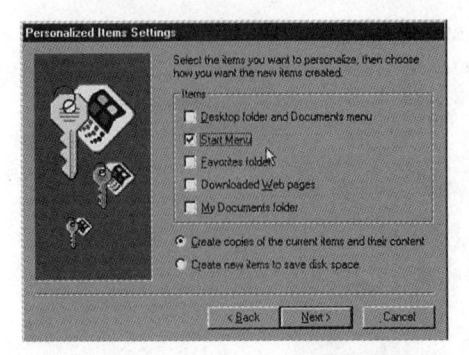

CHAPTER 10
WELCOME TO THE NEIGHBORHOOD: NETWORK, THAT IS...

Figure 10.22 Selecting which items you want to personalize for the new user.

6. The Personalized Items Settings screen appears with all of its check boxes blank, meaning that none of the items listed are created. You need to pick and choose those items that seem appropriate to your environment, by clicking the check boxes once to make your selection. On the radio button option at the bottom of the screen, decide whether you want to copy the information from the default user (the first user created) or if you want new items created with no entries inside them. When you have completed this task, click on the Next> button to continue to the Ready to Finish screen, as shown in Figure 10.23.

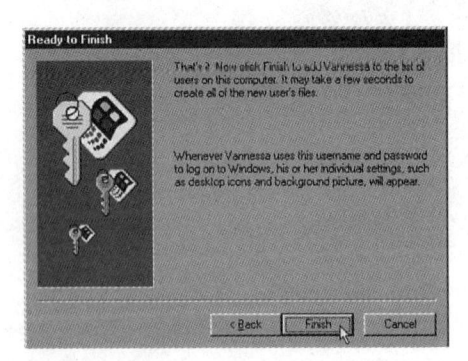

Figure 10.23 Finishing the new user creation process.

7. After you have read the information presented, click the Finish button to complete the process and return to the User Settings screen with this new user added, as shown in Figure 10.24.

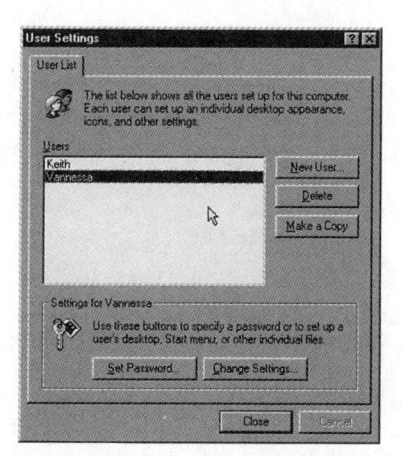

Figure 10.24 Reviewing the user list for your Windows 98 PC.

8. It is on this screen that additional users can be created or the settings for existing users might be altered. In addition, you are able to delete the configurations for a user's work environment. Click the Close button when you are finished configuring and modifying your user group(s).

The work that you have done here in configuring your system for use with multiple users is just the start. If you have a Windows NT Server somewhere on your organization's network, you can implement system policies that work with the Windows 98 multiple user configurations to aid in the better management of your user community. For further information on the concept and technology known as System Policies, consult Chapter 15, "Network Management," of this book.

COMPLEXITY
INTERMEDIATE

10.4 How do I... Add new network adapters?

Problem

I have just finished installing a new physical NIC in my Windows 98 PC. How do I install and configure the network software adapter so that it works with my network? In addition, I need to install a virtual (logical) network adapter on my Windows 98 PC. How can this be accomplished?

Technique

Windows 98 provides a common interface method for installing all its networking components, whether they are network adapters, network clients, network services, or networking protocols. The approach used is similar to the one that you used to install your network software clients. To get started, follow the next set of instructions.

Steps

1. To access the Windows 98 Control Panel, click the Start button, the Settings menu option, and then the Control Panel menu selection.

2. This takes you into the Control Panel screen where you need to double-click the Network icon to reveal the Network Configuration screen, as shown in Figure 10.25. Alternatively, you can quickly go to this same screen by holding down the Alt key on your keyboard and double-clicking the Network Neighborhood icon on the Windows 98 desktop (assuming, of course, that you have at least one networking software client already installed; otherwise, there will not be a Network Neighborhood icon the desktop).

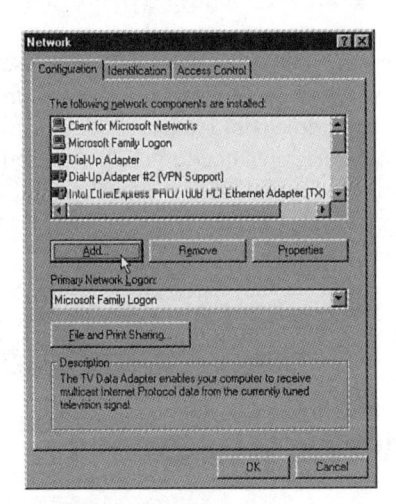

Figure 10.25 Accessing the Windows 98 Network Configuration screen.

This screen contains lots of useful information, the most important of which is a complete listing of all the existing NICs that are already installed on your PC, which are denoted by the icon that looks like a small network card with a fuzzy letter P on the right side of it. Keep in

10.4
ADD NEW NETWORK ADAPTERS

mind that these NICs can be real, physical cards that are physically installed inside your PC or they might be virtual (logical devices) that are software-created cards that exist only in your computer's memory systems.

4. To continue, click the Add... button above the Primary Network Logon text label. This takes you to the Select Network Component Type screen, as shown in Figure 10.26.

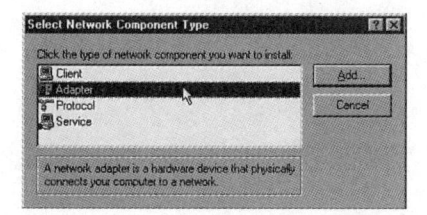

Figure 10.26 The Select Network Component Type screen.

5. Click once on the Adapter network component option to highlight it, and then click on the Add... button to continue to the Select Network Adapters screen, as shown in Figure 10.27.

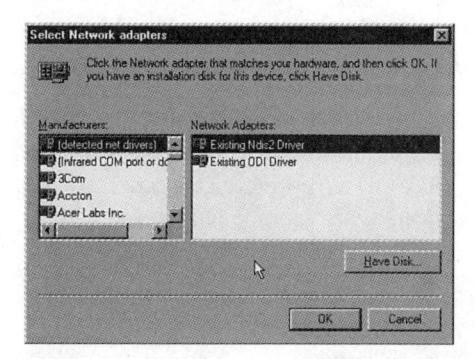

Figure 10.27 Adding a new network adapter component.

6. This screen is used to add the appropriate networking adapter component to your Windows 98 PC. Choose the manufacturer of the adapter in the left windowpane by clicking that vendor's name. Then, all of the available Network Clients for that particular vendor appear in the right windowpane (under the text label of the same name).

This means that you could click once on the Microsoft name under the Manufacturers windowpane, and then click once on the Microsoft Virtual

Private Networking Adapter selection under the Network Clients windowpane to select it. This would permit you to add support for the Microsoft PPTP (Point-to-Point Tunneling Protocol) encryption solution to your system. Keep in mind that you do not really have a physical VPN network adapter card installed in your PC, rather, this is one of those logical software-based networking adapters.

Moreover, it might be that your physical network adapter card came with its own installation disk (or perhaps your network adapter card manufacturer or the adapter itself is not even listed in the appropriate windowpane). In this case, you need to click once on the Have Disk... button, which reveals the Install From Disk screen shown in Figure 10.28.

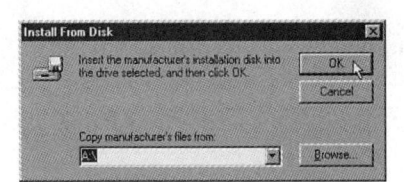

Figure 10.28 Installing network adapter drivers from a manufacturer's disk.

7. This screen permits you to plop the vendor-supplied floppy disk, CD-ROM, or tape into the appropriate drive location, and then have the Windows 98 networking installation process install from one of those locales. After you have put the disk into the correct location and entered that location into the drop-down list box under the Copy manufacturer's files from text label, click OK to continue. This causes the Select Network Adapters screen to appear, as shown in Figure 10.29.

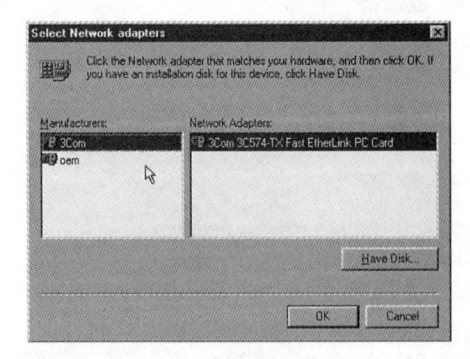

Figure 10.29 Choosing the correct network adapter driver from a vendor-supplied disk.

10.4
ADD NEW NETWORK ADAPTERS

NOTE

Most third party-supplied disks will not present the dilemma that this one from 3Com does (as seen in the example). You need to select the appropriate manufacturer for the network adapter you want to install. It usually has a single name in the Manufacturers windowpane, and one or more network adapters listed in the Network Adapters windowpane. This disk from 3Com is backward to this logic, which makes it more difficult to figure out which adapter to install (and, of course, the vendor's printed documentation is less than desirable). In cases such as this, you might have to just guess.

8. Choose the manufacturer of the adapter in the left windowpane by clicking on that vendor's name. Then, all the available network clients for that particular vendor appear in the right windowpane (under the text label of the same name). Select the one that you want to install by clicking it to highlight it, and then click OK to continue. This causes the Copying Files message status box to appear, which presents a status of the files being copied onto your computer system. Be patient, as this might take a few minutes to complete. When the copying process is complete, the message box automatically closes and returns you to the Network dialog box, as shown in Figure 10.30.

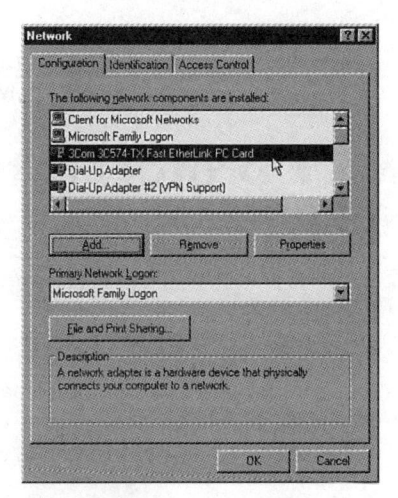

Figure 10.30 Viewing your newly added network adapter.

9. When you return to the Network screen, you need to click OK to finalize the installation process for your newly installed network adapter, as well as to finish the software installation process that might be required using the Windows 98 CD-ROM.

10. If you are prompted to insert your Windows 98 CD-ROM into your CD-ROM (or DVD-ROM) drive, do so, in order for the new networking-related files to install properly into your Windows 98 computer system. After the file installations are complete, the System Settings Change message box appears, as shown in Figure 10.31.

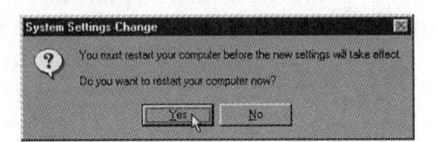

Figure 10.31 Deciding whether to reboot your Windows 98 PC.

11. Click Yes to permit Windows 98 to restart so that the changes you have made take effect. The primary reason for needing to restart the system is that the Windows 98 software drivers need to properly bind to the NIC that you have just installed in your PC.

12. After your PC has restarted and the appropriate network cables are attached to your computer, you are ready to begin using this new network adapter.

COMPLEXITY
INTERMEDIATE

10.5 How do I...
Add new network protocols to my Windows 98 PC?

Problem

I have been using my PC for the basic stuff, and now I want to connect to the Internet. I have installed all the other components necessary, but I have been told I need a networking protocol to make this connection happen. What is this item, which one do I need, and how do I add it to my Windows 98 computer system?

Technique

There are several issues covered within this single topic, but luckily they are all very related. A *networking protocol* is the software transport layer that carries the little data information packets back and forth across the physical wires (network cables, telephone lines, or wireless) between one or more computers.

10.5 ADD NEW NETWORK PROTOCOLS TO MY WINDOWS 98 PC

The basis for the Internet is a protocol known as TCP/IP(Transmission Control Protocol/Internet Protocol). The TCP/IP networking protocol comes with the base Windows 98 operating system. Additionally, Windows 98 provides a common interface method for installing all its networking components, including its networking protocols. The approach used is similar to the one you would use to install your network software clients or network adapters. To get started, follow these steps.

Steps

1. To access the Windows 98 Control Panel, click the Start button, the Settings menu option, and then the Control Panel menu selection.

2. This takes you into the Control Panel screen where you need to double-click the Network icon to reveal the next screen, as shown in Figure 10.32. Alternatively, you can quickly go to this same screen by holding down the Alt key on your keyboard and double-clicking the Network Neighborhood icon on the Windows 98 desktop (assuming, of course, you have at least one networking software client already installed; otherwise, there is not a Network Neighborhood icon on your desktop).

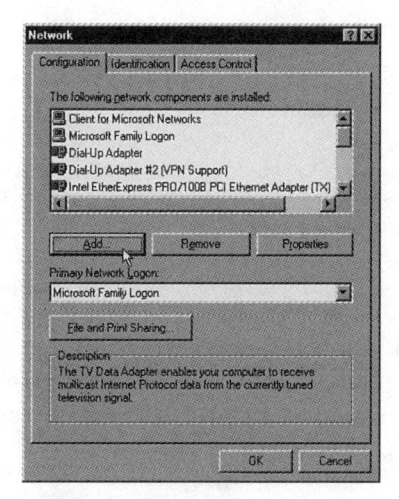

Figure 10.32 Accessing the Windows 98 Network Configuration tab.

3. This screen shows you all the networking protocols that are already installed on your PC. A graphical picture that looks like a small cable that has a plug in the middle of it marks the various network protocols that are installed. Although Windows 98 comes with four network protocols, there are nine listed when you click the Microsoft vendor name.

CHAPTER 10
WELCOME TO THE NEIGHBORHOOD: NETWORK, THAT IS...

- *ATM Call Manager*—This is the Asynchronous Transfer Mode (ATM) User Network Interface (UNI) transport call manager, version 3.1, that is used to perform signaling on an ATM network. This call manager software complies with the ATM Forum's UNI specifications. Try not to confuse the term ATM with automated teller machine, as they have nothing at all in common. However, if you are still confused, see the descriptive note on ATM that appears later in this chapter.

- *ATM Emulated LAN*—This is the LAN Emulation (LANE) module service, version 1.0, which is used to establish network communications with an ATM switch so that it can translate the appropriate Ethernet addresses into ATM addresses. What this means is that you are able to use LAN-based applications and protocols transparently with an ATM network. ATM networks can transport data packets as fast as 655Mbps, which is roughly 6 1/2 times the speed of Fast Ethernet (or roughly 424 T-1 lines)—-not too shabby.

- *ATM Emulation Client*—This is the LAN Emulation (LANE) client software that permits your Windows 98 PC to communicate directly with an ATM LAN. Review the ATM Emulated LAN protocol for more details on this subject.

- *Fast Infrared*—Used with an infrared port on a PC that permits wireless connectivity to various devices such as printers and other computers.

- *IPX/SPX-compatible*—Used most commonly for connectivity to Novell NetWare servers and LANs.

- *Microsoft 32-bit DLC*—The 32-bit version of the DLC protocol that you would use to connect a Windows 98 PC to many types of IBM host systems such as an AS/400, a 3090 mainframe, and so forth. The 32-bit version of this protocol permits direct communication to mainframe systems using third-party host emulation software. Additionally, you might use the same network adapter to communicate with multiple different host systems simultaneously using this protocol.

- *Microsoft DLC*—The 16-bit version of the DLC protocol that you would use to connect a Windows 98 PC to various IBM host systems. This version is not recommended for use because it limits you to using a single network adapter for each connection you want to establish.

10.5 ADD NEW NETWORK PROTOCOLS TO MY WINDOWS 98 PC

- *NetBEUI*—Microsoft's version of the NetBEUI protocol (it originates from IBM, introduced to the market in 1985) is optimized for great performance on single segment LANs and peer-to-peer networks. It is not routable, which means that you cannot use it for data packet transport between LANs that have routers in-between them (although it can be configured for support with bridged LANs).

- *TCP/IP*—The protocol of the Internet, Microsoft's version of the TCP/IP stack, allows you access to UNIX-based systems, other Microsoft networking clients and servers, as well as some IBM mainframes.

NOTE

The ATM protocols are complex in nature and this book does not come close to explaining them in any real detail. For further information on this hot topic you should obtain a copy of Dan Blacharski's book *Maximum Bandwidth* (Que Corporation, 1997) and check out Chapter 2, "Asynchronous Transfer Mode (ATM)," which covers this technology in all the gory details that are required to understand it. Another great book on this topic is Stan Schatt's book *Linking LANs* (McGraw-Hill, 1995).

In addition to these by Microsoft, your ability to install other third-party networking protocols is practically limitless because there are literally dozens made just for Windows 98 alone. And, most of the networking protocols that worked with Windows 95 all work fine with Windows 98. For further details on those protocols, you might want to contact the third-party vendor directly (or visit its appropriate Internet Web site).

4. To continue, click Add... above the Primary Network Logon text label. This takes you to the next Select Network Component Type screen, as shown in Figure 10.33.

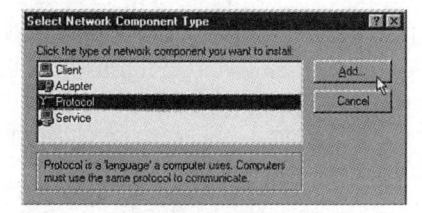

Figure 10.33 The Select Network Component Type screen.

5. Click the Protocol Network Component option to highlight it, and then click Add... to continue to the Select Network Protocol screen, as shown in Figure 10.34.

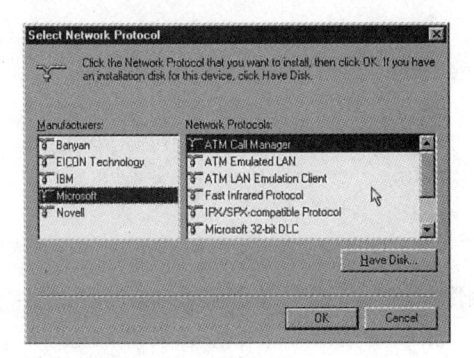

Figure 10.34 Adding a new network protocol component.

6. This screen is used to add the appropriate networking protocol component to your Windows 98 PC. Choose the manufacturer of the adapter in the left windowpane by clicking that vendor's name. Then, all the available Network Protocols for that particular vendor appear in the right windowpane.

This means you could click the Microsoft name under the Manufacturers windowpane, and then click the IPX/SPX-compatible Protocol selection under the Network Protocols windowpane to select it. This permits you to add support for the IPX/SPX-compatible networking protocol to your system. Remember: This is the protocol that you would use for connectivity with a Novell NetWare Server or LAN, but it could also serve as a peer-to-peer networking protocol as well (although it would be roughly 30 percent slower than TCP/IP and probably half as fast as the Microsoft NetBEUI protocol).

However, it is possible that the network protocol that you want to install came with its own installation disk (or perhaps your network adapter card manufacturer or the adapter itself is not even listed in the appropriate windowpane). In this case, you need to click the Have Disk... button, which reveals the Install From Disk screen, as shown in Figure 10.35.

7. This screen allows you to put the vendor-supplied floppy disk, CD-ROM, or tape into the appropriate drive location, and then have the Windows 98 networking installation process install from one of those locales. After

10.5
ADD NEW NETWORK PROTOCOLS TO MY WINDOWS 98 PC

you have put the disk into the correct location and entered its locale into the Copy manufacturer's files from drop-down list box, and click OK to continue.

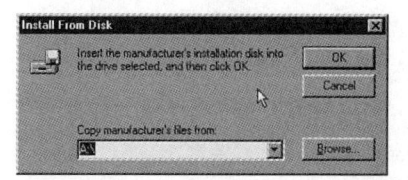

Figure 10.35 Installing a network protocol from a manufacturer's disk.

> **NOTE**
>
> Most third party-supplied disks usually have a single name in the Manufacturers windowpane, and one or more network adapters listed in the Network Protocols windowpane. Select the protocol you want to install, and then Click OK to begin the software installation process. When the installation is complete, you are prompted to restart your computer, which you should do to ensure that everything is installed correctly.

8. Because you are going to install a Windows 98-provided networking protocol, you will not be using the Have Disk method presented earlier. You have an alternative to the Microsoft-provided networking protocols.

9. Therefore, as you did in step 6, you must first choose the manufacturer of the adapter in the left windowpane by clicking vendor's name. Then, all of the available Network Protocols for that particular vendor appear in the right windowpane. Select the one that you want to install by clicking it once to highlight it, and then click OK to continue. This causes the Copying Files message status box to appear, which presents a status of the files being copied onto your computer system. Be patient, as this might take a few minutes to complete. When the copying process is complete, the message box automatically closes and returns you to the Network Configuration screen as shown in Figure 10.36.

10. After you return to the Network screen, you need to click OK to finalize the installation process for your newly installed network protocol(s), as well as to finish the software installation process that might be required using the Windows 98 CD-ROM.

11. If you are prompted to insert your Windows 98 CD-ROM into your CD-ROM (or DVD-ROM) drive, do so, in order for the new

CHAPTER 10
WELCOME TO THE NEIGHBORHOOD: NETWORK, THAT IS...

networking-related files to install properly into your Windows 98 computer system. When the file installations are complete, the System Settings Change message box appears, as seen in Figure 10.37.

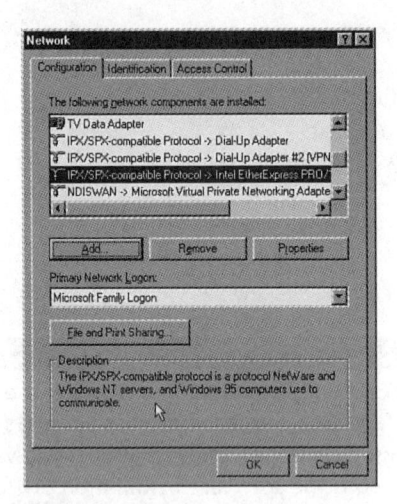

Figure 10.36 Viewing your newly added network protocols.

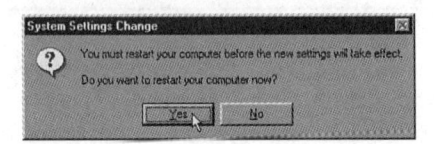

Figure 10.37 Deciding whether to reboot your Windows 98 PC.

12. Click Yes to permit Windows 98 to restart, so that the changes you have made take effect. The reason for needing to restart the system is that the newly installed Windows 98 network protocols need to properly bind to the network interface card that you have just installed in your PC.

13. After your PC has restarted you are ready to begin using this new network protocol.

10.6 How do I...
Configure TCP/IP for use on my Windows 98 PC?

COMPLEXITY
INTERMEDIATE

Problem

I have installed the base Microsoft TCP/IP networking protocol on my Windows 98 PC, along with a network adapter to use it with, but I still cannot get it to work with my network. What do I need to do in order to properly configure the TCP/IP protocol stack for use on my Windows 98 PC?

Technique

Most of the network protocols that you install, fortunately, do not require the intensive configuration that the TCP/IP protocol might need. If you are able to utilize a technology known as DHCP (Dynamic Host Configuration Protocol) for dynamically assigning TCP/IP addresses on your network, by all means do so. This limits the nightmare you are going to have to endure whenever you need to manually assign and track TCP/IP addressing schemes. Assignment of TCP/IP addresses, other than by DHCP servers, is never a pleasant task regardless of whether your client computers are running the Windows 98, Windows 95, X-Windows, or other UNIX-based operating systems.

> **NOTE**
>
> DHCP is a technology that originated in the UNIX world but was popularized by Microsoft, and is used to dynamically assign TCP/IP addresses on a network. Windows 98 computers can automatically be assigned IP address from any Windows NT Server computer (version 3.5 or later). Keep in mind that Windows 98 PCs cannot act as DHCP servers; you must use a Windows NT Server for this purpose. One of the best features (in this author's opinion) of DHCP is that you can move your Windows 98 PC from subnet to subnet across a global organization and still have a valid TCP/IP address automatically assigned to your PC. Also, most of the Internet service providers that you run into use DHCP as their way of managing their own TCP/IP address distributions.

continued on next page

CHAPTER 10
WELCOME TO THE NEIGHBORHOOD: NETWORK, THAT IS...

continued from previous page

For more information on the guts of DHCP, you should refer to RFC 1541 (an Internet Request for Comments standards document). Ohio State University provides a nice entry point for retrieving the RFC documents from the Internet (http://www.cis.ohio-state.edu/hypertext/information/rfc.html) at no cost to you. If you want to FTP all the RFCs down to your Windows 98 PC, use the NIC.DDN.MIL Internet FTP site and look in the RFC directory.

I think I know what you might be thinking at this point: What if I am a small business person who cannot afford the luxury of having an extra computer sit around and dole out TCP/IP addresses to my vast workforce of four people? DHCP sounds like a great technology, but how can a small group of Windows 98 users take advantage of it without enduring undue costs? The answer is a technology new to the Windows 98 operating system: Automatic Private IP Addressing.

> **NOTE**
>
> In the Windows 98 world, if you are on a peer-to-peer LAN or workgroup, a new Windows 98-specific technology known as Automatic Private IP Addressing can be used. With Automatic Private IP Addressing those client computers that have been configured as DHCP clients are capable of automatically assigning themselves a TCP/IP address if the DHCP server cannot be located on the network. This can occur even if you never created a DHCP server, which permits you to fool Windows 98 computers into thinking that they should assign themselves an IP address because they could not find the fictitious DHCP server.

The implementation of Automatic Private IP Addressing is not as difficult as you might think. It requires you to set everyone's TCP/IP address configuration as a DHCP client, which results in an Automatic Private IP Addressing scheme's range of valid IP addresses to be in the 169.254.x.x range. Do not worry, after you follow these next steps, this will make more sense to you. Also, regardless of whether you are using Automatic Private IP Addressing, normal DHCP addressing, or the old-fashioned way of assigning Static IP addresses, these instructions guide you on your way to properly configuring the TCP/IP protocol for use on your Windows 98 PC.

Steps

1. The first thing to do is analyze your community of users. How many PCs are there on your organization's network(s)? For that matter, how many networks and network segments are there? Does everyone use Windows 98 as their client operating system, or are there Windows 95, Windows 3.x, DOS, or even UNIX-based clients on your network that must all

10.6 CONFIGURE TCP/IP FOR USE ON MY WINDOWS 98 PC

communicate with each other? Also, what types of server operating systems are in use? Do your Windows 98 users have to communicate with UNIX servers, IBM hosts, and Novell NetWare servers? All these questions must be answered before you can really begin the task of deciding how to assign TCP/IP addresses to your Windows 98 client computers.

2. Technically, if your answer to the number of users is less than 65,536 and they all exist on the same network segment, you could get away with pure Automatic Private IP Addressing; although this would be a bad idea for a number of reasons: It would be a very, slow LAN, network management would be a disaster, and there would be a lot of really unhappy users.

3. There are a few things that you should keep in mind when you are making your decision as to how to configure the TCP/IP protocol on your Windows 98 client computers. First, are there any routers on your network? If the answer is yes, Automatic Private IP Addressing cannot work correctly on your network, meaning that you will either have to use DHCP or you must assign static IP addresses. Likewise, if you are connecting your network directly to the Internet without using either a proxy server or a NAT, Automatic Private IP Addressing cannot be used to solve your IP addressing problems.

4. The rule of thumb on using Automatic Private IP Addressing is that this is best used on small LANs that have 25 or fewer individuals using all Windows 98 PC clients. This is because Windows 98 PCs that are taking advantage of the Automatic Private IP Addressing feature cannot communicate across subnets, other network hubs, or non-Automatic Private IP Addressing computers.

5. If your organization's network clients exceed 250, you should strongly consider using a DHCP server to dynamically assign TCP/IP addresses. The reason for this is that any number of client computers above that number is not cost-effective to manage manually. In this day and age of TCO (total cost of ownership) mayhem, a network administrator who attempts to spend the organization's monies on manually managing IP addressing schemes is just looking for trouble from the organization's financial controllers.

6. Presumably, by now, you have determined the method of IP address assignment for your Windows 98 client computers. So, to get started, you need to access the Network Configuration tab for the Windows 98 PC.

7. To access the Windows 98 Control Panel, click the Start button, the Settings menu option, and then the Control Panel menu selection.

CHAPTER 10
WELCOME TO THE NEIGHBORHOOD: NETWORK, THAT IS...

8. This takes you into the Control Panel screen where you need to double-click the Network icon to reveal the Network dialog box, as shown in Figure 10.38. Alternatively, you can quickly go to this same screen by holding down the Alt key on your keyboard and double-clicking the Network Neighborhood icon on the Windows 98 desktop (assuming, of course, that you have at least one networking software client already installed; otherwise, there is not a Network Neighborhood icon on the desktop).

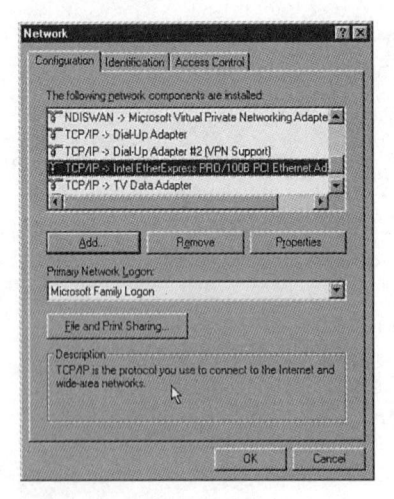

Figure 10.38 Accessing the Windows 98 Network Configuration tab.

9. When the Network screen appears with the Configuration tab shown, use the scrollbar along the right side to scroll down to the TCP/IP protocol that is installed for your network adapter. Click that protocol, and then click the Properties button to reveal the TCP/IP Properties dialog box, as shown in Figure 10.39.

10. Peculiarly, this screen opens with the last tab, the IP Address screen, shown as the default view. This might be because this is the most commonly accessed tab when you are configuring TCP/IP for use with a Windows 98 PC. You have two choices on this screen: Obtain an IP address automatically (use the services of a DHCP server), or Specify an IP address (manually assign a Static IP address). Click the radio button to the left of the option that you want in order to select it.

11. If your choice is to obtain an IP address automatically through the use of a DHCP server, you are finished configuring this tab and are ready to

10.6
CONFIGURE TCP/IP FOR USE ON MY WINDOWS 98 PC

move on to the next step (the WINS Configuration tab). However, if you opt to specify an IP address yourself by manually assigning a Static IP address, continue on to step 12.

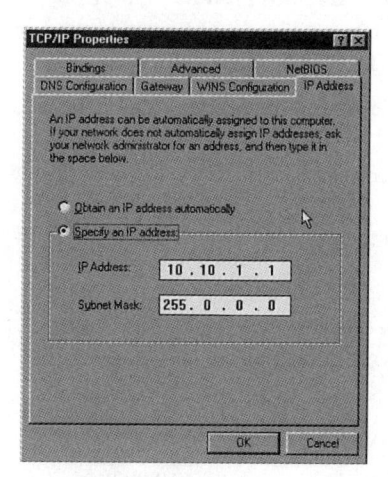

Figure 10.39 Accessing the IP Address tab of the TCP/IP Properties screen.

12. First, you need to enter an IP address into the box of the same label. IP addresses consist of a series of four octets (or 32-bits). Thus, an address within your firm might be something such as this: 130.130.10.57 (essentially, you can pick any number for each octet, provided those numbers range from 1–254). Keep in mind that you cannot use a zero as one of the octets. The address 127.0.0.1 is reserved for loopbacks (meaning you cannot use it); and it is considered good practice to go in order.

NOTE

An *octet* consists of eight binary bits, represented as ones or zeros (1s or 0s). In modern day language on Windows 98 PCs, it is safe to assume that one octet equates to a single byte of information. For example, the octet number 127 is represented in its binary form as 01111111. Kind of ugly, huh? The discussion of binary numbering systems, octets, and 7- versus 8-bit bytes goes way beyond the scope of this book. If you really want to impress your friends and coworkers, you need to spend a week at a Microsoft Education Center taking course #688 on this topic known as Internetworking with Microsoft TCP/IP on Microsoft Windows NT 4.0 (which will probably set you back about $1,200–$1,500). If you do not have that type of cash laying around, I would suggest that you purchase

continued on next page

continued from previous page

a copy of the Windows 98 Resource Kit (available from Microsoft Press for about $70), and consult the TCP/IP topics there (the kit contains basic information, but might be helpful for the TCP/IP beginner). As most modern computer systems today use an 8-bit byte, as an octet does, the issue of 7- versus 8-bit bytes should not arise in your organization (unless you have some old DEC systems hanging around on your network).

13. The next field you need to complete is the Subnet Mask. A *subnet mask* is a 32-bit value that is used to further segment a network so that an IP data packet can distinguish the difference between the network and host ID portions of an IP address.

14. Type your subnet mask into the open field, using a standard Internet addressing scheme, as shown in the Table 10.1.

Table 10.1 Standard Internet Address Numbering Schemes

IP CLASS	FIRST OCTET VALUE (K VALUES)	NETWORK ID	HOST ID	NUMBER OF AVAILABLE NETWORKS	NUMBER OF AVAILABLE HOSTS PER NETWORK	SUBNET MASK
A	1-126	k	l.m.n	126	16,777,214	255.0.0.0
B	128-191	k.l	m.n	16,384	65,534	255.255.0.0
C	192-223	k.l.m	n	2,097,151	254	255.255.255.0

> **NOTE**
> In the Network and Host ID areas, the lettering scheme shown is meant to relate directly to an IP address. For example, the letter *k* is the first octet, the letter *l* is the second octet, the letter *m* is the third octet, and the letter *n* is the fourth octet (that is, *k.l.m.n* could be translated as 130.130.5.1).

15. Creating the actual IP addressing scheme with the appropriate subnet masks is probably the most difficult part of using TCP/IP on your organization's networks. If you get it wrong, it can be a nightmare to change, assuming of course that it worked at all.

> **NOTE**
> If you are planning on using these IP addresses in conjunction with direct connectivity to the Internet, you need to first purchase a license

10.6
CONFIGURE TCP/IP FOR USE ON MY WINDOWS 98 PC

to use this address from the InterNic (for connectivity originating inside the United States of America). Do not plan to purchase any Class A or B licenses, as there are none available. Amusingly enough, this government-created organization was created on April Fools' Day 1993, with the purpose of managing the distribution of IP address and domain names within the USA.

16. After you have made your entries, click the WINS Configuration tab to move to that screen, as shown in Figure 10.40.

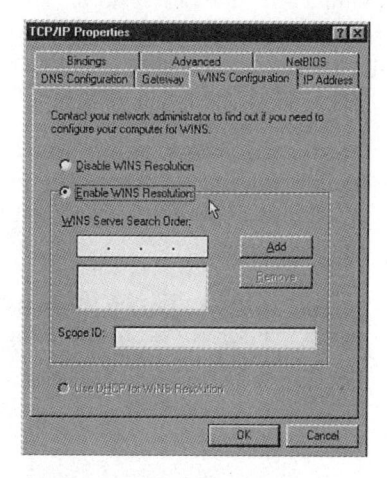

Figure 10.40 Accessing the WINS Configuration tab of the TCP/IP Properties screen.

17. WINS is an acronym that means Windows Internet Naming Service, and is used for the resolution of NetBIOS names to IP addresses. If you are manually assigning IP addresses, you are probably not using this service, in which case this screen can be left blank. This means that you would click the Disable WINS Resolution radio button to disable this feature.

18. Another way to determine whether you might require the use of a WINS server is to see if there are any Windows NT servers in use on your network. If the answer is no, there are no WINS server services available as this is strictly a Microsoft technology (which is similar in nature to a Domain Name Server (DNS) technology). The first thing you need to do is figure out whether you even want to use this technology before you can determine how to use it.

19. If you want to use WINS and have a Microsoft Windows NT DHCP server on your network, the ideal method to deploy WINS information is via the

DHCP server. To do this, click the Use DHCP for WINS Resolution radio button.

20. Otherwise, you need to manually enter the WINS Resolution server information. To do this, click the Enable WINS Resolution radio button, which causes that entire area to no longer be grayed out.

21. Next, type in the IP address for the WINS server that exists somewhere on your network in the box under the WINS Server Search Order text label. Use the *xxx.xxx.xxx.xxx* format, however, do not use leading zeros on any of the numbers (for example, the number 10 would be shown as a .10 and not as a .010). Then, click the Add button, which moves that server's IP address down to the bottom box, meaning that the number is now a part of this Windows 98 client's WINS configuration.

22. The Scope ID box can remain blank, unless your network requires communication based on the NetBIOS over TCP/IP protocol. In general, most networks do not use this, so when in doubt, try leaving it blank to start.

23. After you have made all your selections and entries on this screen, click once the Gateway tab to proceed to that screen, as shown in Figure 10.41.

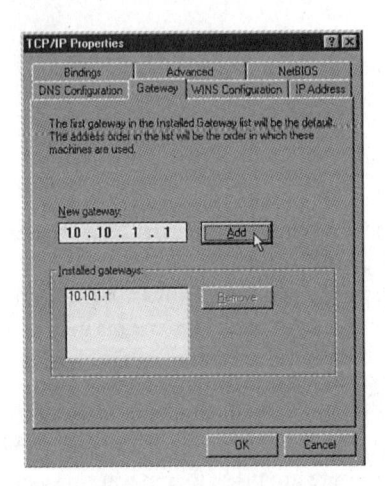

Figure 10.41 Accessing the Gateway tab of the TCP/IP Properties screen.

10.6
CONFIGURE TCP/IP FOR USE ON MY WINDOWS 98 PC

24. A *gateway IP address* is the initial destination where the TCP/IP data packet is sent, in order for it to be properly routed over a large network. In most cases, this would be the IP address for the router that is closest to this Windows 98 PC, which means that you probably cannot use the same gateway address for all the Windows 98 PCs on your network, making this yet another administrative nightmare. You are permitted to have more than one gateway address, but you should enter them in the order that you want this Windows 98 PC to access them.

25. To enter a gateway IP address, type the IP address into the box under the New Gateway Text label using the *xxx.xxx.xxx.xxx* format. Again, do not use leading zeros on any of the numbers. Then, click Add, which moves that gateway's IP address into the Installed Gateways box, meaning that the number is now a part of this Windows 98 client's WINS configuration.

26. If you should ever want to delete an existing gateway, click it once to highlight it, and then click Remove.

27. When you have made all your selections and entries on this screen, click the DNS Configuration tab to proceed to that screen, as shown in Figure 10.42.

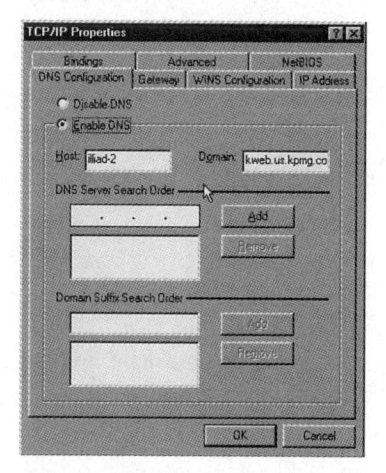

Figure 10.42 Accessing the DNS Configuration tab of the TCP/IP Properties screen.

28. DNS is an Internet standard that has been developed over time through two RFC documents known as RFC 1034 and RFC 1035.

29. The purpose of a DNS server is to resolve IP addresses to host names (pretty much in the same way that a WINS server resolves IP addresses to NetBIOS names). However, while the purpose of both these technologies is similar, the means in which they carry out their duties is very different. A WINS server uses a flat name space, which means that all the NetBIOS names exist in a single domain); whereas a DNS server uses a hierarchical domain name space, which basically means that it resembles a tree with multiple branches.

> **NOTE**
> In Windows NT Server 4.0, a DNS server requires static (manual) maintenance of IP addresses for resolution to host names, whereas a WINS server is capable of performing this similar duty for NetBIOS names on a dynamic or automatic method. In Windows NT Server 5.0, this all changes with the advent of Dynamic DNS; something to keep in mind as you move forward with Microsoft technologies.

30. It is decision time again. If you are not making any type of connection to the Internet or to any internal UNIX hosts, you probably do not need to configure DNS for use with your Windows 98 PCs. Also, if you are on a small mixed Microsoft and Novell NetWare network or a large one that consists purely of Microsoft technologies, there is not a need for DNS for your organization either. If you decide not to use DNS, you need to make sure that the Disable DNS radio button is marked and the rest of the screen is grayed out.

31. Otherwise, click the Enable DNS radio button to gain access to the rest of the screen.

32. Next, you need to enter the host name for this Windows 98 PC along with the fully qualified domain name (FQDN) for your organization. The host name is typically the same as the computer name for your Windows 98 PC. Actually, it is recommended that you maintain this sort of relationship, which makes any future troubleshooting that much easier.

To select the FQDN, you need to type in the name using the proper naming convention. For example, Bill Gates' Windows 98 PC might have the following FQDN: god.executive.microsoft.com (where god equates to his computer's name, executive is the department that he works in, microsoft is the name of the organization he works for, and com is the top-level domain structure that has been assigned to Microsoft by the InterNIC).

10.6
CONFIGURE TCP/IP FOR USE ON MY WINDOWS 98 PC

33. Next, you might want to include a DNS Server Search Order for each of your Windows 98 client PCs. To assist your PC in finding the proper DNS server assigned to it, type the IP address into the box under the DNS Server Search Order text label using the *xxx.xxx.xxx.xxx* format. As with the other TCP/IP properties tabs, be sure not to use leading zeros on any of the numbers.

34. Then, click the Add button, which moves that DNS Server Search Order's IP address into the box below it, which means that that IP address is now a part of this Windows 98 client's DNS Server Search Order configuration.

35. If you should ever want to delete an existing DNS Server Search Order, click it to highlight it, and then click once on the Remove button.

36. Next up is the Domain Suffix Search Order. This option works very much like the DNS Server Search Order feature. Type in the domain's suffix name (your organization's domain name), and click Add to push that name into the box just below it, which means that this domain name is now a part of this Windows 98 client's Domain Suffix Search Order configuration. A domain suffix is the microsoft.com of the preceding Bill Gates example. For the example presented in Figure 10.42, it would be kpmg.com (if you are using DNS Server Search Orders then it is recommended that you also use a Domain Suffix Search Order).

> **NOTE**
> If you would like to avoid configuring DNS on each Windows 98 PC and you already have a WINS server as well as a DNS server present on your Windows NT 4.0 network, there is a way. What you need to do is configure the server so that it uses the feature DNS with WINS Lookup. This permits your Windows NT DNS server to query the WINS server for the NetBIOS names of the computers on your network, and then using that information to create a name that can be used on the Internet (or internally with one of your UNIX host computers).

37. After you have made all your selections and entries on this screen, click the NetBIOS tab to proceed to that screen, as shown in Figure 10.43.

38. This is the easiest tab to configure of the seven presented. If you are using Microsoft's TCP/IP stack, this option is grayed out, but with a check mark in the box. There are no other options on this screen. If you do not want to enable NetBIOS over TCP/IP, try another vendor's IP stack.

39. When you have made all your non-selections on this screen, click once the Advanced tab to proceed to that screen, as shown in Figure 10.44.

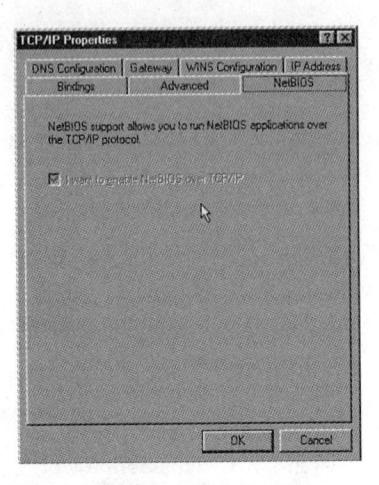

Figure 10.43 Accessing the NetBIOS tab of the TCP/IP Properties screen.

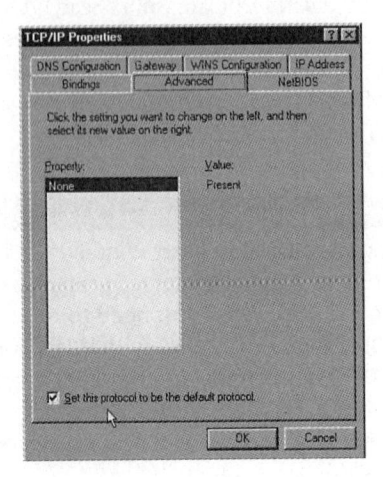

Figure 10.44 Accessing the Advanced tab of the TCP/IP Properties screen.

40. Another easy configuration screen. The only thing that you should consider changing here is whether to make the TCP/IP protocol suite the default protocol for your Windows 98 PC. If the answer is yes, click the check box next to the text label Set this Protocol to be the Default Protocol. Otherwise, make sure that the check box is empty.

41. After you have made all your selections and entries on this screen, click the Bindings tab to proceed to that screen, as shown in Figure 10.45.

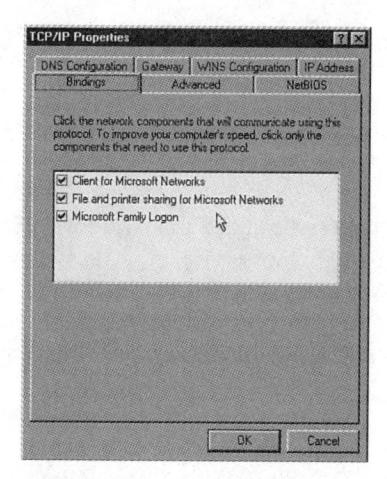

Figure 10.45 Accessing the Bindings tab of the TCP/IP Properties screen.

42. Windows 98 computers run faster if they have fewer networking protocols installed and bound to their network adapters. Therefore, if you do not need or want to use a network protocol with a specific logon request or networking service, by all means remove it from use via this screen.

43. In the example shown, you can see that there is a check mark in the box to the left of the Microsoft Family Logon option. This is a waste of system resources, as there is no technical reason why you would need to bind the TCP/IP protocol to the Microsoft Family Logon option. Thus, to remove this binding, you need to click the check box that appears just to the left of the Microsoft Family Logon text. This removes it from the computer's bindings, but it still appears in this list (in case you want to add it back at some future point).

44. After you have made all your selections on this screen, click OK to return to the Network screen where you started this entire process.

45. Click OK to save all your settings and exit the Network screen completely. If you are prompted to restart your Windows 98 PC, click Yes to reply affirmatively. When your computer restarts, all your changes and entries take effect for the first time.

COMPLEXITY
INTERMEDIATE

10.7 How do I...
Know when to add new network services?

Problem

There are many network services that can be added to a Windows 98 PC, such as File and Printer Sharing or the Novell NDS service. How do I know which ones are good to use and which ones waste system resources for my implementation of Windows 98? Can I use third-party network services with my Windows 98 PC without affecting my configuration in some dire manner?

Technique

There are very few network services that can possibly affect your Windows 98 PC in a dire manner, with perhaps the possible exception of the File and Printer Sharing for either Microsoft or Novell NetWare networks. And even this service, in and of itself, poses no threat to your Windows 98 computer. Rather, it is the implementation and use of this service that might pose a security risk to your PC, should you implement it without careful thought. You need to consider the consequences of installing each network service, weighing carefully the pros and cons of each service. Additional consideration must also be given to the amount of system resources each new network service might want from your PC.

Windows 98 provides a common interface method for installing all its networking components, including that of network services. The approach used is similar to the one that you use to install new networking client software or protocols. So, to get started, follow these steps, which walk you through this process of potential minefields.

Steps

1. First, you need to decide which network services you want to install onto your Windows 98 PC. Some of these are easy decisions. For instance, if you want to be able to share files with other users on your network, you must enable the File and Printer Sharing feature. The only question here becomes: "On what kind of network do you want to perform this function?" That is, there is a File and Printer Sharing service for Microsoft Networks and Novell NetWare networks. You cannot have both enabled simultaneously, so you must pick one or the other. In addition, depending on which one you select, you must also set that network type's client software as the Primary Network Logon.

10.7
KNOW WHEN TO ADD NEW NETWORK SERVICES

2. Likewise, if you want to share a printer that is physically connected to your Windows 98 PC, you must also enable the File and Printer Sharing feature. Here again, you must choose between the File and Printer Sharing for Microsoft networks and the File and Printer Sharing for NetWare networks.

3. Next, assuming that you require connectivity to a Novell NetWare network server, you need to determine what type of connection you are making. That is, is it a bindery connection or do you require access to an NDS tree (a Novell Directory Services directory structure)? If it is a bindery-based server, your Windows 98 PC does not require any special services installed.

4. However, if it is an NDS tree that you need to be authenticated by, you might want to consider installing the Service for NetWare Directory Services (or, of course, you could just install Novell's 32-bit client software for Windows 95, which works okay with Windows 98). This service is installed in the same manner that all the other Windows 98 networking services are installed (go to step 9 of this topic, if you are in a hurry to get started). This service allows you to log onto an NDS system by setting a default context and preferred NDS tree, which then grants you access to NDS-based files and printers.

5. Like anything else that is installed via the Configuration tab on the Network screen, each additional network service consumes additional system resources. It is for this reason that you will want to limit the sheer number of network services that you install on any one Windows 98 PC.

6. Another network service that comes with the Windows 98 operating system is the Microsoft Network Monitor Agent. This service does not install with the Windows 98 operating system, nor does it normally appear in the Select Network Service window that you will see a bit later in these steps. In fact, you just need to know that it exists on the Windows 98 CD-ROM, in case you want to install it on your Windows 98 PC.

7. The purpose of the Microsoft Network Monitor Agent is a simple one. It works with the Network Monitor to provide remote data packet capture capability for the Microsoft Systems Management Server product. So, obviously, if your organization does not own or is planning to implement the Microsoft Systems Management Server product, installing this Windows 98 network service would be a waste of your system resources.

8. However, in case the Microsoft Network Monitor Agent service is what you are looking for, these upcoming steps help you walk through the process of installing this important network service. Additionally, these

CHAPTER 10
WELCOME TO THE NEIGHBORHOOD: NETWORK, THAT IS...

steps also assist you in the installation of the File and Printer Sharing for Microsoft Networks network service as well.

9. So, to get started, you need to access the Windows 98 Control Panel by first clicking the Start button, and then when the Settings menu appears, click the Control Panel menu selection.

10. This takes you into the Control Panel screen where you need to double-click the Network icon to reveal the next screen, as shown in Figure 10.46. Alternatively, you can quickly go to this same screen by holding down the Alt key on your keyboard and double-clicking the Network Neighborhood icon on the Windows 98 desktop (assuming, of course, that you have at least one networking software client already installed; otherwise, there is not a Network Neighborhood icon on the desktop).

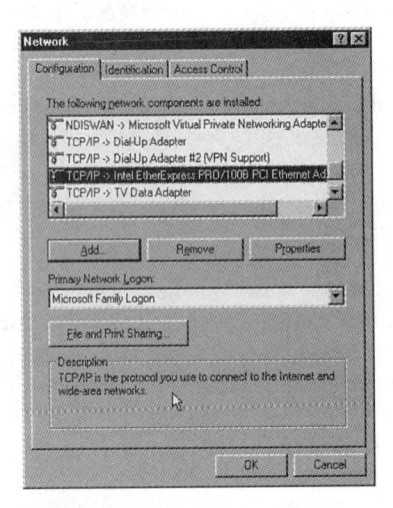

Figure 10.46 Accessing the Windows 98 Network Configuration area.

11. To add a new service (or any new networking component for that matter), you need to click once on the Add... button. This accesses the Select Network Component Type window, as shown in Figure 10.47.

12. Next, click the Service component type to highlight it. Then, click Add.... This brings up the Select Network Service window, as shown in Figure 10.48.

10.7
KNOW WHEN TO ADD NEW NETWORK SERVICES

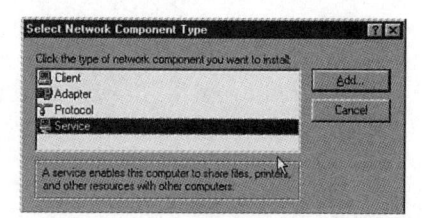

Figure 10.47 Selecting a new network service component.

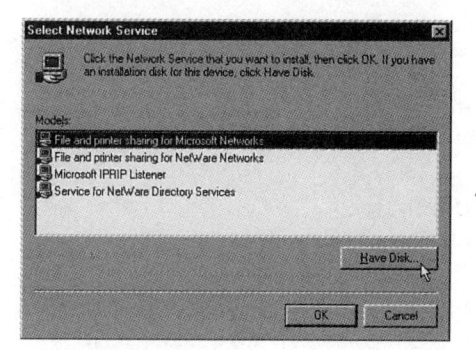

Figure 10.48 Adding a network service.

13. In the middle of this screen is a box with the text label Models. Inside the box are the various networking services that presently are available for installation onto your Windows 98 PC. If you want to install one of these, highlight the one you want, and then click on OK. However, if you want to install another non-listed network service, you need to use another method. Click once on the Have Disk... button to move to the Install From Disk screen, as seen in Figure 10.49.

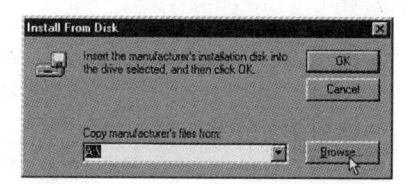

Figure 10.49 Installing a network service from a vendor's disk or the Microsoft Windows 98 CD-ROM.

14. If you already know the precise path to the installation files for this new networking service, you can type that path into the Copy manufacturer's files from drop-down list box. Otherwise, use the Browse... button to go to the Open dialog box, to search your computer or local network for the necessary files (see Figure 10.50).

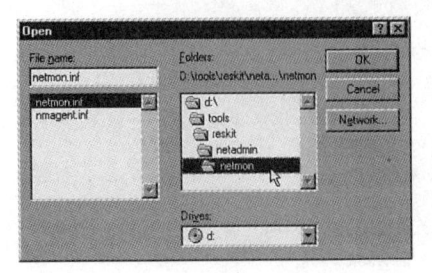

Figure 10.50 Browsing the Microsoft Windows 98 CD-ROM for the appropriate network service's installation files.

15. The Windows 98 CD-ROM contains a few additional Network Services that most home or casual users of Windows 98 would never care to use, much less even have the financial backing to install fully and correctly. This Microsoft Network Monitor Agent service is one of those types of services. Browse to the CD-ROM drive of your computer, and then go down through the Windows 98 CD's folder structure to the netmon folder (\tools\reskit\netadmin\netmon\).

16. All you need to do is open the netmon folder by clicking it, and then clicking OK to start the installation process for this networking service. The necessary files are installed and you are returned to the Configuration tab of the Network screen, as shown in Figure 10.51.

17. Just for fun, let us assume that you also want to install a File and Printer Sharing network service. To do this, without having to first reboot our Windows 98 PC, you should once again click Add... on the Configuration tab of the Network screen.

18. As you recall, this takes you to the Select Network Component Type window where you need to again select the Service component, and then click the Add... button.

19. This takes you into the Select Network Service window, as shown in Figure 10.52.

10.7 KNOW WHEN TO ADD NEW NETWORK SERVICES

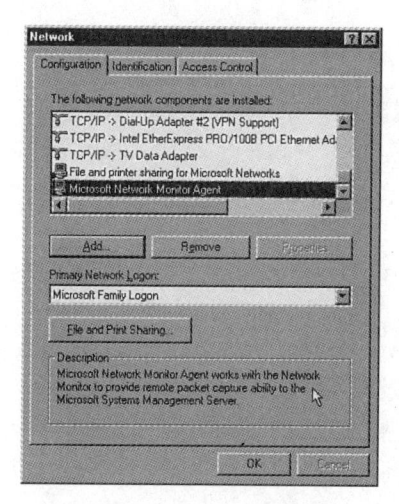

Figure 10.51 Reviewing the installed network services.

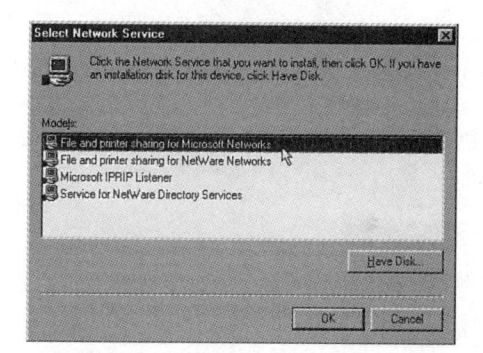

Figure 10.52 Adding a network service.

20. In the middle of this screen you see the Models box. Inside the box are the various networking services that presently are available for installation onto your Windows 98 PC. The very top one is the one you are seeking, as you have a local Windows 98 peer-to-peer workgroup network that you want to share your files with.

21. So, to install the File and Printer Sharing for Microsoft Networks network service, highlight it by clicking it once. Then, click OK to begin the installation process of the necessary networking files. You are automatically returned to the Configuration tab of the Network screen, as shown in Figure 10.53.

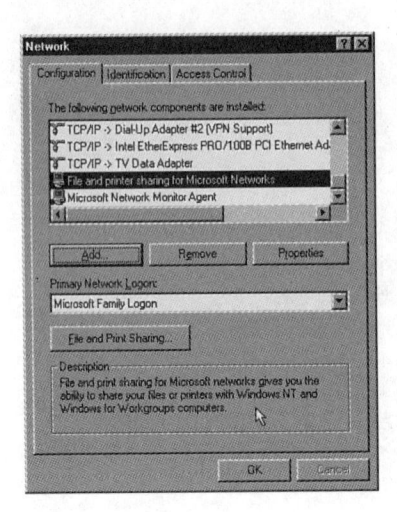

CHAPTER 10
WELCOME TO THE NEIGHBORHOOD: NETWORK, THAT IS...

Figure 10.53 Reviewing the newly installed network services.

22. After you have installed all the network services that you want, click OK to complete the process and save all your changes. When the network services software files are completely installed, the System Settings Change message box appears as seen in Figure 10.54.

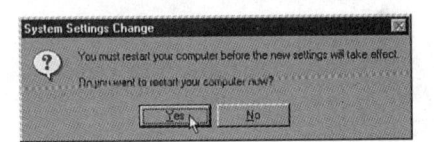

Figure 10.54 Deciding whether to reboot your Windows 98 PC.

23. Click Yes to permit Windows 98 to restart, so that the changes you have made take effect. The reason for needing to restart the system is that the newly installed Windows 98 network services do not start up until your PC has completed a full reboot process.

24. After your PC has restarted you are ready to begin using your newly installed networking service(s).

10.8 How do I...
Configure File Sharing?

COMPLEXITY
BEGINNER

Problem

I have already installed the File and Printer Sharing for Microsoft Networks network service, as well as the necessary hardware for actually making a physical connection to my local workgroup. How do I configure File Sharing on my Windows 98 PC and what are some of the consequences? In addition, does this have anything to do with network browsing, and if so, what?

Technique

Configuring a Windows 98 PC for File and Printer Sharing is a very easy task, and one that does not consume too much of your time. If you need more assistance on Printer Sharing, refer to Chapter 11, "Printer Management," for more details. What is not always so apparent is that the common practice of File Sharing also opens a gigantic security hole if it is done in a haphazard or careless manner. This helps you to understand the common mistakes many professionals make. Also, this section assists you in fine-tuning the browser configuration of your Windows 98 PC so that you are able to browse across your network in a more organized and efficient manner.

This next set of instructions walks you through the process, and provides you with a few tips and tricks of the trade. Ultimately, you will want to take a hard look at your File Sharing strategies to make certain that you are not unduly risking your computing resources, as well as creating too much of a costly burden on your organization's networks.

Steps

1. First, the easy stuff. Configure your Windows 98 PC so that it is capable of sharing files with other Microsoft networking clients and servers. Click the Start button, select the Settings menu option, and then click the Control Panel.

2. This takes you into the Control Panel screen where you need to double-click the Network icon to reveal the Network dialog box, as shown in Figure 10.55.

3. Alternatively, you could quickly go to this same screen by holding down the Alt key on your keyboard while double-clicking the Network

CHAPTER 10
WELCOME TO THE NEIGHBORHOOD: NETWORK, THAT IS...

Neighborhood icon on the Windows 98 desktop. Obviously, you have at least one networking software client already installed; otherwise, there won't be a Network Neighborhood icon on the desktop.

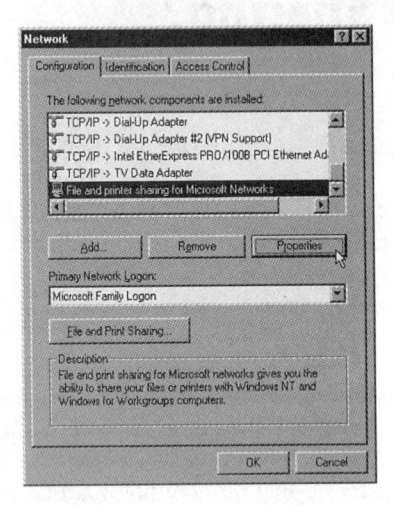

Figure 10.55 Accessing the Windows 98 Network Configuration screen.

4. Scroll down to the bottom portion of the network components listing where you find the entry for the File and Printer Sharing for Microsoft Networks network service. If it does not exist, you still need to add it to your Windows 98 PC. Refer to the previous topic in this chapter, which discusses the installation of additional network services.

5. After you see this entry, click it once to highlight it, and then click once on the Properties button. Doing this causes the File and Printer Sharing for Microsoft Networks Properties screen to appear, as shown in Figure 10.56.

6. There are only a few properties that you need to configure here, but they have far reaching implications--be careful when making your choices. As you can see, there is only a single tab on this screen: the Advanced tab. The screen is broken into two parts, the Property box on the left and the Value drop-down list box to the right. Whenever you make a selection in the Property box, the available selections in the Value drop-down list box change accordingly.

7. Click once on the Browse Master property, and then you can see that there are three possible Value selections that you can make for this property: Automatic, Enabled, or Disabled.

10.8
CONFIGURE FILE SHARING

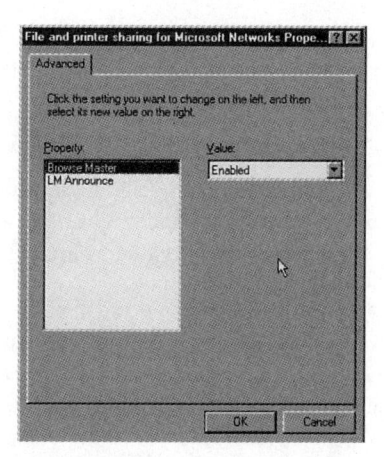

Figure 10.56 Accessing the File and Printer Sharing for Microsoft Networks Properties screen.

8. To make your choice, click the Value selection (for example, Enabled) that you want and it appears as the only value seen in that drop-down list box.

9. Two of the three choices, Enabled and Disabled, are straightforward as to their meaning. The third choice, Automatic, is a bit more complex.

NOTE

Windows 98 incorporates a technology known as *Browsing* into the operating system. Browsing enables your Windows 98 PC to query a known list of computers so that it is capable of finding those computers across the network. It uses a technology known as a *Master Browse Server* to create and maintain this listing by responding to queries from other client computers. The Windows 98 browsing technology is based on the same thing that is used by the Windows NT operating system. When your Windows 98 PC boots onto a network, it automatically seeks out the Master Browse Server for information. If there is no Master Browse Server present, it forces an election (assuming, of course, that it has either the Enabled or Automatic value set in its Advanced Properties box). This election process is based on many complex items, but the end result is simple: a new Master Browse Server is chosen for your Windows 98 network. For all the details on the specifics of this technology, refer to the Windows NT Resource Kit for Windows NT Server version 4.0 (or newer).

10. If your Windows 98 PC has a value of Automatic, it automatically attempts to become a Master Browse Server provided that one does not already exist on the network. If you are on a peer-to-peer LAN, then a setting of Automatic is a good thing.

11. However, if your Windows 98 PC is one of many client computers on a vast Windows NT network, a setting of Automatic might be okay, but you definitely do not want to set the Browse Master value to Enabled.

12. Finally, if you happen to be running a local workgroup such as in a school environment, where you do not necessarily want everyone else in the workgroup to be able to see the other Windows 98 PCs (via the Network Neighborhood desktop icon), you will want to set the Browse Master value to Disabled.

13. The rule of thumb is that if a PC is not generally connected to the network (such as a mobile laptop PC) normally has few spare system resources (such as memory) or is connected to the network via a slower LAN link than is standard, you will always want to set the Browse Master value to Disabled.

14. Keep in mind that a Browse Master value setting of Enabled means that your Windows 98 PC maintains the Browse Master Server listing, if the Windows 98 operating system thinks that it is necessary to do so. In general, this is a bad idea unless you are on a small workgroup LAN where it is okay for everyone to see everyone else and each Windows 98 PC has plenty of computing horsepower built into it.

15. The other property setting on this screen is for something known as *LM Announce* (LAN Manager Announce). This property setting controls whether a Windows PC that is running the File and Printer Sharing for Microsoft Networks service can be seen by LAN Manager version 2.x client computers.

16. LAN Manager is a much older networking technology that probably does not exist anywhere on your networks. So, when in doubt, make this setting a resounding No unless you are positive that there is a LAN manager domain somewhere on your organization's networks.

17. After you have finished configuring the network services properties, click OK to complete the process and save your changes.

18. This causes the Network configuration screen to disappear, leading to the appearance of the System Settings Change message box, as shown in Figure 10.57.

10.8 CONFIGURE FILE SHARING

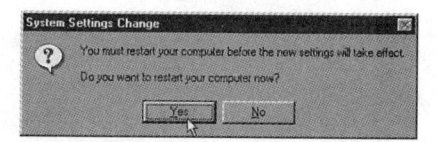

Figure 10.57 Deciding whether to reboot your Windows 98 PC.

19. Click Yes to permit Windows 98 to restart, so that the changes you have made take effect. The reason for needing to restart the system is so that your network services configurations can be fully processed by your Windows 98 PC.

20. After your PC has restarted you are ready to begin using your newly configured networking service.

21. It is time to actually share out a file resource. Sharing is done at the folder level, with the security set in one of two ways: a share-level or a user-level.

> **NOTE**
> On the Access Control screen, if the selection is Share-level Access Control, the Windows 98 PC user uses passwords to protect each resource that is made available on his or her own computer. If the selection is User-level Access Control, the access is controlled at an individual level and not at via a password method. For example, in a User-level type of control you would grant Robin access to a printer or folder, rather than Robin having to know the password for accessing that printer or folder resource. It is important to note that User-level access control is possible only if your network permits it and you have preconfigured the network's Windows NT servers to support it.

22. These settings are made via the Access Control screen, which is accessed from the Network screen. Click the Start button, and then select the Settings menu option. When that menu appears, click the Control Panel menu selection.

23. This takes you into the Control Panel screen where you need to double-click the Network icon to open that screen.

24. Then, click the Access Control tab to reveal that screen, as shown in Figure 10.58.

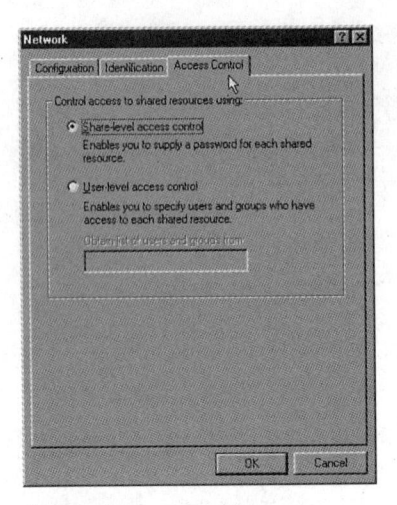

CHAPTER 10
WELCOME TO THE NEIGHBORHOOD: NETWORK, THAT IS...

Figure 10.58 Accessing the Access Control Area of the Network screen.

25. The default setting is the top method of Share-level Access Control for accessing your computer's resources. If you want to change this selection, click once on the radio button next to the User-level Access Control option. Also, you will need to input the NetBIOS domain name for the computer that will be providing the list of valid users and groups for your Windows 98 PC.

26. After you make your choice, click OK to save your configuration and exit the Network screen.

27. If you did not make any changes to the default settings, you can proceed directly to the next step. Otherwise, you are required to restart your Windows 98 PC in order for these changes to take effect.

28. To share a folder, you need to browse to that folder. Double-click the My Computer icon on your desktop, as shown in Figure 10.59.

29. If you see a tiny, outstretched hand underneath any of your drives (floppy, hard, or otherwise), that drive letter has already been shared. For the purposes of this example, you will share your primary hard drive: the C:\ drive (labeled as Home Office in the example given).

30. To share any drive (or folder) click that drive letter to highlight it, and then click again with your secondary mouse button to reveal a small menu, shown in Figure 10.60.

10.8
CONFIGURE FILE SHARING

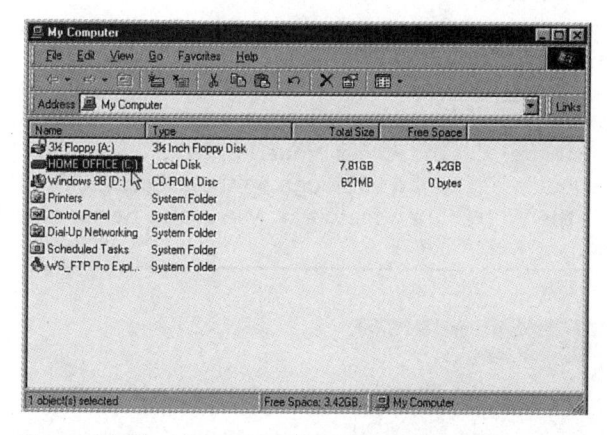

Figure 10.59 Accessing the Access Control area of the Network screen.

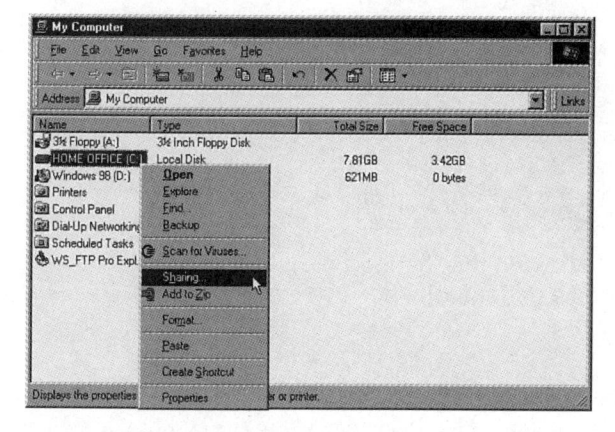

Figure 10.60 Accessing the Sharing Menu option.

31. Move your mouse pointer to the Sharing... menu selection and click once to select it. This reveals the Properties menu for that drive (or folder, if you are trying to share a Windows 98 folder), as shown in Figure 10.61.

32. This screen always defaults to the top radio button option of Not Shared, provided that you have not already shared this drive or folder. To begin sharing this folder, click the Shared As radio button.

> **NOTE**
>
> Regardless of whether you are sharing a drive or a folder, the options shown on the Sharing tab are always exactly the same. What is different, however, is the number and types of tabs available on the
>
> *continued on next page*

continued from previous page

entire Properties screen. On the Drive Properties screen you see at least three tabs: General, Tools, and Sharing (on the example there are two more: one for Web Sharing--a feature of Microsoft's personal Web service, and one for my antivirus application--Cheyenne antivirus and protection software). On the Folder Properties screen you see at least two tabs: General and Sharing (although on the example given there is one more for the Web Sharing feature of Microsoft's personal Web service).

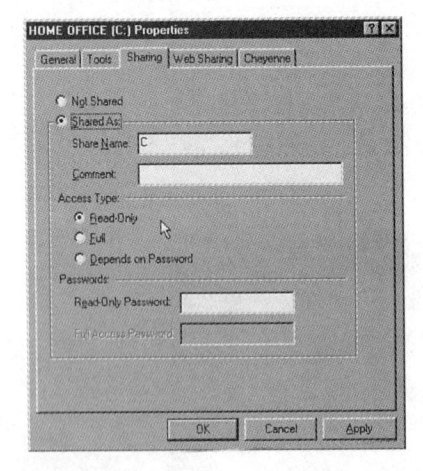

Figure 10.61 Viewing the Sharing tab of the [Home Office (C:)] Properties screen.

33. The Share Name is the name that other users see when they access your computer. If you add a dollar sign ($) to the end of your share name, it will be a hidden share. This means that others using the Network Neighborhood feature of a 32-bit Windows client or server will not be capable of seeing that share in their window. This adds some level of security on its own to your computer system. Likewise, if you use any spaces in your share name, DOS-based computers will not be capable of accessing your computer either, which is great if you are just trying to share your computer's files with others on your Windows 98 peer-to-peer network.

34. The Comment box allows you to store some descriptive text about the share that you are creating. This text can be seen by others using the Network Neighborhood feature to surf your computer.

35. The Access Type area is the most important area, in my opinion. This is where many first-time users of Windows 98 get into trouble because they

10.8
CONFIGURE FILE SHARING

assume that if they make all their shares hidden, they do not need to password-protect their computer systems. Likewise, others will select the Depends on Password access method, but then forget to put any passwords on either the Full or Read-Only access types, which is not a good thing.

36. Click once on the radio button next to the Access Type that you want to use. For the purposes of this example, you will use the Depends on Password access method.

37. When you click on this access method's radio button, both the boxes in the Passwords area open. This permits you to add one password for the Read-Only access users, while putting a completely different one in for Full Access users. In fact, you are prompted by Windows 98 to select different passwords, if you attempt to enter the same one for either Read-Only or Full Access users.

38. When you have made all your entries, click OK to accept your changes. Immediately, the Password Confirmation screen appears, requiring you to reenter each password for each access method. Windows 98 does this so that you know exactly which password you typed in for a particular resource access method type.

39. When you can confirm your passwords correctly, click OK to accept your password choices and to close this screen.

40. This forces your sharing selections to take effect immediately, as shown in Figure 10.62.

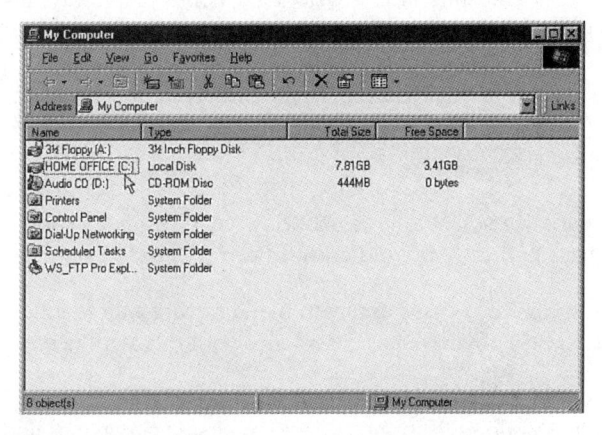

Figure 10.62 Viewing the newly shared Home Office (C:) drive.

41. After reviewing the My Computer screen again, you now see the tiny, outstretched hand underneath your C: drive. This means that this drive letter has been shared out correctly.

COMPLEXITY
INTERMEDIATE

10.9 How do I... Automatically log on to my network, using the proper user ID and password?

Problem

I manage a number of Windows 98 computers that function as print servers for several small offices within my organization. Occasionally, through power fluctuations or outages, these computers reboot, and then someone has to enter the Windows NT network ID and password in order for them to gain the appropriate rights on the network. How can I make this happen automatically, so I do not have to explain to some secretary (for the fortieth time) how to log in with the correct user ID and password?

Technique

Within the Windows 98 Resource Kit there is a very popular utility known as *Tweak UI* (or Tweak User Interface). Tweak UI contains many ways for you to better manipulate the Windows 98 OS without having to directly modify the Windows 98 Registry directly. It is the Network section within this utility that provides the functionality that is necessary for resolving this problem.

Steps

1. Obtain the Microsoft Windows 98 Resource Kit from your local bookstore or purchase it directly from Microsoft Press.

2. Install the CD-ROM that came with the kit, being sure to follow the prompts closely. If you require assistance with this step, review Chapter 1, "Installation Tips."

3. Access the Windows 98 Control Panel by first clicking Start and choosing the Settings menu option. When that menu appears, click once on the Control Panel menu selection.

10.9
AUTOMATICALLY LOG ON TO MY NETWORK

4. This takes you into the Control Panel screen where you need to double-click the Tweak UI icon to reveal that screen, as shown in Figure 10.63.

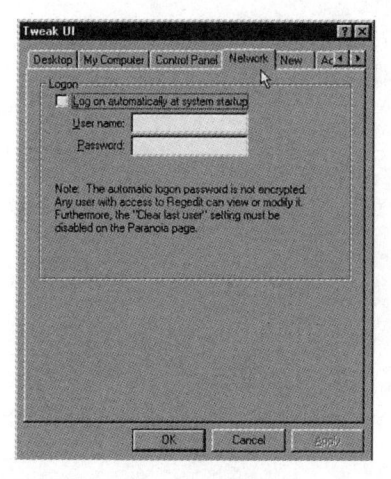

Figure 10.63 Viewing the Network tab of the Tweak UI utility.

5. Using the triangular-shaped arrowheads found on the upper-right corner of the screen, scroll the tabs over to the right until you see the one marked Network. Click this Network tab to select it.

6. Click once on the check box located just to the left of the text label Log on Automatically at System Startup. This enables the auto-logon feature.

7. Next, type in the exact username and password in their respective boxes. These are the username and password fields that are automatically passed along to the network server that you want to log on to each time the server reboots.

8. Keep in mind that this information is not encrypted in any way, so anyone with physical access to this Windows 98 PC can use the Registry Editor to look up the user ID and password data.

9. Also, you need to scroll over to the Paranoia tab, as shown in Figure 10.64.

10. The fifth item in the Covering Your Tracks box is the Clear Last User at Logon option. Make sure that the check box for this option is not marked. Otherwise, the automatic logon feature that you just configured will not work correctly.

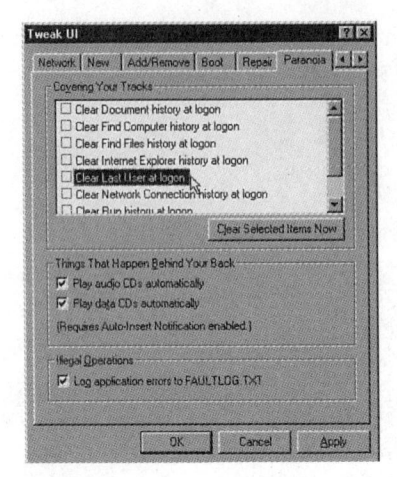

Figure 10.64 Viewing the Paranoia tab of the Tweak UI utility.

COMPLEXITY
BEGINNER

10.10 How do I...
Change either the computer name or workgroup name for my Windows 98 PC?

Problem

My computer came pre-installed with the Windows 98 operating system. Of course, neither the computer name nor the network's workgroup names were set correctly for me. However, as I am a bit new to Windows 98, I do not know how to change either of these names. How can these names be altered and are there any restrictions to keep in mind when making these changes?

Technique

Like most of the other networking configurations that need to be performed in the Windows 98 OS, the system identification parameters are also set from inside the Network screen. These changes take effect after restarting the Windows 98 PC. The total time it takes to change either or both of these screens is about five minutes (and that would be on a bad day), so follow these steps:

10.10 CHANGE THE COMPUTER NAME OR WORKGROUP NAME FOR MY PC

Steps

1. The first thing you need to do is access the Windows 98 Control Panel. Click the Start button, and then choose the Settings menu option. When that menu appears, click once on the Control Panel menu selection.

2. This takes you into the Control Panel screen where you need to double-click the Network icon to reveal the Network dialog box, as shown in Figure 10.65.

3. Alternatively, you can quickly go to this same screen by holding down the Alt key on your keyboard while double-clicking the Network Neighborhood icon found on the Windows 98 desktop. Obviously, you have at least one networking software client already installed; otherwise, there is not a Network Neighborhood icon on the desktop.

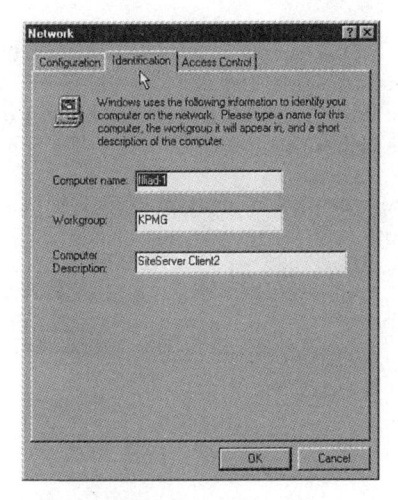

Figure 10.65 Accessing the Windows 98 Network Configuration area.

4. When the Network screen appears, you need to move to the Identification tab by clicking on that tab.

5. You are presented with the opportunity to modify three options: the Computer Name, the Workgroup name, and the Computer Description.

6. The name of the computer must be unique, not exceed 15 characters (numbers and letters are acceptable), and should probably be representative of the computer that it represents. For example, you might want to set your user's user IDs as the computer name. However, for security reasons you might want to set some frivolous naming convention for the Computer Name field.

7. The name of the workgroup should be the same as the networking domain that you most often connect to, or it should be the same as the domain of the server that authenticates you to the network. As with the computer name, it too cannot exceed 15 characters (numbers and letters are acceptable).

> **NOTE**
>
> It is very important that you do not attempt to set the computer name and the workgroup name as the same. Windows 98 does not permit these two fields to contain the same name, as this would be a violation of its internal workings.

8. The Computer Description field is an informational field that should contain a descriptive comment for this user or PC. Keep in mind that while it does not have to be filled in, you should probably put in some text that most accurately describes the user or computer for consistency.

9. After you have made all your changes and entries, click OK to save your changes and exit the Network screen.

10. You are prompted to restart your Windows 98 computer system. Click Yes to permit the restart process to begin. When your system finishes rebooting, you will discover that your newly configured computer and workgroup names have now taken effect.

CHAPTER 11
PRINTER MANAGEMENT

11

PRINTER MANAGEMENT

How do I...

11.1 Add a network-based print device to My Computer?

11.2 Capture a printer port in Windows 98?

11.3 Share a print device?

This chapter covers the brief topic area of printing under the Windows 98 operating system, along with a few of the more advanced features of Windows 98 printing services such as print sharing and adding network printing devices.

11.1 Add a Network-based Print Device to My Computer

Although this topic is practically useless for most home users of Windows 98, most everyone will need to either install or connect to a network-based printer at some point in their professional life. This How-To assists you in that process.

11.2 Capture a Printer Port in Windows 98

This is not a big deal if you live in a completely Windows 98/Windows NT world, but if happen to use DOS-based programs then this topic is for you.

11.3 Share a Print Device

The focus of this How-To is on sharing printers from your Windows 98 PC so that you can allow others to use the printer connected to your Windows 98 computer.

CHAPTER 11
PRINTER MANAGEMENT

COMPLEXITY
INTERMEDIATE

11.1 How do I...
Add a network-based print device to my computer?

Problem

I just purchased a new printer for my Windows 98 PC. What is the best way to install the software drivers for a print device into the Windows 98 operating system, and how do I perform this task?

Technique

Windows 98 provides two excellent methods for installing new printer hardware and software for use with the operating system. The most common method for adding new hardware and its associated device driver software is via the Add New Hardware Wizard from within the Control Panel. While this is the preferred method for all other hardware devices, there is one that is better for print devices only. That method is to use the Add Printer Wizard that is part of the Printers folder, which is accessed from the Settings menu, off the Windows 98 Start button. To use this method, follow the steps provided here.

Steps

1. Click the Settings menu option from the Windows 98 Start button, and then click again on the Printers menu selection. This opens the Printers screen shown in Figure 11.1.

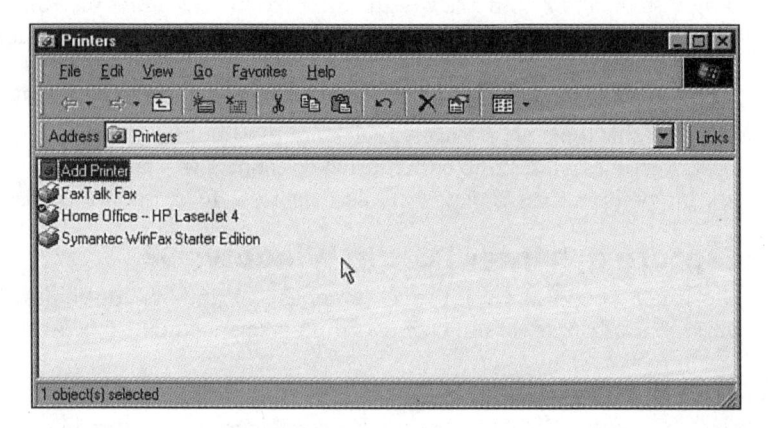

Figure 11.1 The main Printers screen.

11.1
ADD A NETWORK-BASED PRINT DEVICE TO MY COMPUTER

2. All your Windows 98-based printers and fax devices are managed from the Printers screen. You will see a listing of all the printer and fax devices that you already have installed on your PC. If the screen is empty, you have not yet installed any of these types of devices.

3. You will use this screen to add, modify, or delete printers, as well as to capture printer ports. To start the wizard, click Add Printer to go to that wizard, as shown in Figure 11.2.

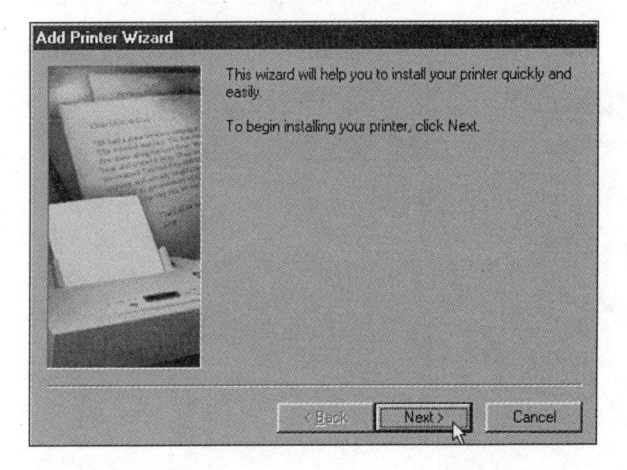

Figure 11.2 Starting the Add Printer Wizard.

4. This first screen of the Add Printer Wizard contains only information. Read it if you want, and then click Next> to continue the installation process. The screen shown in Figure 11.3 appears.

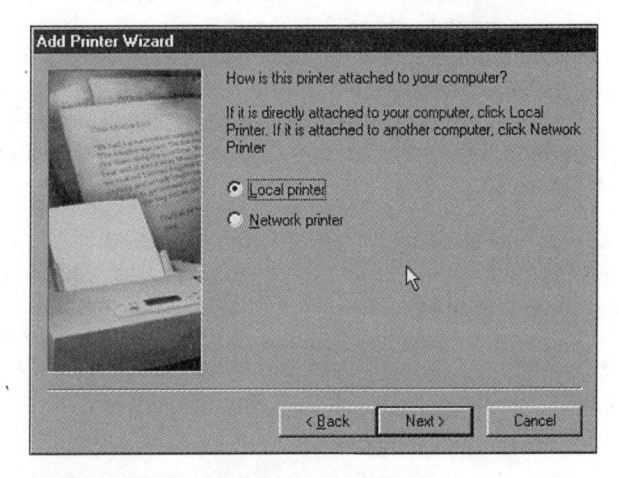

Figure 11.3 Determining the printer connection method.

5. On this screen you must decide if the new printer will be a local one (it is attached to the back of the PC via a parallel printer cable), or if it is a network printer (all printing to it will be accomplished through the network card in your PC). For the purposes of this example, assume that the printer is network-based.

6. After you have made the appropriate selection, click once on the radio button next to that printer type to select it. Then click Next> to continue the installation process. The next wizard screen appears, as shown in Figure 11.4.

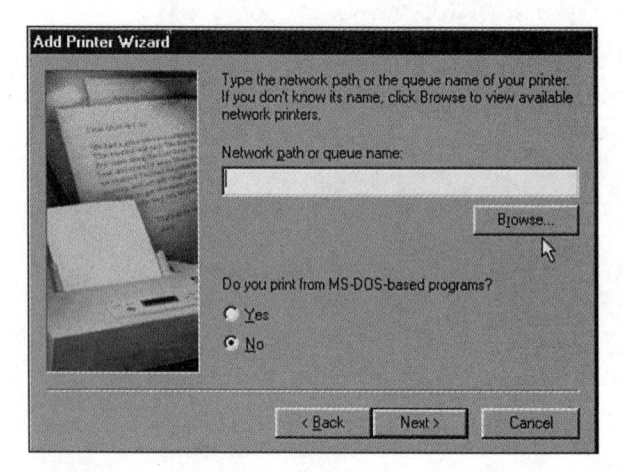

Figure 11.4 Inputting the network path of your Windows 98 printer.

7. It is on this screen that you need to enter the network path of the printer that you are attempting to install. UNC paths are acceptable, and are actually preferred, but you must be precise in your spelling and punctuation for the name and location of the printer you are installing. For this reason it is suggested that you click the Browse... button to search the network for the printer you want in the Browse for Printer dialog box, as shown in Figure 11.5.

8. A browse view that starts with your Network Neighborhood appears inside the Browse for Printer screen. It is from here that you can either scour the entire network or search the computers that you have already been authenticated to or by. For this example, you will use the one PC that you have already been authenticated by (Illiad-1). Open it by clicking the plus symbol next to the computer's name.

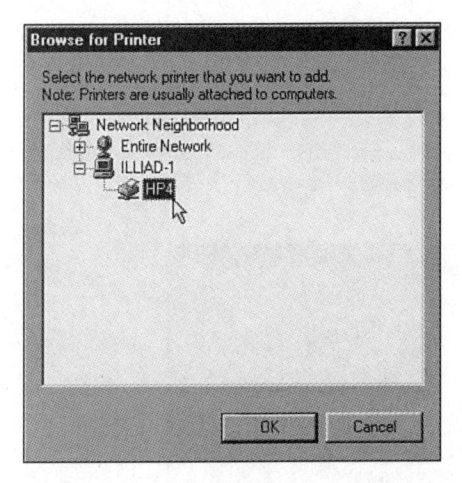

11.1
ADD A NETWORK-BASED PRINT DEVICE TO MY COMPUTER

Figure 11.5 Browsing for the precise printer location (path).

9. Click the shared printer that you want to connect to (in this case it is labeled HP4), in order to highlight it first, and then click OK to return to the Add Printer Wizard screen shown in Figure 11.6.

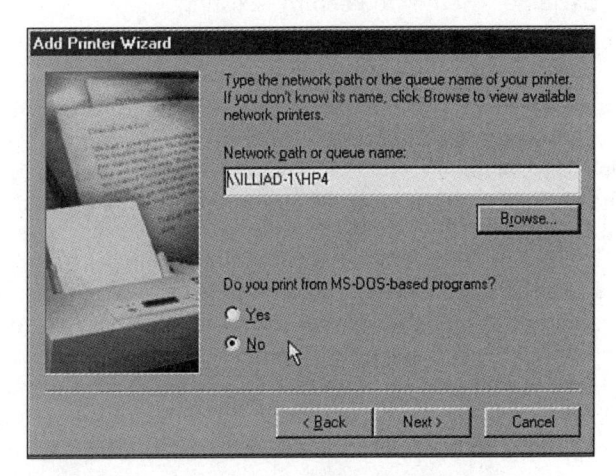

Figure 11.6 Reviewing the Path "pulled-back" by the network printer browse method.

10. The question at the bottom of this screen is rather misleading. By clicking Yes you are actually enabling a *capture* of your printer LPT1: printer port; meaning that all your information you print via that port is automatically rerouted over to this new network-based printer that you are installing.

In most cases, this is not a problem. However, if you already have a different local printer installed on your LPT1: port...; well, you see the problem. If you click the No radio button, the capture process is disabled.

11. After you have made your selections, click Next> to continue to the next screen in the installation process, as shown in Figure 11.7.

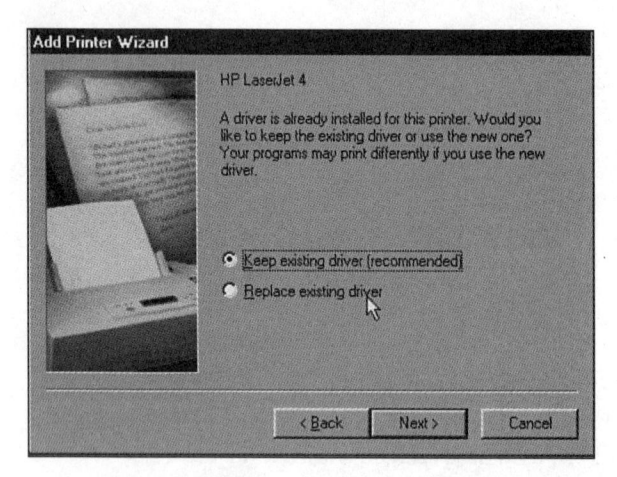

Figure 11.7 Deciding whether to keep the existing printer driver.

12. If you have already installed a printer that uses this same driver, the screen you see here appears. Unless there is a compelling reason for replacing the existing driver (such as you have an updated driver disk from the manufacturer), it is strongly recommended that you leave the original one installed.

13. If this is a new printer, you see a screen with two windowpanes. On this type of screen, first pick the name of the printer manufacturer from the left windowpane by clicking on that manufacturer's name. Then select the printer to be installed by clicking once on the name of the printer. For example, if you chose HP (Hewlett-Packard) as the manufacturer, only HP printers are listed in the right windowpane.

14. When you have made your selections, click Next> to continue the installation process. The wizard box in Figure 11.8 is where you will name your printer.

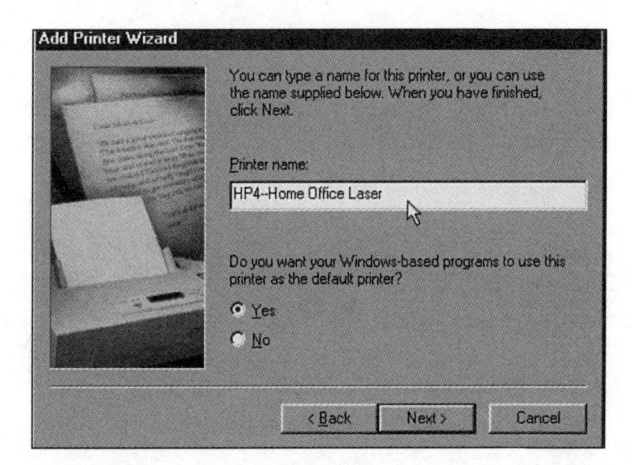

11.1
ADD A NETWORK-BASED PRINT DEVICE TO MY COMPUTER

Figure 11.8 Naming your printer.

15. Try to give your newly installed printer a descriptive name if possible—because this makes it easier for you to remember what its purpose is—by typing that name in the Printer name box. Otherwise, you can just accept the default printer name listed. Then decide whether you want this new printer to be the default one used automatically by all applications. If this is your primary printer, answer affirmatively by clicking Yes (otherwise, click No). Click the Next> button to continue to the next screen in the installation process, as shown in Figure 11.9.

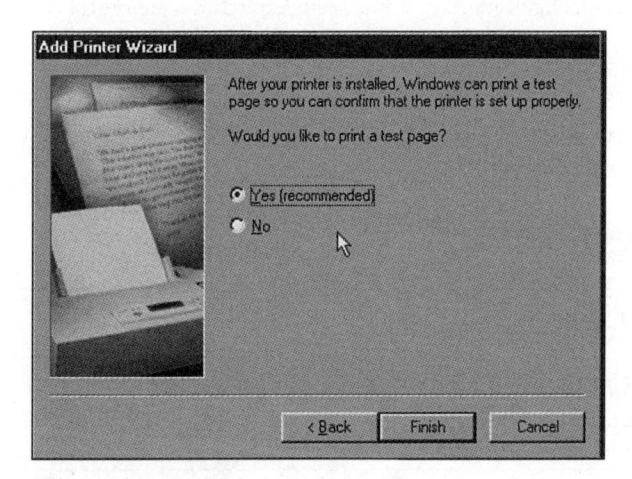

Figure 11.9 Deciding whether to print a test page.

16. If this is a new printer, it is advisable that you accept the default setting of Yes to print a test page from this newly installed printer. If you can read the output, the printer has been installed properly. Click the Finish button to complete the installation process and return to the main Printers screen, as shown in Figure 11.10.

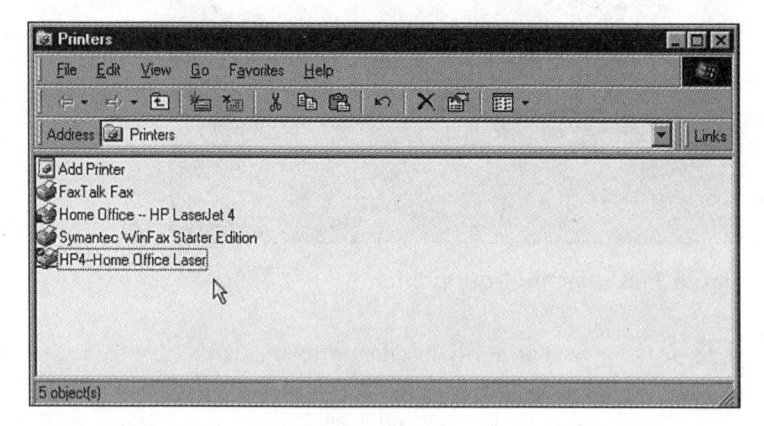

Figure 11.10 Reviewing your newly installed network print device.

17. The newly defined network printer is now installed and should be shown in the listing of print devices, usually at the bottom of the list. You will see a small check mark in a black circle next to it if you told the Add Printer Wizard that this new print device is to be the default printing device. Also, you should notice that this new device looks like it has a wire running underneath it. This signifies the printer is network-connected. Printers that are locally-connected do not have the wire under them. That is all you need to do.

COMPLEXITY
INTERMEDIATE

11.2 How do I... Capture a printer port in Windows 98?

Problem

I have previously installed a network printer, but did not mark that printer as one that required the printer port to be captured. How do I do this now that

11.2 CAPTURE A PRINTER PORT IN WINDOWS 98

475

the printer has already been installed? Does this mean I need to reinstall my print device?

Technique

Windows 98 permits you to redefine printer settings at any time following the use of the Add Printer Wizard. All the print and fax devices, as mentioned previously, are stored within the Printers folder. It is from here that you access that printer's properties and make the necessary changes.

Steps

1. Click the Settings menu option from the Windows 98 Start button, and then click again on the Printers menu selection. This opens the Printers screen.

2. From the Printers screen, all your Windows 98-based printers and fax devices are managed. Click the device that you want to set the captured port for, in order to highlight that print device.

3. Next, click again on that device with your secondary mouse button to reveal a small menu. At the bottom of that menu is the Properties selection.

4. Click once on that menu selection to enter the properties screen for that print device. Click once on the Details tab to reveal the screen shown in Figure 11.11.

5. In the middle of this screen is a button labeled Capture Printer Port.... Click this button to cause the Capture Printer Port window to appear as shown in Figure 11.12.

6. Type in the full network path to the printer that you are attempting to capture this port for (*Hint:* This is the same data path that was shown in the Print to the following port drop-down list box on the previous Details tab screen). Click on the check box next to the Reconnect at logon option only if you want this printer port capture to be "remembered" by Windows 98 every time you are authenticated to the server that controls this print device.

7. After you have entered the correct information and made your selections, click OK to accept this port capture effort and return to the previous Details tab screen.

8. Other options on this screen permit you to alter the timeout settings for this port, as well as to add or delete an existing port. When you finished making your selection(s), if any, click OK to save your changes and exit this screen.

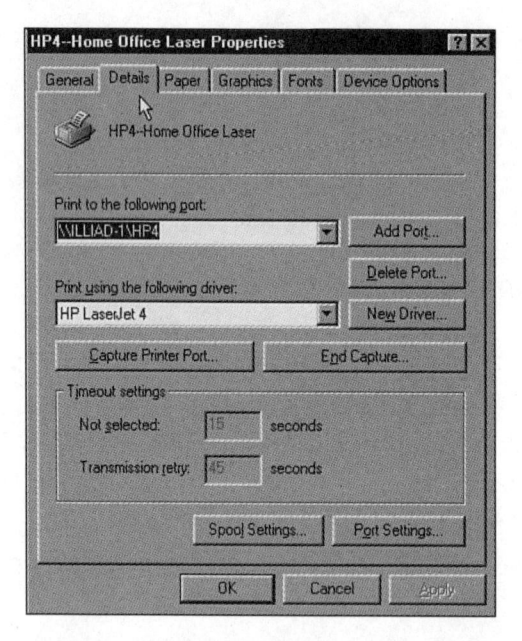

Figure 11.11 Reviewing the Details tab of the Printer Properties screen.

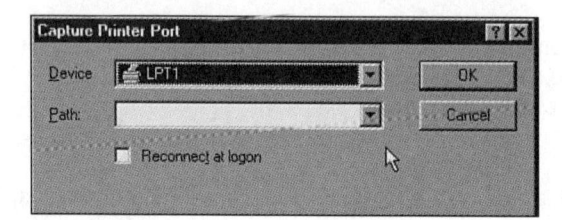

Figure 11.12 Inputting a network path to the printer used with the capture process.

COMPLEXITY
BEGINNER

11.3 How do I...
Share a print device?

Problem

I want to be able to share a printer on my Windows 98 PC so that another person in my organization can use my printer without walking over and bothering me with a floppy disk full of information. How do I do this without purchasing any additional software?

Technique

The capability to share a printer is based on a few premises. First, you must be connected to a network and be using the client for Microsoft networks. Next, you must already have File and Print Sharing enabled from within your Network Properties dialog box. Finally, you should have already installed the print device you want to share with your officemate(s). After these provisions have been fulfilled, sharing a printer becomes a relatively straightforward task. Keep in mind, though, that not all printers are sharable using the procedures listed in this section(such as the Lexmark 2050), so you might want to consult your printer's documentation prior to attempting any sharing procedures.

You will use the Printers folder dialog box to access the Sharing configuration tab for your print device. From there, a few housekeeping items must be attended to, and then you will be finished. Follow these steps:

Steps

1. Click the Settings menu option from the Windows 98 Start button, and then click again on the Printers menu selection. This opens the Printers screen.

2. Your Windows 98-based printers and fax devices are managed from the Printers screen. Click on the device that you want to configure as the shared device, in order to highlight that print device.

3. Next, click again on that device with your secondary mouse button to reveal a small menu. In the middle of this menu is the Sharing... selection.

4. Click that menu selection to enter the Properties screen for that print device directly at the Sharing tab, which reveals the screen shown in Figure 11.13.

5. To share this device, click the radio button next to the Shared As label. This causes the remainder of the screen to reveal itself.

6. In the first box, Share Name, you need to enter a descriptive name for the device that you are sharing. Because this is the same name that others will type in when they are attempting to access this print device, you might want to keep it short and simple.

7. The Comment box is just that. Type a descriptive comment here to help others, who might want to use your printer, figure out the purpose of this print device.

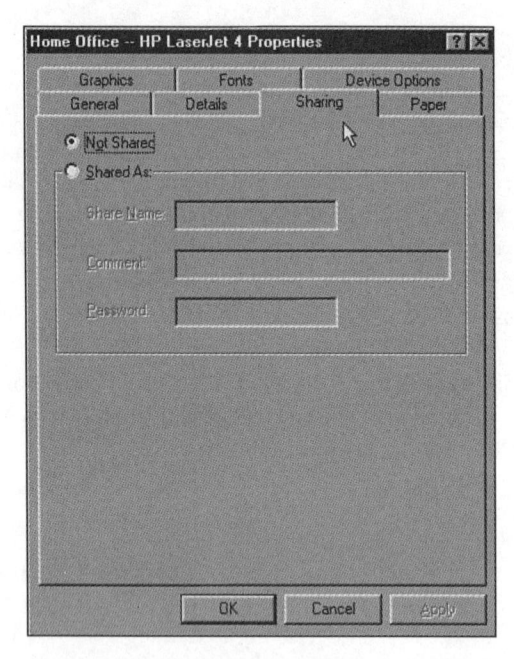

Figure 11.13 Accessing the Sharing tab of the Printer Properties screen.

8. The Password box is important. If you want to protect your print device and limit its use to only authorized persons, you should use a password. Leaving this box blank is like not having a password at all. Use a meaningful password that is not too difficult to remember, but also not too easy to guess. Type that password in this box.

9. Click OK when you have made all your entries, to return to the Printers folder screen, as shown in Figure 11.14.

10. You will see that your print device now has a small hand outstretched underneath it holding it up. This means that you have successfully shared your printer for others to connect to and use.

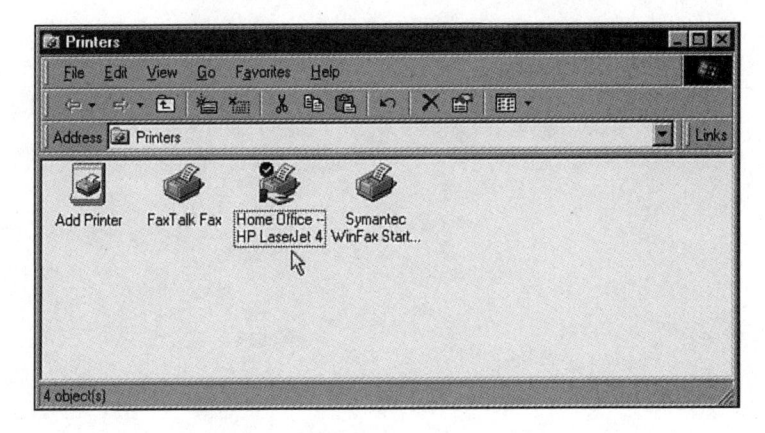

Figure 11.14 Reviewing your newly shared printer device.

CHAPTER 12
THE INTERNET AND WEB BROWSING

12

THE INTERNET AND WEB BROWSING

How do I...

12.1 Install any updates to Internet Explorer?

12.2 Configure Microsoft Internet Explorer?

12.3 Obtain the Microsoft Internet Explorer Administration Kit and why would I want to use it?

12.4 Configure and use the Microsoft Profile Assistant and Microsoft Wallet?

The Internet is a booming topic. Known as the Information Superhighway, Cyberspace, the Net, or any one of a number of other pseudonyms, the Internet is really nothing more than a collection of diverse networks that are connected to one another. The language of the Net is a networking protocol known as *TCP/IP*, which permits different systems (IBM hosts, Microsoft Windows NT, UNIX, Macintosh, and so on) to all "talk" or communicate their data bits with one another. There is, of course, more detail behind this, but at a high level this is how it works.

CHAPTER 12
THE INTERNET AND WEB BROWSING

Although there are four primary ways to *surf*, or use the Internet, the one everyone seems to know is also the most immature technology: the *World Wide Web*, which is also known as the Web or by its abbreviation of WWW. The other ways include Telnet, FTP, and Gopher (of which, really only FTP is still used a lot these days). The Web, as you know it, has only been around since early 1994, but its growth has been exponentially. This chapter discusses the tool that you need to surf with, a *Web Browser*, as well as a few other tools that will make your surfing process a whole lot easier and perhaps more enjoyable. The Web Browser tool discussed is, of course, Microsoft's Internet Explorer version 4.x and not that one made by that evil (smile) company across the parking lot in Mountain View, California.

12.1 Install any Updates to Internet Explorer
This How-To focuses on helping you update the version of Internet Explorer that is built into the Windows 98 operating system.

12.2 Configure Microsoft Internet Explorer
After you have Internet Explorer installed and updated, it would be helpful to know how to configure it for maximum security and usability. This How-To focuses precisely on this area.

12.3 Obtain the Microsoft Internet Explorer Administration Kit and Why Would I Want to Use It
The purpose of this How-To is to help you better manage a mass deployment of Internet Explorer across your organization's computing enterprise.

12.4 Configure and Use the Microsoft Profile Assistant and Microsoft Wallet
This How-To helps you to configure the Profile Assistant and the Microsoft Wallet, which are used in conjunction with Internet Explorer and electronic commerce transactions.

COMPLEXITY
INTERMEDIATE

12.1 How do I...
Install any Updates to Internet Explorer?

Problem
I understand that the Internet Explorer Web browser is built into the Windows 98 operating system, but there are going to be periodic updates to this application

12.1
INSTALL ANY UPDATES TO INTERNET EXPLORER

or its suite of components. How do I access these updates, and then install them onto my PC?

Technique

Microsoft Corporation provides multiple ways to updating the Windows 98 operating system: the Windows Update Web site and their traditional route of paid subscription CD-ROMs. The Windows Update Web site is the best place to obtain these updates, as well as a great way to install them. As such, this method is discussed in the steps presented here. Of course, for those of you who subscribe to the TechNet support CD-ROMs, available from Microsoft at a cost of about $300 per year, you have that avenue of support for obtaining these same updates as well (although the Windows 98 Windows Update Web site provides more timely access to the software patches). Follow these instructions and you will be on your way to updating your Internet Explorer Web browser.

Steps

1. Click the Start button then click the Settings menu option followed by a click on the Windows Update menu selection, as shown in Figure 12.1.

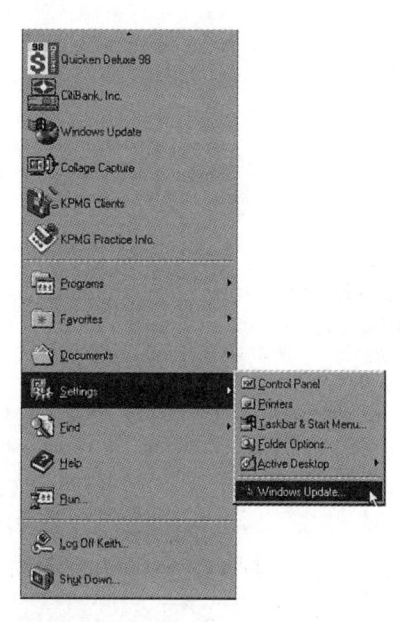

Figure 12.1 Accessing the Windows Update Selection from the Settings Menu option.

CHAPTER 12
THE INTERNET AND WEB BROWSING

2. Alternatively, you could have clicked on the Start button, and then clicked again on the Windows Update menu selection, as shown in Figure 12.2.

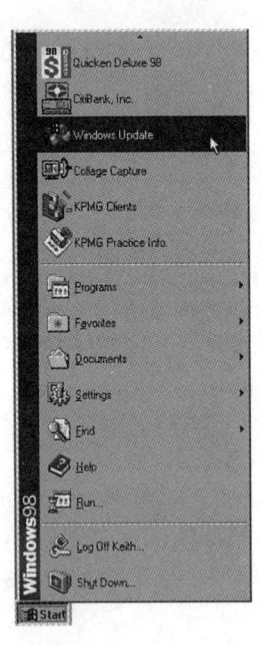

Figure 12.2 Accessing the Windows Update Option from the Windows 98 Start menu.

3. The use of either of these menu options takes you to the Microsoft Windows Update Web site, which is located at the following URL: `http://windowsupdate.microsoft.com` (all lowercase characters), as shown in Figure 12.3.

4. If you look along the left side of the screen you will see a box marked Product Updates, which has a small hand holding a tiny disk as its graphical icon. Click this menu option to start the access to the Product Updates screen.

5. The Windows Update message box appears, prompting you to permit it to automatically check your PC to see what, if any, updates your installation of Windows 98 requires. This is actually to your benefit, provided that you are trying to update just your own PC. If you are accessing the Windows 98 Windows Update site to gather electronic bits that you will then use for many users' computers internally within your organization,

12.1
INSTALL ANY UPDATES TO INTERNET EXPLORER

then you might want to just skip this automatic checking process. If you do want the Web site to check your PC for you, click Yes, as shown in Figure 12.4.

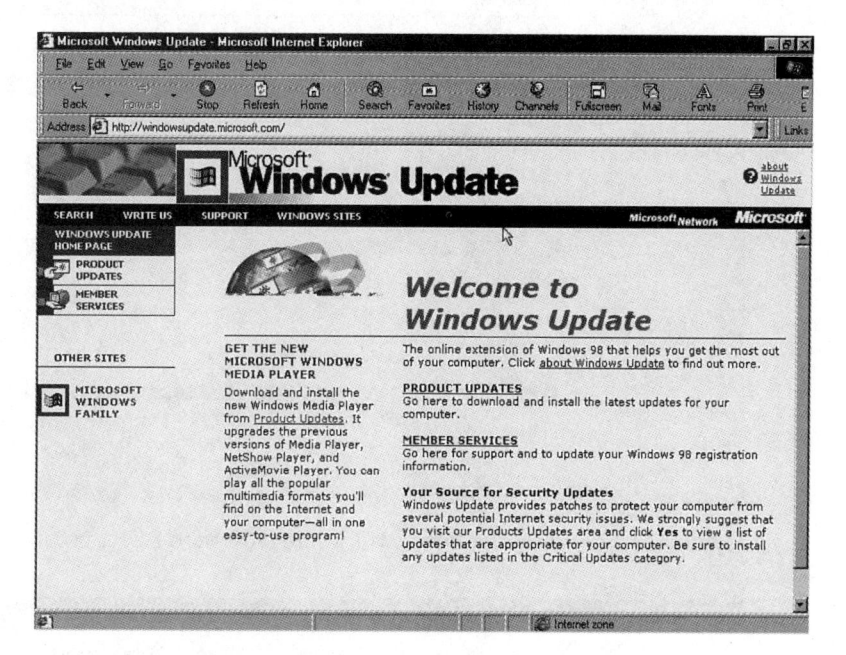

Figure 12.3 Accessing the Windows Update Web site.

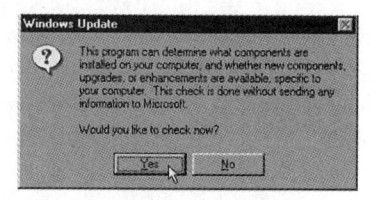

Figure 12.4 Permitting the Windows Update Process to examine your PC.

6. Clicking on either the Yes or No button brings you to the screen shown in Figure 12.5; but if you used the Yes button you would not be bothered with all the updates that you have downloaded previously.

7. If you want to view all the Windows Update files that you have already downloaded at one time or another, click the Download History button. To view every possible update file that is available to the general Microsoft Windows 98 users, click the Show All button.

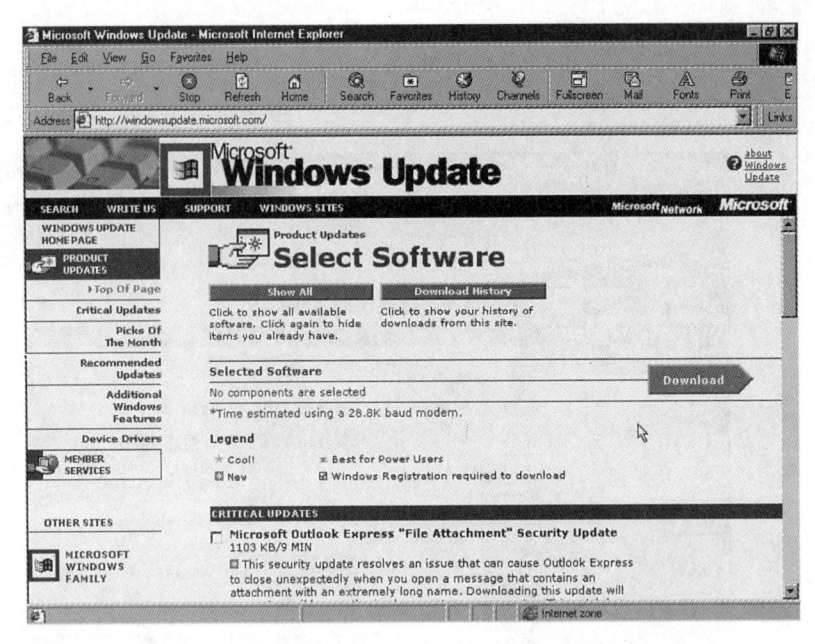

Figure 12.5 Viewing the Products Update' Software Selection area.

> **NOTE**
> You must be running the retail built version of Windows 98 in order to successfully access this Web site. Do not fool yourself into thinking that you can run Windows 95, even if you have the Internet Explorer 4.x browser, and access this site to download updates for the Windows 98 users in your organization that you must support. You will not find it possible to do so. This can be important in organizations that have "renegade" power users who update to the latest operating systems, but still believe that they are entitled to full technical support from their IS department.

8. This screen is split into five sections:

- *Critical Updates*—These will usually consist of security patches to the Internet Explorer browser and the Microsoft Outlook Express POP3 email package. This should be the first place you look when trying to find updates to the Internet Explorer browser and its built-in components.

- *Picks of the Month*—These are special updates to Windows 98, such as the recently released Microsoft Windows Media Player, which is a suite-type upgrade to the older versions of Media Player; NetShow player; and ActiveMovie player, which came with the Windows 98 operating system. (Refer to this topic in Chapter 16, "Multimedia Basics," for more details.) The only real drawback to the typical Pick of the Month update, is that they tend to be rather large in size (2+MB) and thus take a long time to download on a 28.8 Kbps modem.

- *Recommended Updates*—These are typically software patch releases to the non-critical parts and pieces of the Windows 98 operating system. Recent entries in this category have included the Microsoft DirectX Technology Update and the Microsoft Active Accessibility Update. This is not to say that these updates are not critical to your version of Windows 98, it just means that many people never need these updates because they never utilize these features within the Windows 98 operating system.

- *Additional Windows Features*—This section of the Windows Update screen is very large and has several subsections, including one for the Internet, one for International Language Support, System Utilities, Fun and Games, and Preview Versions. The variety of these updates is huge, and is definitely worth a visit or two every now and then. You might just be pleasantly surprised.

- *Device Drivers*—This section of the Windows Update screen is setup very strangely. That is, while it falls under the Product Updates section, you will not find it at the bottom of the Select Software screen. You actually need to click on this menu option separately in order to access this area (which is demonstrated a little bit later on, so keep reading).

9. So, using the scrollbar on the right side of the screen, scroll down so that you can see the Critical Updates title bar across the page, as shown in Figure 12.6.

10. Because the only thing you are concerned about at present is the Internet Explorer browser, you should only select the two software updates that deal with it. To select any software product update, click the check box that is located just to the left of the item in question.

11. Located under the title of each item is a total download size along with an estimated download time, which assumes that you are using a 28.8 Kbps modem to download these items with. Obviously, if you have a network connection to the site, your download time should be considerably shorter.

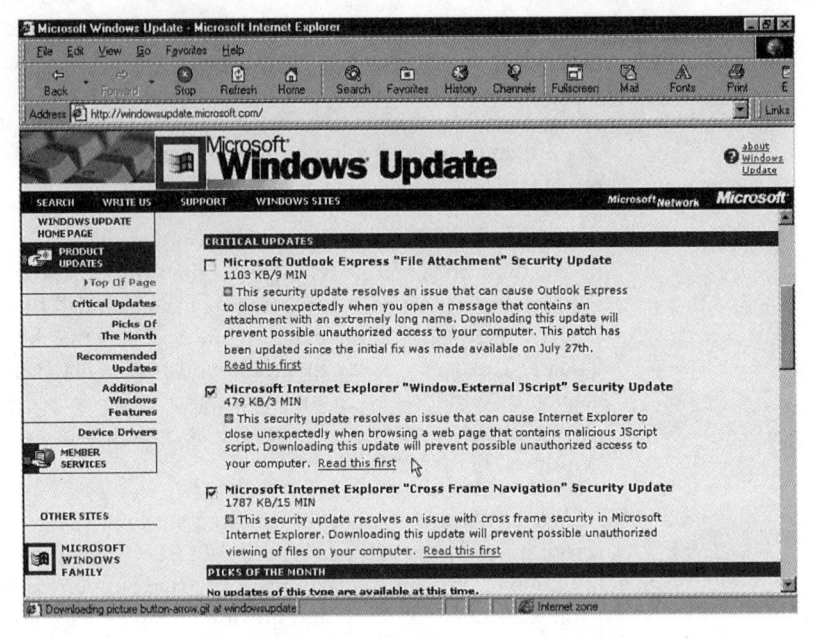

Figure 12.6 Critical Windows 98 Software Update selections.

12. Below each download time estimation is a short description of the item itself, along with a small graphical icon. This icon is Microsoft's way of sometimes telling what the purpose of this item is. For example, if there is a star symbol ☆ next to the item description, this means that this is a cool software update (also known as a waste of time, energy, and resources, but fun to play with or look at). If it is an asterisk * in a small box, it means that this is a newly released software update from Microsoft and they have not yet decided if it is cool or useful. A small, sideways-looking lightening bolt represents a software update that should be useful to your power users, such as the update to Microsoft NetMeeting;, the Windows 98 teleconferencing component that provides electronic whiteboards, video conferencing, online chats, and so on. The final icon graphic representation is a square box with a check mark in it. This means that you must register with Microsoft in order to download it from the Windows Update Web site. These are usually updates that you might find if you had purchased the Microsoft Windows 98 Plus! 98 software package (see Chapter 19, "Giving Windows Special Powers," for more details on Microsoft Plus! 98).

13. At the end of each description is a hyperlink to a Read Me file for that product update. To access this file, click the hyperlink, which takes you to that Product Update's informational file, as shown in Figure 12.7.

12.1
INSTALL ANY UPDATES TO INTERNET EXPLORER

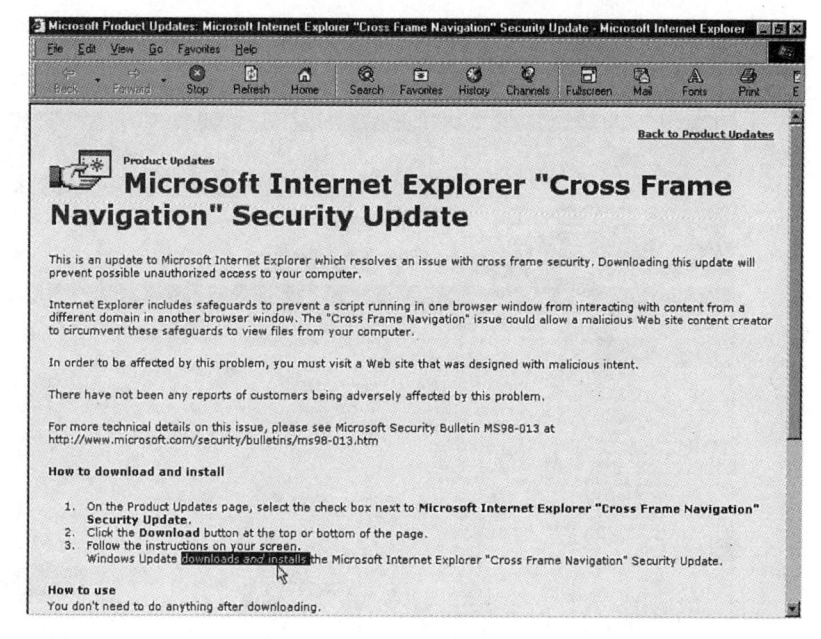

Figure 12.7 Accessing the Software Product Update Read Me area.

14. It is strongly recommended that you click on the Read This First hyperlink for each software update that you want to download, because these files contain quite a bit of useful information. When you do click it, it starts a new browser session that is separate from the one you are in now, so do not be worried about losing your place on the Microsoft Windows Update Web site. For instance, in the example shown you see instructions on how to download and install this file, some additional information on precisely what this update will do for you, and sometimes there is even information on how to access more of the technical details regarding this product update as well. I highlighted the section near the bottom of the screen to help you notice that the Windows Update process will not only download the file in question, but it will automatically apply this update to your PC. After you are finished looking at this file, close this entire browser window.

15. After you make all your selections, return to the main Windows Update Software Selections screen and scroll down to the bottom. This lets you see a total estimate for both the size of the file(s) that you want to download as well as estimated download time, as shown in Figure 12.8.

16. If you do not agree with the time it will take to download these items (as in it is far too much time than you have available right now), scroll up the screen and revise your download selections. When you have an agreeable download size and time, click the Download button to begin the process, as shown in Figure 12.9.

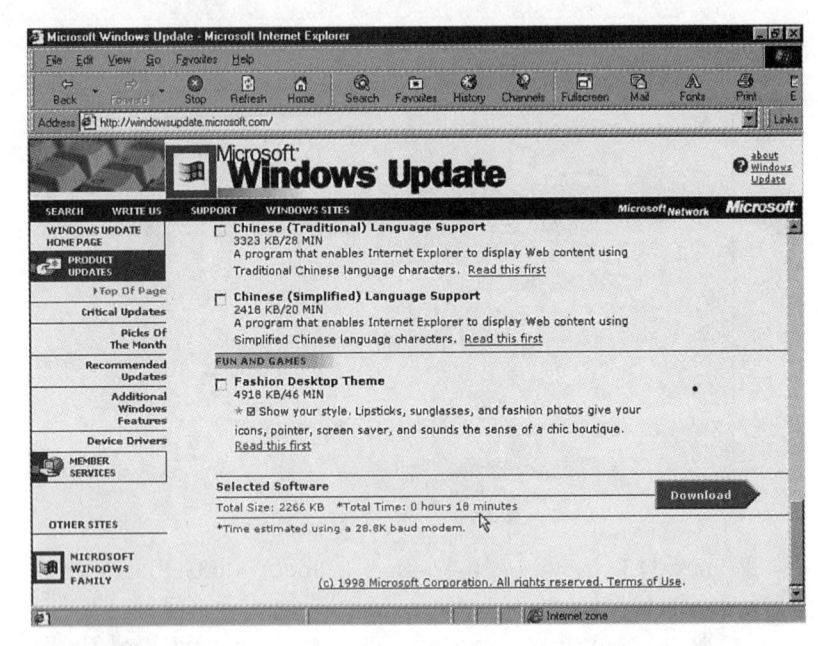

Figure 12.8 Viewing the approximated download size and time.

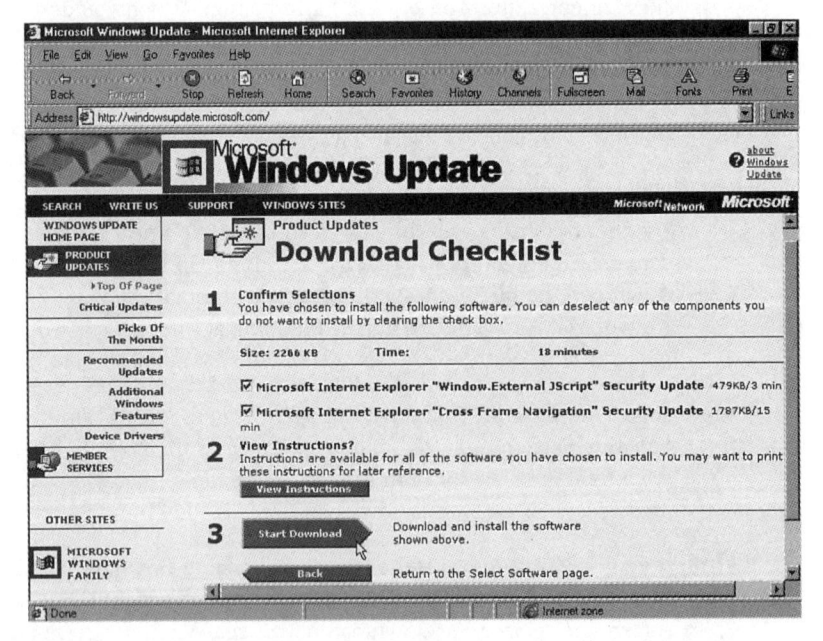

Figure 12.9 Finalizing and reviewing your download selections.

12.1
INSTALL ANY UPDATES TO INTERNET EXPLORER

17. This is basically the last time to change your mind, so do not hesitate here. There are three parts to this screen: the first is meant to permit you to review your selections; the second is to re-review any of those Read This First hyperlinks for each software update that you have chosen; and the last is to actually start the download process itself.

18. So, after you have made your last-minute decisions, click the Start Download button to begin the process. This causes the Windows Update status box to appear, as shown in Figure 12.10.

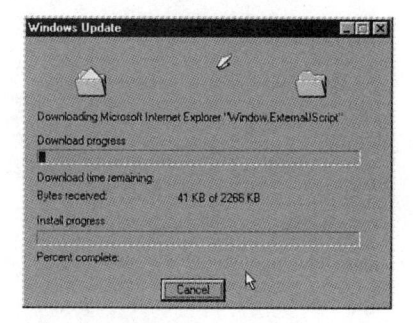

Figure 12.10 Watching the download process.

19. This is a very useful status message box, because it provides a real-time view of the actual download process, as well as letting you know exactly which file is being downloaded at any given moment in time. There is also an estimate of the time remaining in the download process, as well as a status of the bytes received and how many left are remaining to be retrieved.

20. After the download is complete, the message box changes slightly, as shown in Figure 12.11.

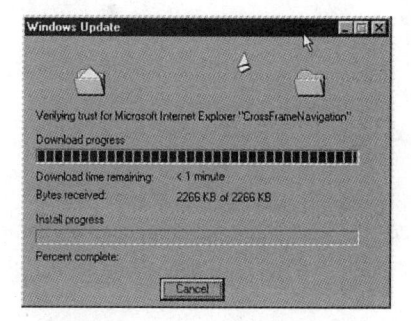

Figure 12.11 Verifying the trust for the download process.

CHAPTER 12
THE INTERNET AND WEB BROWSING

21. When the download of the files themselves is complete, the Windows Update process automatically verifies the trust for each Windows 98 component that has been downloaded to your PC. This is good for you because it ensures that a corrupted component has not been sent down to your PC installation.

22. After the trust levels have been assured, the Windows 98 Windows Update process automatically begins the installation of the components that have just been downloaded (provided, of course, that they are components that require installation).

23. When the download and installation processes are complete, a message box to this affect appears, as shown in Figure 12.12.

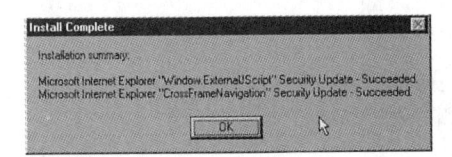

Figure 12.12 Reviewing the Install Complete message summary box.

24. The Install Complete message box appear, which provides you with a summary of the software download and installation process. When you have finished reviewing this information, click OK to complete this process.

25. Almost immediately, another Windows 98 message box appears. This time it is the Windows Update message box prompting you to permit it to restart your Windows 98 PC, as shown in Figure 12.13.

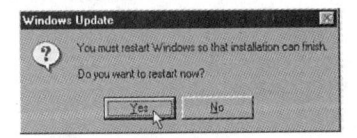

Figure 12.13 Deciding whether to restart your Windows 98 PC.

26. It is strongly recommended that you click Yes to allow this to happen, because your computer system must be restarted to allow it the capability of properly installing and initiating all the components in your PC.

27. After rebooting your PC, the installation of the items that you downloaded is complete. This, by far, is the easiest manner in which to update your Windows 98 version of Internet Explorer.

COMPLEXITY
ADVANCED

12.2 How do I... Configure Microsoft Internet Explorer?

Problem

I understand the basics of Internet Web browsing and how to use my Internet Explorer Web browser as it is when Windows 98 installs. What I do not completely understand are the ins and outs of configuring the Internet Explorer browser. For instance, my company uses a specific proxy server port to access the Internet, but I do not know how to change this setting within Internet Explorer. How do I configure my Internet Explorer Web browser so that I can specify which port to use for access to the Internet? In addition, how do I set a new Web page as my default home page?

Technique

Microsoft's Internet Explorer Web browser is the Internet/intranet/ extranet Web browser that is fully integrated into the Windows 98 operating system. Although you can very easily install and configure a different Web browser such as Netscape's Communicator or Navigator Web browsing products, this book only deals with the Microsoft browser because it comes with the Windows 98 operating system.

Configuration of Internet Explorer can be both very easy and very complex. Although it is very easy to access the configuration settings area for the Microsoft Internet Explorer Web browser, if you make a mistake in flipping a switch or maintaining a setting you might make your Windows 98-integrated Web browser cumbersome to use or perhaps even inoperable. These instructions help you to understand some of the tricks to configuring your Microsoft Internet Explorer Web browser, and maybe even a few things that can be used with the other Web browsers on the market today.

Steps

1. To start, you need to access the Internet Properties screen. This screen can be accessed in one of two ways. The first is to open your Internet Explorer Web browser, click the View menu option, and then click the Internet Options... menu selection, as shown in Figure 12.14.

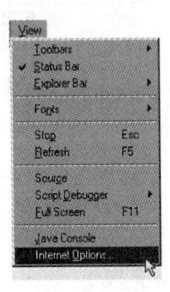

Figure 12.14 Accessing the Internet Explorer Internet Options screen via the Internet Explorer Web browser.

2. The second way to access the Internet Properties screen is to click the Start button, click the Settings menu option, and then click the Control Panel menu selection. After the Windows 98 Control Panel appears, double-click the Internet icon, as shown in Figure 12.15.

3. Regardless of the method utilized to get here, the Internet Properties screen is where everything takes place. From within the Internet Explorer Internet Properties screen you are able to perform any of a number of tasks such as:

- Change a default home page
- Set the location of your temporary Internet files
- Change the language for your browser
- Modify the security level of your browsing activities
- Define the connection method
- Specify what content your children can access or not access on the Internet

12.2
CONFIGURE MICROSOFT INTERNET EXPLORER

- Add your credit cards to a virtual wallet for use during your Internet shopping sprees

- Set an electronic certificate that identifies yourself as *you* on the Internet.

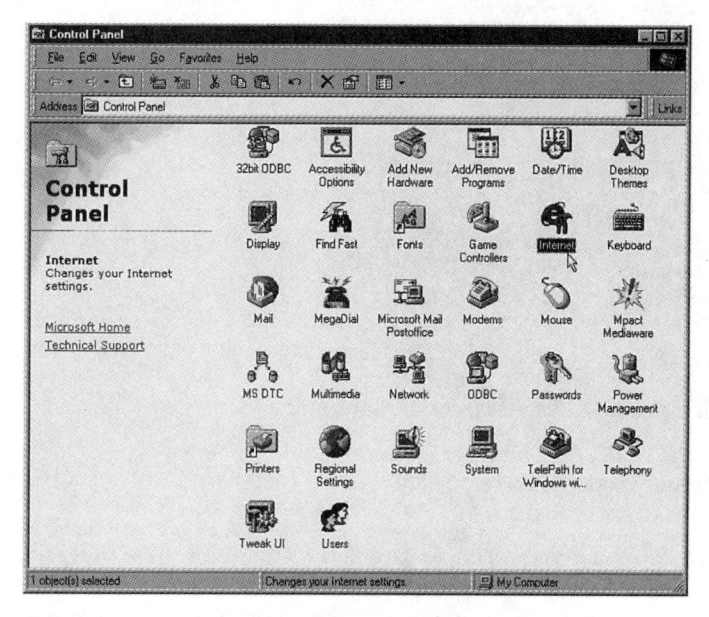

Figure 12.15 Accessing the Internet Explorer Internet Properties screen via the Windows 98 Control Panel.

So, despite the method you used to access the Internet Properties screen, you will see the screen shown in Figure 12.16.

4. The configuration area for the version of Internet Explorer that is integrated into the Windows 98 operating system is actually split into six different "tabbed" sections: General, Security, Content, Connection, Programs, and Advanced. The purpose of each section is thoroughly discussed in order for the remainder of these steps, beginning with the General tab.

5. The General tab is split into three parts: Home Page, Temporary Internet Files, and History. Each of these sections deals with the basic configuration of your Internet Explorer Web browser. The top part, Home Page, permits you to set a specific Web site as your default location. That is, when you start the Internet Explorer browser, you are taken to this spot. For many organizations, this would most likely be your default.html page on your organization's intranet. Of course, if your group does not have an intranet then perhaps this might be a location on the Internet such as http://www.nasdaq.com (in case your group is traded publicly on this stock exchange).

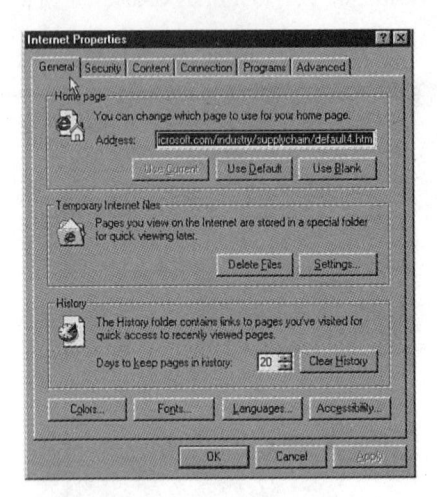

Figure 12.16 The Internet Explorer Internet Properties screen.

6. To set a home page, you have a few choices. Keep in mind that you will want to keep the Internet Properties screen open and start up the Microsoft Internet Explorer Web browser. Then, aim your Internet Explorer Web browser at a particular location. You will need to click the Use Current button, which causes that Web site's location to be automatically placed into the Address box that appears near the top of the General tab. This site is now your default location. To return to the original site that was configured by Windows 98 (http://home.microsoft.com/) when you installed the operating system, you need to click the Use Default button. If you do not want a Home page setting at all, click the Use Blank button.

7. If you happen to know the URL that you want to set as the default, you can type it into the open Address box. Regardless of the method you use to set or not set a default home page, you need to click the Apply button at the bottom of the screen to implement your selection.

8. To delete the many dozens, hundreds, or even thousands of temporary files that have accumulated on your PC due to countless access to the Internet or your organization's intranet, you need to use the Delete Files button in the Temporary Internet Files section. Therefore, if you click the Delete Files button, you are presented with a Delete Files message box, as shown in Figure 12.17.

12.2
CONFIGURE MICROSOFT INTERNET EXPLORER

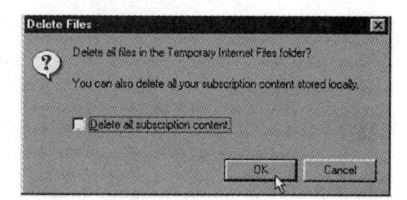

Figure 12.17 Deciding whether to delete all your temporary Internet files.

9. To delete all the temporary Internet/intranet/extranet files on your computer, which are stored in the Temporary Internet Files folder, click OK. If you would like to remove all the Internet/intranet/extranet file content as well, make sure that you have clicked the Delete All Subscription Content check box to select it first before you click OK. Keep in mind though, that if you are a heavy Internet user that repeatedly visits the same Web sites, performing this step actually works against you because you will be re-downloading the same information repeatedly.

10. After deleting the temporary Internet/intranet/extranet files that you no longer want, you will be returned to the Internet Properties screen. If you want to change the configuration of the Temporary Internet Files section, click the Settings... button. This takes you to the Settings screen, as shown in Figure 12.18.

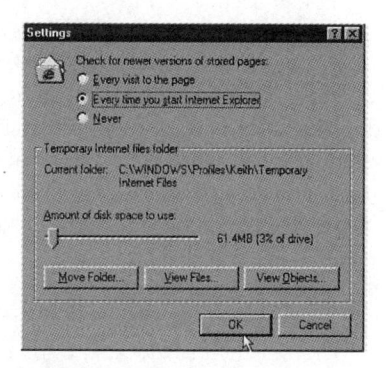

Figure 12.18 Configuring the Temporary Internet Files section.

11. The Settings screen is broken into two areas: the top part lets you decide how often you want your browser to check for newer versions of Web pages, whereas the bottom section deals with the actual physical location of your temporary Internet files, as well as how much space these files are permitted to occupy.

12. Although you can decide to spend time checking and downloading newer versions of a stored page every time you access that Web location, you might want to do it each time you start your Internet Explorer Web browser. The reasoning for this is simple. Chances are, are that you will close your browser each time you have finished locating and using the particular site that you require information from. Because of this, you will be checking for a newer version of the stored (cached) Web page.

If you are one of those persons who starts their Internet Explorer browser at the start of each business day and does not close it until you go home each night, you might want to click the radio button for the Every Visit to the Page option. However, I'm guessing that you, like most people, open and close the browser when you need it, just as you do for most of the other software applications on your computer.

The final option available, Never, is rarely used. This radio button option means that if there is a cached version of the Web page that you need, regardless of its age (that is, it does not matter how old or out-of-date it is), the Internet Explorer browser should open that page in its screen for your viewing pleasure. This might be useful to some of you who have an older 9,600bps modem who can take the chance of not downloading all the pages on a site that they already have cached locally. Instead, this type of person only updates those that they deem fit by clicking the Internet Explorer's Refresh button.

13. In the Temporary Internet Files Folder section of this screen, you are able to precisely set the total amount of space that these types of files might occupy on your PC. This setting is dependent on the user, so if you have more than one user permitted for this PC you might have multiple Temporary Internet Files folders and sizes allocated. Keep this in mind when determining the total amount of disk space that you want to allocate on your computer. To change the amount of disk space allocated, click and hold on the slider bar, and then drag it to either the left or the right. If you go right, you are increasing the total amount of disk space allocated, and if you go left then the amount decreases. To the right of the slider bar is an indicator that tells you how much space in megabytes, as well as a percentage of the total drive, which is allocated to this purpose.

14. If you want to move the Temporary Internet Files Folder to another location, you will need to use the Move Folder… button. If you have multiple users all accessing the same computer, then you might want to move everyone's temporary Internet files folder to be the same place. That way, you will be able to always know how much space is being taken at any

12.2
CONFIGURE MICROSOFT INTERNET EXPLORER

one time, as well as being able to quickly and easily delete these files from a single location. To begin the moving process, click once on the Move Folder... button, which brings you to the Warning! message box shown in Figure 12.19.

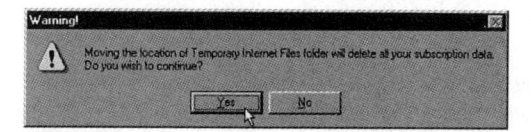

Figure 12.19 Caution is necessary when moving the Temporary Internet Files folder.

15. This box is Windows 98's way of informing you that any move will automatically invalidate any Internet subscriptions and delete the subscription data stored to date. If this is alright with you, click Yes to continue the process. Otherwise, click No to halt the process. If you click Yes button to continue, you will be prompted with a Windows Explorer-type screen that helps you in finding the new location for your temporary Internet files folder. After you have used an existing folder or created a new one, you will be returned to the temporary Internet files Settings screen.

16. If you want to view the files that are contained within the temporary Internet Files folder, click once on the View Files... button to reveal the screen shown in Figure 12.20.

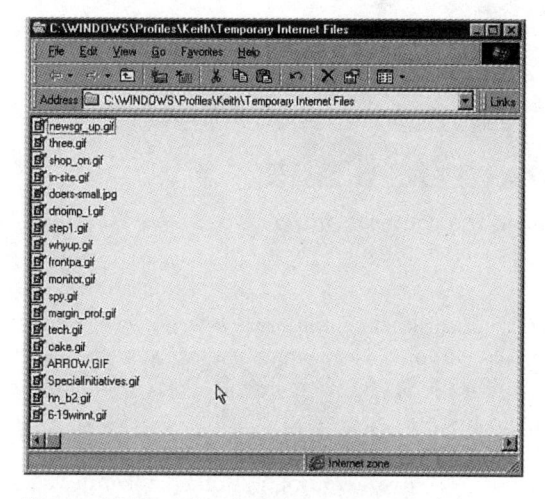

Figure 12.20 Viewing the contents of the Temporary Internet Files folder.

17. As you can see, the majority of the temporary files stored on your computer will be graphics files such as those with the .GIF or .JPG picture formats. If you want to delete any files at this point, you can click the file or files that you want to delete to select them, and then click the secondary mouse button on the Delete menu selection to actually remove these files from your hard drive.

18. After you are finished reviewing your temporary Internet files, close this window and you will again see the temporary Internet Files Settings screen.

19. The final option on this screen is to view the various object files that have been downloaded to your computer from the Internet or intranet that you have connected to at least once. These objects are also known as the Temporary Internet Program Files. To see these objects, click the View Objects... button to reveal the screen shown in Figure 12.21.

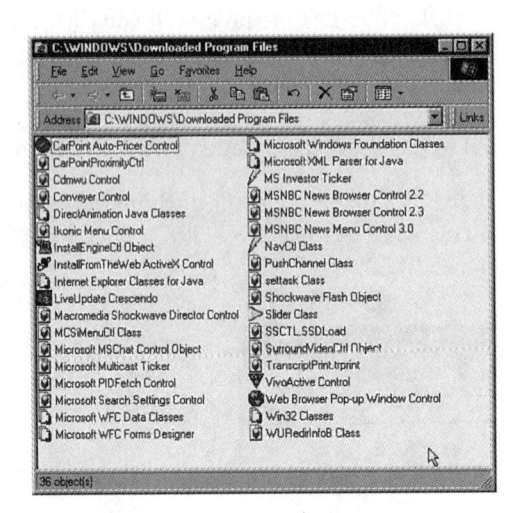

Figure 12.21 Viewing the contents of the Downloaded Program Files folder.

20. This screen works just like the Temporary Internet Files folder. You can delete programs at will on this screen or you can just review them to see what kinds of applications you have downloaded (usually unbeknownst to you) during an Internet or intranet connection session. These temporary programs might be used to run a specific instance of part of a Web site (such as a special ActiveX control, multimedia feature, and so on). If you do not know exactly what a specific program does, you might not want to arbitrarily delete it. When you have finished reviewing this screen, close the window and you again see the temporary Internet files Settings screen.

12.2
CONFIGURE MICROSOFT INTERNET EXPLORER

21. Click OK to accept all your changes, which returns you to the Internet Properties screen with the General tab displayed.

22. The final section of the General tab is used to modify the history that has been accumulated on the Web pages that you have visited for the past xx number of days. To change the number of days that you retain the history of the sites you visit, click the up or down scrollbar arrows. Clicking the up arrow increases the total number of days for which you retain history, while clicking the down arrow decreases the total number of days for which you retain history. Or, if you are impatient, you can click the number that appears in the Days to Keep Pages in History: box and type in a new number such as 0 (meaning do not keep any history) or 60 (keep two months worth of history).

23. If you would like to delete all the existing history of visits to various Web pages, click the Clear History button to reveal the screen shown in Figure 12.22.

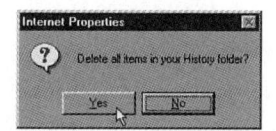

Figure 12.22 Erasing the contents of the History folder.

24. On this screen you should click the Yes button to proceed with the deletion of all your history files, or click the No button to stop the deletion process of your history files. Either way, after you click a button, you are returned to the Internet Properties screen (if you selected Yes, there would be a bit of a delay because Windows 98 is processing the deletion of all your history files).

25. Along the bottom portion of the General tab is a series of basic configuration options that you might use to modify the colors, fonts, languages, and accessibility features of the Microsoft Internet Explorer Web browser. For example, if you click the Colors... button, you will be taken to the Colors modification screen, as shown in Figure 12.23.

26. This is a very straightforward screen. If you want to change the color of your text or background, use the Colors section of this screen. Otherwise, if you want to change the colors of visited versus unvisited links, use the Links section. When you are finished, click OK to confirm your choices and return to the Internet Properties screen.

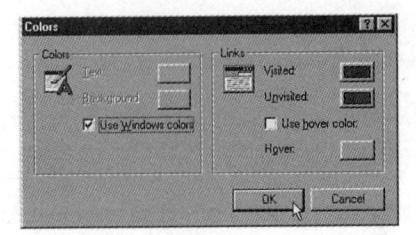

Figure 12.23 Changing the colors of the Internet Explorer browser.

27. Click the Fonts... button to reveal the Fonts screen, as shown in Figure 12.24.

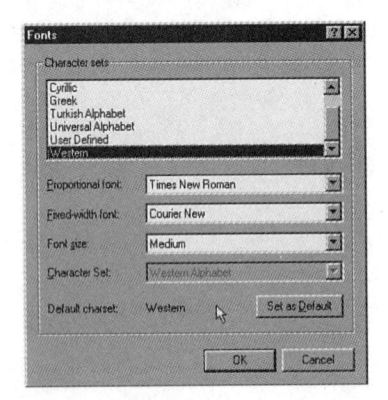

Figure 12.24 Modifying which fonts are used with the Internet Explorer browser.

28. The default character set for your browser is shown in the top box of this screen. To modify it, use the scrollbar and click on the character set that you want. Then, click the Set as Default button.

29. The proportional and fixed-width fonts can also be specified, using the next two drop-down list boxes on this screen. If you do not understand the uses of these fonts, do not play with them. This might cause you a bit of grief and heartache down the road when wacky things—such as distorted writings on your screen—begin to happen.

30. When you have finished making any changes to this screen, if any, click OK to confirm your selections and return to the Internet Properties screen.

12.2
CONFIGURE MICROSOFT INTERNET EXPLORER

31. Sometimes you will find a Web site that appears in another language and your browser does not seem to handle it just right. This is probably due to the single language setting of your browser: English (United States), if you have purchased a USA-version of Windows 98. To modify this, click the Languages... button to reveal the screen shown in Figure 12.25.

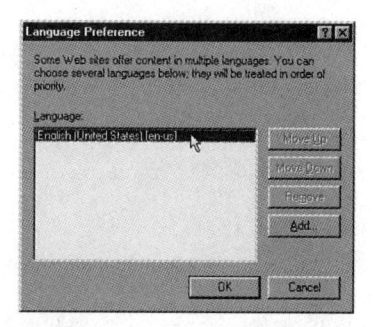

Figure 12.25 Modifying the languages used with the Internet Explorer browser.

32. When the Language Preference screen appears, you are able to review those language(s) that have already been configured for use on your Windows 98 PC. If you want to add another, click the Add... button to go to the Add Language screen, as shown in Figure 12.26.

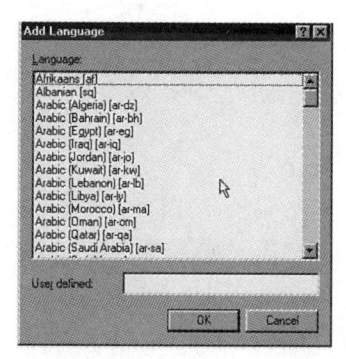

Figure 12.26 Adding a new language for use with the Internet Explorer browser.

33. As you can readily see, there are dozens of additional languages that can be added for use with the Internet Explorer browser. In the brackets to the right of the language type's name is the country(ies) where these languages are most prominently used (such in the case of Arabic, which is slightly different amongst the various Arabic-speaking peoples of the world). Click the language that you want to add, and then click OK. This returns you to the Language Preference screen.

34. On the Language Preference screen, you can now modify the order in which the Internet Explorer browser will use a specific language when it hits a Web site. Keep in mind that the more languages your browser needs to review, the longer it might take for you to surf a particular Web site.

35. When you have made your selections, click OK to return to Internet Properties screen.

36. The final button on the General tab is permits you to alter the Internet Explorer browser for persons with disabilities, in accordance to previous options that you might have set using the Accessibility icon in the Windows 98 Control Panel.

37. To access this area, click the Accessibility... button in the lower-right corner of the General tab, which reveals the screen shown in Figure 12.27.

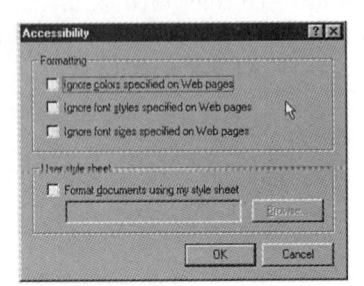

Figure 12.27 Modifying the Accessibility options of the Internet Explorer browser.

38. These are very simplistic options that are available on the Accessibility screen that deal with the formatting of Web pages. To force the Internet Explorer browser to ignore the colors, font styles, and font sizes found on a specific Web page, you need to click the check box next to the appropriate option, which then selects that option. If an option is selected, that option's topic will be ignored on all Web pages you access.

39. The bottom section of this screen permits you to define a specific style sheet for use with each Web page you encounter. To choose one, click the

12.2 CONFIGURE MICROSOFT INTERNET EXPLORER

check box next to the label Format documents using my style sheet, which will then un-gray the Browse... button and the style sheet entry box. Browse your computer to find the style sheet that you want to use, and then click OK to confirm your choices. This returns you to the Internet Properties screen.

40. That was the final topic of the General tab. It is now time for you to move on to the sensitive topic of Internet browser security. To do this, click the Security tab as shown in Figure 12.28.

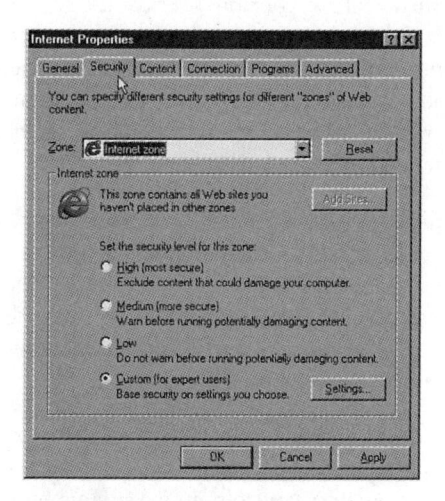

Figure 12.28 Accessing the Internet Explorer browser Security tab.

41. The options found on this tab are the most complex to configure, and also the most important. If you make a mistake in configuring some of these options, you might expose yourself to others who could easily take advantage of your weakness to destroy your computer's data or access your sensitive data without your knowledge or consent.

It is also in this area of configuring the Microsoft Internet Explorer Web browser that things tend to get a little ugly. That is, a change that you make in one area might result in another change being made or required to be made in a completely different area. This can make configuration difficult at best, and downright confusing for the first time user of these screens. Therefore, a little background is needed on the terminology that is used.

There are actually five different levels of security that can be assigned within Internet Explorer. These levels are known as *zones* and are as follows:

- *Local Intranet Zone*—the purpose of the Local Intranet Zone is to provide an area where just your organization's intranet Web sites are found. The default security setting for this zone is Medium, which means that users will be warned before inherently detrimental content might be executed.

- *Trusted Sites Zone*—This zone is where you should store the URLs for those sites that are proven trustworthy. Obviously, it is up to you to determine the trustworthiness of a site, as you will need to manually add a trusted site to your browser (or use the Microsoft Internet Explorer Administration kit to change this setting for a large user community of Internet Explorer browsers; review that topic in this chapter for further details). The default security setting for this zone is Low, which means that users will be warned before inherently detrimental content might be executed.

- *Internet Zone*—This zone is where all site URLs are stored, that do not already exist in other zones. That is, unless a site specifically appears in another zone, it will default to the Internet Zone automatically. The default security setting for this zone is Medium, which means that users will be warned before inherently detrimental content might be executed.

- *Restricted Sites Zone*—This zone contains the URLs of those sites that you believe to contain potentially harmful content, such as Java applets, HTML code, ActiveX controls, an executable binary, and so on that were designed to hurt others. The default security setting for this zone is High, which means that users will be warned before inherently detrimental content might be executed.

- *My Computer Zone*—This zone has no default security setting. It is here that some of the ugliness exists. Although there is a My Computer Zone, you are unable to configure or alter its security state through this process (I guess Microsoft still does not completely trust us users just yet).

Each zone provides a distinct and separate purpose within Internet Explorer and should be handled with care, so to speak. Do not place a site within your organization into the Trusted Sites Zone just because that site is inside your organization. It is estimated that nearly 90 percent of the hacker attempts against a Web page or site come from *within* an organization, as opposed to some orchestrated outside attack from outside your group. You need to be sure before you actually place something within the Trusted Sites Zone. Keep this in mind as you plan your Internet Explorer zone strategies.

12.2
CONFIGURE MICROSOFT INTERNET EXPLORER

42. So, to get started, click the drop-down list box that is located next to the Zone label, as shown in Figure 12.29.

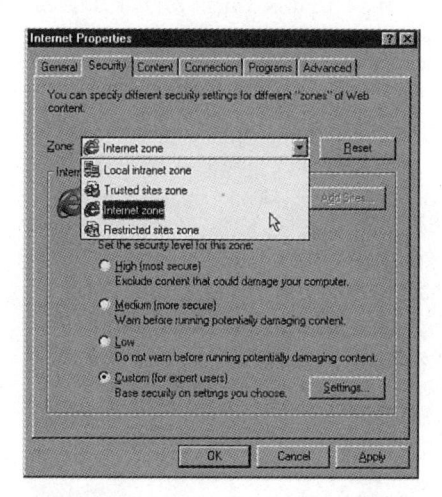

Figure 12.29 Accessing the various Internet Explorer Security Zones.

43. To make things easier, explore each of these zones in order, beginning with the Local Intranet Zone on top. Click that zone to select it. Next, you will see four radio buttons in the Internet Zone section on the Security tab screen: High (most secure); Medium (more secure); Low (not very secure at all); and Custom (you make the choices—meaning that this is either the most secure zone or the least protected zone). Click once on the setting that you require, which moves the radio button selection dot to be inside that security level's option. The detailed settings for the Custom selection is discussed a bit later in this section (go to step 53 if you want to read it now).

44. To actually add a site to a zone, click the Add Sites… button. After clicking this button, you will see the screen shown in Figure 12.30.

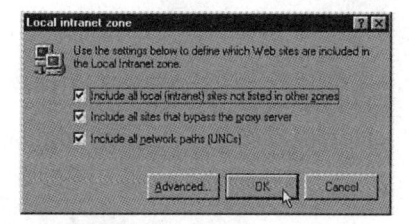

Figure 12.30 Adding sites to the Local Intranet Security Zone.

45. This part of the Local Intranet Zone screen is used to decide which site configurations are or are not included within this security zone. To select a zone configuration, click the check box next to that zone option.

46. To actually add a specific URL to this zone, you need to use the Advanced Options screen. To access this screen, click the Advanced... button to reveal the screen shown in Figure 12.31.

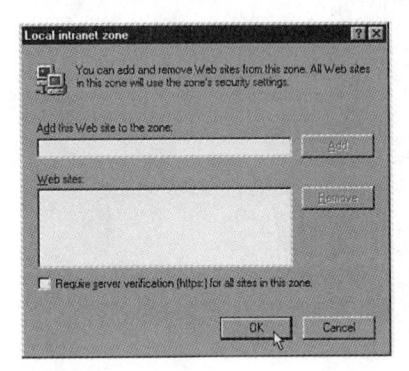

Figure 12.31 Specifying URLs for the Local Intranet Security Zone.

47. To actually add a Web site to this zone listing, you must type in the exact uniform resource locator (URL) address for that Web site into the top box. After the URL has been entered, click the Add button to move that site to the bottom box, which means that it is now a permanent member of this zone until you remove it, that is.

48. If you want to require the use of a server verification process via a process such as the Secured Sockets Layer (SSL) encryption method, click the Require Sever Verification (https) for All Sites in This Zone check box. After you have made all your entries, click OK to return to the Internet Properties screen.

49. To add Web sites to either the Trusted Sites Zone or the Restricted Sites Zone, you need to use the drop-down list box to select that particular zone. Then, click the Add Sites... button to access the necessary screen for either of these two zones, as shown in Figures 12.32 and 12.33.

50. The entry process for both of these zones works the same as the Advanced Options screen for the Local Intranet Zone. As you can see, you need to enter the exact URL in the top box on either screen, and then click the Add button to move that site to the bottom box, which means that it is now a permanent member of this zone—until you remove it, that is.

12.2
CONFIGURE MICROSOFT INTERNET EXPLORER

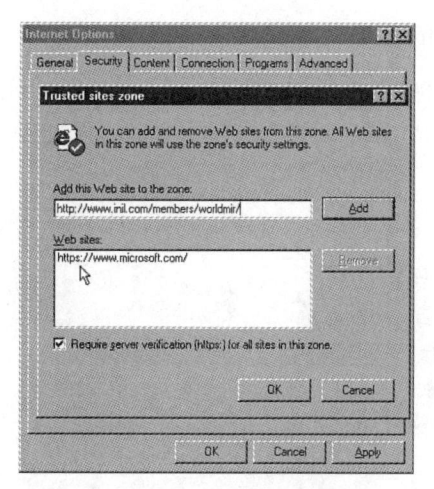

Figure 12.32 Specifying URLs for the Trusted Sites Security Zone.

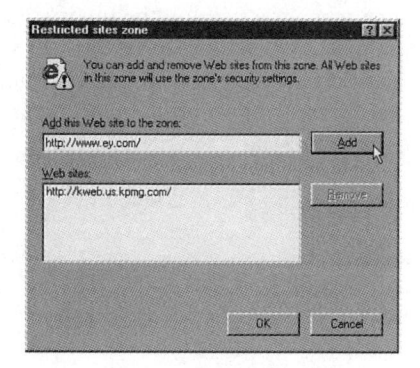

Figure 12.33 Specifying URLs for the Restricted Sites Security Zone.

51. If you want to require the use of a server verification process via a process such as the SSL encryption method, click the Require Sever Verification (https) for All Sites in this Zone check box. After you have made all your entries, click OK to return to the Internet Properties screen.

52. The final section on the Security tab of Internet Properties screen that you need to review is the Settings... button that is found next to the Custom (for expert users) radio button. This is where the real fun begins, because a mistake here can cost you your computer system.

53. To begin, click the Settings... button, which reveals the screen shown in Figure 12.34.

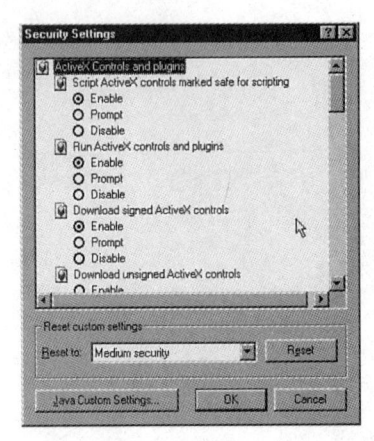

Figure 12.34 Accessing the custom Security Settings screen.

54. This screen is chock-full of options and switches that can make or break the security of your computer, whenever you use the Internet Explorer browser to access Web sites. You can lock down your browser so that ActiveX controls, Java applets, and other executables do not run, as well as making sure that unwanted fonts or files are not inadvertently downloaded to your computer from a Web site.

55. The top box of this screen is broken into several sections:

- ActiveX Controls and Plug-ins
- Java
- Scripting
- Downloads
- User Authentication
- Miscellaneous

56. Each of these sections has subsections, which are all indented underneath each of these main titles. When this discussion progresses to the Java subsection, we will discuss the use of the Java Custom Settings... button found at the bottom of this screen.

57. To instantly go back to the default settings, as defined by Microsoft, for any of the Internet Explorer security levels (High, Medium, or Low) you need to select that particular setting in the drop-down list box. Then, you

12.2
CONFIGURE MICROSOFT INTERNET EXPLORER

must click once on the Reset button to actually make those changes. If you are an occasional or entry-level user of Windows 98, Medium is the best choice for you. However, if you are in a large corporation and your system administrator has *not* specified a custom one for you, you should also select Medium as your security level setting.

58. Seeing how you are still reading, you must be interested in the details of each of the radio button options that appear within each subsection on this screen. So, why not begin?

59. Within the ActiveX Controls and Plug-ins section, there are a series of three radio buttons: Enable, Prompt, and Disable. Enable means that that particular option automatically occurs without your immediate knowledge or timely consent. Prompt means that you want the Internet Explorer browser to let you know when someone or something is attempting to send you something or attempting to execute something on your PC. Disable means that you do not want this feature to occur no matter what.

60. So, going from the top, you have an option known as Script ActiveX controls marked safe for scripting, which, means that you are giving permission for an authenticated Web site to configure ActiveX scripts for use on your computer.

61. Next, comes the capability to actually run those ActiveX controls and plug-ins. This capability can be a real pain if you mark it as Prompt, because just about every Web site these days seems to use ActiveX controls. This means that you will forever be clicking Yes on the prompt message box saying that it is okay for this script or that script to execute. Keep in mind that if you say No to any one control or script that the remainder of a Web page might fail to load properly.

62. Next is the capability to Download Signed ActiveX Controls. A signed control is one that has been digitally signed (you should review the sections on Digital Signatures and the Signature Verification Tool in Chapter 13, "Email and News," for more details on digital signing). Likewise, just beneath that option is the one to Download Unsigned ActiveX Controls.

Your decision is required on both of these. A basic rule of thumb is to accept all signed controls and content, and to prompt on all unsigned controls and content. While this is not a sure-fire way to protect yourself on the corporate intranet and on the open Internet, it makes life a whole lot easier because you will not constantly be clicking a Prompt message box.

63. As you scroll down the Security Settings screen, you will see even more radio button options, as shown in Figure 12.35.

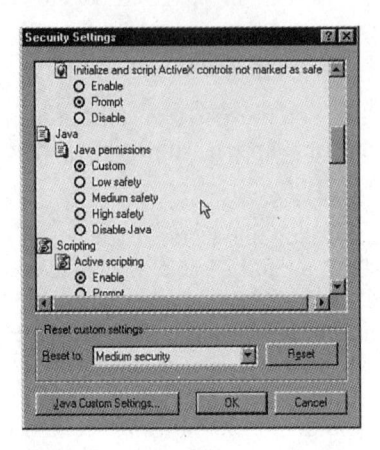

Figure 12.35 Making changes to the Security Settings screen.

64. One option is to Initialize and script ActiveX controls not marked as safe; another for Java; and a third for the use of scripting, such as Visual Basic Scripting, on your PC.

65. Of these, the Java permissions subsection is probably the most important, given the inherent security holes that the Java language brings with it to the Microsoft Internet Explorer browser operating environment. Within this subsection are the same self-explanatory radio button options that you found previously in the Internet Explorer browser: Low Safety; Medium Safety; High Safety; and the option to disable the use of Java entirely on your computer. The final option, Custom, is not so clear.

Custom presents you with the capability to run Java applets in the mainstream portion of your PC, which means that these applets work much in the same way that ActiveX controls might and could work. However, within the Internet Explorer security model, you are presented with the capability to Sandbox Java. *Sandboxing* is a slang computer term that means to run in a test environment. That is, while it might appear that you are running Java in such a manner that it can run amuck on your computer, it actually is operating in a "secure" play area...a sandbox, so to speak.

66. To modify the custom Java permissions section of the Internet Explorer browser, click the Java Custom Settings button to reveal the screen shown in Figure 12.36.

12.2
CONFIGURE MICROSOFT INTERNET EXPLORER

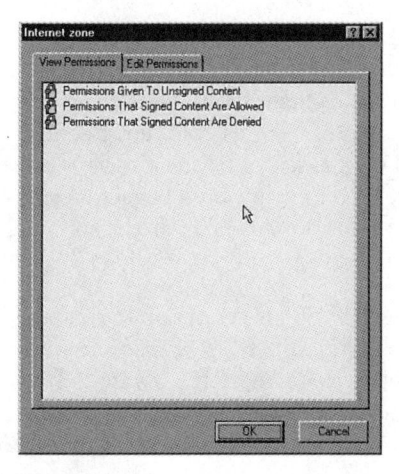

Figure 12.36 Accessing the Java Custom Settings Configuration area.

67. On the Internet Zone screen that appears there are two tabs: View Permissions, and Edit Permissions. The View Permissions is more of an informational screen. It tells you which permissions have been assigned thus far. The important screen is the editing screen. To get there, click the Edit Permissions tab, which reveals the screen shown in Figure 12.37.

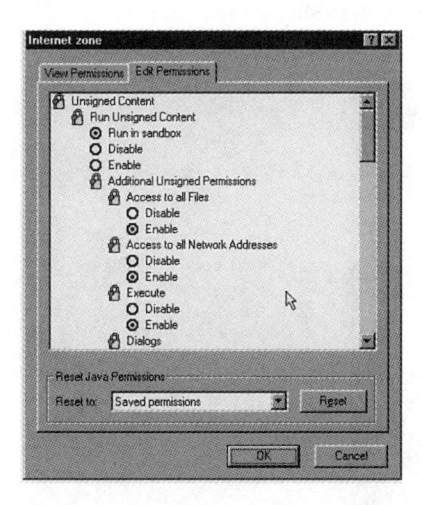

Figure 12.37 Modifying the Java Custom Permissions.

68. The Edit Permissions tab is split into two parts: Unsigned Content and Signed Content. Essentially what you need to do is determine the permitted settings for Web site content that is digitally signed and for content that is not digitally signed. Sounds easy enough anyway. What is missing and sorely needed on this screen for most users is access to Windows-based help—any kind of help would benefit most people, because not everyone will be able to remember all the specific terms and nuances that appear on this screen.

69. Within the Unsigned Content section is the option to run all of it in a Sandbox. If you are uncertain as to the types of Web sites that you will be pointing your Internet Explorer browser at, it is a wise to run all unsigned content that might contain Java code or applets in the protected, "test" area known as the sandbox. As the old adage goes, it is better to be safe than sorry.

70. A subsection within the Unsigned Content section is a radio button option that grants additional access to unsigned content. For example, you can set up the capability for content to access all the files on your computer system, access to all your network addresses (this is especially important if your PC is connected to the corporate networks), and execute programs on your computer. If you scroll down the screen, as shown in Figure 12.38, you can also grant access to your computer's System Information, the capability to Print, access to the Protected Scratch Space, as well as to User Selected Files.

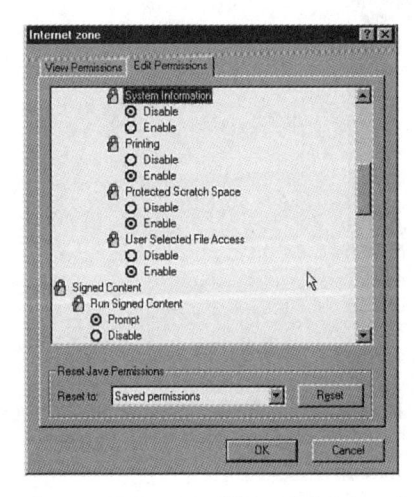

Figure 12.38 Modifying additional unsigned content permissions for Java content.

12.2
CONFIGURE MICROSOFT INTERNET EXPLORER

71. All these options are selected by a single-clicking the radio button next to either the Disable or Enable radio button options.

72. You are able to make a similar set of choices for Signed Content. The first decision you need to make is whether to Run Signed Content on your PC. If you decide is yes, you need to click the Enable radio button below this option's text label. If you decide no, click the Disable radio button. You might, of course, click the Prompt radio button, which forces the Internet Explorer browser to prompt you every time signed Java content is accessed through this browser.

73. Assuming that you have chosen either the Prompt or the Enable radio buttons, you now have more choices to make, as shown in Figure 12.39.

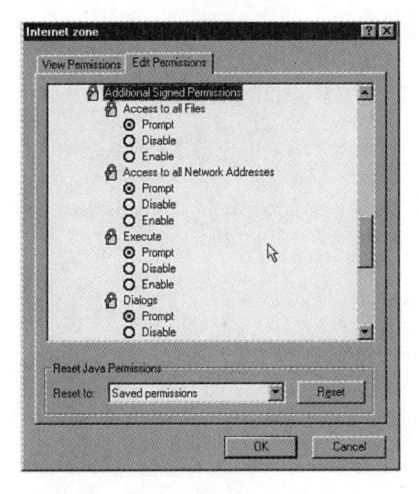

Figure 12.39 Modifying Additional Signed Permissions for Java Content.

74. Just like in the Unsigned Content Permissions area, there are several options in the Additional Signed Permissions section. You are able to bequeath the possibility for Java content to access all your files, access to all your network addresses (again, this is especially important if your PC is connected to the corporate networks), execute programs on your PC, and execute Dialogs on your PC. As you scroll down the screen, as shown in Figure 12.40, you are also able to grant access to your computer's System Information, to Printing, to the Protected Scratch Space, and to the User Selected File Access.

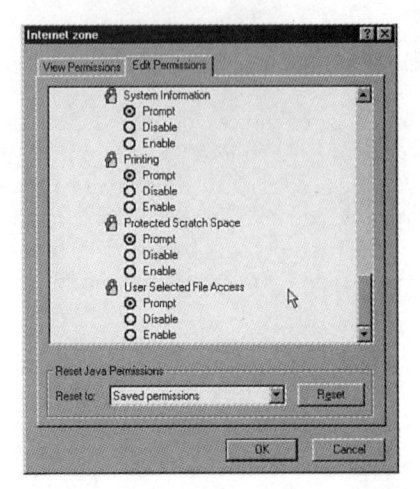

Figure 12.40 Modifying Additional Signed Content Permissions for Java content.

75. When you have made all your changes, click OK to return to the main Security Settings screen, as shown in Figure 12.41.

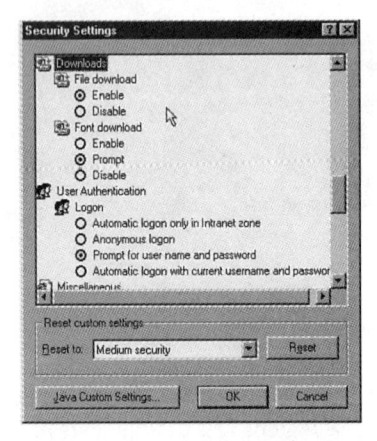

Figure 12.41 Accessing more permissions for use with the Internet Explorer Web browser.

76. The next two sets of permissions deal with the capability to download fonts and files to your PC. If either of these sections are marked as disabled, you will not be able to use your Internet Explorer browser to download that particular subject That is, if you click the Disable radio button under the File Download section, you cannot download files, and so on.

12.2
CONFIGURE MICROSOFT INTERNET EXPLORER

77. The final set shown on this screen has to do with user authentication on those Web sites where you must log in, such as on one of Microsoft's secure sites: the Value Chain Initiative's private area on the Supply Chain site (`http://www.microsoft.com/industry/supplychain/default4.htm`). If you want to automatically log in, click the Automatic Log on with Current Username and Password. However, this can be dangerous if your current username and password do not match what the private Web site is expecting, because these are the current username and password identifiers that you use on your organization's internal systems.

> **NOTE**
>
> For example, you might work in the payroll department for your company, but you are attempting to download a "free" copy of Microsoft Outlook and so you must register with Microsoft's Web site. If you used this automatic log-on feature, you might inadvertently send your private user ID and password to Microsoft or some other company. This is bad, especially because many Web sites track exactly which combinations of user IDs and passwords have been attempted on their sites. The result? Your private username and password are now part of their records.

78. The Anonymous Logon selection automatically sends the username of anonymous and the password of the default email address for your PC, leaving it blank if there is not one).

79. If you scroll down the screen, you will see the first part of the Miscellaneous security settings topics as shown in Figure 12.42.

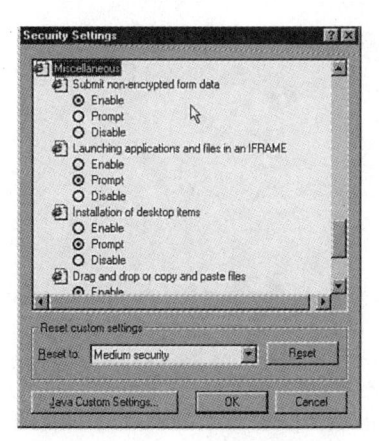

Figure 12.42 Accessing the Miscellaneous Internet Explorer Security Permissions.

80. The ability to submit non-encrypted form data is not really a feature, per say, instead it should be viewed as the ability to perform a not-so-wise act. This means that your information will pass essentially in a clear-text format so that people who want to read it may do so, provided they have the basic tools required to see the data (such as a sniffer or other network monitoring device). If you work entirely on a private intranet, this is not such a bad thing. However, if you are passing data on the open Internet, you should really think this through before continuing this unsafe practice.

81. The next three options, Launching Applications, Installing Desktop Items, and Enabling the Drag-and-Drop Features of Internet Explorer are easy to understand. If you click the Enable button for any of these options, you will be able to perform these tasks. Otherwise, click the Disable button and you will no longer be able to perform that specific task. The Prompt button does the same as the Enable button, except you will be notified prior to the system being capable to perform the task at hand.

82. When you make the changes to these three areas, use the scrollbar to move down to the final option on this screen, as shown in Figure 12.43.

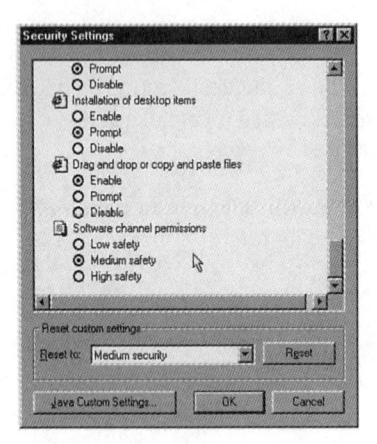

Figure 12.43 Reviewing and modifying Miscellaneous Security Permissions.

83. The final option within the Security Settings screen is concerned with the permissions for *software channels*. Software channels, as you might recall, are software-based distribution mechanisms by which program files and applications may be installed, distributed, or updated from a centralized location, such as a Web or file server, to an individual's PC. This technology is based on the *Push* technology that has become so prevalent over

12.2
CONFIGURE MICROSOFT INTERNET EXPLORER

the past few years. The settings for the Channel option are arranged into a Low, Medium, and High format, just as the Security Levels for the Security Zones are defined.

84. After you make your selections, click OK to return to the Security tab of the Internet Properties screen.

85. Next up is the Content screen. To access this screen, click the Content tab, as shown in Figure 12.44.

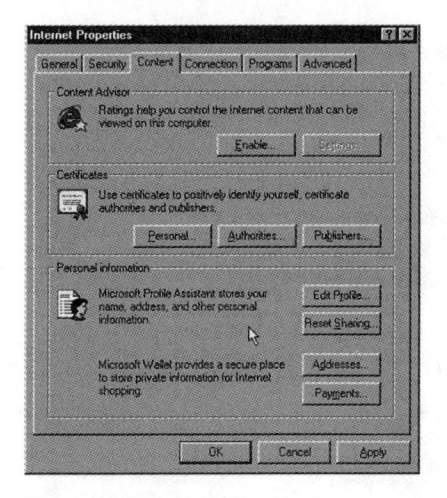

Figure 12.44 Reviewing the Content tab options.

86. This screen is split into three areas: the Content Advisor, Digital Certificates, and Microsoft Personal Assistant/ Microsoft Wallet. The first two are covered here. You should review the topic that appears later in this chapter for more details on both the Microsoft Personal Assistant and the Microsoft Wallet technologies. The Content Advisor utility is a function of Internet Explorer that permits you to control a user's access to content on the Internet; your organization's intranet, or some other extranet Web site. Or, to put it another way, its purpose is to censor content so that the users of this Internet Explorer Web browser cannot see everything that might be harmful to them on the Internet.

The only area where this might be useful is for those home users who have young children using their home PC for Internet connections. Other than this type of an example, it is plain censorship. To enable use of the Internet ratings system using the Content Advisor, click the Enable... button, and you will be prompted for a password, as shown in Figure 12.45.

CHAPTER 12
THE INTERNET AND WEB BROWSING

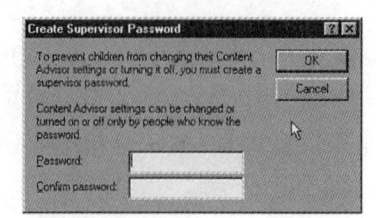

Figure 12.45 Creating a supervisor password.

87. This password prevents unauthorized users from accessing non-authorized Web sites, such as pornography-filled pages. When you have entered a password and confirmed it in the second box, click OK to proceed, as shown in Figure 12.46.

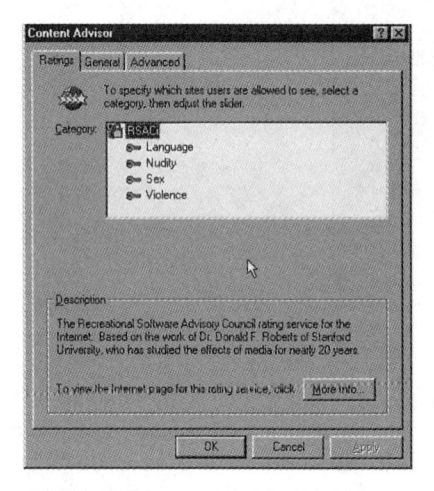

Figure 12.46 Reviewing the Content Advisor screen.

88. There are four main ratings topics that are configurable via this screen: Language, Nudity, Sex, and Violence. To modify the settings for any one of these areas, click the Category name, as shown in Figure 12.47.

89. There are four levels that may be set for each of these four options. Level 1 is the lowest or tamest setting, whereas Level 4 is the highest or most explicit setting—there is no censorship using a Level 4 setting. In the description box near the bottom of this screen there is a brief reference to the setting that you have selected.

12.2
CONFIGURE MICROSOFT INTERNET EXPLORER

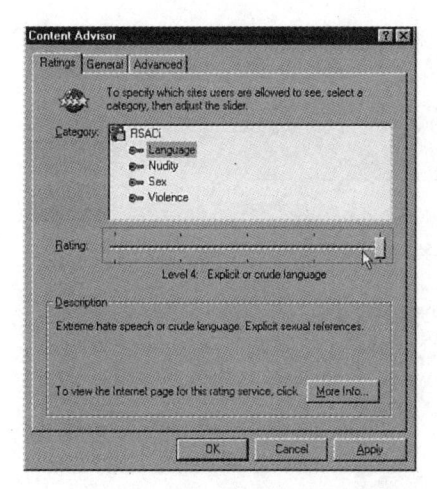

Figure 12.47 Modifying the Language category settings.

90. After you make all your selections, you cant click the More Info... button to both test your settings and gather more data on this topic from the Recreational Software Advisory Council for the Internet (RSACi). Remember that you should have already made your connection to the Internet prior to clicking this button.

91. Almost immediately, the Content Advisor message box shown in Figure 12.48 appears.

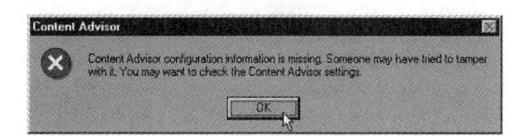

Figure 12.48 A Content Advisor error message.

92. This error message occurs because although you have made a series of settings, you have not yet officially saved them into the Internet Explorer browser. Click OK to return to the previous Content Advisor screen for the Ratings configuration tab. Click either the Apply button or OK to make your changes take effect, which then displays the screen shown in Figure 12.49.

93. When this message appears, click OK to continue. You may now click the More Info... button to test your settings and to gather more data on the RSACi. After doing so, the next Content Advisor message window appears, as shown in Figure 12.50.

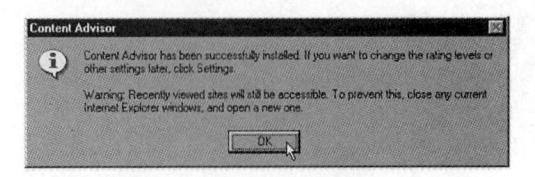

Figure 12.49 The Content Advisor successful configuration message box.

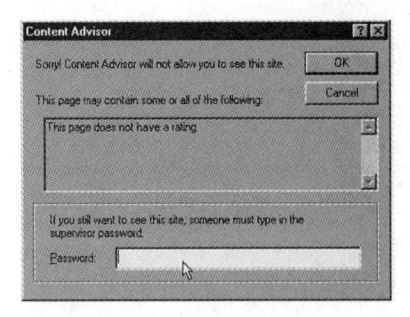

Figure 12.50 A Content Advisor blocking message box.

94. This message box appears because the Web site page that you are attempting to access does not have a rating. This is the case in countless numbers of Web sites, which is the primary pitfall to using rating systems software such as the Content Advisor that is built into the Internet Explorer browser software—many porn sites are learning not to rate their Web site pages. Anyway, click OK after you enter the Supervisor's password, which reveals the Web site screen shown in Figure 12.51.

95. If you do not know the password, you will be blocked from accessing this Web site unless you have disabled this feature in the General tab. Otherwise, you are presented with the Internet Explorer browser pointed at the RSACi Web site.

96. When you have finished reviewing and playing with the RSACi Web site, close the Internet Explorer browser window and disconnect from the Internet (if it was a Dial-Up Networking session). If you had exited the Content Advisor configuration area, return to it now as well.

97. Click the General tab to move to that section of the Content Advisor settings, as shown in Figure 12.52.

12.2
CONFIGURE MICROSOFT INTERNET EXPLORER

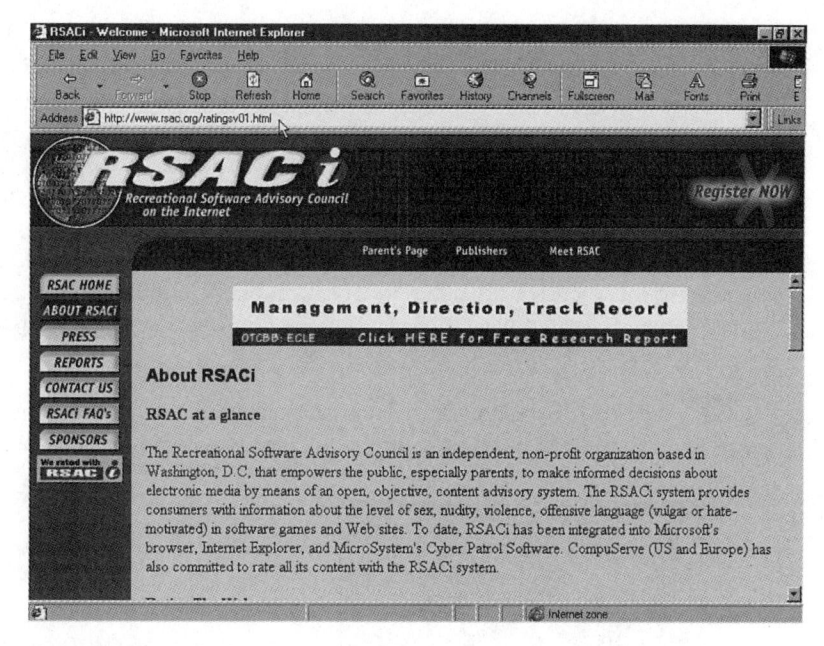

Figure 12.51 The home page of the RSACi Internet Web site.

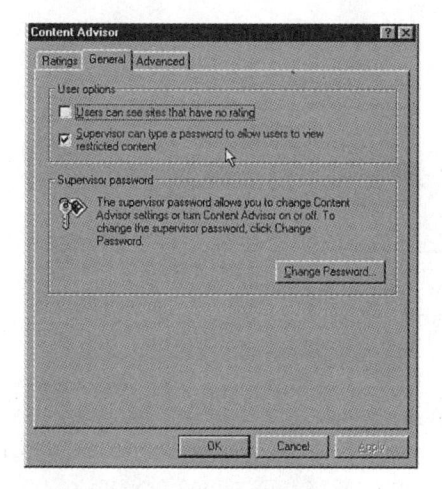

Figure 12.52 Reviewing the options on the General tab of the Content Advisor screen.

98. This screen permits you to change the supervisor password, and allow users to see Web sites that have no rating. While this is a good idea most of the time, there are several pornography and violence-oriented sites that cater to children that do not have ratings. Keep this in mind if you are planning to use the Content Advisor as a means of protecting your children from the Internet. If you are a network administrator scheming to keep your corporate users from accessing these same types of site...well, you need to be performing your real job duties instead of goofing off trying to censor others in the organization. Also found on this screen is a check box that permits you to type in the supervisor password and thus see an otherwise restricted Web site.

99. When you have finished making your alterations on this screen, click the Advanced tab to progress to that screen, as shown in Figure 12.53.

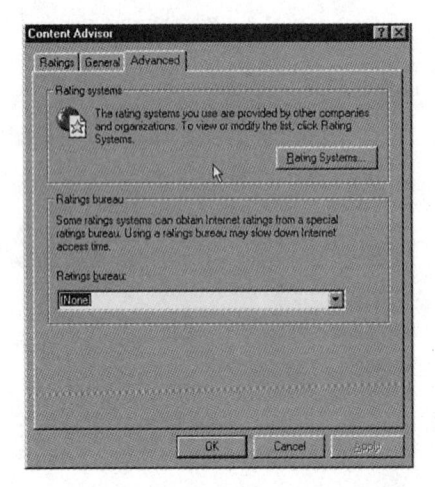

Figure 12.53 Reviewing the options on the Advanced tab of the Content Advisor screen.

100. This screen deals strictly with rating systems and bureaus that you might use with the Internet Explorer Web browser to restrict content access on a Web site. To view or modify the existing Rating Systems list, click the Rating Systems...button to access that screen, as shown in Figure 12.54.

101. To add a new ratings system, click the Add... button and follow the Windows Explorer-type screen to the location (such as the A:\ drive; your floppy disk drive) that contains your ratings files. Likewise, if there is a ratings system in use that you want to get rid of, click it to highlight it, and then click the Remove button.

12.2 CONFIGURE MICROSOFT INTERNET EXPLORER

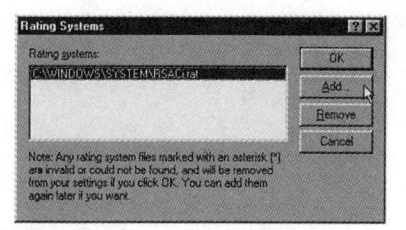

Figure 12.54 Reviewing the Content Advisor Ratings Systems in use.

102. After you make your changes, click OK to return to the Advanced tab.

103. The ratings bureau in use for your Internet Explorer browser is found inside the drop-down list box near the bottom of the screen. Click this drop-down list box to change the selection if you want. When you have finished making your alterations on this screen, click OK to return to the Internet Properties screen, as shown in Figure 12.55.

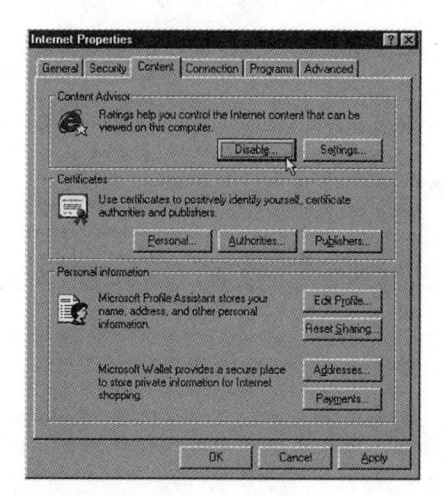

Figure 12.55 Reviewing the Internet Properties screen.

104. If, after all that configuring, you have decided not to use the Content Advisor, you can turn it off by clicking the Disable... button, which takes you to the screen shown in Figure 12.56.

105. Click OK to accept the disablement of the Content Advisor, and you are returned to the Internet Properties screen.

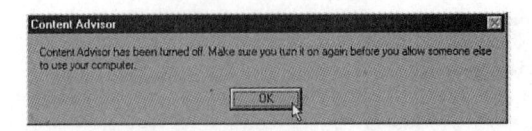

Figure 12.56 Reviewing the Content Advisor message box.

> **NOTE**
>
> If you choose not to use the built-in Content Advisor software that comes with the Microsoft Internet Explorer Web browser, you might still want to pursue other options for content monitoring. To this end, you might want to check out various third-party software providers such as CyberPatrol or GuardiaNet. In any event, there are much stronger methods of protecting (or censuring) your users from the various content types that you might openly view on today's Internet.

106. Next up is the Certificates section of the Internet Properties screen. There are three primary uses of a digital certificate: to identify yourself to others, to identify certificate authorities (to ensure that their content is real), and to identify publishers of content. To add or modify the list of digital certificates that are valid for your computer, click the Personal... button to reveal the Client Authentication screen shown in Figure 12.57.

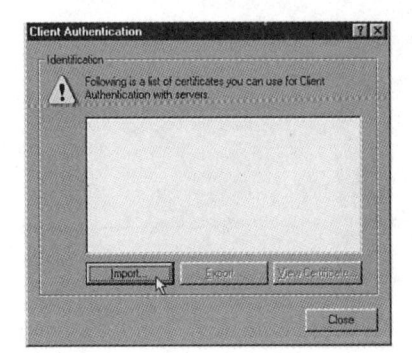

Figure 12.57 Reviewing the Client Authentication screen.

107. More than likely this screen is blank on your computer. Very few people have gone to groups such as VeriSign and obtained a personal certificate. I know I have not, because a few hundred bucks for others to know who I am digitally is not worth it yet. However, if I were a business, I am sure my attitude toward digital signing would quickly change.

12.2
CONFIGURE MICROSOFT INTERNET EXPLORER

108. Assuming you have already acquired a certificate, you might import it into this screen by using the Import... button. There is nothing special to do here, other than finding the certificate using a Windows Explorer-type screen to discover the location, such as the A:\ drive; your floppy disk drive, which contains the certificate file(s).

109. After you have finished making your alterations on this screen, click OK to return to the Internet Properties screen.

110. To modify the list of digital credentials that your computer should trust as being valid for your computer, click the Authorities... button, which reveals the screen shown in Figure 12.58.

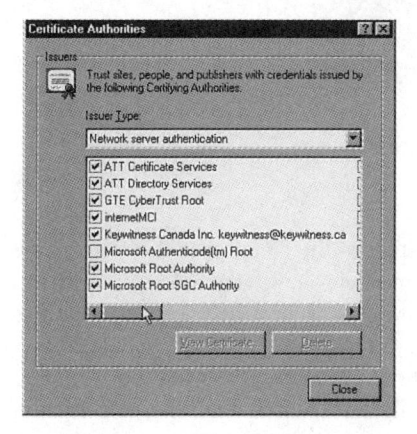

Figure 12.58 Reviewing the Certificate Authorities screen.

111. This screen contains a listing of the credentials that various sites, people, and publishers have presented electronically to you in the past. Those certificates that have a check mark in the box next to them are considered to be valid, and thus can be used on your PC.

112. To remove any certificate from this listing, click it to highlight it, and then click the Delete button to remove it.

113. To view the details of any certificate, click on that certificate to highlight it, and then click the View Certificate... button to review its details.

114. When you have finished making your alterations on this screen, click the Close button to return to the Internet Properties screen.

115. The final type of certificate that you might want to review is that of the Publishers certificate. To review the list of software developers and publishers as well as credential agencies that your computer should trust as being valid for your computer, click the Publishers... button in order to reveal the screen shown in Figure 12.59.

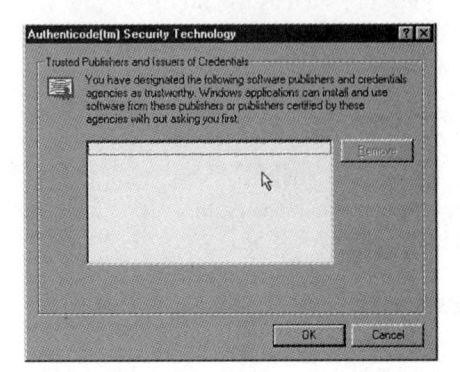

Figure 12.59 Reviewing the Authenticode™ Security Technology screen.

116. This screen contains a listing of the credentials that various software publishers or credentials agencies have given electronically to you in the past, which you have marked as trustworthy. Those certificates that appear in this list are considered to be valid, and thus can be used on your PC at any time without your consent at the time of execution. To remove any of these certificates, click that certificate to first highlight it, and then click the Remove button to delete that certificate from your computer system.

117. When you have finished making your alterations on this screen, click OK to return to the Internet Properties screen.

118. Because you have finished making your changes to this section, click the Connection tab to move to that screen as shown in Figure 12.60.

119. The purpose of this tab is to provide a means to configure the manners in which your Internet Explorer Web browser may be connected to the Internet, as well as your organization's intranet sites (if you have any).

The top section of this tab is where you can access the Internet Connection Wizard that makes it virtually impossible for someone not to be able to access the Internet (assuming, of course, that you do have a connection of some sorts as well as the correct equipment). To access this wizard click the Connect... button, which tosses up the splash screen shown in Figure 12.61.

12.2
CONFIGURE MICROSOFT INTERNET EXPLORER

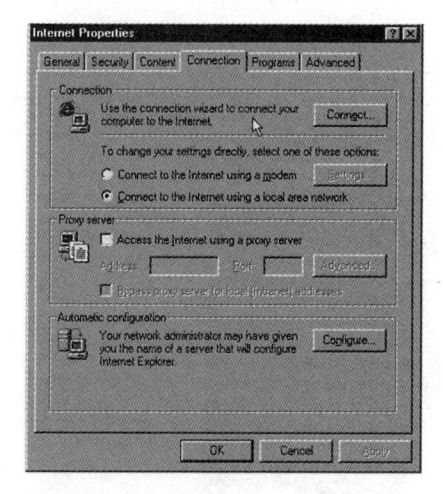

Figure 12.60 Reviewing the Connection screen.

Figure 12.61 Viewing the Internet Connection Wizard's splash screen.

120. This screen stays on your screen for only a few seconds before automatically proceeding to the screen shown in Figure 12.62.

121. There are three options presented as part of the Internet Connection Wizard: to sign up and configure your PC as part of a Dial-Up Networking session, which requires a telephone line and a modem; to gain admittance to an existing Internet account using a LAN or network-based Internet connection access point; or to do nothing, meaning that you already have configured your PC and do not want to do so again. As the content of these wizard screens is very basic, and not really intended for this book, I will skip the review of this wizard. Either complete this wizard or click Cancel to return to the Internet Properties screen.

122. The next section of the Connection tab allows you to change your Internet connection settings directly. The top radio button allows you to

change your connection method to use a modem, and the bottom radio
button alters your connection method to a LAN- based link. If you select
a modem-based connection method, you are able to change the default
settings as shown in Figure 12.63

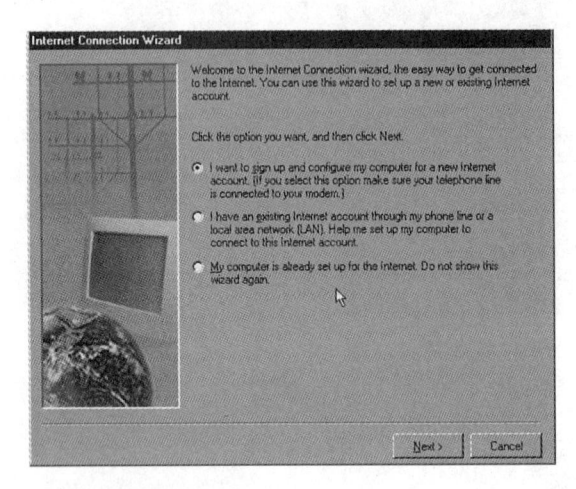

Figure 12.62 Reviewing the Internet Connection Wizard.

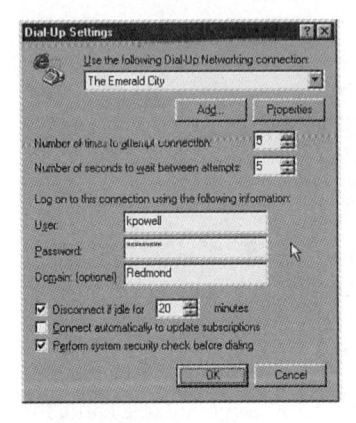

Figure 12.63 Altering the Dial-Up Settings for a modem-based connection.

123. The Dial-Up Settings screen contains the base information you might encounter using the more formal Windows 98 Dial-Up Networking configuration screens. From this single screen you are able to determine which Windows 98 Dial-Up Networking client you want to use, and set the number of connection attempts and the default user ID and password (along with a Windows domain, if required).

12.2
CONFIGURE MICROSOFT INTERNET EXPLORER

124. The other options on this screen are self-explanatory with the possible exception of the Perform System Security Check Before Dialing check box. What this means is that Internet Explorer checks to see if you have File and Printer Sharing enabled on your computer. And if so, it prompts you to disable this feature and restart your system so that the disablement takes effect, before you actually connect to the Internet via a Dial-Up Networking connection. The reason for this, is that if you have a drive or folder shared with no password, just about anyone on the Internet will be able to access your computer because the Internet is nothing more than a giant LAN/WAN combination of networks that you are now a part.

125. After you make your selections or changes, click OK to confirm your choices and return to the Internet Properties screen.

126. The Proxy Server section allows your organization to use a technology known as a *proxy* to dole out access to the Internet in a shielded manner. To put it another way, a proxy server can be used in conjunction with a firewall to form a security barrier between your organization's users and non-company networks such as the Internet. You might also use the proxy server to cache URLs that are used a lot, which makes end-user performance that much faster. To configure a proxy server for use with your Internet Explorer browser, click once the Access the Internet Using a Proxy Server check box to select it.

127. Doing this un-grays the remainder of the proxy area, where you need to enter the Address (name or number) and the Port number for your proxy sever into the appropriate box. The Address can be either a server's name such as *ITGproxy*, or it can be an IP address such as *10.10.1.54*. In most organizations a name is used, usually because it is easy to remember and there will be fewer mistakes when entering a short name as opposed to a TCP/IP address.

128. If your organization has an intranet, which does not require the use of a proxy server, you should click the Bypass Proxy Server for Local (intranet) Addresses check box to select it.

129. If your organization uses multiple proxy servers or just different ports on the same proxy server for the various Internet tools, such as FTP, Telnet, Web, and so on, you will need to perform a few advanced steps. To do this, click the Advanced... button, which reveals the screen shown in Figure 12.64.

130. If you had entered an Address name and number and a Port number on the previous screen, you will see that combination of Address and Port replicated into every area on this screen. If you did nothing on the previous screen, all these address and port boxes would be blank. The top portion of this screen is very self-explanatory, because you need to enter the Address name and number into that field and a Port number into the port box. In the Exceptions area, things can get a bit tricky.

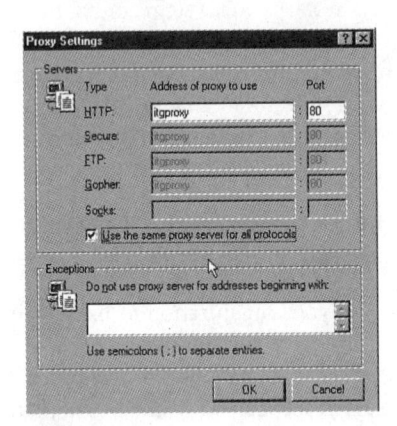

Figure 12.64 Configuring Advanced Proxy Server settings.

131. The purpose of the Exceptions box is to avoid using the proxy server for the partial URLs or IP numbers that exist here. You need to place a semicolon (;) between each entry, so that Internet Explorer can see where one exception ends and the next one begins.

For example, assume you work for an accounting firm that wants to keep its own internal sites from using the proxy server. To do this, you would enter the string *.kpmg.com* into the Exceptions box followed by a semicolon. Keep in mind that you probably have a few people who might actually know the IP address scheme to enter, so you will want to input the IP address as well to keep those users from using the proxy server to access the same site (such as *130.130*.**).

132. When you have made all your selections, click the OK to return to the Connection screen.

133. The final section of the Connection screen is the Automatic Configuration area. This section permits your users to configure their versions of Internet Explorer by clicking a single button and typing in an URL, which in turn accesses an INS file that was created with the IEAK Profile Manager. To access this area, click the Configure... button to reveal the screen shown in Figure 12.65.

12.2
CONFIGURE MICROSOFT INTERNET EXPLORER

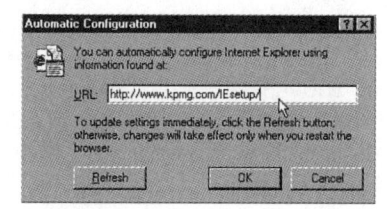

Figure 12.65 Accessing an Automatic Internet Explorer configuration.

134. You, as the network IEAK administrator, can set the URL to be any address you want, including just an IP address if you want. It is suggested that you use an alias name such as IEconfig or something like that to help your users perform this task; because many of them will get it wrong anyway, this might help to lessen the numbers of support calls made to your organization's help desk.

135. When you make your entry, click OK to return to the Configuration screen.

136. As that was the last entry for that screen, you need to advance to the next tab. To do this, click the Programs tab to access the screen shown in Figure 12.66.

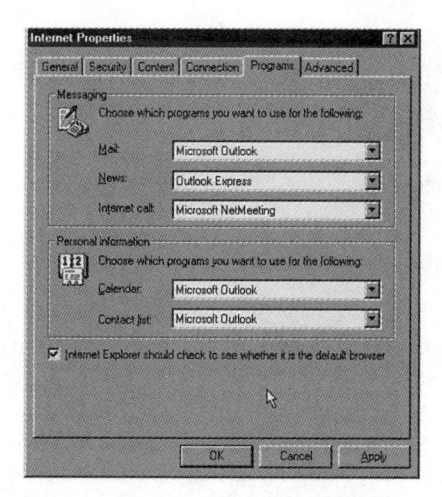

Figure 12.66 Reviewing the Internet Explorer Programs configuration tab.

137. The purpose of this screen is to allow you the ability to make sure that the email, calendar, (or whichever) application that you want to use, is set as the default program for each specific area. Although this screen is split by the Messaging and Personal Information areas, it all works the same. Click the drop-down list boxes in each area to make your choices. When you make all your selections, click the Apply button to make those choices take effect.

138. If you want Internet Explorer to check to see whether it is the default browser on your computer system each time it starts, click once on the check box at the bottom of this screen to activate this feature.

139. Because this is the last entry for the Programs screen, click the Advanced tab to access that screen, as shown in Figure 12.67.

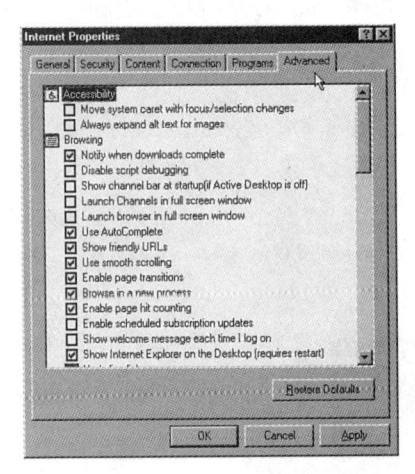

Figure 12.67 Reviewing the Internet Explorer Advanced configuration tab.

140. Within the Internet Properties screen, this is probably the area that you will visit most often. It contains the tweaks and nuances that make Internet Explorer a great browser, and gives you much more precise control over your browser than you might have previously known possible. This screen is split into several areas: Accessibility, Browsing, Multimedia, Security, Java VM (the Java virtual machine), Printing, Searching, the toolbar, and HTTP 1.1 Settings (the Hypertext Transfer Protocol, version 1.1 configuration area).

141. To select any option, click the check box next it. To unselect any option, click again on the check box to remove the check mark from the box. As

12.2
CONFIGURE MICROSOFT INTERNET EXPLORER

you review the options shown in Figure 12.67, you realize that most of these options are self-explanatory. However, there are a few that you should pay a little more attention to:

- *Disable Script Debugging*—This means that if you encounter a Visual Basic script, a Java script, or a Visual InterDev script file, you will not be able to debug that script file on-the-fly. This is probably a very good idea for the vast majority of your user community, but some of your software developers will definitely not like you for doing this. This is because Internet Explorer provides the capability for a script to be debugged on an as needed basis. It will automatically start your Visual Studio or Visual C++ debugging tool and load the script into for your examination, thus saving quite a few steps for a developer-type to review a script gone bad.

- *Use AutoComplete*—This permits your Internet Explorer users to start typing in an URL, and then have Internet Explorer automatically complete the Web site address for those sites, which your users have already visited at least once. I strongly recommend the use of this Internet Explorer feature because it makes for a more enjoyable surfing experience and makes the browsing process simpler for non-typing experts.

- *Browse in a New Process*—This is great for users of Internet Explorer that want to start a new browser window for each URL or HTML document that they access. This is also beneficial to software developers who might have a particularly unstable file open in one browser window and who want to check out a different HTML document in another window.

142. Scroll down the window to the next screen-full of advanced topics, as shown in Figure 12.68.

143. Continuing the review process, you will notice that most of these options are self-explanatory. However, there ones that you might need a little help with, including the following from the Security section:

- *PCT 1.0*—This is the first version of the Personal Communications Technology software, which was created as part of a consortium effort including the likes of Visa, MasterCard, Microsoft and others. Use of this software feature will ensure that your Internet Explorer transactions across your organization's intranet or the Internet will remain private. It is strongly recommended that you use activate this option.

- *SSL 2.0*—This is version 2 of the Secure Socket Layer (SSL), which provides secure communications between the Internet Explorer Web browser and a Web site that has been configured to use SSL. Like PCT, SSL provides for secure, encrypted transactions across the Internet, which might include electronic commerce, banking, and even e-cash transactions. It is strongly recommended that you use activate this option.

- *SSL 3.0*—This is version 3, the latest and greatest version, of the SSL privacy protection protocol, which provides secure communications between the Internet Explorer Web browser and a Web site that has been configured to use SSL. Like PCT, SSL provides for secure, encrypted transactions across the Internet, which might include electronic commerce, banking, and even e-cash transactions. You should try to use SSL 3.0 whenever possible, as it has a few more bug fixes and patches applied to it than version 2.0 had incorporated. It is strongly recommended that you use activate this option.

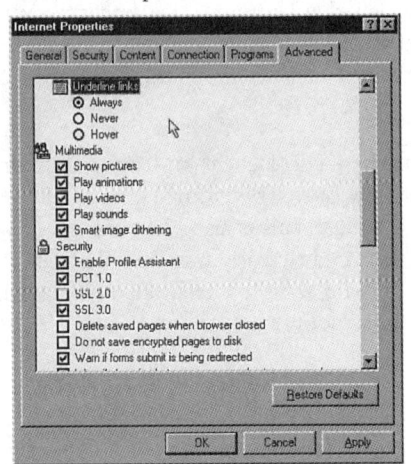

Figure 12.68 Reviewing Internet Explorer Advanced options.

144. Using the scrollbar, slide the window down to the next screen-full of advanced topics as shown in Figure 12.69.

145. Continuing the review process, you will notice that the majority of these options are self-explanatory. Within each of these sections, however, a few topics do need more of an explanation:

12.2
CONFIGURE MICROSOFT INTERNET EXPLORER

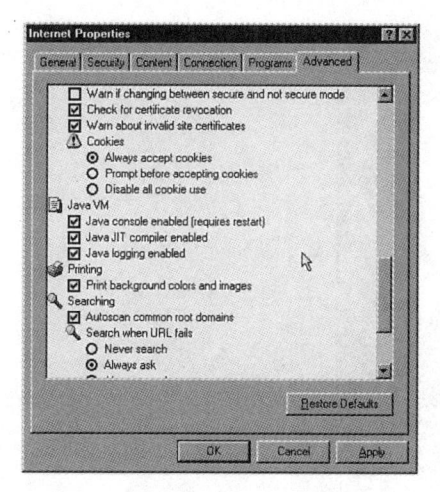

Figure 12.69 Reviewing more Internet Explorer Advanced options.

- *Cookies*—A cookie is a piece of software that stores information about a particular Web site connection, such as an Internet shopping cart order or the personalization features of a Microsoft Web site connection. While it might seem that configuring your system to not use cookies would be a good thing, it in fact limits your Web site productivity as many sites will refuse to do business with you. In addition, the option to receive a prompt before accepting a cookie might initially look like a good choice, there is no real way of telling a good cookie from a bad one. Therefore, you might as well set this option to Always Accept Cookies, by clicking that radio button.

- *Java Console Enabled (requires restart)*—Enabling this option allows you to run the Java console that is built into Internet Explorer. It is recommended that you enable this feature only if you are a software developer or other professional that understands how to use Java. Otherwise, this feature will waste your Windows 98 and Internet Explorer system resources.

- *Java JIT Compiler Enabled*—This permits Java applets to download and be processed for execution on your Internet Explorer browser's Java VM on an as needed basis. This means that Java byte code is compiled on-the-fly so that applets run faster on your machine.

146. When you make your changes or selections, use the scrollbar to slide the window down to the remaining advanced topics, as shown in Figure 12.70.

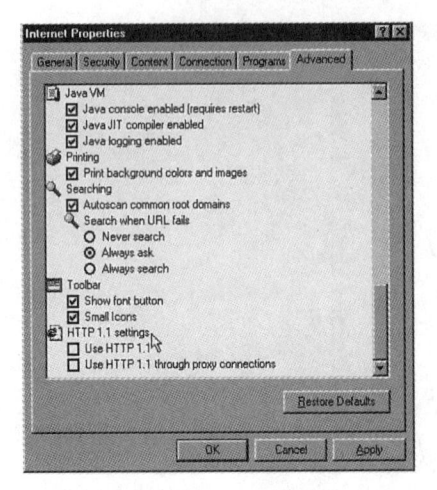

Figure 12.70 Reviewing the last of the Internet Explorer Advanced options.

147. The final selections on this screen concern the Internet Explorer toolbar and the HTTP 1.1 Settings. You should check for the use of the HTTP 1.1 settings options prior to actually using them with your Internet Explorer browser, because not many sites these days require the use of this older HTTP standard. In fact, many sites, such as the Microsoft Certified Professional Web site, prohibit the activation of the version 1.1 settings of HTTP (you are unable to properly use this entire site with either of these check boxes marked).

148. After you make all your changes or selections, click OK to confirm your choices and exit the Internet Properties screen.

149. There are a few more items that you might want to examine on your Internet Explorer Web browser. Open your Internet Explorer browser without first accessing a connection to the Internet, so that you will reveal a screen similar to the one shown in Figure 12.71.

150. This error message box appears whenever Internet Explorer cannot find a particular Web site. In most cases, this message box shows up because your connection to the Internet was never established (or was inadvertently dropped). To clear this message box, click OK and proceed into the Internet Explorer browser, as shown in Figure 12.72.

151. Because the default home page is not locatable, the Internet Explorer browser displays a Navigation Canceled message. As you remember from earlier in this section, it is also possible to set your default home page to this about:NavigationCanceled Web site address too.

12.2
CONFIGURE MICROSOFT INTERNET EXPLORER

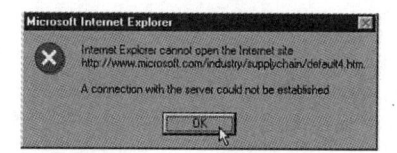

Figure 12.71 An Internet Explorer error message box.

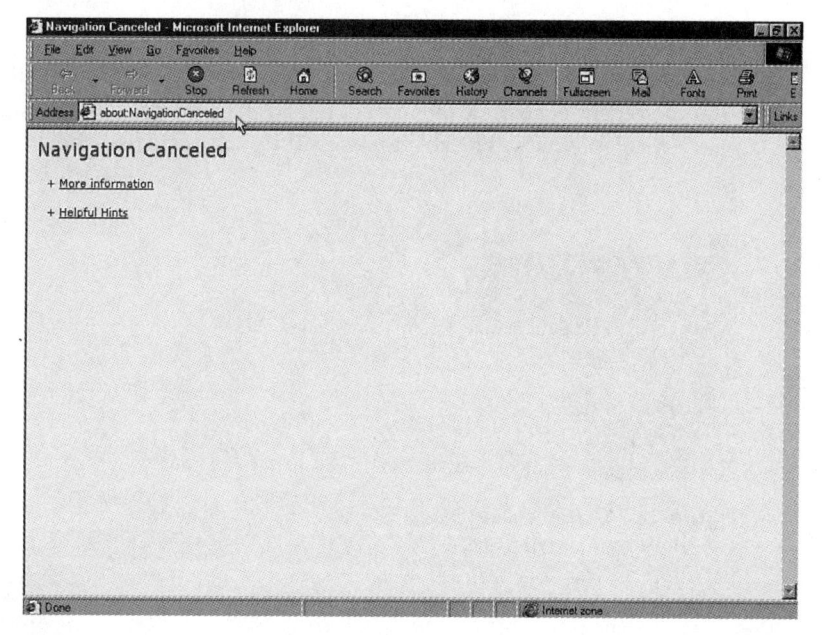

Figure 12.72 The main screen of the Internet Explorer Web browser.

152. Along the top row of the Internet Explorer window is a series of drop-down menus: File, Edit, View, Go, Favorites, and Help. If you click File, you reveal the menu structure, as shown in Figure 12.73.

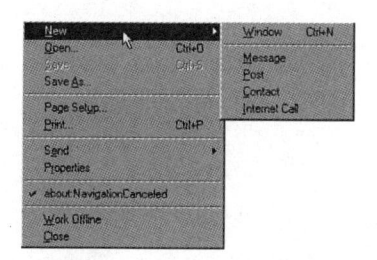

Figure 12.73 Reviewing the Internet Explorer File menu structure.

153. Although all these menu options are self-explanatory, you might want to pay particular attention to the New menu selection. This reveals a submenu with the Window option on the top and the Message, Post, Contact, and Internet Call options on the bottom.

154. The Window option allows you to open multiple copies of the Internet Explorer browser simultaneously. This is a powerful option, especially in the hands of an Internet software developer. All the options on the bottom-half of the menu are Internet messaging related and self-explanatory.

155. If you click the View menu option, and then click the Toolbars menu selection, you will be able to access the menu structure shown in Figure 12.74.

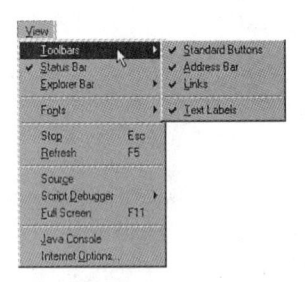

Figure 12.74 Reviewing the View menu structure, focusing on the Toolbars menu selection.

156. Use the Toolbars menu selection to add or change the format of the toolbars that you see within Internet Explorer. Text labels can be added or removed using this menu topic, as well.

157. If you click the Explorer Bar menu selection, you will see the submenu shown in Figure 12.75.

158. The Explorer Bar menu selections includes access to the Internet Explorer Search, Favorites, History, and Channels areas. Of course, you might click None to avoid seeing any of these four menus selections from appearing along the left side of the Internet Explorer screen.

159. If you click the Script Debugger menu selection, you will see the submenu shown in Figure 12.76.

12.2 CONFIGURE MICROSOFT INTERNET EXPLORER

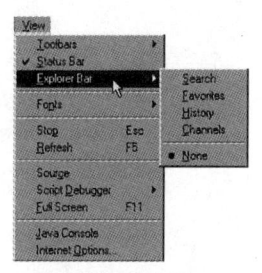

Figure 12.75 Reviewing the View menu structure, focusing on the Explorer Bar menu selection.

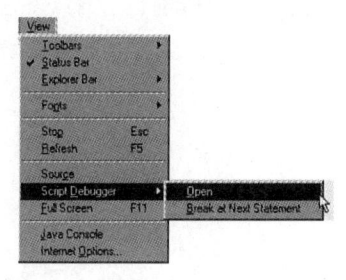

Figure 12.76 Reviewing the View menu structure, focusing on the Script Debugger menu selection.

160. The Script Debugger menu selection includes the capability to Open your Script Debugging tool or the option to halt the execution of the script, which requires debugging, at its next statement. For most people, this is not an option they would use. Rather, this feature appears to be aimed at the software developers who utilize the Microsoft Internet Explorer browser in their development process.

161. Moving over to the Go menu option, as shown in Figure 12.77, you are able to quickly jump to one of the many other features found within the Internet Explorer browser.

162. Just as it does in many of its other software applications, Microsoft has provided a menu-driven way to quickly access most of the items that are available as buttons on the main window of the Internet Explorer browser. The ones that you will not find specific button icons for are the My Computer, Address Book, Calendar, and Internet Call features. However, if you type any local address (such as \) you will quickly go to that folder address on your computer. A single backslash (\) takes you to the root directory of your system's home drive (usually c:\).

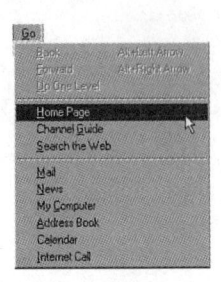

Figure 12.77 Reviewing the Go menu structure.

163. On the Favorites menu option, as shown in Figure 12.78, you are able to quickly go to one of your saved URLs, any folder on your computer, or another HTML document file.

Figure 12.78 Reviewing the Favorites menu structure.

164. This Favorites menu structure is identical to the one found off the Windows 98 Start menu button (because it is accessing the same area on your hard drive). You can add to this listing at any time or modify it by using the Organize Favorites menu selection.

165. On the Help menu option, shown in Figure 12.79, you are able to quickly go to one of the many other features found inside the Internet Explorer browser as well as to the Internet.

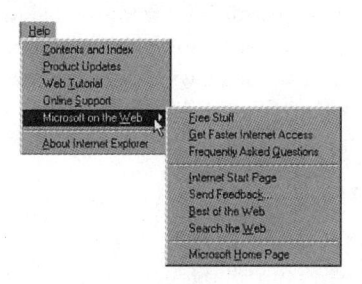

Figure 12.79 Reviewing the Help menu structure.

166. Use this menu selection if you require assistance with your computer, the Internet Explorer Web browser itself, or just about any other topic. The Product Updates option takes you to the Internet Explorer product updates area and not the Windows 98 Windows Update file area—keep this in mind. Additional features include promotional content for freebies, modems (the Get Faster Internet Access menu selection), and a frequently asked questions (FAQs) area. To check to see exactly what version of Internet Explorer you are running, click the About Internet Explorer menu selection found at the bottom of the main Help menu option.

COMPLEXITY
ADVANCED

12.3 How do I...
Obtain the Microsoft Internet Explorer Administration Kit and why would I want to use it?

Problem

I have heard that I need to use the Microsoft Internet Explorer Administration Kit to ensure that all the Internet Explorer users in my organization have a standard way to access the Internet. If this is true, how do I obtain, install, and use this kit?

Technique

The tool that you actually need to use is the Internet Explorer Profile Manager. There is a standalone version of this tool that comes with the Internet Explorer Administration Kit (IEAK), which can be downloaded from the Microsoft Web site at no cost (after you register its use with Microsoft). You might also obtain the Profile Manager from the CD-ROM that comes with the Windows 98 Resource Kit (review Chapter 1, "Installation Tips," for more details). You will need this Profile Manager application to customize Internet Explorer configurations, which are then saved to a specialized file that has an .INS file extension.

These specialized files are then used when you need to install and configure Internet Explorer on more than one PC at a time. This .INS file lets you force your organization's configurations down onto all the users in your organization in a uniform manner, meaning that everyone has the same installation version. The primary benefit then becomes your ability to centrally manage the dozens, hundreds, or even thousands of Internet Explorer users that might exist in your organization. There are three types of .INS files:

- *Per-user profiles*—Used for individual users with a file naming format of the *UserName*.INS format.

- *Group profiles*—Used for groups of users with a file naming format of the *GroupName*.INS format.

- *Default profiles*—This profile should contain the profile scheme that is used for any users that are not covered by either a per-user or group profile.

After you have created these files, you are able to use them for distribution to your organization's Internet Explorer user community. To learn how to obtain and install the Profile Manager, as well as basic usage of this tool, follow these steps.

Steps

1. Obtain a copy of either the Internet Explorer Administration Kit from the Microsoft Internet Explorer add-on utilities Web site pages, which can be found at the following URL: `http://www.microsoft.com/ie/corp`, or you will need to copy the Internet Explorer Profile Manager off of the Windows 98 Resource Kit CD-ROM. Because this can be a rather slow download (the full kit is about 187MB whereas the Profile Manager is 1.6MB), I will focus on using the Windows 98 Resource Kit CD-ROM as

12.3
OBTAIN THE MICROSOFT INTERNET EXPLORER ADMINISTRATION KIT

my source instead of the Microsoft Web sites.

2. Open the Windows Explorer and navigate your way to the Windows 98 Resource Kit CD-ROM, and go into the folder structure so that you are

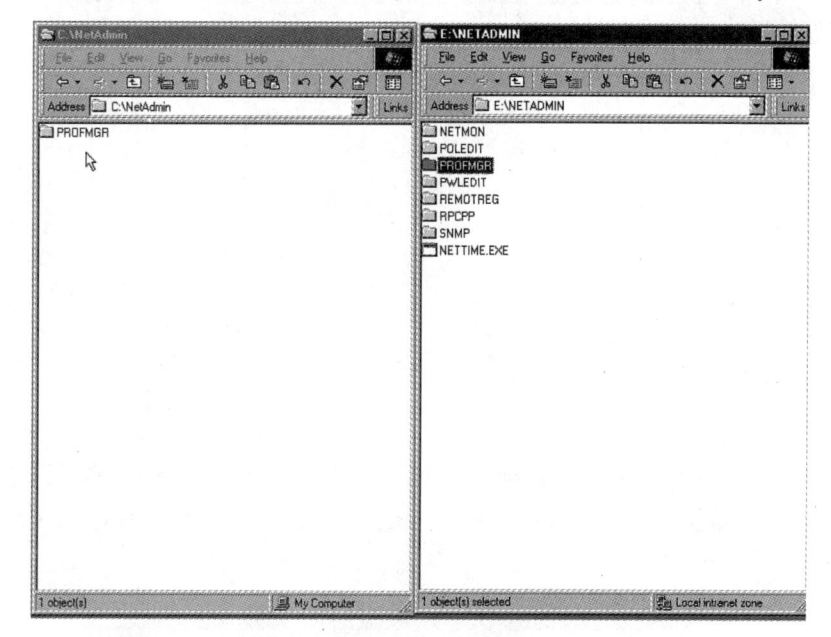

Figure 12.80 Finding the Internet Explorer Profile Manager.

inside the NETADMIN folder, as shown in Figure 12.80.

3. Drag and drop the entire set of contents within the \PROFMGR folder that you see inside the NETADMIN folder on the CD-ROM. After you copy it over to your hard drive (try to maintain the same folder structure, placing it inside a folder named NETADMIN on your root drive), you should have a structure that resembles the screen shown in Figure 12.81.

4. The Internet Explorer Profile Manager is now installed on your computer (ugly install process, isn't it?).

5. To start the Profile Manager application, double-click the PROFMGR.EXE file found inside the \NETADMIN\PROFMGR folder (this is where you put the rest of the Profile Manager application files) to reveal the screen shown in Figure 12.82.

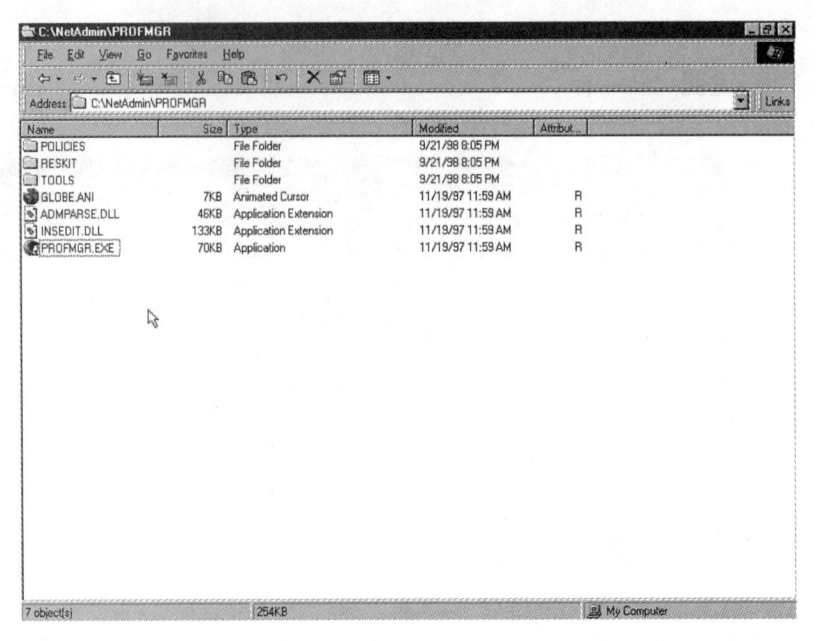

Figure 12.81 Reviewing the Internet Explorer Profile Manager folder structure.

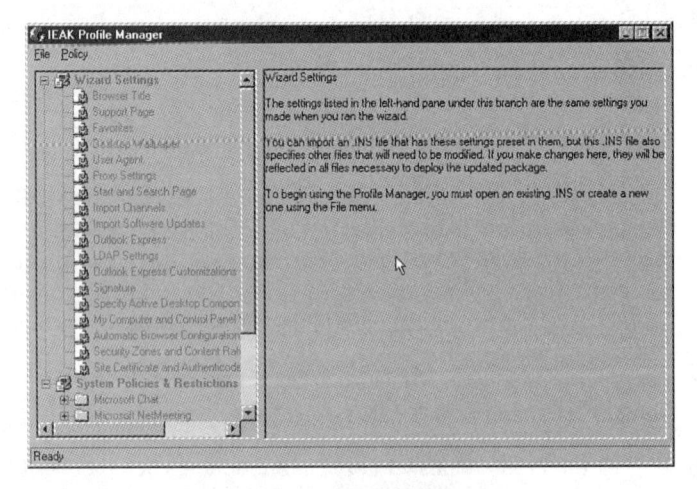

Figure 12.82 Using the IEAK Profile Manager application.

6. When the main screen of the IEAK Profile Manager appears most of the information will be grayed-out, which means that you are unable to access those areas. The best way to use this utility, is to create a new profile for your Internet Explorer browser that you want to customize. To

12.3
OBTAIN THE MICROSOFT INTERNET EXPLORER ADMINISTRATION KIT
549

start, click the File menu option, and then click again on the New menu selection, which starts you on your way to customizing the Internet Explorer browser for your users, as shown in Figure 12.83.

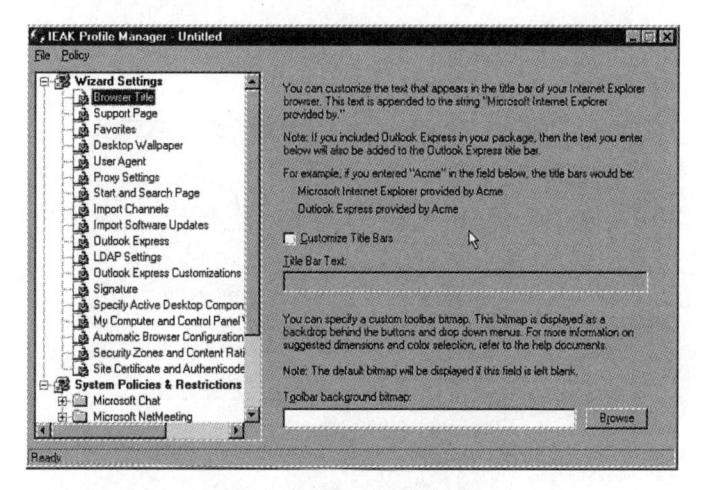

Figure 12.83 Creating a new IEAK profile.

7. There are two parts of the Profile Manager that you need to familiarize yourself with: the Wizard Settings and the System Policies and Restrictions section. If you click once on each of the options under the Wizard Settings section, you will be able to configure that option using the right side of the Profile Manager screen. Refer to Figure 12.83 and you will see a lot of text that describes the Browser Title option and the options to configure that aspect of the Wizard Settings section.

8. If you click on each of the remaining options under the Wizard Settings section, you will see various configurable options appear to the right of the scrollbar. Most of these you have seen before, but there are a few you might want to focus on more carefully. Click the Outlook Express option, as shown in Figure 12.84.

9. As you well know, Outlook Express is an email/Newsgroup/directory service utility that is built into the Internet Explorer browser software. In most organizations, the incoming and outgoing mail servers, as well as the Internet news server are all the same for everyone, so it makes sense to configure them within the IEAK Profile Manager.

Also, the default settings for this section is to *not* make Outlook Express either the default mail or news client, but you might want to change this setting by clicking each check box next to each of these items. Whether you use the Secure Password Authentication (SPA) process during the authentication process of your users, is entirely up to you. The SPA is used to encrypt your passwords so that they do not cross the wires (your LANs, WANs, the Internet, and so on) in an open or clear-text format. Because there are many other ways to accomplish this same thing, you might not want to check this box.

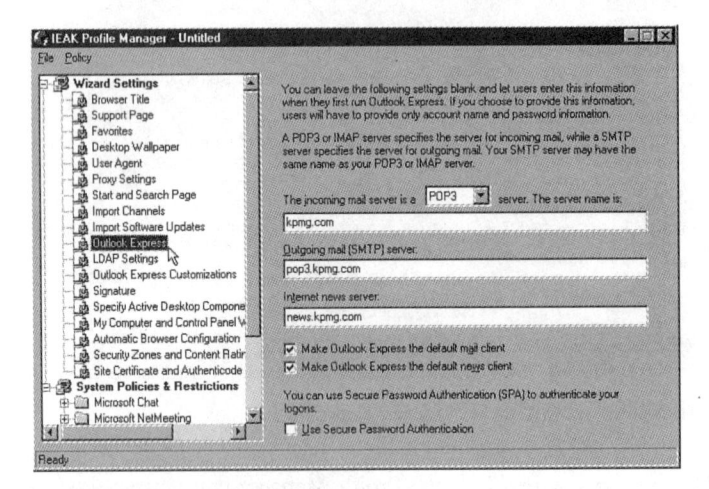

Figure 12.84 Modifying the Outlook Express Wizard setting option.

10. The last topic within the Wizard Settings section that you might want to review is that of the Site Certificate and Authenticode Settings area, as shown in Figure 12.85.

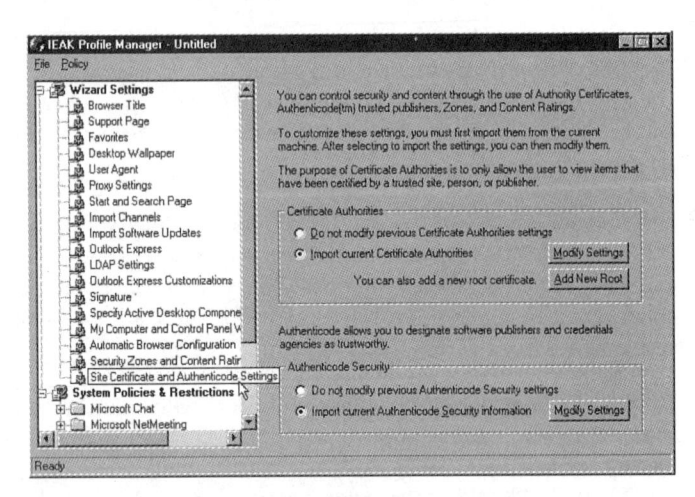

Figure 12.85 Modifying the Site Certificate and Authenticode Settings option.

12.3
OBTAIN THE MICROSOFT INTERNET EXPLORER ADMINISTRATION KIT

11. This option permits you to import your Certificate Authorities and Authenticode Security information, both of which are necessary for maintaining a strictly confidential business environment. Keep in mind that if you have mobile users, you might want to be careful how you implement both Certificate Authorities and your Authenticode Security information because this technology can pick up and leave the building at any time.

12. The next segment that you need to review and change is the System Policies and Restrictions section. To get there, click the System Policies and Restrictions icon, as shown in Figure 12.86.

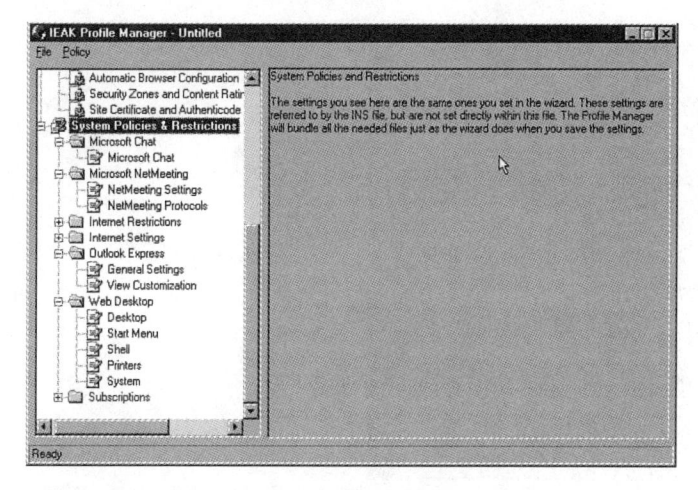

Figure 12.86 Reviewing the System Policies and Restrictions section.

13. If you click the folder for any of the topics within this section, you will see a few paragraphs that explain that topic a bit further. To actually modify the sub-sections within an area, click the plus symbol (+) that is located to the left of each folder, such as on the Microsoft NetMeeting folder.

14. There are literally hundreds of possible combinations for restricting a user's Internet Explorer browser, as well as hundreds more when you toss in the various add-on components that are available for Internet Explorer, so be very careful when you process your selections.

NOTE
Keep in mind that if you have mobile users you might want to be careful how you implement system policies and restrictions, because

continued on next page

continued from previous page

these technology users might pick-up and leave the building at any time. If you are configuring the Internet Explorer browser and its add-on components for users who must travel to outside client sites, your restrictive policies that work fine inside your organization can spell disaster for those who work outside the boundaries of your perfect little glass house.

15. When you have set all the configurations that you want to use, click the File menu option, and then the Save menu selection, which reveals the screen shown in Figure 12.87.

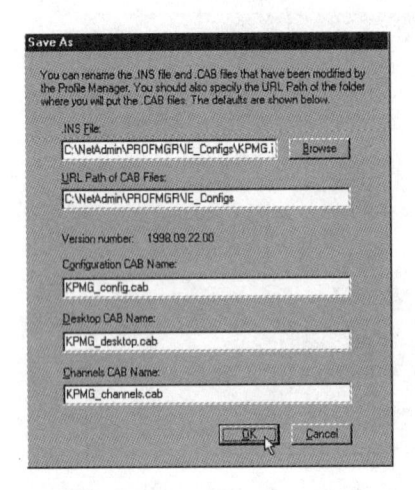

Figure 12.87 Saving your IEAK .INS and .CAB files.

16. After the Save As screen appears, you should search for a path to place these newly created .INS and .CAB files. It is strongly recommended that you create a new folder somewhere on your computer to store these files, because there will be more than one file created. When you have entered the correct path and filenames, click OK to continue. This starts the profile save process, as shown in Figure 12.88.

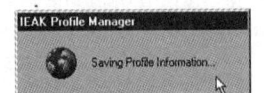

Figure 12.88 The IEAK Save process.

12.3
OBTAIN THE MICROSOFT INTERNET EXPLORER ADMINISTRATION KIT

17. As soon as the save process is complete you will be left with the IEAK Profile Manager screen showing, except you will now see the path and filename of your newly created file along the top window bar of this screen. To confirm that you have created all the proper files, open the My Computer icon and go to the path that you configured in step 16, as shown in Figure 12.89.

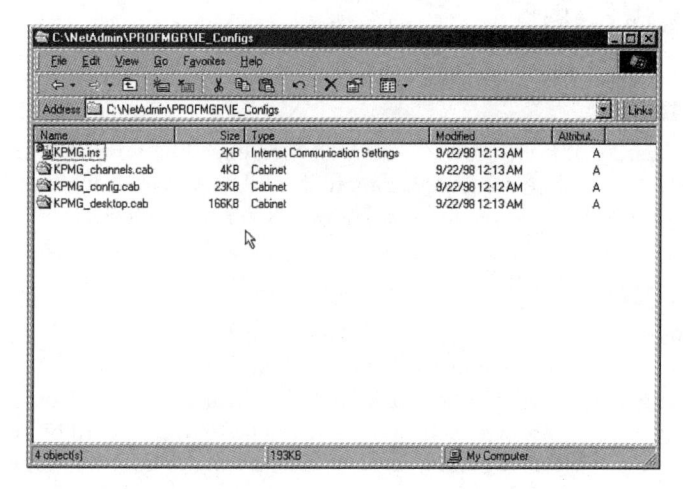

Figure 12.89 Reviewing the results of the IEAK Save process.

18. This screen contains at least one more file than the number of sections that you altered during your use of the IEAK Profile Manager. For example, in your walk through of the process, you touched on sections in the Internet Explorer Channels, configuration, and desktop areas. In this screen you can see a .CAB file for each of these areas, as well as a master .INS file for the organization's default Internet Communications Settings file. Remember that it is this .INS file that you connect to within Internet Explorer to grab a new configuration for your Internet Explorer browser--this file is usually stored on a file server that is centrally located within your organization, or it is distributed to several file servers within your organization.

12.4 How do I...
Configure and use Microsoft Wallet and the Microsoft Profile Assistant?

COMPLEXITY
INTERMEDIATE

Problem

I have heard that it is possible to store the contents of my physical wallet, such as credit card and personal information, inside the Microsoft Internet Explorer Web browser. Is this true, and if so, how do I perform this feat?

Technique

To store credit card information, you must configure the Microsoft Wallet option that is available within the Internet Explorer Web browser. Personal information is stored in close proximity by using another technology within Internet Explorer known as the Microsoft Profile Assistant. Both of these technologies are easily configurable and are done using the Internet Properties screen of the Microsoft Internet Explorer Web browser. To do this, go through this next set of instructions.

Steps

1. To start, you need to access the Internet Properties screen of the Microsoft Internet Explorer Web browser. To find this screen, click the Windows 98 Start button, and then click again on the Settings menu option, followed by another click on the Control Panel menu selection.

2. When the Windows 98 Control Panel appears, double-click the Internet icon. This causes the Internet Properties screen of the Microsoft Internet Explorer Web browser to appear.

3. Next, you need to click the Content tab to reveal the screen shown in Figure 12.90.

4. Both the Microsoft Wallet and the Microsoft Profile Assistant technologies are maintained using the bottom section of this screen, which is labeled as the Personal Information area. To create or modify a profile, you need to click the Edit Profile..., which reveals the screen shown in Figure 12.91.

12.4
CONFIGURE AND USE MICROSOFT WALLET AND PROFILE ASSISTANT

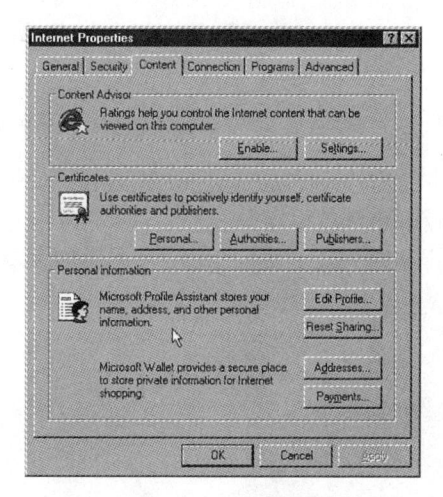

Figure 12.90 Reviewing the Content tab of the Internet Properties screen.

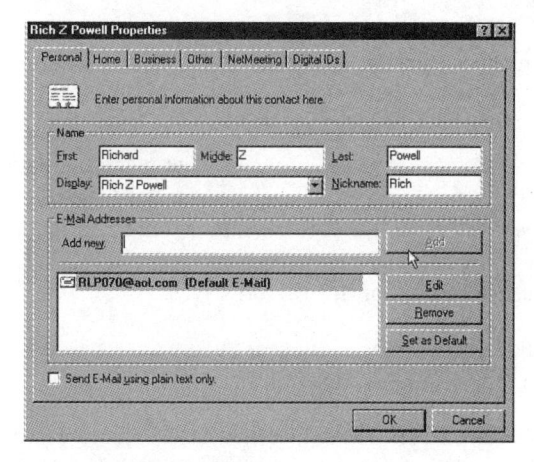

Figure 12.91 Editing a profile within the Microsoft Profile Assistant.

5. The first Microsoft Profile Assistant screen to appear is the Personal tab. This is where you enter information about your contact, such as their first, middle, and last names as well as their Internet email address. If this Internet Explorer browser is for your use only, this is where you enter your own personal information.

6. To add an Internet email address, type the address into the Add New box, and then click the Add button. Your email address information automatically drops down to the box below, and if this is the first address to be entered, it automatically is set as the default email address.

7. To continue, click the Home tab to move to that screen, as shown in Figure 12.92.

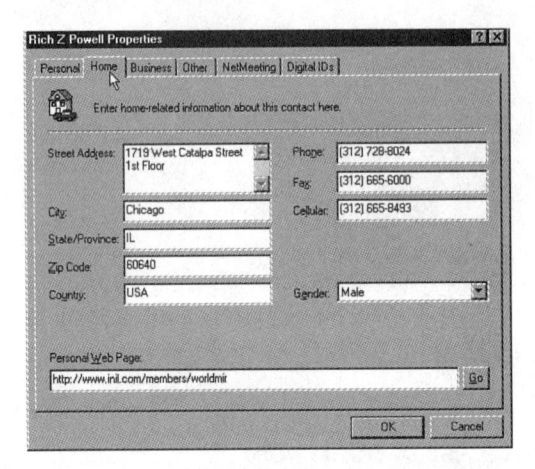

Figure 12.92 Editing the home information within a person's profile.

8. This Profile Assistant screen is used to enter data regarding your contact, such as full address (including the street address, city, state, Zip code, and country), as well as their telephone, fax, and cellular information. Additionally, you are able to specify the person's gender as well as specifying a personal Web page for this person.

9. When you make all the changes or entries you want, click the Business tab to move to that screen, as shown in Figure 12.93.

10. This Profile Assistant screen is used to enter information regarding your contact's employer, such as the full company name and address (including the street address, city, state, Zip code, and country), as well as their telephone, fax, and cellular information. Additionally, you are able to specify the person's position information as well as specifying their employer's Web page.

11. After you make all the changes or entries you want, click the Other tab to move to that screen, as shown in Figure 12.94.

12.4
CONFIGURE AND USE MICROSOFT WALLET AND PROFILE ASSISTANT   557

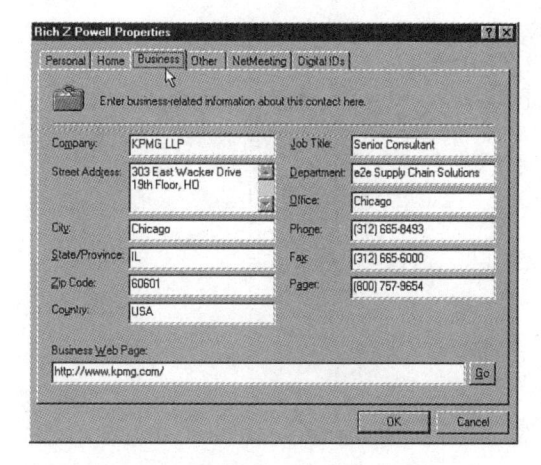

Figure 12.93 Editing the business information within a person's profile.

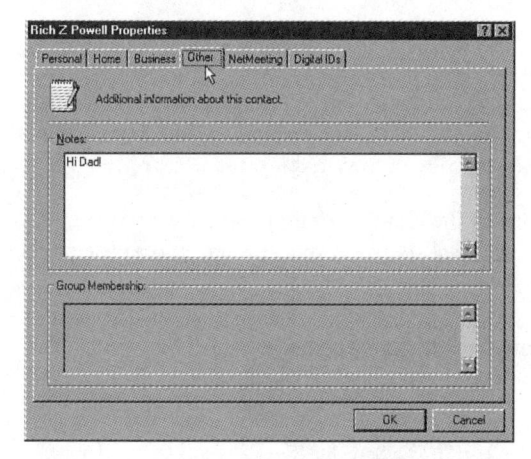

Figure 12.94 Editing other miscellaneous information within a person's profile.

12. This Profile Assistant screen is used to enter miscellaneous information regarding your contact, such as personal notes. Anything else you want to add can be noted here. The box at the bottom of the screen is where a listing of the groups that this person belongs to are noted.

13. When you make all the changes or entries you want, click the NetMeeting tab to move to that screen as, shown in Figure 12.95.

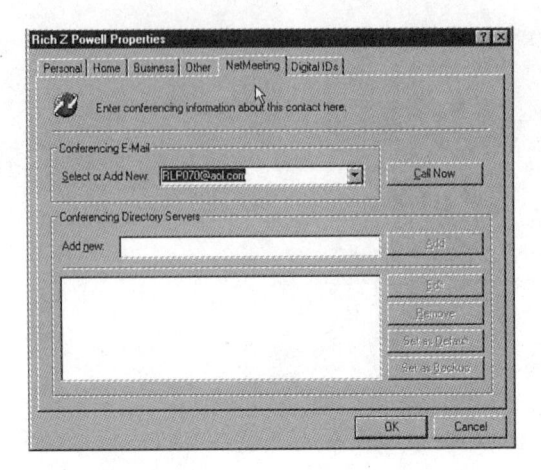

Figure 12.95 Editing the NetMeeting information area within a person's profile.

14. This Profile Assistant screen is used to select or enter details regarding your contact's conferencing information, such as their email address, and all the Conferencing Directory Servers through which this person can be contacted using the Microsoft NetMeeting technology, which is an add-on component to Microsoft Internet Explorer.

15. When you make all the changes or entries you want, click the Digital IDs tab to move to the final screen in this configuration process, as shown in Figure 12.96.

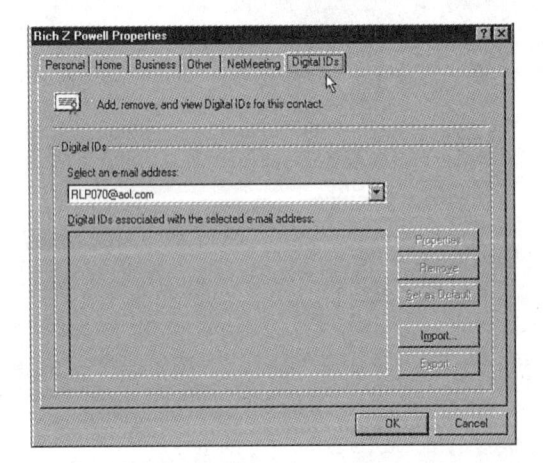

Figure 12.96 Editing the Digital IDs information area within a person's profile.

12.4
CONFIGURE AND USE MICROSOFT WALLET AND PROFILE ASSISTANT

16. This final Profile Assistant screen is used to select or enter digital IDs that are to be associated with the email address that you selected from the drop-down list box. Most persons probably do not have a digital ID, but over the next year or so you will see this become a much more popular phenomenon, especially among private individuals.

17. After you make the changes or entries you want, click OK to confirm all your changes and return to the Internet Properties screen.

18. One option that you might want to know more about is the Reset Sharing button that appears below the Edit Profile button in the Microsoft Profile Assistant area. To access more details behind the use of this button, click the question mark that appears in the upper-right corner of the Internet Properties screen, and then click the Reset Sharing button, as shown in Figure 12.97.

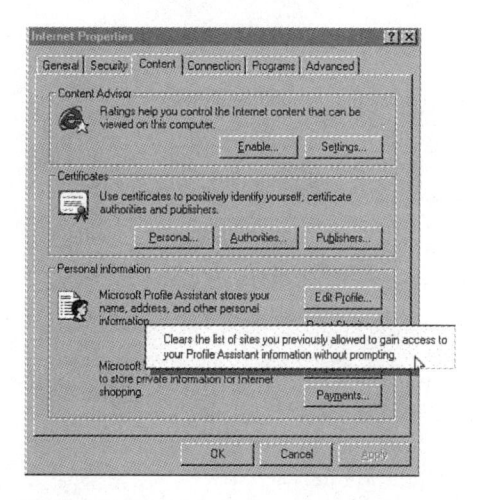

Figure 12.97 Obtaining more information on the Reset Sharing utility.

19. This button revokes any access that a Web site might have once had to your personal information that is stored within the Microsoft Profile Assistant. To activate this option, click the Reset Sharing button, which prompts you with the message box you see in Figure 12.98.

20. If you want to go through with the revocation of access, click OK. Otherwise, click No and return to the Internet Properties screen immediately. Even if you had clicked Yes you would be returned to the Internet Properties screen, but only after all the access rights have been revoked from the various Web sites that once had access.

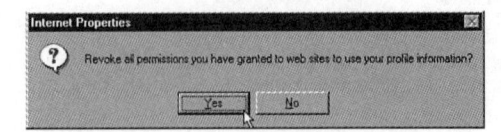

Figure 12.98 Deciding whether to revoke access to your private information.

21. That is all you need to do to configure the Microsoft Profile Assistant. Next up is the Microsoft Wallet. To access this area, click the Addresses... button, to bring up the Address Options screen, as shown in Figure 12.99.

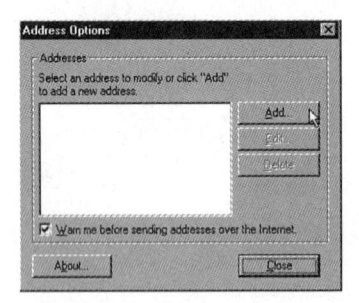

Figure 12.99 Accessing the Address area of the Microsoft Wallet.

22. This screen contains the various addresses that are valid for use with the Microsoft Wallet feature of the Internet Explorer browser. If no addresses appear, you need to add one. To do this, click the Add... button, which reveals the screen shown in Figure 12.100.

23. The layout of this screen should look very familiar to you; it is the same one that you saw in the Microsoft Profile Assistant section. You can either enter all the information here, or you can quickly grab an existing address from the Windows address book, which is actually the Microsoft Profile Assistant. To do it the easy way, click the Address Book... button to bring up the screen shown in Figure 12.101.

12.4
CONFIGURE AND USE MICROSOFT WALLET AND PROFILE ASSISTANT   561

Figure 12.100 Adding a new address for use with Microsoft Wallet.

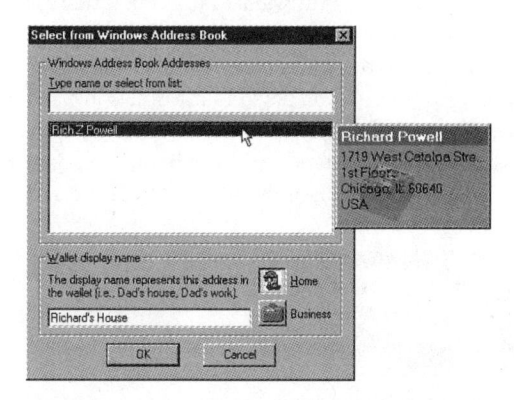

Figure 12.101 Retrieving an address from the Microsoft Profile Assistant's address book.

24. The Microsoft Profile Assistant's address book appears from which you are able to snag one of the addresses that exist. If you double-click one of the addresses that appear in the middle box, then a large, colorful version of that person's address appears in a pop-up box to the right of the screen. Now comes a neat little feature of this option: If you click the Business icon found in the Wallet Display Name area, you will automatically go to the address that appears in that large, colorful version of the highlighted person's address box as shown in Figure 12.102.

CHAPTER 12
THE INTERNET AND WEB BROWSING

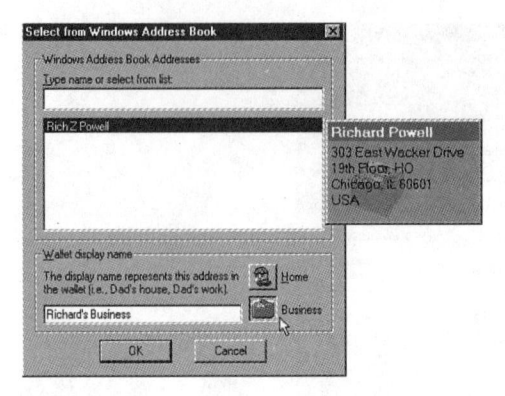

Figure 12.102 Displaying a business address in the Microsoft Profile Assistant's address book.

25. After you make the address that you want to use, click that person's name, and then modify the Wallet Display Name for that person's address. Then, click OK to return to the Add a New Address screen (the previous one), which automatically pulls this person's information back. Something interesting happens here. Although you had a valid country name listed within the Microsoft Profile Assistant's Address Book, you are prompted for an entry into the Country field, as shown in Figure 12.103.

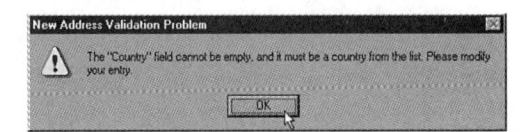

Figure 12.103 Retrieving an address from the Microsoft Profile Assistant's address book.

26. This message box seems to appear regardless of how you might have entered an address' country name, click OK to get rid of this message box.

27. Doing this reveals the screen shown in Figure 12.104, where you will find it necessary to change the Country/Region field.

28. Once you have made the required change to the Country/Region field, you are able to alter any of the other contents of this screen as well. After you have made all the alterations you want, click once on the OK button to have Microsoft Wallet accept all your changes and return to the Address Options screen shown in Figure 12.105.

12.4
CONFIGURE AND USE MICROSOFT WALLET AND PROFILE ASSISTANT

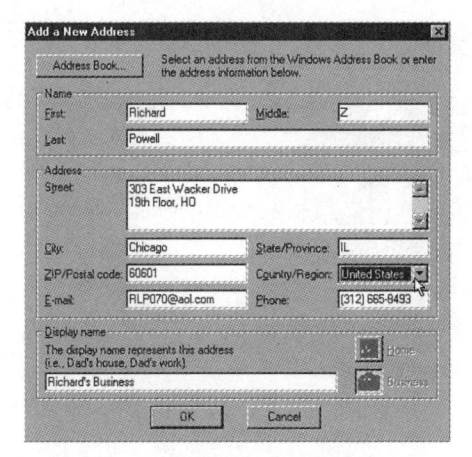

Figure 12.104 Modifying the Country/Region entry for an address.

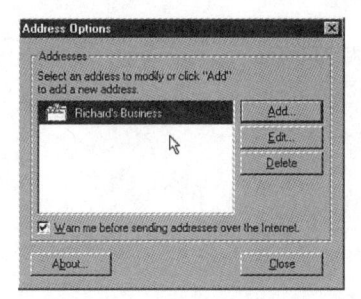

Figure 12.105 Reviewing the Address options screen.

29. Click the Close button after you are satisfied with the address that you have chosen for use with your electronic Microsoft Wallet. This returns you back to the Internet Properties screen of Internet Explorer.

30. Now you need to add some credit card information. To do this, click the Payments button, which takes you to the screen shown in Figure 12.106.

31. When the Payment Options screen appears, you need to scan it to see if you already have any credit cards installed (that is, look to see if one of your card's data has already been added to the Microsoft Wallet). If not, then you need to add one. To do so, click the Add... button, which drops down a listing of the available credit card types that you might use. Currently, this list is limited to adding Visa, MasterCard, American Express, and Discover credit cards, but presumably Microsoft is hard at work to add Diner's Club to this listing in some future release of Internet Explorer.

CHAPTER 12
THE INTERNET AND WEB BROWSING

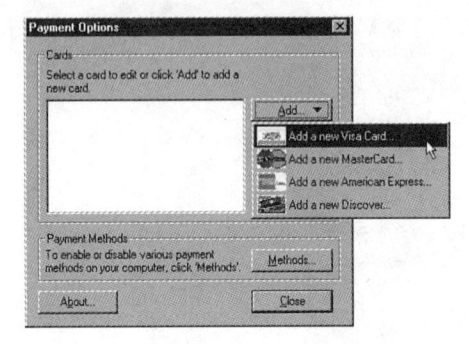

Figure 12.106 Adding a credit card to the Microsoft Wallet.

32. Select one of these existing credit card types by clicking it once. This automatically takes you to the starting screen of the Add a New Credit CardWizard, as shown in Figure 12.107.

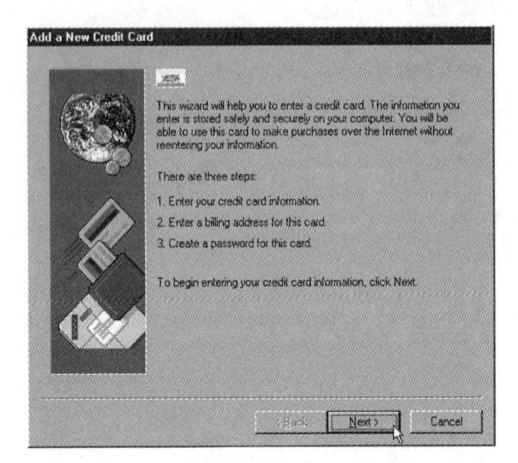

Figure 12.107 Starting the Add a New Credit Card Wizard.

33. For the purposes of this demonstration, I have selected a new Visa card. The first Add a New Credit Card Wizard screen that appears is strictly informational. It succinctly explains the steps that are required to add a new credit card, as well as explaining why you really want to do this.

34. To continue the wizard, click the Next> button, which takes you to the screen shown in Figure 12.108.

12.4
CONFIGURE AND USE MICROSOFT WALLET AND PROFILE ASSISTANT

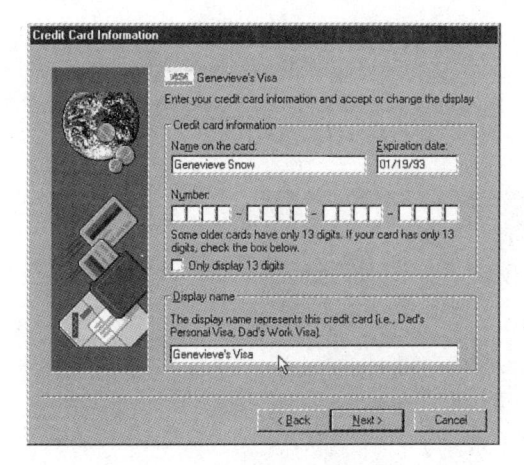

Figure 12.108 Adding the important credit card information.

35. You should enter the name on the card exactly as it really does appear on your credit card. The expiration date and the actual credit card number fields are obviously the most important ones on this screen. If you make a fatal mistake, such as an invalid credit card number or a bad date, the Microsoft Wallet software is smart enough to detect it and warn you to correct it. In fact, if you do not correct your errors, you will not be able to progress to the next screen in the wizard, as demonstrated by the error message boxes shown in Figures 12.109 and 12.110.

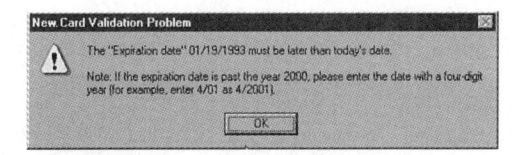

Figure 12.109 A message box telling you that you have entered an invalid date.

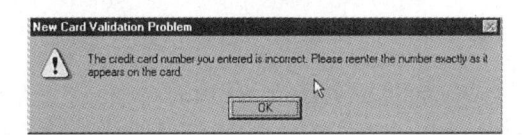

Figure 12.110 A message box telling you that you have entered an invalid credit card number.

36. Click OK for each of these error message boxes, if they occur during your entry process. When you have completed the valid entry of the data required on this screen, click Next> to proceed to the Credit Card Billing Address screen shown in Figure 12.111.

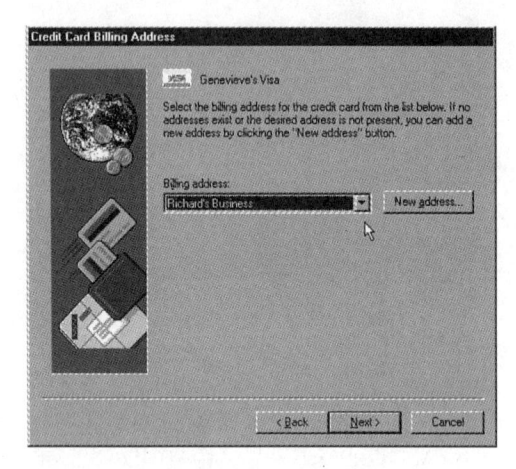

Figure 12.111 Adding the important credit card information.

37. To select a billing address, click the drop-down list box that appears on this screen. If you want to add a new address click the New Address button, which appears to the right of this drop-down list box.

38. The New Address button takes you through a series of screens just like the ones you saw during the configuration of the Microsoft Profile Assistant.

39. After you have completed the valid entry of the data required on this screen, click the Next> button to proceed to the screen, which is shown in Figure 12.112.

40. You should enter a non-word password in order to properly protect your credit from fraudulent use. That is, do not select a word from a dictionary or use one of your children's' or relatives' or pets' names. Instead, try to use a combination of upper- and lowercase letters, along with a number or two, in addition to a special character (such as an asterisk, a dollar sign, and so on).

41. When you have entered and confirmed a valid password on this screen, click the Finish button to proceed to the Payment Options screen, shown in Figure 12.113.

12.4
CONFIGURE AND USE MICROSOFT WALLET AND PROFILE ASSISTANT

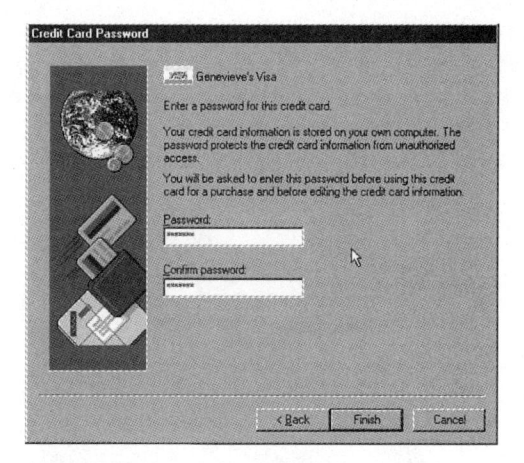

Figure 12.112 Adding password protection to your credit card information.

Figure 12.113 Reviewing your credit card options.

42. Click the Close button to exit the Payment Options screen and return to the Internet Properties screen.

43. To finalize the configuration of the Microsoft Profile Assistant and Microsoft Wallet features of Internet Explorer, click OK. This closes the Internet Properties screen and returns you to the Windows 98 desktop.

44. To use the Microsoft Profile Assistant and Microsoft Wallet features of Internet Explorer, you will be prompted for them at a Web site such as one that might be found in an electronic virtual mall on the Internet. All you need to do is click your virtual wallet and present one of your credit cards; the information that you enter here will filter through to the appropriate destinations. Ensure that you are accessing a Web site that takes advantage of either the PCT or SSL 3.0 levels of Web site encryption technologies, so that you do not wind up sending your personal financial information over a public network, such as the Internet, in an open, clear-text fashion.

CHAPTER 13
EMAIL AND NEWS

13

EMAIL AND NEWS

How do I...

13.1 **Install the Internet email and newsgroup components of Windows 98?**

13.2 **Configure and use the Outlook Express email client?**

13.3 **Configure and use the Outlook Express newsreader component?**

13.4 **Configure Outlook Express when I have multiple users on the same PC?**

13.5 **Perform Outlook Express maintenance tasks?**

13.6 **Use the Outlook Express address book?**

13.7 **Configure a digital signature and why would I want to use one?**

This chapter delves into the electronic mail (email) and electronic newsgroups (news) software access tools that are built into the Windows 98 operating system. What this means is that you take an in-depth look at the Microsoft Outlook Express software application. Though Outlook Express could very easily survive on its own as a standalone email and newsgroup product, Microsoft chose to first integrate it into its Internet Explorer Web browser (for use with Windows 95) and then further integrate it into the Windows 98 operating system.

CHAPTER 13
EMAIL AND NEWS

Before you start the How-To process, you want to make sure that you have obtained all the latest and greatest updates to Outlook Express, which presently are available on the Windows 98 Windows Update Web site (`http://windowsupdate.microsoft.com/`). If you do not know how to use the Windows 98 Windows Update process, review the section, "How do I Install any Updates to Internet Explorer?" in Chapter 12, "The Internet and Web Browsing," because it explains this very important process.

For this chapter the two most important updates that you can download from the Windows Update Web site are the Outlook Express update itself (1.5MB) and the Outlook Express file attachment security update (1.1MB). The security update resolves an issue with file attachments. Downloading this update means that you're able to prevent possible unauthorized access to your computer; that is, you can prevent a hacker from running malicious code on your computer. The other fix contained in this second patch fixes a problem that might otherwise occur when you open a message that contains an attachment with an extremely long name, which could possibly make Outlook Express terminate without warning. Additional information on this patch is available within the Microsoft Security Bulletin MS98-008, found at `http://www.microsoft.com/security/bulletins/ms98-008.htm` (on Microsoft's Web site), should you want more details before downloading the security update.

After you have these two updates installed (the Windows Update utility does the download and installation at the same time, so you do not have to worry about it), you're ready to proceed with the remainder of this chapters. If you do not have access to the Internet or do not want to download either of these updates, you can also proceed, but keep in mind that it is possible a few things might not work as correctly on your PC as they do in the examples given.

13.1 Install the Internet Email and Newsgroup Components of Windows 98

This section of the chapter gets you started. If you do not have the Outlook Express software accessory installed, none of the remaining How-To topics work for you.

13.2 Configure and Use the Outlook Express Email Client

This How-To is focused on sending, receiving, and reviewing electronic mail messages on your computer. This is one of the two core components of Outlook Express, which is integrated into Windows 98.

13.3 Configure and Use the Outlook Express Newsreader Component

This How-To is focuses on downloading, reviewing, and sending messages between your computer and the newsgroups area of the Internet. This is the other core component of Outlook Express.

13.4 Configure Outlook Express when I Have Multiple Users on the Same PC

Many times you find yourself wanting to have more than one distinct user needing his or her own address book, mailbox, and private email functions within Outlook Express. This How-To shows you how it is possible to very easily configure Outlook Express for use with multiple users on the same Windows 98 PC.

13.5 Perform Outlook Express Maintenance Tasks

During the use of the Outlook Express accessory, you might want to know how to use the compacting tool; how to import email messages, address books, and other mail account settings; how to export email messages and address books; or how to configure the Inbox Assistant. This How-To covers all these topics and more.

13.6 Use the Outlook Express Address Book

There is a very nice contacts Address Book built into Outlook Express. The purpose of this How-To is to assist you in the configuration and possible uses of this address book.

13.7 Configure a Digital Signature and Why Would I Want to Use One

You have probably heard a lot about digital signatures. You might even find yourself wanting to use one. This How-To discusses digital signatures including why you might want to use one and how to obtain and configure one for use with Outlook Express.

COMPLEXITY
BEGINNER

13.1 How do I...
Install the Internet email and newsgroup components of Windows 98?

Problem

I have heard so much about using an Internet Service Provider (ISP) such as the Microsoft Network (MSN) or Internet Illinois to send and receive email and access the thousands of Internet newsgroups that exist. How can I install the proper components within Windows 98 to permit me to do these types of things? Do I need to purchase any add-on software to perform either of these tasks?

Technique

Windows 98 has numerous built-in utilities and applications that can be added or dropped at any time. In the case of Outlook Express, if you performed a full installation of Windows 98, you already have this Internet tool installed. Otherwise, you can easily check to see whether it is installed, and if not, it is simple to install; these steps quickly walk you through the process.

Steps

1. To start, you should check to see whether the Microsoft Outlook Express tool is installed. There are two ways to accomplish this task. The first is to try to run it from the menus within Windows 98. For instance, click the Start button, move to the Programs menu option, select the Internet Explorer menu option, and then click the Outlook Express menu selection, as shown in Figure 13.1.

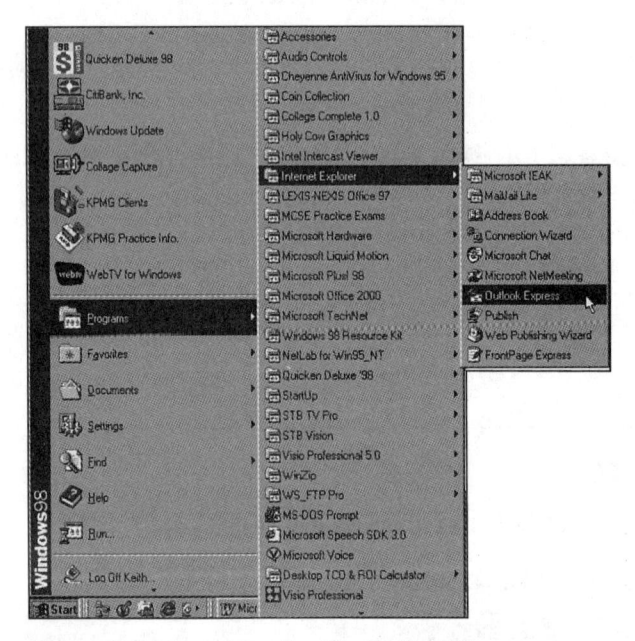

Figure 13.1 Searching for the Outlook Express menu selection.

2. If you get to the Internet Explorer menu option and there is no Outlook Express menu option, that is a hint that perhaps you do not have Outlook Express installed on your PC. Furthermore, if you click the Outlook Express menu option and nothing happens, it is a strong indicator as well that you might not have Outlook Express installed on your PC.

13.1
INSTALL THE INTERNET EMAIL AND NEWSGROUP COMPONENTS

3. The next place to look is on the Windows 98 Windows Setup screen. To get there, click the Start button, select the Settings menu option, and then click the Control Panel menu selection. This takes you directly into the Windows 98 Control Panel.

4. Next, double-click the Add/Remove Programs icon to reveal the Add/Remove Programs Properties screen. After this screen opens, click the Windows Setup tab to reveal the screen shown in Figure 13.2.

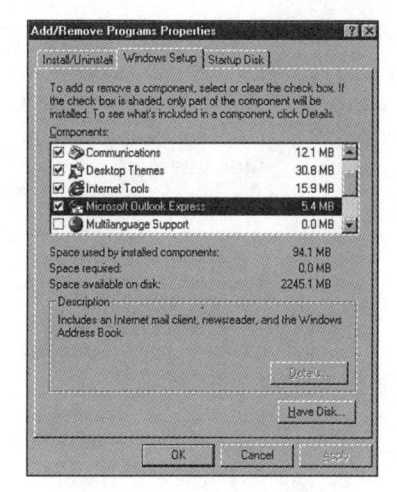

Figure 13.2 Reviewing the available options within the Windows Setup screen.

5. After this screen appears, use the scrollbar to move down the screen until you get to the Microsoft Outlook Express option. If there is a check mark in the box next to this option, it is already installed. If the box is empty (and the size is 0.0, instead of the 5.4MB size shown), this means that the Microsoft Outlook Express option has not been installed yet.

6. To install the option, assuming that the box was empty, click the box to mark it. Then, click OK to confirm your choice and begin the software installation process. You need your Windows 98 CD-ROM for this part of the process.

7. After the software has finished installing (the option for Microsoft Outlook Express includes both the email and newsgroup components), you might be prompted to restart your PC. If so, click Yes to confirm your choice. After the PC has restarted, you're ready to start the configuration process.

CHAPTER 13
EMAIL AND NEWS

COMPLEXITY
INTERMEDIATE

13.2 How do I...
Configure and use the Outlook Express email client?

Problem

Okay. I have successfully installed Outlook Express. I want to use it now, so that I can connect to my ISP's POP3 (Post Office Protocol, version 3.0) email system. What do I need to do to configure Outlook Express so that it can be used for Internet email? Also, after it is configured, how do I use Outlook Express for sending and receiving email across the Internet?

Technique

Configuring Microsoft Outlook Express for use with a POP3 email service provider, such as your ISP, is not difficult and requires about 5–10 minutes of your time. A POP3 email account is one that has long been associated with sending and receiving Internet-based email for quite some time. Although POP3 has long been the Internet's email standard, the newest Internet email protocol offering is IMAP4 (Internet Message Access Protocol, version 4.0). With IMAP4, it is possible to search through email messages via a set of keywords while the messages are still on the mail server, which means that you can review them before actually downloading them to your PC. Like POP3, IMAP uses SMTP (Simple Mail Transfer Protocol) for communication between the email client and server. If you want to review more information regarding the IMAP protocol, visit `http://www.imap.org/whatisIMAP.html`.

Begin this section by starting up Outlook Express. Use the configuration screens to create a new account for your ISP connection. After you finish, I walk you through the basic steps for composing, sending, receiving, and reading all your email messages.

Steps

1. To begin using Outlook Express, click the Start button, select Programs, choose Internet Explorer, and then finally click the Outlook Express menu selection. This takes you into the first screen of the Microsoft Outlook Express configuration process, as shown in Figure 13.3.

2. Choose a folder in which to place your Outlook Express files (your eventual email and newsgroup information, account data, and so on). After you have made your selection by clicking on the destination folder, click OK to continue.

13.2 CONFIGURE AND USE THE OUTLOOK EXPRESS EMAIL CLIENT

Figure 13.3 Configuring the location for the Outlook Express email and newsgroup data files.

3. This takes you directly into Outlook Express, as shown in Figure 13.4.

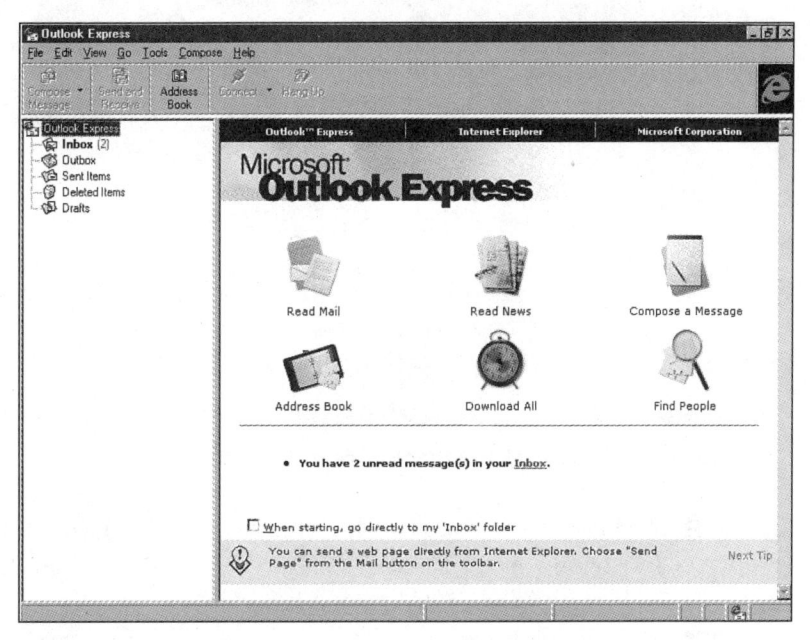

Figure 13.4 The opening screen of Outlook Express.

4. After the primary screen of Outlook Express opens, you can quickly figure out the basics by looking at it. Over to the left is a tree-like structure that permits quick access to all the folders within the application: Inbox, Outbox, Sent Items, Deleted Items, and Drafts (a *draft* is a message that you composed and closed but did not send yet).

CHAPTER 13
EMAIL AND NEWS

5. In the window to the right you see the high-level topic known as Microsoft Outlook Express, which is a graphical way to access those very same folders in the tree structure. Obviously, by clicking the Outlook Express folder option (at the top of the folder tree on the left), you are able to see this top-level GUI presentation of your Outlook Express folder options. Each time you click one of the folders, whether it is in the Inbox, the Drafts, and so on, that folder's contents appear in the window to the right.

6. Click the Tools menu option, and then click again on the Accounts... menu selection, as shown in Figure 13.5.

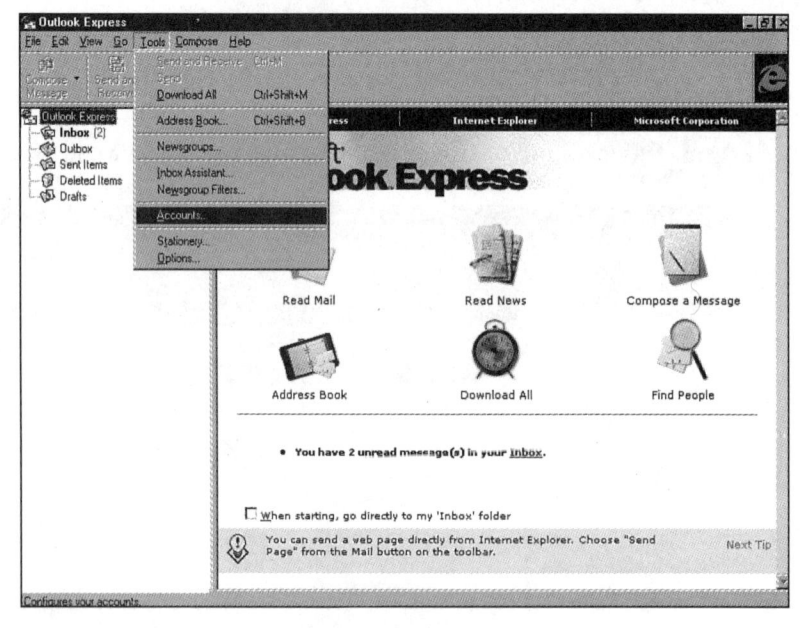

Figure 13.5 Using the Outlook Express menu options.

7. The Internet Accounts window appears. After it opens, click the Mail tab to be taken to that screen (the Internet Accounts windows opens with the Mail tab showing), as shown in Figure 13.6.

8. Click Add to reveal a small menu, which contains three options: Mail..., News..., and Directory Service... (all three of these menu selections are used to create new mail, news, or directory service accounts). Click the Mail... menu selection, which reveals the screen shown in Figure 13.7.

13.2
CONFIGURE AND USE THE OUTLOOK EXPRESS EMAIL CLIENT

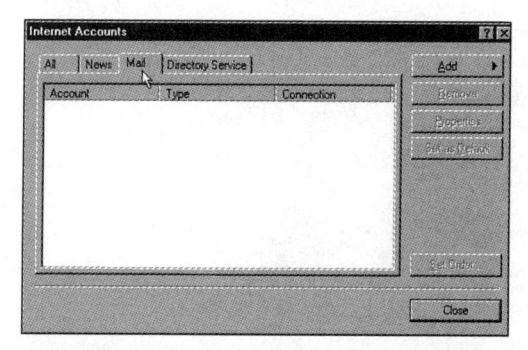

Figure 13.6 The Mail tab of the Internet Accounts window.

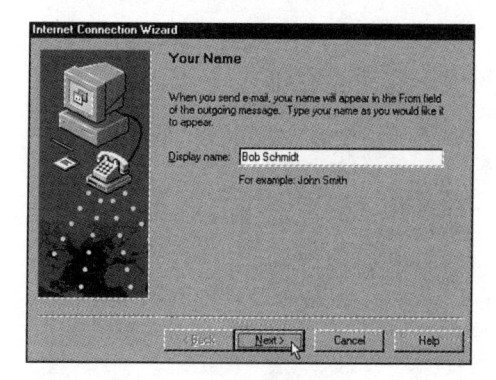

Figure 13.7 The opening screen of the Internet Connection Wizard.

9. On this first screen of the Internet Connection Wizard you need to fill in a descriptive name for the new Internet email account that you are creating. I usually put in the name of the ISP or the person that uses it most used. After you have input the text that you want, click the Next> button to continue the process. This takes you to the screen shown in Figure 13.8.

10. On this screen you need to type the complete Internet email address that your email administrator or ISP assigned to you. After you have input the text that you want, click the Next> button to continue the process. This takes you to the screen shown in Figure 13.9.

11. At this point you need to determine whether the Internet email account you are configuring is of the POP3 or IMAP type. When in doubt choose POP3, because the vast majority of Internet email accounts use this version. The most popular IMAP messaging system is Microsoft Exchange Server, so select this one if you are certain that this the type of email system to which you are connecting.

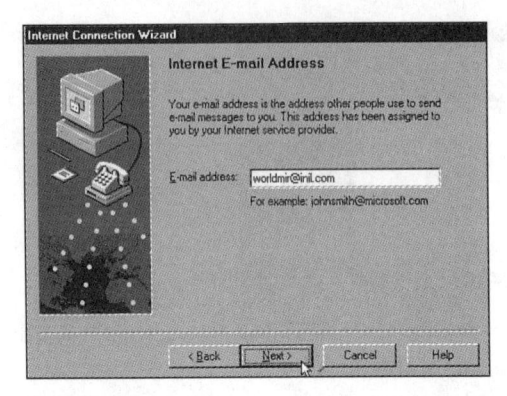

Figure 13.8 Entering your full Internet email information.

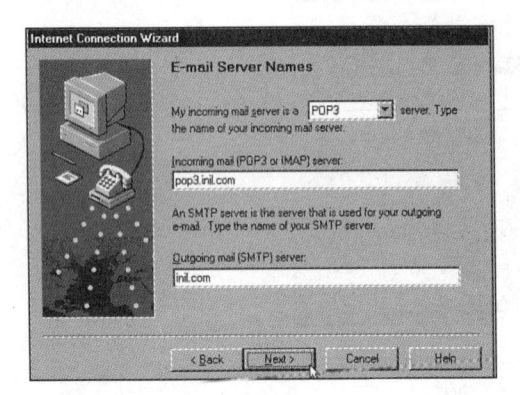

Figure 13.9 Entering your email server names.

12. Use the drop-down list box to make your incoming Internet mail server type selection. Then enter the full name of your POP3 or IMAP incoming mail server in the top box and the outgoing SMTP mail server's name in the lower box.

> **NOTE**
>
> An SMTP mail server handles the Simple Mail Transfer Protocol, which has long been the de facto Internet messaging protocol standard. SMTP is part of the POP3 protocol that is defined in Internet RFC (Request for Comment) 1939. POP3 contains only eleven commands, is designed for offline message usage, and uses SMTP for its message submission and LDAP (Lightweight Directory Access Protocol) for its address resolution. LDAP is used as part of the directory service that is also built into Outlook Express. IMAP is a client/server protocol that is based on

13.2
CONFIGURE AND USE THE OUTLOOK EXPRESS EMAIL CLIENT

RFC 2060, is designed for online use, provides access to multiple or shared folders, is able to retrieve just portions of messages, and, like POP3, uses SMTP for its message submission and LDAP for its address resolution.

13. After you have input the data required, click the Next> button to continue the process. This takes you to the screen shown in Figure 13.10.

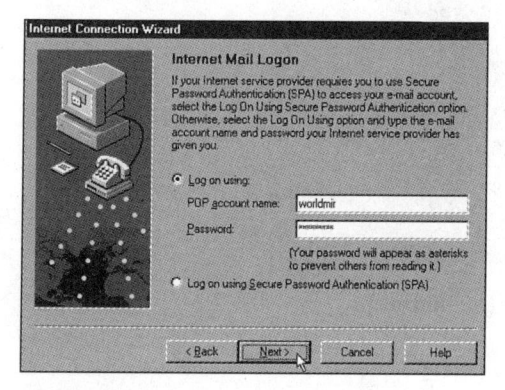

Figure 13.10 Entering your Internet email logon information.

14. Typically you need to enter your user ID and password in the top two boxes, which then permit you to be authenticated by your ISP's Internet servers. However, if you are connecting to a non-POP3 email server, you need to click the bottom radio button. This enables you to log on using the Secure Password Authentication.

15. Make your entries as necessary, and click the Next> button to continue the process. This takes you to the screen shown in Figure 13.11.

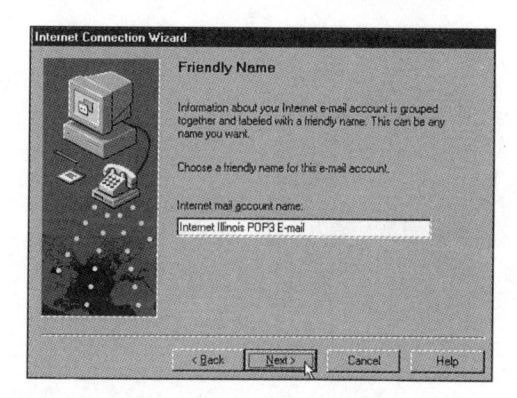

Figure 13.11 Creating a friendly name.

16. A friendly name is simply a descriptive name that you use to describe your newly created Internet email account. After you have input the text that you want, click the Next> button to continue the process. This takes you to the screen shown in Figure 13.12.

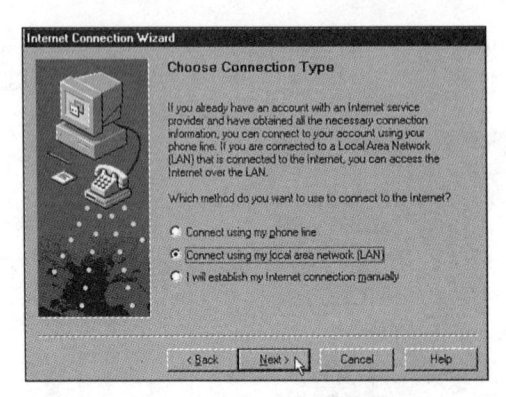

Figure 13.12 Selecting an Internet connection type.

17. The Internet Connection Wizard continues by prompting you to select an Internet connection type. To choose one, click the radio button next to the type that is required for you to connect your PC to the Internet. The top choice requires the use of a telephone, whereas the second means that you are using a network connection, and the third signifies that you do not want to change a selection that you already have in place—that is, you need to manually establish your own connection every time you want to use Outlook Express.

18. After you have made your selection, click the Next> button to continue the process. This takes you to the screen shown in Figure 13.13.

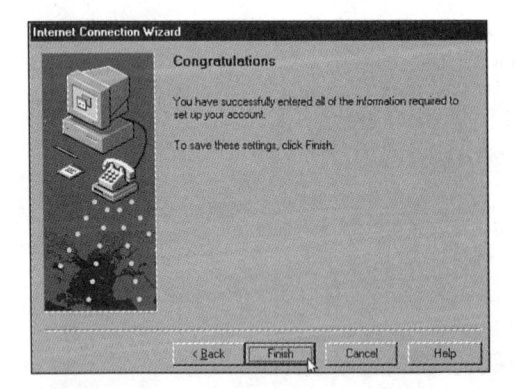

Figure 13.13 Completing the wizard.

13.2
CONFIGURE AND USE THE OUTLOOK EXPRESS EMAIL CLIENT

19. Review the information on this screen and then click the Finish button to end the wizard. This takes you to the screen shown in Figure 13.14.

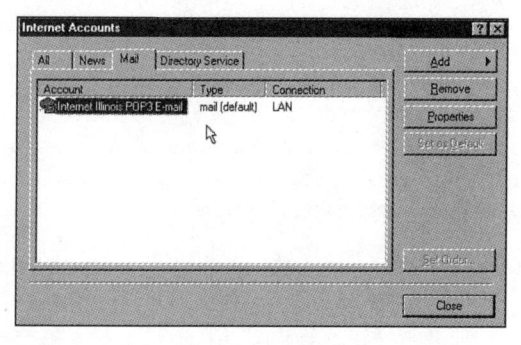

Figure 13.14 Reviewing configured Outlook Express mail accounts.

20. To continue forward into the advanced configuration process, click to select the email account that you just established. Next, click the Properties button, which takes you to the screen shown in Figure 13.15.

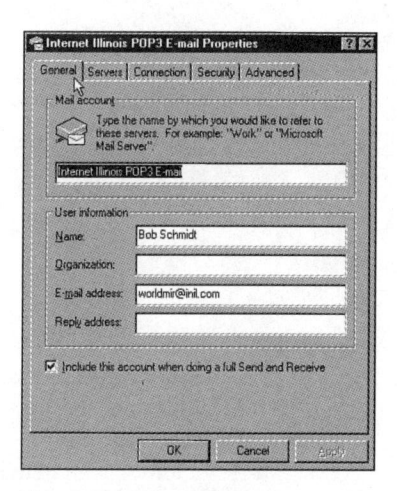

Figure 13.15 Reviewing general information for the email account.

21. This first screen contains mostly descriptive or informational data. Most of this screen already has information in the various boxes, due to the responses you made during the wizard setup of this email account. However, you should pay close attention to the check box located near the bottom of this screen. It is labeled Include This Account when Doing a Full Send and Receive, which means that when you click the Send/Receive button or menu option, your computer tries to send and receive all the messages associated with this email account. When you have six or eight accounts configured at any one time, you find yourself waiting around a lot for all your accounts to automatically be checked during the Send/Receive process. Therefore, the rule of thumb for someone with fewer than three accounts is to leave this option checked, while someone with four or five accounts might want to carefully examine the need for including any one account, and someone with more than five accounts might want to avoid using this option on all their accounts.

22. After you have made your changes, if any, click the Servers tab to proceed to the screen shown in Figure 13.16.

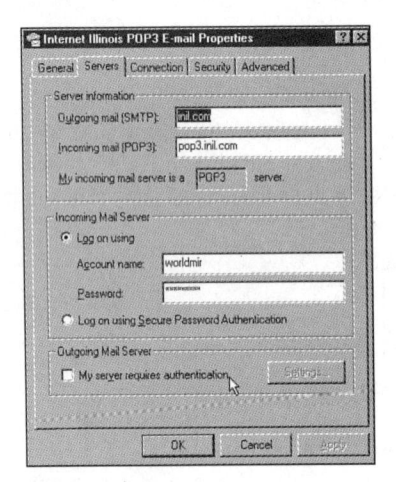

Figure 13.16 Reviewing server entries for an email account.

23. The purpose of this screen is for you to be able to review the various server entries that you made during the initial setup of this email account. You can change any of the server settings, as necessary, with the only new area of information being the possible use of additional authentication required for your outgoing mail server. During the initial setup and configuration process, Outlook Express assumes that you want to use the same level of security for your outgoing mail server as you defined for the incoming mail server. However, by checking this box, you are able to configure your outbound email server to authenticate using a different user ID and password, as well as to use the SPA (secure password authentication) process. Chances are that you never use this feature unless you work for some ultrasecret defense agency or some other Dilbert-like organization.

13.2
CONFIGURE AND USE THE OUTLOOK EXPRESS EMAIL CLIENT

24. Click the Connection tab to continue. This takes you to the screen shown in Figure 13.17.

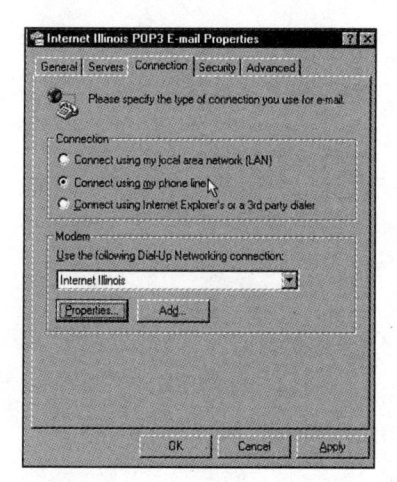

Figure 13.17 Reviewing email account connection options and settings.

25. On this tab you are able to alter the default connection type for this specific email account. If you click the radio button next to the Connect Using My Phone Line option, you are able to specify a default Dial-Up Networking connection type in the drop-down list box in the following section.

26. If you have not yet created a Dial-Up Networking session on your PC, you should click the Add... button to do so (follow the prompts or review Chapter 9, "Dial-Up Networking").

27. If you need to make any changes to the Dial-Up Networking session, click the Properties button. This button takes you into the Dial-Up Networking properties area, where changes can be made. If you require more information on how to make these types of alterations, refer to Chapter 9.

28. Click the Security tab to continue. This takes you to the screen shown in Figure 13.18.

29. This screen permits you to configure a digital signature for use with your Outlook Express email account. To add one, click the top check box to select it, and then fill in the box located below this section (it has the Digital ID... button to its left). If you do not understand why you might need a digital ID or where to get one, you should review these topics later in this chapter (in section 13.7, "How do I configure a digital signature and why would I want to use one?").

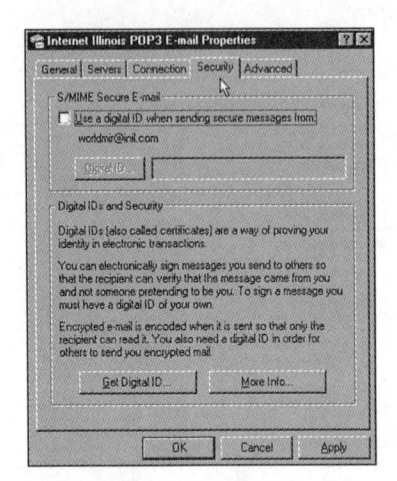

Figure 13.18 Reviewing email account security options.

30. Click the Advanced tab to continue. This takes you into the screen shown in Figure 13.19.

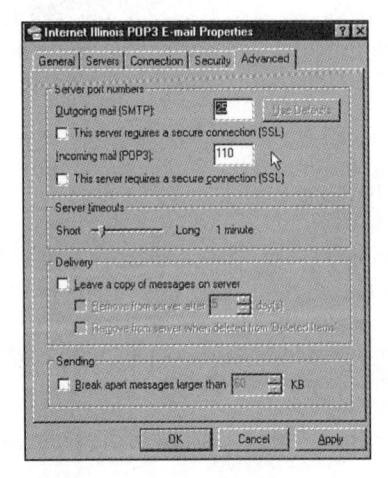

Figure 13.19 Reviewing the advanced email account options.

13.2
CONFIGURE AND USE THE OUTLOOK EXPRESS EMAIL CLIENT

31. The majority of these options are self-explanatory, but the top ones can usually use more of an explanation. These permit you to change the port numbers of your incoming (POP3) or outgoing (SMTP) email servers. Typically, you do not need to change either of your port addresses, but if it does become necessary it is nice to know where this setting is made. Also, you are able to designate the use of SSL (Secure Sockets Layer) for either or both of these email servers. SSL is a level of encryption that provides for the secure transfer of email between your PC and the email server you are connecting to. (Your server must already provide this capability; it is not a one-sided affair.)

> **NOTE**
> When you transfer information via the Internet, such as via Outlook Express or Internet Explorer (using SSL), you want to use the 128-bit encryption level wherever possible. Now, obviously, Internet Explorer comes with this level of encryption as part of Windows 98, but you might want to obtain a digital signature for use with Outlook Express. To do that you might want to review the topic on digital signatures, which is found near the end of this chapter (in section 13.7).

32. To continue on, click the OK button to complete the advanced configuration process. This finally gets you to the main Microsoft Outlook Express screen. Well, almost, anyway. Chances are, if this is your first time to run Outlook Express or if you have another email package installed on your PC, you are encountering the message box shown in Figure 13.20.

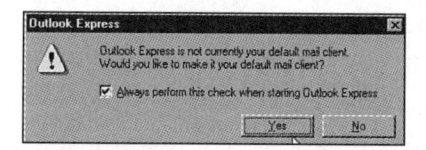

Figure 13.20 Determining whether to make Outlook Express your default email messaging client software.

33. If you want Outlook Express to become your default messaging client software, click the Yes button. Otherwise, click No. In either case, click the check box to select if you want Outlook Express to automatically check to see whether it is still the default email package on your PC every time you start Outlook Express. Make sure that you check (or uncheck) this box, *before* you click either Yes or No. After you make your selection, you then come to the main Outlook Express screen.

34. If you do not now have and never have had any other email software packages installed, you come directly into the main screen of Outlook Express. If you have previously installed other email packages, Outlook Express detects them and attempts to convert that software's address book and existing messages. Of course, if it is an old or very proprietary package, Outlook Express is unable to make these conversions work. Otherwise, you see the first screen of the Outlook Express Import Wizard, as shown in Figure 13.21.

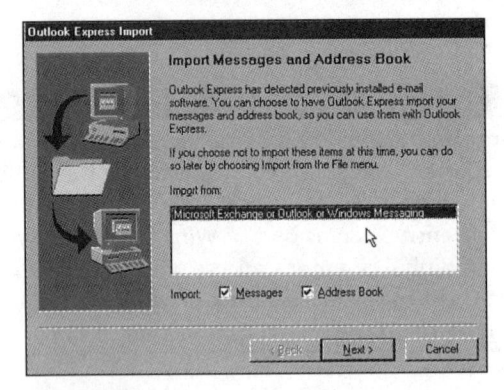

Figure 13.21 Deciding which systems to import from and what to import.

35. If you want to import both messages and addresses from your existing email system, leave both of the check boxes marked (as is the default). Otherwise, to unselect either or both of these, click the option that you want to unmark. After you have made your decisions, click the Next> button to continue to the Choose Profile dialog box, shown in Figure 13.22.

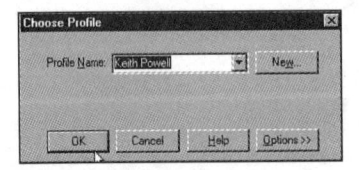

Figure 13.22 Choosing the Microsoft Outlook profile to import.

13.2
CONFIGURE AND USE THE OUTLOOK EXPRESS EMAIL CLIENT   589

> **NOTE**
> These next few screens all assume that you are converting an existing Microsoft Outlook account (this is the client email package that comes with both Microsoft Office 97 and Microsoft Exchange Server). If you are performing a conversion from one of the many other software packages that the Outlook Express Import utility supports, follow the prompts as shown on the screen. The options for those packages are similar to this demonstration, so you still want to try to follow along.

36. On this screen, use the drop-down list box to select the Microsoft Outlook profile from which you want to convert the messages and address book. After you make your selection, click OK to continue the process. This takes you to the screen shown in Figure 13.23 (depending on whether your Microsoft Outlook account is set to prompt you for an online or offline connection).

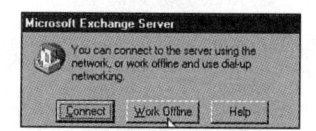

Figure 13.23 Choosing the Microsoft Outlook type.

37. You can make either selection, to work online or offline, provided that you have a local mailbox. Otherwise, you need to select the Online mode if your mailbox is stored only on your messaging server. After you make your decision, follow the few short prompts that follow (it is all wizard based). On completion, you are taken directly to the main screen of Outlook Express, as seen in Figure 13.24.

38. On opening the primary screen, you are taken into the inbox for the Outlook Express package. There you notice two email messages. These are the two default messages that Microsoft automatically places inside everyone's Outlook Express email mailbox, which tout the security and messaging features of Outlook Express. If you double-click one of these, such as the Welcome message, you are taken into that message as shown in Figure 13.25 (which, by the way, is how you access any email message in your Outlook Express inbox).

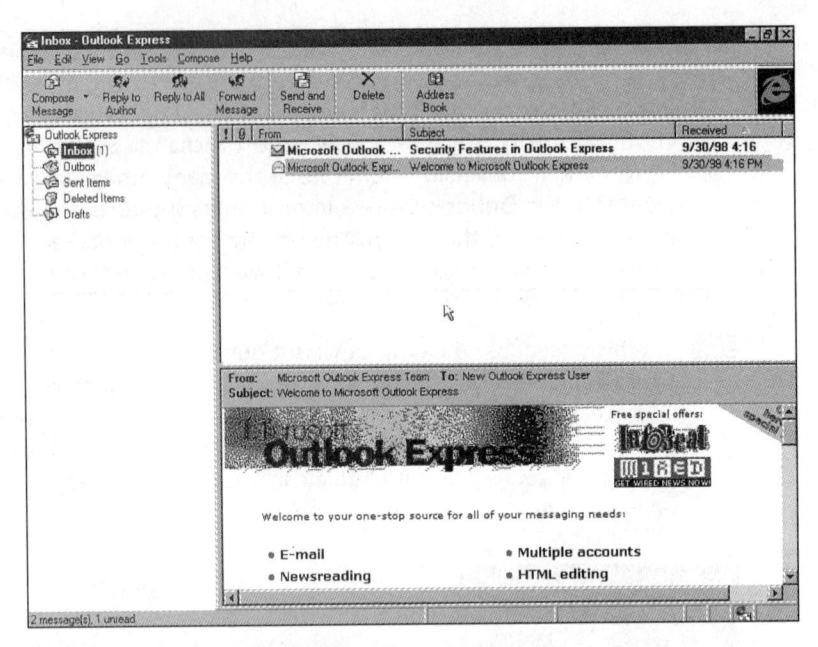

Figure 13.24 The main Outlook Express screen.

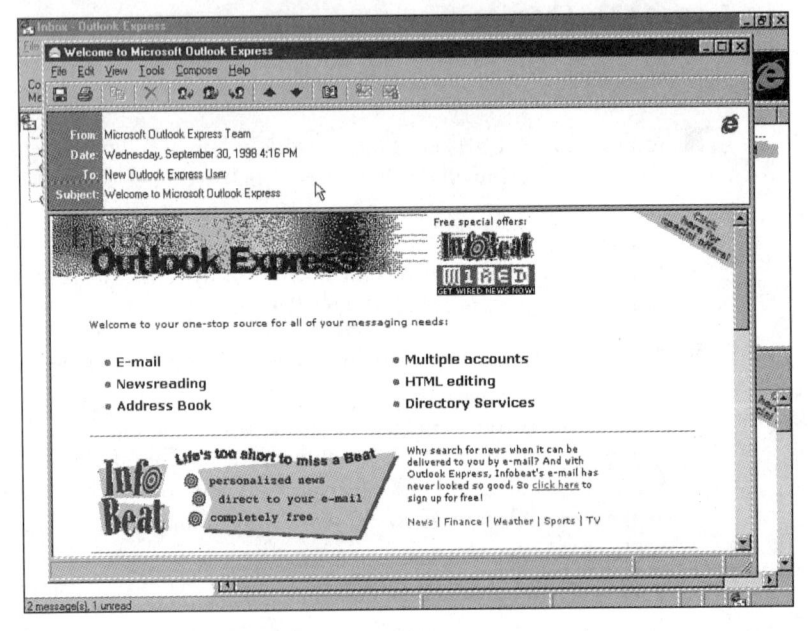

Figure 13.25 Reading an Outlook Express message.

13.2
CONFIGURE AND USE THE OUTLOOK EXPRESS EMAIL CLIENT

39. After you have read this message, close it as you would close any Windows 98 message window. After you are back in the main Outlook Express window, click the Compose Message button's drop-down list box down arrow, as shown in Figure 13.26.

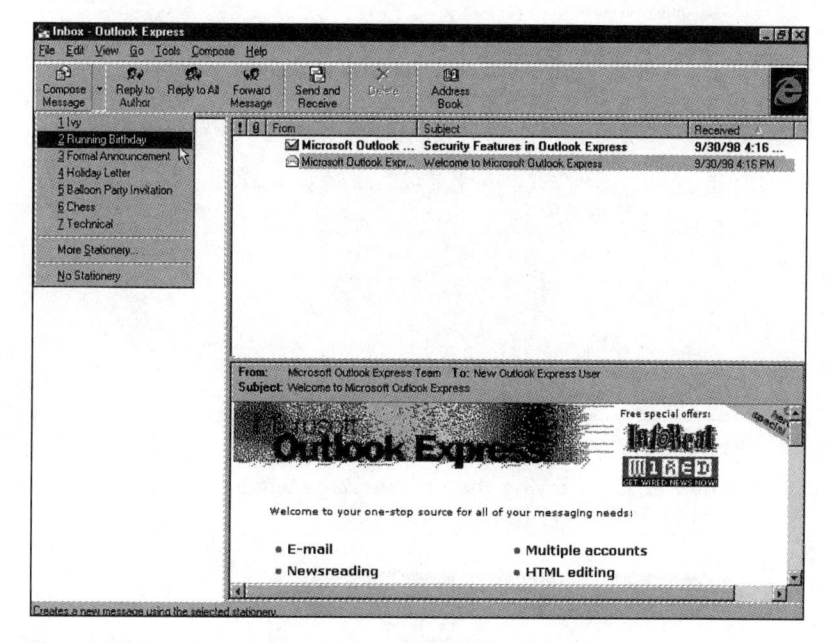

Figure 13.26 Composing a new Outlook Express message.

40. A drop-down menu appears, where you are able to create a new message using either the special stationery that comes with Outlook Express or no stationery at all. Click the option that you want (if you want stationery, select the type you want), which then takes you into a new message window with that stationery shown in the background of the New Message window as seen in Figure 13.27.

41. The first step in composing any new message is deciding whom you want to send the message to. So, click the To area so that you can enter the recipient(s) name(s), which must be separated by a semicolon or a comma.

42. You can, of course, click the little index card icon located at the start of the To area, which enables you to select recipient name(s) directly from the Outlook Express Address Book, as shown in Figure 13.28.

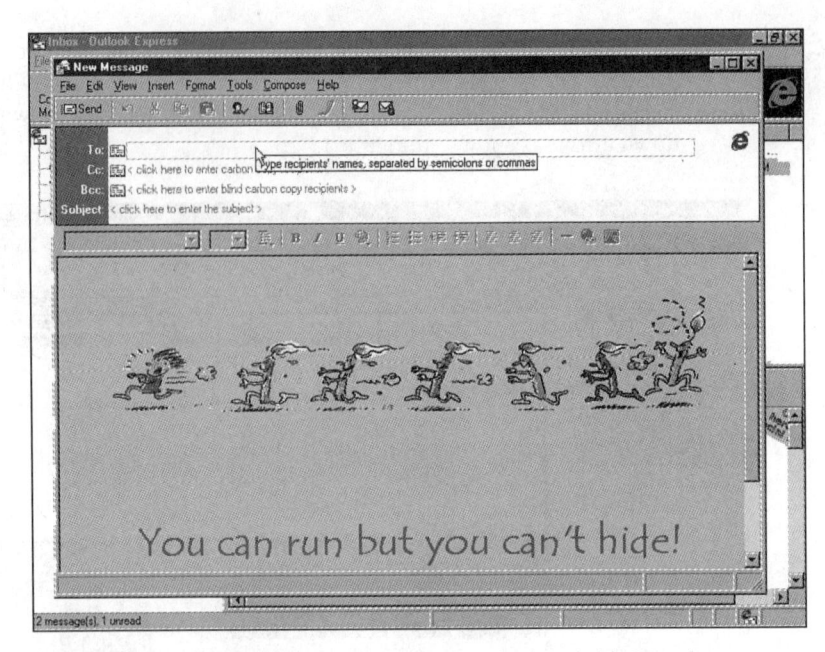

Figure 13.27 Viewing the new message window with Running Birthday stationery background.

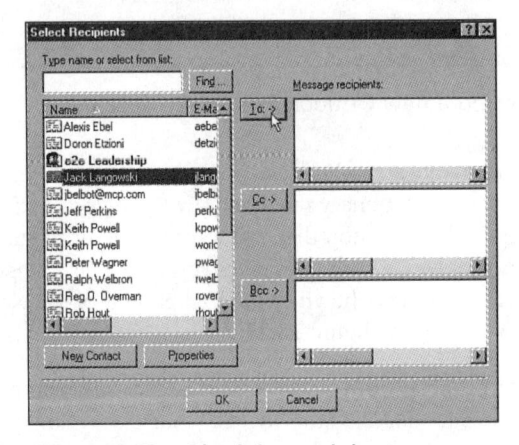

Figure 13.28 Obtaining recipient names from the Outlook Express Address Book.

43. To select a recipient, click that person's name to select it, and then click the appropriate button (the To:, Cc:, or Bcc: buttons). A Cc: means that you want a carbon copy (that is, a copy of the message) to be sent to the person in the Cc: field. A Bcc: means the same thing, except that the original recipients of the message (the ones in the To: field) don't know that you have copied these persons on this message.

13.2
CONFIGURE AND USE THE OUTLOOK EXPRESS EMAIL CLIENT

If you need more information regarding the use of the Address Book, you might want to see section 13.6, "How do I use the Outlook Express Address Book," for further details.

44. After you have made all your selections, click OK. This takes you back to your new message, but with the names of all the recipients that you selected, as shown in Figure 13.29.

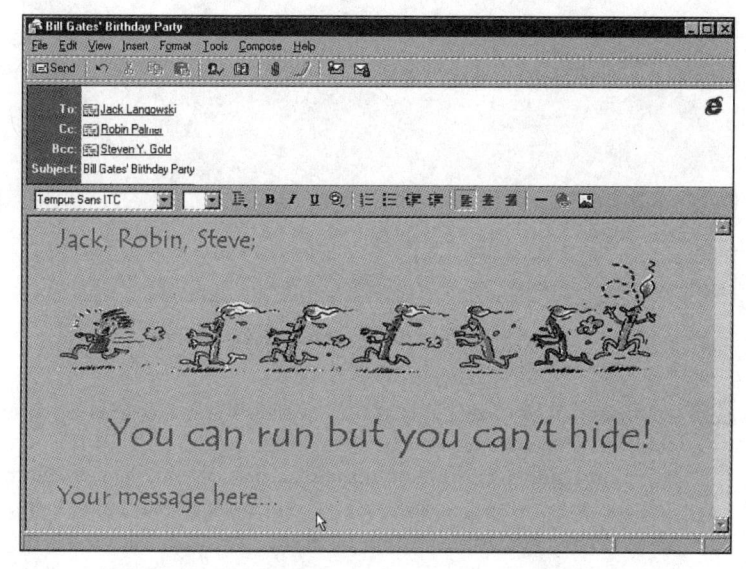

Figure 13.29 Reviewing your recipient name(s) selections.

45. From this point, all you need to do is type a Subject (this is an optional field, though) and the message itself, and then click the Send button (located near the top-left side of the New Message window). However, before you actually send your newly created message, you might want to set a few extra Outlook Express features for this message.

46. To set additional message options, click the Tools menu option, and then click again on the Set Priority menu selection as shown in Figure 13.30.

47. You are able to set a High, Normal, or Low priority for every message you send. This is actually a priority level for your use only, as it does not really set a delivery schedule priority for the recipient of the message. However, it can be useful to you for those times when you review your dozens or hundreds of sent email messages. Make your selection, if any, before continuing on.

Figure 13.30 Setting a priority for your new message.

48. Assume that you decide that the stationery you chose is not quite right for you or your occasion. To change it requires a few quick menu selections, instead of a complete reconstruction of your new email message. To change your message's background, click the Format menu option, and then click again on the Apply Stationery menu selection as shown in Figure 13.31.

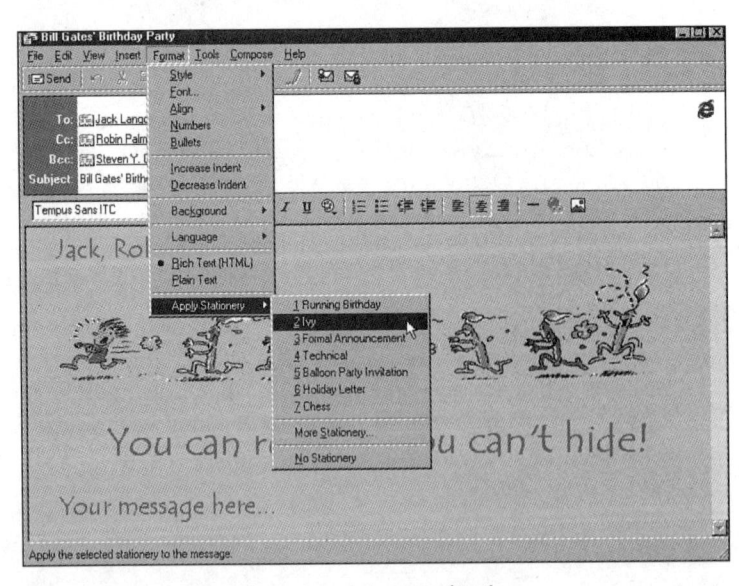

Figure 13.31 Changing a stationery selection.

13.2
CONFIGURE AND USE THE OUTLOOK EXPRESS EMAIL CLIENT

49. As you can see by looking at Figure 13.32, the change in the stationery's format occurs instantly. However, the strange thing about the way the change process works is that it simply overlays the new background directly on the old one.

Figure 13.32 Reviewing a stationery change.

50. Okay, enough of the frivolous picture background changes. Something that everyone with an email package needs is the capability to send one or more file attachments. And to do that you need to click the Insert menu option, and then click again on the File Attachment... menu selection. Or, you could click the Paper Clip icon, which permits you to do the same thing only faster.

51. Next, you see a Windows Explorer–type window appear, where you need to find and select the file that you want to attach to your email message. After you have located the file, click that file, and then click the Attach button.

52. This returns you to the message that you are editing, with the attached file. If you want more than one file attachment for this message, repeat this attachment process. After you are finished, you are ready to send the message.

CHAPTER 13
EMAIL AND NEWS

> **NOTE**
>
> If you send two or more file attachments in the same email message, they are sent in the .MIM format. Sometimes, if these files are not automatically extracted, the files might require some sort of decompression software. WinZip claims to not officially support this file format type, but it does work (see http://www.winzip.com/ to purchase a copy of their very valuable utility software).

53. To quickly send the message, click the Send button, which is located on the upper-left side of the message screen. However, if you so desire, you can send this message at a later time or date, depending on your needs. You do this by clicking the File menu option, and then clicking again on the Send Later menu selection. Doing this merely sends the message to your outbox. However, the message isn't actually sent anywhere until you connect to your email service provider (such as your organization's LAN/messaging server or an ISP) and click the Send and Receive button that is found along the top toolbar of the Outlook Express application.

54. A neat feature of Microsoft Outlook Express is that it can automatically detect your default email message type for the recipients that you have entered into your Address Book. For example, if you have some Internet-based recipients who can receive only plain text (ASCII) messages, sending that type of person an HTML-based file would be pretty worthless. Luckily, the Outlook Express application that comes with Windows 98 takes care of all this techy stuff behind the scenes automatically, as shown in Figure 13.33.

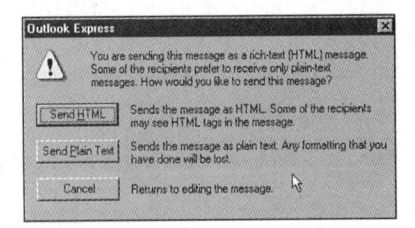

Figure 13.33 Deciding on an email message send format.

55. If this screen appears, you must decide whether to send the message in either HTML or plain text. It would be wise to always go with the lowest common denominator, which means that if even a single person requires plain text then everyone should be sent a plain text file. A better method is to group your recipients by message format type so that you can send HTML files to HTML people and plain text messages to the others.

13.2
CONFIGURE AND USE THE OUTLOOK EXPRESS EMAIL CLIENT

56. After you have sent a file, it is moved to the Microsoft Outlook Express Outbox as seen in Figure 13.34.

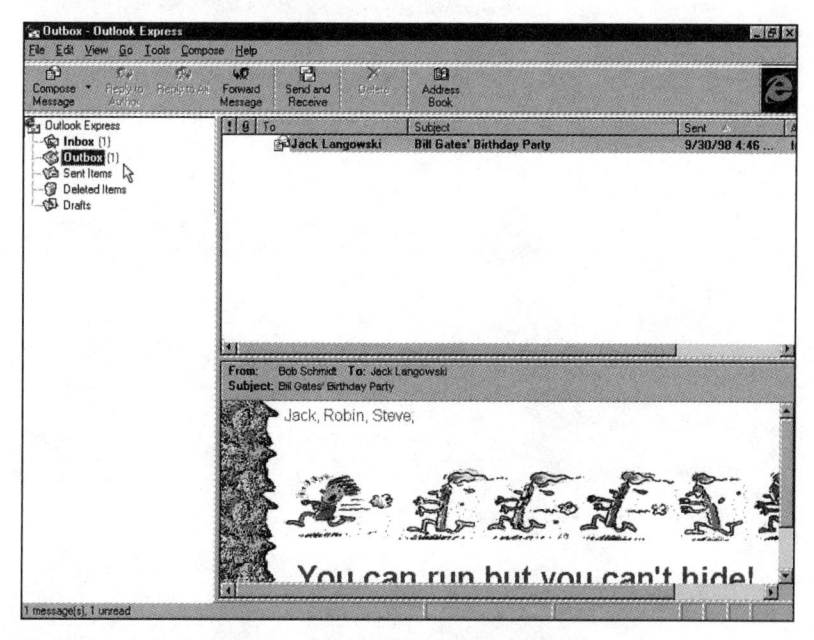

Figure 13.34 Reviewing outgoing message headers.

57. The number in the brackets to the right of the label Outbox represents the total number of messages waiting in your outbox for transmission to their ultimate destinations. After those messages are sent, these messages automatically disappear from the outbox.

58. If you click the Sent Items icon in the Outlook Express tree (in the column on the left, below the Outbox icon), you are taken to the screen shown in Figure 13.35.

59. All the items in this screen have already been sent via your messaging server on their way to their ultimate destinations. Underneath the column header Sent, you see the exact time and date that the message was transmitted from your PC and started its journey towards its destination.

60. If you highlight a message and then either press the Delete key on your keyboard or drag it over to the Deleted Items icon, that message is removed from your system. Well, almost, anyway. You guessed it! That message now resides in the Deleted Items area of Outlook Express, as shown in Figure 13.36 and remains there until you empty your trash.

CHAPTER 13
EMAIL AND NEWS

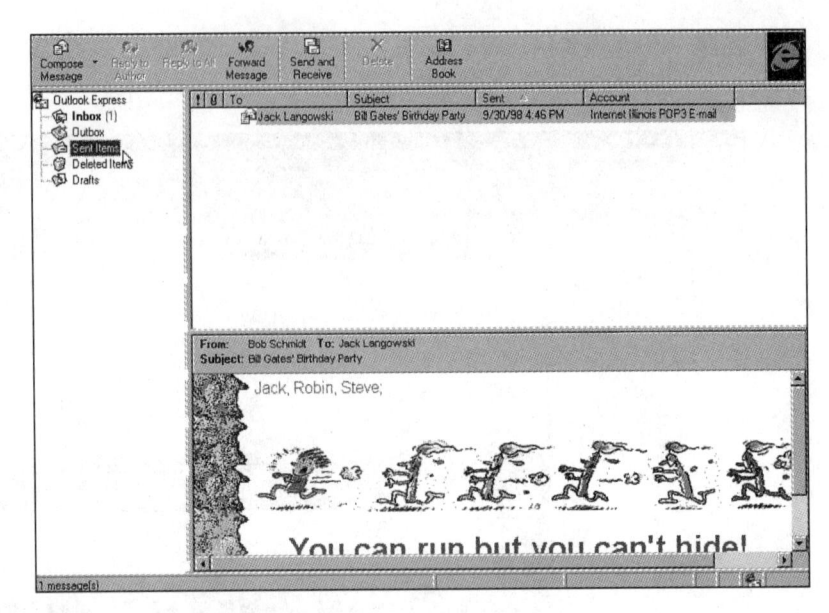

Figure 13.35 Reviewing sent messages.

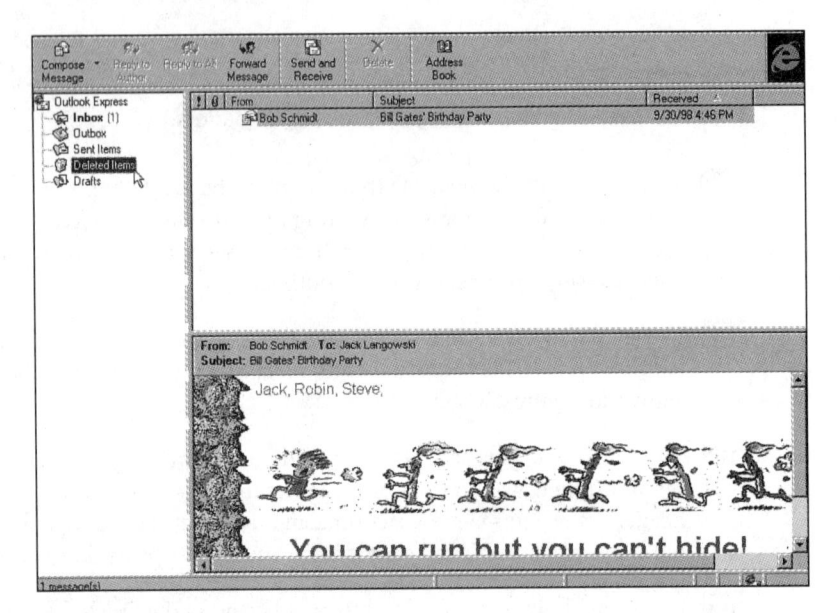

Figure 13.36 Reviewing deleted items.

61. There is one final feature that you should be aware of when working with email in the Outlook Express environment: forwarding mail. To forward any message, you need to first select it by clicking to highlight it. Keep in mind that although the example shown might make it appear that you

13.2
CONFIGURE AND USE THE OUTLOOK EXPRESS EMAIL CLIENT

can only forward messages out of the Inbox, you can actually forward messages from any of the icon placeholders in the Outlook Express tree (Inbox, Outbox, Sent Items, Drafts, or Deleted Items).

62. So, to forward an item, click it once to highlight it and then right-click that same item to reveal the menu shown in Figure 13.37.

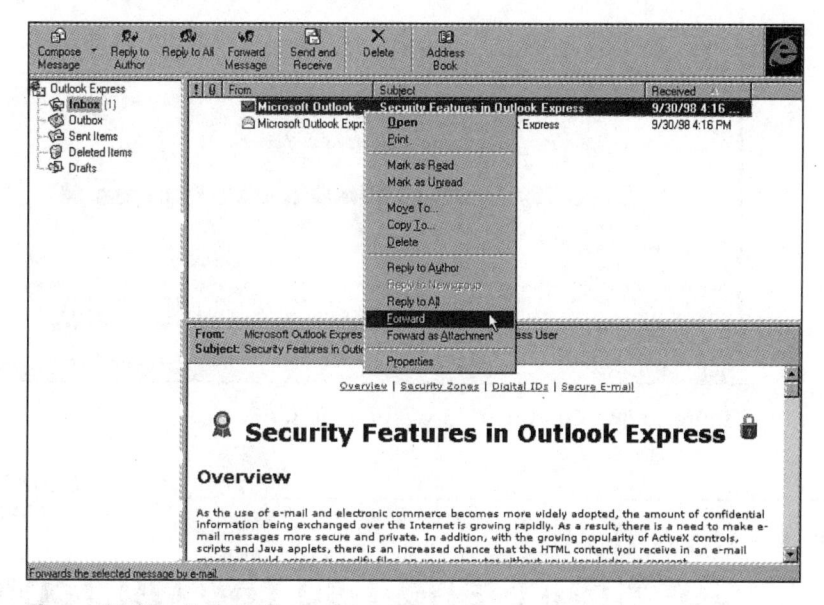

Figure 13.37 Forwarding a message.

63. Move your mouse pointer all the way down to the Forward menu selection and click it. This opens a new message area with your original subject already inside the Subject area and your original message in the text area, as shown in Figure 13.38.

64. Fill in the blanks (the To:, Cc:, and Bcc:) and change the Subject line if you want. Add any text you want to the message body and then click the Send button to forward this message to its intended recipient(s).

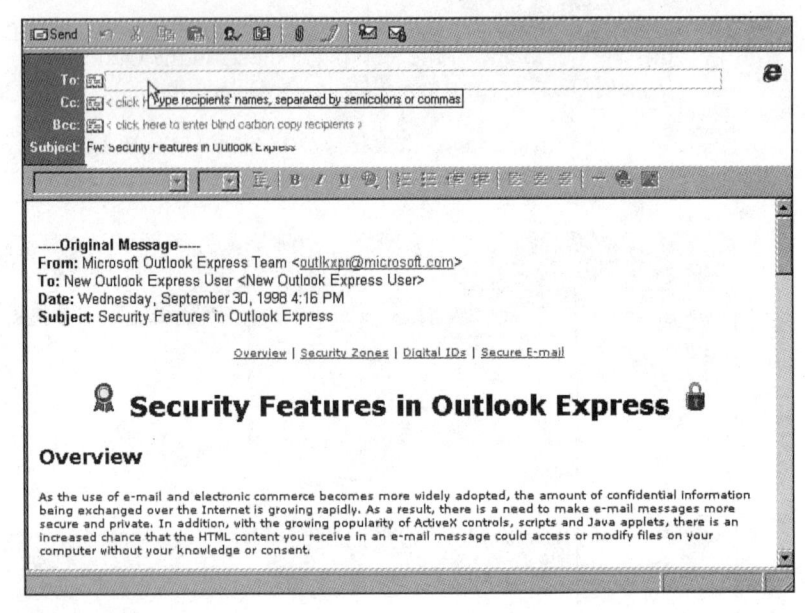

Figure 13.38 Creating a forwarded message.

COMPLEXITY
INTERMEDIATE

13.3 How do I...
Configure and use the Outlook Express newsreader component?

Problem

Okay. I have successfully installed the Microsoft Outlook Express software. I want to use it now, so that I can connect to Internet newsgroups. What do I need to do to configure Outlook Express so that it can be used for Internet newsgroups, and then what are some basic ways to use newsgroups?

Technique

Configuring Outlook Express for use with newsgroups, such as those offered via your ISP, is not a difficult task. An Internet account is required and should be provided by your ISP or your organization's network administrator (though many companies do not permit access. to Internet newsgroups via the corporate network, through the firewall). You begin access by starting the Microsoft Outlook Express application and then using the configuration screens to create a new account for your newsgroups connection. After this is finished, there are a few things you should know about when using Internet newsgroups, which are discussed within this discussion thread.

13.3 CONFIGURE AND USE OUTLOOK EXPRESS NEWSREADER COMPONENT

Steps

1. To begin using Outlook Express, click the Start button, select the Programs menu option, choose the Internet Explorer menu option, and then click once more on the Outlook Express menu selection.

2. This takes you directly into the Microsoft Outlook Express application, as shown in Figure 13.39.

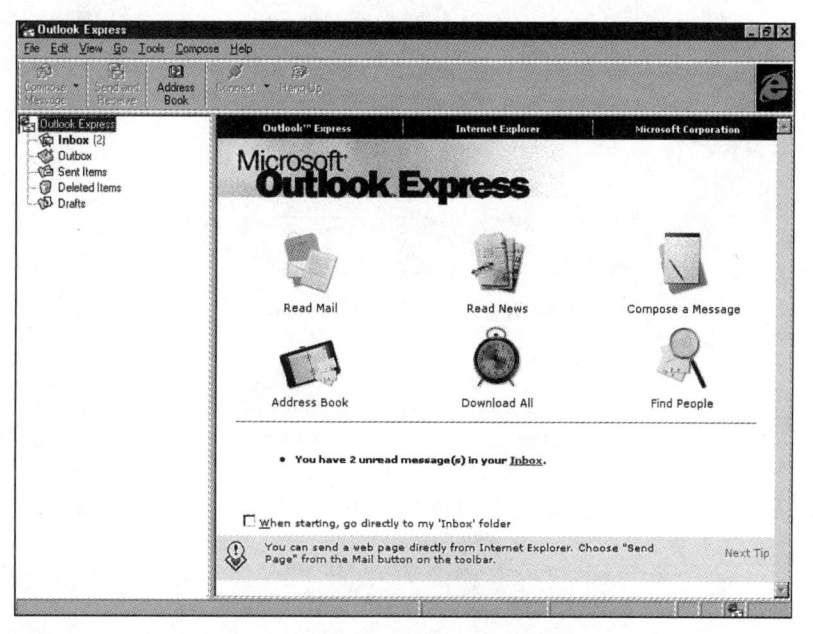

Figure 13.39 The opening screen of Outlook Express.

3. After the primary screen of Outlook Express opens, you can quickly figure out the basics by looking at it. Over to the left is a tree-like structure that permits quick access to all the folders within the application: Inbox, Outbox, Sent Items, Deleted Items, and Drafts (a draft is a message that you composed and closed, but haven't sent yet).

4. In the window to the right you see the high-level topic known as Microsoft Outlook Express, which is a very graphical way to access those very same folders in the tree structure. Obviously, by clicking once on the Outlook Express folder option (at the top of the folder tree on the left), you are able to see this top-level GUI presentation of your Outlook Express folder options. Each time you click one of the folders—whether it's the Inbox, the Drafts, and so on—that folder's contents appear in the window to the right.

5. Moving on, you want to click the Tools menu option and then click again on the Accounts... menu selection.

6. The Internet Accounts window appears. After it opens, click the News tab to be taken to that screen (the Internet Accounts window opens with the All tab showing), as shown in Figure 13.40.

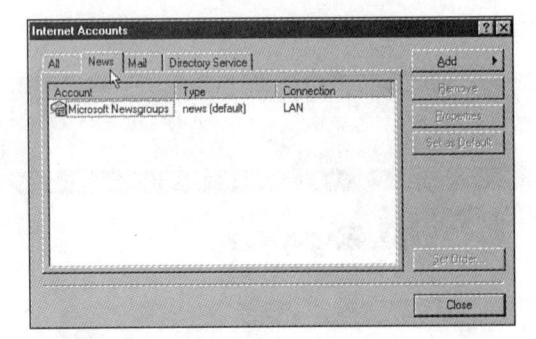

Figure 13.40 The News tab of the Internet Accounts window.

7. Click the Add button to reveal a small menu, which contains three options: Mail..., News..., Directory Service... (these menu selections are used to create new mail, news, or directory service accounts). Click the News... menu selection, which reveals the screen shown in Figure 13.41.

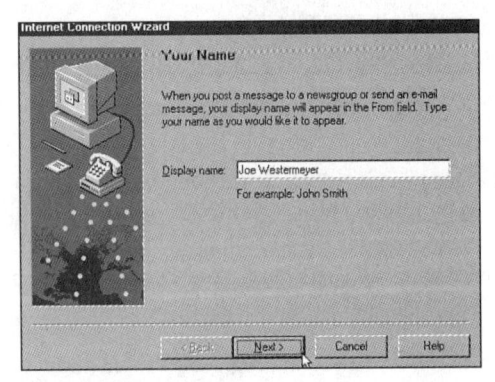

Figure 13.41 The opening screen of the Internet Connection Wizard.

8. On this first screen of the Internet Connection Wizard you need to fill in the name that appears whenever you post a message to a newsgroup. I strongly recommend that you do not use your real name, much less your full name, and perhaps instead use the name of someone else such as an

13.3
CONFIGURE AND USE OUTLOOK EXPRESS NEWSREADER COMPONENT 603

old drinking buddy or someone famous (as in the example shown). After you have input the text that you want, click the Next> button to continue the process. This takes you to the screen shown in Figure 13.42.

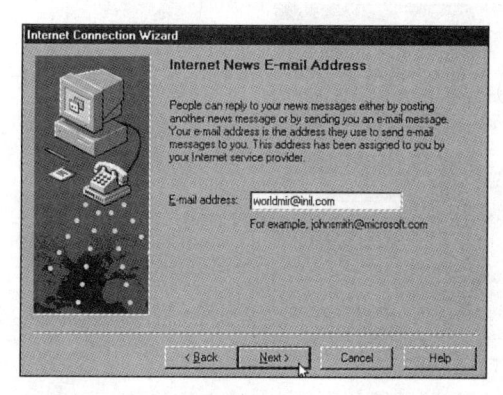

Figure 13.42 Entering your full Internet email address.

9. On this screen you need to type in the complete Internet email address that was assigned to you by your email administrator or ISP. After you have input the text that you want, click Next> to continue the process. This takes you to the screen shown in Figure 13.43.

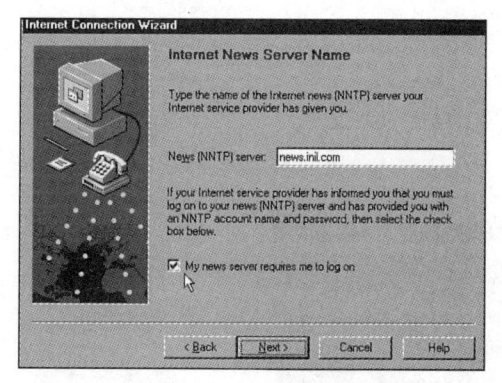

Figure 13.43 Entering a news server name.

10. At this point you need to determine whether the Internet newsgroup account you are configuring requires you to log on to it or not (the vast majority of news servers do not). To use a logon ID and password with a news server, click the check box near the bottom of the screen to select it.

11. After you have input the name of the news server, click Next> to continue the process. This takes you to the screen shown in Figure 13.44.

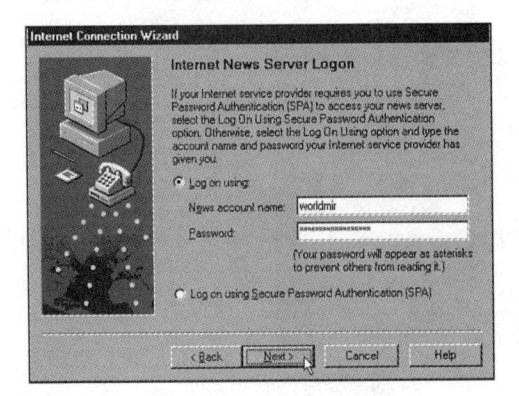

Figure 13.44 Selecting an authentication method.

12. If you did not request a news server that requires logon information, this screen doesn't appear during your use of the Internet Connection Wizard. However, because you did request one, you need to click one of the two radio buttons. The top one forces you to input a user ID (it calls it a News account name) and a password. The bottom option uses the SPA option. In both cases you must have been preassigned an account and password of some sort in order to use either of these two options correctly.

13. After you have input the necessary information, click Next> to continue the process. This takes you to the screen shown in Figure 13.45.

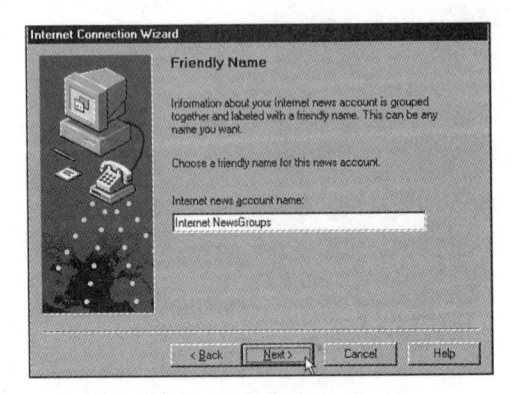

Figure 13.45 Selecting a friendly name for the Internet news account.

13.3 CONFIGURE AND USE OUTLOOK EXPRESS NEWSREADER COMPONENT

14. On this screen you need to create a descriptive name for your Internet news account. This should be a name that helps you to remember exactly what is in this news server's newsgroups. However, you are able to type about anything you want, so feel free to take as great a poetic license as you want. After you have input the friendly name, click the Next> button to continue the process. This takes you to the screen shown in Figure 13.46.

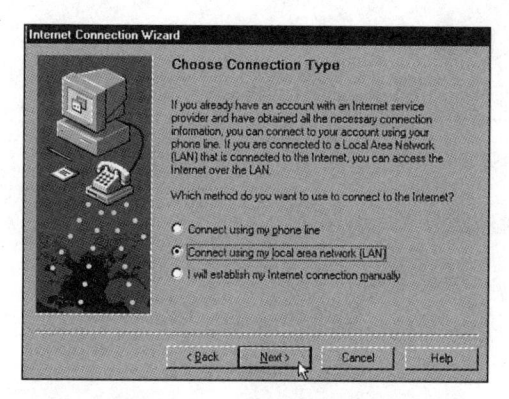

Figure 13.46 Choosing an Internet connection type.

15. The Internet Connection Wizard continues by prompting you to select an Internet connection type. To choose one, click the radio button next to the type that is required for you to connect your PC to the Internet. The top choice requires the use of a telephone, while the second means that you are using a network connection, and the third signifies that you do not want to change a selection that you already have in place (that is, you need to manually establish your own connection each time you want to use the Outlook Express newsgroups).

16. After you make your selection, click Next> to continue the process. This takes you to the screen shown in Figure 13.47.

17. Review the information on this screen, and then click Finish to end the wizard. This returns you to the Internet Accounts screen, as shown in Figure 13.48.

18. To complete the configuration process, click Close to exit this screen. You then find yourself in the main Outlook Express screen.

19. You might want to make certain that you have already established a connection to the Internet. If you have not done so, establish that connection to the Internet first (refer to Chapter 9 for more details).

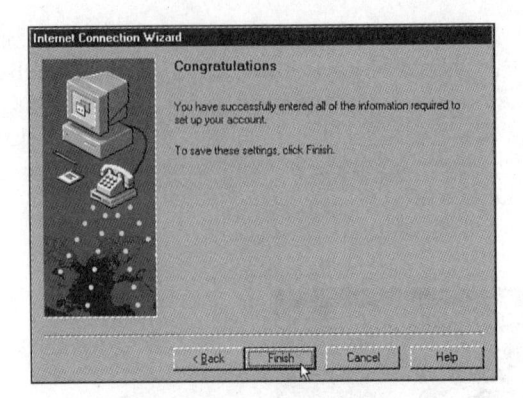

Figure 13.47 Completing the wizard.

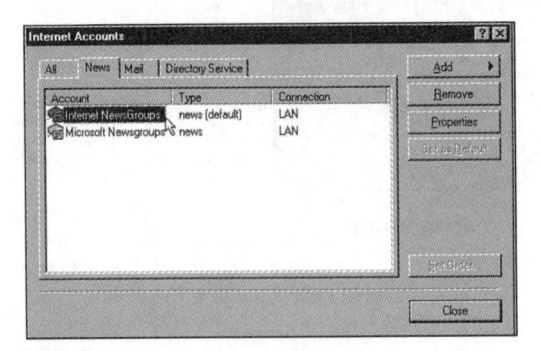

Figure 13.48 Reviewing your newly created news account.

20. Click the newsgroup account that you made, and then click the Newsgroups icon in the center of the top toolbar of this Outlook Express screen. This takes you into the Newsgroups screen shown in Figure 13.49.

21. All your news server accounts appear in the column on the left, and their active newsgroups appear in the center window area on the right. If there is a little newspaper icon to the left of a newsgroup's name, this means that you have already subscribed to that newsgroup. Otherwise, there is no icon, which means that the newsgroup has not yet been subscribed to—you must first subscribe to a newsgroup before you can download and read its contents.

22. Subscribing is easy. Click the newsgroup you want and click the Subscribe button. You can also double-click any newsgroup, which has the same effect.

13.3
CONFIGURE AND USE OUTLOOK EXPRESS NEWSREADER COMPONENT

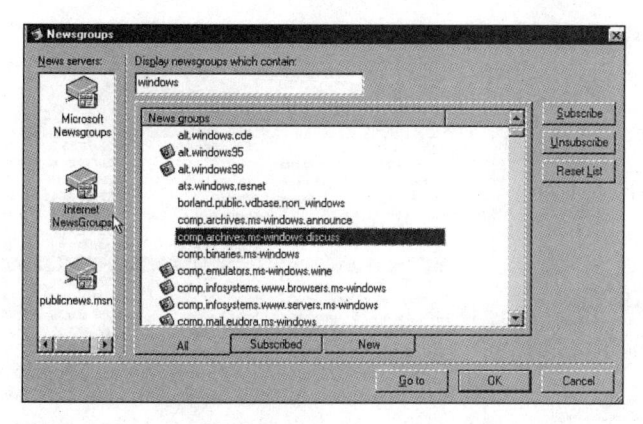

Figure 13.49 Selecting newsgroups to review.

23. To select all the newsgroups at once, click the top one, and then while holding the Shift key down, go to the bottom of the list and click the bottom newsgroup. Then, click the Subscribe button.

24. The Unsubscribe button does that very thing—it unsubscribes you from a newsgroup. The Reset List button automatically resets the listing of newsgroups so that it becomes up-to-date with all the correct newsgroup names and descriptions. After you make all your selections, click OK to exit this screen.

25. After you return to the main Outlook Express screen, click any newsgroup in the left column to reveal its contents, as shown in Figure 13.50.

26. If you examine the various newsgroups in the left column, you see a number inside a set of brackets to the right of each newsgroup name. This number is the total number of items that are contained within that newsgroup's discussion thread. However, this does not necessarily mean that you have already downloaded the contents of that entire newsgroup. For example, if you look in the right column you see that a message has been highlighted, but the contents appear to be missing. The statement, "This message is not cached," means that you have not yet downloaded this newsgroup message.

27. A quick way to determine whether a message has been downloaded yet is to closely examine its icon. Look at the highlighted message. The icon appears to only be a tiny note with two lines of text, which means that the full message has not been downloaded (only the header, which you are reading, has been downloaded). Now look at the message two above the highlighted message. The icon resembles a full page of text, which means that this message has been completely downloaded.

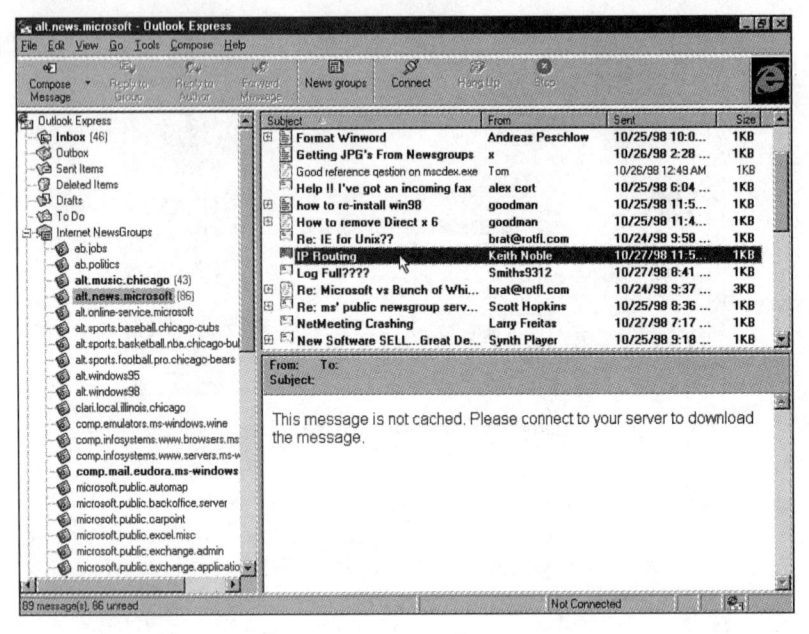

Figure 13.50 Reviewing newsgroup contents.

28. Moving on, if you first right-click the name of the newsgroup in the left column, and then click the Properties menu option on the small pop-up menu that appears, you see the Properties screen for that particular newsgroup as shown in Figure 13.51.

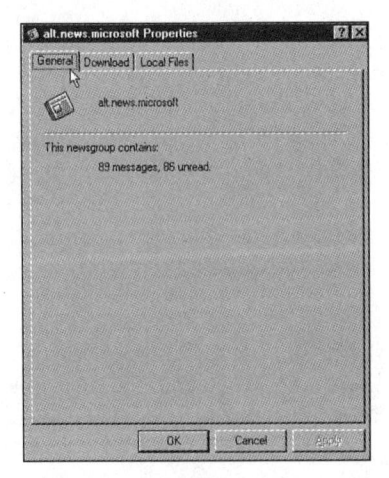

Figure 13.51 Reviewing a newsgroup's properties screen.

13.3 CONFIGURE AND USE OUTLOOK EXPRESS NEWSREADER COMPONENT

29. The first screen that appears is the General tab. This gives you the full name of the newsgroup and the number of messages that are contained within it, as well as how many of these messages you have yet to read. This is an informational screen only.

30. Click the Download tab to reveal the contents of that screen, as shown in Figure 13.52.

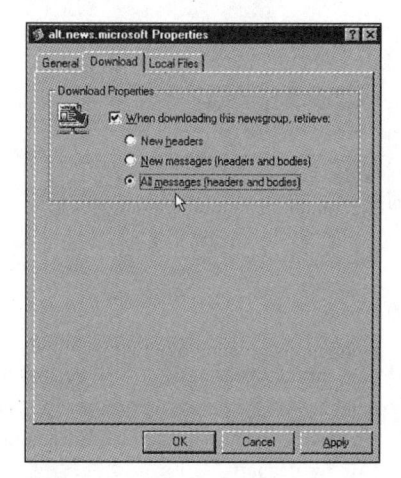

Figure 13.52 Reviewing newsgroup download options.

31. This is where you can specify how much information is automatically downloaded with each newsgroup. Click the top check box to select it, which then un-grays all the radio button options. Then, select how much data you would like to download for this particular newsgroup.

32. After you make your selection, click the Local Files tab to reveal the contents of that screen, as shown in Figure 13.53.

33. The purpose of this screen is to help you minimize the amount of storage space a newsgroup occupies on your computer. As you read, download, delete, and respond to messages, you create some wasted space on your PC that can only be reclaimed using a processes known as compaction. Click the Compact button to do that. The File Information area at the top of this screen informs you of how much space is being wasted by this newsgroup.

34. Click the Remove Messages button to delete all the message bodies that you have previously downloaded to your PC. This is helpful if you have not used this newsgroup in quite some time and want to see the most recent information in the discussion threads anyway.

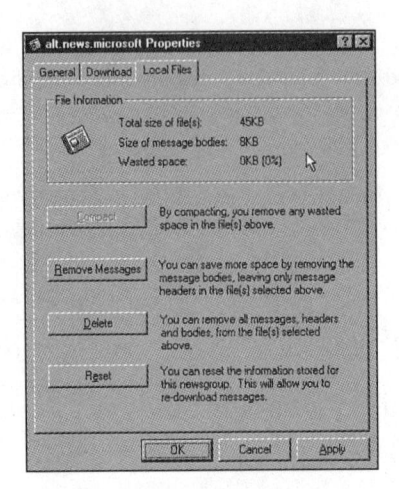

Figure 13.53 Reviewing newsgroup message compaction and deletion options.

35. Click the Delete button to delete all the messages—the headers as well as the bodies—that you have previously downloaded to your PC. This is useful if you have not used this newsgroup in quite some time and want to get a completely fresh start using it again.

36. Click the Reset button to restore the default information for this newsgroup. You can then download all the messages (this is similar to adding the newsgroup for the first time).

37. After you make your selections, click OK to close this screen and return to the primary Outlook Express screen.

38. The remaining area that is of any importance for using newsgroups with Outlook Express is the Tools menu option, as shown in Figure 13.54.

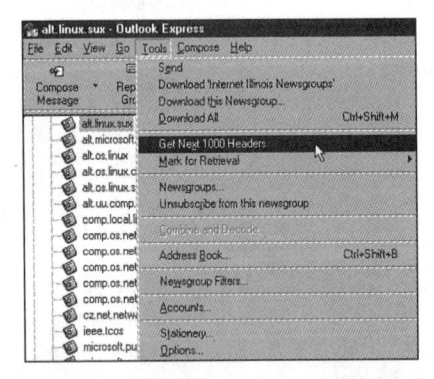

Figure 13.54 Reviewing tools menu options.

39. Use the Tools menu option to access the Accounts area, to download a particular newsgroup or all of them at once, and to mark specific newsgroups for retrieval purposes (done during a "Download All" download session). Newsgroups can be filtered so that you do not see postings from particular individuals or messages that do not fall within a specific date range. About the only real special item on this menu is the Get Next 1000 Headers menu selection, which enables you to download the next 1,000 header messages for a particular newsgroup. (However, if you download this many, you have way too much free time on your hands.)

COMPLEXITY
INTERMEDIATE

13.4 How do I... Configure Outlook Express when I have multiple users on the same PC?

Problem

Several people in my family want to use the family PC for sending and receiving email. However, it is agreed that everyone needs their own account, stored in a separate location on the hard drive so that no one can accidentally delete someone else's email and newsgroup data. Is there a way to configure this type of setup with Windows 98, without having to purchase any additional software or extra hardware?

Technique

The answer is yes. It is very simple to configure, and it's much easier than most people would ever expect. The first thing you need to do is configure your Windows 98 PC for multiple users (review section 10.3, "How do I configure my system for multiple users?" in Chapter 10, "Welcome to the Neighborhood: Network, That Is" for instructions on doing this). Next, you must install Outlook Express, if you haven't already done so. Follow the steps in section 13.1, "How do I install the Internet email and newsgroup components of Windows 98?" for details on how to do this. Finally, logon to your PC and examine the configurations. To do this, follow the next set of instructions.

Steps

1. Configure your PC for multiple users, preferably using the Microsoft Windows 98 "Family Logon" networking service.

2. Install Outlook Express.

3. Examine your PC to ensure that the proper folder structure has been established. You need to sign on to your computer at least twice, using at least two different users, This then creates at least two folder structures, so you can more easily examine what is actually being created by Windows 98.

4. To view your system, use Windows Explorer and maneuver your way over to the \Windows\Profiles directory (found on the Windows 98 boot drive; usually the C:\ drive), as shown in Figure 13.55.

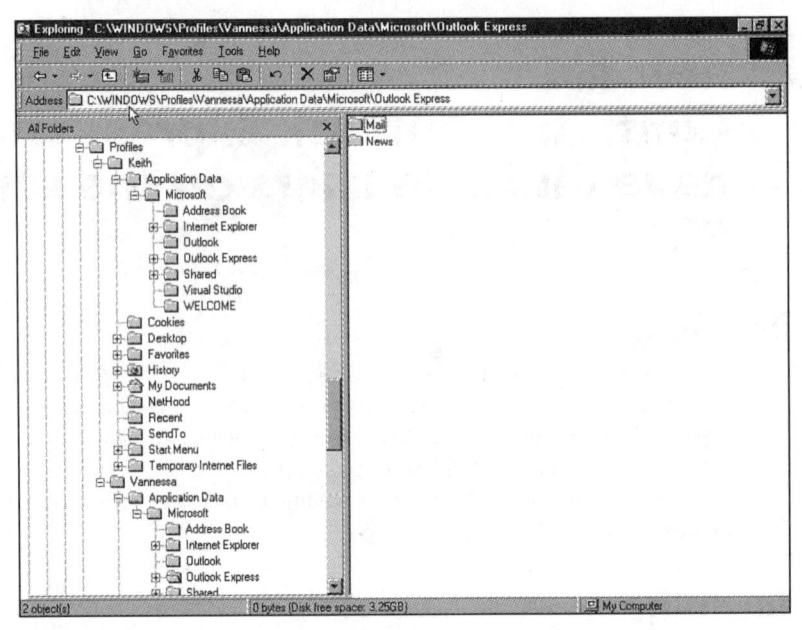

Figure 13.55 Reviewing a multiuser configuration for Outlook Express messaging.

5. Directly below the Profiles folder are folders for each of the users on this PC: Keith and Vannessa. (Follow the lines straight down to see how the folder structure really plays out.) Within each of these Windows 98 users are the same folder structures that Windows 98 automatically creates for you (see, I told you this would be really easy). And, finally, down inside the \Microsoft folder are the Internet and messaging applications (such as Outlook Express) folders. Within the Outlook Express folder you see two more folders: one for Mail and one for News. This is where your Microsoft Outlook Express email files and newsgroups data messages are stored. No mess, no confusion—one distinctly separate set of folders for each Windows 98 user. It is that simple.

COMPLEXITY
INTERMEDIATE

13.5 How do I...
Perform Outlook Express maintenance tasks?

Problem

What, if any, are the maintenance items that must be performed within Outlook Express on a periodic basis? Additionally, how do I use Inbox Assistant to help me maintain a better organized Outlook Express operating environment?

Technique

There are a few maintenance items that should be attended to within Outlook Express. Failure to perform these maintenance items doesn't necessarily result in the crash of your Windows 98 PC, even after months or years of neglect, but they might cause your computer to operate a bit more sluggishly than it otherwise would. All these maintenance items are started from within the main Outlook Express screen, using the general toolbar that is at the top of this application. Additionally, the Inbox Assistant is simple to use, after you are comfortable with the rest of the Outlook Express application.

Steps

1. To begin using Outlook Express, click the Start button, select the Programs menu option, choose the Internet Explorer menu option, and then click the Outlook Express menu selection.

2. This takes you directly into Outlook Express, as shown in Figure 13.56.

3. It is from this initial screen that everything happens within Outlook Express, whether it's email, newsgroups, or general Outlook Express maintenance items. If you click the File menu option, and choose the Folder menu selection, another sub-folder appears, as shown in Figure 13.57.

4. After you arrive at this menu, you need to decide whether you want to compact only the folder you had highlighted (immediately before you accessed this menu tree) or all your Outlook Express folders. I suggest that you compress them all, regardless of which ones you compressed the last time you ran the compaction option.

5. After you have completed the compaction process, click the View menu option, and then click again on the Layout... menu selection. This takes you into the screen shown in Figure 13.58.

CHAPTER 13
EMAIL AND NEWS

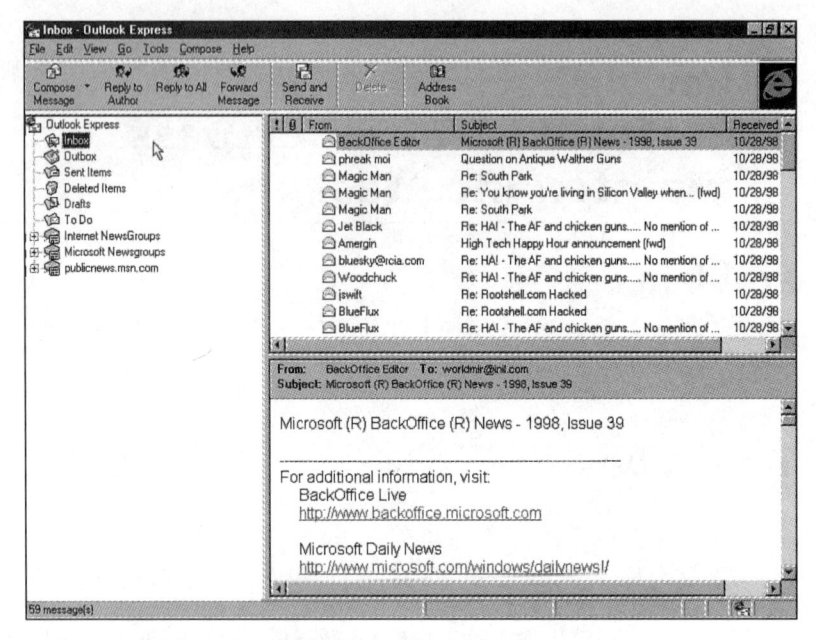

Figure 13.56 The opening screen of Outlook Express.

Figure 13.57 Accessing the compaction area of Outlook Express.

6. The Window Layout Properties screen is used to modify the existing Outlook Express menus and customize the toolbar that appears near the top of this screen.

7. Make the choices that you deem appropriate, and then continue to the next part of this configuration screen by clicking the Customize Toolbar... button. This takes you into the screen shown in Figure 13.59.

13.5 PERFORM OUTLOOK EXPRESS MAINTENANCE

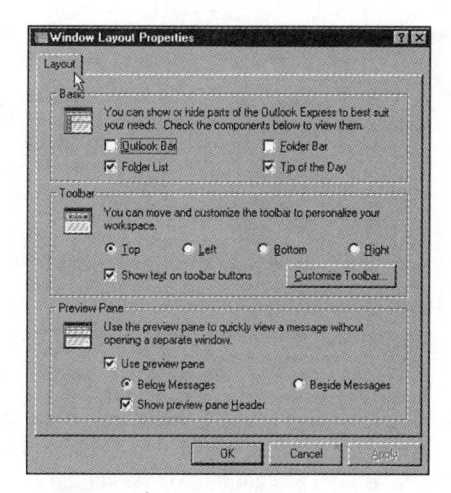

Figure 13.58 Changing the menu and toolbar views for Outlook Express.

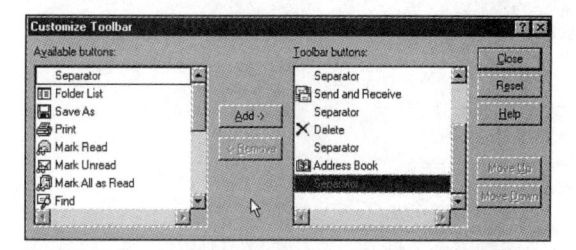

Figure 13.59 Modifying the Outlook Express toolbar.

8. The focal point of this screen is to modify the manner in which the Outlook Express toolbar is presented to users. Click an item in the left window, and then click Add to move it over to the right window, which means that it now appears on the Outlook Express toolbar. After you make the selections you want, click Close to return to the previous page. From there, click OK to return to the primary Outlook Express screen.

9. The next item you might want to examine is the Inbox Assistant, which is used to filter messages, perform automatic replies and forwards, move and copy messages to other specific Outlook Express folders, and perform specific server-side messaging functions. To access the Inbox Assistant, click the Tools menu option, and then click again on the Inbox Assistant... menu selection to reveal the screen shown in Figure 13.60.

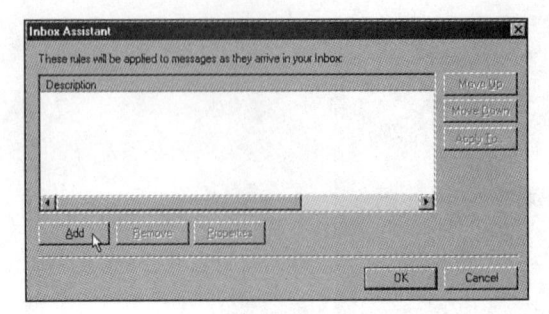

Figure 13.60 Using the Inbox Assistant.

10. This first screen displays a list of all the active messaging rules that presently are applied to your Inbox as messages arrive there. Most likely, the window shown is blank as you probably have not added any rules yet. To add one click Add, which takes you to the Properties window shown in Figure 13.61.

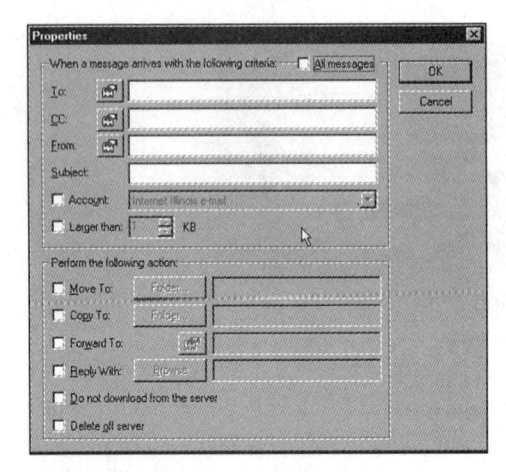

Figure 13.61 Adding a rule to the Outlook Express Inbox.

11. The top half of the window is used to define where the messages are originating that require a rule definition; the bottom half of this window is where you define precisely what you want done to a message, a specific group of messages, or all messages.

12. For example, you might click the To: icon, which takes you into the Outlook Express Address Book, where you can then select a specific individual's email address. Next, you return to this Properties window where you can specify that all messages that arrive from that person should automatically be moved to a To Do folder (which you must first create) and forwarded to another one of your email addresses (perhaps a work address or a personal ISP address). The options that you have are endless, as you can mix and match any and all these options in any manner you want. These rules are very straightforward to create. After you are finished making your selections, click OK to save your changes, activate them, and return to the main Inbox Assistant window, where you can view a descriptive listing of all your Inbox Assistant rules.

COMPLEXITY
BEGINNER

13.6 How do I...
Use the Outlook Express Address Book?

Problem

Okay, I have successfully installed Outlook Express. I want to use it now, but I do not understand why I need a separate address book, much less how to use it. So, what are some basic ways to use the Address Book and how can I best benefit from its use?

Technique

Using the Outlook Express Address Book is not difficult, because most of the content that you need to fill in is based on common sense (now, if you do not have any common sense, it might be a little bit more difficult). Go through this next set of instructions and soon you will be an expert Outlook Express Address Book user.

Steps

1. To begin using Outlook Express, click the Start button, select the Programs menu option, choose the Internet Explorer menu option, and then click once more on the Outlook Express menu selection.

2. This takes you directly into Outlook Express, as shown in Figure 13.62.

3. From here, accessing the Outlook Express Address Book is easy: Click the Address Book icon that appears on the Outlook Express toolbar. When you click the Address Book button, you might be prompted with a default vCard viewer message box as seen in Figure 13.63.

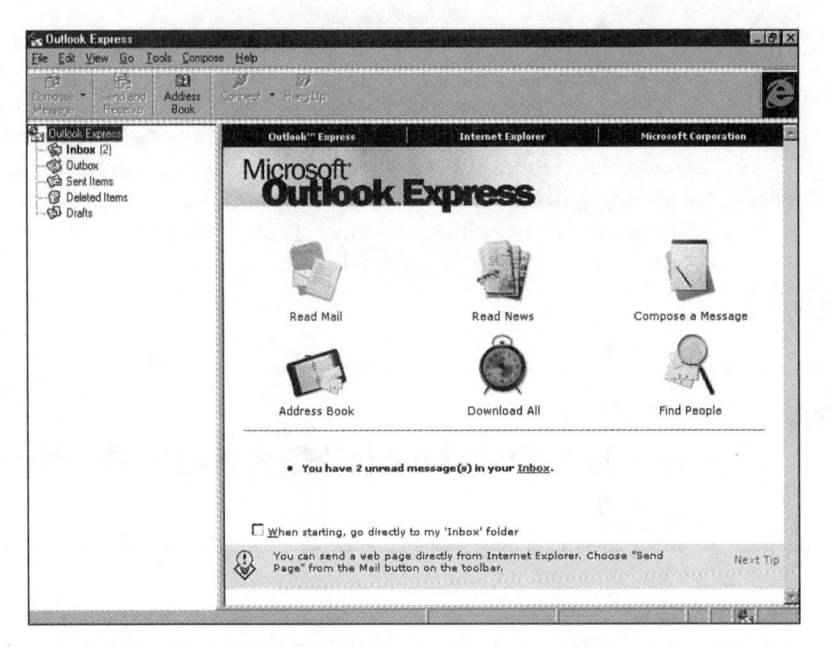

Figure 13.62 The opening screen of Outlook Express.

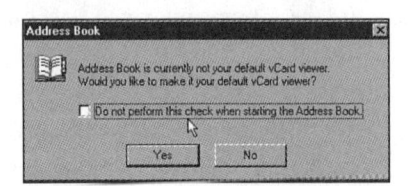

Figure 13.63 Determining whether to set the Outlook Express Address Book as the default vCard viewer.

4. If Outlook Express is the only messaging application on your PC, you will probably not see this message box. However, if you use the full-blown Microsoft Outlook client application for connecting to Exchange Server or as a Personal Information Manager tool, you are prompted to set it as the default. I recommend that you do not make this Address Book the default for your computer system, especially if you use your other messaging application for work or other specially developed applications. If you click the check box, you will no longer see this prompt regardless of the answer that you give now.

5. To continue, click either Yes or No, which takes you directly to the main screen of the Outlook Express Address Book, as shown in Figure 13.64.

13.6
USE THE OUTLOOK EXPRESS ADDRESS BOOK

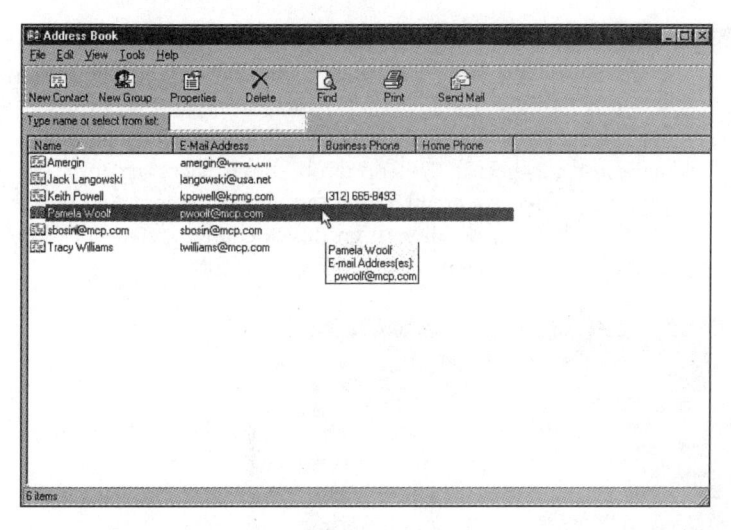

Figure 13.64 Reviewing the Outlook Express Address Book.

6. To view information about a name listed in your Address Book, click the name, which then displays a small box with that person's full name and email address.

7. To add someone new to the Address Book, click the New Contact button (the one on the far left side of the toolbar), which takes you into Properties screen for an Address Book contact. Keep in mind that these next six screens are the identical ones that you would see if you had clicked on the Properties button (the third button on the toolbar) for a particular entry in your Address Book. In either case, the first screen that you see is the Personal tab as shown in Figure 13.65.

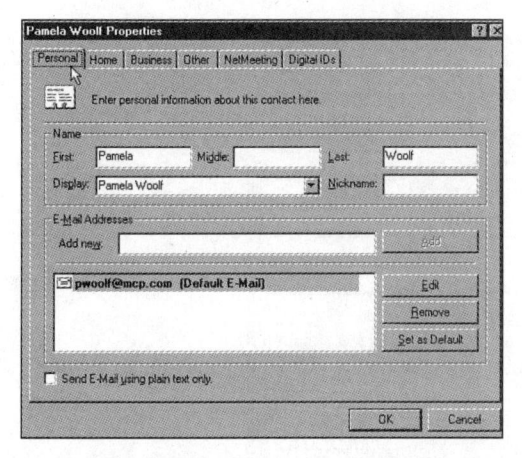

Figure 13.65 Adding personal information to an Address Book entry.

CHAPTER 13
EMAIL AND NEWS

8. This screen is used to enter the basic person/data information that can be saved along with someone's email address. An important option on this screen is found in the lower left-hand corner, and is labeled as Send E-mail Using Plain Text Only. Click this box, which then places a check mark in it to select it. This option becomes necessary for those recipients who cannot receive email in any format except as plain text (or ASCII). After you have made all your entries or changes, click the Home tab to continue to the screen shown in Figure 13.66.

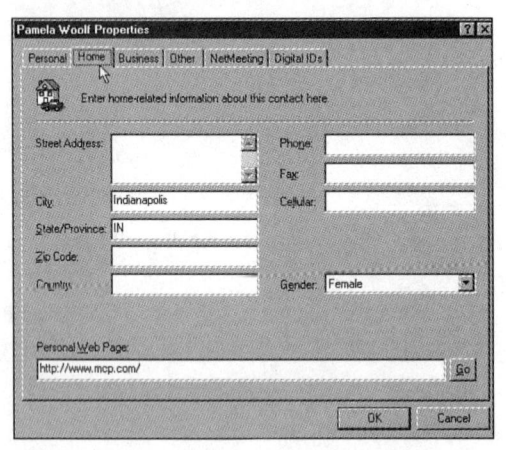

Figure 13.66 Entering home information.

9. On this screen you can enter information regarding your Address Book contact's home address; phone, fax, and cellular numbers; personal Web page; and gender. All this information is optional, so enter only the data that you want. After you have made all your entries and changes, click the Business tab to continue to the window shown in Figure 13.67.

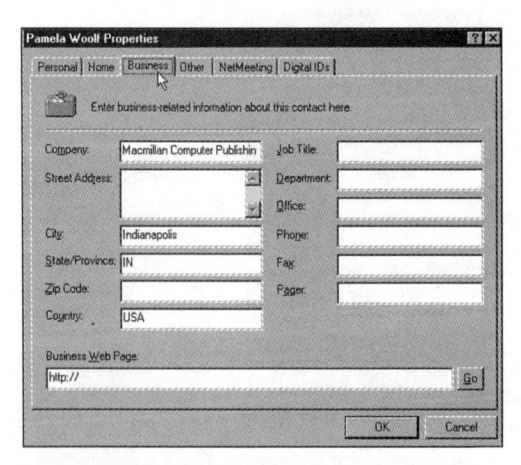

Figure 13.67 Entering business information.

13.6
USE THE OUTLOOK EXPRESS ADDRESS BOOK

10. On this screen you can enter information regarding your Address Book contact's business address, telephone numbers, business Web page, and job title. All this information is optional, so enter only the data that you want. After you make all your entries and changes, click the Other tab to continue to the window shown in Figure 13.68.

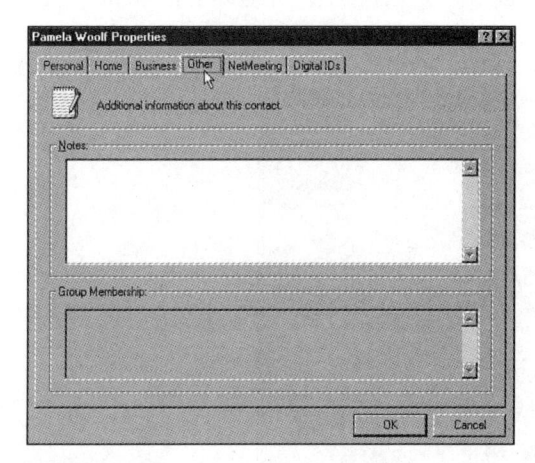

Figure 13.68 Entering other information.

11. On this screen you can enter notes regarding your Address Book contact. Anything you want to enter here is optional, so enter whatever you want. After you make all your entries and changes, click the NetMeeting tab to continue to the window shown in Figure 13.69.

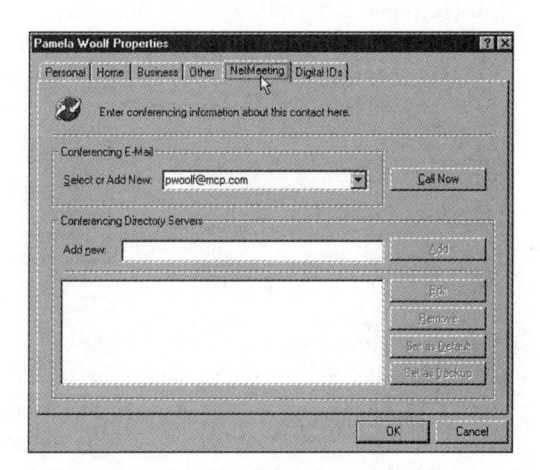

Figure 13.69 Entering NetMeeting information.

12. This screen permits you to define a default NetMeeting server as well as a listing of all other NetMeeting servers that are available for meeting up with this contact. To help you understand what NetMeeting is and why you would want to use it, refer to Chapter 18, "Teleconferencing the Multimedia Way," for more details. After you have made all your entries and changes, click the Digital IDs tab to continue to the window shown in Figure 13.70.

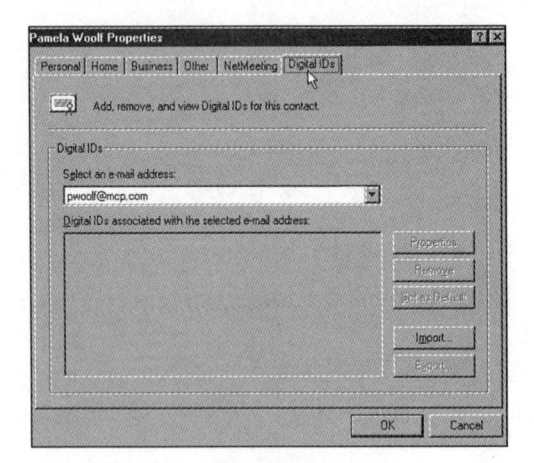

Figure 13.70 Entering digital ID Information.

13. Select an email address to use with your digital ID information and then click the Import button to add a digital ID for use with this account. If you do not understand what a digital ID is or how to get one, refer to section 13.7, later in this chapter. After you have made all your entries and changes, click OK to complete the process and return to the main Address Book screen.

14. The next topic that you might want to review is the use of distribution groups—known as Groups in Outlook Express terminology. To create one, click the New Group icon found on the toolbar. This takes you to the Editors Properties screen, as shown in Figure 13.71.

15. Creating a distribution list (Group) for use with your Outlook Express Address Book is very easy. Click the New Contact button to add brand-new contacts (using the screens you just saw), or click the Select Members button to add people from your existing Address Book lists. After you make your entries, click OK to save your new list and return to the primary Address Book screen.

13.6
USE THE OUTLOOK EXPRESS ADDRESS BOOK

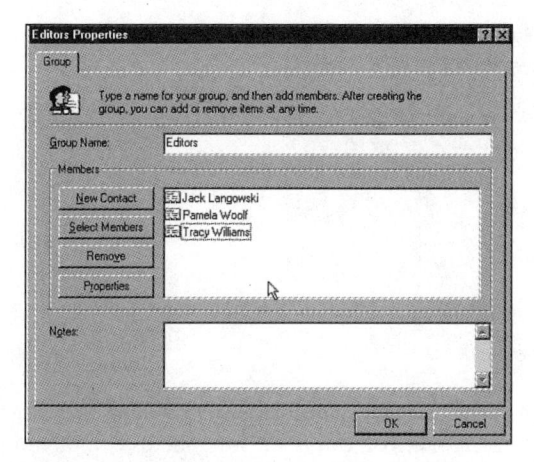

Figure 13.71 Creating a new Address Book group.

16. If you click the new distribution list that you just created, you see its descriptive name along with a complete listing of all the members of this new group, as shown in Figure 13.72.

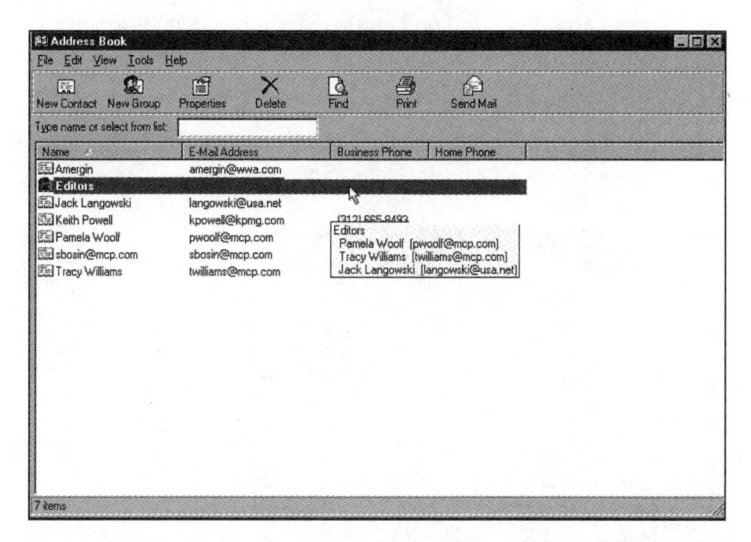

Figure 13.72 Reviewing your new Address Book group.

17. Next up is using the Find button from the primary Address Book screen. If you click this button on the toolbar, you are taken to the Find People screen shown in Figure 13.73.

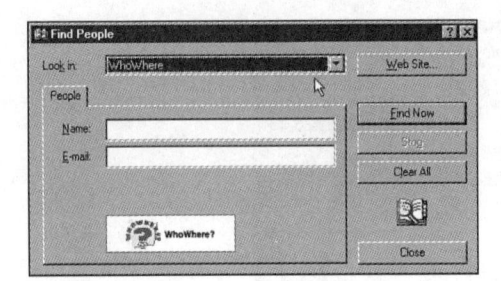

Figure 13.73 Finding people via the Internet.

18. The Find People screen appears, with a drop-down list box for the Look In area. From that list box you can select any one of a number of search areas (their logos are displayed on the bottom of this screen), which is where this search engine focuses its search. Of course, if you click the Web Site... button for any of these Look In locations, you are taken to that group's Internet Web site (assuming you have already established a connection to the Internet) where you can then search for people using a variety of other possible attributes (city, state, Zip code, telephone number, partial email address, and so on). After you have made all your entries and selections and completed your search efforts, click the Close button to return to the main Address Book screen.

19. If you click the Tools menu option, and then click again on the Accounts menu selection, you enter the Internet Accounts screen shown in Figure 13.74.

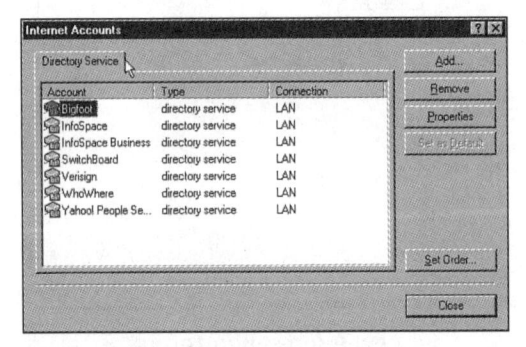

Figure 13.74 Reviewing and modifying existing directory service accounts.

20. A directory service account is actually an LDAP-formatted account, which means that it is readily accessible from an Internet messaging system such as Outlook Express. Additionally, as an Internet standard (RFC 2252) that

13.6
USE THE OUTLOOK EXPRESS ADDRESS BOOK

was last updated in December 1997, LDAP provides a standardized manner in which applications can access directory structures and information therein.

21. It is most likely that you will never need to add a new directory, as all the popular ones have automatically been added already for you. Chances are, though, that if you do need to add a new one, it is due to some change at your place of employment. In that case, click the Add... button and follow the few short prompts. When you are finished adding to or reviewing your directory services, Click Close to return to the main Address Book screen.

22. A quick way to send someone mail from your Outlook Express Address Book is to click that person to select him or her, and then right-click once to reveal a small pop-up menu as shown in Figure 13.75.

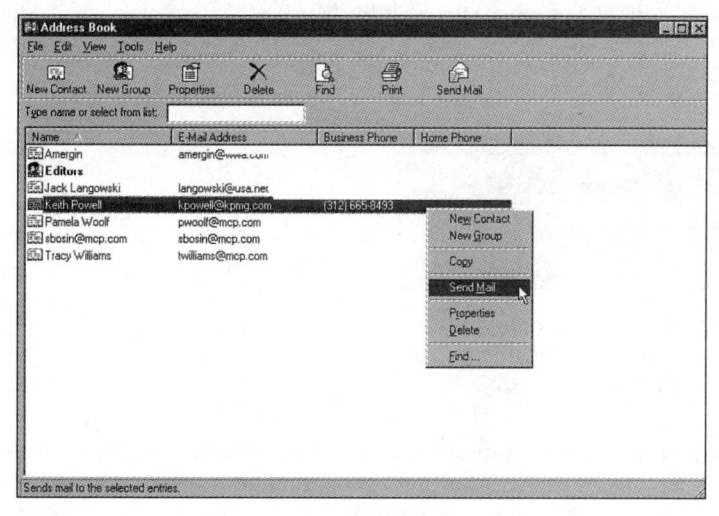

Figure 13.75 A fast way to send email.

23. Next, click the Send Mail menu selection, which takes you directly into a New Message screen where you see this Address Book contact already inputted into the To address box. Complete the text, add an attachment if necessary, and click the Send button; you are finished!

24. Another nifty feature of the Outlook Express Address Book is its capability to import contact information from other address books that might already exist on your computer's hard drive. To start the import process, click the File menu option, choose the Import menu selection, and click the Address Book menu selection. This reveals the screen shown in Figure 13.76.

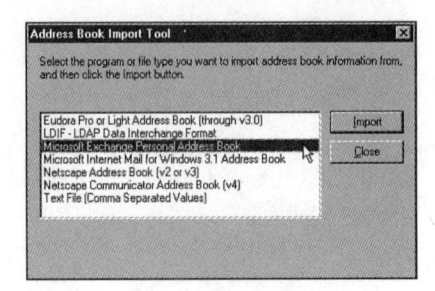

Figure 13.76 Using the Address Book Import tool.

25. Select the origin of the Address Book data that you want to import by clicking it once to highlight it. Then click the Import button and the process commences immediately. If you are attempting to import Address Book data from a Microsoft Exchange Server client (such as Microsoft Outlook 97 or 98), you might be prompted by a Choose Profile screen like the one shown in Figure 13.77.

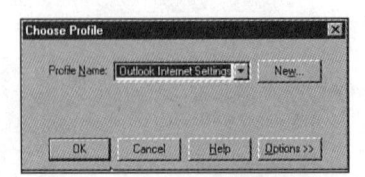

Figure 13.77 Selecting an Exchange client profile to use for the import process.

26. If you are not importing from an Exchange Server client software package, chances are you see no notification of the progress of the import process. However, when the process is complete, you are notified by an Address Book Import message box as shown in Figure 13.78.

Figure 13.78 Receiving notification of the completed Address Book Import process.

13.7 CONFIGURE A DIGITAL SIGNATURE

27. As soon as the process finishes, click OK to signify your notice of the end of the import process and close this message box. You now see all your newly imported Address Book contacts inside the Outlook Express Address Book.

COMPLEXITY
ADVANCED

13.7 How do I...
Configure a digital signature and why would I want to use one?

Problem

I use Outlook Express for my Internet email, which includes sending credit card information and other data that I deem very private. How can I keep this type of information private while on the Internet, and would I use one of those digital signatures to do so? Also, if a digital ID is the answer, how do I obtain and use one?

Technique

A digital signature or ID is an electronic method by which you can protect confidential data that you send across public networks such as the Internet. Like many aspects of your busy life, it is becoming important to know that your messages cannot be read or accessed by anyone other than those persons you originally intended. Along these same lines, would you not want to also protect your electronic cash documents that can be sent via email such as checks and credit card numbers? By using the digital ID feature of Outlook Express, you can secure your data, and, at the same time, prove to others that you are who you say you are, even though you are present only in an electronic sense to that other person or business.

A digital ID contains three parts: a public key, a private Key, and a digital signature. The way this works is that you send others your digital ID, which actually contains your public key. This permits those persons to be able to send you encrypted mail which only you can decrypt and read, because you have the private key. The digital signature part of a digital ID essentially becomes your electronic driver's license (or whatever ID card you use to prove your identity). The digital signature portion of the digital ID verifies for the message recipient that you are indeed the creator or originator of the message, which means no one other than you has tampered with or forged the message at hand.

In order to do all these whiz-bang things, you must first get a digital ID from a certifying authority (such as VeriSign, BelSign NV-SA, and so on), and then

CHAPTER 13
EMAIL AND NEWS

you must install it for use with Outlook Express. To do all these things, walk through the following set of instructions. However, keep in mind that you can obtain a free digital ID only for a 60-day trial period. After that, expect to pay at least $9.95 (USD) per year to receive and maintain this digital ID.

Steps

1. To begin using Outlook Express, click the Start button, select the Programs menu option, choose the Internet Explorer menu option, and then click once more on the Outlook Express menu selection.

2. This takes you directly into Outlook Express, as shown in Figure 13.79.

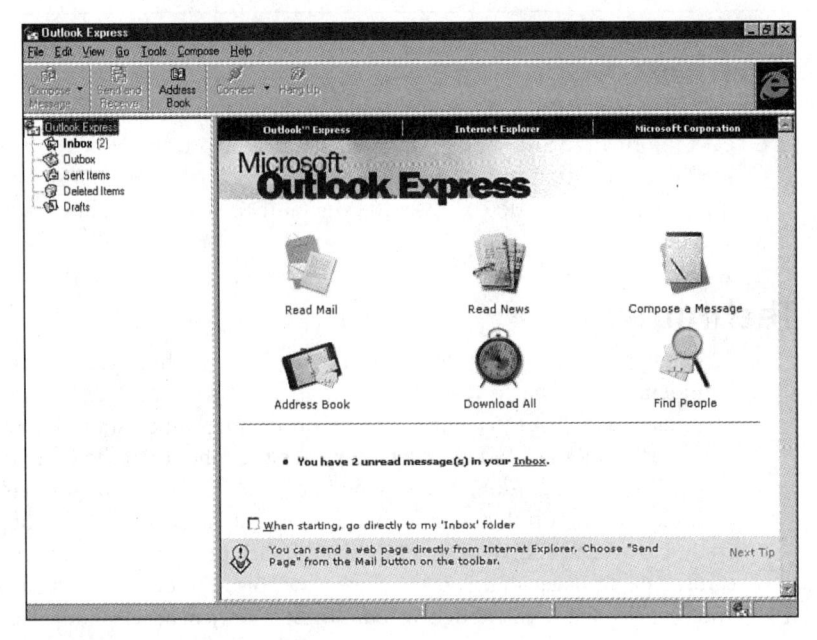

Figure 13.79 The opening screen of Outlook Express.

3. From the main screen, click the Tools menu option, and click again on the Options menu selection. After the Options screen appears, click the Security tab to reveal the screen shown in Figure 13.80.

4. After the Security tab appears, you need to pay close attention to the bottom two parts of this screen: the Secure Mail and the Digital IDs areas. If you want to digitally sign or encrypt all outgoing messages sent from your PC, you need to mark the check boxes as you deem appropriate. Keep in mind that if you do not have a digital ID, checking either of these boxes does no good until you have obtained and installed your digital ID.

13.7 CONFIGURE A DIGITAL SIGNATURE

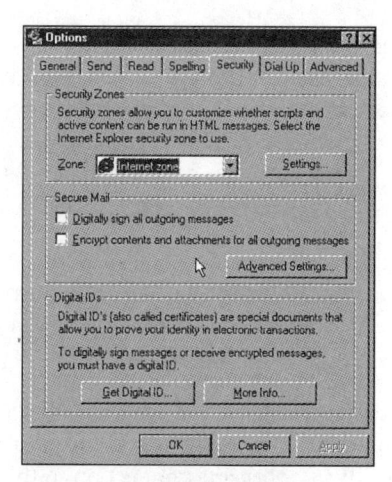

Figure 13.80 Accessing the Security tab of the Options screen of Outlook Express.

5. For an additional layer of security, click the Advanced Settings... button to reveal the screen shown in Figure 13.81.

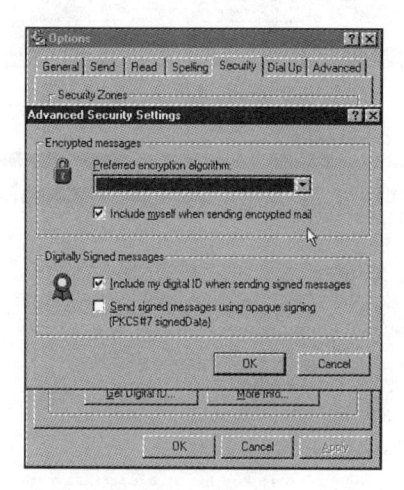

Figure 13.81 Accessing the Advanced Security Settings for data encryption options.

6. The top option permits you to select a preferred encryption algorithm (this drop-down list box is empty if you have not yet obtained a digital ID from a certifying authority). You can also decide to include yourself when sending any encrypted mail.

7. The bottom half of this screen deals with the use of digital IDs, whenever you are sending signed messages. Select the options you deem necessary by clicking each one once (or none of them), which places a check mark into the appropriate box. When you have finished making your selections, click OK to save your changes and return to the Security Options screen.

8. If all this security and digital ID stuff still seems to baffle you, you might want to click the More Info... button located near the bottom-right side of this screen. This starts the Windows 98 Help window, which contains quite a bit more details (in a much more simplified fashion) that should help you better understand this complex topic.

9. However, assuming you know what a digital ID is and that you want one, make sure that you have already established a connection to the Internet, and then click the Get Digital ID button. Doing this starts Internet Explorer and takes you directly to the Microsoft Outlook Express Digital IDs Web page, as shown in Figure 13.82.

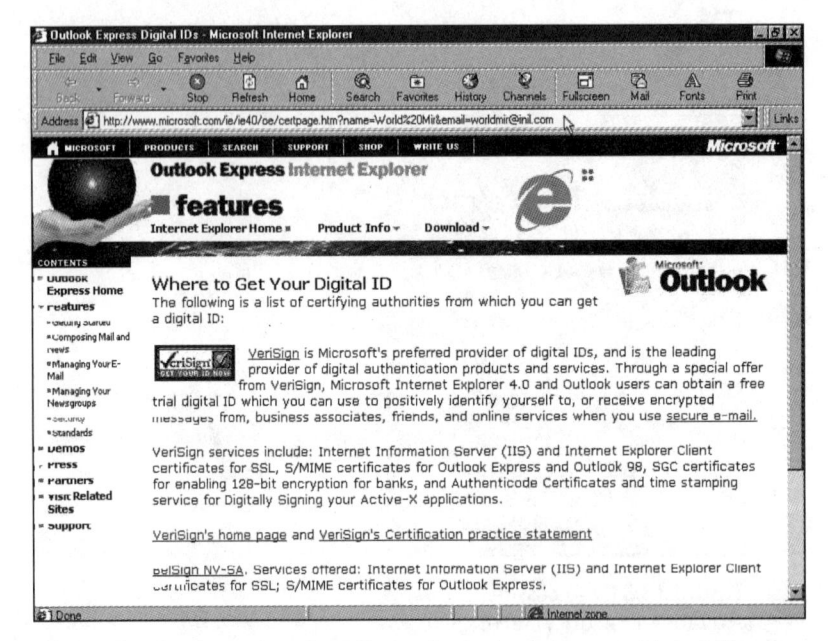

Figure 13.82 Accessing the Microsoft Outlook Express Digital IDs Web site.

10. On this page, near the top center, you are able to click a few URL hotlinks that take you to the appropriate certifying authority's Web site, where you are able to obtain a complete digital ID.

13.7
CONFIGURE A DIGITAL SIGNATURE

11. I recommend that you use VeriSign as your digital ID supplier—at least until you get your feet wet, so to speak—because they are the easiest vendor to work with. VeriSign does have a 60-day trial period for obtaining and using digital IDs, which is a nice feature as well. To hop on over to the VeriSign site, click the hotlink that appears at the very start of the first paragraph within the VeriSign section. This takes you directly to their Web site, as shown in Figure 13.83.

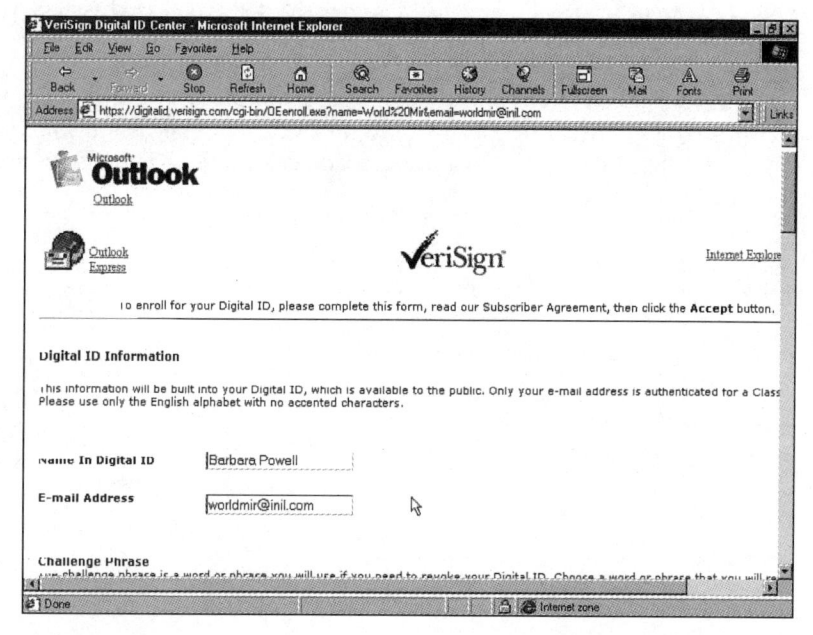

Figure 13.83 Accessing the VeriSign digital ID Web site.

12. After you reach this site, fill in all the information required on this screen, including your real email address and birth date (these fields are used to generate an accurate digital ID, so it works against you to fabricate information here).

13. Also, you must create a Challenge Phrase, which is basically a password for your digital ID (so that only you can use it, unless you spread your secret Challenge Phrase around town). This Challenge Phrase is required by VeriSign to cancel or revoke your digital ID in the event that it is compromised in some way. (VeriSign does not revoke or cancel a digital ID for you, if you cannot produce this Challenge Phrase, so do not lose it!)

14. If you only want to test drive this digital ID, you do not owe VeriSign any money. Otherwise, be prepared to fork over $9.95 (USD) via the use of a credit card. (There is no need to worry, VeriSign's Web site is SSL 3.0 protected.)

15. After you have paid your money (or skipped over that section because you want to get a free 60-day trial digital ID), click the Accept button found at the very bottom of this Web page. This begins the RSA key creation process, which takes a few minutes. After it completes, you are shown a message box that affirms that the digital ID has been generated. You soon receive an email message that tells you exactly where you need to go to download your newly created digital ID.

16. After you receive this email message, download your digital ID, and then install it using the instructions provided by VeriSign. You will see this digital ID and its signature appear inside Outlook Express automatically.

CHAPTER 14
INTERNET PUBLISHING

14

INTERNET PUBLISHING

How do I...

14.1 Install the Internet publishing components, such as FrontPage Express, the Web Publishing Wizard, and the Personal Web Server?

14.2 Use FrontPage Express?

14.3 Use the Web Publishing Wizard?

14.4 Use the Personal Web Server?

The focus of this chapter is how to publish information to the Internet and your local intranet. Internet publishing is accomplished through the use of two primary tools: FrontPage Express and the Web Publishing Wizard. Windows 98 provides a third utility known as the Personal Web Server, which can be used as a testing facility for you to test your Web site and HTML page designs before you actually publish them someplace public (such as the Web site that your ISP hosts for you).

Neither the publishing tools nor the Personal Web Server are automatically installed for you when you install Windows 98, so the first topic of this chapter explains the process of installing these three items. Three quick sections then follow that topic on how to use each of these tools: FrontPage Express, the Web Publishing Wizard, and the Personal Web Server. As you go through each of these tools, keep in mind that although there are much better ways to do all this same stuff (such as through the use of the full-blown Microsoft FrontPage 98 or the Microsoft Visual InterDev products), these Windows 98–provided tools are meant to be starting points for you to get acquainted with Web publishing and hosting requirements. To put it another way, do not expect these tools to satisfy all your needs, because they will probably come up short in many respects, which is why there are full-blown Web development tools available from Microsoft and others for these very same topics.

14.1 Install the Internet Publishing Components, Such as FrontPage Express, the Web Publishing Wizard, and the Personal Web Server

This topic focuses on the steps for installing these three Web publishing-related tools onto your Windows 98 PC. This is a very quick How-To discussion because this is a relatively simple and straightforward task to perform.

14.2 Use FrontPage Express

This How-To discusses some of the quick ways you can get up to speed on the use of the FrontPage Express Web page development tool, and it offers some tips on how you can eventually grow into using a real Web page development tool such as FrontPage 98 or Microsoft Visual InterDev, or perhaps even a non-Microsoft tool such as ColdFusion.

14.3 Use the Web Publishing Wizard

This How-To discusses some of the quick ways you can get up to speed on the use of the Web Publishing Wizard posting tool, and it offers some tips on how you can eventually get comfortable using an enterprise-level sufficient tool such as the Microsoft Visual InterDev.

14.4 Use the Personal Web Server

This How-To discusses some of the quick ways you can get up to speed on the use of the Personal Web Server, which is a miniaturized version of a real Internet Web server. Additional tips are given on how you can eventually learn to use a real Web site tool such as the Microsoft Windows NT-based Internet Information Server Web server platform.

14.1 How do I...
Install the Internet publishing components, such as FrontPage Express, the Web Publishing Wizard, and the Personal Web Server?

COMPLEXITY
BEGINNER

Problem

I want to be able to use the various Internet publishing components that come with Windows 98, but I do not know where to get them or how to install them. What do I need to do in order to accomplish these tasks?

Technique

Windows 98 ships with three very useful Internet publishing tools: FrontPage Express, the Web Publishing Wizard, and the Personal Web Server. All three of these tools come built into Windows 98, but it is very likely that you will need to install each of these tools because many organizations and computer vendors will not install any of these tools by default. To perform the installations, use this next set of steps to quickly walk through the short process. You will need to have your Windows 98 CD-ROM handy for the installation process.

For the FrontPage Express and the Web Publishing Wizard tools, though, you might want to rummage through the Windows 98 Windows Update Web site after you have performed this first round of installations, so that you can download the updates to both these tools. At the time of this writing, both of these products have substantial updates available to the general Windows 98 computing public at the Microsoft Windows Update Web site.

Steps

1. To begin the installation process, insert the Windows 98 CD-ROM into your CD-ROM drive.

2. Next, open the Windows 98 Control Panel and double-click the Add/Remove Programs icon. This takes you into the Add/Remove Programs Properties screen, where you need to click the Windows Setup tab to access the screen shown in Figure 14.1.

CHAPTER 14
INTERNET PUBLISHING

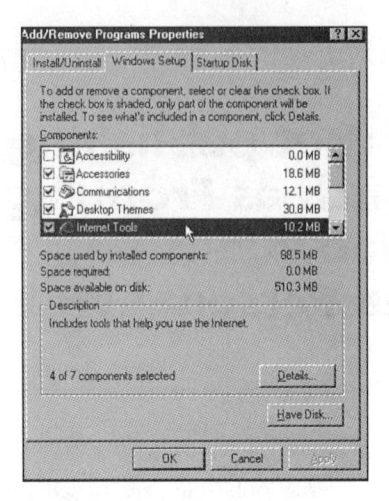

Figure 14.1 Reviewing the Windows Setup Components options.

3. Click the Internet Tools selection, and then click the Details button, which takes you into the selection screen for the Internet Tools features of Windows 98, as shown in Figure 14.2.

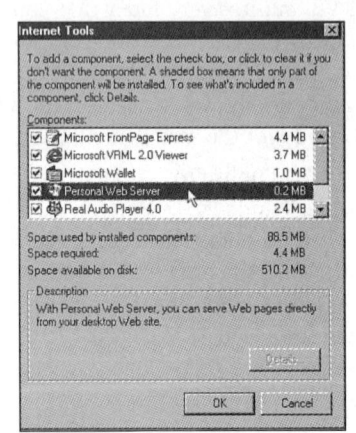

Figure 14.2 Selecting the appropriate Internet tools to install.

4. Click the check boxes that are located to the left of each option: Microsoft FrontPage Express, Personal Web Server, and the Web Publishing Wizard. After you have selected all three of these items, click OK to confirm your selections. This returns you to the main Windows Setup screen.

14.1
INSTALL THE INTERNET PUBLISHING COMPONENTS

5. At this point, click OK and the software installation process commences, as shown in Figure 14.3.

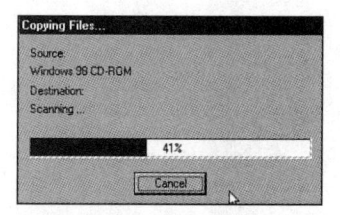

Figure 14.3 Watching the Windows 98 files installation process.

6. When the process completes, you are left with the Windows 98 desktop showing. Now, the naive person would believe that they were all done—that everything was installed just perfectly. Not! This is when the fun is just beginning.

7. If you were to access the Personal Web Server icon from the Start menu tree, you would be presented with a Web page that tells you there are more steps remaining for this Windows 98 software tool. To complete the installation of the Personal Web Server, click the Start button and choose Run.

8. Then enter the exact path to your Windows 98 CD-ROM and to the Personal Web Server setup program, using the `x:\add-ons\ pws\setup.exe` format (where *x* equates to the drive letter for your CD-ROM device). Then click the OK button to start the installation process.

9. The first screen of the installation wizard is informational in content only, as shown in Figure 14.4.

10. Click the Next> button to continue, which brings you to a screen that enables you to select the installation type, as shown in Figure 14.5.

11. Select the type of installation that best suits your needs. Although the Typical installation will work best for most people, you will choose the Custom option so that you can see what additional Internet components are available with the Windows 98 Personal Web Server. After you make your choice by clicking the installation type, you are automatically taken to the next screen (you do not need to use the Next> button, unless you used the Tab key to select the installation type). The Select Components screen appears, as shown in Figure 14.6.

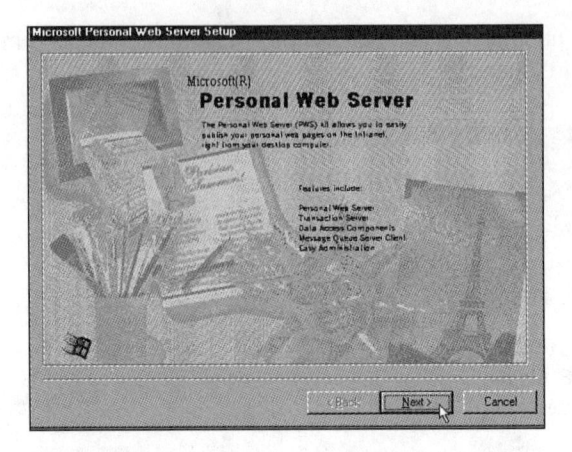

Figure 14.4 Starting the Personal Web Server installation process.

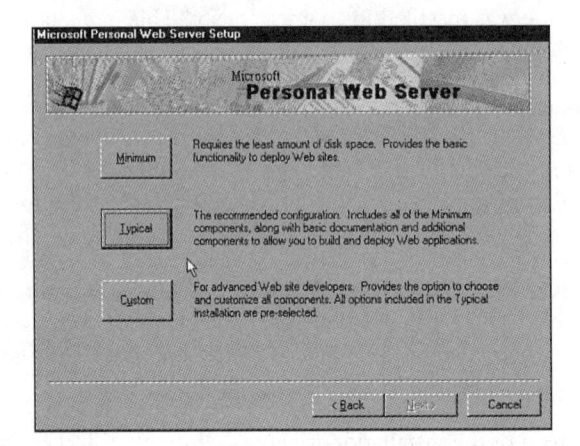

Figure 14.5 Selecting an installation type.

12. The Microsoft Personal Web Server Setup screen lists all the components that you can select to install—use the scrollbars to view the list in its entirety. Click the check box that corresponds with the components you want to install. Click the Show Subcomponents button to view the subcomponents of the highlighted component.

13. For example, scroll down the screen until you find the Personal Web Server (PWS) option, and then click the Show Subcomponents button to reveal the screen shown in Figure 14.7.

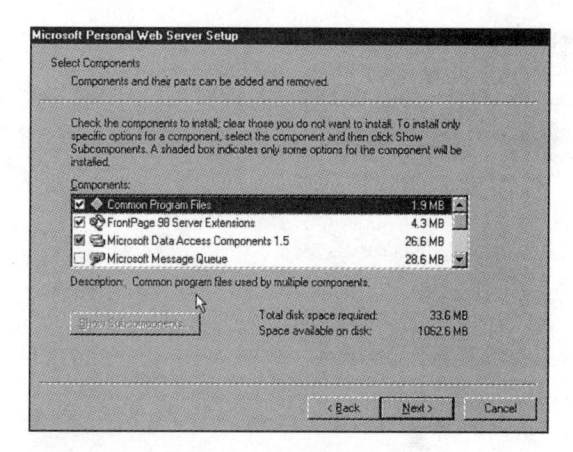

14.1
INSTALL THE INTERNET PUBLISHING COMPONENTS

Figure 14.6 Choosing Specific Personal Web Server components to install.

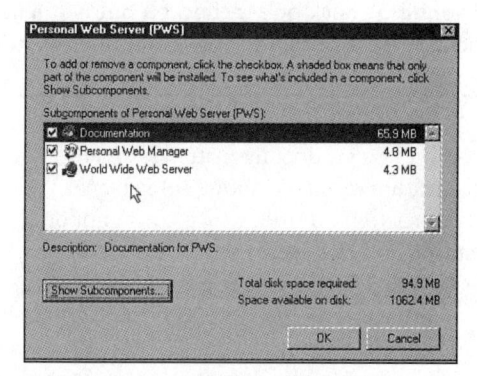

Figure 14.7 Drilling down into the Personal Web Server option.

14. The first screen of the Personal Web Server subcomponents contains the three features of this option: lots of documentation, the Personal Web Manager (which is what you need to use to configure and run the Personal Web Server), and the World Wide Web (WWW) Server. However, when you click the Documentation option, you notice that the Show Subcomponents button is not grayed out. This means that there is more to this option, so click the Show Subcomponents button to reveal these additional options, as shown in Figure 14.8.

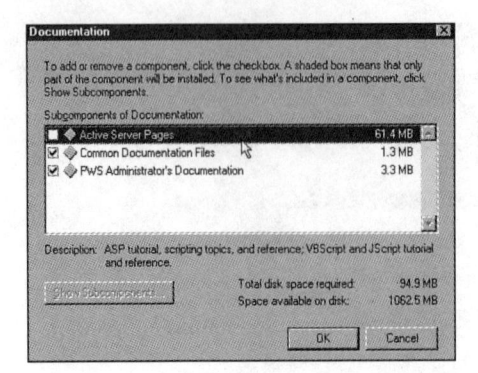

Figure 14.8 Drilling down into the PWS Documentation option.

> **NOTE**
>
> If a component's corresponding check box is checked but is still partially grayed out, it is an indication that not all of that component's subcomponents have been installed.

15. Although the Active Server Pages documentation is great to have and it represents a very nice feature of the Windows 98 Personal Web Server, it is also a pig when it comes to hard drive space consumption. I recommend that you select this option if disk space is not a concern, otherwise this might be one feature that you forgo for now. After you make your selections, click OK to return to the previous Personal Web Server components screen. Then, click again on the OK button to return to the main Personal Web Server Setup components selection screen, as shown in Figure 14.9.

16. At the very bottom of the Personal Web Server Setup components listing is an option for the Visual InterDev RAD Remote Development Support. This permits others on your organization's LAN/WAN or others within your local peer-to-peer network, to connect to your Personal Web Server and post Web pages to it. Although this is a very powerful option, keep in mind that it can be both a security risk and a potential resource drain on your Windows 98 PC because Windows 98 does not quite make a perfect server just yet.

17. After you have made all your component selections, click the Next> button to move to the next screen, as shown in Figure 14.10.

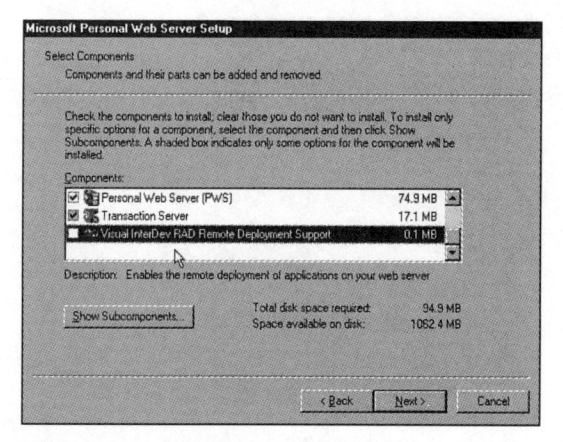

14.1
INSTALL THE INTERNET PUBLISHING COMPONENTS

Figure 14.9 Deciding whether to implement Visual InterDev RAD Remote Development Support.

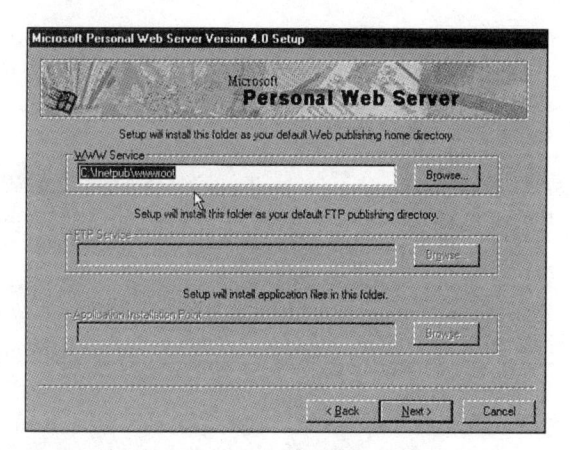

Figure 14.10 Determining the physical installation location.

18. The screen shown enables you to set or change the default folder destinations for any of the services on the screen (those options that are grayed out are the Personal Web Server components that you chose not to install). If you want to change any of these destinations, enter the new folder path in the appropriate box.

19. After you make your selections, click the Next> button to continue, which takes you to the screen shown in Figure 14.11.

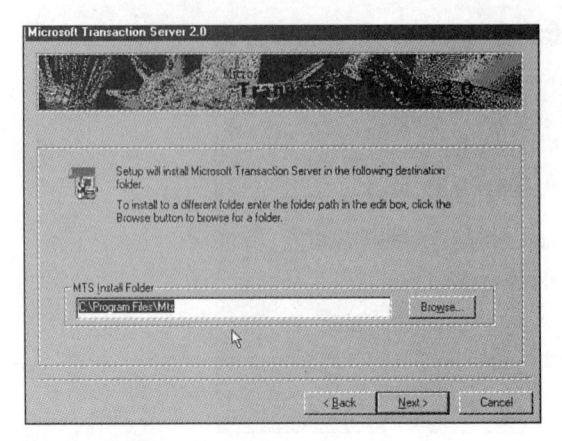

Figure 14.11 Determining the physical installation location for the Microsoft Transaction Server (MTS) component.

20. This screen enables you to specify where the Microsoft Transaction Server (MTS) will be installed. Either accept the default location or change it to one that better meets your needs, and then click Next> to continue.

> **NOTE**
>
> **MTS** is a component-based transaction processing system that enables you to develop, deploy, and manage high-performance, scalable, server-based applications. MTS defines a programming model; it also provides a runtime environment and graphical administration tool for managing enterprise applications.

21. The progress bar shown in Figure 14.12 keeps track of the installation's progress. When the installation is complete, click Next>.

22. When the Personal Web Server installation process finishes, the screen shown in Figure 14.13 appears.

23. After seeing this screen, you need to click Finish to complete the installation process. As soon as you do this, you are prompted to restart your computer, as shown in Figure 14.14.

24. Click Yes to reply affirmatively to this prompt. After your PC reboots, the installation process for all three of these Internet publishing tools is finally complete.

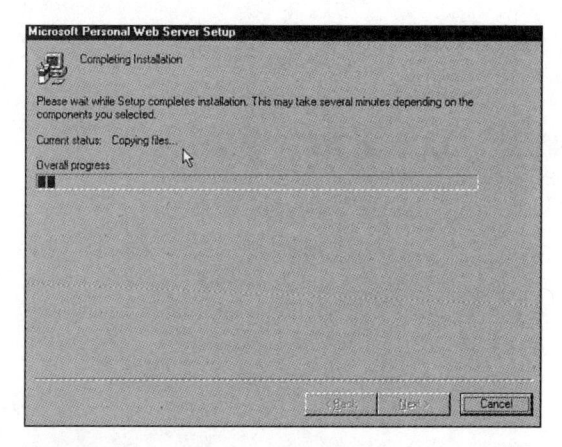

14.1
INSTALL THE INTERNET PUBLISHING COMPONENTS

Figure 14.12 The Personal Web Server installation status bar.

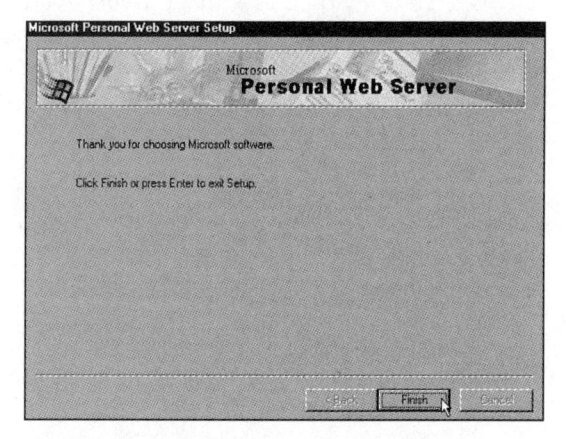

Figure 14.13 Completing the Personal Web Server installation.

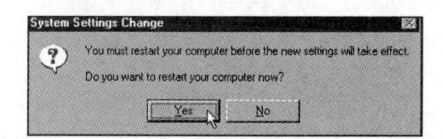

Figure 14.14 Deciding whether to restart your PC.

14.2 How do I... Use FrontPage Express?

COMPLEXITY: INTERMEDIATE

Problem

I installed the FrontPage Express Web tool, but I have no idea how to use it. What are some of the ways that I can use FrontPage Express to create Web pages without turning myself into an HTML guru?

Technique

FrontPage Express is a tool for creating Web pages. Based on the full-blown Microsoft FrontPage98 Web development tool, FrontPage Express makes it easy for first-time Web authors to create Web pages without having to learn the HTML programming language. For established Web authors, FrontPage Express is a great way to edit and enhance existing HTML documents. There are a few quick things you should understand about FrontPage Express, and then the rest is up to you!

Steps

1. To get started with this tool, click Start, choose the Programs menu selection, select the Internet Tools menu folder, and then click the FrontPage Express menu option.

2. This starts the FrontPage Express Web development tool, as shown in Figure 14.15.

3. If you are an HTML programming wizard, you can start typing and create a Web site. However, if you are like the rest of us, you will probably find it easier to modify an existing Web site to get the hang of things. To open a Web site, click the File menu option, and choose the Open menu selection, which reveals the screen shown in Figure 14.16.

> **NOTE**
> Remember that all the text and graphical contents of commercial and personal Web sites belong to their owners and copyright and trademark laws do apply. Therefore, although I suggest that you use other Web sites for learning purposes, I strongly recommend that you never ever use anyone else's work on your own Web site. The only time that it is even slightly acceptable to borrow from other Web sites is if you have obtained that Web site's written permission to do so. Failure to do this is a bad idea at best.

14.2
USE FRONTPAGE EXPRESS

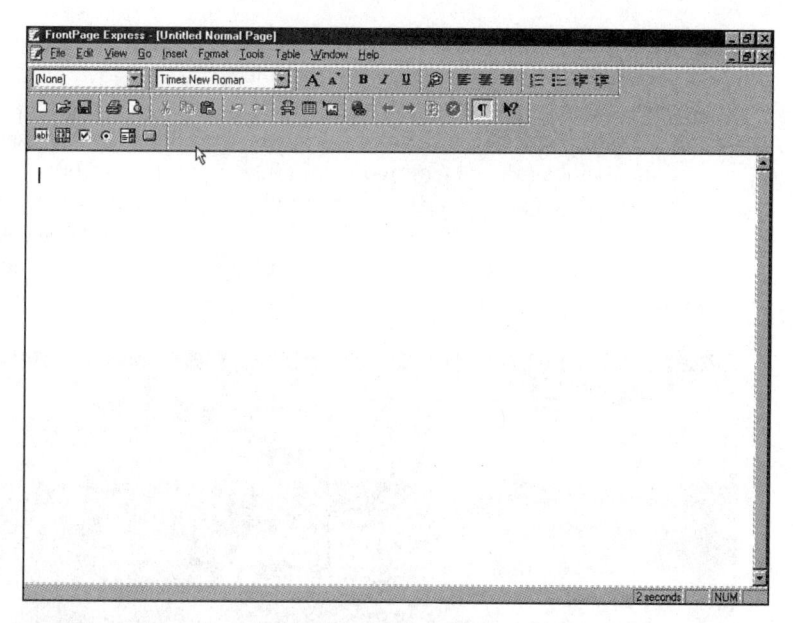

Figure 14.15 Accessing the FrontPage Express Web development tool.

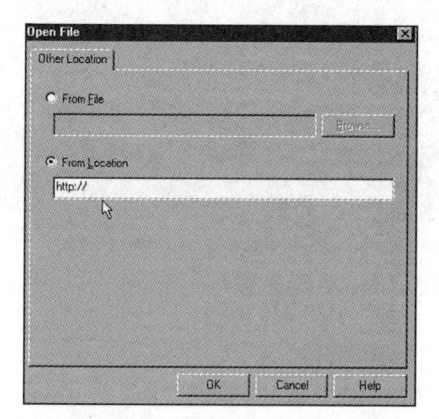

Figure 14.16 Accessing an existing Web site.

4. The Open File dialog box, as shown in Figure 14.17, is displayed on your system's monitor. If you want to find an existing Web page or site on your local computer or network, select the From File radio button and then enter the pathname to the file in the corresponding text box (click Browse if you don't know the pathname).

5. Select the From Location radio button if you want to pull a copy of a Web page from the Internet or from an intranet/extranet. However, if this is your decision, you must manually (yuk!) type the exact URL of the site you want to access. In the example given, the URL used was the one for Carson's Ribs (a great Chicago restaurant for you rib lovers): http://www.ribs.com/index.html (all lowercase text). After you enter this URL and click OK, you will retrieve the home page for whatever URL you choose, directly into the FrontPage Express tool, as shown in Figure 14.17.

Figure 14.17 Accessing the Carson's BBQ ribs restaurant home page.

6. To examine the HTML code that makes the graphical features of the site possible, click the View menu option and then select the HTML menu selection. This reveals the screen shown in Figure 14.18.

7. The View or Edit HTML window appears. Examine the contents of this window to get a feel for how HTML operates.

> **NOTE**
> HTML code is neither as difficult nor as complex as it looks, because HTML uses tags to format text and other elements of a Web page. For example, to place a title on your Web page, you will use the <title></title> format. To use this format, simply add in whatever

text you want to appear in your title between these two. All the first <title> piece means is that you want to start your title here. The second </title> means that you have completed your title and want to end it. That's all there is to basic HTML. Take a closer look at various Web pages for ideas on how to format your own Web pages or pick up one of the many *Sams Teach Yourself* books on the topic.

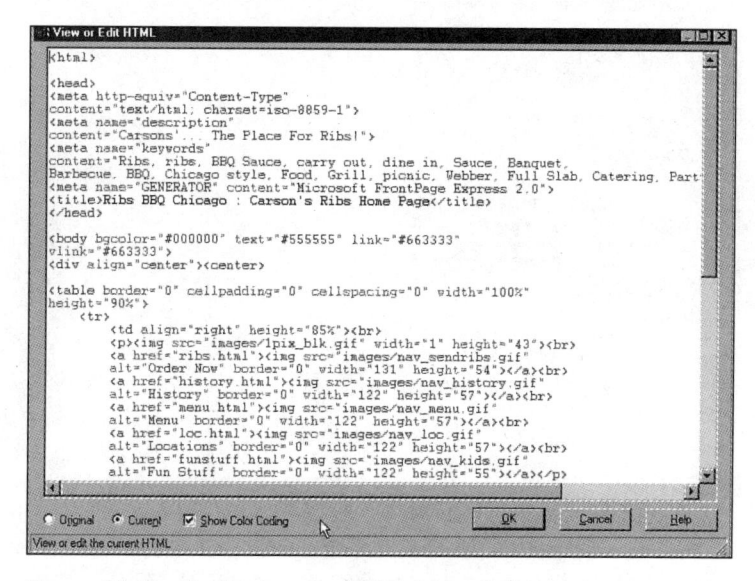

Figure 14.18 Reviewing the HTML text of the Carson's home page.

8. There are literally hundreds of specialty items and options found throughout this application (and this is considered the "express" version!). To get a feel for all of them would take most of this book, and even then someone who did not already fully understand VB and Java scripting, HTML, Active Server Pages, or WebBot components would require even more tutelage and training. For example, if you look at Figure 14.19, you will see an indication of some of the other components you are able to insert into a Web page via the FrontPage Express tool.

NOTE

If your goal is to quickly and easily create your own Web sites, I strongly urge you to purchase a whole book on HTML and upgrade to the full Microsoft FrontPage 98 software package, which provides many of the very advanced features found in Web sites around the Internet. For beginners, I would recommend the book *Using HTML 3.2, Second Edition*, by Todd Stauffer (Que Corporation, 1996); whereas for more

continued on next page

continued from previous page

technical users, David Cohn and Justin Higgin's book, ***Web Designer's Guide to FrontPage97*** (Hayden Books, 1997), is excellent even though it is one version old. For those persons wanting a quick introduction all the way through to advanced Java scripting and development, you might wish to check out ***Microsoft Visual J++ 6.0 Deluxe Learning Edition*** (Microsoft Press, October 1998).

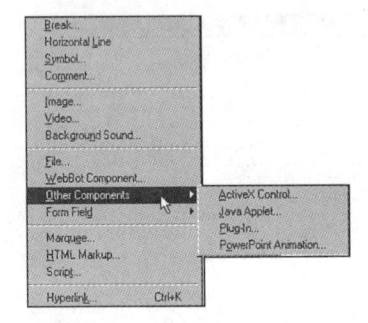

Figure 14.19 Inserting other components into your Web page.

9. However, there are a few quick things you can pick up. First, if you click a picture (graphical image) to select it, and then right-click that same item, a small menu appears. Click the Properties menu selection to reveal the Image Properties screen, as shown in Figure 14.20.

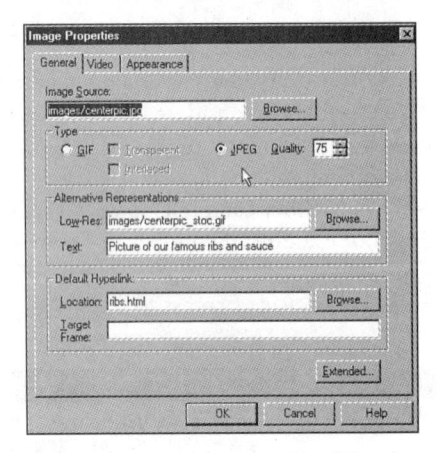

Figure 14.20 Accessing an image's properties.

14.2
USE FRONTPAGE EXPRESS

10. This screen can be used to quickly change a graphical image that presently appears on this Web site, as well as to play with the quality of this same picture. There are two other tabs on the Image Properties set of screens, both of which permit you to add or change video clips and alter the general appearance of a specific image that appears on your Web site.

11. To save your changes and exit this screen, click OK.

12. Next, you can save your work by clicking the File menu option, and then by clicking once more on the Save As menu selection to reveal the screen shown in Figure 14.21.

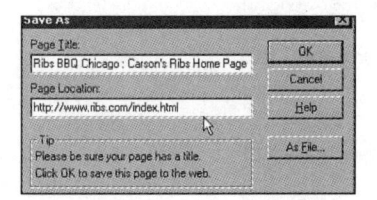

Figure 14.21 Saving your work.

13. This screen permits you to save your work directly back to the Web site that you grabbed it from, assuming that you have the proper permissions, of course. Additionally, you can save this Web site to another location, which then automatically activates the Web Publishing Wizard (refer to this topic later in this chapter, if you do not understand how to use it). Your final choice on this screen is to save your work under a completely new name somewhere locally on your hard disk drive.

14. After you have finished with your selections, click OK to save your page's title and location and return to the main FrontPage Express screen.

15. Another screenful of information that you might want to examine is the Page Properties screen, which can be accessed by clicking the File menu option, and then clicking the Page Properties menu selection. Doing this takes you directly into the Page Properties screen, as shown in Figure 14.22.

16. This screen permits you to alter the base location and default target frame for this Web page. You can also set a background sound (and a few sound options) for this page. After you make your selections, click the Custom tab found on this same screen (the Background and the Margins tabs are very self-explanatory and thus do not require any further detailing). Doing this takes you into the Custom screen, as shown in Figure 14.23.

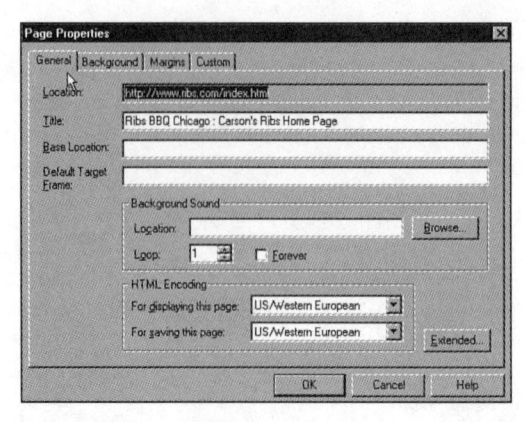

Figure 14.22 Accessing the Web Page Properties screen.

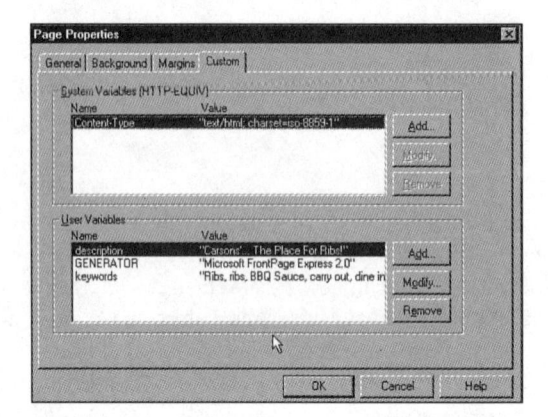

Figure 14.23 Changing the Custom Web Page Properties.

17. This screen is used to set the system and user variables for this Web page. A system variable is usually something that permeates the entire Web site, whereas the user variable is used to set basic descriptors and keywords for this particular Web site. After you have finished with your review and changes, click OK to save your alterations and exit this screen.

18. When you have finished working on your Web page, either save it or discard as an interesting learning experience.

COMPLEXITY
INTERMEDIATE

14.3 How do I...
Use the Web Publishing Wizard?

Problem

I have created a couple of great Web pages that fit together into a nice Web site. Now that all the hard work is finished, how can I publish my work to the Internet or my organization's intranet?

Technique

Within Windows 98 is a little-known Web publishing tool known as the Web Publishing Wizard. This tool provides experienced users an easy way to post their own Web sites to an Internet/intranet Web server. The wizard automates the process of copying files from your computer to the Web server, because you will be using a systematic set of computer-generated instructions. The great thing about the Windows 98 Web Publishing Wizard is that not only can you publish your pages to the Internet (via your local ISP), but you can also post your data directly to Microsoft's Internet Information Server (a Windows NT–based Internet Web server), America Online, CompuServe, GNN, and Sprynet, as well as perhaps other intranet/extranet Web servers that might exist elsewhere within your organization's LAN/WAN operating environments.

Steps

1. Click Start, choose the Programs menu option, select the Internet Explorer menu folder, and then click the Web Publishing Wizard.

2. The first screen of the Web Publishing Wizard provides information about the wizard, as shown in Figure 14.24.

3. Because this first screen of the Web Publishing Wizard is for informational purposes only, click the Next> button to continue to the Select a File or Folder screen, shown in Figure 14.25.

4. Select the file or folder that you want to publish to the Web in this screen. If you do not know the entire path to the folder or file, click either the Browse Folders... button or the Browse Files... button (if you want to publish a single file, use the Browse Files... button; the Browse Folders... button lets you publish an entire directory at once).

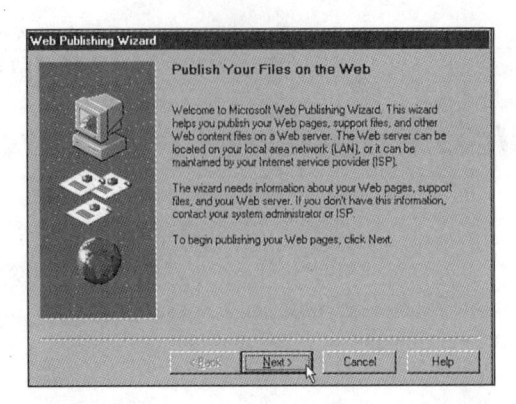

Figure 14.24 Starting the Web Publishing Wizard.

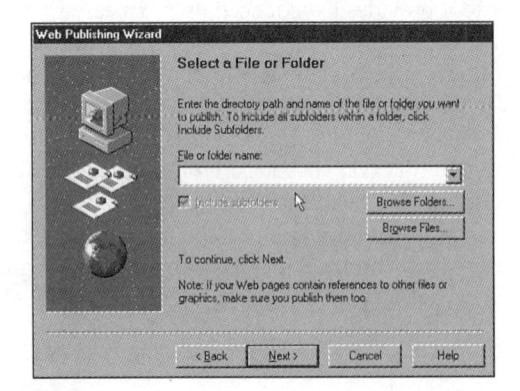

Figure 14.25 Selecting the files or folders to publish.

5. After the file or folder name is in place, click Next> to reveal the Web server selection screen, as shown in Figure 14.26.

6. On the Select a Web Server screen, you need to enter the full URL for the Web server on which you are planning to publish your Web content. Typically, this is the full name of your ISP's Web site for its members or users. After you have accessed the correct name via the drop-down list box, you should click Next> to continue (you should now go to step 8). If the location that you want to put your Web site is not listed in the drop-down list box, click New to reveal the screen shown in Figure 14.27.

7. In the Name the Web Server screen you need to type a descriptive name for your Web server. After you have finished this, click Next> to proceed to the screen shown in Figure 14.28.

14.3
USE THE WEB PUBLISHING WIZARD

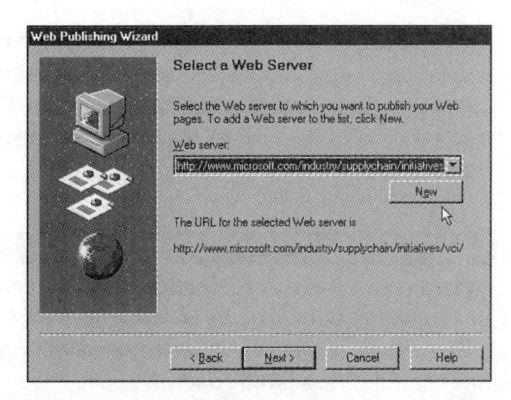

Figure 14.26 Selecting a Web server.

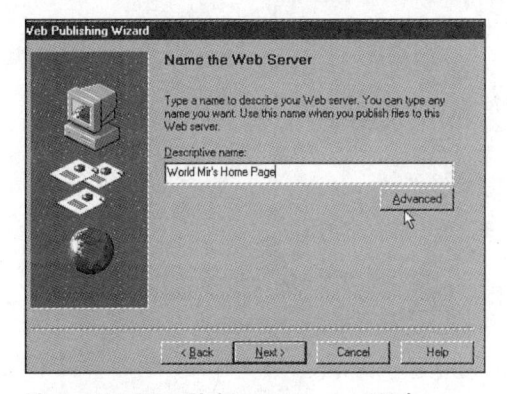

Figure 14.27 Giving your new Web server a descriptive name.

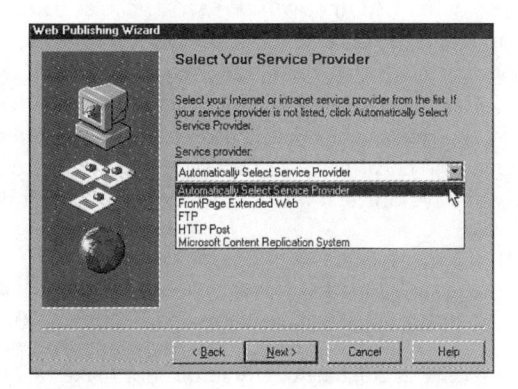

Figure 14.28 Selecting the service provider.

8. Specify your Internet or intranet service provider's publishing type by using the drop-down list box. After you make a selection (use the Automatically Select Service Provider if you are unsure about which one to use), click Next> to proceed to the Specify the URL and Directory screen, shown in Figure 14.29.

> **NOTE**
>
> It is very important that you select the correct service provider; failure to do so might result in your page being shown incorrectly or not at all. When in doubt, select the Automatically Select Service Provider option. This might alleviate some troubles down the road.

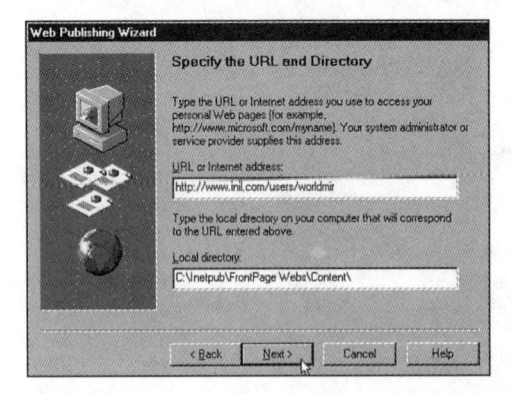

Figure 14.29 Specifying the destination URL and the content origination location.

9. In the top box, specify the URL that will be used to access your new Web site. In the bottom box, labeled Local Directory, you need to input the local folder on your hard drive where all the Web site's content exists (that is, the folder where you created all your Web page stuff). In other words, the URL is the Web address that is used to locate the Internet or intranet site, whereas the Local Directory is used to locate files on your hard drive. After you have finished this, click Next> to proceed with the wizard.

10. If you input the wrong URL in the top box, you will be hit with a Web Publishing Wizard error message box, as shown in Figure 14.30.

11. As soon as you correct your mistake or if you did not make this error, you will arrive at a password prompt, as shown in Figure 14.31.

14.3
USE THE WEB PUBLISHING WIZARD

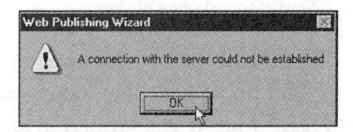

Figure 14.30 The results of an incorrect URL.

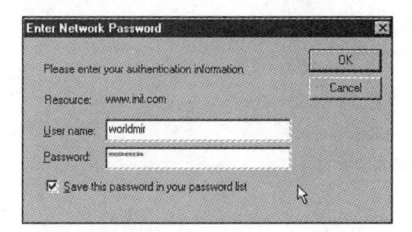

Figure 14.31 Authenticating to your Web server.

12. Just about everyone should encounter this message box, because this is where you insert your username and password for accessing your Web site's location. If you do not need to do this, there is a possible security gap in your Web server. (This is something to check, anyway). If you will be posting to this location multiple times, you might want to click the check box to select the password saving feature, which means that you no longer need to enter your password every time you want to post something. After you type the correct username and password, click OK to proceed. This brings you to the final screen of the Web Publishing Wizard, as shown in Figure 14.32.

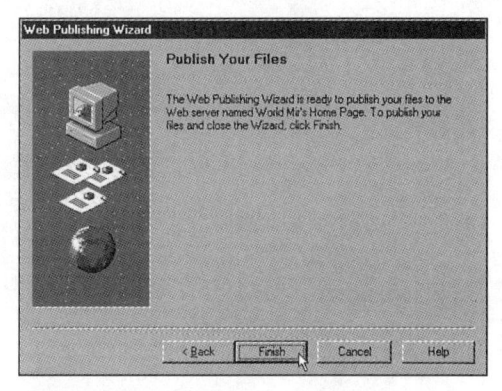

Figure 14.32 Completing the Web Publishing Wizard process.

CHAPTER 14
INTERNET PUBLISHING

13. Click Finish to post the site to the server and complete the Web Publishing Wizard process. You should now be able to view your Web site on either your intranet or the Internet, depending on where you published it. After you click the Finish button you will see a results message box similar to the one in Figure 14.33.

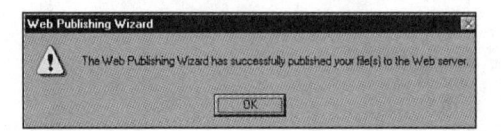

Figure 14.33 Notification that the Web Publishing Wizard has completed successfully.

14. To check out your new Web site, reestablish your connection to the Internet or your intranet (depending on where you published it) if you had previously dropped your connection. You can then open your new Web page, as shown in Figure 14.34.

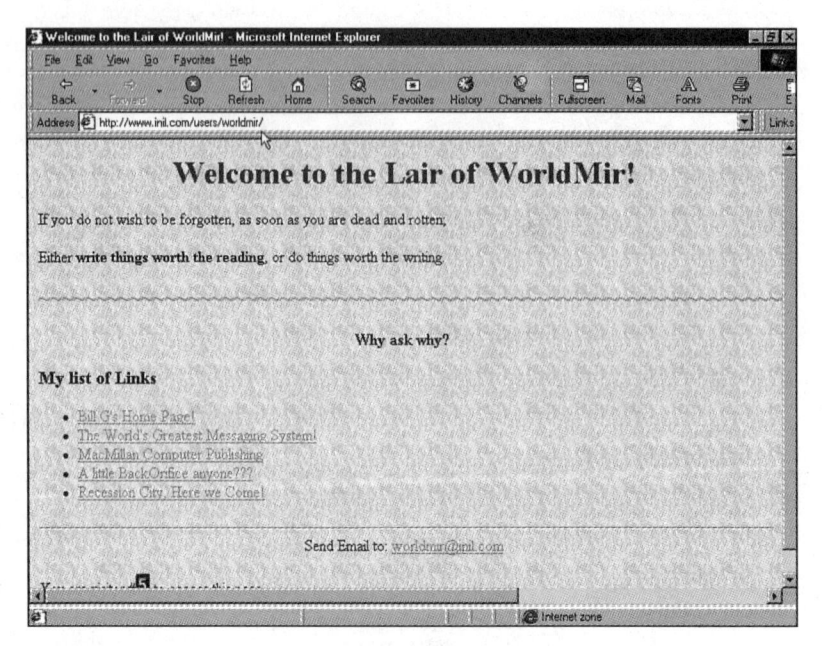

Figure 14.34 Reviewing your Web site.

COMPLEXITY
INTERMEDIATE

14.4 How do I...
Use the Personal Web Server?

Problem

I have heard that the Web server software that comes with Windows 98 is supposed to function much like a real Internet Web server, such as Microsoft's Windows NT-based Internet Information Server (IIS). Is this true, and, if so, how do I use the Personal Web Server tool so that it functions much like IIS?

Technique

The Windows 98 Personal Web Server enables you to quickly create and display Web pages and sites on your own computer. A nifty wizard application helps you create your first Web site, which can then be copied to another server (maybe your ISP's), where it can be accessed via the Internet. The Personal Web Server is meant to be a work area for those persons who do not have their own Windows NT–based IIS to play with (this would probably be most of us). Do not try to get too fancy with it, in that if you attempt writing CGI scripts or extensive Java scripts, you will find that it is not nearly as robust as an IIS server would be. Also, it is silly to try to use a Personal Web Server as your organization's Web server (use IIS instead), because the Personal Web Server was designed for single person usage only; putting more than one person on the same Personal Web Server is going to require a very good sense of humor when it comes to response times.

Steps

1. To begin using the Personal Web Server Manager application, which is the tool that you use to work with the Personal Web Server, double-click the Publish icon that appears on your Windows 98 desktop. It was placed there by the Personal Web Server setup program, as shown in Figure 14.35.

2. After you enter the Personal Web Manager application, you are prompted with the Tip of the Day (these tips are really basic), as shown in Figure 14.36.

3. To eliminate seeing this in the future, click the Show Tips at Startup check box to clear it. After you have finished reviewing the tip, click Close to reveal the main Personal Web Manager screen, as shown in Figure 14.37.

CHAPTER 14
INTERNET PUBLISHING

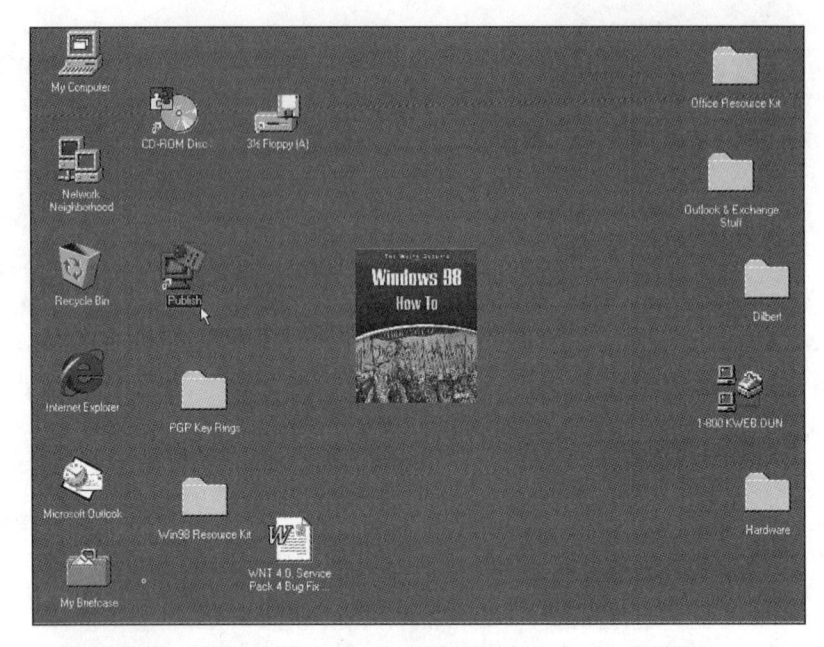

Figure 14.35 Starting the Personal Web Manager application.

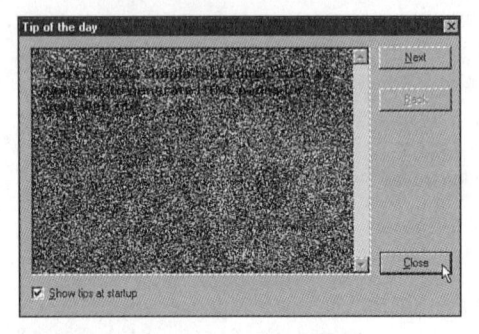

Figure 14.36 Reviewing the Personal Web Manager Tip of the Day.

4. The right side of this screen contains a wealth of information, including your default home page (on the Personal Web Server), the home directory for that page, and several connection statistics regarding your Web site on the Windows 98 Personal Web Server.

5. To continue, click the Publish icon found in the left windowpane, which reveals the screen shown in Figure 14.38.

14.4
USE THE PERSONAL WEB SERVER

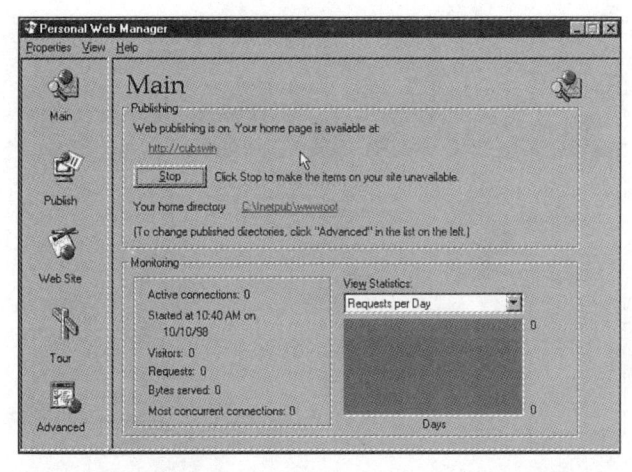

Figure 14.37 Reviewing the primary Personal Web Manager screen.

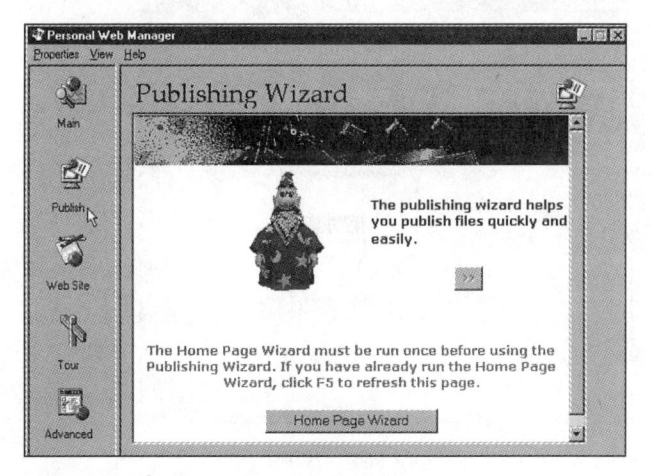

Figure 14.38 Starting the Publishing Wizard.

6. In order to work with the Publishing Wizard you must have run the Home Page Wizard at least once. Because you have not done that yet, do so by clicking the Home Page Wizard button found at the bottom of this screen. This takes you into the starting screen for the Home Page Wizard, as shown in Figure 14.39.

7. This first screen has only informational content, so after you review it, click the double-arrow (>>) button to move to the next screen, shown in Figure 14.40.

Figure 14.39 Starting the Home Page Wizard.

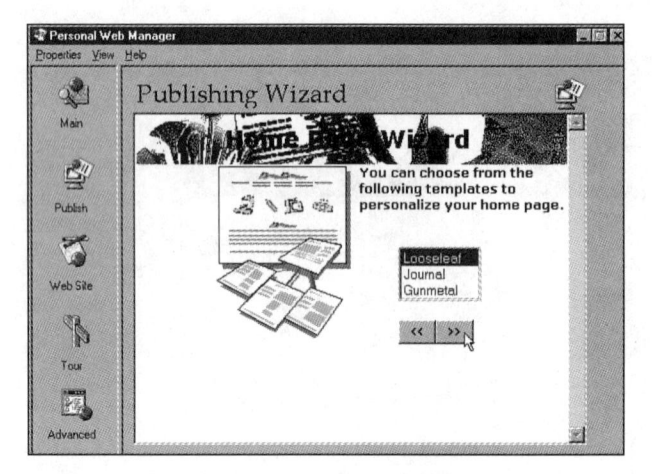

Figure 14.40 Choosing a Web Page theme.

8. On this screen you need to select a theme or background for your home page. To do this, click any of the three styles that appear in the box just above the double-arrow buttons. After you make your selection, click the double arrow (>>) button to move to the guest book screen, as shown in Figure 14.41.

9. This screen prompts you to select one of the two radio buttons, which determines whether you will use a guest book on your home page. The default is Yes, which is what you will choose as well. To continue, click the double-arrow (>>) button to move to the drop box screen, as shown in Figure 14.42.

14.4
USE THE PERSONAL WEB SERVER

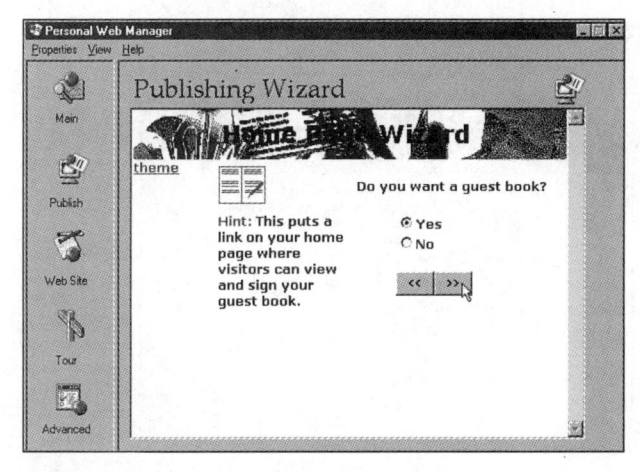

Figure 14.41 Deciding whether you want a guest book.

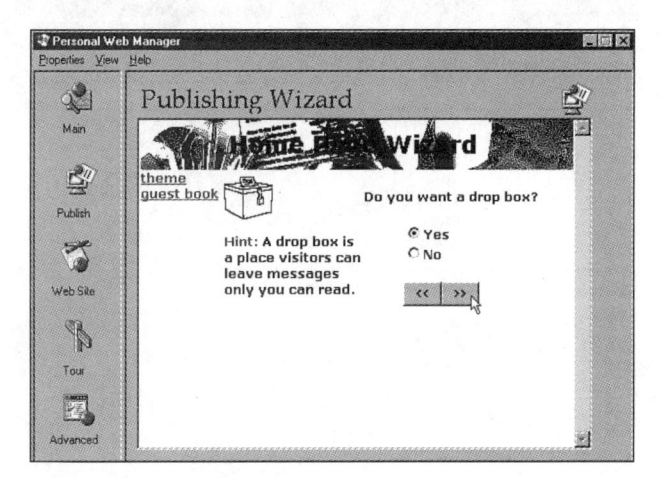

Figure 14.42 Deciding on a drop box.

10. This screen prompts you to select one of the two radio buttons, which determines whether you will use a drop box on your home page. The default is Yes, which is what you will choose as well. To continue, click the double-arrow (>>) button to move to the completion screen, as shown in Figure 14.43.

11. This screen informs you that the Home Page Wizard has completed. To continue, click the double-arrow (>>) button to move to the next screen. You are prompted to make a few more changes to your Web page via Internet Explorer, as shown in Figure 14.44.

Figure 14.43 The completion screen.

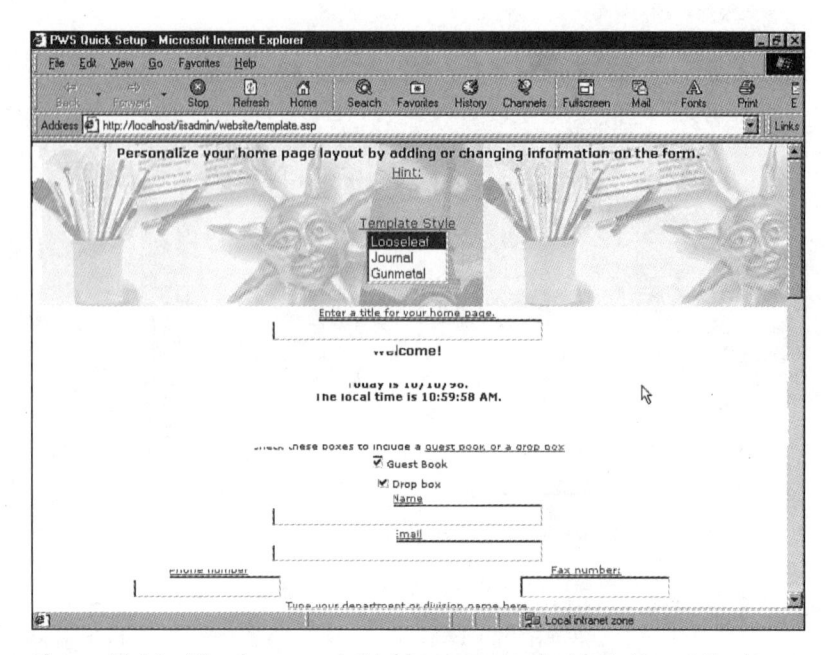

Figure 14.44 Viewing your initial home page inside Internet Explorer.

12. On this screen you can enter additional information regarding your new default home page. All the boxes accept content from you, so feel free to go wild here. When you finish making your changes (the screen scrolls up and down, so be sure to look all over for boxes), scroll down to the bottom of the browser window, as shown in Figure 14.45.

14.4
USE THE PERSONAL WEB SERVER

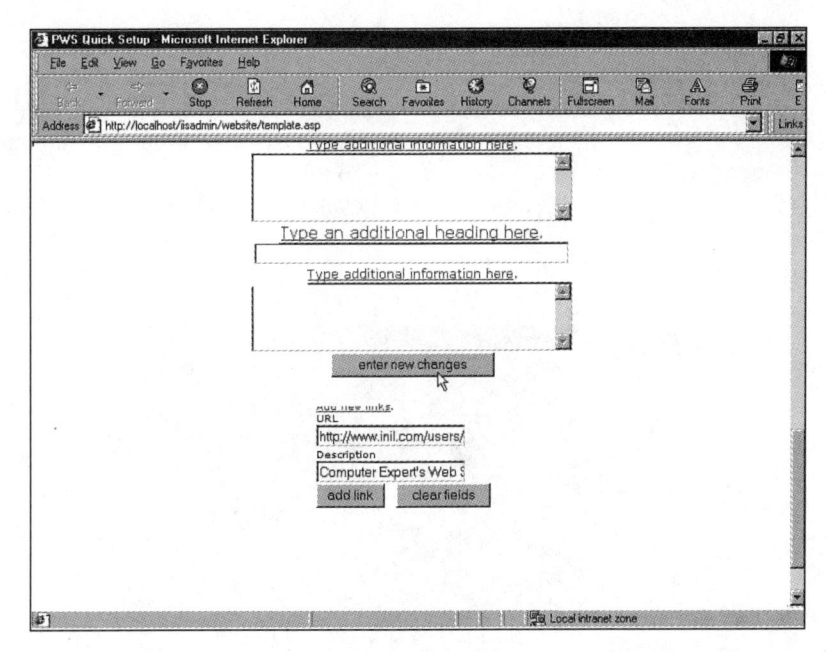

Figure 14.45 Saving changes to your home page via Internet Explorer.

13. Click the Enter New Changes button, found near the bottom of this screen, which saves your changes. After you have done this, close Internet Explorer. When you return to the Personal Web Manager screen, click the Web Site icon, as shown in Figure 14.46.

Figure 14.46 Viewing the Publishing Wizard options.

14. Now that you have used the Home Page Wizard at least once, you will be able to finally use the Publishing Wizard. Essentially, all you are doing is modifying choices that you made during the Home Page Wizard screens, so don't go looking for the details, so to speak. (You won't find them using this tool, because you need to use either FrontPage98 or FrontPage Express to get down into the details). After you have finished your changes or your review, click the Tour icon, which begins the Product Tour, as shown in Figure 14.47.

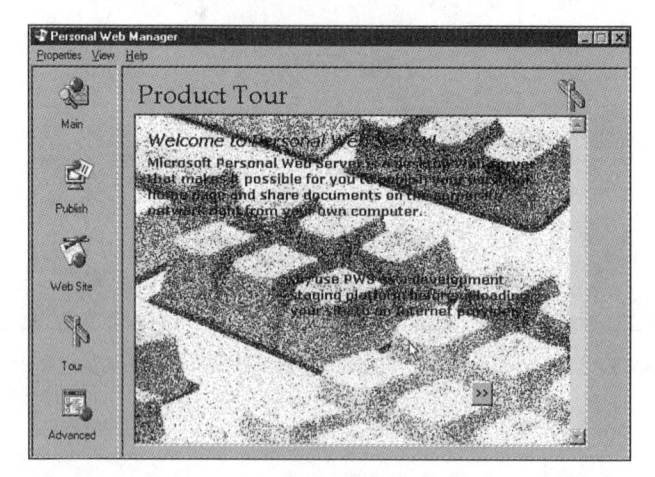

Figure 14.47 Using the Personal Web Manager tour.

15. If you have never used a Web site manager of any kind before, the Personal Web Manager Tour screen really should be used first. However, the information found in this screen is so basic that you would think that you were reading some *Dick and Jane* book. If you need help this badly, you should pick up a beginners' book on the Internet and Web sites.

16. To continue, click the Advanced icon to continue to the Advanced Options screen shown in Figure 14.48.

17. This screen shows you the nuts and bolts of your Web site. Use the browser-looking window under the Virtual Directories label to review all the Web sites you have created to date. If you have the <Home> directory highlighted and click the Edit Properties button, you will see the Edit Directory screen, as shown in Figure 14.49.

18. This screen sets the local folder on your hard drive for your default home page, and it also permits you to change the base permissions for this Web site. If you permit use of the Execute feature, it is possible for you (or others) to run VB or Java scripts on your Web site. After you finish making your changes, if any, click OK to return to the previous screen.

14.4
USE THE PERSONAL WEB SERVER

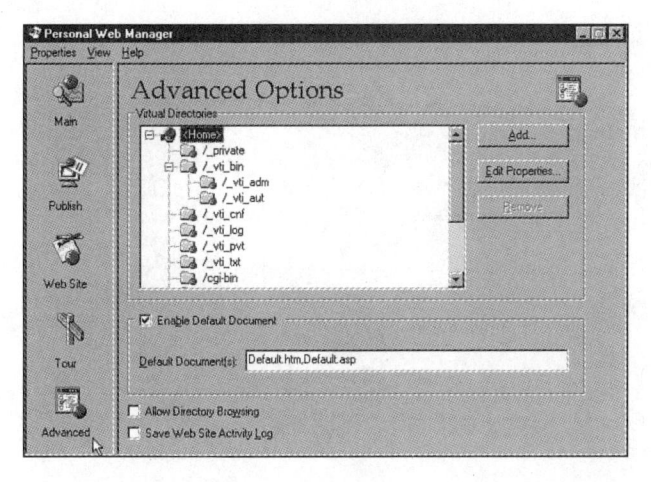

Figure 14.48 Accessing the advanced options of your Web page.

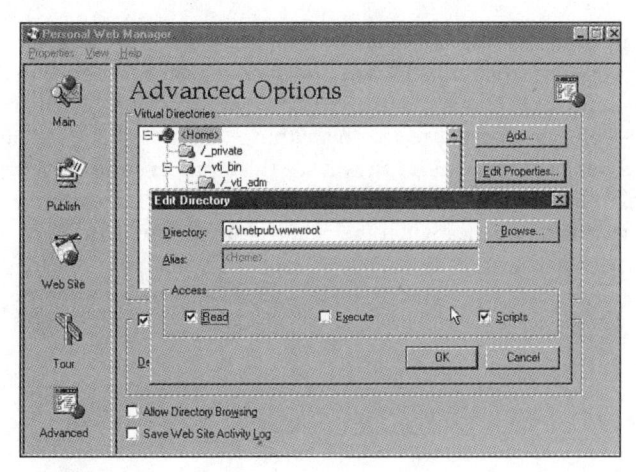

Figure 14.49 Editing the directory properties of your home page.

19. When you return to the Advanced Options screen, click the Main icon (found in the left windowpane) to return to the screen where you originally started your Personal Web Manager journey, as shown in Figure 14.50.

20. If you look again at the Monitoring section of this screen, you will notice that the numbers have changed to reflect the usage of your Web site (by you during the use of the various wizards).

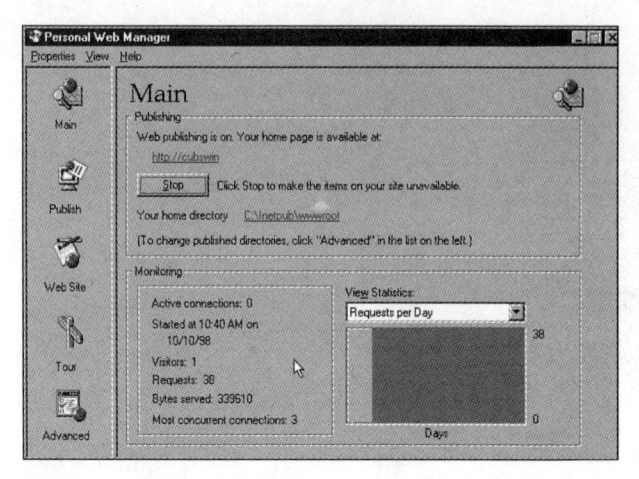

Figure 14.50 Reviewing the usage statistics for your Web page.

21. The most interesting tidbit, and usually the most surprising for people, is the Bytes Served counter. If you look closely, you will notice that you have already served-up nearly 340,000 bytes worth of information. Huh—but you did not really do anything! Exactly. After you start using your Web site in earnest, you will see this number jump astronomically. Keep in mind that this amount is pretty much the same number that others will experience when they are trying to view your Web site via the Internet (or your organization's intranet), so you should try to keep this number as low as possible.

CHAPTER 15
NETWORK MANAGEMENT

15

NETWORK MANAGEMENT

How do I...

15.1 Create and configure a Windows 98 peer-to-peer network?

15.2 Take advantage of the Microsoft Zero Administration Initiative (ZAIW) for Windows?

15.3 Install and configure the Windows 98 Web-based Enterprise Management (WBEM)?

15.4 Install Simple Network Management Protocol (SNMP)?

15.5 Use system policies?

This chapter helps to walk you through the messy area of network management. If you are a home PC user, this chapter probably is not for you; it is meant for corporate network/desktop managers who are responsible for 10 to 100,000 Windows 98 computer systems. The primary focus of the discussion within this chapter is on that hot topic better known as *total cost of ownership* *(TCO)*. There are countless ways to lower your organization's TCO when it comes to using large numbers of Windows 98 PCs, and this chapter presents some of the more popular methods.

Managing large numbers of computers has never been easy, but with the advent of the GUI operating system it has actually gotten much more difficult. The end user community has become more sophisticated and more willing to try new things at the expense of the organization and its networks (usually, this is done unknowingly by the individual, but it happens nonetheless). People have begun to "own" the PC that sits on their desk at work and do not take kindly to the "geeks" in the information services (IS) department who are attempting to "control" them. Thus, a lot of desktop management techniques do occur behind the scenes, which in part allows the IS group to keep end users from "helping out" and "fixing things" for IS staffers.

Moreover, on top of all this, you have year 2000 (Y2K) concerns, which thankfully inside the Windows 98 operating realm are not as bad as those being encountered in the Novell NetWare world. The largest Y2K issues with Windows 98 come not with the OS itself, but with the numerous Y2K-compliant software that runs on top. What's that, I thought you just said everything was compliant? Well, it is, but users tend to write their own quick and dirty macros (especially inside Microsoft Excel and Lotus 1-2-3) that tend to not be compliant. Unfortunately, there is little you can do from a network management perspective to prevent this from happening, but using tools such as Systems Management Server you can find out who in your organization (on the desktop level, anyway) are creating macros. From there, you can work with those individuals on a one-on-one basis. This chapter presents you with a little more detailed information on the Microsoft Systems Management Server tool.

15.1 Create and Configure a Windows 98 Peer-to-Peer Network

The purpose of this topic is to introduce the reader to non-server network configurations. Many times in small organizations and companies, the local computer store's sales representative sells the non-computer literate company president (or other executive staff member) on the idea that you must have a server on a local area network (LAN). While a corporate network or systems administrator would be cognizant of this fact, in a smaller organization where the computer person is also the bookkeeper and the receptionist, this fact tends to get hidden in the shuffle. This topic is aimed at those types of individuals who might not have the LAN knowledge necessary to perform their duties in the best way possible.

15.2 Take Advantage of the Microsoft Zero Administration Initiative (ZAIW) for Windows

The Microsoft Zero Administration Initiative (ZAIW) for Windows does apply to Windows 98, although there is no specific Zero Administration Kit (ZAK) for the Windows 98 operating system. This How-To is geared at bringing up your level of knowledge on this purely Microsoft technology, with the aim to lower the TCO for your desktop and laptop computers throughout your organization. Additional discussion is given to the Microsoft Systems Management Server tool, which can also be used to help you lower TCO for your Windows 98 desktop operating environment.

Additional information within this How-To introduces the reader to the world of Web-based network systems management. This section helps you understand how WBEM can be used throughout your organization on such diverse non-Microsoft technologies such as Cisco routers and UNIX servers. In addition, the simple network management protocol (SNMP) is discussed.

15.3 Install and Configure the Windows 98 Web-based Enterprise Management (WBEM)

Now that you know what WBEM is, and why you need it, you need to know how to install and configure it. This How-To is geared precisely at that.

15.4 Install SNMP

Now you know what SNMP is and why you need it. This How-To tells you how to install it.

15.5 Use System Policies

Many individuals do not understand how system policies can come into play, especially as a tool to better manage your Windows 98 PCs that might exist all over your organization. Coupled with the power of Windows NT servers, system policies do make it much easier for you to better control your own network operating environments.

COMPLEXITY
INTERMEDIATE

15.1 How do I...
Create and configure a Windows 98 peer-to-peer network?

Problem

I only have about 10 people working in my small law firm office. Is there some way that I can create a network through which all the lawyers, secretaries, and research assistants can share files, printers, and initiate a small email operating environment? And if so, how do I go about doing something like this?

Technique

Windows 98 incorporates into itself a technology known as *peer-to-peer networking*. Peer-to-peer networking was first originated in the Microsoft Windows world with the advent of the Windows for Workgroups, which was an add-on to the Windows 3.1 GUI. Windows for Workgroups was released in October 1992, as version 3.1, and required at least MS-DOS version 3.31 to work. In March 1993, version 3.11 was released (and is the version that most everyone remembers). Windows for Workgroups 3.11 became the basis for the peer-to-peer networking in Windows 95 and now in Windows 98. Of course, there have been major modifications and improvements made to peer-to-peer networking by Microsoft over the years, but the core technology is still the same.

You should select a single networking protocol to use, a cabling strategy (for example, thinnet versus twisted-pair), a topology (for example, Ethernet versus token ring), and a level of security to utilize. Additionally, you should assess your current requirements then try to envision your future needs, and put them all together for a cohesive networking strategy. This type of up-front planning allows your network to grow with your business. Too many times, small business owners quickly and cheaply slop something together only to pay a fortune when they wind up replacing stuff piecemeal to make their peer-to-peer network grow up into a real network. With the right strategy, your peer-to-peer network can easily grow into a real LAN, and you can save most of your existing technology as you grow forward into the future. Use these steps to help you walk through the process, and soon you will be on your way to your first peer-to-peer network.

Steps

1. The first thing you should do is to count the number of users in your organization then assess the PC computing power that exists (Windows 98 versus Windows 95 versus Windows 3.1 PCs). Make a chart with all this information (preferably in Microsoft Excel or another spreadsheet program), which can then grow as you add more data and complexity to it.

2. Next, you need to select a security model to start with. This is very easy to do, and you do not need to be a computer expert to make this decision. All you need to do is exercise some common sense. So first, you need to decide if one of your Windows 98 computers acts as a server. In a peer-to-peer network, a Windows 98 PC can act as both a client and a server at the same time (which is why it is called peer-to-peer networking), which means that you do not need to sacrifice a valuable computer to sit around and play server all day. Or, conversely, none of your Windows 98 PCs has to be *the* server as they all can act as the server. With a small professional office, such as a law firm, medical office, or a similar business, it is recommended that you permit all Windows 98 computers to be both a client and a server in your peer-to-peer network.

3. Next, you need to decide on a network topology. This means, will you use *Ethernet* or *token ring* technology. You might want to examine their pros and cons before you get hung up on the technical terminology. *Ethernet* (invented by Bob Metcalf in 1973, founder of 3Com Corporation) comes in two varieties (*thinnet* and *twisted-pair*, which are actually cabling technologies) and is the cheaper of the two to install, maintain, upgrade, and is easier to use. Ethernet comes in a variety of speeds, which are measured in megabits per second (Mbps):

- 2Mbps (2Base-T)—This is typically a thinnet speed.
- 5Mbps (5Base-T)—This can also be a thinnet speed.
- 10Mbps (10Base-T)—This is typically a twisted-pair speed, using category 3 or 5 cabling.
- 100Mbps (100Base-T, 100VG-AnyLAN, or (100Base-Tx)—This is typically a twisted-pair speed, using category 5 cabling.
- 1,000Mbps (Gigabit Ethernet)—This is typically a twisted-pair speed, using category 5 or fiber-optic cabling.

Token Ring (invented by IBM in 1984) is usually viewed by mainframe IS folks as being the real enterprise level networking technology. Token ring is very expensive to deploy, costs a lot to maintain, likes to fail in dirty and dusty manufacturing environments (it does much better in clean offices), has a limited upgrade path (from purely a bandwidth perspective), and is harder to use. Token ring comes in two speeds, which are also measured in Mbps:

- 4Mbps
- 16Mbps

A big thing to remember with token-ring technology is that you cannot mix network card speeds (and thus token speeds) on the same LAN, which means that either everyone on your peer-to-peer network operates at 4 or 16Mbps—no half-and-half stuff permitted here.

After that lambasting, what choice do you have but Ethernet? Ethernet is by far the best choice for peer-to-peer networking.

4. Next up is the network protocol. In a small (for example, less than 25 users) peer-to-peer networking environment, Microsoft's NetBEUI is the best selection. If at some future point you decide to expand your network, you can always add an additional network protocol such as TCP/IP (for accessing the Internet or your organization's new intranet) or IPX/SPX (for accessing Novell NetWare servers). If you have a need to build an intranet from the start of using your peer-to-peer network, your choice should be TCP/IP. Whatever your choice, make sure to note it on your chart.

In a peer-to-peer networking environment, where all the peers (client PCs) are running Windows 3.11 (WFW) or later, NetBEUI is the best choice because it is low maintenance. For example, you do not have to assign any numbers or addresses, like you have to with TCP/IP because it is the fastest protocol available for a Microsoft Windows 98 peer-to-peer network (20 percent faster than TCP/IP and 50 percent faster than IPX/SPX, on an average basis). If you need more input on making this decision, review Chapter 10, "Welcome to the Neighborhood: Network, That Is," for more information on this topic.

5. Next, you need to pick a cabling strategy. If you are in an office environment, Unshielded twisted-pair (UTP) is the choice for you. UTP, which comes in a variety of category levels, looks like thick telephone wire and is assembled in much the same manner. In fact, you can very easily buy UTP cabling at your local computer store, in varying lengths, which means that installing it becomes a breeze. However, the downside to UTP cabling is that it does not fare well in a dirty manufacturing environment or other places that have a lot of electronic interference present, because it likes the cleanliness of offices (besides, it really is not all that durable).

The category level of UTP helps to determine the total length a cable can be without using a device known as a repeater. If you need one of these, you should not be building a peer-to-peer network anyway. Because the top of the line level is category 5, and because that level is so cheap to purchase (retail is around $.10 a foot), you really should only invest in this category level. This means that you can have a distance of up to 100 meters (326 feet) between your PC and the peer-to-peer network's hub device—the distance between the front office and the back work area can really be up to 200 meters apart, roughly 650 feet. Not too shabby for a peer-to-peer network, huh? UTP can be used with either Ethernet or token ring, so it does not affect your topology decision.

Thinnet (also known as thin Ethernet or thin coax) is the easiest way to string a peer-to-peer network together. No network hub is required (it costs roughly $100 for a 16-port hub, whereas one port equates to one user on your peer-to-peer network) and uses a daisy-chain approach to

15.1
CREATE AND CONFIGURE A WINDOWS 98 PEER-TO-PEER NETWORK

677

wiring. Connection to a thinnet network is made via a BNC T-connector (from the Windows 98 computer's network interface card), which is very easy to do. The major downfall to thinnet is that it is inherently slow, especially as you add more users. For example, anything over 10 users on a thinnet peer-to-peer network is too much, and a break in the wire anywhere on the network brings the whole peer-to-peer network down (unlike UTP wiring, where a single break only affects the user that is connected to that wire). The other primary difference between thinnet and twisted-pair (UTP) is in their physical layouts, as you can very easily see in Figure 15.1.

Peer-to-Peer Networks: Physical Layouts

Thinnet Cabling Structure

Twisted Pair Cabling Structure

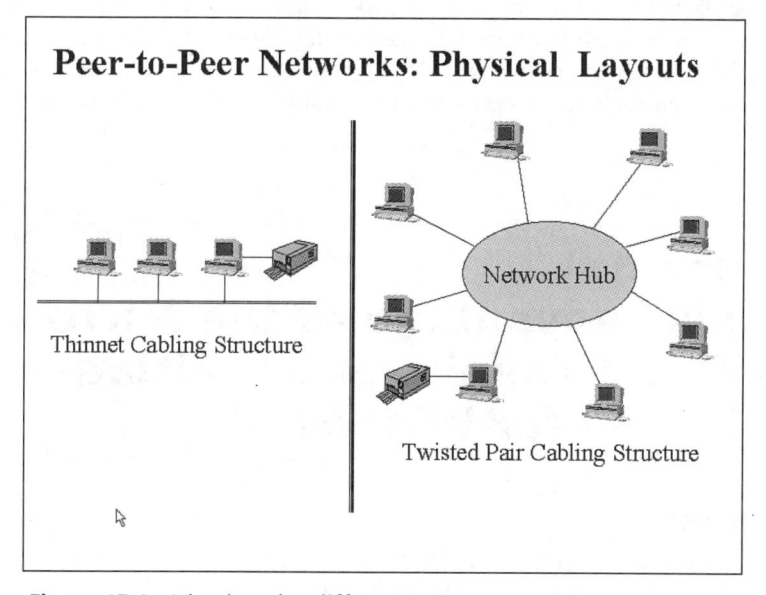

Figure 15.1 Viewing the differences between thinnet and twisted-pair peer-to-peer network wiring schemes.

6. The key to these two cabling structure schemes is the hub in the middle of the UTP peer-to-peer network. Regardless of the cabling scheme, printers are attached to the network in the same manner: via a Windows 98 PC that is acting as a print server. You can have a printer attached to every PC on your network if you want and still be able to have everyone else on the peer-to-peer network connect to that shared print device. Likewise, all your other peer-to-peer network shared devices (modems, fax-modems, and so on) can be used across the network regardless of the cabling type.

7. Now that you know how to create your own peer-to-peer network, your next step is to really do it. If you are a bit wary of doing your own cabling, look in the yellow pages for the dozens of tiny firms that do cable installations. If you decide to go the UTP route, the hub requires your ability to plug a power cable into the wall, and then plug each UTP cable into the hub on one end and the PC's network interface card on the other end. You might want to have a professional install the network cards in your Windows 98 computers. In fact, it is recommended that whomever does your cabling should also do your network interface card (NIC) installations as well. This saves you some money and alleviates the problem of having one vendor point to the other if the peer-to-peer network does not work once the hardware has been installed.

8. Finally, all you need to do is to install the Client for Microsoft Networks software that comes with the Windows 98 operating system. To do this, closely follow the steps that are found in Chapter 10, which discuss precisely how to perform this installation and configuration process.

COMPLEXITY
INTERMEDIATE

15.2 How do I...
Take advantage of the Microsoft Zero Administration Initiative (ZAIW) for Windows?

Problem

I hear so much about how Windows 98 can help me to lower my TCO for the Windows 98 computers on my organization's networks, but there have been very few details discussed on how to actually go about doing this. How do I deploy the various Microsoft ZAIW for Windows 98, and what kinds of benefits can I expect to see from this type of stuff?

Technique

Microsoft's recent foray into the world of network management and lowering the TCO for an organization's deployment of Windows 98 technologies has led it to launch a ZAIW initiative. This initiative actually comprises itself of several software tools including the following:

- *Internet Explorer Administration Kit's Profile Manager*—Review the details on deploying this software, which are found in Chapter 12, "The Internet and Web Browsing."

- *Windows Management Instrumentation* (WMI)—The purpose of the WMI is to provide a basis for instrumentation in future Windows environments

(Windows NT 5.0, Windows Consumer, and so on). This means that the WMI is not quite ready for prime time, especially in the Windows 98 world. However, it does include a set of extensions to the Win32 Driver Model (WDM), which helps to provide hooks to the future (and maybe even later usage of Windows 98) operating systems environments.

- *Microsoft Management Console* (MMC)—This is discussed in the Windows 98 Resource Kit's topic found in Chapter 1, "Installation Tips."

- *Web-based Enterprise Management* (WBEM)—These Web-based network management technologies are discussed in more detail later in this chapter.

- *Microsoft Systems Management Server* (SMS)—A Windows NT BackOffice component that allows for the close management of desktop computers and network devices.

The core focus of ZAIW is to open the infrastructure of Windows 98 to the rest of the world so that organizations can better manage their Windows 98 PCs, as well as to begin the establishment of a management infrastructure for lowering the TCO for a Windows 98 client base (inside a Windows NT server base). Microsoft has announced several other technologies, both hardware and software, that go along with ZAIW, but they have not been officially released to the retail market. This section does not discuss them in any detail (the majority of these technologies are still in the vaporware stage, that is, the idea exists, but the rubber never meets the road). As you step through these technologies, try to visualize where each one of these can aid you in your organization.

Steps

1. The Profile Manager utility, which comes as a part of the Internet Explorer Administration Kit, is excellent at making sure that each of your organization's users are all accessing the Internet in a similar manner. This benefits you when a user contacts your internal help desk (or other support infrastructure) for assistance; everyone should be able to provide a quick and consistent answer to the problem at hand. What this means is that tech support calls should be shorter in length, problems can be more easily resolved, and hopefully, the organization's end user community becomes more satisfied with the IS departments that exist in your company. Refer to Chapter 12 for the nitty-gritty details on installing and using the Internet Explorer Administration Kit's Profile Manager tool.

2. The Microsoft Systems Management Server software, which is sold separately or as a part of the Microsoft BackOffice suite of Windows NT networking products, is an excellent tool for managing your Windows 98 desktop client computers. Systems Management Server (SMS) excels at the following capabilities:

- Monitors client computers.

- Takes hardware and software inventories of those same PCs.

- Performs mass deployments of software (such as Microsoft Office and Windows 98).

- Assists corporate help desks with its remote control capabilities, where a help desk staff person can literally take control of a Windows 98 user's PC and see exactly what that user has done to "fix" their environment so that it no longer works correctly.

- Identifies and fixes Y2K issues.

3. The Windows Management Instrumentation (WMI) came about in part due to the whole NetPC debate and initiatives. WMI is optimized for the Windows platform. When coupled with WBEM, WMI provides an instrumentation mechanism within the Windows 98 platform that provides backward compatibility with legacy management instrumentation technologies, such as the Desktop Management Initiative (DMI). In theory, the WMI technology takes off when Microsoft releases its Windows NT Server 5.0 technology.

4. WBEM comes with the Windows 98 operating system and needs to be installed separately, because it does not install with the full installation of Windows 98 (probably because most people would never know what to do with it). Refer to the next section, "How do I install and configure Web-based Enterprise management (WBEM)?", which explains how to install Web-based enterprise management for Windows 98. WBEM is an industry-wide initiative (launched in July 1996, which included the likes of Cisco, Microsoft, Compaq, Intel, BMC Software, 3Com, Bay Networks, Dell, Hewlett-Packard, Tivoli Systems, Sybase, Symantec, Zenith, Attachmate, and Platinum Technologies) that includes a number of standards designed to allow management of systems, networks, and users through the use of Internet technologies. It defines schemas and protocols and is open and extensible. The Desktop Management Task Force (DMTF) has now ratified parts of it as the Common Information Model (CIM).

5. The MMC feature does not come with the Windows 98 operating system, but is a part of the Microsoft Windows 98 Resource Kit (refer to Chapter 1 for more details on that collection of tools). The purpose of the MMC is to provide a standard framework display for hosting administration tools, which are built as MMC snap-ins by Microsoft and other third-party software vendors. The MMC has the potential to be used from within an existing enterprise console or to launch enterprise consoles. Unlike some

of the other enterprise consoles on the market today, the MMC imposes no protocol dependencies or object repositories; these remain the responsibility of each snap-in. By allowing administrators to create their own views and by removing technology discipline boundaries, it is possible to create appropriate displays of network, systems, and user information. This, in turn, provides a single point of management that is integrated, comprehensive, and easy to use.

This might sound great, but again there is a lot of vaporware present in this technology. Microsoft is working hard on the MMC as part of the Windows NT 5.0 operating system. It has released miniaturized versions of the MMC as part of other applications (IIS 4.0, the Windows 98 Resource Kit, Site Server 3.0, etc.), but it still is not fully real for the whole world to see and use on a stable, daily basis.

COMPLEXITY
INTERMEDIATE

15.3 How do I...
Install and configure the Windows 98 Web-based Enterprise Management (WBEM)?

Problem

I have heard so much about the Web-based Enterprise Management (WBEM) initiative and its associated software, but even though I did a full installation of Windows 98 it is no where to be found. How do I install and configure the Windows 98 version of WBEM, so that I can then better manage my Windows 98 computers?

Technique

WBEM is a new feature to the desktop Windows world. It includes the components necessary for system administrators and technical support personnel to provide remote problem tracking and systems administration. This is not a feature for a home computer, nor was it designed for technicians other than those who possess advanced knowledge of the Windows 98 operating system. However, you should probably know if it has been installed on your PC (for those of you on corporate networks), so that you do not accidentally delete it because you want more hard drive space available for your games. Therefore, the first set of steps is aimed at showing you whether it has been installed on your PC. The instructions following demonstrate how to install it, and then these are followed-up with brief configuration explanations.

Steps

1. After starting the Windows Explorer, maneuver your way over to the C:\Windows\System folder, as shown in Figure 15.2.

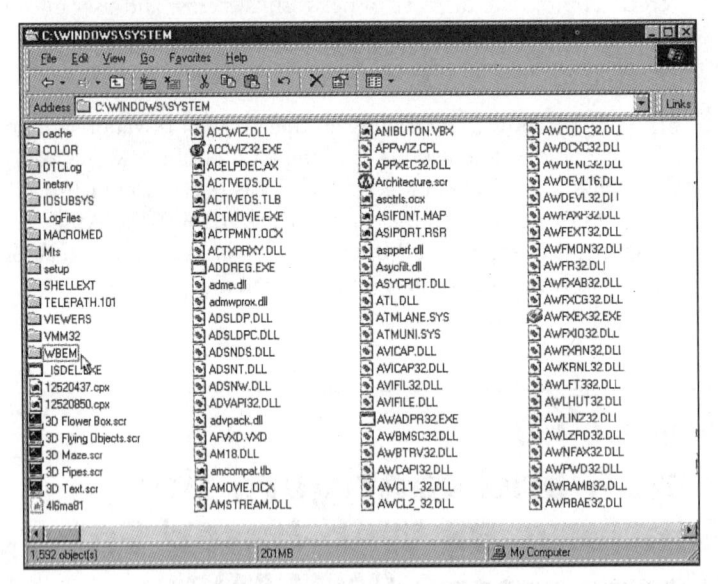

Figure 15.2 Looking for a WBEM installation.

2. You will see a folder called WBEM. Open this folder by double-clicking it to reveal the screen shown in Figure 15.3.

3. That is all there is to it. It would be wise not to delete any of these files and folders, unless you have specific permission from your IS department to do so. If you are the IS department, you should continue through the remainder of these steps.

4. If you had looked on your computer in the `%windowsroot%\system` directory, as was done in step 1, and there was no WBEM folder, it is not installed on your computer. To install it, you need to use the Add/Remove Programs icon from within the Windows 98 Control Panel.

5. Next, go to the Windows Setup tab by clicking it. From there, click once on the Internet Tools selection to highlight it.

6. Click once on the Details... button to move to the Internet Tools selection area, as shown in Figure 15.4.

15.2
INSTALL AND CONFIGURE WBEM

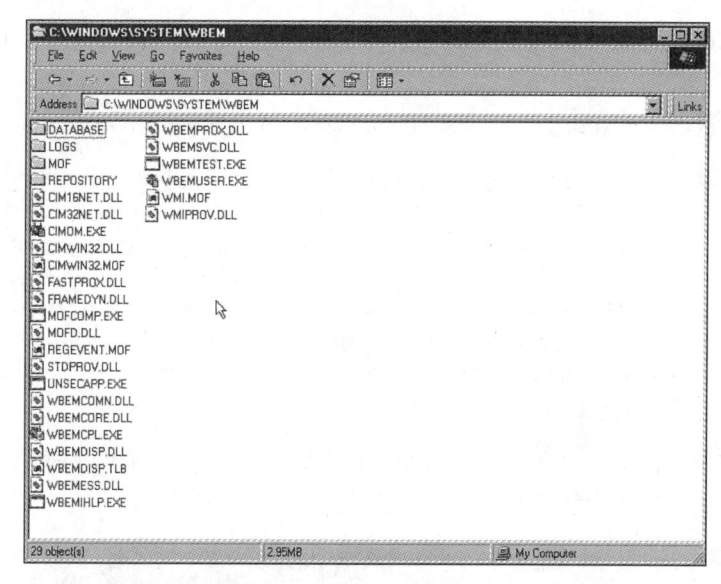

Figure 15.3 Reviewing a WBEM installation.

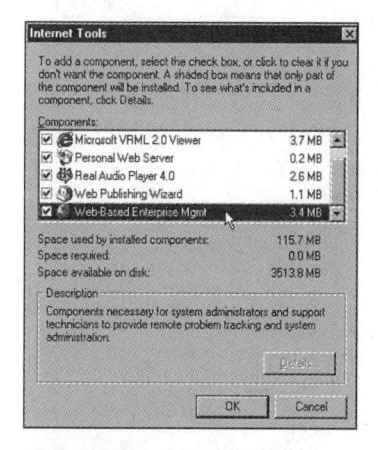

Figure 15.4 The Internet Tools selection area.

7. Scroll down to the bottom of this screen, where you see the Web-Based Enterprise Mgmt selection. Select it by placing a check mark in the box just to the left of this option.

8. Click OK to return to the previous Windows Setup screen. From there, click OK to accept your changes and selections, at which time the software installation copying process begins.

9. When all the files have copied, you might be prompted to restart your computer. Do so, by clicking Yes.

10. When your PC restarts, you are ready to begin the configuration process.

11. This is where things in today's world are still on what you would term *the ugly side*. Use of WBEM is still heavily dependent on the use of a Windows NT server. If your network does not have one then, at present, there is very little that having WBEM on your Windows 98 PC will do for you. This is because WBEM is dependent on DCOM as its transport mechanism, a technology that Microsoft invented (but has gotten little support outside of the Microsoft world). However, there are a few binaries that you might want to examine.

12. Open the \Windows\System\WBEM folder on your Windows 98 PC and look at the files present, as shown in Figure 15.5.

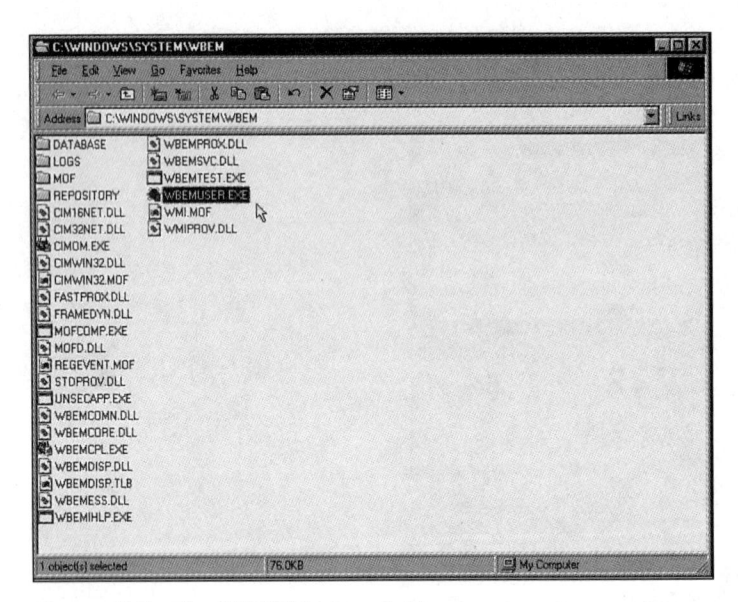

Figure 15.5 The WBEM System folder.

13. By double-clicking the WBEMCPL.EXE file you are able to access the Web-Based Enterprise Management Administrator tool, as shown in Figure 15.6.

14. The purpose of this tool is to configure the frequency of backups of your data repository, as well as to determine the type of logging that is performed. At the bottom of this screen, you are also permitted to set the size and location of your log files.

15.2
INSTALL AND CONFIGURE WBEM

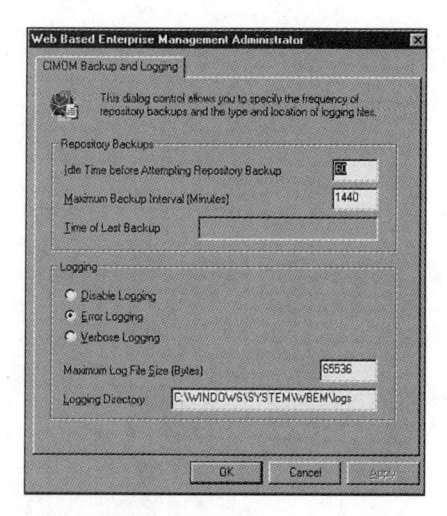

Figure 15.6 Using the Web-Based Enterprise Management Administrator tool.

15. As with all the WBEM software screens found in Windows 98, there is no online help (even when you do see a Help button, there is no code behind it, which means that obtaining immediate help from Microsoft on any of this is out of the question).

16. Click OK to exit and save your changes to the Web-Based Enterprise Management Administrator screen.

17. Then, double-click the WBEMUSER.EXE file to reveal the screen shown in Figure 15.7.

18. This tool works like something out of Windows NT 4.0 (server, that is, the User Manager for Domains utility to be specific). Click the Add New User button or use the User/Add New User menu hierarchy, to reveal the screen shown in Figure 15.8.

19. Enter the user's name (user ID) and the domain in which that user resides (remember that this is a Windows NT domain). The rest of the screen appears to still be for "show" (because the WBEM built into Windows 98 is a beta 2 release). However, in the future, it would make sense that you would be able to enable or disable user attributes and execute methods at will, as well as to be able to edit the security levels for a particular user.

20. Make your changes and additions, and then click OK to return to the main Web-Based Enterprise Management User Manager screen.

CHAPTER 15
NETWORK MANAGEMENT

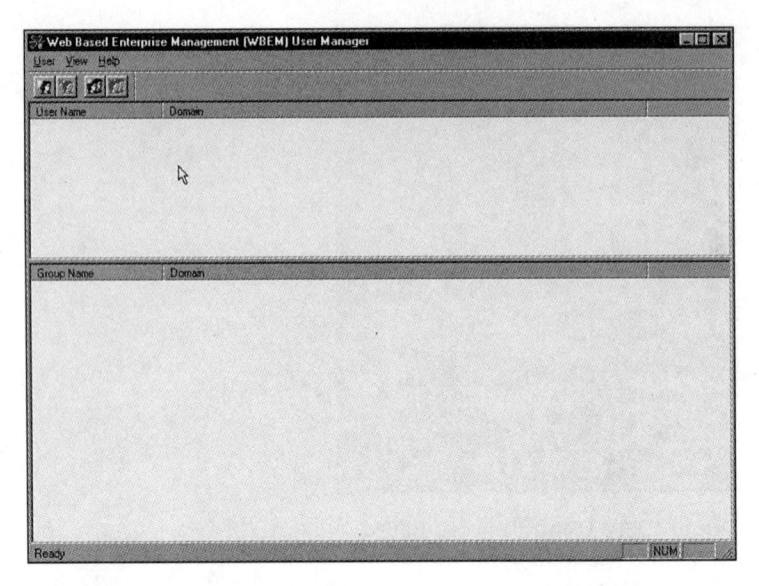

Figure 15.7 Using the Web-Based Enterprise Management User Manager tool.

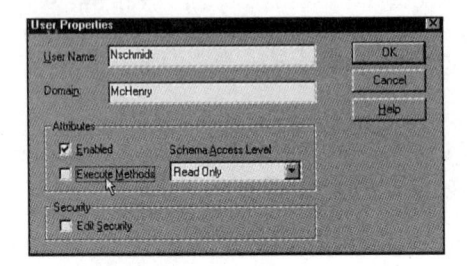

Figure 15.8 Adding a new user to the WBEM User Manager.

21. Next, click the Add New Group button or use the User/Add New Group menu hierarchy, to reveal the screen shown in Figure 15.9.

22. This screen works exactly as the New User screen does, except that there is an additional area on the Group screen. It is in this Type section that you specify the domain for the group, as well as to determine whether it is a Local or Global group. Make your changes and additions, and then click OK to return to the main Web-Based Enterprise Management User Manager screen.

15.2
INSTALL AND CONFIGURE WBEM

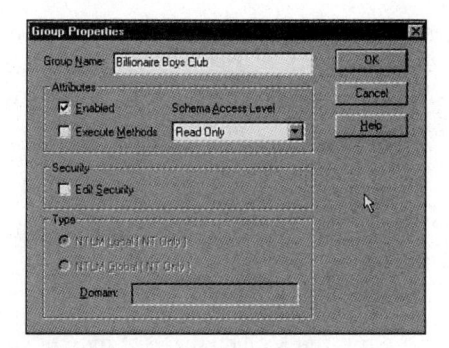

Figure 15.9 Adding a new group to the WBEM User Manager.

23. Close the main Web-Based Enterprise Management User Manager screen with all your changes intact.

24. Next, double-click the WBEMTEST.EXE file to reveal the screen shown in Figure 15.10.

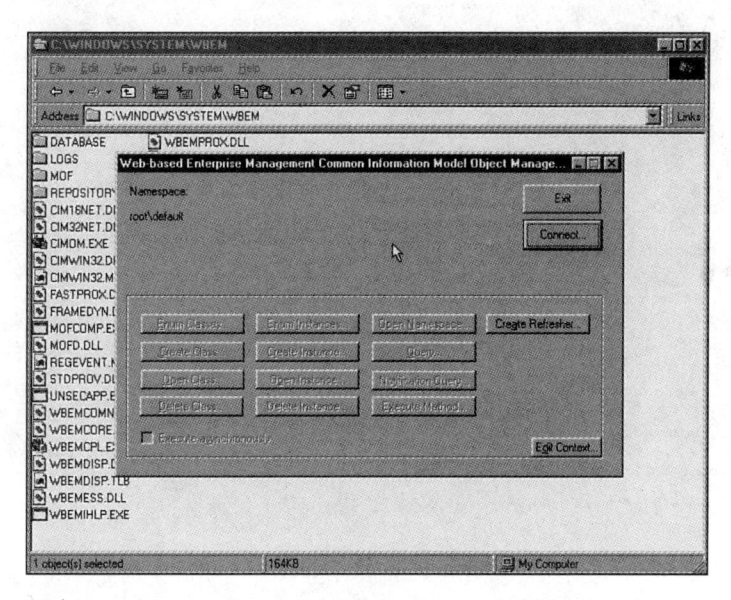

Figure 15.10 Testing the WBEM Common Information Model Object Manager.

25. The use of this tool goes way beyond the scope of this book. This tool is actually part of the *WBEM* Systems Development Kit (the Web-Based Enterprise Management SDK), which is presently coded in Microsoft Visual C++. The gist of this tool is to permit you to test your CIM objects for use with the WBEM. The Connect button allows you to test your DCOM transport connection to your server-based WBEM tools. Click once on the Exit button to close this screen, which again has no online help available.

26. The final Web-Based Enterprise Management tool that comes with the Windows 98 operating system is the MOFcomp.Exe (an SDK compiler), which is not even a GUI tool. To determine the parameter specifications for this tool, run this command in a DOS prompt shell without any parameters attached, as shown in Figure 15.11.

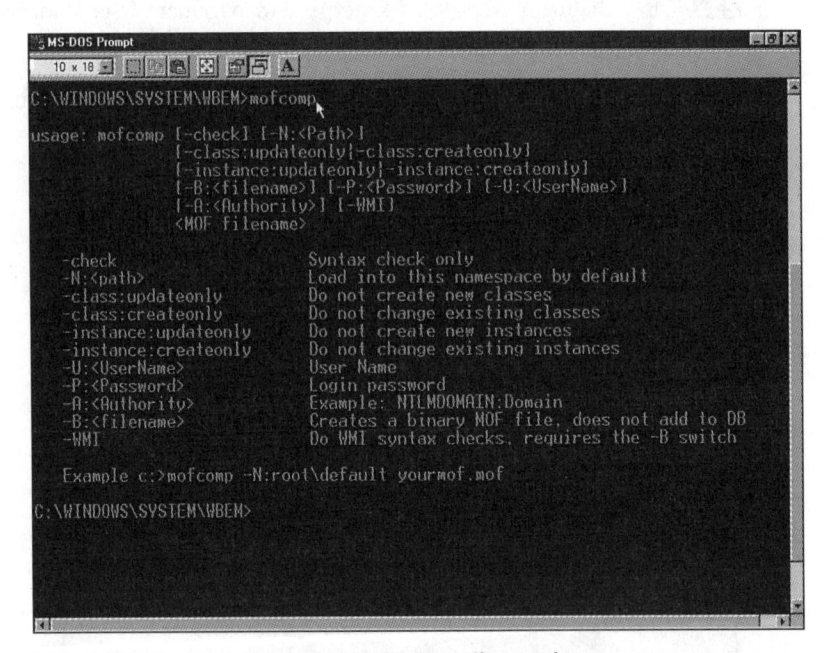

Figure 15.11 Examining the MOF Compiler tool.

27. If you want to test this tool on your system, run the following command inside your DOS prompt shell: `MOFcomp wmi.mof` (any case is fine, because Windows 98 DOS is not case-sensitive), as shown in Figure 15.12.

28. What happens is that the tool parses the WMI file before it stores the results in the Repository, which exists inside folder found within the WBEM folder structure on your PC's hard drive. A success flag is noted when this tool has finished its execution.

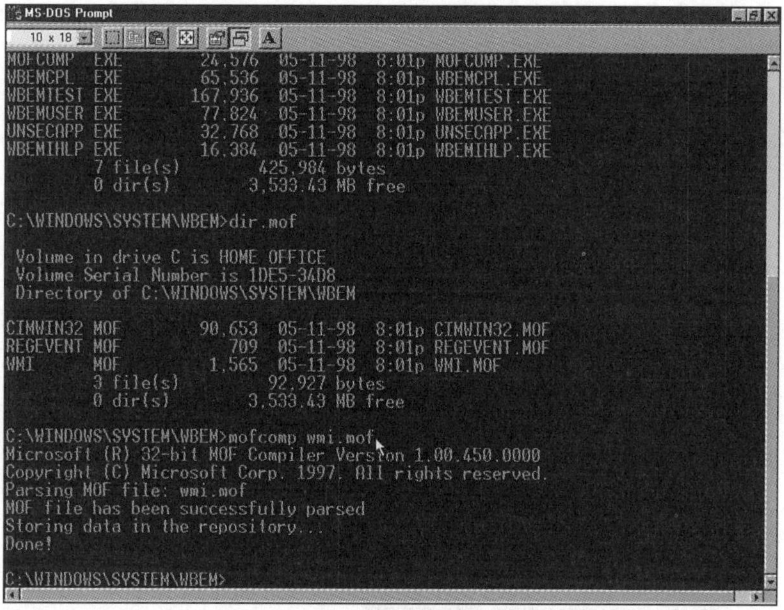

Figure 15.12 Running the MOF Compiler tool.

COMPLEXITY
ADVANCED

15.3 How do I...
Install and configure Simple Network Management Protocol (SNMP)?

Problem

I want to use the SNMP networking management protocol with my Windows 98 PCs that I must manage. How do I install and configure SNMP for use with Windows 98 computers?

Technique

The networking management protocol known as SNMP or Simple Networking Management Protocol, has a client version that comes with the Windows 98 operating system. However, to analyze its results, you must have installed a server-based SNMP software package on your server (which can be Windows NT-based, UNIX-based, or even NetWare-based if you prefer). Keep in mind that nothing like this comes with the Windows NT operating system, so it is up to you to purchase and install one of these packages on your own. After you install the software, there is no configuration to do on the client (the Windows 98) side.

Steps

1. To access the Windows 98 Control Panel, click the Start button, and then click the Settings menu option, followed by a click on the Control Panel menu selection.

2. This takes you into the Control Panel screen where you need to double-click the Network icon to reveal the next screen, as shown in Figure 15.13. Alternatively, you can quickly go to this same screen by holding down the Alt key on your keyboard and double-clicking the Network Neighborhood icon found on the Windows 98 desktop (assuming, of course, that you have at least one networking software client already installed; otherwise, there will not be a Network Neighborhood icon on your desktop).

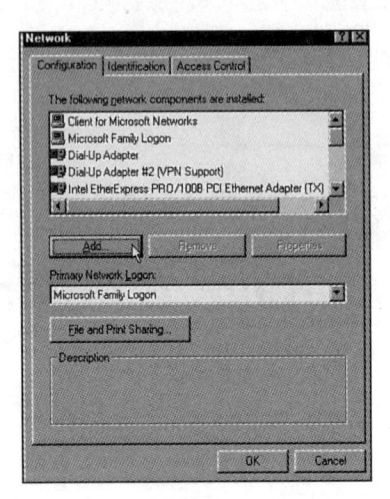

Figure 15.13 Examining the Network Configuration screen.

3. After the Network window appears, you should take a closer look at it because it possesses a wealth of useful information. In the top boxed area, you see a listing of all the networking components that are already installed on your computer. Use the scrollbar along the right side of the box if there are more items listed they appear in the single box's window area. At the top of the listing is all the networking client software. The next set of objects are the various NICs that you have installed on your computer. Below the network adapters are the networking protocols

15.3
INSTALL AND CONFIGURE SNMP

that are already installed on your computer. The final item(s) in the box are the networking services that are already installed on your Windows 98 PC.

4. Continuing on, click the Add... button, above the Primary Network Logon text label, found near the middle of this screen. This takes you to the next screen, as shown in Figure 15.14.

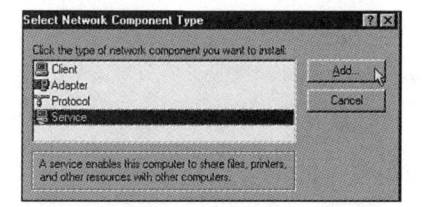

Figure 15.14 The Select Network Component Type screen.

5. Click once on the Service network component option, and then click Add... to continue.

6. When the Select Network Service screen appears, click once on the Have Disk button to proceed to the Install From Disk screen. From here, you need to use the Browse button to locate the proper path on the Windows 98 CD-ROM for the SNMP installation files. Click the Browse button to reveal the screen shown in Figure 15.15.

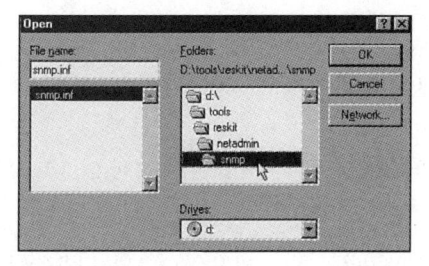

Figure 15.15 Adding the SNMP network service.

7. After you locate the SNMP directory on the Windows 98 CD-ROM (in the \Tools\ResKit\NetAdmin\SNMP folder), click it to highlight it, and then click OK to pull this path information back to the Install From Disk screen, as shown in Figure 15.16.

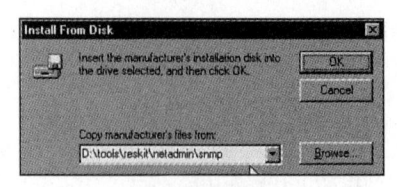

Figure 15.16 Installing the SNMP network service from the Windows 98 CD-ROM.

8. Click OK to proceed with the installation process, as shown in Figure 15.17.

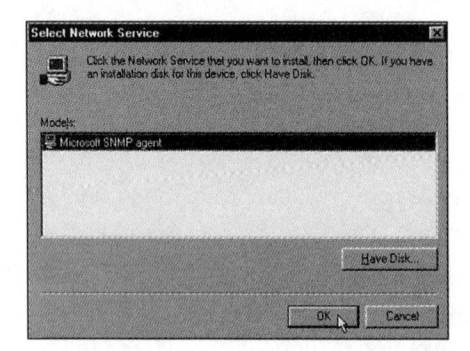

Figure 15.17 Viewing the SNMP network service in the Select Network Service window.

9. Make sure that you are installing the Microsoft SNMP Agent service, and then click OK to return to the Network Configuration screen, as shown in Figure 15.18.

10. Click OK to start the software installation process. Figure 15.19 shows the installation in progress.

11. The Building Driver Information Database process continues for a few minutes. You are prompted to insert your Windows 98 CD-ROM in your CD-ROM drive if you have not already done so, at which time the software driver files for the SNMP software are installed into your Windows 98 PC, as shown in Figure 15.20.

12. When the installation process is complete you are prompted to restart your computer, as shown in Figure 15.21.

15.3
INSTALL AND CONFIGURE SNMP

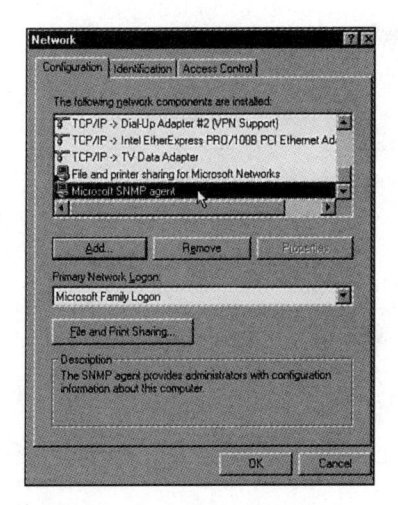

Figure 15.18 Confirming the Microsoft SNMP Agent exists.

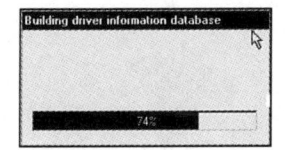

Figure 15.19 Continuing the SNMP network service installation process.

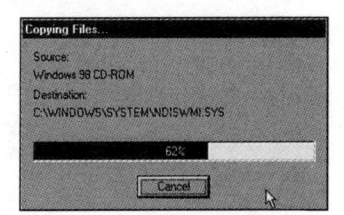

Figure 15.20 Copying the SNMP network service software files.

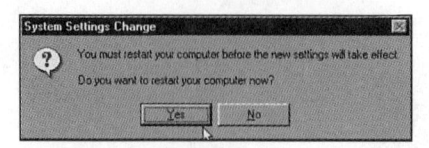

Figure 15.21 Deciding whether to reboot the Windows 98 PC.

13. Click Yes to restart your system.

14. After restarting your PC, you are ready to use the Microsoft SNMP Agent.

COMPLEXITY
INTERMEDIATE

15.5 How do I...
Use system policies?

Problem

Is there some way that I can better control the desktop systems of my organization's users without having to spend thousands of dollars on a specialized software package such as Microsoft's Systems Management Server? If so, how do I do this within the constraints of the Windows 98 operating system?

Technique

The method to the madness that you seek to control is a tool known as the *Systems Policy Editor*. However, there is a caveat to using this tool with Windows 98: It is installed as part of the Windows NT Server 4.0+ operating system, which means that you need a Windows NT Server somewhere on your organization's LAN. This means that while you may completely lock-down the end user's Windows 98 operating environment, a Windows NT Server is required to do so.

Steps

1. The only step here is to ensure that the client for Microsoft networks is installed on each Windows 98 PC on your organization's network that you want to manage using the Windows NT system policies. (Refer to Chapter 10.)

PART IV
THE MULTIMEDIA REVOLUTION

CHAPTER 16
MULTIMEDIA BASICS

16

MULTIMEDIA BASICS

How do I...
16.1 Install the additional Microsoft multimedia tools?
16.2 Use the Windows Media Player?
16.3 Configure and use the Microsoft Comic Chat?

The world of computer-based multimedia continues to spin faster and faster. Things that were completely unheard of only a few years ago continue to thrive in ways that are unimaginable today. Your PC works like the mainframes of yesteryear, while performing like the home movie theatre of tomorrow, using TV studio capabilities that used to cost tens-of-thousands of dollars, all for just $1,500–$2,500 (USD). This chapter introduces you to some of the more graphically-intense features of the Windows 98 operating system including the Windows Media Player, the Microsoft Comic Chat, and the Macromedia Shockwave utilities. One of the coolest features of Windows 98 is the Comic Chat, which is an interactive Internet Relay Chat (IRC)-based tool that permits you to perform teleconferencing via TCP/IP-based networks (both public and private) such as the Internet.

There are a few Windows 98 accessory items that you will need to install to help support the multimedia functions of your Windows 98 PC, but that do not seem to publicly do anything for you. There is no real configuring or direct use of tools, such as the Macromedia Shockwave utilities (both Director and Flash); the VRML 2.0 Viewer; and the RealAudio player (version 4.0), yet, the core multimedia features of Windows 98—the Windows Media Player and the Microsoft Comic Chat—will fail to function properly without these accessory items being installed.

CHAPTER 16
MULTIMEDIA BASICS

So, without further ado, go through the first topic in this chapter for assistance on finding all these items that must be installed for a fully functioning Windows 98 multimedia experience. After the task is complete, you are able to easily tread your way through the Windows Media Player and the Microsoft Comic Chat topics much more smoothly.

16.1 Install the Additional Microsoft Multimedia Tools
This How-To explains the steps necessary for installing the various multimedia tools that come with the Windows 98 operating system.

16.2 Use the Windows Media Player
After the Windows Media Player has been installed, you'll need to know how to use it properly. This How-To addresses this subject.

16.3 Configure and Use the Microsoft Comic Chat
The Microsoft Comic Chat tool that comes with Windows 98 can be a fun communications device for *talking* with others across the Internet. This How-To explains the steps involved in properly configuring this Windows 98 feature, as well as some hints on how to best use it.

COMPLEXITY

INTERMEDIATE

16.1 How do I...
Install the additional Microsoft multimedia tools?

Problem
I am seeking the full Windows 98 multimedia capability so that I can run a full gamut of sounds and videos such as the audio, MPEG, MP3, MIDI, QuickTime, RealMedia, video such as .AVI, and the Microsoft NetShow file types (.asf and .asx formats). How do I do this within Windows 98, and do I need to use more than one tool or can I finally run all these different types of multimedia formatted-files from within the same tool? Finally, how do I install these tools, such as the VRML Viewer, the RealAudio player, the Macromedia Shockwave utilities, the Microsoft Media Player (formerly known as the NetShow Player), and Microsoft Chat and utilities? And, will I have to buy any additional software?

Technique
Most of these tools and utilities are installed from the Add/Remove Programs icon found inside the Windows 98 Control Panel, but you will need to grab a

16.1
INSTALL THE ADDITIONAL MICROSOFT MULTIMEDIA TOOLS

few updates from the Windows 98 Windows Update Web site as well. Moreover, there are no other software packages that you need to purchase, because everything you need comes with the Microsoft Windows 98 operating system.

Steps

1. To begin the installation process, click the Start button then the Settings menu option, and then click the Control Panel menu selection. This takes you into the Windows 98 Control Panel.

2. Double-click the Add/Remove Programs to access the Add/Remove Programs Properties screen. You will enter this screen on the Install/Uninstall tab.

3. Click the Windows Setup tab to proceed to that screen. Keep in mind that Windows 98 will re-search your hard drive at this point to see what options you have installed, so be patient because it might take a few minutes for the screen shown in Figure 16.1 to appear.

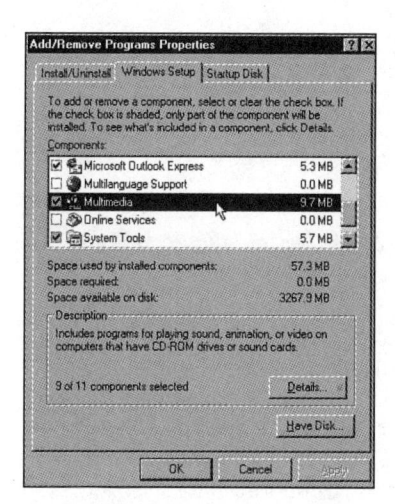

Figure 16.1 Reviewing the Windows Setup Components options.

4. Use the scrollbar to move down to the Multimedia menu option. Highlight it by clicking it once. Then, click the Details... button to move to that screen.

5. Select the Macromedia Shockwave Director, the Macromedia Shockwave Flash, and the Media Player options. You do this by clicking the check box next to each option. After you make your selections, click OK to return to the primary Windows Setup tab.

6. Again use the scrollbar to move downward until you see the Internet Tools option. Highlight it, and then click once on the Details... button to move to that screen, as shown in Figure 16.2.

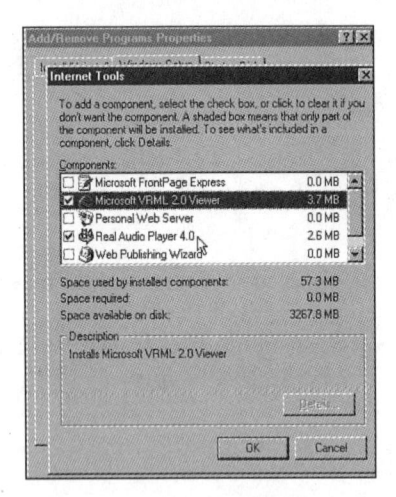

Figure 16.2 Reviewing the Internet Tools components of the Windows Setup screen.

7. Select the Microsoft VRML 2.0 Viewer and the RealAudio Player 4.0 utility by placing a check mark in the box located to the left of each option. You do that by clicking the check box once. If there is already a check mark present, you have already installed that component and do not need to repeat this installation process.

8. After you have selected these two items, click OK to return to the primary Windows Update tab screen. You are getting close now, there is only one more place to go and that is the Communications section.

9. To get there, scroll upward until you see the Communications option. Highlight it by clicking it, and then click the Details... button to move to that screen.

10. Inside the Communications Details screen you will finally see the option for the Microsoft Chat utility. Select it by placing a check mark in the box located to the left of that option. If there is already a check mark present there, you have already installed that component and do not need to repeat this installation process.

11. When you have selected this item, click OK to return to the primary Windows Setup tab screen.

12. You are now finally ready to start actually copying files and performing the installation. Click OK on the primary Windows Setup tab to begin the actual installation of the files from the Windows 98 CD-ROM.

13. When all the files have finished copying, you are just about done. If you are prompted to restart your system, do so. (You might be prompted to reboot if you have never had some of these multimedia tools installed on your PC.)

14. When the restart is complete, if there was one, you are finished and now ready to start the final installation process. This one is completed via the Microsoft Windows 98 Windows Update Web site, where you need to download a few key items that are critical to the multimedia features of Windows 98.

15. If you do not understand how to use the Windows Update Web site, refer to Chapter 12, "The Internet and Web Browsing." When on the Windows Update Web site, there are a few updates that you need to be sure to obtain and install:

- The Microsoft Chat 2.5 Update (or newer, if there is one)
- The DirectX 6.0 Technology Update (or newer, if there is one)
- The Interactive Music Control with MS Synthesizer Update

16. After these updates have been downloaded from the Internet to your PC, they will automatically be installed, so you do not have to worry about that piece. Upon their installations, you need to restart your PC. When your computer finishes its reboot sequence, you will finally be finished with the full Windows 98 multimedia enhancements installation processes.

COMPLEXITY
INTERMEDIATE

16.2 How do I...
Use the Windows Media Player?

Problem

I have successfully installed the new Windows Media Player for Windows 98 (from the Microsoft Windows Update Web site found at:

http://windowsupdate.microsoft.com/, and now I want to use it. The only problem is that I do not know exactly how to do this. What do I need to do to get up to speed on the Windows Media Player, and are there any tips or tricks that I should know about?

Technique

The Windows 98 Media Player enables a user to play several types of files such as ActiveMovie, Mpact MPEG Decoder, Video for Windows, Sound (.WAV), MIDI Sequencer, QuickTime, and CD Audio files. It can also play even more sophisticated multimedia file types, depending on the varying degrees of sophistication of your computer's video and sound system equipment. Starting the application is very easy, as well as using it. To do so, go through this next set of steps and you will be an expert in the ways of Windows 98 multimedia experiences.

Steps

1. To access the Windows Media Player, click Start, Programs, Accessories, Entertainment, and then the Media Player menu selection.

2. This series of mouse movements and clicks causes the Windows Media Player main screen to appear, as shown in Figure 16.3.

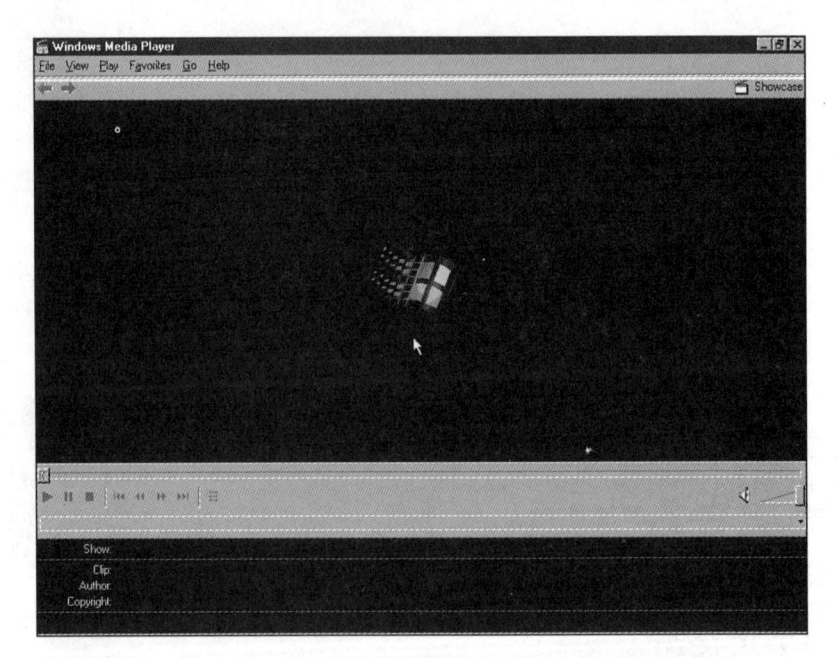

Figure 16.3 Accessing the Windows Media Player.

16.2
USE THE WINDOWS MEDIA PLAYER

3. This newest version of the Windows Media Player is very different from the old one (the one that shipped with Windows 98), not only from the types of media that it plays, but also in its appearance. Much more information is available about a particular media file along the bottom portion of the screen, and there is a volume control on the right side of the screen.

4. To get started with the Windows Media Player, click the File menu option, and then click again on the Open menu selection to reveal the screen shown in Figure 16.4.

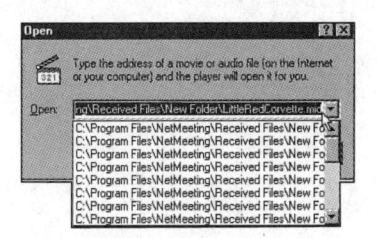

Figure 16.4 Retrieving a media file for use in the Windows Media Player.

5. This open dialog box is very different from the previous versions in that you now have a drop-down list box from which you can select previously-opened media files. Although you cannot see it in the example shown, there is also a Browse button that lets you surf your PC for other new media files that you want to play. After you find the one you want, click OK to open that file in the Windows Media Player, as shown in Figure 16.5.

6. Because you chose a MIDI file for use with your Windows Media Player (LittleRedCorvette.mid, a Prince pop music tune from the early 80s), you will not see a picture of any kind appear in the main portion of the screen, where the Windows logo now appears. Had this file been some sort of a video image, such as an MPEG or AVI file, not only would you see the images but you might also hear the soundtrack for that video (provided, of course, that it has one).

7. If you look along the lower-left portion of this screen, you will notice the traditional looking Play, Pause, Stop, Fast Forward, and Reverse buttons. If you were to place your mouse pointer over any of these buttons, a Windows GUI-standard ToolTip would appear for that particular button.

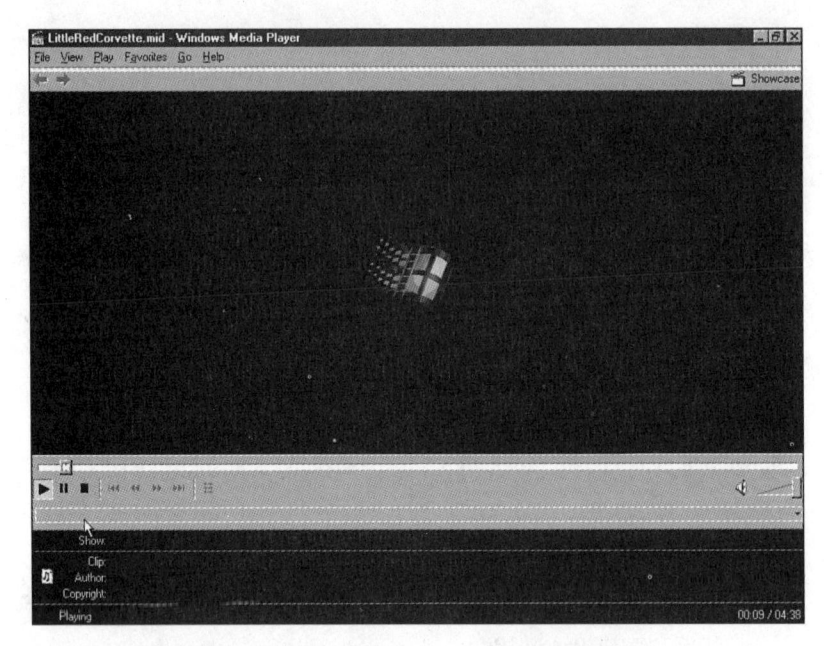

Figure 16.5 Using your first Windows Media Player file.

8. Of course, you probably do not have any video clips that you can play around with. So, the problem becomes, where do you get one or more? The answer is easier than you might otherwise suspect—you can grab them from the Internet. To do this, click the Favorites menu option, and then click the MUSICVIDEOS.COM menu selection (this is added to your Favorites menu by Windows 98, so you will have it on your PC too!), as shown in Figure 16.6.

9. When you click this Favorite, or any Favorite for that matter, you will be taken to the Web site on the Internet for that particular Favorite. It is for that reason, then, that you will want to make sure that you have first established a connection to the Internet (review Chapter 9, "Dial-Up Networking," if you need more assistance doing this).

10. After you have successfully connected to the Internet and clicked the MUSICVIDEOS.COM menu selection, you are taken to that Internet Web site: `http://www.musicvideos.com`, as shown in Figure 16.7.

11. This is a great site for picking up new videos, which you can use to test-out your Windows Media Player. You will need to sign onto the MusicVideos site, but this process goes pretty fast; you just need to fill-in the blanks and follow the site's prompts as you go.

16.2
USE THE WINDOWS MEDIA PLAYER

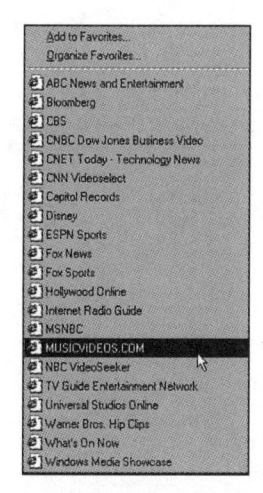

Figure 16.6
Finding video files for the Windows Media Player.

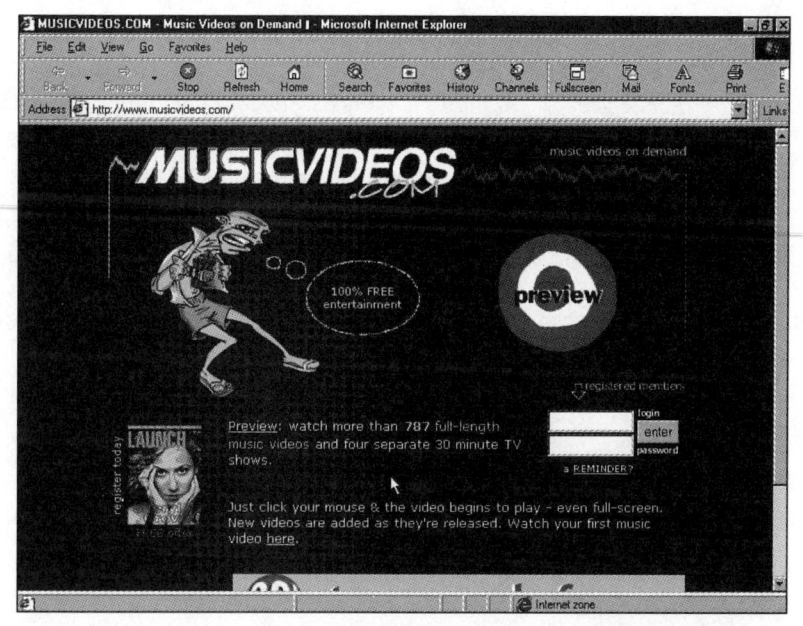

Figure 16.7 Getting Windows Media Player videos from the Internet.

12. Now that you know how to use the Windows Media Player, you should know how to better manipulate this latest Windows 98 software device. To start the configuration process, click the View menu option, and then click the Options menu selection to reveal the Options screen shown in Figure 16.8.

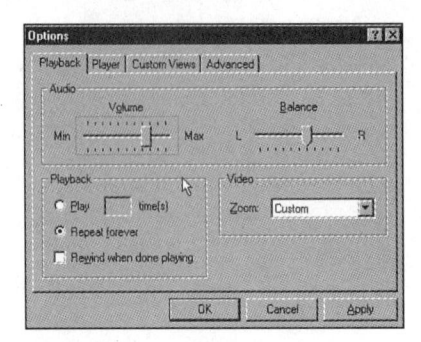

Figure 16.8 Setting the playback options for the Windows Media Player.

13. First up are the audio and other playback settings. Use the slider bars to set the default volume for the audio, as well as the left-right balance of your audio speakers.

14. Next, click the radio button of your choice to determine whether something gets played more than once or if it just continues to play over and over again.

15. The Video section allows you to set the default size of the Zoom view for watching videos on your Windows Media Player. The available options from the drop-down list box are 50%, 100%, 200%, or Custom. Custom permits you to keep your own stretched size of the Windows Media Player screen (set it by clicking and grabbing onto one of the corners of the screen). When you have finished making your selections, click the Player tab to reveal that screen, as shown in Figure 16.9.

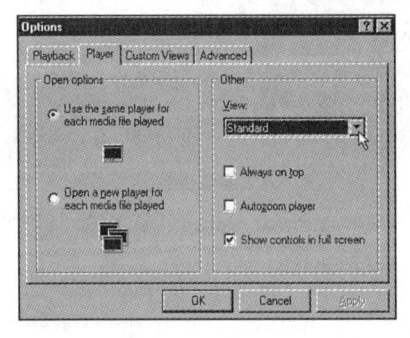

Figure 16.9 Setting the Player options.

16.2
USE THE WINDOWS MEDIA PLAYER

16. The Open Options are simple: If you want to always have just a single version of the Player running, regardless of how many media files you attempt to play, the top radio button (using the same player for each file played) is the correct choice. However, if you want to have multiple occurrences of the Windows Media Player, click the bottom radio button to select that instead.

17. The right side of this screen allows you to set the defaults for how you can view the Windows Media Player. Your choices within the View drop-down list box are Standard, Compact, or Minimal. The other three options can all be selected independently of each other and are activated by placing a check mark in each appropriate box. When you finish making your changes, click the Custom Views tab to reveal that screen, as shown in Figure 16.10.

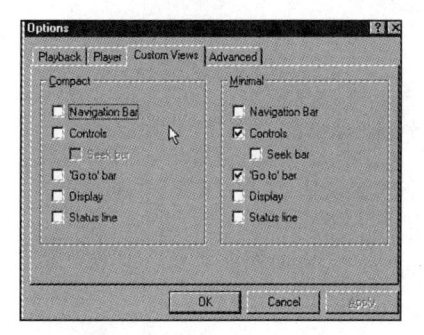

Figure 16.10 Setting the Custom Views options.

18. The options on this screen come into play only if you chose the Compact or Minimal view from the Player tab, otherwise you can skip the options on this tab if you selected Standard. The available options are the same on both sides of the screen, and are self-explanatory. After you finish making your changes, click the Advanced tab to reveal that screen, as shown in Figure 16.11.

19. At present Microsoft provides you with the chance at two advanced options: Streaming Media with RealVideo software, and Windows Media. To set the options for the first one (Streaming Media with RealVideo software), highlight your selection by clicking it once, and then click the Change... button to reveal the screen shown in Figure 16.12.

20. The Transport tab of the Streaming Media with RealVideo window appears first. These options can be pretty tricky, so if you are unsure about any change, it is strongly advised that you do not make any alterations to your settings. The term *transport* means that this screen is referring to the networking protocols that transport your data packets across your organization's networks (either public or private) or via the Internet.

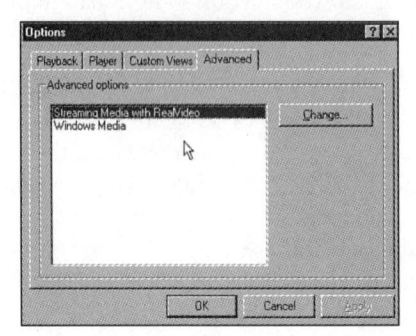

Figure 16.11 Setting the Advanced Windows Media Player options.

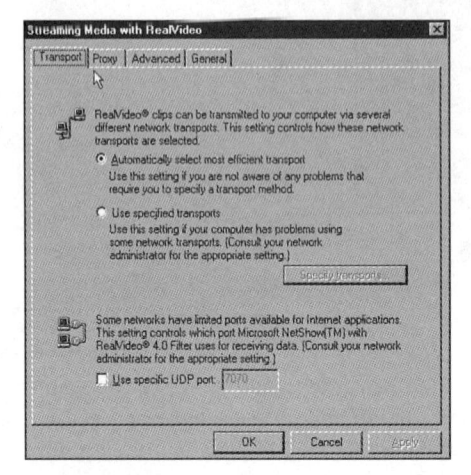

Figure 16.12 Configuring the Transport options for Streaming Media with RealVideo.

21. The top option should not be changed from the default unless you are certain that the transport method chosen by Windows 98 *does not work* for you at the present time. It is more likely that playing with this option and getting it wrong will hurt you much more than the Windows Media Player ever could on its own. Your choices, when you specify the transport mechanisms, include TCP, UDP, and HTTP (consult a TCP/IP technical manual if you do not understand the difference between any of these terms).

16.2
USE THE WINDOWS MEDIA PLAYER

22. The bottom option should be used if you find yourself unable to connect to the Internet using the appropriate RealVideo filter. However, because you will be altering the port number to use with this option, you will want to make sure that the port number you choose (provided that you are the system administrator) is not already in use elsewhere. Keep in mind that this is a UDP port and not a TCP port, so be careful if you are the system administrator doing this, and perhaps opening a hole in your organization's firewall to support it.

23. Click the Proxy tab to gain access to the screen shown in Figure 16.13.

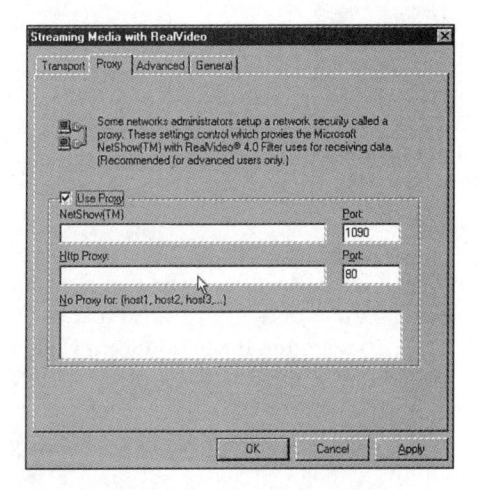

Figure 16.13 Configuring the use of a proxy server with Streaming Media with RealVideo.

24. If you do not use a proxy server within your organization's networks or for connectivity to the Internet, you should skip the options on this screen. However, if you do need to use a proxy server, click the Use Proxy check box to select it. Next, enter the host name (or the IP address) for either (or both) the NetShow player and the HTTP Proxy servers in the box(es) on the left. In the boxes labeled Port, you need to type in the port number for that particular service. Typically, if you are running these services on an intranet, you would not use a proxy server. This is what the bottom area is used for; you type in the host name of the server you want to exclude from the proxy's use, separating each server/host name by a semicolon (in case you have more than one server/host to exclude).

25. If you click the Advanced tab you will be able to access the screen shown in Figure 16.14.

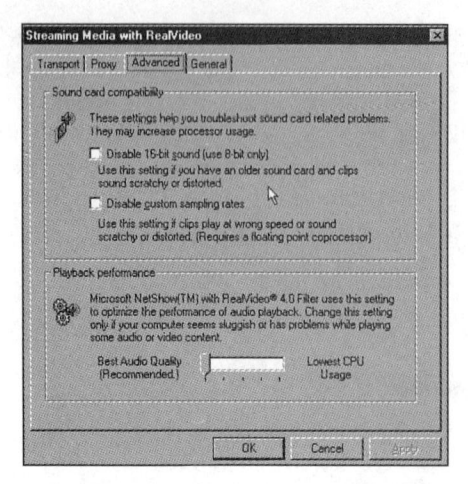

Figure 16.14 Configuring Sound Card Compatibility and Playback Performance options.

26. The top option here is useful for those times when you have an older 8-bit sound card or a 16-bit card that does not work all that well on your computer. The second check box within the Sound Card Compatibility section can be used if your audio clips still do not play correctly. Keep in mind, though, that you must have either a math coprocessor on your 80486 PC or a Pentium-class machine—not too unreasonable, given the state of personal computing technology today.

27. Use the slider bar in the Playback Performance area to reduce the quality of your audio sound if you are experiencing performance problems with your PC. You do this by sliding the bar to the right, which then reduces the impact on your system's processor.

28. Click the General tab to access the final configuration screen, shown in Figure 16.15.

29. This is probably the most important configuration screen for this topic, because the failure to set your bandwidth capabilities correctly usually results in the critical failure of one or more of your system components, which in turn, probably results in your Windows 98 PC locking up or hitting the blue screen of death. The only thing you need to do here is be honest. Do not attempt to trick the system into believing that you have a wider communications pipeline than you really do. This will not benefit you; it can only serve to hurt you.

30. After you make all changes, click OK to save your alterations and return to the Advanced tab of the Windows Media Player Options screen.

16.2
USE THE WINDOWS MEDIA PLAYER

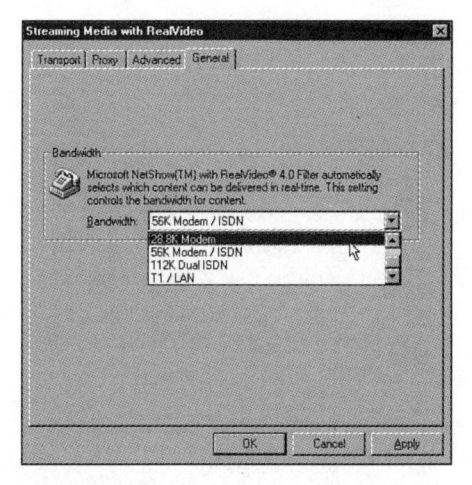

Figure 16.15 Configuring bandwidth requirements for Streaming Media with RealVideo.

31. Click the Windows Media option to highlight it. Then, click the Change… button to reveal the screen shown in Figure 16.16.

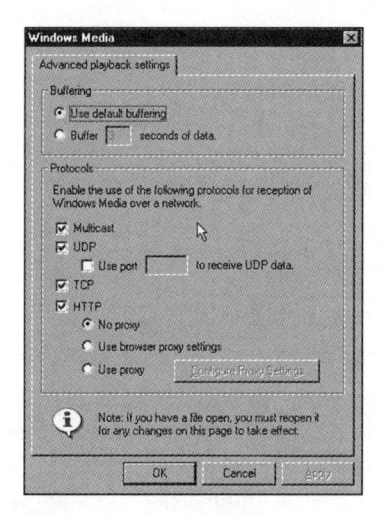

Figure 16.16 Configuring advanced playback settings.

32. This screen is split into two parts: Buffering and Protocols. *Buffering* refers to a process of saving data in a buffer to help the overall performance of the Windows Media Player appear faster. Your choices are to use the default buffering settings—the system default—or to buffer some time quantity of data. To set a buffering limit, click the bottom radio button, and then type in the number of seconds that you want the data to be buffered.

33. The Protocols section of this screen is used to configure the use of Windows Media over a network. Like the Streaming Media with RealVideo options, Windows Media can also be configured to use a proxy server (for use with the HTTP protocol) as well as to use a specific UDP port for communications access. Additionally, you might click the Multicast check box to select it, which makes this networking technology available to you as well. When you make your selections, click OK to save those changes and exit this screen.

34. After you return to the Advanced tab of the Options screen, click OK to save your changes and return to the Windows Media Player main screen.

35. Click the File menu option, and then click again on the Properties menu selection. This takes you to the Properties screen shown in Figure 16.17.

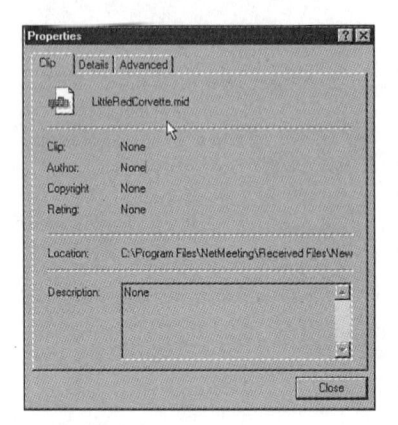

Figure 16.17 Reviewing media clip information.

36. The purpose of this screen is to provide you with information regarding the multimedia file that is presently active on your Windows Media Player. At the top of the Clip tab is the full filename of the media file that is presently active. Just below the faint line is additional information regarding the clip, its author, the copyright date, and its Internet Web rating. Unfortunately, in the vast majority of the time, all these areas will probably have the word "none" input into their respective data areas. A little farther down this tab you will see the location of the active file. This is the physical location of the active file, either on your local PC or whatever network server you opened this file from. At the very bottom of this

16.2
USE THE WINDOWS MEDIA PLAYER

screen is a description area, that typically is also left blank by most files you will see, with the exception of the professionally produced media files. After you finish reviewing this information, click once on the Details tab to reveal the screen shown in Figure 16.18.

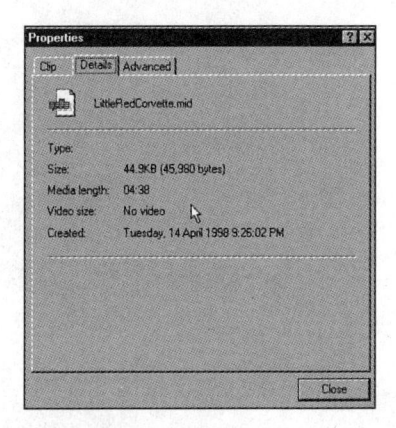

Figure 16.18 Reviewing media clip details of the active media file.

37. This tab shows the media details for the active file, including its length, size, type, and creation date. In the case of video files, it will also contain a video size entry. When you have finished reviewing this information, click the Advanced tab to reveal the screen shown in Figure 16.19.

38. This screen informs you of which media filters are presently being used, as well as those codecs that are in use by this particular media file. After you finish reviewing this information, click OK to return to the main Windows Media Player screen. From there, close the Windows Media Player and you are finished.

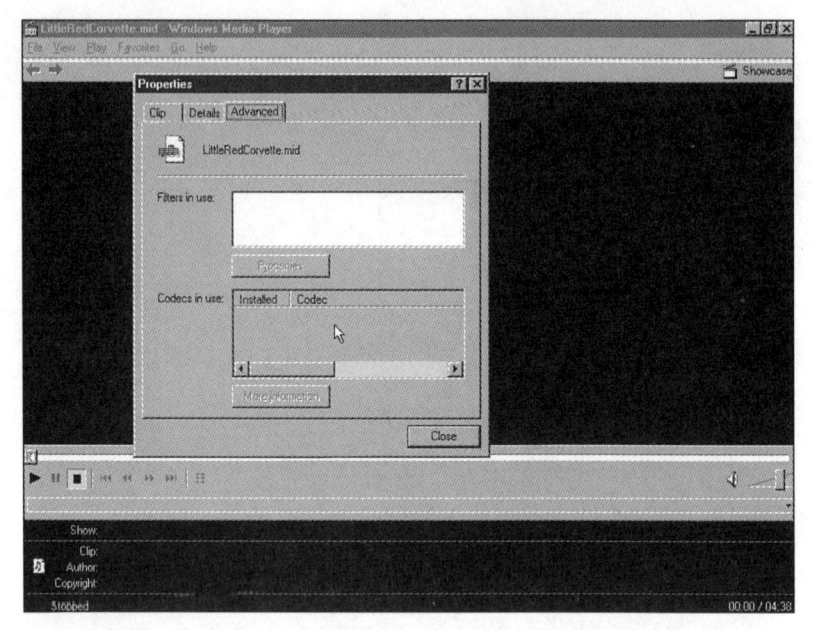

Figure 16.19 Reviewing active filters and codecs for the active media file.

COMPLEXITY
INTERMEDIATE

16.3 How do I...
Configure Microsoft Comic Chat?

Problem

I want to talk to my friends across the country, but I do not want to use a telephone and instead use my computer that is connected to the Internet. What is the best way to accomplish this, and what configuration is necessary to my Windows 98 PC to make this doable?

Technique

There is a tool within Windows 98 known as Microsoft Chat (although you should be using the updated version that is accessible via the Windows 98 Windows Update Internet Web site). Microsoft Chat permits a Windows 98 user to "talk" with others in an Internet chat room. What makes Microsoft Chat so special is that it is very visual. This means that everyone appears as a comic book character (although it is possible to remain in a plain-text format if your computer is not powerful enough to support the comical characters. You can modify your own character to give it a range of emotions, as well as to give it a life of its own. Chat sessions can be saved or printed for future use.

16.3 CONFIGURE MICROSOFT COMIC CHAT

Steps

1. To use the Microsoft Chat application, you need to first connect to the Internet. If you do not know how to do this, you should refer to Chapter 9, "Dial-up Networking," or Chapter 10, "Welcome to the Neighborhood: Network, That Is," for more details. After the connection has been established, click the Start button, move the mouse pointer to the Programs option then over to the Internet Tools option, and then down to the Microsoft Chat menu selection, as shown in Figure 16.20.

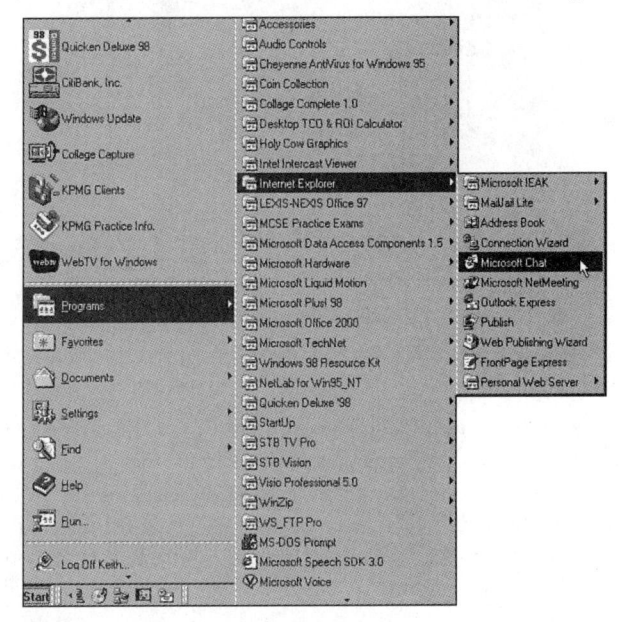

Figure 16.20 Finding the Microsoft Chat application on the Start menu structure.

2. This series of mouse movements and clicks takes you into the Microsoft Chat application. However, because this is the first time that you have used this Windows 98 tool, you will see the Chat Connection window appear, as shown in Figure 16.21.

3. If this is not your first time using Microsoft Chat, you will go directly to the Connect screen.

4. When you first see the Chat Connection screen, you will be on the Connect tab. Unless you know of other chat servers on the Internet, as well as other chat rooms, it is advised that first time users leave the defaults in place. Otherwise, you could click the drop-down list box to access the other Microsoft Chat servers that are available to you.

CHAPTER 16
MULTIMEDIA BASICS

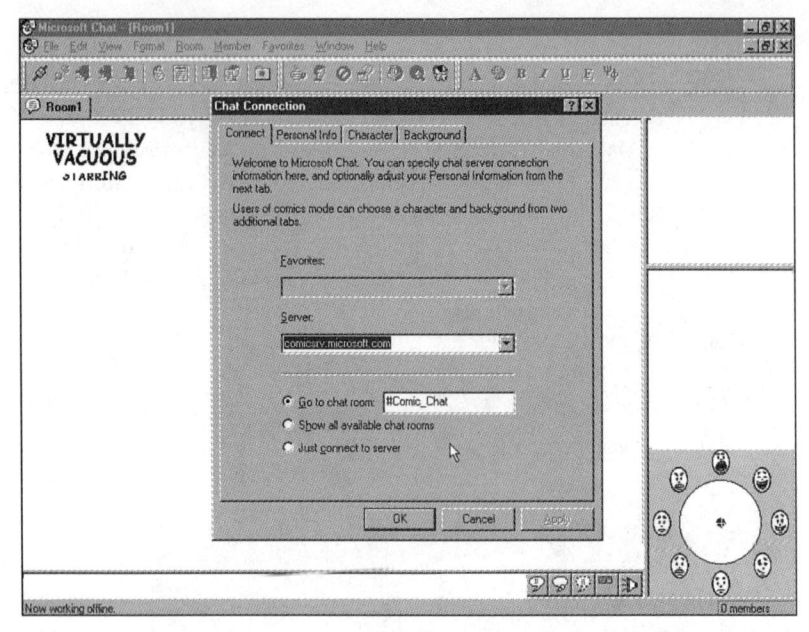

Figure 16.21 Starting the Microsoft Chat program for the first time.

5. These three radio button options at the bottom of this first screen deal with your initial connection. If this is your first time, it is strongly suggested that you leave the default setting of accessing the #Comic_Chat room (this is the top option). You can select from a listing of all the available chat rooms by clicking the middle radio button, or just connect to the server (but not enter any rooms) by using the bottom radio button.

6. When you have made your choices, click the Personal Info tab to reveal the screen shown in Figure 16.22.

7. Type in a name that you feel is descriptive of yourself or your real name, as well as a fun nickname for yourself. It is recommended that you use a real email address in the third box from the top (although you might want to use one that you obtained anonymously from some free site such as `hotmail.com`). Your Internet Web page URL and your email address are optional fields. The Brief Description of Yourself box at the bottom is a good place to put some quote or saying that you like—if you leave this blank, Windows 98 forces a quote in there that says that you are too lazy to write one for yourself.

16.3 CONFIGURE MICROSOFT COMIC CHAT

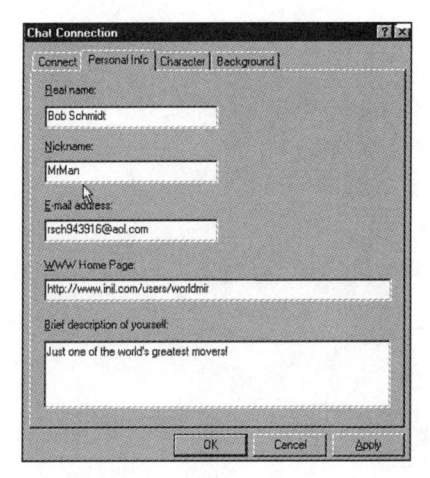

[Screenshot of Chat Connection dialog, Personal Info tab, showing fields: Real name: Bob Schmidt; Nickname: MrMan; E-mail address: rsch943916@aol.com; WWW Home Page: http://www.inil.com/users/worldmir; Brief description of yourself: Just one of the world's greatest movers!]

Figure 16.22 Entering your own and your character's personal information.

> **NOTE**
>
> The Nickname field is the only required entry on the Personal Info tab. There are a few things to remember, though. The chat software does not accept illegal characters such as periods and commas, and will therefore slam you with an error message anytime you try to use those types of characters. It is recommended that you try to limit yourself to only characters and numbers for your nicknames and refrain from attempting to use special characters, spaces, and punctuation marks.

8. Click once on the Character tab to reveal the screen shown in Figure 16.23.

9. This is one of the more useful screens because it permits you to preview your new self. When you click once on any character name in the box on the left, a comic character is previewed in the box to the right. Clicking once on the heads in the circle below enables you to change the face, and thus the mood or emotion, of your character. Placing the mouse pointer on top of each face, but not clicking at all, generates a description of what the mood is for that particular head. In the example, the head selected has the coy face. We know this is the selected head because it has the little dark circle next to it (within the larger white circle that has the + symbol in the middle of it). Choose the character and face to your liking, and then click the Background tab to reveal the screen shown in Figure 16.24.

CHAPTER 16
MULTIMEDIA BASICS

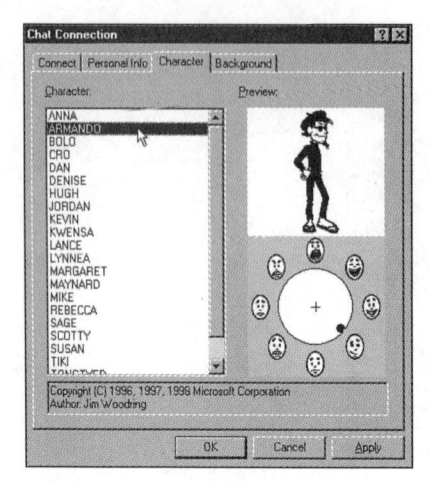

Figure 16.23 Choosing a comic character to represent you in the chat room.

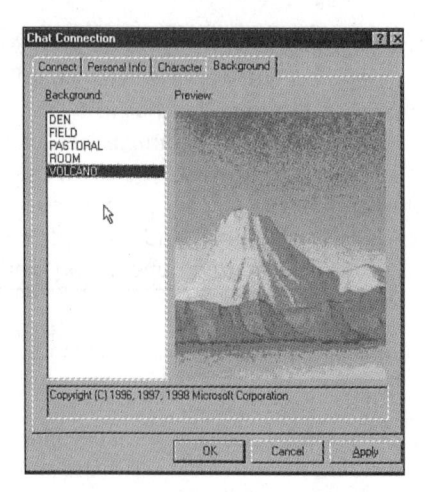

Figure 16.24 Picking a colorful background for your Comic Chat window.

10. At the time of this writing there were only five Microsoft Chat room backgrounds, but this author is certain that more will be coming. Click the background of your choice, and you will see a preview of it in the window to the right. For example, if you click the Background labeled Volcano, you will see a picture of that background in the box to the right.

11. When you have made all your selections, click OK to save all your choices. The Chat Connection window closes and you will finally enter the Microsoft Chat application, as shown in Figure 16.25.

16.3
CONFIGURE MICROSOFT COMIC CHAT

Figure 16.25 Attempting to connect to the Microsoft Chat (an IRC application) room for the first time.

12. When the Microsoft Chat main window appears you will be able to start your chat session. Unfortunately, if you were like me and forgot to connect to the Internet first, this screen will be blank until you establish that critical connection to the Internet. After you make that connection, you will be able to fully use this great application.

13. The first time you do actually connect to the Microsoft Chat application server, (such as the #Comic_Chat server that we chose at the start of this process), you might encounter an Enter New Nickname error message and repair box, as shown in Figure 16.26.

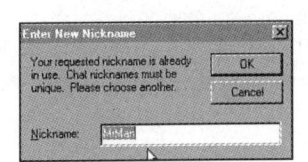

Figure 16.26 Changing your Microsoft Chat nickname.

14. If this error occurs on your system, it only means that someone else has already thought of your uniquely unimaginable Microsoft Chat nickname. So, to fix it you must pick another nickname, because you will not be permitted to connect to the Microsoft Chat servers until you have chosen one that is unique. After you have, click the OK button to finally start using the Microsoft Chat application, as shown in Figure 16.27.

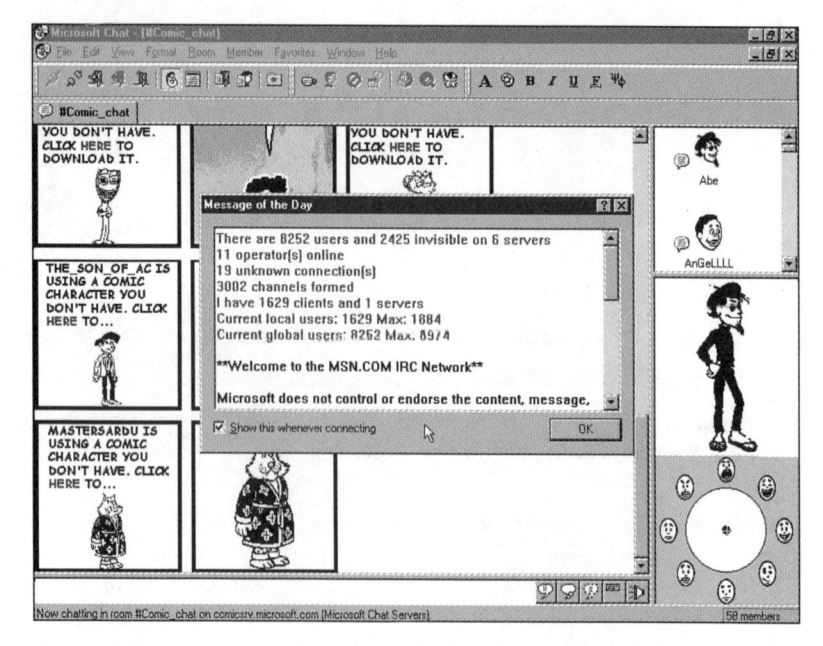

Figure 16.27 Entering the Microsoft Chat (an IRC application) for the first time.

15. When you first connect, you will see the Message of the Day message box appear on your PC. If you like what it has to say, along with its interesting statistics, click OK to make this message box disappear until the next time you enter the Microsoft Chat application. Otherwise, you may click the check box in the lower-left corner of the screen to prevent this screen from ever rearing its ugly head in your presence again. After you have made your decision, click OK to close this screen.

16. You are now an active character within the Microsoft Chat application! To actually see yourself, you need to say something to the chat room. To do this, type your message in the box that appears along the bottom of the screen, as shown in Figure 16.28.

17. When you type your message into the box, click the Say button.

16.3
CONFIGURE MICROSOFT COMIC CHAT
723

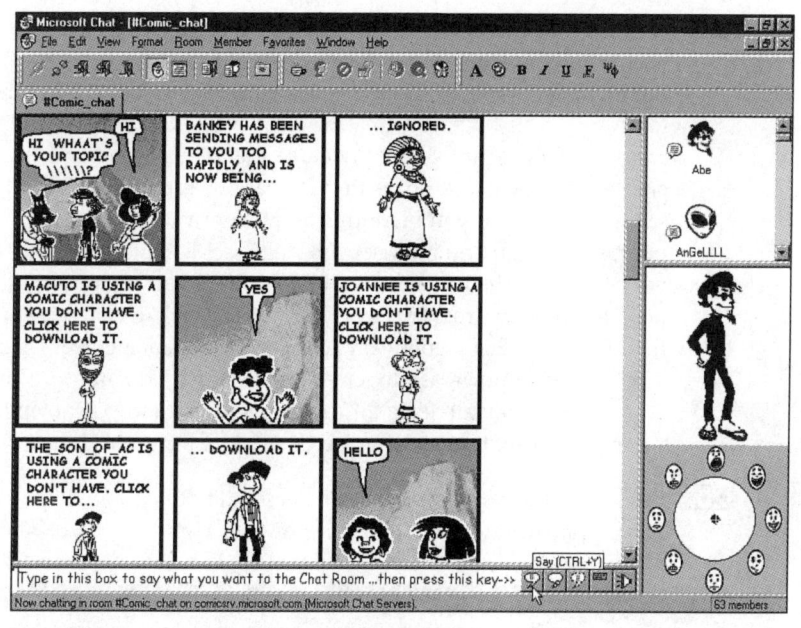

Figure 16.28 Talking to the rest of the Microsoft Chat room.

18. Now that you are in this first primary chat room, you will notice is how fast the message boxes fly by as well as how many duplicate characters there are in the room. It is the duplicate comic characters that make it really tough to figure out who is really talking, because you might see your character talking gibberish only to realize it is someone else speaking. To avoid this confusion, you can create your own personal Microsoft Chat room. To do this, click the Room menu option, and then click again on the Create Room menu selection to access the window shown in Figure 16.29.

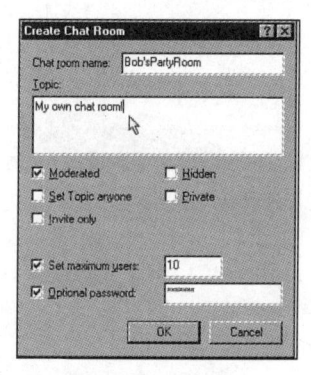

Figure 16.29 Creating your own chat room.

19. At the top of this window is where you type in a descriptive name for the chat room you are creating. Be sure not to use any spaces, so as to make the room accessible to those persons who might be accessing the chat room via a non-Microsoft Chat piece of IRC client software. In the Topic area, enter a descriptive, catchy name that helps to draw people into your chat room. The check boxes provide various functions, most of which are self-explanatory. If you mark this room as private, people need your permission to enter. Likewise, you might set a maximum number of users who can be in the room at one time, and even set a password that people need to know in order to access your chat room. This last feature makes the Microsoft Chat a good way to do teleconferencing over the Internet. The selection known as Moderated, means that you are the room's moderator or essentially a referee for the room—this can be annoying if your room was created just for fun, so be wary of using this option.

20. Click OK after you make your choices and your room will be created with you automatically inside of it, as shown in Figure 16.30.

Figure 16.30 Entering your newly created chat room.

21. You now see yourself as a member in this chat room, by looking at the box in the upper-right side of the screen. The example character is using the name FastFreddy, which is what was assigned to it when the nickname MrMan was already taken.

16.3
CONFIGURE MICROSOFT COMIC CHAT

22. If you look along the top border of the chat room area, you will notice a series of tabs (okay, there are only two present at the moment). These tabs allow you to jump from room to room with a single-click of your mouse. So, because the room is boring (unless you happen to like talking to yourself), click the #Comic_Chat tab to return to the main Microsoft Chat chat room.

23. When you are in a room with many people it would be nice to know who someone is. To do this, click that person's head in the room members' box (the one just above your character's full-size picture, along the right side of the screen) to highlight that person. Next, click the Member menu option, followed by a click on the Get Identity menu selection, as shown in Figure 16.31.

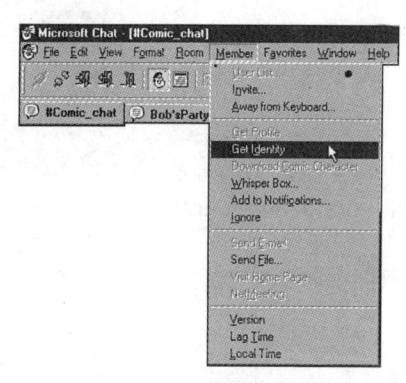

Figure 16.31 Discovering someone's identity profile.

24. After you click on the Get Identity function, you will see (as will everyone else) a character box appear with that person's email address as shown in Figure 16.32.

25. This is the same email address that that person had typed into their Personal Info tab data area.

26. The next area that you might want to know about, is figuring out exactly what version of the Microsoft Chat application you are running. To do this, click the Help menu option, and then click again on the About Microsoft Chat menu selection to reveal the screen shown in Figure 16.33.

27. This information can be especially helpful if you are a system administrator who is tasked with making sure that everyone in your organization is working with the same set of Microsoft Chat features and options. This is a much later build of the software than the one that originally shipped with the Windows 98 operating system.

Figure 16.32 Reviewing another character's identity.

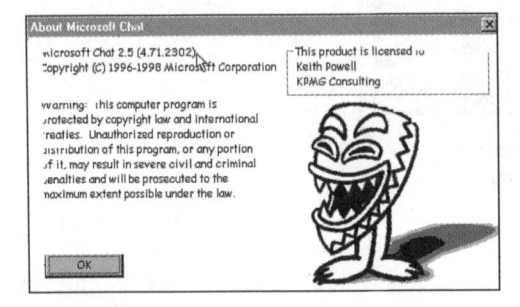

Figure 16.33 Checking the program's version number.

28. Next up are the various View options that are available to you. The Toolbar menu selection permits you to change the way in which the buttons appear along the top part of the screen. Other options available include the capability to see a complete listing of all the members within a chat room (in either a listing format or an icon format), the capability to turn off the sound that occurs when each new comic-book like box appears, and the capability to see the logon notifications of everyone as they log on to this chat room. In a large room this is very annoying, but in a controlled, moderated, chat room (such as for a teleconferencing session conducted by your organization) it can be neat to see who is coming and going from the chat session.

16.3 CONFIGURE MICROSOFT COMIC CHAT

29. The Options menu selection at the bottom of the screen takes you back to the Microsoft Chat Options screen where you are able to modify your Personal Info, Character type, room background, and so on. Within a new Settings tab, though, you can set about a dozen other self-explanatory options including the capability to receive NetMeeting calls via this application.

30. Moving over to the Room menu option, as shown in Figure 16.34, you will see all the chat room options that can be accessed.

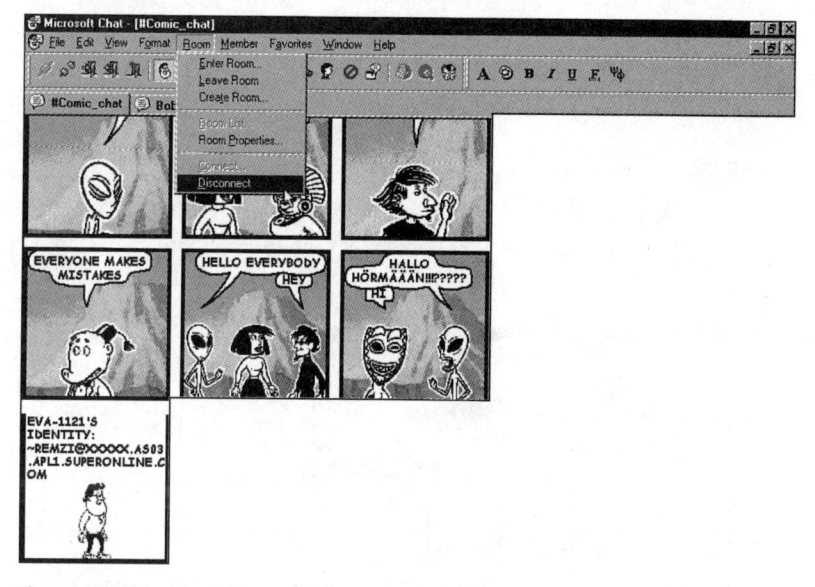

Figure 16.34 Deciding which room-specific option to select.

31. The most important one here is the capability to quickly disconnect your Microsoft Chat chat room experience. Likewise, if you are already disconnected from Microsoft Chat, you may click the Connect menu selection to access a chat room online. The other options on this tab are quite basic and self-explanatory.

32. Click the Member menu option, as shown in Figure 16.35.

33. There are many options available on this menu You might want to play with these different options, and then watch as the results of each option appear inside the chat room window.

34. Within the Format menu option you have the ability to set the various fonts in use, as well as being able to size each of the boxes shown within a chat room screen.

CHAPTER 16
MULTIMEDIA BASICS

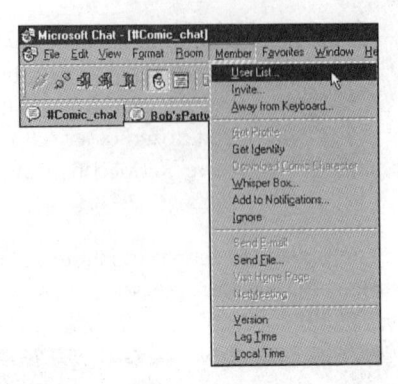

Figure 16.35 Changing member-specific chat options.

35. To quickly go to another chat room when you have more than 10 rooms open (and you do not want to have to scroll through all the tabs along the top of the chat area), click the Window menu option, as shown in Figure 16.36.

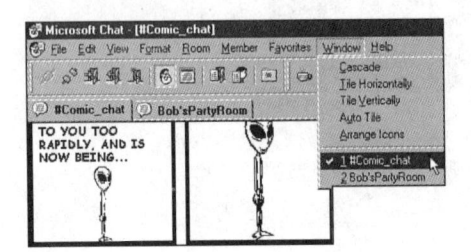

Figure 16.36 Going to another chat room.

36. In the numbered order that you originally entered or created each room, you will see the names of all the rooms at the bottom of this menu option. Click the one you want and you are quickly transported to that room.

37. Finally, to leave the Microsoft Chat session, use the Disconnect feature on the Room menu option or close the Microsoft Chat application.

CHAPTER 17
WEBTV FOR WINDOWS

17

WEBTV FOR WINDOWS

How do I...
17.1 Install WebTV for Windows and its components?
17.2 Configure and use WebTV for Windows?
17.3 Listen to the radio on my Windows 98 PC?
17.4 Configure WaveTop Data Broadcasting?

The world of personal computer technology continues to advance in ways that only a few years ago would have been referred to as science fiction. The capability to watch TV, listen to the radio, or access your public broadcasting station's shows via your PC are all very popular and available technologies today. Of course, the majority of these devices are still limited to desktop computers, as there are additional hardware devices that must be installed in the PC to make it work correctly (and most of these are not small devices...yet).

Like anything else, to use these various broadcasting devices, your computer requires a base minimum of hardware to make it work smoothly. These broadcasting services have a minimum set of requirements:

- An Intel Pentium 166MHz CPU.

- 28.6MB of available hard drive space for WebTV, plus an additional 10.8MB of space for the WaveTop Data Broadcasting.

- 16MB of RAM, although if this is all you have, Windows 98 is not going to run that well either.

- An SVGA monitor that supports a resolution of at least 800×600. Color is preferred, though not truly necessary.

- A two-button mouse or compatible pointing device. Using Windows 98 without one of these is nearly impossible, anyway.

- Sound card with speakers. If you cannot hear what is happening, that would defeat the purpose of using either of these broadcast technologies.

- A TV tuner card. Though many are on the market today, you might want to consult the Windows 98 Hardware Compatibility Listing (HCL) on the Internet to make sure you are purchasing a compatible tuner card.

These broadcasting services have a recommended level of hardware requirements as follows:

- An Intel Pentium 200MHz CPU.

- 28.6MB of available hard drive space for WebTV, plus an additional 10.8MB of space for the WaveTop Data Broadcasting.

- 32MB of RAM.

- A 28.8Kbps or better internal fax modem that is compatible with the AT Command Set.

- Cable TV connection to the TV tuner card.

- An SVGA Monitor that supports a resolution of at least 800×600. Color is preferred, though not truly necessary.

- A two-button mouse or compatible pointing device. Using Windows 98 without one of these is nearly impossible, anyway.

- Sound card with speakers. If you cannot hear what is happening, that would defeat the purpose of using either of these broadcast technologies.

- A TV tuner card. Though there are many on the market today, you might want to consult the Windows 98 Hardware Compatibility Listing (HCL) on the Internet to make sure you are purchasing a compatible tuner card.

Like anything else Microsoft does, you really need the recommended hardware levels to be able to use WebTV and the WaveTop Data Broadcasting services smoothly. Anything less will require you to have one heck of a sense of humor whenever you attempt to use either of these technologies.

17.1 Install WebTV for Windows and its Components

What's that? You want to watch TV on your PC? Well, to do that you will need to install the technology known as WebTV for Windows, and its additional component known as WaveTop Data Broadcasting. Face it: You cannot configure or use something that you have not yet installed. This How-To walks you through the basic steps of installing both WebTV for Windows and WaveTop Data Broadcasting. Additionally, this How-To tells you exactly how to get the latest and greatest updates from Microsoft for these amazing new technologies.

17.2 Configure and Use WebTV for Windows

Now that you have WebTV for Windows installed, wouldn't it be nice to know how to configure it for your viewing pleasure? This How-To shows you how to do that, and shows you the basic steps on how to use it. Additional tips and tricks will be offered up to help you make your use of this technology a little bit more enjoyable.

17.3 Listen to the Radio on My Windows 98 PC

Great, I can watch TV on my PC. However, I have a real job that will not let me get away with watching the Chicago Cubs baseball game every afternoon. Can I listen to the radio instead? And if so, how can I do this? This How-To walks you through the steps required to enable you to listen to your local radio stations while you work.

17.4 Configure WaveTop Data Broadcasting

When the WaveTop Data Broadcasting system is installed, you will need to configure it before you can use it. This How-To shows you how to do that.

COMPLEXITY
BEGINNER

17.1 How do I...
Install WebTV for Windows and its components?

Problem

I have purchased and installed my TV tuner card and installed it properly. I have confirmed this by checking out the Device Manager within the Windows 98 System Properties screen. Now, how do I go about installing the software required for Windows 98 to use my new hardware?

Technique

The installation process for using WebTV for Windows or WaveTop Data Broadcasting is the same as it is for all the other built-in Windows 98 accessories and components: You need to use the Windows 98 Add/Remove Programs icon from within the Windows 98 Control Panel. Follow these steps and you will soon be on your way to watching TV via cable, your antenna, or the Internet.

Steps

1. To check to see whether you have WebTV for Windows or WaveTop Data Broadcasting installed, click the Start button, select the Programs menu option, choose the Accessories menu option, move to the Entertainment folder option, and then look inside to see whether the WebTV for Windows and WaveTop Data Broadcasting menu selections exist. If not, it is safe to assume that you probably have not yet installed either of these yet.

2. To begin the installation process, click the Start button, select the Settings menu option, and then click the Control Panel menu selection. This takes you into the Windows 98 Control Panel.

3. When there, double-click Add/Remove Programs to access the Add/Remove Programs Properties screen. You will enter this screen on the Install/Uninstall tab.

4. Click the Windows Setup tab to proceed to that screen. Keep in mind that Windows 98 will re-search your hard drive at this point to see what options you have installed, so be patient as it might take a few minutes for this screen to appear.

17.1
INSTALL WEBTV FOR WINDOWS AND ITS COMPONENTS

5. When there, use the scrollbar to move down to the WebTV for Windows menu option. Highlight it by clicking on it. Then, click the Details... button to move to that screen.

6. When there, look for the WebTV for Windows and the WaveTop Data Broadcasting options. Select either or both of these by placing a check mark in the box located to the left of the options that you want. You do that by clicking the check box once, as shown in Figure 17.1. If there is already a check mark present in either or both of these boxes, you have already installed the product whose boxed is checked and do not need to repeat this install process.

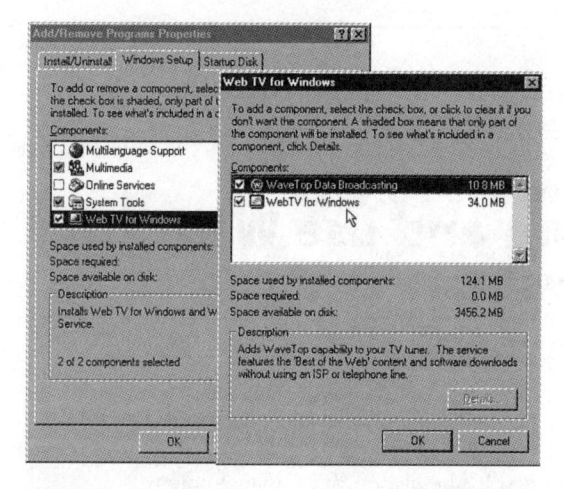

Figure 17.1 Finding the WebTV for Windows and the WaveTop Data Broadcasting options in the Windows Setup screen.

7. When you have selected the items you want, click OK to return to the primary Windows Setup screen. Click OK to begin the actual installation of the files from the Windows 98 CD-ROM.

8. When all the files have copied, you are finished. You will be prompted to restart your system at least twice, and you must do so. If you don't, these services will not install correctly.

9. When the restarts are complete, you are finished and now ready to start the configuration process.

> **NOTE**
> Keep in mind that if you are not using the ATI All-in-Wonder Card or the ATI All-in-Wonder Card Pro for your TV tuner card, you will not be able to use Microsoft's WebTV for Windows until you download and install the updated version of WebTV for Windows from the Windows 98 Windows Update Web site (review the first topic in Chapter 12, "The Internet and Web Browsing," for details on using Windows Update). If your tuner card does not appear in the Windows Update listing, such as the STB TV PCI card, you will not be able to use the Microsoft WebTV for Windows with this tuner card. This means that you are wasting your time if you attempt to install and use WebTV for Windows with your PC.

COMPLEXITY
INTERMEDIATE

17.2 How do I... Configure and use WebTV for Windows?

Problem

I have installed the necessary WebTV for Windows software that came with Windows 98. Now how do I configure WebTV for Windows for use on my PC, and what are some tips in the use of this new technology?

Technique

WebTV for Windows enables your PC to display both standard and interactive television broadcasts, as well as Internet data broadcasts. You can receive the standard and interactive TV broadcasts only if a TV tuner card (a hardware device for receiving television broadcasts) is installed on your PC. The Internet data broadcasts, though, will enable you to capture TV broadcast listings and display them in the Windows 98 program guide that is a part of WebTV.

Although that sounds great, there are a few caveats. A lot of this technology is still in the *vaporware* stage, which means that there are a lot of promises to do a lot of great things but not much reality (that is, Microsoft has both its feet firmly planted in the clouds on this one). To use WebTV for Windows, provided you happen to own one of the only two or three different types of TV

17.2
CONFIGURE AND USE WEBTV FOR WINDOWS

tuner cards in the world that presently work with this technology, follow this next set of steps. Otherwise, you will be able to download your local TV listings very nicely, but when it comes to watching TV you will need your old Zenith or Sony television set.

Steps

1. Click the Start button, choose Accessories, select Entertainment, and then click WebTV for Windows.

2. The WebTV splash screen appears, as shown in Figure 17.2.

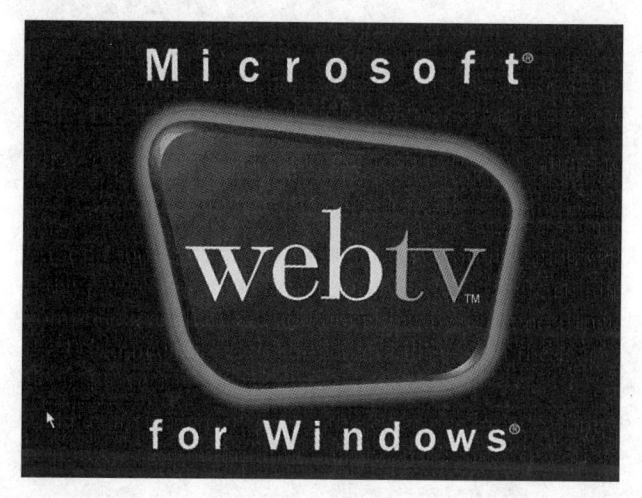

Figure 17.2 Viewing the WebTV for Windows splash screen.

3. Your system will pause here for a few seconds before taking you directly to the WebTV Program Guide screen. Scroll up or down this screen to figure out what television shows are scheduled in your area. Of course, if you installed WebTV for Windows for the first time, there are no listings because you go directly to the WebTV's minitutorial as shown in Figure 17.3. If you are at the program guide, skip down to step 13 to see what else you can do with this program; otherwise, continue on here.

4. These next few screens explain the basics of Microsoft's WebTV technology and help you in downloading your local television listings. To continue, click the Next button to reveal the screen shown in Figure 17.4.

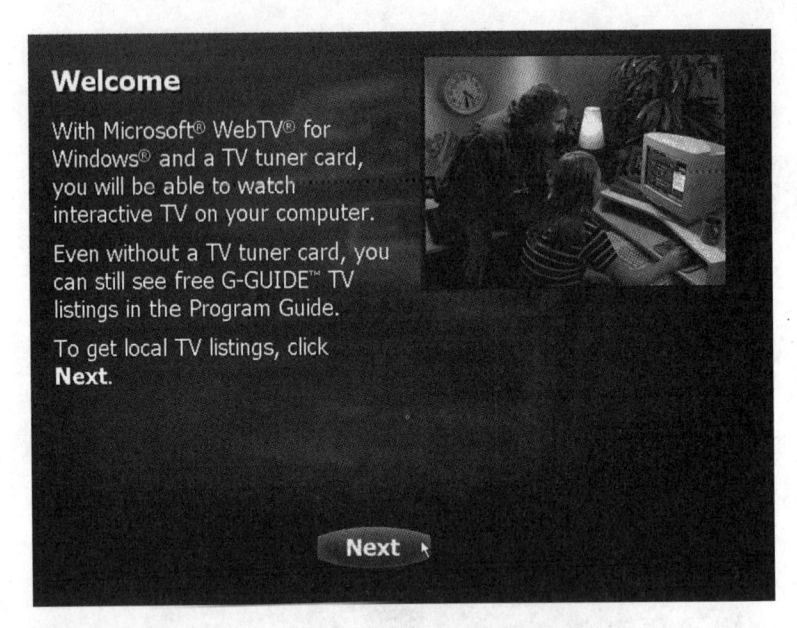

Figure 17.3 The WebTV for Windows Welcome screen.

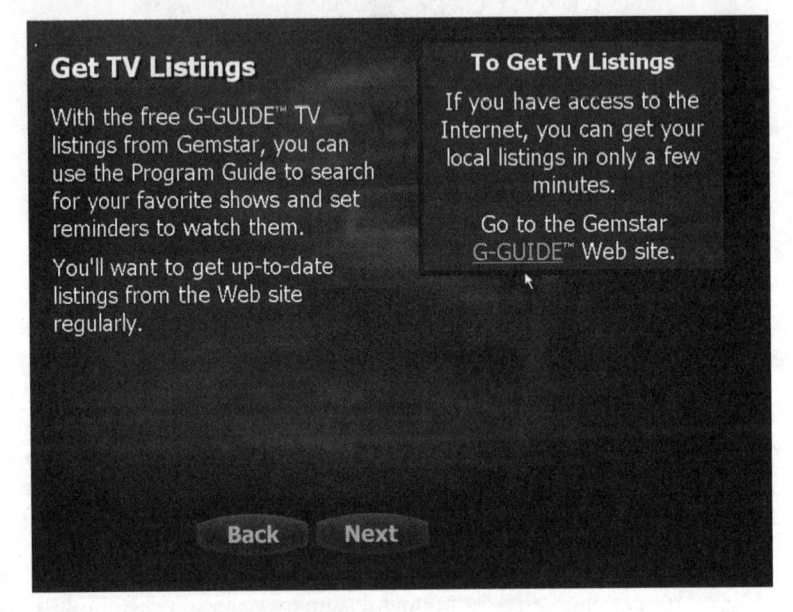

Figure 17.4 How to get local TV listings for use with WebTV for Windows.

2.1 CONFIGURE AND USE WEBTV FOR WINDOWS

5. This screen is where you are able to start your access to the Gemstar Internet Web site (http://broadcast.microsoft.com/epgdata/gemstar/region.htm) where all the broadcast listings are kept. You could jump to this Web site right away by clicking the G-GUIDE hyperlink, but you will skip this step for now. To continue, click the Next button to reveal the screen shown in Figure 17.5.

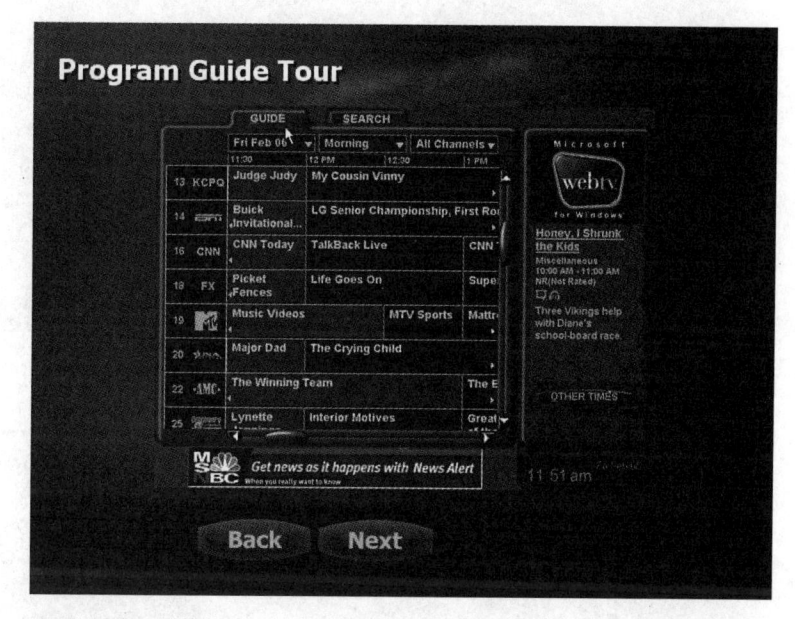

Figure 17.5 Viewing a sample WebTV for Windows program guide.

6. The sample Program Guide Tour window appears where you can see an example of this technology. It is interesting to note that Microsoft has not yet updated their screen shots here, as the program guide shown is from it February 1998 Beta 3 release (roughly six full months before the retail release of the Windows 98 operating system). Click the Next button to reveal the screen shown in Figure 17.6.

7. This screen demonstrates how you can search the Program Guide, when you want to find the particular program that strikes your fancy. Again, it is interesting to note that Microsoft has not yet updated this screen shot either, as the program search guide displayed is from the February 1998 Beta 3 release of WebTV for Windows. Click the Next button to reveal the screen shown in Figure 17.7.

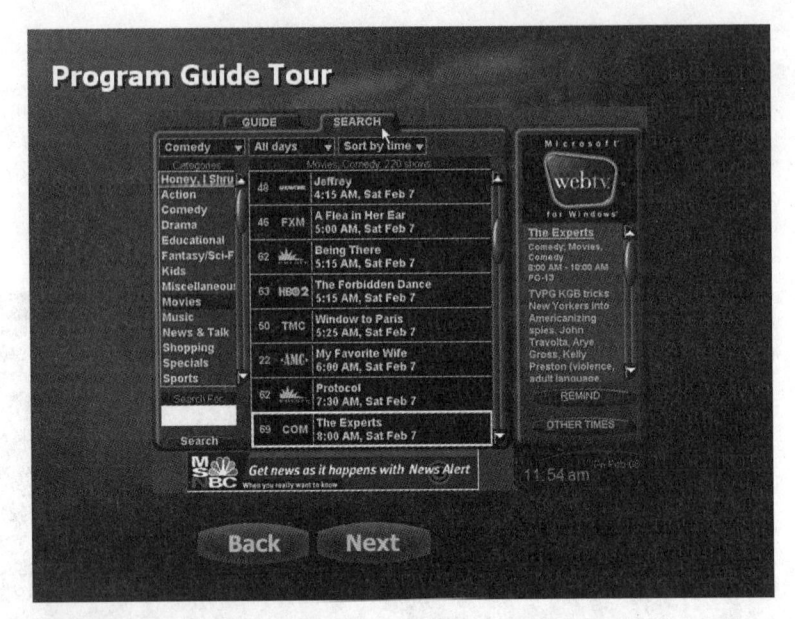

Figure 17.6 Viewing a WebTV for Windows Program Guide Search.

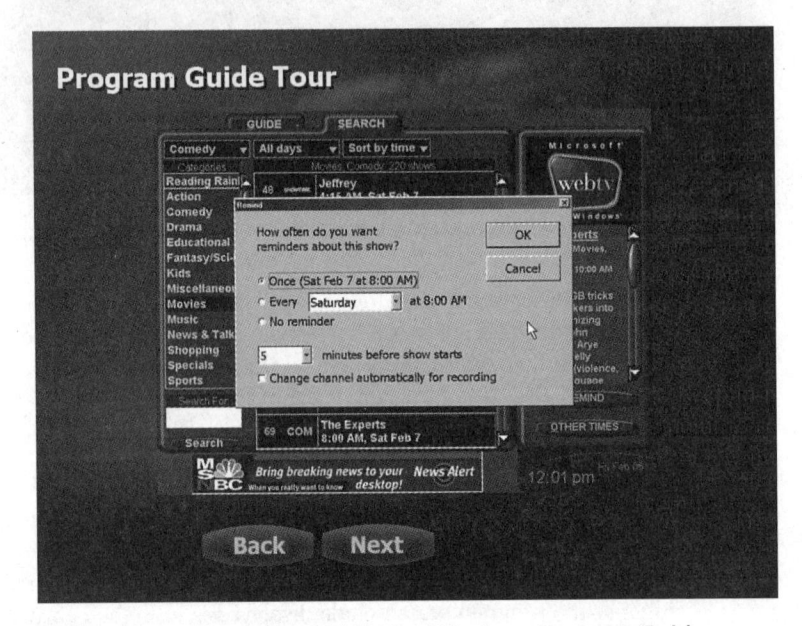

Figure 17.7 Viewing a WebTV for Windows Program Guide reminder box.

17.2 CONFIGURE AND USE WEBTV FOR WINDOWS

8. This screen shows how you can set a reminder for a particular television program (like you need a computer to remind you to spend more of your life in front of the TV). However, this feature does have a few nice options, such as the weekly reminders and the automatic channel changing for recording purposes. Click the Next button to reveal the screen shown in Figure 17.8.

Configuration Complete

Click **Finish** and you'll see the Program Guide.

To get new TV listings at any time, go to the Configuration channel.

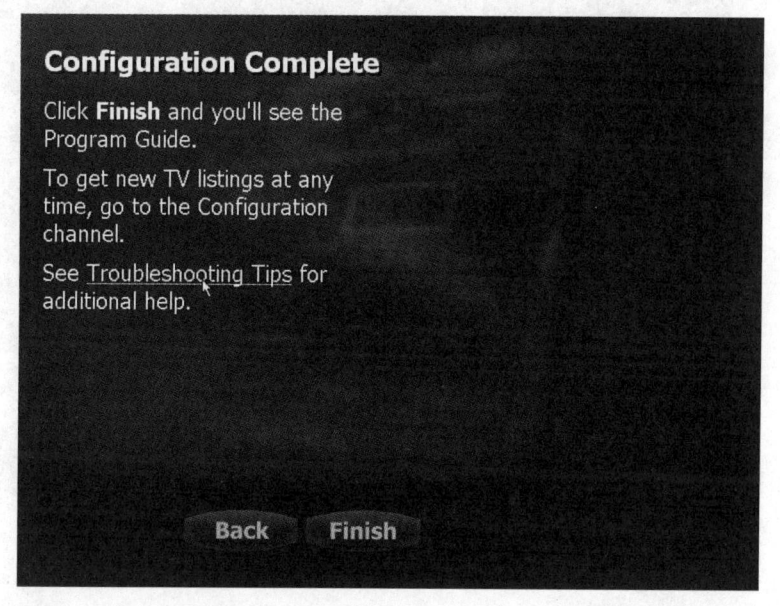

See Troubleshooting Tips for additional help.

Back   Finish

Figure 17.8 Completing the WebTV for Windows tour.

9. The WebTV for Windows tour is now complete. Click Finish and you are taken to the screen shown in Figure 17.9. If there is something within WebTV for Windows that still confuses you, you can click the Troubleshooting Tips hyperlink for more assistance (although it is really basic help and gives you no help with any hardware issues you might be experiencing).

10. This is the standard WebTV for Windows Program Guide that you will see each time you start up this Windows 98 component. Because this is your first time in the WebTV for Windows component since you installed it and you have not yet downloaded your local program listings, this screen consists of two channels: the TV Configuration channel and the Program Guide channel. Neither of these channels can be deleted from your program guide, so get used to them being shown. If you double-click the TV Configuration channel, Channel 96 in the example, you will be taken to the WebTV for Windows tour, as shown in Figure 17.10. (Say what?!? Tell me that is not a confusing thing to do!)

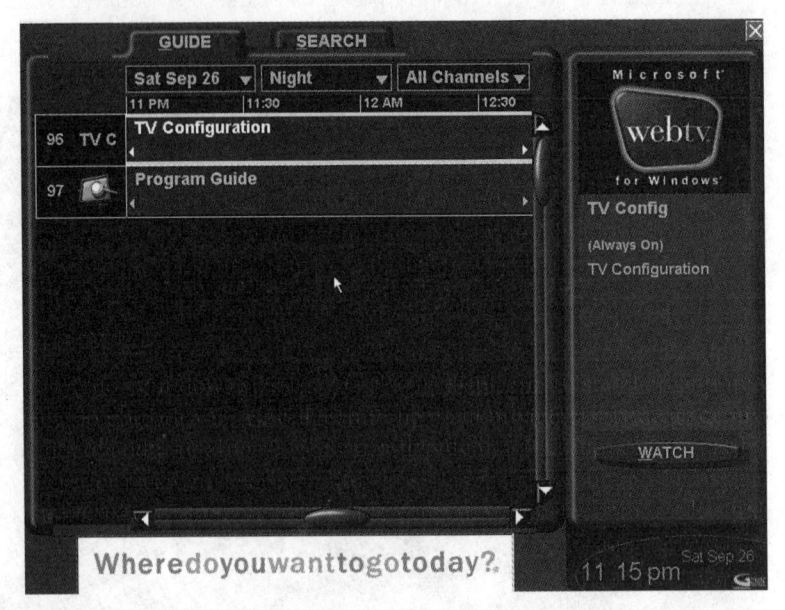

Figure 17.9 The WebTV for Windows Program Guide.

11. This is where WebTV for Windows gets really wacky. You are supposed to automatically know—through osmosis, I guess—that placing your mouse pointer at the top of the screen causes a drop-down menu bar to automatically reveal itself to you. (How about a little information printed clearly onscreen here, Microsoft, instead of hiding it?)

> **NOTE**
> For further assistance, you might want to click the Help button for clarification on some of WebTV's more confusing screens and hidden menus (like the Settings menu). However, there is no Help button back on the main screen; it is located on the hidden Settings menu bar (tell me that is not a less-than-brilliant GUI design).

17.2
CONFIGURE AND USE WEBTV FOR WINDOWS
743

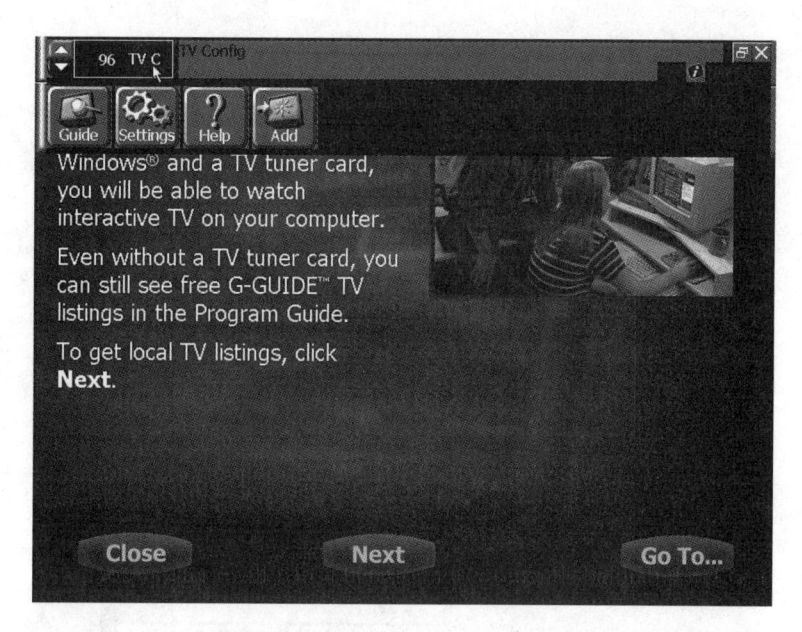

Figure 17.10 Access the WebTV for Windows TV Configuration area from the WebTV for Windows Tour screen.

12. The word *configuration* takes on a whole new meaning with this section of WebTV for Windows. About all you can really do is add or drop TV channels from your program guide here. You are powerless to do anything else, such as modify the order of your channels (numerically is your selection) or change the resolution of your screen. (Most TV tuner cards will require an 800×600 resolution with at least 16-bit color, but you are supposed to know that and already have done this—more osmosis, I guess). When you are finished, click the × in the upper-right corner to close this window, or click the Next buttons until you reach the end.

13. At this point, it makes sense to go out to the Internet and retrieve your local program guide listings. You have two choices here, go back to the WebTV for Windows tour and then take the hyperlink jump to the Gemstar Web site, or access the Internet site directly yourself. I'd vote for the latter. It's much faster and easier than first launching the sluggish WebTV for Windows application, so to get to the Gemstar site enter the following URL:

http://broadcast.microsoft.com/epgdata/gemstar/region.htm

14. This takes you to the first screen within the site, which is where you will be prompted to specify your physical location as shown in Figure 17.11.

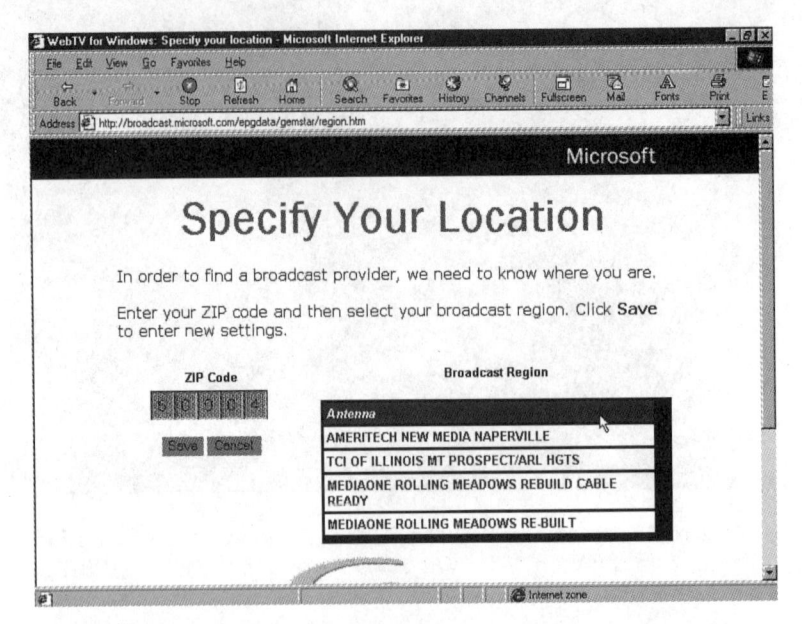

Figure 17.11 Accessing the Gemstar Web site.

> **NOTE**
> As part of the installation process for WebTV, you will be prompted for your Zip code and who is providing your television service (such as your cable or satellite TV company or your rooftop antenna). This is how the software knows where you live.

15. Enter your Zip code for the location where your PC is located, which automatically causes the Web site to then display a listing of the various television broadcasters in your region as shown in Figure 17.12.

> **NOTE**
> Because it is an ActiveX control that performs this little feat of magic, you need to use Internet Explorer to cruise this Web site. The vast majority of Netscape's Web browsers (with the exception of the latest one, which is still in beta testing) do not support ActiveX controls, which means that they will not work. If these controls cannot execute, you will not be able to download the information that you require to run your WebTV for Windows Program Guide.

17.2
CONFIGURE AND USE WEBTV FOR WINDOWS

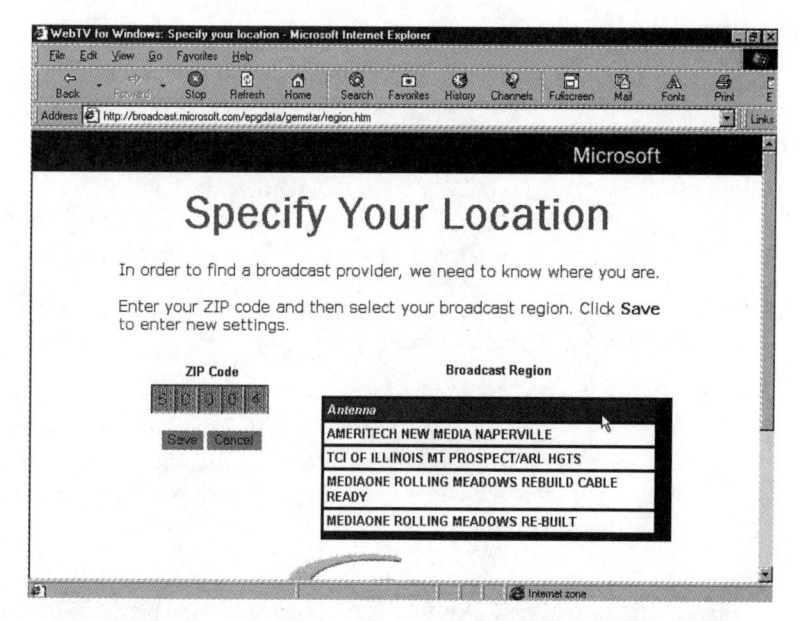

Figure 17.12 Specifying your location for use with the Gemstar Web site.

16. When you have selected your choice, such as a rooftop antenna, click Save to continue, as shown in Figure 17.13.

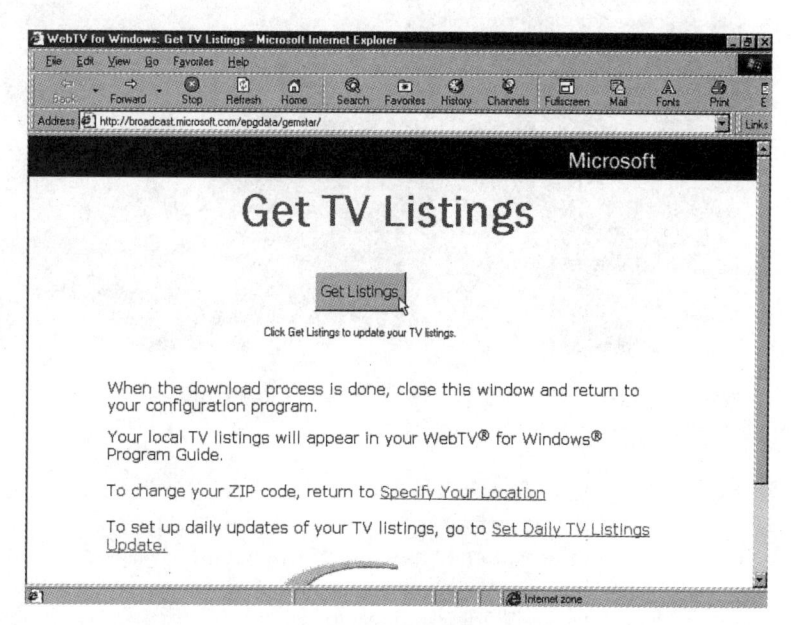

Figure 17.13 Get TV listings from the Gemstar Web site.

CHAPTER 17
WEBTV FOR WINDOWS

17. At this point, you can begin downloading your local television listings from the Gemstar Web site. Click the Get Listings button to initiate this download process.

18. When the download completes, the TV listings are automatically installed into your WebTV for Windows Program Guide. You will receive an update message that appears directly below the Get Listings button that informs you of the success of the download and installation process.

19. Close your Web browser and disconnect from the Internet (if you are on a Dial-Up Networking connection).

20. Start up the Windows 98 WebTV for Windows application, which can be found by clicking the Start button, selecting the Programs menu option, choosing the Accessories folder, moving to the Entertainment folder menu, and then clicking the WebTV for Windows menu selection. This will bring you to the screen shown in Figure 17.14.

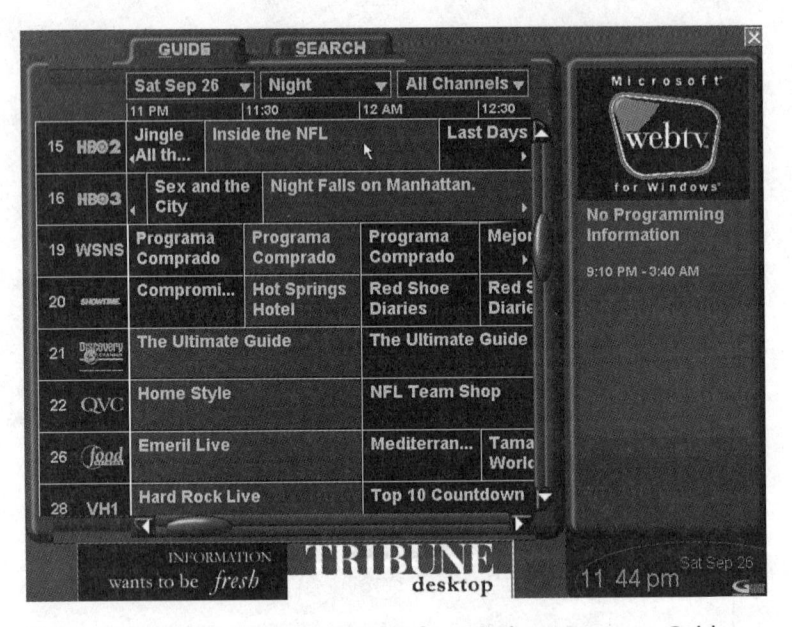

Figure 17.14 Viewing the WebTV for Windows Program Guide Screen.

21. This is the primary screen for the WebTV for Windows Program Guide. You can use the scrollbar to move up and down this screen. For more detailed information on any one program, click that program's box and its information (if any) will appear on the right (directly under the big Microsoft WebTV for Windows logo).

17.2 CONFIGURE AND USE WEBTV FOR WINDOWS

22. Click the Search tab to access the screen shown in Figure 17.15.

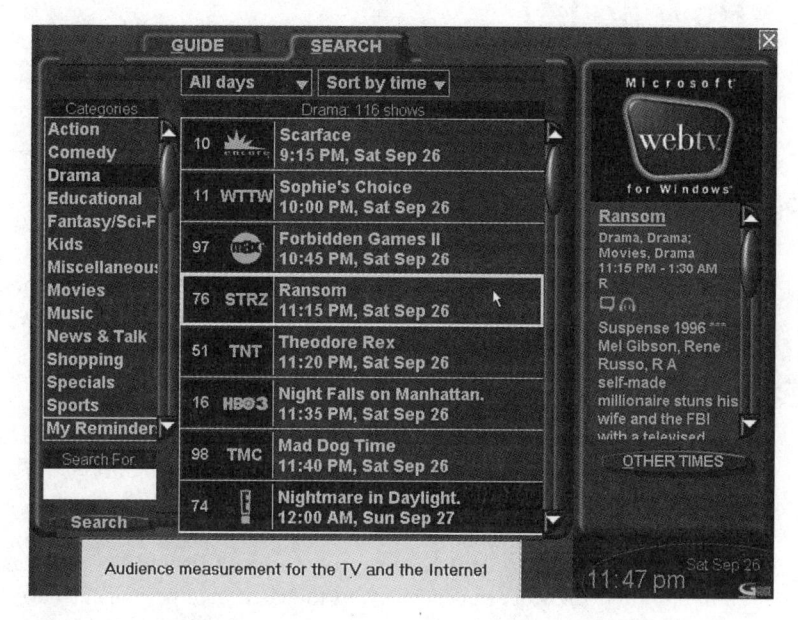

Figure 17.15 Viewing the WebTV for Windows Program Guide Search.

23. Type the text string that you want to search for, and then click the Search button to initiate the search. When you have found the show that you are seeking, click it once to highlight it, and then click the Watch button (on the right side of the screen).

> **NOTE**
>
> The far-left portion of the Search tab features a scrollable Categories list. The television shows are split into areas such as Action or Drama by the WebTV service automatically, and at present, this is not an organizational feature that you can modify.
>
> Think of the Categories listing as a quick way to find a TV show that you want to watch, but are not really sure what the name of it is. What you do with this listing is like "zapper surfing" without actually using your TV remote.

24. To exit this screen and return to the normal program guide simply click the Guide tab at the top of the screen. To end your use of the WebTV for Windows application, click the × located on the upper-right corner of the WebTV for Windows screen.

COMPLEXITY
INTERMEDIATE

17.3 How do I...
Listen to the radio on my Windows 98 PC?

Problem

Great. I can watch TV on my PC. However, I have a real job that will not let me get away with watching the Chicago Cubs baseball game every afternoon. Can I listen to the radio instead? And, if so, how can I do this?

Technique

To listen to the radio on your PC, you will need a TV tuner card that has an AM or FM radio station tuner built into it. Otherwise, you might be able use the RealAudio software that comes with Windows 98 (see this topic in Chapter 16, "Multimedia Basics," for more details). Keep in mind, though, that most network administrators have learned how to block RealAudio broadcasts from jamming their firewall applications and the corporate network, so do not be surprised if you are unable to receive RealAudio broadcasts via your organization's LANs and WANs. This How-To walks you through the steps required to let you listen to your local radio stations while you work, using the physical TV tuner card installed in your PC.

Steps

1. Start up the Windows 98 radio tuner application (such as STB's STB PCI FM tuner), which can be found by clicking the Start button, selecting the Programs menu option, and then clicking the STB FM Pro menu selection. This will bring you to the screen shown in Figure 17.16.

2. Keep in mind that your PC might use a different proprietary software package for use with your TV tuner card. However, that card will probably start much in the same way as the STB card's TV tuner does.

3. When the software starts, it probably has some sort of car stereo-like interface. This makes it much easier to use, as everyone has probably played with their car stereo (or their parents') at one time or another. If you have trouble using your software, click the Help button for that software (or press the F1 key on your keyboard, as many applications still recognize that universal call for help). This reveals the screen (or one like it) shown in Figure 17.17.

17.3
LISTEN TO THE RADIO ON MY WINDOWS 98 PC

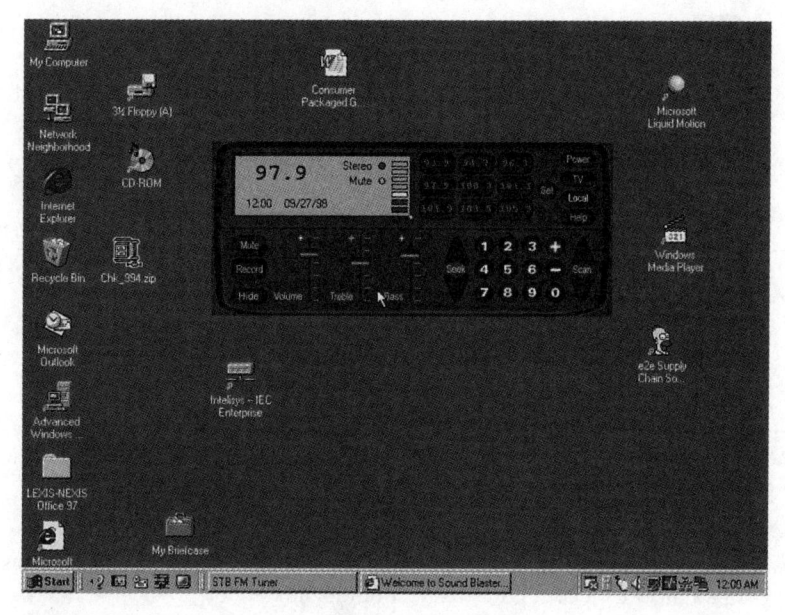

Figure 17.16 Viewing the WebTV for Windows Program Guide screen.

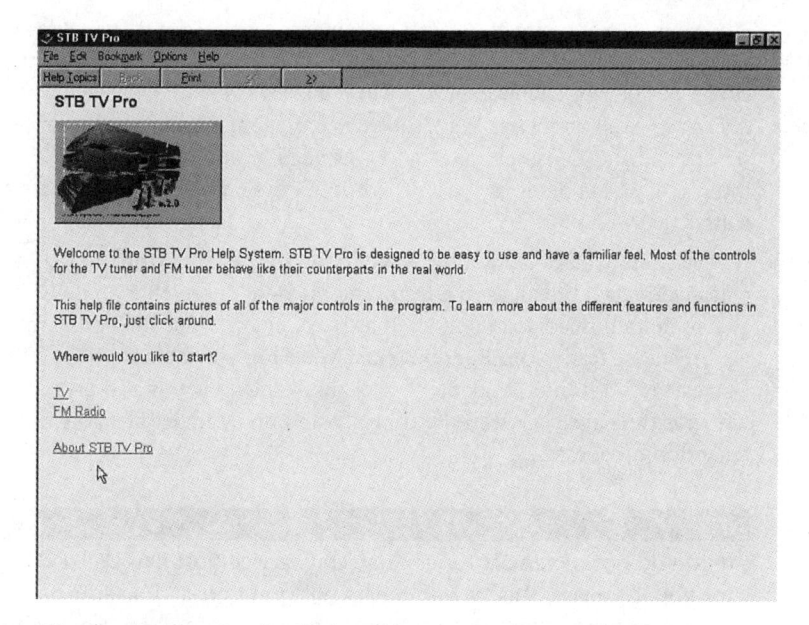

Figure 17.17 Getting help with your AM/FM radio tuner application.

4. Make sure that your PC has its external antenna attached to the back of the TV tuner card, and you should be able to start up your radio just in time to hear the closing moments of the Cubs World Series victory—okay, so that's a dream, but…

COMPLEXITY
INTERMEDIATE

17.4 How do I… Configure WaveTop Data Broadcasting?

Problem

I heard about a way to receive Internet content without having to first find a way to connect and pay for my own connection to the Internet. Is this true, and if so, how do I configure this technology for my own PC?

Technique

WaveTop Data Broadcasting is a new wireless technology that enables you to acquire the "Best of the Web" content and software downloads, without using either an ISP or a telephone line. This almost sounds like a little bit of magic, doesn't it? Well, it's close. WaveTop uses a combination of your local television service and the TV tuner card that is installed in your PC to deliver Internet-based content to your PC without either an ISP or WAN-based Internet connection.

WaveTop, wholly owned by WavePhore, Inc., is an advertising-supported nationwide data broadcast medium, the purpose of which is to deliver electronic multimedia content such as news, magazines, and software to users via broadcast-ready computer systems. WaveTop collaborated with PBS National Datacast to send Internet content over the vertical blanking interval (VBI), which is the pause between the transmission of TV images (that is, PBS's own television broadcasts).

> **NOTE**
> If you do not own a TV tuner card, this service (just like WebTV) is not for you. Likewise, this technology is not quite ready for laptop computer prime time, so to speak, so do not attempt to use it without first possessing a solid knowledge of your computer's hardware and internal components.

17.4 CONFIGURE WAVETOP DATA BROADCASTING

To get started with the WaveTop Data Broadcasting component, go through these steps. Keep in mind that this is a relatively young technology that makes several claims (which are not true) to being available to every household in America, as long as you can receive Public Broadcasting System services. There is a lot of marketing hype in these types of statements, so take them with a grain of salt whenever you hear them.

Additionally, because you need a TV tuner card to make this technology work, you will probably be stuck using a desktop computer. TV tuner technology still is in its infancy when it comes to laptop computer systems (that is, expensive!). Also, the other hardware requirements for this technology are similar to those required for WebTV for Windows, except that you can run WaveTop with only a 90MHz Pentium computer, 2MB of video RAM, and 16MB of system RAM. The infrastructure requirements for using WaveTop are as follows:

- Your PC's TV tuner card must be connected to your cable television provider or to a rooftop or settop antenna.

- A modem or an Internet connection is required for registering and reporting statistics to WaveTop, using a toll-free telephone call.

- Optional: An Internet connection (such as via an ISP or your organization's direct WAN connection) is necessary for using the hyperlinks found within the broadcast pages, which will take you to Internet Web sites.

Finally, you must make sure that your TV tuner card is compatible with the WaveTop Data Broadcasting service. To do this, examine Table 17.1.

Table 17.1 Determining the Compatibility of Your TV Tuner Card

TV TUNER CARD MANUFACTURER	CARD DESCRIPTION	TV TUNER CARD MANUFACTURER'S INTERNET WEB SITE
ADS	Channel Surfer TV	http://www.adstech.com
AIMS Lab	VideoHighway Xtreme	http://www.aimslab.com
AITech	WaveWatcher NE TV-PCI	http://www.aitech.com
ATI	All-in-Wonder	http://www.atitech.com
	All-in-Wonder Pro	
AVerMedia	TVPhone	http://www.aver.com
Diamond Multimedia	DTV-2000	http://www.diamondmm.com
Hauppauge	Win TV models, including:	http://www.hauppauge.com

continued on next page

continued from previous page

TV TUNER CARD MANUFACTURER	CARD DESCRIPTION	TV TUNER CARD MANUFACTURER'S INTERNET WEB SITE
	WinCast/TV	
	WinCast/TVdbx	
	WinCast/TV-Radio	
	WinTV-PCI	
	WinTV-PCI with FM	
	DBX-TV stereo	
	WinTV-PCI with	
	DBX-TV stereo	
IXMICRO	Turbo TV	http://www.ixmicro.com
Miro	miroMEDIA PCTV	http://www.miro.com
STB	TV-PCI Tuner	http://www.stb.com
Zoltrix	TV Max	http://www.zoltrix.com

If your TV tuner card does not appear in this table, chances are that it will not work with the WaveTop Data Broadcasting service. However, you might want to visit the WaveTop Data Broadcasting service's own Internet Web site (http://www.wavetop.net/) for more details on what does and doesn't work with their technologies.

> **NOTE**
>
> ADS, Aims Lab, AITech, AVerMedia, Diamond Multimedia, IX Micro, MiroMedia, STB, and Zoltrix are working on new Windows 98-compatible drivers. At present, only the Hauppauge Win TV WDM tuner card (whose software drivers can be downloaded from the WaveTop Web site), and the ATI All-in-Wonder WDM drivers (which come with the Windows 98 CD-ROM) are fully compatible with Windows 98. All the other manufacturers are busy working on compatible drivers, so be sure to check out their Web sites before you purchase one of these other TV tuner cards.

Steps

1. To start the WaveTop Data Broadcasting service, click the Start button, choose the Programs menu option, select the Accessories menu folder, and then click the WaveTop icon to reveal the screen shown in Figure 17.18.

2. To start the WaveTop Network Initialization process, click Yes to proceed to the screen shown in Figure 17.19.

17.4
CONFIGURE WAVETOP DATA BROADCASTING

Figure 17.18 Accessing the WaveTop Data Broadcasting Welcome screen.

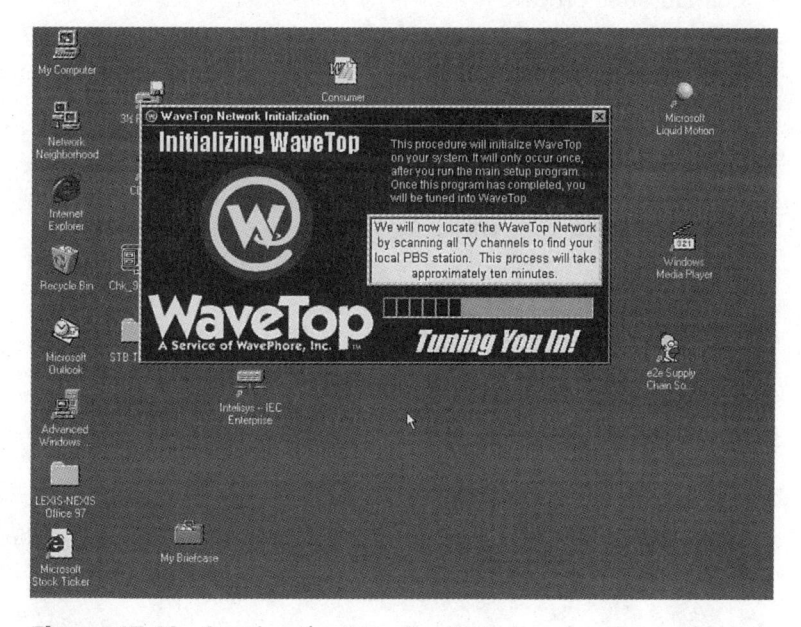

Figure 17.19 Starting the WaveTop Data Broadcasting initialization process.

3. This portion of the configuration process (when it works) takes roughly 10 minutes to complete. The WaveTop software continues its configuration process by scanning all the TV channels in your viewing area to find the local PBS station. During this process, the WaveTop Receiver Channel Scan window automatically appears, as shown in Figure 17.20.

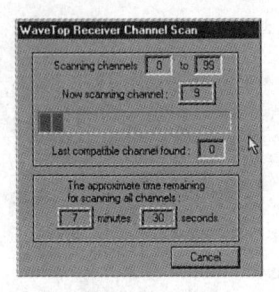

Figure 17.20 The WaveTop Data Broadcasting Configuration process.

4. This screen does a pretty good job of estimating the time remaining for the scanning process. Unfortunately, as shown in Figure 17.21, most of the time you receive an error message stating that a compatible WaveTop channel could not be found.

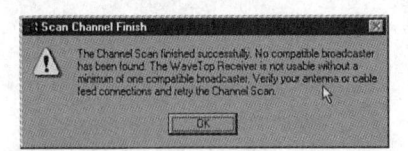

Figure 17.21 A WaveTop Data Broadcasting configuration error message.

5. To clear this error message, click OK. This takes you back to the Initializing WaveTop screen shown in Figure 17.22.

17.4
CONFIGURE WAVETOP DATA BROADCASTING

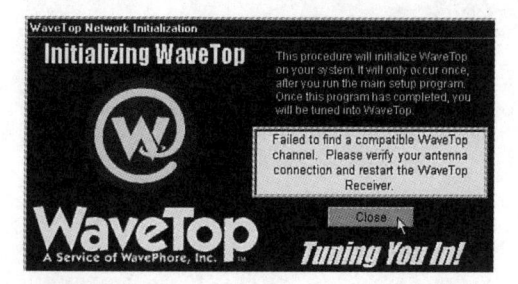

Figure 17.22 Initialization WaveTop error message.

6. This should in no way discourage you from continuing to try to use this service. This is an idea that is conceptually way ahead of its time, and as such, will probably take a bit more time for it to work on a regular basis (like the early days of cellular telephones). Click Close to close this screen and exit the WaveTop Data Broadcasting system.

7. I recommend that you continue to try your configuration efforts, because you might one day find that you are able to access your local PBS station's broadcasts. However, if you are attempting to use nonstandard TV tuner equipment, you will want to look for more up-to-date drivers for this hardware or consider purchasing new hardware that is compatible with the WaveTop Data Broadcasting system.

CHAPTER 18
TELECONFERENCING THE MULTIMEDIA WAY

18

TELECONFERENCING THE MULTIMEDIA WAY

How do I...
18.1 Install Microsoft NetMeeting?
18.2 Configure and use Microsoft NetMeeting?

The Internet continues to thrive in ways that only a few years ago were completely unheard of. Not only are you able to send and receive all types and sizes of data and graphical files, you can now transmit your voice via the Internet using a technology known as *Voice over IP*. As this type of technology progresses into the future, an offshoot of it is appearing: voice and video conferencing via the Internet.

Within Windows 98 is a tool known as *Microsoft NetMeeting*. This tool permits you to host or join virtual meetings across the Internet, without having to incur the expense of long-distance telephone calls or purchase additional software. The future is now. NetMeeting allows you to make video or voice or even online chat conference calls over the Internet (or your corporate LAN/WAN infrastructure). While on a call with one or more people you are able to share files, including sending them back and forth to one or more people; use a shared whiteboard that everyone can see, provided you dole out permission; and share applications across the wire, even if the application was not specifically designed for multiuser use.

This chapter discusses how you install, configure, and use this exciting new technology from Microsoft, which is built into the Windows 98 operating system (OS) and installs automatically during a full installation method. If you did not do a full installation of Windows 98, you might need to install Microsoft NetMeeting manually using the Add/Remove Programs feature of Windows 98.

Before you get started you should confirm that your computer hardware is compatible with NetMeeting, especially in the video camera, microphone, and other audio equipment areas. Review these tables (a more up-to-date version might be available on the Microsoft Web site at: `http://www.microsoft.com/netmeeting/`) to determine if you even have the base equipment covered. For further details, you should go to the Web site for each manufacturer's hardware component that you own (and are hoping to use with the NetMeeting tool).

18.1 Install Microsoft NetMeeting

The focus of this How-To is to assist you in the installation process of the Microsoft NetMeeting application.

18.2 Configure and Use Microsoft NetMeeting

After the Microsoft NetMeeting tool has been installed, you need to go through a series of installation steps that, although not too difficult, still mean that you must pay close attention in order to get it right the first time. This How-To ensures that you are able to configure your PC system correctly.

Table 18.1 Audio Component Review for Use with Microsoft NetMeeting

AUDIO EQUIPMENT VENDORS

MANUFACTURER NAME	COMPONENT NAME(S)	MANUFACTURER'S INTERNET WEB SITE
Aztec	Sound Galaxy	http://www.aztechca.com/aztfiles.html
Cirrus Logic	Crystal drivers	http://www.cirrus.com/drivers/audiodrv/
Diamond	Sonic Impact, Monster Sound, Monster Sound M80	http://www.diamondmm.com
Ensoniq	Soundscape, Vivo90, AudioPCI	http://www.ensoniq.com/multimedia/mm_html/html/drivers.htm
ESS	Generic ESS drivers	http://www.esstech.com/faq/faq_sofware.htm

MANUFACTURER NAME	COMPONENT NAME(S)	MANUFACTURER'S INTERNET WEB SITE
Guillemot	Maxi Sound	http://www.guillemot.com
Internet PhoneJACK	Quicknet drivers, version 1.2 or later	http://www.quicknet.net
Soundblaster	SB16, SB32, AWE 32, AWE 64	http://www-nt-ca.creaf.com/wwwnew/tech/ftp/ftp-sb16awe.html
TurtleBeach	Tropez, Daytona PCI, Montego	http://www.tbeach.com/tbs/downloads/scardsdown.htm
VideoLogic	Sonic Storm	http://www.videologic.com
Xitel	Storm3D	http://www.xitel.com
Yamaha	OPL-3SA	http://www.yamaha.com

(Source: Microsoft Corporation, 1998)

Table 18.2 Video Component Review for Use with Microsoft NetMeeting

VIDEO EQUIPMENT VENDORS

MANUFACTURER NAME	COMPONENT NAME(S)	MANUFACTURER'S INTERNET WEB SITE
Aims Lab	Video Highway Extreme	http://www.aimslab.com
ATI	All-in-Wonder, ATI-TV	http://support.atitech.ca/drivers/drivers.html
AVerMedia	MPEG Wizard, EZCapture, TVPhone	http://www.avermedia.com
Compro	D-Cam	http://www.acscompro.com/support/dcamdrv.html
Connectix	QuickCam	http://www.connectix.com/html/quickcam_pc_updates.html
Creative	VideoBlaster	http://www-nt-ok.creaf.com/wwwnew/tech/ftp/ftp-vb.html
Diamond	DVC 1000	http://www.diamondmm.com
Digital Vision	Computer Eyes	http://www.digvis.com/drivers.html
Fast Multimedia	FPS60	http://www.fast-multimedia.com
Hauppauge	Wincast, Cinema Pro, Celebrity	http://www.hauppauge.com/html/free_sw.htm#wcast
Intel	Intel Smart Video Recorder	http://support.intel.com/support/videocapture/

continued on next page

continued from previous page

MANUFACTURER NAME	COMPONENT NAME(S)	MANUFACTURER'S INTERNET WEB SITE
Kodak	DVC300, DVC323	http://www.kodak.com
Miro	Miro DC 10,20,30	http://www.miro.com/support/
Multimedia Access	Osprey 100	http://www.mmac.com
Nogatech	ConferenceCard	http://www.nogatech.com/html/software.html
Orchid	Vidiola Pro/D	http://www.orchid.com/support/digvid/drv-vidiola.html
Philips	EasyCam	http://www.pps.philips.com/support/downloads.html
STB	TV-PCI	http://www.stb.com
Toshiba	JK-VC1	http://www.toshiba.com
USRobotics	BigPicture	http://www.usr.com/home/online/
VideoLogic	Captivator PCI, Captivator PCI/VC	http://www.videologic.com
Viewcome	Topcam	http://www.viewcome.com
Vista Imaging	ViCam	http://www.vistaimaging.com
Winnov	Videum	http://www.winnov.com
Xirlink, Inc.	XVP-500 USB camera	Drivers found at ftp://xirlink.com

(Source: Microsoft Corporation, 1998)

Table 18.3 Computer Systems Review for Use with Microsoft NetMeeting

COMPUTER SYSTEMS

MANUFACTURER NAME	COMPONENT NAME(S)	MANUFACTURER'S INTERNET WEB SITE
Compaq		http://www.compaq.com
Dell		http://www.dell.com
Gateway 2000	Misc. Audio and Video drivers	http://www.gw2k.com/
IBM		http://www.ibm.com
Packard Bell	Misc. Audio and Video drivers	http://support.packardbell.com/ftp/00index.asp
Toshiba	Misc. Audio and Video drivers	http://www.toshiba.com/tais/csd/support/

(Source: Microsoft Corporation, 1998)

CHAPTER 18
TELECONFERENCING THE MULTIMEDIA WAY

Microsoft NetMeeting has its own set of hardware requirements as well. However, its minimum stated requirements for data and audio conferencing are a joke, as you can see:

- Intel (or compatible) 80486/66MHz CPU—If this is all you have, Windows 98 is going to run kind of slow anyway.

- 5MB of free hard drive space—This had better not be the bottleneck on your system, otherwise you will have many other problems other than not being able to run NetMeeting.

- 8MB of RAM (memory)—If this is all you have, Windows 98 is not going to run that well.

- Sound card with speakers and a microphone—If you cannot hear or talk, that might be a problem.

- A 14.4Kbps analog modem or better—Although NetMeeting can run audio conferences, any heavy use requires at least a 33.6Kbps modem.

Its minimum stated requirements for video conferencing is not much more real either:

- Intel (or compatible) 90MHz Pentium CPU or faster—I find that video is sluggish on this slow of a box (try a 200MHz Pentium Pro or better), especially if you are using a cheap video camera, such as a parallel port unit that will suck the life out of a 90MHz CPU (because it does not have its own video card). That is, when the video usage is processed via software rather than its own hardware, it takes a lot of extra CPU cycles that otherwise would still be free if you had your own video card for your video camera.

- 16MB of RAM—If this is all you have, Windows 98 is going to run a bit slow anyway.

- A 28.8Kbps analog modem or better—Although NetMeeting can run audio conferences with this modem, any heavy use requires at least an ISDN (64k digital) modem or faster. A digital connection, such as a cable modem or T1 leased line, is by far the best solution when using the video conferencing features of NetMeeting.

Microsoft NetMeeting uses the TCP/IP networking communications protocol suite for the transmission of its information, such as across the Internet. It works by using an LDAP server service known as the Microsoft Internet Locator Server (ILS), which permits NetMeeting (version 2.1 or later) users to connect and locate each other on your organization's networks or the company intranet as well as the Internet. Keep in mind that when you use the video conferencing features of NetMeeting, you might create larger volumes of network traffic. This, in turn, can then create delays that lower the quality of service (QoS) of the transmission itself, which means that you will be affecting the real-time capabilities of NetMeeting, which is why you were doing a video conference call to begin with. You might want to consider the use of black-and-white video cameras to lessen network traffic or simply increase the available bandwidth on your LANs/WANs.

COMPLEXITY
BEGINNER

18.1 How do I...
Install Microsoft NetMeeting?

Problem

I want to conduct conference calls using the Internet as my hosting system, and I need to also be able to use a virtual whiteboard during these conference calls. How do I do this, and what software do I need to install?

Technique

The Windows 98 Internet Explorer add-on component known as Microsoft NetMeeting (version 2.1 is the current, but like everything else Microsoft has, it too will increase in version numbers sooner rather than later as the next version is already being readied for a free download to the world). This component is installed during a Full installation of the Windows 98 OS, but for purposes of these examples, assume that you either did not install Microsoft NetMeeting or did and already removed it from your computer system.

Steps

1. To check to see if you have the Microsoft NetMeeting package installed, click Start, move the mouse pointer to the Programs menu option, go to the Internet Tools menu option, and then look to see if the Microsoft NetMeeting menu selection exists. If not, you probably have not yet installed it.

2. To begin the installation process, click the Start button, choose the Settings menu option, and then click the Control Panel menu selection. This takes you into the Windows 98 Control Panel.

3. Double-click the Add/Remove Programs to access the Add/Remove Programs Properties screen. You will enter this screen on the Install/Uninstall tab.

18.1
INSTALL MICROSOFT NETMEETING?

4. Click the Windows Setup tab to proceed to that screen. Keep in mind that Windows 98 re-searches your hard drive at this point to see what options you have installed, so be patient as it might take a few minutes for this screen to appear.

5. Use the scrollbar to move down to the Communications menu option. Highlight it by clicking it once. Then, click the Details... button to move to that screen.

6. Once there, use the scrollbar to move downward until you see the Microsoft NetMeeting option. Select it by placing a check mark in the box located just to the left of this option. You do that by clicking the check box once, as shown in Figure 18.1. If there is already a check mark present, you have already installed the Microsoft NetMeeting product and do not need to repeat this installation process.

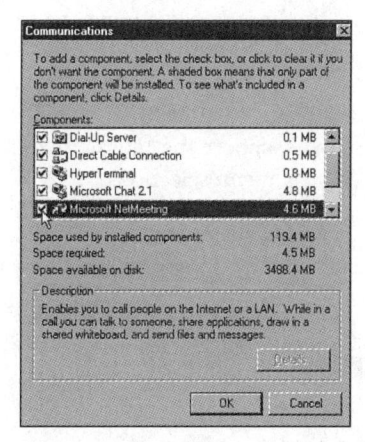

Figure 18.1 Finding the Microsoft NetMeeting option on the Communications page of the Windows Setup screen.

7. After you have selected this item, click OK to return to the primary Communications screen. Click OK there to begin the actual installation of the files from the Windows 98 CD-ROM.

8. When all of the files have finished copying, you are done. If you are prompted to restart your system, do so (you might be prompted to reboot if you have never had NetMeeting installed on your PC).

9. When the restart is complete, if there was one, you are finished and now ready to start the configuration process.

COMPLEXITY
INTERMEDIATE

18.2 How do I...
Configure and use Microsoft NetMeeting?

Problem

I have already installed the Microsoft NetMeeting software. How do I configure this software in the best way possible for use with my computer system?

Technique

The Microsoft NetMeeting product begins with its own Configuration Wizard. Follow these steps closely, and you are on your way to communicating with others across your organization, across the Internet, or around the world.

Steps

1. To start, click Start, choose Programs, choose the Internet Explorer menu folder, and then click the NetMeeting menu selection.

2. This series of mouse movements and clicks causes the initial Microsoft NetMeeting Configuration Wizard window to appear, as shown in Figure 18.2.

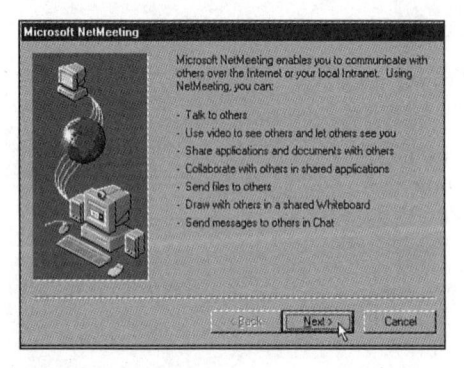

Figure 18.2 Starting the Microsoft NetMeeting Configuration Wizard.

3. This is an informational screen of the wizard; it describes the various functionalities of the Microsoft NetMeeting product. Click Next> to continue to the next wizard screen, which is shown in Figure 18.3

18.2
CONFIGURE AND USE MICROSOFT NETMEETING

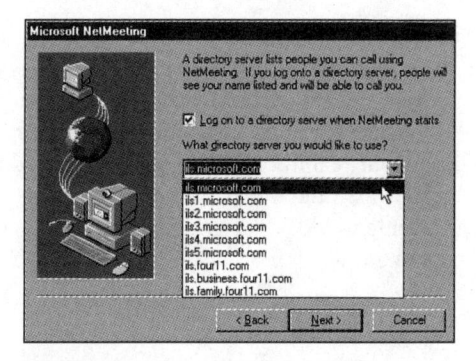

Figure 18.3 Choosing an Internet Locator Service (ILS) server for use with NetMeeting.

4. The directory server entry is very important. It is the name of the computer that will be hosting the Internet conference call meeting, and must be the same one that all the intended meeting participants use. It is suggested that you use the default server provided by Microsoft Corporation until you find or create others for your own purposes. To create your own ILS Server, you may download the version 2.1 software from the Microsoft Web site:
(`http://www.microsoft.com/netmeeting/`). (Keep in mind that Microsoft is discontinuing support for this version.) Microsoft wants you to purchase the Microsoft SiteServer 3.0 product (one of the Microsoft BackOffice products), which has the newest official ILS server included in it.

5. Click Next> to move to the next screen, shown in Figure 18.4.

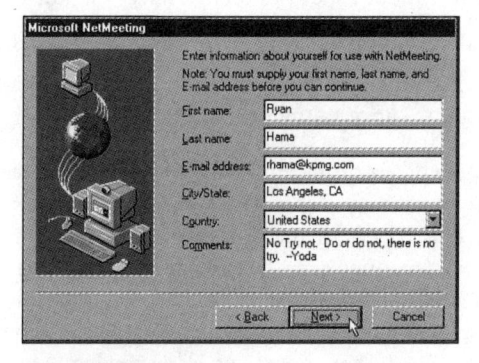

Figure 18.4 Entering your personal information for use with NetMeeting.

CHAPTER 18
TELECONFERENCING THE MULTIMEDIA WAY

6. The personal information screen contains information that you input about yourself, in order to identify you to the other participants on this same meeting server. Before you get excited about putting your personal information out on the Internet for all to see, remember that it is only a suggestion that you place your real information here. You could always input Chicago Cubs as your first and last name and WorldSeries@1998 (always a great thought, I might add) as your email address if you want. It is meaningless content, but so what!

7. Click Next> to move to the next screen, the wizard as shown in Figure 18.5.

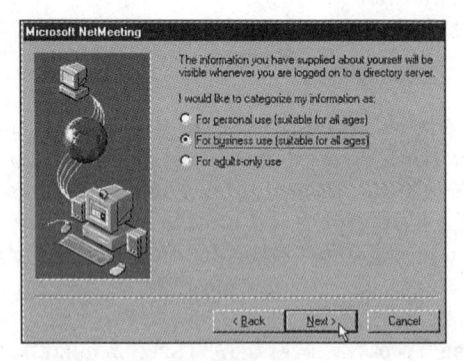

Figure 18.5 Categorizing your personal NetMeeting information.

8. The categorization area is an important one. If you select For Adults-Only Use you will see several NetMeeting participants whose only purpose appears to be the sale or discussion of pornography. What this means is that those of you with children should perhaps select the For Personal Use [Suitable for All Ages] radio button option.

9. Click once with the mouse on the radio button of your choice, and then click the Next> button to move to the next screen, shown in Figure 18.6).

10. The speed of your network connection for the Microsoft NetMeeting calls is very important. If you specify a speed that is too fast for your modem, additional graphics and content might be forwarded to you in a manner that your slower modem cannot handle. This, in turn, might lead to loss of information for you. Therefore, click the radio button for the speed that truly, most closely represents your network or Internet/intranet connections. For example, if you are using a cable modem, your connection choice will be Local Area Network, because a cable modem is much faster than any of the other radio button options.

18.2
CONFIGURE AND USE MICROSOFT NETMEETING?

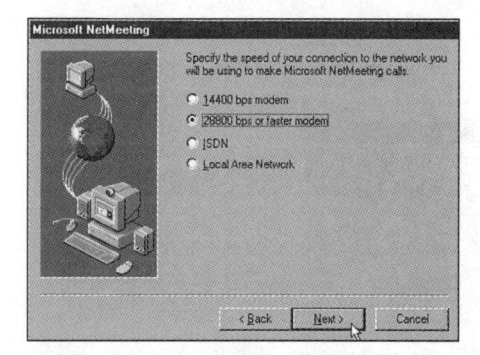

Figure 18.6 Specifying a connection speed to be used when making NetMeeting calls.

11. Click Next> to move to the next screen in the wizard, which is shown in Figure 18.7.

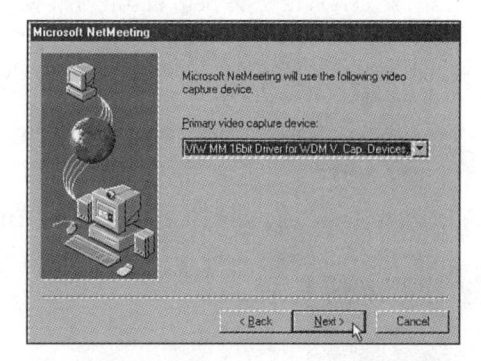

Figure 18.7 Determining which video capture device to use.

12. A video capture device is used to display your picture to others within the NetMeeting conference call.

> **NOTE**
> A better known name for a video capture device is camera, such as a camcorder for instance. You are capturing real-time video and pushing it out through the Microsoft NetMeeting software to the other NetMeeting users in your conference call or chat session. In the computer world people like techy terms instead of plain English, but it can be tough making the connection between the technical jargon and the normal terms.

13. Choose your main camera (video capture device), and then click Next> to move to the Audio Tuning Wizard screen, as shown in Figure 18.8.

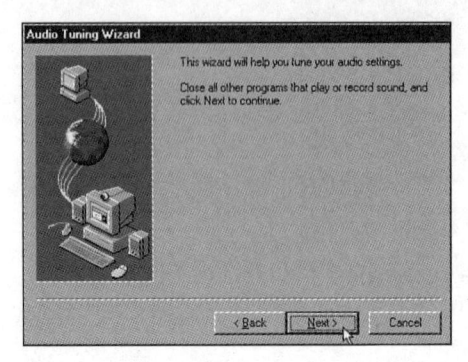

Figure 18.8 Beginning the Audio Tuning sub-Wizard for NetMeeting.

14. The Audio Tuning Wizard screen is used to help ensure that when you speak into your microphone your voice sounds as it does in person (or as close as possible). A quick note: You must close all your other applications that play or record sounds, such as the CD Player or Sound Recorder, prior to starting the Audio Tuning Wizard. Otherwise, you will receive error messages in the process.

15. Click Next> to move to the volume test screen, as shown in Figure 18.9.

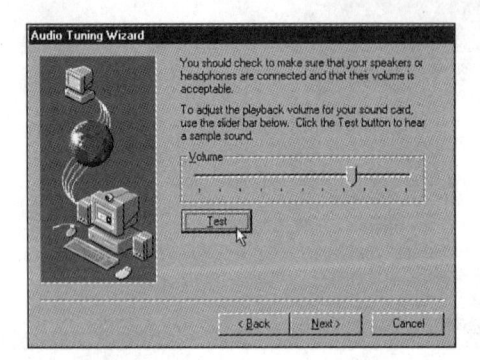

Figure 18.9 Tuning your Computer's Audio Systems for use with NetMeeting.

16. On this screen you tune the volume for the computer speakers and headphones that are used during any NetMeeting calls. Click the Test button after you think you have positioned the slider bar correctly. Note that the

18.2
CONFIGURE AND USE MICROSOFT NETMEETING?

Test button changes into a Stop button while the test is underway. When you have achieved the volume level that is musically pleasing to your ears, click Stop to stop this test.

17. As soon as you are satisfied with the results of your testing, click Next> to move to the record volume, as shown in Figure 18.10.

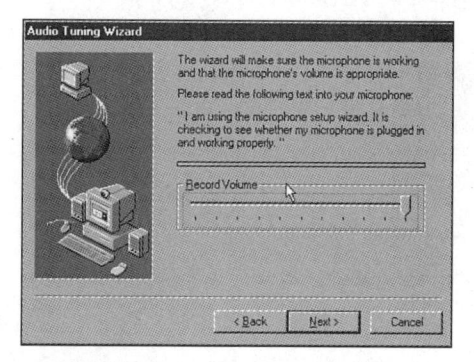

Figure 18.10 Tuning the PC microphone levels for use with NetMeeting.

18. Now that you have tuned your audio output, you must tune the sound input levels. As such, pick a spot on the Record Volume slider bar, and then begin speaking into the microphone. Chances are that you need to play with the settings until you find one that is acceptable to you. Do not yell into the microphone, but instead use your normal speaking voice. Also, even the cheapest of microphones, such as the $10 ones that come from the cow people in South Dakota (great PCs, cheap microphones) will almost always work just fine with your normal speaking voice.

19. Click Next> to move to the final screen of the wizard, shown in Figure 18.11.

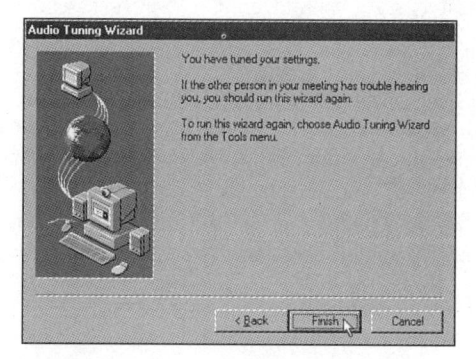

Figure 18.11 Completing the NetMeeting Configuration Wizard.

20. Congratulations! You have made it to the closing screen of the NetMeeting configuration Wizard. This screen is another informational one that can be closed by clicking the Finish button, which takes you directly into the primary Microsoft NetMeeting screen.

21. Immediately after entering the NetMeeting application, you are prompted with a Microsoft NetMeeting message box, as seen in Figure 18.12.

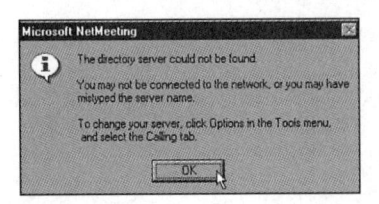

Figure 18.12 NetMeeting ILS Connection Error message box.

22. This message box appears if you have not yet established a network connection to the NetMeeting ILS server, such as a dial-up connection to the Internet for the public ILS servers or a LAN connection to your corporate ILS servers.

23. After you click OK to clear the error message box, which you can do even if you have not yet established a proper connection to the ILS server, you notice that you are not yet connected to any conference calls or directory servers, as shown in Figure 18.13.

24. In the center of the screen are two drop-down list boxes—one for the Category of the calls, and the other for the Server (directory) to be called. The categories available presently are simplistic: business, personal, and for pleasure. The business and personal categories are for persons of all ages and tastes. The pleasure category is also known as the Adult-content category, and is definitely not for children. Choose the category you want by clicking it.

25. Next, click the Server list box to determine where you want to connect. Until you become more familiar with Microsoft NetMeeting, I recommend that you stay with one of the default Microsoft servers (lots of great content here). You can click once on the giant drop-down list box labeled, Directory: ILS *ServerName* (where ILS *ServerName* equates to the presently selected server), which reveals the directory tree view, as shown in Figure 18.14.

18.2 CONFIGURE AND USE MICROSOFT NETMEETING?

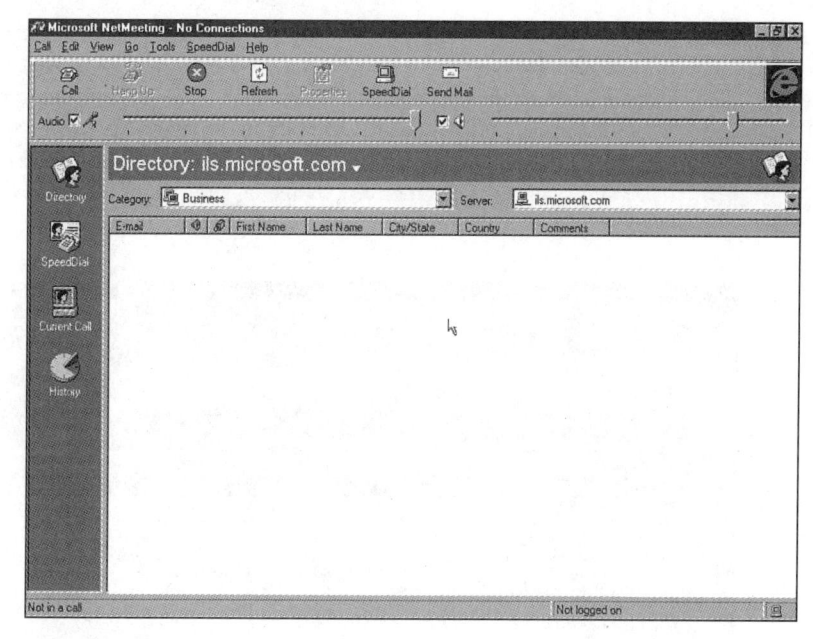

Figure 18.13 Welcome to the main NetMeeting screen.

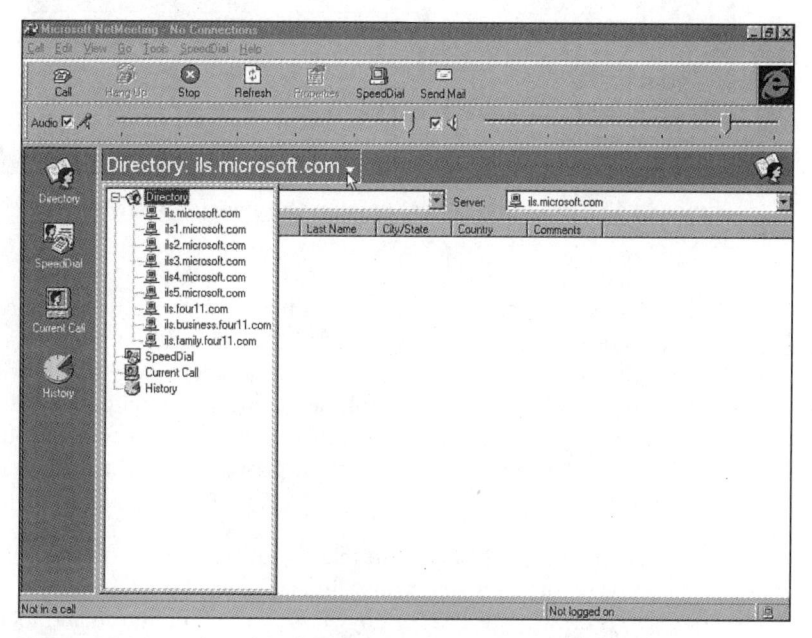

Figure 18.14 Using the directory tree to select a NetMeeting Server.

26. After you click on the server of your choice, press Enter to initiate the connection. Please note, however, that you must already have established a connection to the Internet, if the server you are attempting to contact is located somewhere else out in cyberspace, otherwise confirm your connection to your organization's LAN/WAN infrastructure. Performing these steps causes the screen to change, as you begin to see all the other users on this same directory server, as shown in Figure 18.15.

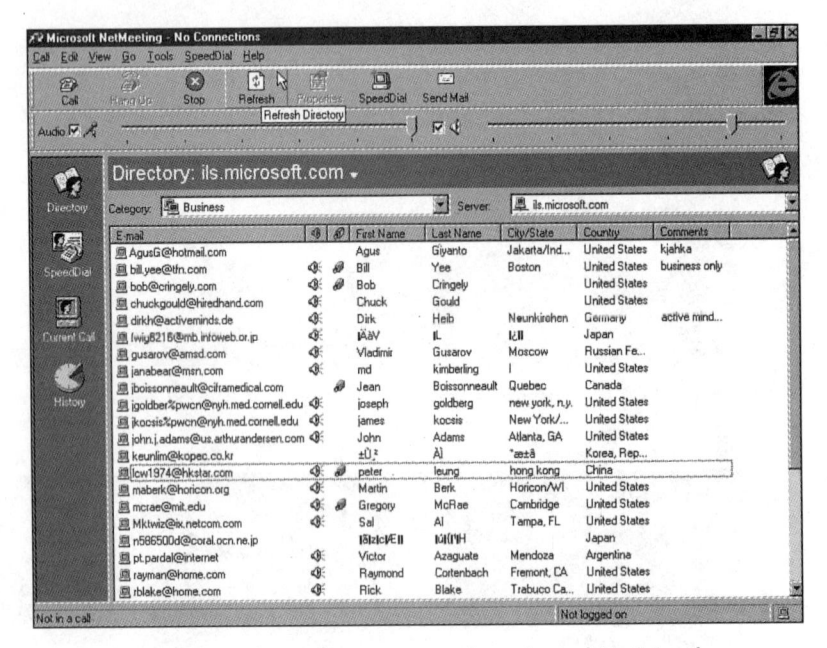

Figure 18.15 Browsing other users on the selected NetMeeting Server.

27. Although you have contacted the directory server of your choice, you still are not a part of any conference call. To join a call in progress, double-click any of the directory entries (for example, a person) who already has an asterisk * on the left side of their computer monitor icon (this means that that person is connected and "live" as well). Of course, you may try to contact anyone, but do not be surprised if a lot of contact tries end up in failure.

28. Also, the people in a call can reject your entry to that conference, so do not be surprised if you cannot find a call to join. Likewise, you can always create your own call by clicking the Call button and following those simplistic prompts.

18.2
CONFIGURE AND USE MICROSOFT NETMEETING?

29. However, before you do make that call, click the Call menu option, and then click again on the Change My Information menu selection, as shown in Figure 18.16.

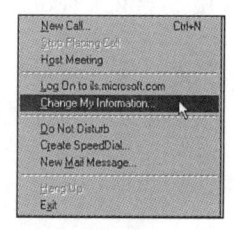

Figure 18.16 Changing your NetMeeting information.

30. This takes us into the NetMeeting Options screens, with the My Information tab appearing first as shown in Figure 18.17.

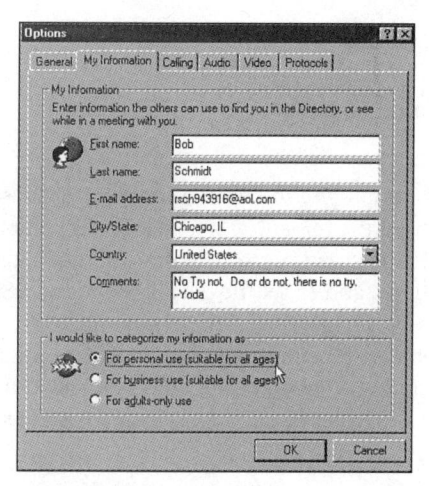

Figure 18.17 Changing data on the My Information tab.

31. On this screen, people should enter their own contact information, along with choosing a category (at the bottom) for their personal data. The information that does appear here is the same as what was entered during the initial Configuration Wizard. Looking at the example, you notice that I changed the original data that was entered and instead took the name of a very famous character in Chicago history (yep, a cousin) instead of

CHAPTER 18
TELECONFERENCING THE MULTIMEDIA WAY

using my own data. If you are using NetMeeting within your organization's communications environment, you might want to check with the marketing or IS departments for company standards and guidelines.

32. To continue, click the General tab to access that configuration screen, as shown in Figure 18.18.

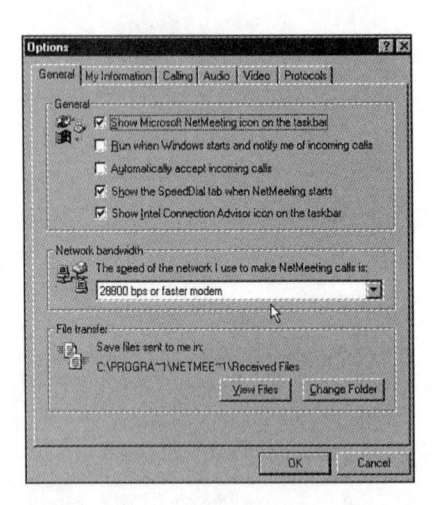

Figure 18.18 Changing data on the General tab.

33. The General tab options permit you to reconfigure many of those same options that were set during the initial NetMeeting Configuration Wizard. Again, you are able to set the speed of the network/Internet connection, basic NetMeeting operations, and to set the default Windows 98 folder location (displayed in an 8.3 file format) for receiving files transmitted to you during the course of a NetMeeting conference call. Use the mouse pointer and click those options that you want, and then click the Calling tab to continue with the Options configuration screen, as shown in Figure 18.19.

34. The Calling tab is primarily used to set the name of the directory server that should be used after entering NetMeeting. Another very useful option is the capability for you to hide your email address from the directory listing, which anyone can readily access and view. People can still contact you, but they must already know your email address. After making the appropriate selections on this screen, click the Audio tab to continue to that screen, as shown in Figure 18.20.

18.2 CONFIGURE AND USE MICROSOFT NETMEETING?

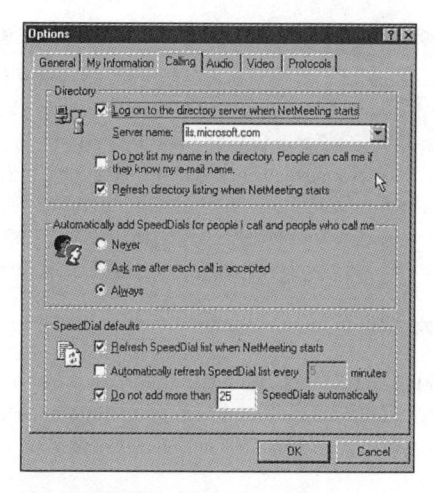

Figure 18.19 Changing data on the Calling tab.

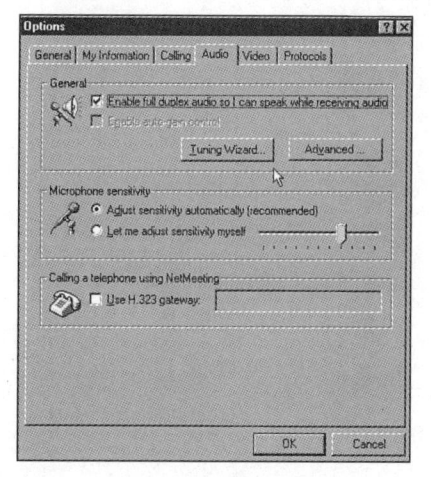

Figure 18.20 Changing data on the Audio tab.

35. It is recommended that the options on this screen not be modified unless you are an advanced computer user or professional, with the exception of rerunning the Audio Tuning Wizard, which everyone runs the first time they enter Microsoft NetMeeting. If you do run this wizard by clicking the Tuning Wizard button, upon its completion you are brought back to this Options tab where you left off.

> **NOTE**
>
> The last option on this screen refers to using an H.323 Gateway. This is the International Telecommunication Union's (ITU) standard for audio and video conferencing. The H.323 Gateway allows a Microsoft NetMeeting user (version 2.1 or newer) to access the Internet and place a telephone call using the Public Switched Telephone Network (PSTN). What all this means is that you can use NetMeeting to make telephone calls—the whole voice over IP technologies that you read and hear so much about.

36. To manually modify your audio *codecs* (see the following note for a description) you need to use the Advanced... button on the top part of this tab. Click the Advanced... button to reveal that screen, as shown in Figure 18.21.

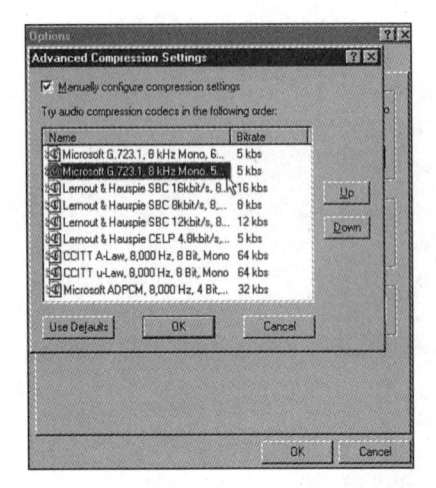

Figure 18.21 Manually configuring audio compression codecs.

37. To modify the order of your codecs, click the Manually Configure Compression Settings check box to select it. This un-grays the rest of this screen, at which point you can modify the order of your codecs. After you have made your modifications, click OK to return to the Audio tab.

> **NOTE**
>
> The term codec means Compression/Decompression. A codec is used for audio and video files in such a manner that it permits your computer to more effectively manage its multimedia functions. You as a user do not need to worry about codecs because the operating system will do this

18.2
CONFIGURE AND USE MICROSOFT NETMEETING?

for you automatically, but if you are the system or desktop administrator for your organization then you might have to deal with this issue. However, if you are seeking to impress your friends by talking about codecs, one of the more popular codec formats is that of the MPEG format.

38. As soon as you have completed all your modifications, if any, click the Video tab to move onto that screen, as shown in Figure 18.22.

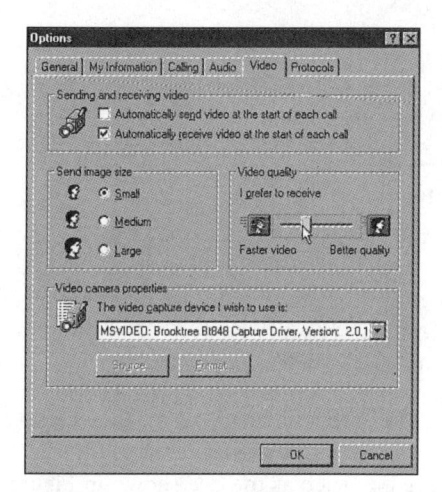

Figure 18.22 Configuring the NetMeeting video options.

39. If you do not have a camera attached to your PC, some of these options obviously do not pertain to you. The better the quality and size of the video images sent and received, the slower the NetMeeting call might appear to operate. So, unless you have a high-speed network connection, you might want to set your preferences to Faster Video instead of Better Quality on the receiving side, and a Small or Medium image size. The drop-down list box in the bottom section allows you to select an alternative video capture device (assuming you have more than one installed on your PC).

40. After you have made your modifications, if any, click the Protocols tab to access this last screen, as shown in Figure 18.23.

41. Make the appropriate selections on this tab, such as choosing the Null Modem as the protocol (not a great idea, by the way). To select or deselect any protocol, click the check box next to that protocol's text label.

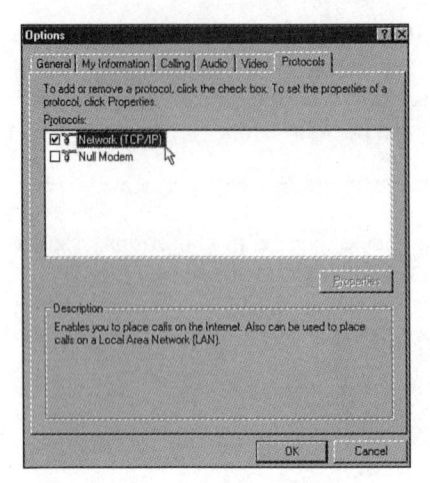

Figure 18.23 Configuring the NetMeeting Protocol Options tab.

42. When you are finished with this screen and want to accept all changes made to any of theses Options screen tabs, click OK. Doing this returns you to the primary Microsoft NetMeeting window.

43. Again, if you are not logged in to a directory server (maybe because you are not on the Internet or your corporate network), you receive a NetMeeting error message box such as the one shown in Figure 18.24.

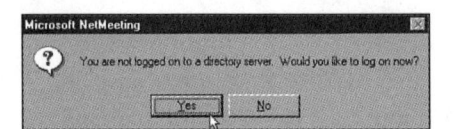

Figure 18.24 Reviewing a NetMeeting Error Message box.

44. Click Yes to connect to a directory server or click No to decline.

45. Another section of NetMeeting that you need to be aware of, is the capability for you to host your own NetMeeting (for example, an audio, video, or chat conference call). To do this, click the Call menu option, and then click again on the Host Meeting menu selection, which takes you to the message box shown in Figure 18.25.

46. If you click once on the Don't Show Me This Message Again check box to select it, the next time you click on the Host Meeting option you bypass this message box entirely. Click OK to begin your hosting of a NetMeeting conference call, which takes you to the screen shown in Figure 18.26.

18.2
CONFIGURE AND USE MICROSOFT NETMEETING?

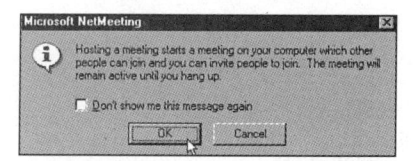

Figure 18.25 Starting the NetMeeting conference call hosting process.

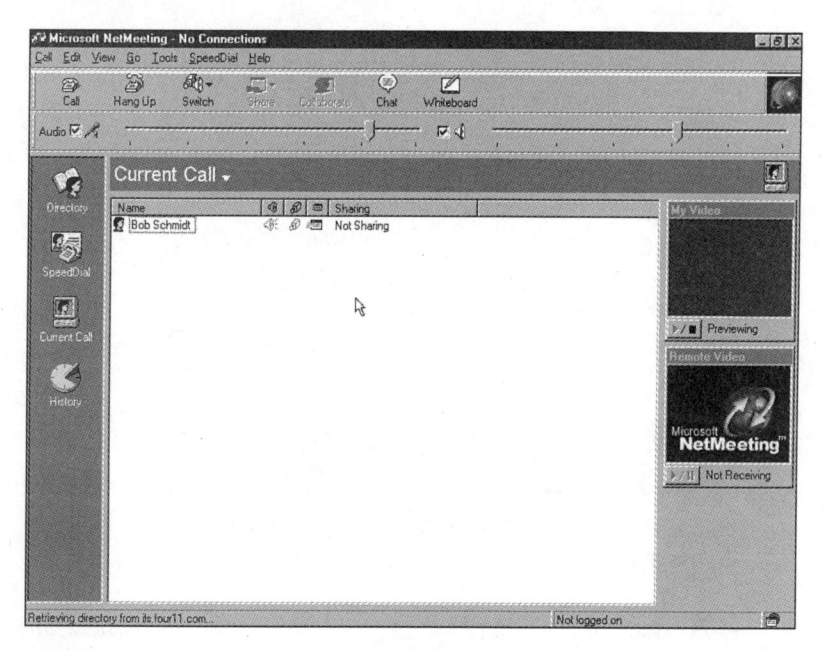

Figure 18.26 Hosting your own NetMeeting conference call.

47. Whenever you start to host a conference you go to the Current Call screen; this is also where you should wind up after you connect to someone else's conference call.

48. Return to the main screen by clicking the Directory button found on the left side of the screen. Do this so that you can access the Tools menu options. To access any of these tools, click the Tools menu option, as shown in Figure 18.27.

49. From this menu you can click the tool of your choice, including switching the audio and video features, a few more video choices, sharing another application, an interactive chat, a virtual whiteboard, and the file transfer mechanisms. The Tools menu also provides another way in which to access the Audio Tuning Wizard as well as the NetMeeting Options screens. If you click the Whiteboard menu selection, you are taken to the screen shown in Figure 18.28.

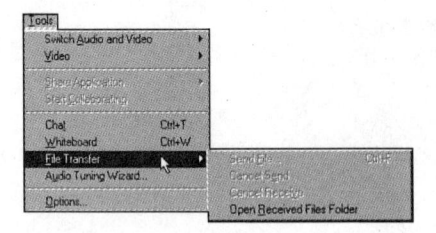

Figure 18.27 Accessing the various optional NetMeeting tools.

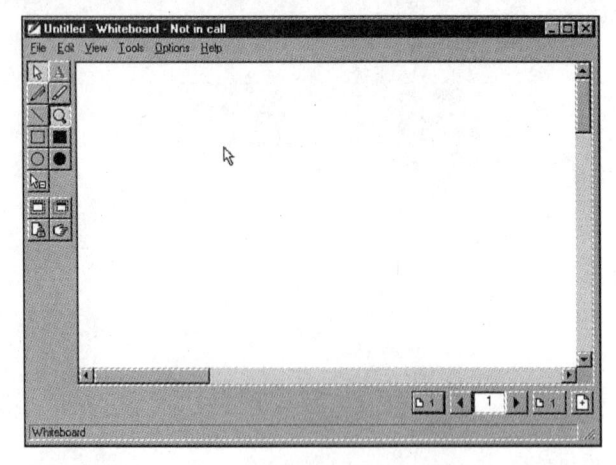

Figure 18.28 Using the NetMeeting virtual whiteboard tool.

50. Think of this tool literally as an electronic version of the whiteboard that you have probably used dozens of times in your business office, at school, or maybe even in your home office. Conceptually, it works very much in the same way. If you are good at drawing in Microsoft Paint, you are going to be a wizard with this tool (which works very similarly to this Whiteboard tool). To exit the whiteboard and return to the general directory screen, click the File/Exit menu selections. Note that you can switch back and forth between all the NetMeeting tools at will, without losing data in any of them.

51. If you had clicked once on the Chat menu selection, you are taken to the screen shown in Figure 18.29.

52. This chat is about as basic as it gets. You type in your message, and then either press Enter or click the button that has an icon on it that looks like a full piece of paper. You see everyone else's messages fly by in the big white box above this area. One neat option that this chat tool has, which

18.2
CONFIGURE AND USE MICROSOFT NETMEETING?

most of the Internet relay chat (IRC) tools still do not have, is the capability to "whisper" to someone else in the chat session. This essentially means that you can send a private message to someone else in the group, without everyone else seeing that message appear on their chat screens. To exit the Chat tool and return to the general directory screen, click on the File/Exit menu selections. Note that you can switch back and forth between all the NetMeeting tools at will, chat included, without losing data in any of them.

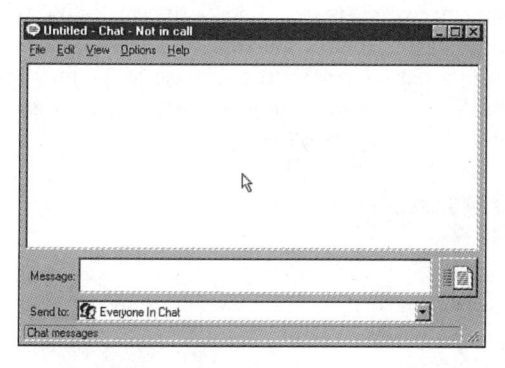

Figure 18.29 Using the NetMeeting Chat tool.

53. Another interesting feature within the NetMeeting application is the SpeedDial capability. This works like a speed dial button would on a telephone, making the usability of NetMeeting just that much easier. To add someone to the SpeedDial feature is very easy as well. All you need to do is select the person you want to add from the main Directory screen, by clicking on that person after to select him or her.

54. Next, right-click the secondary mouse button to reveal the small menu, as shown in Figure 18.30.

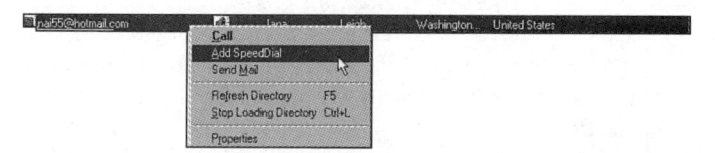

Figure 18.30 Accessing the NetMeeting pop-up menu.

55. After this menu appears, move your pointing device to the Add SpeedDial menu selection and click on it once. And voilà, your friend/coworker/acquaintance is now automatically added to your

SpeedDial area. Note that this person does not necessarily have to be active on NetMeeting when you want to add them to your SpeedDial area, which is another nice aspect of this capability.

56. From this same menu, which was shown in Figure 18.30, you have the capability to send an email message using your default email application such as Microsoft Outlook Express or the full Microsoft Outlook 9x product.

57. Also on this menu, shown in Figure 18.30, is the capability to review the properties of others on the NetMeeting Directory. Highlight the person whose NetMeeting properties you want to review, and then click the Properties menu selection from that pop-up menu. This reveals the screen shown in Figure 18.31 for that NetMeeting user.

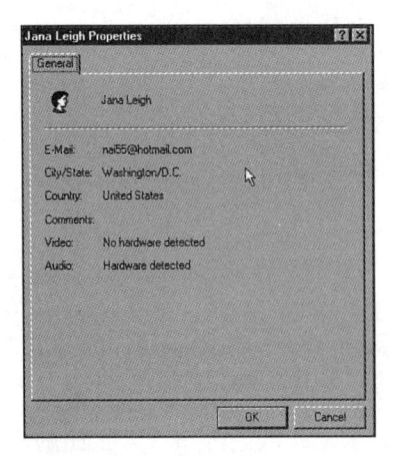

Figure 18.31 Reviewing another NetMeeting user's properties.

58. If you want to suddenly contact this person whose properties you just reviewed and if that person is a member of your SpeedDial section, you can do this very quickly. Click the SpeedDial button located along the left side of the NetMeeting screen, which takes you to the screen shown in Figure 18.32.

59. After you reach the SpeedDial screen, double-click the NetMeeting user you want to contact and you will be connected (provided, of course, that they are logged in to the same ILS server as you).

60. Occasionally, when contacting someone else, you will receive an error message box like the one in Figure 18.33.

18.2
CONFIGURE AND USE MICROSOFT NETMEETING?

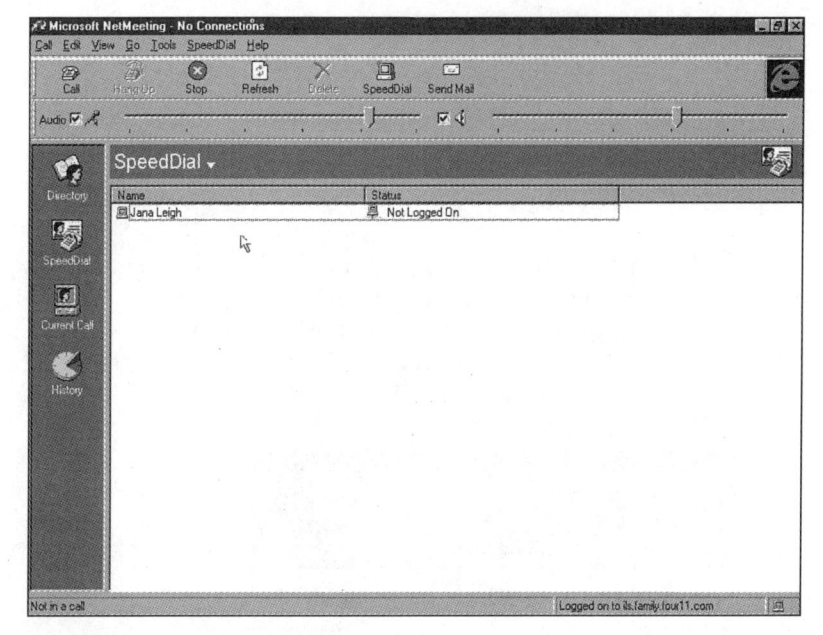

Figure 18.32 Using the SpeedDial feature of NetMeeting.

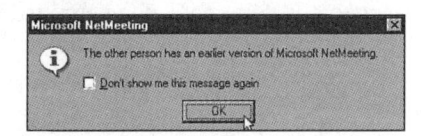

Figure 18.33 Reviewing a NetMeeting error message box.

61. This error message appears any time you encounter someone who does not have the same version of NetMeeting that you are using. Hopefully you are using version 2.1 or newer, as this is the version that shipped with Windows 98. If another NetMeeting user is on an older version, you might find that that person is unable to perform some or most of the conferencing tasks such as whiteboarding, chatting, or video transmissions. No problem, just send this person an email message and tell them to download the latest and greatest version of NetMeeting from the Microsoft Windows Update Web site. And if they are not running Windows 98 yet, tell them to get with the times and update.

62. If you try to connect to someone and receive the error message box that you see in Figure 18.34, don't panic.

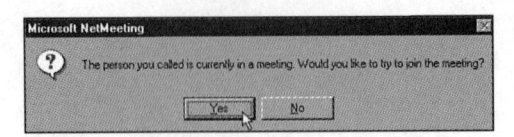

Figure 18.34 Reviewing a NetMeeting error message box.

63. This means that the person you are trying to contact is already actively participating in a NetMeeting conference call. If that person (or in some calls anyone can do this) invites you in, you will be permitted to join. Otherwise, you will be prompted with another error message box like the one shown in Figure 18.35.

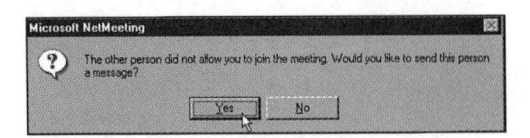

Figure 18.35 Reviewing a NetMeeting error message box.

64. This error message box means that you are not being permitted to join the conference that is already in progress. You are given the option to send this person an email message using your default email system if you would like.

65. One final note. The NetMeeting product can be misleading in that it appears very easy to use initially, but there are many options and features that can quickly make it a very complex software application. So, some of the best advice there is, is that you might need to play with it to figure things out (or, of course, you can cheat and buy a whole book that is dedicated to nothing but the Microsoft NetMeeting application). If you do want to obtain a book that is dedicated solely to Microsoft NetMeeting, I suggest the *Official Microsoft NetMeeting Book* by Microsoft Press. It came out in mid-1998, and is very good. There might still be some excerpts of this book on the Microsoft NetMeeting (http://www.microsoft.com/netmeeting/) or the Microsoft Press (http://www.microsoft.com/mspress/) Web sites.

CHAPTER 19
GIVING WINDOWS SPECIAL POWERS

19

GIVING WINDOWS SPECIAL POWERS

How do I...

- **19.1** Use the Make Compatible utility?
- **19.2** Use the WinAlign utility?
- **19.3** Change or fix file associations?
- **19.4** Install and use the Microsoft Plus! 98 software add-on for Windows 98?
- **19.5** Obtain additional security tools for Windows 98?

This is one of those interesting chapters, which means that it covers some of the more esoteric tools and utilities that are built into the Windows 98 operating system (OS) and its associated Resource Kit but never really documented by anyone. Microsoft gives a few pages worth of stuff to a few of these tools, but only because they were the ones that came with the Windows 98 Resource Kit. Additional coverage is given to the Windows 98 Plus! 98 add-on application mostly because it has a few enhancements to the utilities that are already built into the base Windows 98 OS.

CHAPTER 19
GIVING WINDOWS SPECIAL POWERS

19.1 Use the Make Compatible Utility
This How-To focuses on the definition and possible uses for the MKCOMPAT.EXE file that is found in the \Windows\System folder.

19.2 Use the WinAlign Utility
This How-To focuses on the definition and possible uses for the WINALIGN.EXE file that is found in the \Win98RK\Powertoy folder (or wherever you might have installed the Windows 98 Resource Kit).

19.3 Change or Fix File Associations
Many times you will install new software and it changes the association with a file extension that another application requires to work properly. This How-To helps you to change existing file associations and repair broken file associations.

19.4 Install and Use the Microsoft Plus! 98 Software Add-on for Windows 98
Great. You have purchased the Microsoft Plus! 98 software add-on for Windows 98, but now have no idea how to install it. This How-To helps explain the installation process, and explains why this was a good purchase.

19.5 Obtain Additional Security Tools for Windows 98
This How-To focuses on the various other security tools that exist for Windows 98, and why you might want to acquire and use them.

COMPLEXITY
ADVANCED

19.1 How do I...
Use the Make Compatible utility?

Problem
I have an older Windows 3.1 application that I really like, but it will not print properly under Windows 98. I heard that there was some tool that Microsoft insiders used to make older software work correctly with Windows 98. Does this tool really exist and, if so, how can I get a copy of it to use? Oh, and by the way, how would I use it?

Technique
The tool you're looking for is the Make Compatible tool, which already exists on your computer's hard drive in the \Windows\System folder on your hard

drive; it is the file labeled MKCOMPAT.EXE (not case-sensitive). Using this tool can help you make that old screen capture utility work fine under Windows 98, or let you use that older 16-bit version of QuickBooks with Windows 98 (because now it will print correctly). Keep in mind though, that you should not be using this tool to try to get old, non-compliant application development debugging tools as well as disk utilities to work with Windows 98. The side effects of doing such a thing can be devastating not only to your application, but perhaps even your entire Windows 98 computer system.

Steps

1. Maneuver your way to the \Windows\System folder on your hard drive and look for the MKCOMPAT.EXE, as shown in Figure 19.1.

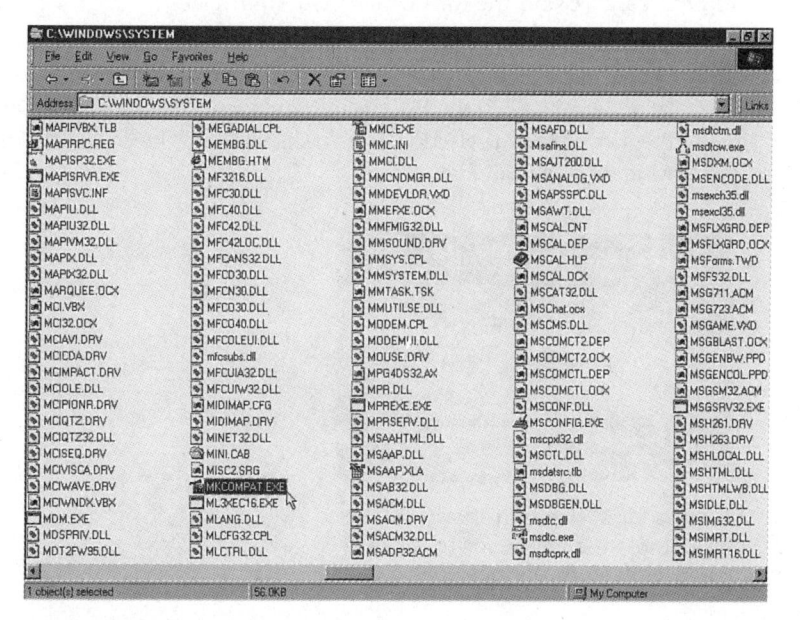

Figure 19.1 Finding the MKCOMPAT.EXE file.

2. After you find the Make Compatible utility double-click it to execute it. This takes you into the main screen for this tool, the Make Compatible utility, as shown in Figure 19.2.

3. The first thing you need to do is select an executable file to use this with. This means that you need to discover which file runs your application. In the example, you are using a program known as Collage Capture (version 1.0), which was made by Inner Media, Inc. in 1993. Although it is an excellent screen capture program, its compatibility out-of-the-box with Windows 98 is questionable at best.

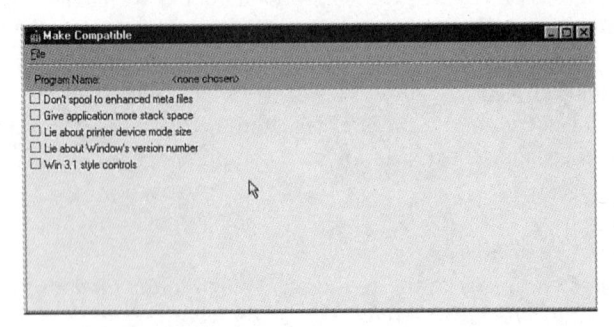

Figure 19.2 Using the MKCOMPAT.EXE file.

4. To find the executable program you want to make compatible with Windows 98, click the File menu option, and then click the Choose Program... menu selection. This takes you into the &Choose Program window shown in Figure 19.3.

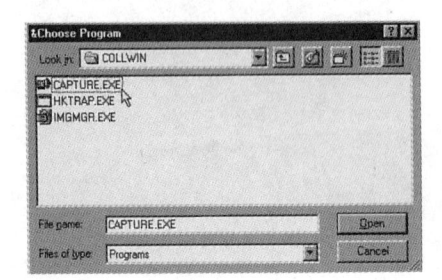

Figure 19.3 Finding the executable file you want to make compatible with Windows 98.

5. Maneuver your way through your Windows 98 PC's folders until you find the program you need. This part might be a guessing game, especially if you have never developed software (and thus have no feel for figuring out which program does what for a specific application). When you have located the file you want to use, click that file to select it, and then click the Open... button to pull that file into the Make Compatible program, as shown in Figure 19.4.

19.1
USE THE MAKE COMPATIBLE UTILITY

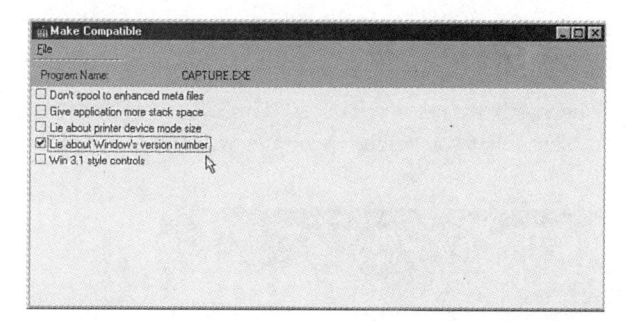

Figure 19.4 Selecting from the basic Make Compatible options.

6. The three most popular choices on this screen are the bottom three:

- Lie About Printer Device Mode Size—This is great for those applications that blow up whenever you try to print from within them.

- Lie About Window's Version Number—This is an overall nicety, which fools older programs into thinking that they are still running in a Windows 3.x environment.

- Win 3.1 Style Controls—Not every program out there can handle the Minimize, Restore, and Close options found in the upper-right corner of every Windows 95/Windows 98 screen.

7. To select any of these options, click the box next to the option you want, which places a check mark in that box.

8. After you have everything you want, click the File menu option, followed by a click on the Save menu selection.

9. However, sometimes these options are not enough. To locate all the additional settings that the Make Compatible application has available, click the File menu option, followed by a click on the Advanced Options menu selection. This causes the advanced features to be displayed, as shown in Figure 19.5.

10. Several of these are great for older applications, especially the old DOS programs that you might have developed yourself years ago in FoxPro 2.0, Turbo Pascal, or Visual Basic for DOS. My favorites include:

- Enable 3.x UI Features—Pretty obvious what this one does.

- Disable EMF Spooling—This is a printer feature.

- Increase Stack Size—This should get you around those invalid stack size error messages that you see a lot with DOS programs.

- Windows 3.1 palette behavior—This aids in colors resolution problems that you might encounter with some graphics packages.

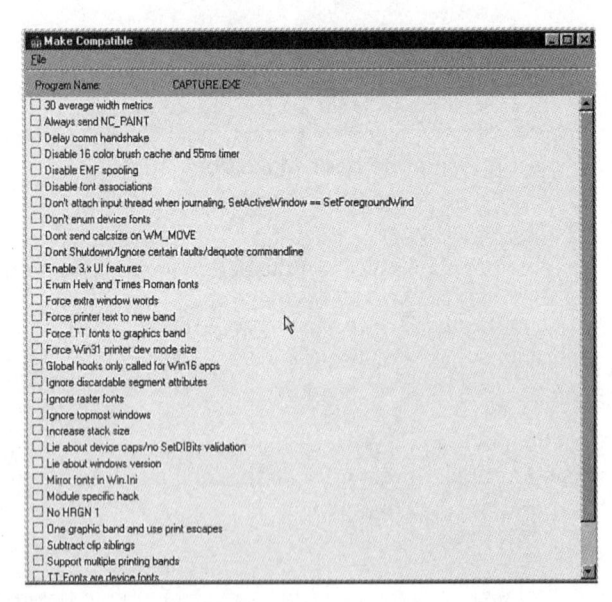

Figure 19.5 Selecting from the advanced Make Compatible options.

11. After you have everything you want, click the File menu option, followed by a click on the Save menu selection to save your work. Otherwise, you can always click the Close button in the upper-right corner of the screen (it looks like an X), which immediately attempts to close this utility. If you have not yet saved your work, you will be prompted to do so by the Make Compatible message box shown in Figure 19.6.

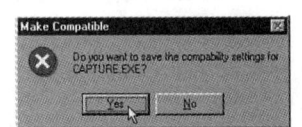

Figure 19.6 Deciding whether to save your Make Compatible selections.

12. If you want to save your work click *Yes*, otherwise choose No.

19.2 · How do I...
Use the WinAlign utility?

COMPLEXITY
ADVANCED

Problem

It seems like my programs do not process as fast as they could on my PC. Is there a tool from Microsoft that you can use to optimize the performance of Windows programs for use with Windows 98? Does this tool exist and, if so, how can I get a copy of it to use?

Technique

The tool that you need is known as *WinAlign*, which comes as a part of the Windows 98 Resource Kit (to obtain and install this kit, refer to this section back in Chapter 1, "Installation Tips". There is also a different version of WinAlign that comes with the Windows 98 operating system, known as WALIGN.EXE (this one uses an .INI file to keep track of the files it will be aligning).

Using the WinAlign tool can help you optimize your program's executables, because it automatically formats sections of the binary files along 4Kb boundaries, which happens to be the same size as the Intel x86 chip's memory pages. The way WinAlign works is by utilizing the *MapCache* feature of Windows 98 to arrange executable sections of that application directly to its memory pages. MapCache is a Windows 98 feature that permits programs to consume less memory. Keep in mind that you should not be using this tool to try to get old, non-compliant application development debugging tools and disk utilities to work with Windows 98. The side effects of doing such a thing can be devastating not only to your application, but perhaps even your entire Windows 98 computer system.

> **NOTE**
> *Caution: If you use WinAlign on an application that has already been aligned or is incompatible with WinAlign, you might make that application completely inoperable.* Moreover, not all mistakes can be reversed using the WinAlign -r command-line statement, which means that you might wind up reinstalling one or more of your applications, and perhaps the entire Windows 98 operating system as well. Be very careful about what applications you use this tool with.

Steps

1. Maneuver your way over to the folder on your hard drive where you installed the Windows 98 Resource Kit and look for the WINALIGN.EXE, as shown in Figure 19.7.

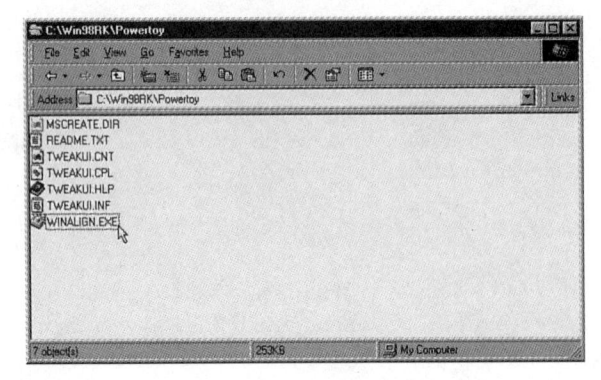

Figure 19.7 Finding the WINALIGN.EXE file.

2. After you find the Windows Alignment utility (WINALIGN.EXE) make a note as to where it is. Do not double-click it in an attempt to execute it. If you do, you will see the error message box shown in Figure 19.8.

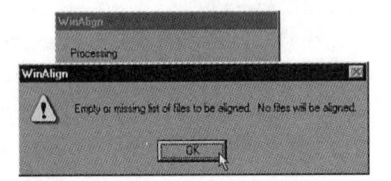

Figure 19.8 WinAlign error message box.

3. Open an MS-DOS window and change directories so that you are inside the folder where the WINALIGN.EXE file exists, as shown in Figure 19.9.

4. You can run the WinAlign tool by typing in the command:
WinAlign \FileApplicationPath\FileName.exe (using this type of format), as shown in Figure 19.10.

5. For further assistance on using this utility, check out the Help file found inside the Performance Tools folder of the Microsoft Management Console, as shown in Figure 19.11.

19.2
USE THE WINALIGN UTILITY

Figure 19.9 Viewing the WinAlign application in the Resource Kit folder.

Figure 19.10 Using the WinAlign application from the Resource Kit folder.

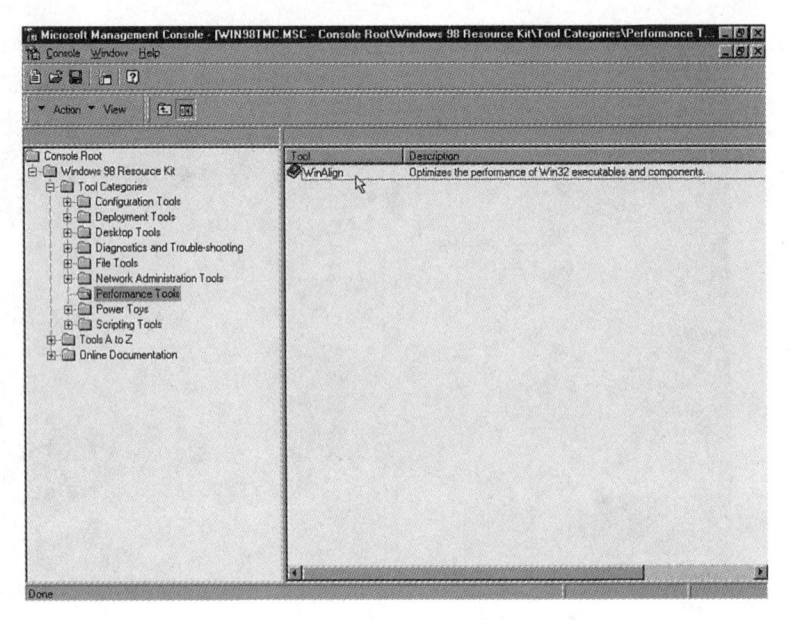

Figure 19.11 Obtaining more WinAlign help from inside the Resource Kit.

6. If you double-click the WinAlign Help option, you are taken directly into the Windows 98 Resource Kit Tools Help application, as shown in Figure 19.12.

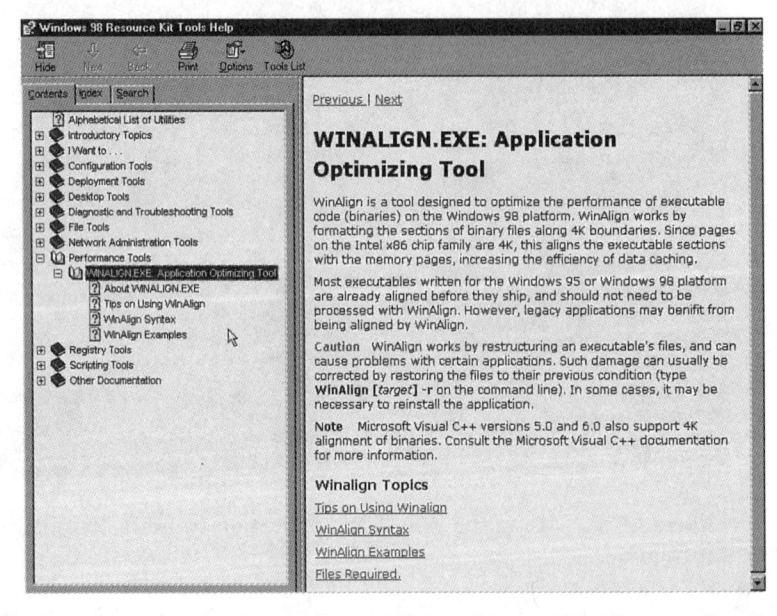

Figure 19.12 Getting additional help with the WinAlign application.

COMPLEXITY
INTERMEDIATE

19.3 How do I...
Change or fix file associations?

Problem

I just installed a different Web browser, and now whenever I open a Web page it automatically uses that browser instead of the Microsoft Internet Explorer browser that came with Windows 98. How do I alter the HTML file association so that it once again is associated with the Internet Explorer browser and not the Mosaic browser?

Technique

There are probably dozens, if not more, file types configured on your Windows 98 PC. These file type configurations are better known as File Associations, which means that if you attempt to open a file directly it will "call" the file type association to see which application is used to open this file. For example, if you double-click on a *.PPT file, then the Microsoft PowerPoint application will start up and then open the file that you just double-clicked on. Changing a file association is a lot easier than you might think, and to do so just walk through these steps.

Steps

1. Double-click the My Computer icon found on your Windows 98 desktop, which takes you into window shown in Figure 19.13.

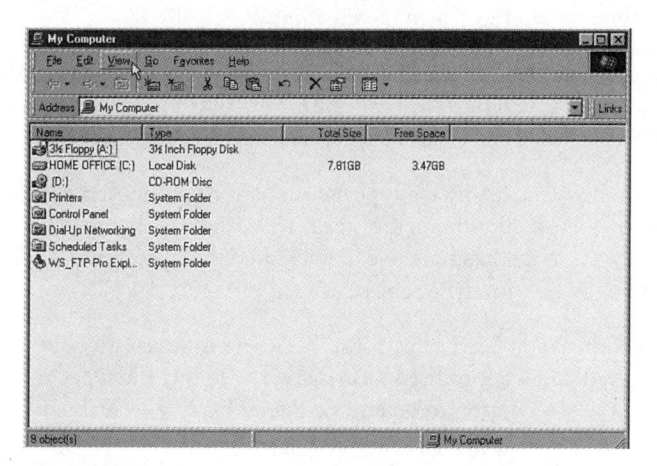

Figure 19.13 Accessing the My Computer window.

2. Click once on the View menu option, and then click once on the Folder Options... menu selection to access the Folder Options screen. From there, click the File Types tab to reveal the screen shown in Figure 19.14.

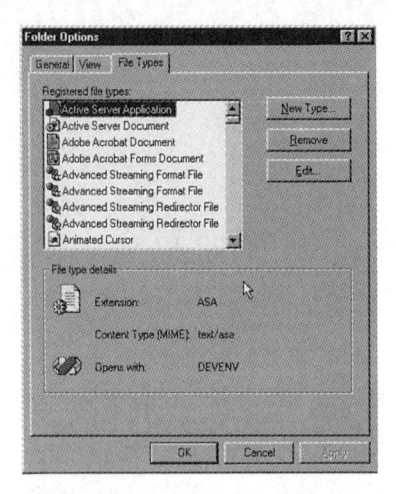

Figure 19.14 Accessing the File Types tab of the Folder Options screen.

3. From this screen you can add new file associations (types) and delete existing ones. The option you are most interested in is the modification of existing file types.

4. The first thing you need to do is locate the Registered File Type that you want to modify (the URL: Hypertext Transfer Protocol, in this case) by scrolling down the screen, as shown in Figure 19.15.

5. Next, select this file type by clicking it. Then, to access that file type's associations, you need to click the Edit... button, which takes you to the Edit File Type screen, as shown in Figure 19.16.

6. To modify an existing file type association, click the Action type shown in the box on the bottom half of the screen, such as the open action displayed in the example. Next, click the Edit... button to reveal the Editing Action for Type screen, as seen in Figure 19.17.

7. The application used to perform the action is a nice way of asking which program you want to use in association with this file type. You can use the Browse... button to determine the path and executable file that you want to use with this particular file type. In the example, shown back in

19.3 CHANGE OR FIX FILE ASSOCIATIONS

Figure 19.17, notice that there are double quotes around the entire path and filename statement, while the additional, undocumented parameter for this program's executable file (Microsoft's Internet Explorer Web browser) is actually used outside of the double quotes.

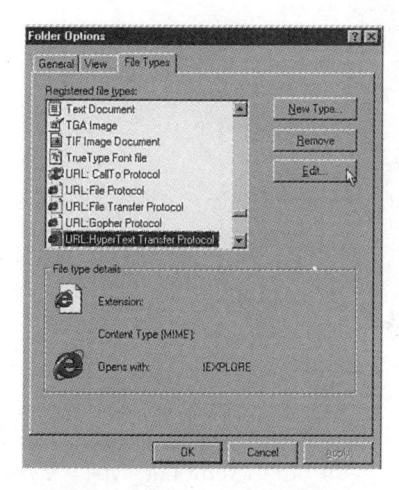

Figure 19.15 Accessing the default file types.

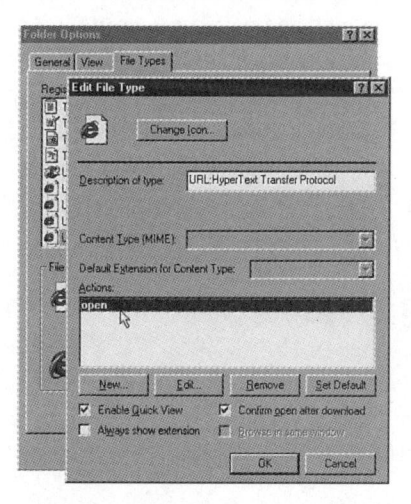

Figure 19.16 Accessing the Edit File Types screen.

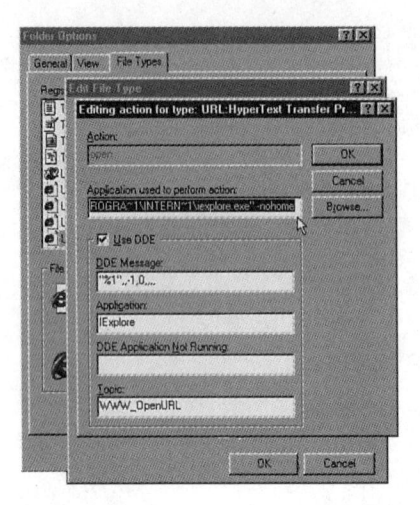

Figure 19.17 Changing a file association.

8. After you have made your changes and selections, click OK to save your changes to this file type and return to the Edit File Type window.

9. If you want a new action to be associated with a particular file type, you can do so from here as well. For instance, while many of the common actions are Open, Close, New, and so on, you can create just about anything you want, as is demonstrated by the New Action, shown in Figure 19.18.

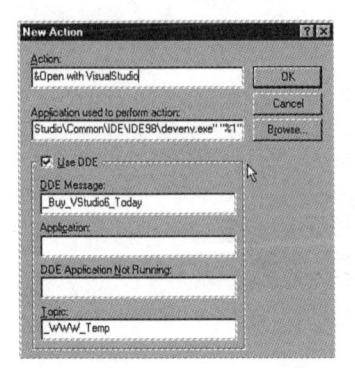

Figure 19.18 Adding a New File Association.

10. Give your new action a name in the Action box (most actions are one word in length, such as Open, Close, Run, Edit), and then enter the exact path and filename for the executable to be run. Next, decide whether you will be using DDE (Dynamic Data Exchange) with this new action. If so, click the Use DDE check box to select it. This un-grays the rest of the DDE section, where you can make your entries as required (and specified) for your application.

11. When you have finished making your entries, click OK to save your changes and return to the Edit File Type window.

12. From there, click OK to exit the Folder Options screen, and return to the My Computer window or wherever you originally started this whole process. Close that window and you are finished.

COMPLEXITY
BEGINNER

19.4 How do I...
Install and use the Microsoft Plus! 98 software add-on for Windows 98?

Problem

I purchased the Microsoft Plus! 98 software package that I am supposed to be able to use with Windows 98. How do install this package, and is there anything I should be on the lookout for?

Technique

Just like Windows 95, there is a Plus! package for the Windows 98 OS named Microsoft Plus! 98. This is where the similarity between the Windows 95 and Windows 98 versions end. The Microsoft Plus! 98 package, when fully installed, requires nearly 190MB of hard disk drive space (it can only be purchased in a CD-ROM format). The old Windows 95 Plus! Package, however, came on six floppy disks and took less than 30MB of disk space.

Microsoft Plus! 98 comes with a whole lot of neat little utilities, more games, screen savers, and even an antivirus package. The components are as follows:

- *Compressed folders*—This works just like WinZip.

- *Deluxe CD player*—A much better version than standard Windows 98 CD-ROM player, in that it has a lot of niceties such as a Play List that can automatically be downloaded from the Internet.

- *Desktop themes*—How does another 95MB worth of pictures, themes, noises, and graphics sound?

- *Disk cleanup add-ons*—This extends the feature set of the Disk Cleanup utility that comes with the base Windows 98 operating system, including new disk space recovery and uninstall options.

- *Golf 1998 Lite*—This scaled-down version of Microsoft Golf is not too bad, although it consumes a lot of hard disk space.

- *Lose Your Marbles*—Another addictive game that quickly becomes one of your favorite Windows games.

- *Maintenance Wizard*—This feature offers additional scheduling capabilities that are not found in the base Windows 98 operating system's Maintenance Wizard utility.

- *Organic art screen saver*—This is just what you would think it is.

- *Picture It! Express*—This is a scaled-down version of this very good photographic modification tool.

- *Spider Solitaire*—Another very addictive Windows Solitaire game; and perhaps one of the best reasons for getting the Plus! 98 package (if you are a gamer, that is).

- *Virus Scan*—The McAfee antivirus software package.

Steps

1. Loading the Plus! 98 software is very easy. Place the Plus! 98 CD-ROM in your disc drive and run the SETUP.EXE file. Follow the prompts. All you need to do is click the check boxes next to the components you want to install, and then click on the Next> button, which starts the installation process.

2. After completing the software installation process, restart your PC when prompted to do so.

3. Something you might want to keep alert for is the Install All option. If you already have an antivirus program installed, you might want to make sure that you don't overwrite anything by selecting the McAfee Antivirus utility that comes with the Plus! 98 software.

COMPLEXITY
INTERMEDIATE

19.5 How do I...
Obtain additional security tools for Windows 98?

Problem
I want to be able to secure my Windows 98 PC better than just using the capabilities that are built into the Windows 98 operating system. How do I do something like this? Are there any specific resources that I can use to bolster my level of security on my Windows 98 PC?

Technique
There are literally thousands of different methods, techniques, and products that you can use to better safeguard your Windows 98 PC. These include direct folder and file encryption devices and software packages; retina, fingerprint, and voice authentication devices; and software-based password protection for your entire PC, at both at the file and folder level. For more information on these and other security technologies, you might want to consult one or more of the following Internet Web sites:

- `http://lockdown2000.com/`—This firm specializes in protecting Windows 95, Windows 98, and Windows NT software applications.

- `http://www.l0pht.com/l0phtcrack/download.html`—This site is focused on helping you to find the cracks in your own Windows 98 and Windows NT computers.

- `http://www.intrusion.com/`—This firm focuses on protecting Windows NT and Novell NetWare networks.

- `http://www.cs.hut.fi/crypto/software.html`—This Web page contains a catalog of software packages related to cryptography.

- `http://www.nai.com/default_pgp.asp`—This is where you can find a copy of PGP (Pretty-Good-Privacy), which is an excellent email encryption tool that works great with the Microsoft Outlook software package.

PART V
HELP!

CHAPTER 20
WHERE DID I GO WRONG AND HOW DO I FIX IT?

20

WHERE DID I GO WRONG AND HOW DO I FIX IT?

How do I...

- **20.1** **Use the Windows 98 online help?**
- **20.2** **Approach a troubleshooting strategy when addressing problems with Windows 98?**
- **20.3** **Know who to call for assistance?**
- **20.4** **Know where to obtain other means of problem resolution?**
- **20.5** **Obtain Microsoft TechNet and why would I want to use it?**

The sole purpose of this chapter is to assist you in locating additional help with Windows 98 and its many built-in utilities and tools. Many people, when they run into trouble with their PC, will almost always want to run and pick up a telephone with the expectation that the person on the other end can and will fix their problem(s). However, Windows 98 comes much closer to reaching that utopian level of a self-healing software application. That is, its levels of sophistication when it comes to built-in help wizards, troubleshooting guides, and other assistance tools, Windows 98 allows its users to help themselves instead of having to rely on others. In fact, in many cases, Windows 98 detects and sometimes solves its own problems before they become known issues to most users.

This chapter starts with learning how to access the various Online Help sections and wizards, and then progresses into more troubleshooting techniques and processes. From there it shows you how to contact more experienced troubleshooting and help resources and finally culminates in an introduction to one of the many paid subscription programs—which are designed to help you find the answers you need—that Microsoft offers to users of its operating systems and applications. Although users of Windows 98 in your organization have someone to call—you—you might not have anyone to turn to. This chapter provides you with the knowledge to either solve those problems outright or at least give you someone to turn to for assistance.

20.1 Use the Windows 98 Online Help

This section gets you started with using the various Microsoft Windows 98 help topics and sources that are built directly into the Windows 98 operating system.

20.2 Approach a Troubleshooting Strategy When Addressing Problems with Windows 98

Before you address a problem with Windows 98, you should have a consistent strategy in place to do it. Otherwise, you wind up spinning your wheels and reinventing the wheel every time you approach a problem with the Windows 98 operating system. This How-To walks you through a base set of steps that you can use to avoid the more common pitfalls when approaching this topic and gives you a jump start to creating your own organization's help desk strategy.

20.3 Know Who to Call for Assistance

Well, even if you do all the right things, walking through the problems in a logical, precise order, and looking for assistance from the various Microsoft technical resources, you might still not be able to solve your problem(s). In this case, you need to call someone for help. This How-To gives you the important telephone numbers and base information that you need to get a Microsoft technical support engineer on the line to help you through one of your darker moments in working with the Windows 98 operating system.

20.4 Know Where to Obtain Other Means of Problem Resolution

What's that? You need more help, but you do not want to pay for it? If this were the Novell or Sun world you would be in for a shock. No pay; no help. Well, with Microsoft, there is still a solution. Microsoft's extensive Internet Web site, with its amazing Online Support section, might just get you the answers that you need. There is an extensive search engine that is detailed in this How-To so that you can find the assistance you want when you want it.

20.5 Obtain Microsoft TechNet and Why Would I Want to Use It

The purpose of Microsoft TechNet is to keep you off the Internet and on your own PC. This incredible wealth of knowledge bases, software drivers and patches, resource kits, training and technical information, as well as a 60,000+ pages of technical information network is well worth its annual cost. This How-To takes you into the world of Microsoft TechNet, explaining what you get, how to get it, and what it will cost you to obtain it.

COMPLEXITY
BEGINNER

20.1 How do I...
Use the Windows 98 online help?

Problem

I keep getting stuck with various Windows 98 issues, such as technical difficulties with my printers, wacky problems with the various built-in tools, knowing which ones to use when, and so on. Is there some way to locate and then search through some Windows 98 online knowledge base that can help me find the answers I need?

Technique

Windows 98 has a variety of Online Help tools including a mini-knowledge base, which is indexed and searchable, as well as an online Getting Started book that you might want to always point your new Windows 98 users to (that is, make sure they know it exists and show them how to get there). Additionally, it is through this Online Help that you can access a Support Online Web site on Microsoft's Internet Web site that has the latest up-to-the-minute facts and tidbits about the Windows 98 operating system. Follow these steps to find solutions for those hard-to-solve problems sooner than you might originally have thought possible.

Steps

1. To start your foray into the world of online Windows 98 help, click on the Start button then click on the Help menu selection. This takes you to the screen shown in Figure 20.1.

CHAPTER 20
WHERE DID I GO WRONG AND HOW DO I FIX IT?

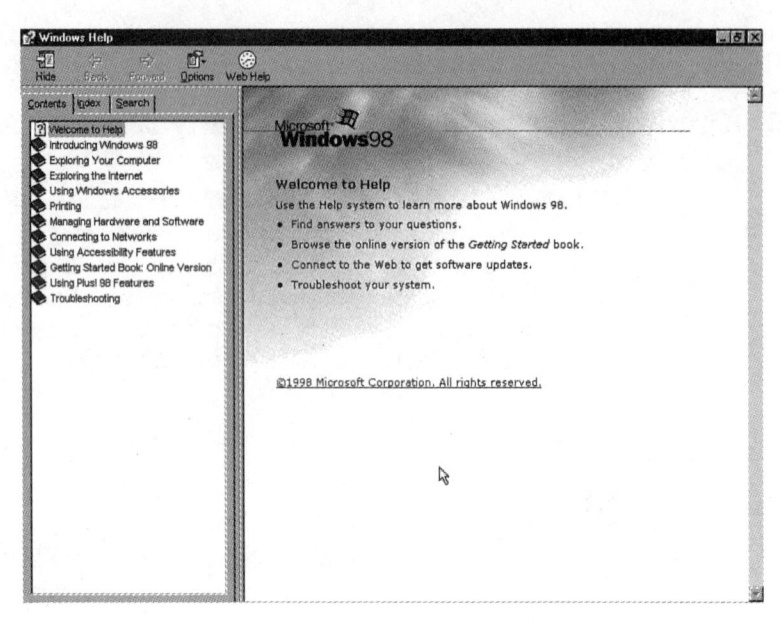

Figure 20.1 Welcome to Windows 98 online help.

2. Because this is a help screen, its complexity is nonexistent. That is, if you need to access help to use a help screen then that help would probably be rather worthless to you. Some simple buttons exist along the top row. The first, labeled Hide, hides the left column of this screen (the one with the three tabs, Contents, Index, and Search). If you click it once then that column disappears, and a Show button appears on top of the screen (in place of the Hide button). Click that button once and you will again see this left column and all its contents.

3. Within the left column are a series of tabs:

- *Contents*—The Contents tab shows what is essentially a table of contents for the Windows 98 Online Help System. Each "book" opens when you click on it, thus revealing its contents. The titles of these books get right to the point. Obviously, the one labeled Printing discusses nothing but how to connect and use printers with the Windows 98 operating system. These 11 books cover the basic topics, which most every Windows 98 user needs to use at some point. The Getting Started Book: Online Version, is an electronic version of the help manual that you usually receive when you purchase the Windows 98 operating system.

20.1
USE THE WINDOWS 98 ONLINE HELP

- *Index*—The Index tab is where you can type in either a partial word or string of words and the Windows 98 Help automatically sorts through its cross-reference listing of topics in an attempt to find a topic or series of topics on the subject that you are seeking.

- *Search*—The Search tab allows you to enter a partial word or string of words, and then click on the List Topics button, which reveals an indexed listing of topics that hopefully cover the topic(s) on the subject that you are seeking.

4. These three tabs are all you need to find quick bits of information on various Windows 98 topics, as well as from where to start most of the troubleshooting wizards that are built into the online Help System. For example, on the Index tab, shown in Figure 20.2, you start typing a topic and the Help System starts to jump toward the topic you are entering (it is in alphabetical order).

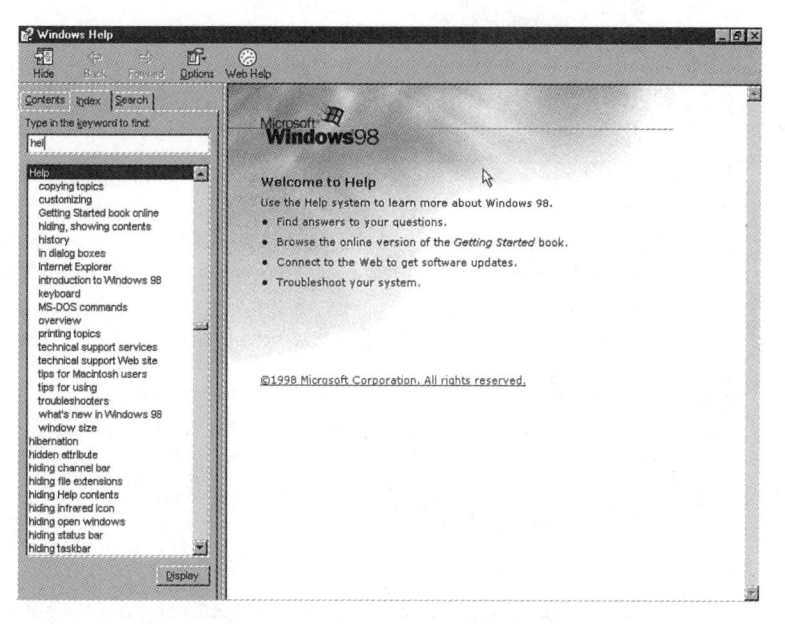

Figure 20.2 Using the Index tab of Windows 98 Online Help.

5. If you click once on the Search tab, you are taken to that portion of the Windows 98 Help System. There you can find the built-in help wizards. For example, if you enter the search word *registry* in the keyword box, and then click the List Topics button, you see the screen shown in Figure 20.3.

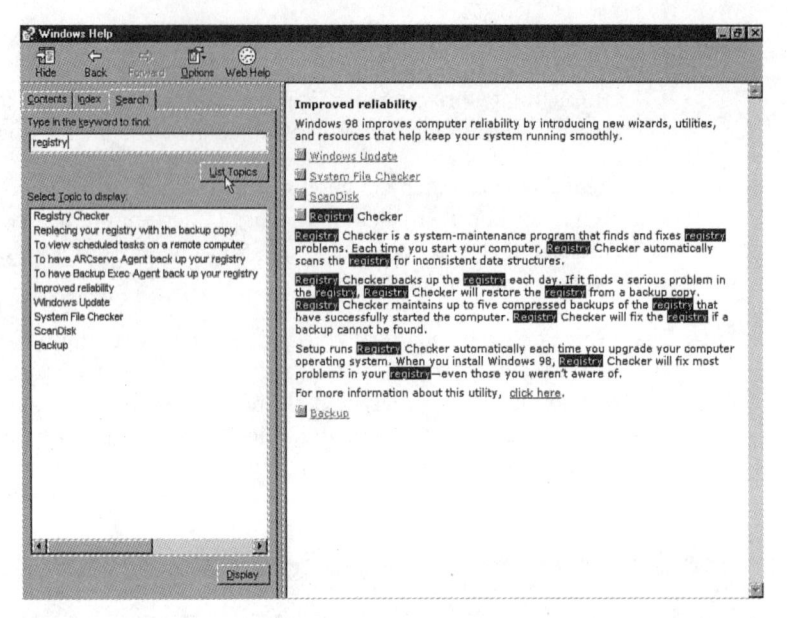

Figure 20.3 Using the Search tab to Find the Registry Help Wizards.

6. Something interesting occurs on this screen. As you can see, the word registry is highlighted everywhere it appears on this screen. This is due to the Options setting of Search Highlight On being activated. To turn it off, click the Search Highlight Off menu selection from this same Options button. Although it is a bit much on this screen, on other more esoteric topics this might actually be a rather nice feature.

7. Another new feature on this screen is the items that have small boxes located to the left of these underlined items. These underlined items are jumps to other areas of the Windows 98 Online Help. In many instances, these jumps take you into the start of one of the many Windows 98 Online Help wizards.

8. One final item you need to know about is the Web Help button found at the top of the screen. If you click this button, you are brought to an informational screen that further explains the Internet Help options, as well as giving you the jumping point for accessing the Microsoft Support Online Web site, as shown in Figure 20.4.

9. If you click once on the Support Online hyperlink, shown at the bottom of this screen's text, you are transported to the Support Online Web site found on Microsoft's Internet Web site.

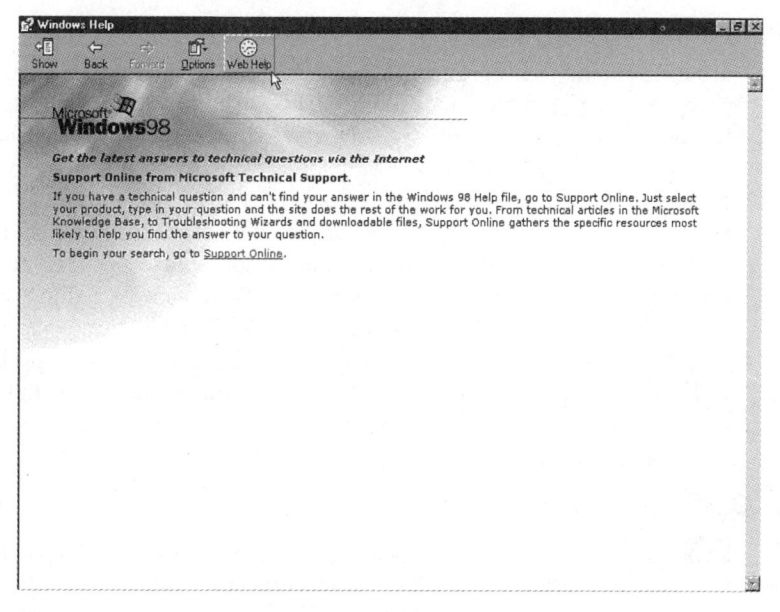

Figure 20.4 Locating access to the Microsoft Support Online Web site.

10. Keep in mind, though, that you must have first connected to the Internet (if you are using Dial-Up Networking) or have a LAN-based connection established to the Internet for this feature to work.

COMPLEXITY
INTERMEDIATE

20.2 How do I...
Approach a troubleshooting strategy when addressing problems with Windows 98?

Problem

My organization seems to flounder a lot when it comes to solving Windows 98 issues with users. The help desk seems confused most of the time, with only some of the support personnel being very effective at problem solving while the rest of them seem like beginners, although they have been working here a long time. Is there a strategy for starting the Windows 98 troubleshooting process? And if so, how can I apply this to my organization?

Technique

Troubleshooting techniques and strategies have been around for eternity, with a new one being invented almost daily. The best thing to remember when troubleshooting any system, especially a Windows 98 PC, is to always take an even and logical approach to the problem. Be sure to document everything you do so that the next time another user is experiencing similar difficulties you (or someone else on your technical support staff) can quickly figure the problem out and resolve it more efficiently than the first time. The steps involved in creating your strategy are simple: Document everything you do and make sure that your team shares information both electronically and physically; communicate with each other and the users; and always take a logical, level-headed approach to all problems—there is no sense in panicking, because it will not make the problem go away any faster.

Steps

1. Talk to the person who is experiencing the problem. Listen to their explanation of the problem and document it completely.

2. Make sure the problem is reproducible. If it is not then document the issue fully and place it in an unresolved category. However, do not waste time theorizing about what might have gone wrong and agonizing over it. If it cannot be reproduced then it cannot be fixed.

3. Write down, verbatim, the exact steps that are necessary in order to reproduce the problem. Make sure that you have a screen shot (picture) of the exact text of the error message (if there is one), which might have resulted from the problem.

4. Make sure that you know precisely when the problem started to occur, how long it has been occurring, and what the user does when the problem occurs.

5. Find out what the user did to try to fix the problem. For example, if the problem is with a piece of hardware, such as the PC speakers stopped working then did the user try to delete and then reinstall the sound system hardware from inside the Windows 98 Device Manager? Information such as this is critical.

6. Take a quick inventory of the open applications on the user's PC, including any TSRs (terminate-and-stay residents) that might be active.

7. Find out whether the user contacted some other Windows 98 "expert" that is local to that user, such as his or her office mate. If another expert

was used, interview that person(s) to find out exactly what they did to further "fix" the problem; ensuring the veracity of the expert's statements might be a very difficult and delicate task.

8. Inform the user of an estimated time that it will take to resolve the problem, going from a worst-case scenario. Be sure to include and base this estimate quite a bit on the Service Level Agreements (SLAs) that you have in place between the help desk and the user community.

9. After you have determined the actual cause of the problem, make sure that the help desk support person documents this problem on a systematic basis, including how a solution was determined.

10. Solve the problem for the user and document everything you can about the issue. What was the original complaint? What was found to be the problem? What was done to resolve the problem? How long did it take to fix it? How many support personnel were involved and who were they? Were any outside sources involved, such as Microsoft TechNet, the Support Online Web site, or a direct telephone call to Microsoft's paid support line ? All these questions must be answered each time a problem call is made to the help desk so that they can build their own repository of problems and solutions. This makes them a much more efficient group on a going-forward basis.

COMPLEXITY
BEGINNER

20.3 How do I...
Know who to call for assistance?

Problem

I just cannot figure out a problem with Windows 98. The system crashes repeatedly, and even the Safe Mode does not work well enough for me to troubleshoot what is going wrong. Is there someone at Microsoft I can talk to who might be able to assist me?

Technique

Microsoft provides many avenues for supporting its Windows 98 operating system. There is a lot of free online support and support wizards built into the Windows 98 OS. There are many third-party sources as well as an annual paid subscription from Microsoft that includes many of its own Windows 98 knowledge base resources. However, if or when that fails, you can always call a Microsoft technical support engineer.

Steps

1. To reach a Microsoft technical support engineer, you have three options:

- *Standard No-Charge support*—This means that you get technical support that you do not have to pay for, for 90 days after the first time you contact Microsoft Technical Support regarding a Windows 98 problem (not a bad deal). In the United States, this means that you must call (425) 635-7222, Monday-Friday, no holidays allowed, between the hours of 6 a.m. to 6 p.m., Pacific Standard time; in Canada, you can call (905) 568-4494 (5 a.m. to 5 p.m. Pacific Standard time, Monday-Friday). Actually, you do have to pay any long-distance charges you incur for dialing a Redmond, Washington area code (425), but if you live in Seattle then this is a pretty good deal. Also, keep in mind that only the base Windows 98 operating system and its Personal Web Server (PWS) component are covered by this deal. The other major Personal Web Server components, such as Microsoft Transaction Server, Microsoft Message Queue Server, and the Microsoft Data Access components are not included in this freebie.

> **WARNING**
> If your copy of Windows 98 was preinstalled or distributed with your computer system, that PC manufacturer is responsible for providing your product support. What this means is that if you bought your PC from Gateway 2000, you need to call Gateway 2000 for any free technical support of the Windows 98 operating system. Microsoft will not provide it to you. Wait, it gets worse. Even if you did purchase your copy of Windows 98 at a local retailer or directly from Microsoft, the free technical support might be limited if you are running Windows 98 on hardware which does not appear on the Windows 98 Hardware Compatibility List. (Refer to Microsoft's Web site, which contains this listing, to check out your hardware components.)

- *Pay-per-Incident support*—This is for those times when you want Microsoft technical support after normal business hours, which is after 6 p.m. (Pacific standard time) and before 6 a.m.

(Pacific standard time); if your 90 days of free time have expired; or if you need support for the Microsoft Transaction Server, Message Queue Server (MSMQ), or Data Access Components of Windows 98. The cost of this service is $35 USD ($45 Canadian) for Windows 98 and the Personal Web Server, Data Access Components questions are $95 each USD, whereas questions regarding all other components are $195 USD per incident. (If it takes Microsoft six telephone calls to answer the same question, you will only pay one fee.) On the plus side, you get a toll-free number to call (800) 936-5700 or (900) 555-2000 in the United States, 24 hours a day, seven days a week, including holidays. However, if you are in Canada, you must call (800) 668-7975, 5:00 a.m. to 5:00 p.m. Pacific time zone, Monday-Friday, and no holidays permitted.

- *Priority Annual support*—This, by far, can be the most expensive, but really is the best option for large organizations that expect a fair number of technical support calls. Like the Pay-per-Incident support you do get a toll-free number to call, so there are no long-distance telephone charges. What you do get for your $295 USD are 10 support incident calls, which work out to $29.50 each.

2. You can, of course, submit all your technical support questions via the Internet using the Web Response, provided that you (or your organization that is making the request) reside in either the United States or Canada. Keep in mind, though, that you still need to pay any charges that would have been applicable had you used a voice telephone instead of the Internet.

3. Microsoft uses a pay as you go payment plan. This means that you must have a Visa, MasterCard, or an American Express (including Optima) credit card handy, in order to purchase technical support for the 1-800 telephone calls. If you dial a 1-900 number, the technical support charges are automatically charged directly to your telephone bill.

4. If you reside outside of the United States or Canada, do not worry. There are many Microsoft technical support facilities outside of these countries, so you should just contact your local Microsoft subsidiary for more information and details.

CHAPTER 20
WHERE DID I GO WRONG AND HOW DO I FIX IT?

COMPLEXITY
INTERMEDIATE

20.4 How do I...
Know where to obtain other means of problem resolution?

Problem

I cannot find the solution to my Windows 98 problem and I do not want (or cannot afford) to pay Microsoft for additional support. Is there any other place I can look for solutions to my Windows 98 issues and is that location searchable? If so, how do I perform these types of support searches?

Technique

You can go down many avenues when searching for assistance with the Microsoft Windows 98 operating system. The ones that are built into the Windows 98 OS (Online Help, the Getting Started Book, and so on) the ones that you can pay extra for (Pay-per-Incident support and the Priority Annual support), and the free telephone support are all very good paths in and of themselves. However, there are more places to look, and they all can be found on the Internet at no additional cost to you, other than your Internet connection.

Steps

1. To begin, you need to establish a connection to the Internet, either via your organization's LAN/WAN or your own ISP using the Dial-Up Networking feature of Windows 98 (see Chapter 9, "Dial-Up Networking," for more details).

2. Start your Web browser, such as the Microsoft Internet Explorer Web browser that is integrated into the Windows 98 operating system.

3. Proceed to the Microsoft Windows 98 Web site on the Internet (located at http://www.microsoft.com/windows98/), as shown in Figure 20.5.

4. When the Web site appears you will notice a menu bar listing of site topics along the left side of the window, with a little point coming out on the topic that is highlighted and active. For instance, looking at the example shown, you will see the topic Windows 98 Home highlighted with the point coming out at that topic.

20.4
KNOW WHERE TO OBTAIN OTHER MEANS OF PROBLEM RESOLUTION

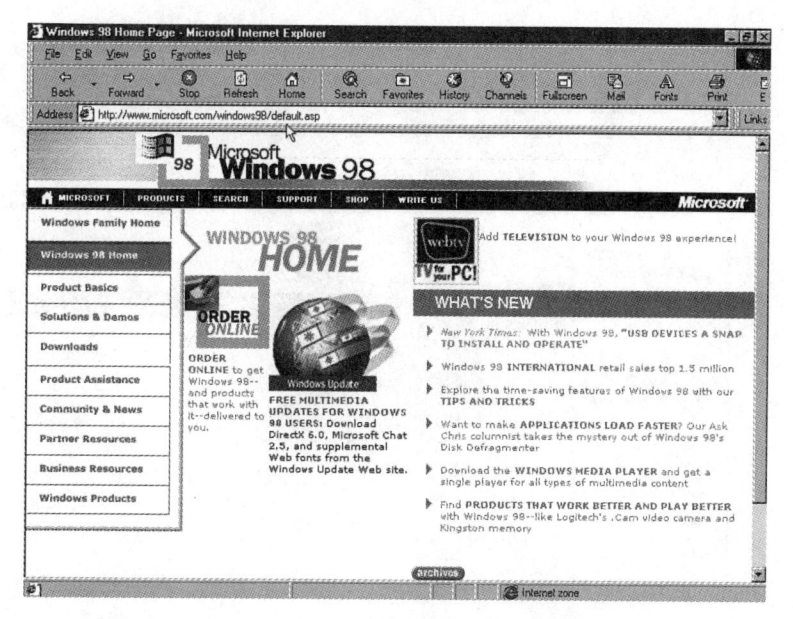

Figure 20.5 Accessing the Microsoft Windows 98 Web site.

5. Staying inside that menu bar you will want to click once on the Product Assistance topic, which opens up to display a subset of topics as shown in Figure 20.6.

6. In all the submenus that you will discover on this page, as well as others on the Microsoft Web site, the formatting works about the same. You click the larger menu topic, which then opens to reveal its contents inside. You then click the topic that you want, such as the one labeled Support, which takes you automatically to that Web page, as shown in Figure 20.7.

7. Although there is a lot of great information on this page, its purpose is aimed at Windows 98 beginners and not intermediate-to-advanced product users such as yourself. Therefore, you need to drill one level deeper into the support resources. To do this, click the Support Online topic that appears at the top of the More Resources listing.

8. After you click on that option, you are taken to the Web page shown in Figure 20.8.

CHAPTER 20
WHERE DID I GO WRONG AND HOW DO I FIX IT?

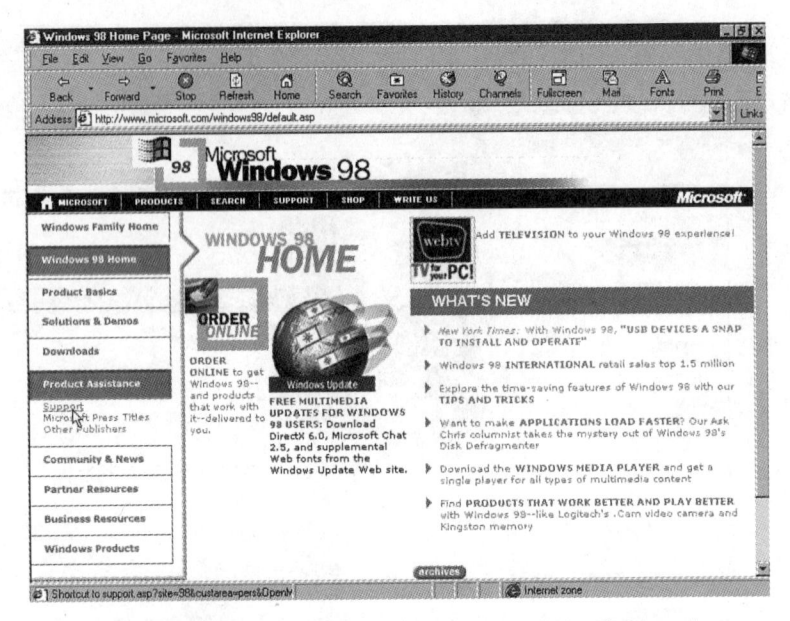

Figure 20.6 Opening the Product Assistance menu bar section.

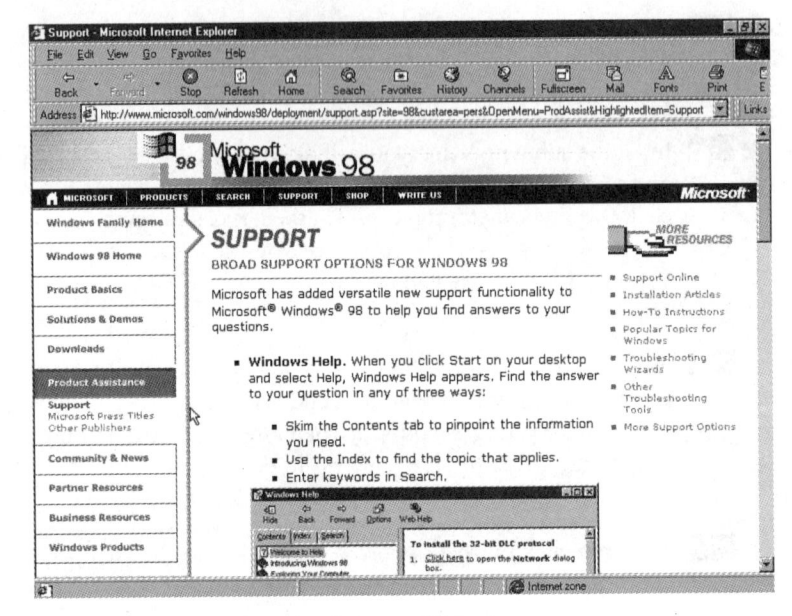

Figure 20.7 Opening the Support Web page.

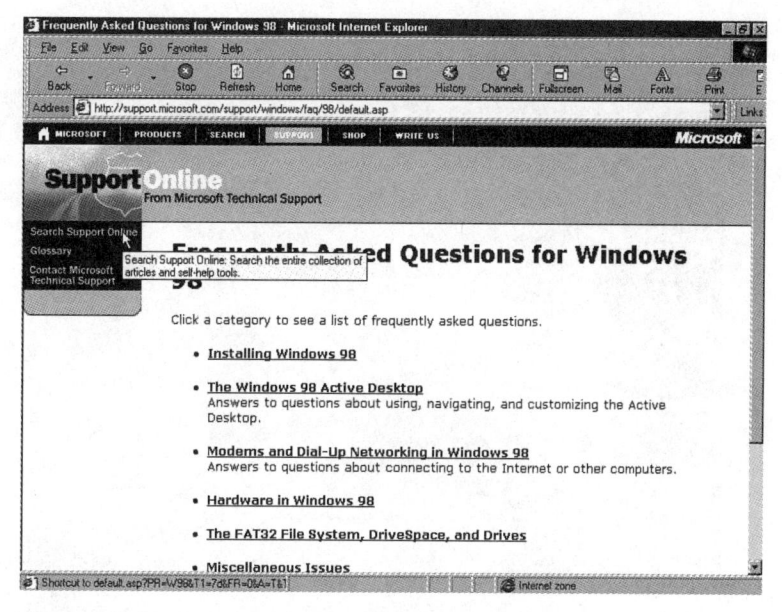

20.4
KNOW WHERE TO OBTAIN OTHER MEANS OF PROBLEM RESOLUTION

Figure 20.8 Opening the Microsoft Support Online Web site.

9. The key to this site is the capability for you to search the entire site quickly and easily. To do this, you need to click the Search Support Online menu option that is located just under the main site title of Support Online From Microsoft Technical Support (look at where the arrow pointer is positioned).

10. Click once on the Search Support Online menu option and you go to the Support Online Search window.

11. There is an underlined option near the top right side of this window that takes you to the Advanced view. Click once on this underlined option and you will see the screen reapply itself, as shown in Figure 20.9.

12. The art of searching this site for the information you require is as simple as 1-2-3. In step one, you need to tell the Microsoft Support Online what your primary topic is. To do this, click the drop-down list box to reveal the names of the many Microsoft applications, operating systems, and development tools. Make sure you choose Windows 98 as your selection here.

13. For step 2, set your search to the top radio button of Keyword, which is also the default search method.

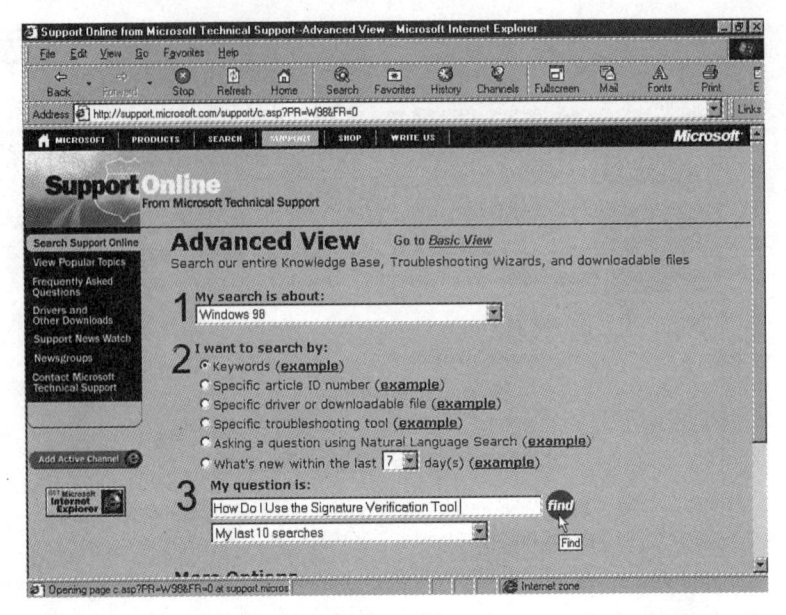

Figure 20.9 Using the Advanced view format of the Support Online site's searching page.

14. Type in your question in step 3, which should be in a normal English sentence. In the example given, the Microsoft Support Online Web site is being asked to show you how to use the Windows 98 Signature Verification tool (of course, you do not need to really search on this, because you have probably already read all about this topic in Chapter 13, "Email and News."

15. When you have made your three entries/selections, click once on the find button that is located to the right of the box in step 3.

16. Doing this takes you to the Search Results Web page, as shown in Figure 20.10.

17. All the results that the Support Online Web site's search engine was capable of finding are displayed on this page. Click the underlined title for the answer that you want to review, which takes you to the details for that item. For example, you will click the first one, because the short synopsis that you see for that one sounds like it bests fulfills our need for the information you see. Clicking the underlined portion of number 1, Description of the Signature Verification Tool, reveals the screen shown in Figure 20.11.

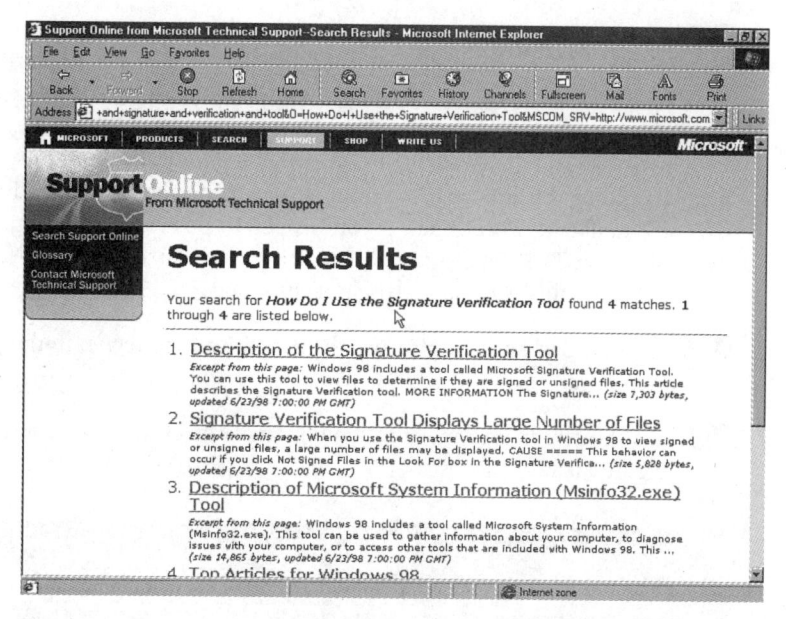

Figure 20.10 Reviewing the Search Results Web page.

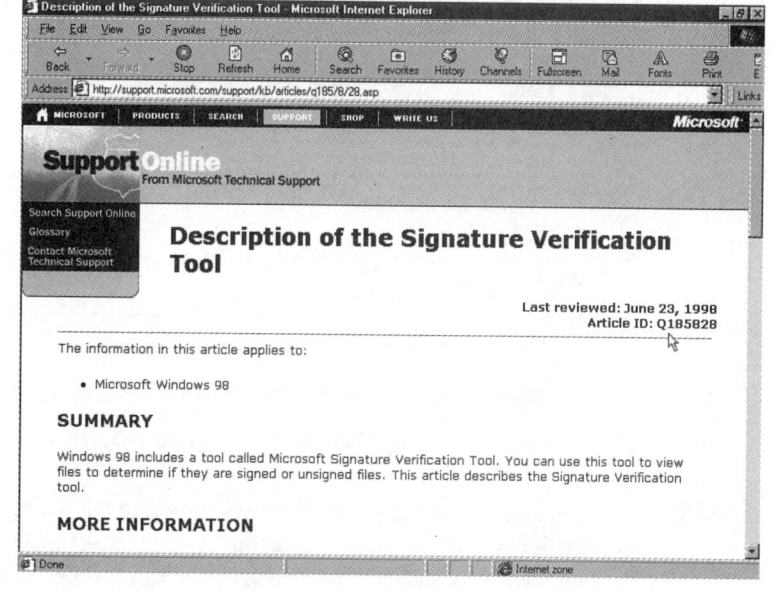

Figure 20.11 Reviewing the Detailed Search Results Web page.

18. A detailed Web page appears that shows a quick summary of the answer, which is then followed by all the many details, that you might need to answer your questions and concerns. If you look to the upper-right portion of this page, you will see both a date as to when this page was last reviewed and an Article ID number that comes in handy for re-finding this article at some future date (yes, you can search by article ID numbers). In addition, if you happen to possess a subscription to the Microsoft TechNet solutions CDs, you might search the Knowledge Base CD using this very same Article ID number.

19. Hit your Backspace key or use the Back button to return to the previous Web page.

20. Use the scrollbar to move to the bottom of this screen, as shown in Figure 20.12.

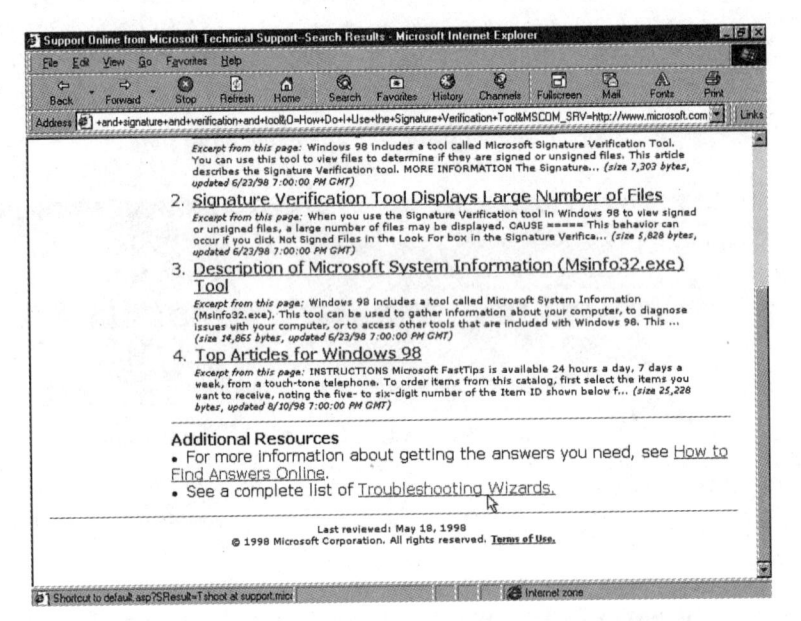

Figure 20.12 Finding a list of the troubleshooting wizards.

21. At the very bottom of this screen is a hyperlink that takes you to a Web page, which contains the complete listing of all Microsoft troubleshooting wizards presently available. Click this hyperlink to proceed to the screen shown in Figure 20.13.

22. Use the drop-down list box to find the Troubleshooting Wizards listing for the Windows 98 operating system. Then, click the Next>> button to move to the screen, as shown in Figure 20.14.

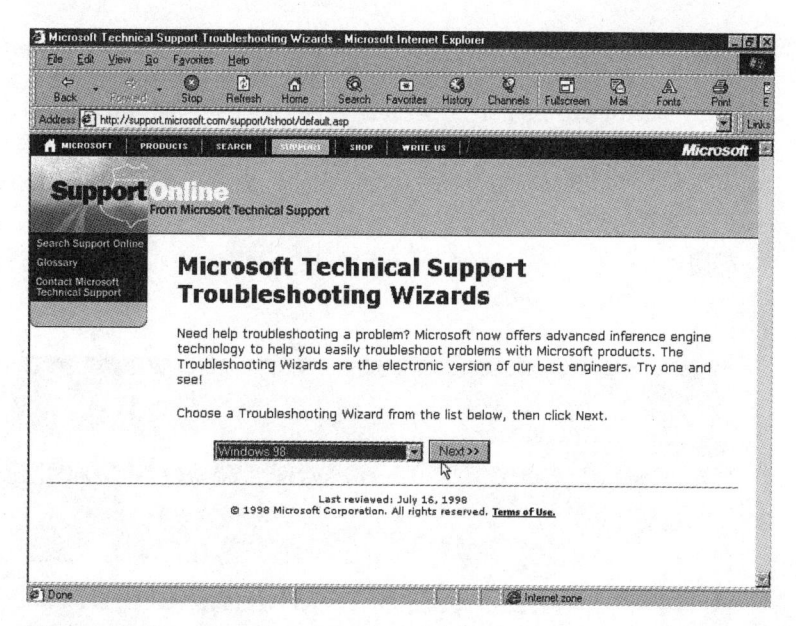

20.4
KNOW WHERE TO OBTAIN OTHER MEANS OF PROBLEM RESOLUTION

Figure 20.13 Accessing the Microsoft Technical Support Troubleshooting Wizards Web page.

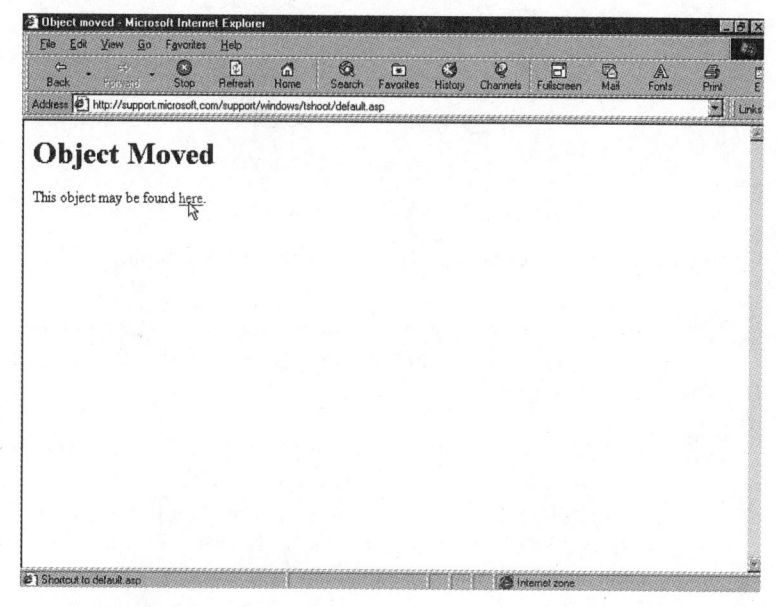

Figure 20.14 Hitting a Microsoft Web site semi-error Web page.

23. Whoops! Occasionally, you are confronted with one of Microsoft's infamous Object Moved Web pages. This means that the previous screen's hyperlink does not work exactly the way it should. All you need to do to find the correct page (which is the one that you originally were seeking), is click the underlined hyperlink that is associated with the word "here" (refer to Figure 20.14).

24. Then, click once on the word "here," which will take you to the screen shown in Figure 20.15.

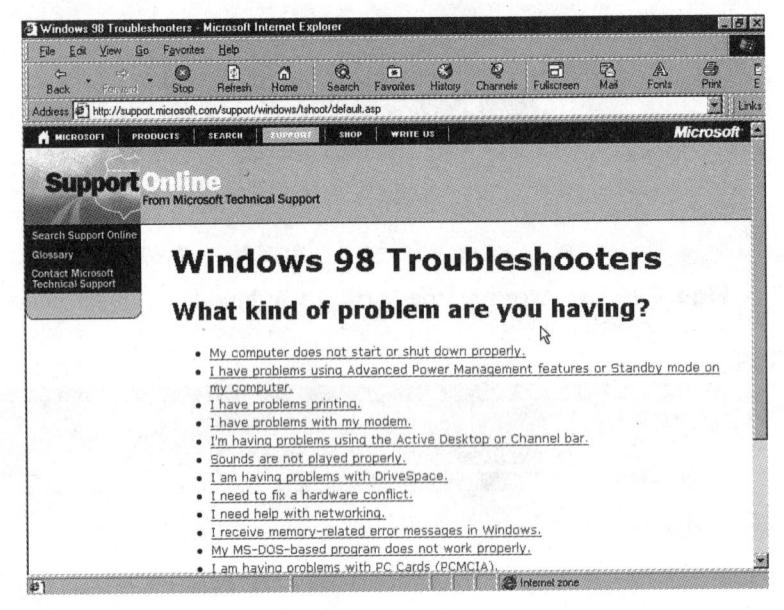

Figure 20.15 Reviewing the Search Results Web page.

25. After you arrive on the Windows 98 Troubleshooters, you will have a complete listing of all the Windows 98 troubleshooting wizards that presently exist.

26. To actually begin using any one of these wizard topics, click once on any of the wizard topics shown. For example, click on the second one from the top, which deals with problems concerning the Windows 98 Advanced Power Management system features. This takes you to the screen shown in Figure 20.16.

27. A detailed listing screen appears for the topic that you chose on the previous Web page. It is possible that sometimes the Windows 98

20.4
KNOW WHERE TO OBTAIN OTHER MEANS OF PROBLEM RESOLUTION   831

Troubleshooting Wizard starts running immediately. This is because some of the topics are so narrow in focus that there are no multiple wizards for that specific help topic.

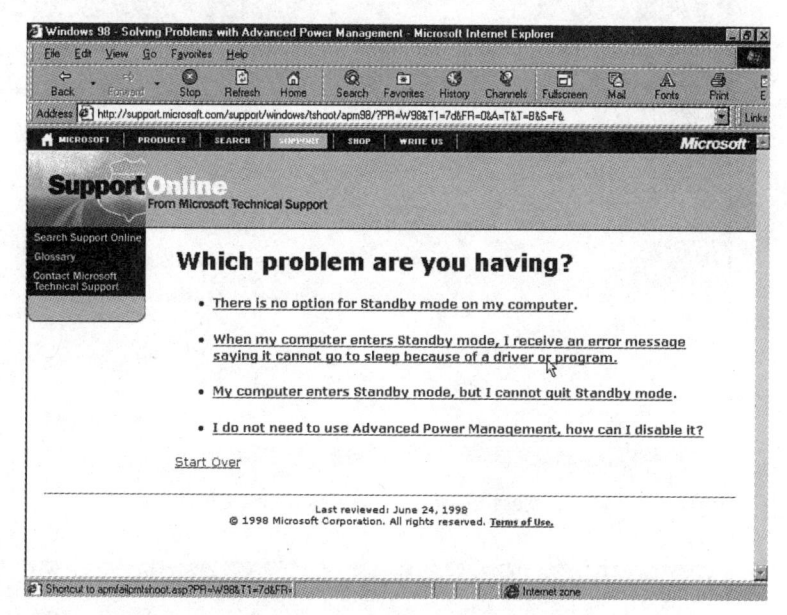

Figure 20.16 Accessing a Windows 98 Wizard.

28. To actually use any of these wizards, click the wizard that you believe will best meet your needs.

29. Also on this screen, or just about any of the other Support Online Web pages, is access to the Support Online Glossary, as shown in Figure 20.17.

30. To access this very detailed and useful glossary, click n the hyperlink that makes up that menu option's name (Glossary).

31. Doing this takes you to the Glossary Web page, as shown in Figure 20.18.

32. To find any definition, just click once on the starting letter of that topic. For example, you probably will want to know a bit more about *Digital Signatures*, since this is the technology that is used along with the *Signature Verification tool* that you asked for assistance on at the start of this topic.

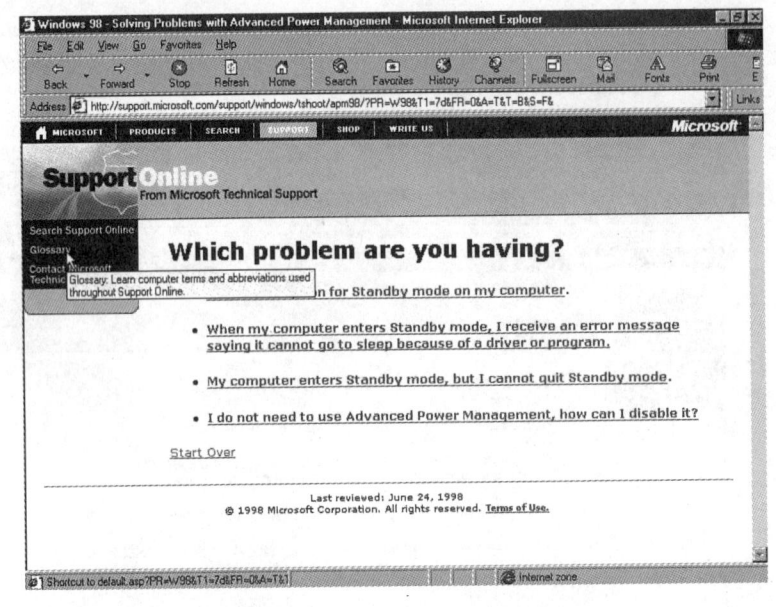

Figure 20.17 Accessing the Support Online Glossary.

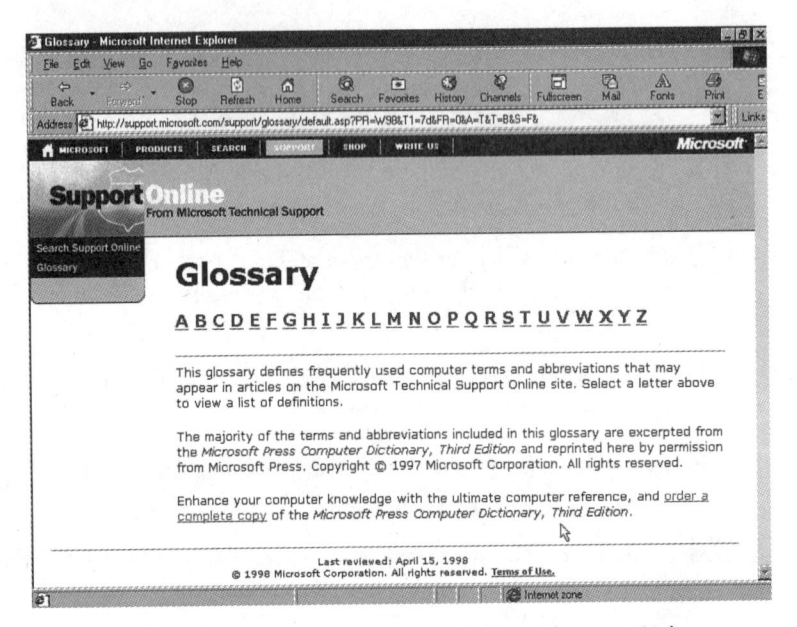

Figure 20.18 Reviewing the Support Online Glossary Web page.

33. To find this topic, click once on the letter D, which takes you to the Web page shown in Figure 20.19.

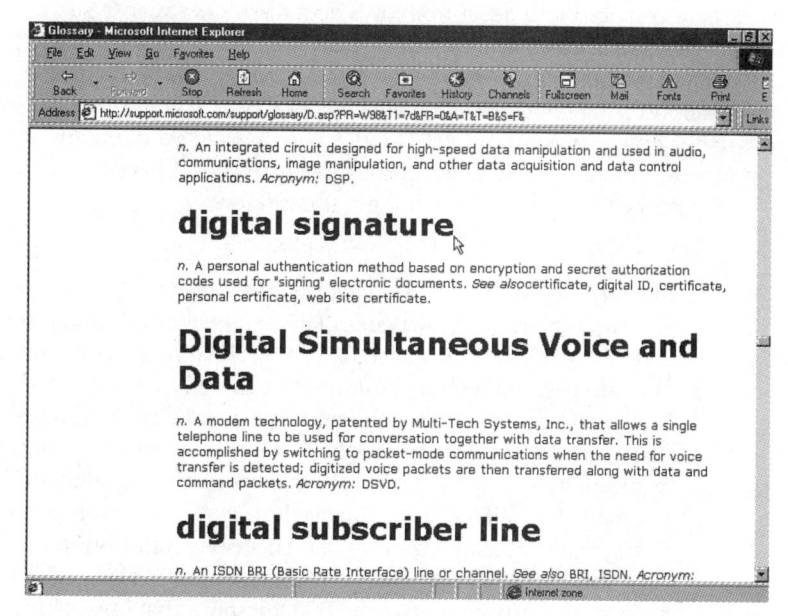

Figure 20.19 Reviewing a Glossary's definition.

34. As you can see, a one or two paragraph explanation is given for most of the topics that are stored in the Support Online Glossary. After you are finished examining this screen, close your Web browser and exit your Internet connection.

COMPLEXITY
BEGINNER

20.5 How do I... Obtain Microsoft TechNet and why would I want to use it?

Problem

I have heard a lot about the Microsoft TechNet program and all the neat things that it is supposed to be capable of providing me. However, why would I want or need to ever use it? How do I obtain a copy of Microsoft TechNet, and is it expensive or is it free?

Technique

This section explains some of the benefits of Microsoft TechNet, as well as where you need to order it from. It is about $299 per year to subscribe to, although sometimes you might get "deals" in the mail from Microsoft, which offer slight discounts to you because you are important to them. It consists of a small, two-ring binder that contains the 19 CDs that come with the initial starter pack. Several of these CD-ROMs are updated every month, which means that each month you receive at least three new ones (I have received as many as nine at one time) that replace last month's editions.

The CD-ROMs are broken into four categories:

- *Monthly Issues*—This section usually consists of three CD-ROMs: Technical Information Network (TIN), Supplemental Drivers and Patches, and the Microsoft Knowledge Base. The TIN disc is where you find over 300,000 pages of technical information as well as detailed case studies. The Supplemental disc has the most recent software drivers and patches that Microsoft has issued over the past several years for its software applications and operating system (sure beats downloading them from the Internet). The Microsoft Knowledge Base is still my favorite; remember the previous topic on searching the Microsoft Online Support Web site? Now you have your very own copy of that site's answers. This disc contains the answers to over 60,000 questions that others in your position have faced using Microsoft products.

- *Utilities*—There are several CD-ROMs here including all the Microsoft Resource Kits (Windows 98, Windows 95, Windows NT Server and Workstation, and so on). Additionally, the Software Library Archive disc has all the older software patches and drivers issued since 1991 (for the recent edition of these drivers, refer to the Supplemental Drivers and Patches CD found in the Monthly Issues section of TechNet). There is a Client and a Server CD-ROM, each of which contain numerous training utilities and Resource Kit utilities for Windows 95 and Windows 98, including a mass Windows 95 deployment plan that you would use with Microsoft Project, which of course could very easily be converted into a Windows 98 deployment plan of attack. Furthermore, there are several security updates to the various Internet tools that work with Windows 98, including those specifically for Windows 98 itself.

- *Service Packs*—There are usually 7–10 CD-ROMs in this section, which contain the Exchange Server 4.0, 5.0, and 5.5; the Small Business Server; all the Windows NT Server and Workstation; the Windows 98; Windows

95; Internet Explorer 4.01; Office 97; Site Server 2.0; Systems Management Server 1.1 and 1.2; SNA Server 2.11, 3.0, and 4.0; Microsoft SQL Server 6.0 and 6.5; Microsoft Transaction Server; and the Visual Studio 97 service pack and service releases.

- *Extras*—These are usually the demo or sample editions of software, such as the Microsoft BackOffice products evaluation CD-ROM. However, other very useful discs include the Windows NT 4.0 Option Pack CD-ROM, which includes Internet Explorer 4.01 and the Internet Information Server 4.0 for Windows NT.

Steps

1. To obtain a copy of Microsoft TechNet, you may do so by telephone in either the United States or Canada by calling Microsoft directly at 1-800-344-2121, extension 3118, from 6:30 a.m. until 5:30 p.m. (Pacific standard time). If you reside outside either of these two nations, contact your local Microsoft subsidiary for more information. Of course, if you want to call Microsoft in the United States to obtain a copy of TechNet you may do so by dialing this telephone number, 510-275-0826 to subscribe.

2. The cost of this technology is $299 USD or $399 CAN and can be purchased either via the Internet or by telephone. The path via telephone is explained in step 1; using the Internet requires a slightly different approach.

3. First you need to establish a connection to the Internet and start your Web browser, such as the Microsoft Internet Explorer, which is integrated into the Windows 98 operating system.

4. You need to access this URL: http://www.microsoft.com/technet/subscription/ordernow.htm (all lowercase), which takes you to the start of the ordering process. Keep in mind that this is for USA or Canadian folks, if you reside outside of these two nations, you should visit the How to Order hyperlinked section of this Web site.

5. Follow the prompts and in two to four weeks, you will be enjoying these CD-ROMs, while saving on your Internet connection costs; as you are no longer downloading those 6+ MB patches and drivers.

6. Another technology that can help you along these same lines is known as the Microsoft Developer Network (MSDN). The MSDN annual subscription process is similar to that of TechNet; you can ask the TechNet folks about picking up an MSDN subscription at the same time you get your TechNet subscription. There are three levels of MSDN, Standard, Professional, and Universal, which range in price. At the bottom level you get most of the Microsoft software products ($1,299), whereas the Universal subscription gives you everything (it is $1,999 when you can get it on sale) from the Windows 98 Device Development Kit to a full copy of Windows 98 and Plus! 98. Of course, if you are seeking to support a Windows 98 deployment and not to develop Windows 98-based software products, TechNet should be the subscription of choice.

INDEX

A

access (file sharing), 455-456
Access Control tab (Batch 98 Network Options screen), 337-338
Accessibility options (Internet Explorer), 506-507
Accounts area (newsgroups), 611
Active Desktop
    Channel Bar, 98, 100
    Classic Desktop, 64-65
    configuring, 69-72, 74
    defined, 62
    icons, 97-98, 100
ActiveX Controls and Plug-ins (Internet Explorer security settings), 513
Add a New Credit Card Wizard, 564, 566
Add New Connection icon, 356
Add New Hardware Wizard, 192
    CD-ROM and DVD-ROM drives, 247-249
    printers, 468
Add New User Wizard, 416-419
Add Printer Wizard
    changing printer settings, 475
    installing printers, 468-470, 472-474
Add/Remove Programs utility, 270-272
Additional Clients tab (Batch 98 Network Options screen), 338
Additional Files tab (Batch 98 Advanced Options screen), 344
Address Book (Outlook Express), 617-627
addresses
    gateway, 334
    gateway IP, 439
    TCP/IP protocol, 434-437
ADS Web site, 751
advanced configuration (Outlook Express), 583-585, 587-589
Advanced configuration tab (Internet Explorer), 536-540
advanced playback settings (Media Player), 713-714

Advanced Troubleshooting Settings window, 140
Aims Lab Video Highway Extreme Web site, 761
AIMS Lab Web site, 751
AITech Web site, 751
Amazon Web site, 30
Animated Cursor Editor, 35
Application Performance Optimizer, 36
applications. *See also* utilities
    GHOST, 98, 349
    troubleshooting, 284-285, 287
Area Code Rules dialog box, 359
Artisoft LANtastic server, 401
Artisoft Web site, 401
AS/400 computer, 402
ASD (internal Automatic Skip Driver agent), 136-137
    launching, 137
    running (manually), 137-139
assigning
    security levels, 507-511
    specific drive letters, 245-246
    TCP/IP address, 434-437
Associate Resource Kit tool, 36
ATI All-in-Wonder, ATI-TV Web site, 761
ATI Web site, 751
ATM protocols, 426-427
attachments (email), 595-596
audio. *See also* broadcasting
    conferencing (NetMeeting), 778
        another user's properties, 784
        audio codecs, 778
        audio components, 760-761
        audio options, 777-779
        calling options, 776
        computer systems, 762
        Configuration Wizard, 766-772
        configuring, 766-772, 774
        email, 784
        error message box, 784-786

    hardware requirements, 763
    hosting conference calls, 780-781
    ILS (Microsoft Internet Locator Server), 763
    information, 775-777
    installing, 764-765
    joining calls in progress, 774
    main screen, 772
    protocol options, 779-780
    server connection, 772, 774
    SpeedDial, 783-784
    tools, 781-783
    version 2.1 download Web site, 767
    video components, 761
    video options, 779
    Web site, 760, 786
  radio, listening to, 748-749
Audio Tuning Wizard, 770-771
Automated .INF Installer, 36
Automatic Configuration setting (Internet Explorer), 534
Automatic Private IP Addressing, 432-433
automating tasks, 306-309, 311
AVerMedia MPEG Wizard, EZCapture, TVPhone Web site, 761
AVerMedia Web site, 751
Aztec Sound Galaxy Web site, 760

B

backing up data, 251-258, 260
Backup Wizard, 253-256
Banyan Web site, 401
Barnes and Noble bookstore Web site, 30
Batch 98, 323
  Advanced Options screen, 344
  Display screen, 340
  General Setup Options screen
    Desktop tab, 330
    Install Info tab, 327
    MRU Locations tab, 330
    Printers tab, 330
    Regional Settings tab, 329
    Setup Prompts tab, 328
    User Profiles tab, 331
  installing, 323-324
  installing Windows 98, 324-330, 332-336, 338-341, 343-348
  Internet Explorer Options screen, 341, 343

  Internet Explorer screen, 340
  Network Options screen
    Access Control tab, 337-338
    Additional Clients tab, 338
    Clients tab, 336-337
    Protocols tab, 332
    Services tab, 335-336
  Optional Components screen, 339
  primary msbatch.inf screen, 339-340, 343
  TCP/IP Options screen
    DNS Configuration tab, 332
    Gateway tab, 334
    IP Address tab, 335
    WINS Configuration tab, 334
Batch File Wait Resource Kit tool, 36
Batch Processing of Files Resource Kit tool, 36
binary values, 157
binding protocols, 443
boot process. *See* startup
bridged networks, 398
broadcasting. *See also* audio
  hardware recommendations, 732-733
  hardware requirements, 731-732
  radio stations, listening to, 748-749
  WaveTop Data Broadcasting, 734-736
  WebTV for Windows, 737
    configuring, 742-743
    installing, 734-736
    launching, 737, 746
    local program guide listings, 743-744, 746
    Program Guide, 741, 746
    Program Guide search, 747
    quitting, 747
    sample Program Guide Tour, 739, 741
    tuner cards, 736
    Welcome screen, 737
Browse Master property (file sharing), 452-454
Browser tab (Batch 98 Internet Explorer Options screen), 341
browsing, 453
buffering, 713
Bulk Configuration Utility, 36
buttons (mouse), 67, 197

C

.CAB files, 552-553
cabling (networks), 676
calling Microsoft technical support engineers, 820-821

INDEX

calling cards (Dial-Up Networking connection), 361-371
    calling card sequence, 365-368
    dialing sequence, 370
    dialog box, 363
    PIN numbers, 369-370
    selecting types, 363, 365
    Sequence dialog box, 365
    telephone number to be dialed, 370
cameras, 769
capturing printer ports, 475
CD-ROM drives, 247-249
CD-ROMs (TechNet), 834-835
changing
    audio codecs (NetMeeting), 778
    character typing speed, 179-180
    default view (My Computer icon), 83, 86
    file associations, 799-800, 802-803
    NetMeeting
        audio options, 777-779
        calling options, 776
        information, 775-777
        protocol options, 779-780
        video options, 779
    startup modes, 116-127
Channel Bar (Active Desktop), 98, 100
character information (Microsoft Chat), 718-720
character typing speed (keyboards), 179-180
chatting (Microsoft Chat), 722-723
    character information, 718-720
    Chat 2.5 Update, 703
    connecting, 721-722
    entering, 722
    first time launching, 717-718
    Format menu, 727
    identity profiles, 725
    installing, 701-703
    launching, 717
    Member menu, 727
    Options menu, 727
    personal Chat room
        creating, 723-724
        entering, 724-725
    quitting, 728
    Room menu, 727
    version numbers, 725

    View options, 726
    Window menu, 728
Checklinks, 80-83
Cherry Corp. Web site, 174
Cirrus Logic Crystal drivers Web site, 760
Classic Desktop
    Active Desktop, compared, 64-65
    configuring, 66-68
    defined, 62
click rates (keyboards), 179-180
clients software (networks), 407-410, 412-415
Clients tab (Batch 98 Network Options screen), 336-337
Clip Resource Kit tool, 37
Clipboard Buffer Tool, 37
Clipboard Organizer, 37
cloning installation, 348-349
CODEC (compression/decompression), 282
codecs, 778
colors
    Internet Explorer background and text, 503
    monitors, 185-186
combining
    modems, single Dial-Up Network connection, 389-392
    network connections and modems, 377-379
Communications folder (Dial-Up Networking), 356
compaction (newsgroups), 609-610
Compaq Web site, 401
components (network), 420-424
Components header (System Information utility), 281-282
Compound File Layout User Tool, 37
compressing hard drives, 216-219
Compression Options window, 217
compression/decompression (CODEC), 282
Compro D-Cam Web site, 761
conference calls. *See* NetMeeting
configuring
    Active Desktop, 69-72, 74
    Classic Desktop, 66-68
    Disk Cleanup utility, 224-231
    disk compression tool (DriveSpace 3), 216-218

Disk Defragmenter, 233-236
File and Printer Sharing, 451-460
    Browse Master property, 452-454
    drive sharing, 456-457
    file sharing, 451-455
    LM Announce property, 454
    passwords, 459
    security access, 455-456
Internet Explorer, 495
Media Player, 708-709
Microsoft Wallet, 560-562, 564, 566-568
monitors, 183-192
    colors, 185-186
    default profile, 190-191
    graphics acceleration speed, 189-190
    refresh rate, 188
    screen area (resolution), 186
    screen font size, 186-187
    video card, 186
mouse/pointer devices, 195-200
Multilink, 390-392
multiple monitors, 192-193
multiple users, 415-419
NetMeeting, 766-772, 774
newsgroups, 600-606
Outlook Express, 576-579, 581-582
    advanced options, 583-585, 587-589
    multiple users, 611-612
peer-to-peer networks, 674-678
    Ethernet, 675
    thinnet cabling, 676
    token ring, 675
    UTP cabling, 676
playback settings (Media Player), 713-714
primary mouse button, 197
Profile Assistant, 554, 556, 559-560
ScanDisk, 236-239
single-click mode (desktop icons), 101-103
TCP/IP protocol, 432-434
    address, 434-437
    binding protocols, 443
    default protocol, 442
    DNS server, 439-441
    DNS Server Search Order, 441
    Domain Suffix Search Order server, 441
    gateway IP addresses, 439
    NetBIOS, enabling, 441
    subnet masks, 436
    WINS, 437-438
Temporary Internet Files Folder section (Internet Explorer), 500-502
Temporary Internet Files section (Internet Explorer), 499-500
timing arrangement (Dial-Up Networking telephone calls), 365-368
User Profiles, 415-419
VPN Adapter, 380-381, 383-384
WaveTop Data Broadcasting, 752, 754-755
WBEM, 681, 683-685, 688
WebTV for Windows, 742-743
connecting to
    Internet. See Dial-Up Networking
    Microsoft Chat server, 721-722
    NetMeeting server, 772, 774
    network connections and modems combinations security, 377-379
    other networks, 397-406
        Artisoft LANtastic server, 401
        AS/400, 402
        DECnet protocol, 401
        DLC (Data Link Control) protocol, 400
        IBM Mainframe systems, 400
        IBM OS/2 LAN and Warp servers, 401
        Microsoft Windows NT servers, 400
        Novell NetWare servers, 400
        Samba servers, 403
        UNIX systems, 400
        VINES server, 401
Connection tab (Internet Explorer Properties screen), 530
    Automatic Configuration, 534
    Dial-Up settings, 532-534
    Internet Connection Wizard, 530
Connectix QuickCam Web site, 761
Content Advisor (Internet Explorer), 521-524, 526-528
Content tab (Internet Explorer, Internet Properties screen), 521
    Content Advisor, 521-524, 526-528
    digital certificates, 528-530
Contents tab (Online Help), 814
converting hard drives to FAT32, 220-223
Create New Compressed Drive window, 218
Create Shortcut Wizard, 96-97

INDEX

Create StartUp Disk window, 218
Creative VideoBlaster Web site, 761
credit cards
    information, storing, 554, 560-562, 564, 566-568
    Dial-Up Networking, 361
cryptography software packages catalog Web site, 806
cursor blink rate, 179-180
custom security settings (Internet Explorer), 511-514, 516-518

D

Data Link Control protocol (DLC), 400
Daylight Savings Time Resource Kit tool, 37
DbSet utility, 347
dead shortcuts, 80-83
DECnet protocol, 401
Default Printer Resource Kit tool, 37
Defragmenter utility, 212
deleting
    dead shortcuts, 81-83
    newsgroups, 609-610
    system icons, 76-79
    temporary Internet files, 498-499
Dell Web site, 762
Dependency Walker Resource Kit tool, 37
deployment. *See* installing
desktop
    Active
        Channel Bar, 98, 100
        configuring, 69-72, 74
        defined, 62
        hiding all icons, 97-98, 100
    Classic
        configuring, 66-68
        defined, 62
    icons, 101-103
    modes, compared, 64-65
    My Computer icon, 83, 86
    system icons, 76-79
Desktop tab (Batch 98 General Setup Options screen), 330
DHCP (Dynamic Host Configuration Protocol), 431
diagnostic startup, 116-118
dial properties, 359

Dial-Up Networking, 355-356, 359, 361-362
    calling cards, 362-371
        calling card sequence, 365-368
        dialing sequence, 370
        PIN numbers, 369-370
        selecting types, 363, 365
        telephone number to be dialed, 370
    dial properties, 359
    Multilink, 389-392
    tweaking (more productivity), 372
        GUI changes, 372-373
        Registry modifications, 373-376
    VPN, 379-380
        Adapter, 380-381, 383-384
        connection, 385-388
        Dial-Up Networking session, creating, 385-388
Dial-Up settings (Internet Explorer), 532-534
Dialing Properties dialog box, 359
dialing sequence (Dial-Up Networking), 370
dialog boxes. *See also* windows
    Area Code Rules, 359
    Calling Card, 363
    Calling Card Sequence, 365
    Dialing Properties, 359
    Dr. Watson options, 287
    Network, 423, 434, 451, 463
    Open, 448
    Printers folder, 477-478
    Select Network Adapters, 380
    TCP/IP Properties, 434
        Advanced tab, 441-442
        Bindings tab, 443
        DNS Configuration tab, 439-441
        Gateway tab, 438-439
        IP Address tab, 434-437
        NetBIOS tab, 441
        WINS Configuration tab, 437-438
Diamond Web sites
    DVC 1000, 761
    Multimedia, 751
    Sonic Impact and Monster Sound, 760
digital certificates (Internet Explorer), 528-530
digital IDs, 627-632
Digital Vision Computer Eyes Web site, 761
DirectX, 185
DirectX 6.0 Technology Update, 703

disabling
    encrypted password Registry setting, 403-406
    user access, 162-163, 165-167
Disk Cleanup utility, 224
    cleaning up hard drives, 212
    configuring, 224-231
disk compression
    FAT32, compared, 213, 215
    tool (DriveSpace 3)
        compressing hard drives, 216-219
        configuring, 216-218
        installing, 216
Disk Defragmenter, 223, 233-236
Disk Defragmenter Settings window, 233
disk drives
    finding and repairing errors, 236-239
    management tools and utilities, 209, 211
disk operating systems. *See* DOS
disks (startup), 143-144
Display Properties window, 71, 98, 183, 193
Display screen (Batch 98), 340
displaying
    DOS prompts, 128, 130-134
    identity profiles (Microsoft Chat characters), 725
    media clip properties (Media Player), 714-715
    newsgroup properties, 608
    Startup Menu, 131
DLC (Data Link Control) protocol, 400
DNS (Domain Name Server)
    Configuration tab (Batch 98 TCP/IP Options screen), 332
    Server Search Order, 441
    servers, 439-441
Domain Suffix Search Order, 441
DOS (disk operating systems), 94
    prompts, 128, 130-134
    window, 94-97
dot pitch, 181
downloading
    Internet Explorer security settings, 518
    newsgroup options, 609
    local program guide listings, 743-744, 746
Dr. Watson, 98, 109, 277
    startup files, 110-115
    launching, 110

options dialog box, 287
troubleshooting application faults, 284-285, 287
Drive Converter (FAT32), 220-223
drives
    CD-ROM, 247-249
    DVD-ROM, 247-249
    hard
        managing, 240-244
        removable devices, 250-251
    removable media
        assigning specific drive letters, 245-246
        managing, 244-246
    sharing, 456-457
DriveSpace 3
    compressing hard drives, 216-219
    configuring, 216-218
    installing, 216
Duplicate File Finder Resource Kit tool, 38
DVD-ROM drives, 247-249
DWORD (double-word) value, 157
Dynamic Host Configuration Protocol (DHCP), 431

E

Edit String window, 158
editing
    MSDOS.SYS file, 131-134
    Registry
        disable user access, 162-163, 165-167
        launch applications (startup), 153-154, 156-160
    system files, 135
email
    NetMeeting, 784
    Outlook Express
        Address Book, 617-627
        advanced configuration, 583-585, 587-589
        attachments, 595-596
        configuring, 576-579, 581-582
        creating messages, 591, 593, 595
        digital IDs, 628-632
        forwarding messages, 598-599
        Inbox, 589
        Inbox Assistant, 615, 617
        installing, 574-575
        Internet Connection Wizard, 579-583

INDEX

  maintenance tasks, 613-617
  multiple users, configuring, 611-612
  newsgroup configuration, 600-606
  newsgroups, 607-611
  Outbox, 597
  reading messages, 589
  sending messages, 596
  Sent Items icon, 597
 protocols, 576, 580
enabling
 File and Printer Sharing, 444
 NetBIOS, 441
encrypted password setting (Registry), 403-406
Ensoniq Web sites
 Soundscape, 760
 Ensoniq Vivo90, AudioPCI, 760
entering
 Microsoft Chat, 722
  character information, 718-720
  personal Chat room, 724-725
 PIN numbers (calling cards), 369-370
enumerating, 136
Environment Setting Utility, 38
error message box
 Internet Explorer, 540
 NetMeeting, 784-786
Error Message Translation Resource Kit tool, 38
ESS drivers Web site, 760
Ethernet, 675
executing MSBATCH.INF file, 348
Expand for Windows Resource Kit tool, 38

F

Fast Infrared (network protocol), 426
Fast Multimedia FPS60 Web site, 761
FAT12, 206
FAT16, 206-208
FAT32, 207
 Conversion Information Resource Kit tool, 38
 Conversion Information window, 214
 disk compression, compared, 213, 215
 Drive Converter, 220-223
 FAT16, compared, 207-208
FDisk utility, 240-242
File and Directory Comparison Resource Kit tool, 38

File and Printer Sharing
 configuring, 451-460
  Browse Master property, 452-454
  drive sharing, 456-457
  file sharing, 451-455
  LM Announce property, 454
  passwords, 459
  security access, 455-456
 enabling, 444
 file sharing, 455-460
 network services, 446-450
file associations, 799-800, 802-803
File Compress Resource Kit tool, 39
File Locating Resource Kit tool, 39
File Version Resource Kit tool, 39
File Wise utility, 39
files
 altered since installation, 288-292
 .CAB, 552-553
 corrupted, 288-292
 .INS, 546, 552-553
 MSBATCH.INF, 348
 MSDOS.SYS, 131-134
 Registry, 148-149
 sharing, 455-460
  Browse Master property, 452-454
  configuring, 451-455
  drive sharing, 456-457
  LM Announce property, 454
  passwords, 459
  security access, 455-456
 startup, 110-115
 system, 134-135
 temporary Internet, 498-499
finding
 altered files, 288-292
 corrupted files, 288-292
 dead shortcuts, 81-83
 malfunctioning device drivers, 116-127
 system files, 134-135
 system resources, 267
 video clips (Internet), 706
Finding Executable Type Resource Kit tool, 38
folders
 Communications, 356
 Recent Documents, 88-90
fonts
 Internet Explorer, 504
 screen size, 186-187

forcing Safe Mode startup, 140, 142
Format menu (Microsoft Chat), 727
forwarding email messages, 598-599
FQDN (fully qualified domain name), 440
Free Disk Space Resource Kit tool, 39
FrontPage Express, 646, 648-652
fully qualified domain name (FQDN), 440

G

Gateway 2000 Web site, 762
gateway addresses, 334
gateway IP addresses, 439
Gateway tab (Batch 98 TCP/IP Options screen), 334
GDI (graphical device interface), 272
Gemstar Web site, 739
General options (Internet Explorer), 497-507
    Accessibility, 506-507
    colors (background and text), 503
    fonts, 504
    history (sites), 503
    home page, 498
    languages, 505-506
    temporary Internet files, 498-500
    Temporary Internet File Folders section, 500-502
    Temporary Internet Program Files, 502
General Setup Options (Batch 98), 327, 330
GHOST, 349
GHOST Web site, 349
Glossary (Microsoft Support Online), 831, 833
graphical device interface (GDI), 272
graphics acceleration speed, 189-190
GRE Protocol Troubleshooting Resource Kit tool, 39
GUI, tweaking Dial-Up Networking, 372-373
Guillemot Maxi Sound Web site, 761

H

H.323 Gateway (audio and video conferencing standard), 778
hacker Web sites, 377
hard drives
    cleaning up, 224-231
    compressing, 216-219
    converting, FAT32, 220-223
    Disk Defragmenter, 233-236
    managing, 240-244
    more space, creating, 212-213
    removable devices, 250-251
    troubleshooting, not enough space, 212-213
hardware
    below standard levels, 28-29
    broadcasting services, 731-733
    NetMeeting requirements, 763
    startup problems, 137-139
    Windows 98 requirements, 17-22, 24, 26
Hardware Compatibility List (HCL), 20-24, 26, 44
Hardware Resources header (System Information utility), 278-281
Hauppauge Web site, 752
Hauppauge Wincast, Cinema Pro, Celebrity Web site, 761
HCL (Hardware Compatibility List), 20-24, 26, 44
help
    calling Microsoft technical support engineers, 820-821
    Internet assistance, 822-823, 825-826, 828, 830-831, 833
    Microsoft Support Online Web site, 823, 825-826, 828
    MSDN (Microsoft Developer Network), 836
    Online Help, 813-814
        Contents tab, 814
        Index tab, 815
        Search tab, 815-816
        Web Help button, 816-817
    TechNet, 834-835
    troubleshooting
        application faults, 284-285, 287
        disk drives, 236-239
        hard drives, not enough space, 212-213
        malfunctioning device drivers, 116-127
        startup hardware problems, 137-139
        techniques and strategies, 818-819
        utilities, 277
        wizards, 828, 830
hertz (Hz), 188
hiding
    icons, 97-98, 100
    Channel Bar, 98, 100
history (Internet sites), 503

INDEX

HKEY_CLASSES_ROOT Registry hive, 150
HKEY_CURRENT_CONFIG Registry hive, 150
HKEY_CURRENT_USER Registry hive, 150
HKEY_DYN_DATA Registry hive, 150
HKEY_LOCAL_MACHINE Registry hive, 150
HKEY_USERS Registry hive, 150
home page (Internet Explorer), 498
Home Page Wizard, 661-663
hosting conference calls, 780-781
HTML (Hypertext Markup Language) tags, 648
Hz (hertz), 188

I

IBM
    Mainframe systems, 400
    OS/2 LAN and Warp servers, 401
    Web site, 402, 762
icons
    hiding, 97-98, 100
    My Computer, 83, 86
    single-click mode, 101-103
    system, 76-79
identification parameters (system), 462-464
identity profiles (Microsoft Chat characters), 725
IEAK Profile Manager (Internet Explorer Administration Kit), 39, 546, 549-553, 679
    installing, 546-547
    launching, 547
    saving .INS and .CAB files, 552-553
    System Policies and Restrictions section, 551-552
    Wizard Settings section, 549-551
ILS (Microsoft Internet Locator Server), 763
Image Editor Resource Kit tool, 39
IMAP (Internet Message Access Protocol), 580
IMAP Web site, 576
IMAP4 (Internet Message Access Protocol, version 4.0), 576
implementing Drive Converter (FAT32), 220-223
Inbox (Outlook Express), 589
Inbox Assistant (Outlook Express), 615, 617
Index tab (Online Help), 815
Install Info tab (Batch 98 General Setup Options screen), 327

installing
    Batch 98, 323-324
    CD-ROM and DVD-ROM drives, 247-249
    disk drive management tools and utilities, 209, 211
    File and Printer Sharing network service, 446-450
    Internet publishing components, 637-639, 641-644
    keyboards, 174
    Microsoft Family Logon software, 407-410, 412-415
    Microsoft Network Monitor Agent, 445-446, 448-450
    Microsoft Plus! 98, 804-805
    mouse/pointer device, 194-195
    Multilink, 390-392
    multimedia tools (Microsoft), 701-703
    NetMeeting, 764-765
    network
        components, 420-424
        protocols, 425-430
        services, 444-446, 448-450
    Novell NetWare LAN software, 407-410, 412-415
    Outlook Express, 574-575
    printers, 468
        Add New Hardware Wizard, 468
        Add Printer Wizard, 468-470, 472-474
    Profile Manager, 546-547
    Resource Kit, 30-35
    Service for NetWare Directory Services, 445-450
    SNMP, 690-692, 694
    System Management tools and utilities, 270-272
    VPN Adapter, 380-381, 383-384
    WaveTop Data Broadcasting, 734-736
    WBEM, 681, 683-685, 688
    WebTV for Windows, 734-736
    Windows 98
        Batch 98 utility, 324-330, 332-336, 338-341, 343-344, 346-348
        cloning, 348-349
        hardware systems below standard levels, 28-29
        network-based, 321-323
        preparations, 26-28

Intel Smart Video Recorder Web site, 761
Interactive Music Control with MS Synthesizer Update, 703
internal Automatic Skip Driver agent (ASD), 136-139
International Telecommunication Union (ITU) audio and video conferencing standard, 778
Internet, 483
    chat rooms. *See* Microsoft Chat
    confidential data, sending, 627-632
    Connection Wizard, 530, 579-583
    Dial-Up Networking, 355-356, 359, 361-362
        calling cards, 362-371
        Multilink, 389
        tweaking (more productivity), 372-376
        VPN. See VPN
    email. *See* email
    publishing
        components, 637-639, 641-644
        FrontPage Express, 646, 648-652
        Personal Web Server Manager, 659, 661-664, 666-668
        Web Publishing Wizard, 653-654, 656, 658
    surfing, 484
    TCP/IP, 483
    temporary files, 498-499
    video clips, 706
    WaveTop Data Broadcasting
        configuring, 752, 754-755
        installing, 734-736
        launching, 752
        requirements, 751
        TV tuner card compatibility, 751-752
    Windows 98 assistance (help), 822-823, 825-826, 828, 830-831, 833
Internet Explorer
    add-on utilities Web site, 546
    Advanced configuration tab, 536-540
    configuring, 495
    Connection settings, 530
        Automatic Configuration, 534
        Dial-Up settings, 532-534
        Internet Connection Wizard, 530
    Content options, 521
        Content Advisor, 521-524, 526-528
        digital certificates, 528-530
        error message box, 540
    General options, 497-507
        Accessibility, 506-507
        colors (background and text), 503
        fonts, 504
        history (sites), 503
        home page, 498
        languages, 505-506
        temporary Internet files, 498-500
        Temporary Internet Files Folder section, 500-502
        Temporary Internet Program Files, 502
    .INS files, 546
    menus, 541-543, 545
    Microsoft Profile Assistant, 554, 556, 559-560
    Microsoft Wallet, 554, 560-562, 564, 566-568
    Programs configuration tab, 535-536
    Security options, 507
        ActiveX Controls and Plug-ins, 513
        custom settings, 511-514, 516-518
        downloads, 518
        Java permissions subsection, 514-517
        levels (zones), assigning, 507-511
        miscellaneous, 519-520
        software channel permissions, 520-521
        user authentication, 519
    updating, 485-495
Internet Explorer Administration Kit (IEAK). *See* IEAK Profile Manager
Internet Explorer Options screen (Batch 98), 340
Internet Message Access Protocol, version 4.0 (IMAP4), 576
Internet PhoneJACK Quicknet drivers Web site, 761
InterNic (government Internet connectivity organization), 437
.INS files, 546, 552-553
IP Address tab (Batch 98 TCP/IP Options screen), 335
IP Packet Size, 372-373, 375
IPX/SPX (network protocol), 426
ITU (International Telecommunication Union) audio and video conferencing standard, 778
IXMICRO Web site, 752

J - K

Java permissions (Internet Explorer security settings), 514-517
joining NetMeeting calls in progress, 774

kernal, 273
Keyboard Properties window, 175, 179
keyboards
    character typing speed, 179-180
    default language, 175-179
    installing, 174
    languages, 178
    selecting, 173
    shortcuts, DOS window, 95-97
Kodak Web site, 762

L

LAN Manager Announce, 454
languages
    keyboards, 175-179
    Internet Explorer, 505-506
launching
    Add New Hardware wizard, 247
    Add New User Wizard, 416
    Add Printer Wizard, 469
    ASD, 137
    Batch 98, 325
    Checklinks, 81
    Disk Defragmenter, 233
    Dr. Watson for Windows 98, 110
    Dr. Watson utility, 285
    FrontPage Express, 646
    Maintenance Wizard, 298
    Make Compatible utility, 791
    Make New Connection Wizard, 385
    Media Player, 704
    Microsoft Chat, 717-718
    Microsoft Windows 98 Backup utility, 252
    Net Watcher utility, 302
    NetMeeting Configuration Wizard, 766
    Online Help, 813
    Outlook Express, 576, 613, 617, 628
    Personal Web Server Manager, 659
    Profile Manager, 547
    Registry Checker, 160
    Registry Editor, 153, 162, 374
    ScanDisk, 236
    Scheduled Task Wizard, 307-310
    Scheduled Tasks utility, 307
    System Configuration utility, 115-117, 140
    System File Checker, 288
    System Information tool, 116
    System Monitor utility, 293
    Tweak UI, 76, 461
    WaveTop Data Broadcasting, 752
    Web Publishing Wizard, 653
    WebTV for Windows, 737, 746
    WinAlign, 796
LDAP (Lightweight Directory Access Protocol), 580
Lightweight Directory Access Protocol, 580
Link Check Wizard, 40, 81-82
links, 80
listening to, radio, 748-749
LM Announce (LAN Manager Announce), 454
local program guide listings (WebTV for Windows), 743-744, 746
Log Time Resource Kit tool, 40
logging on networks, 460-461
Long Filename Utility, 40

M

Macromedia Shockwave Director, 701, 703
Macromedia Shockwave Flash, 701, 703
maintenance
    Outlook Express, 613-617
    scheduling
        tasks, 306-309, 311
        utilities, 297-301
Maintenance Wizard, 297-301
Make Compatible utility, 790-794
Make New Connection Wizard, 356, 385-387
managing
    hard drives, 240-244
    networks, 671-672. *See also* ZAIW
    removable media drives, 244-246
    system resources, 312-313
Master Browse Server, 453
media clip properties, 714-715
Media Player, 704-706, 708-712, 714-715
    configuring, 708-709
    finding video clips, 706
    installing, 701, 703
    launching, 704

media clip properties, viewing, 714-715
playback settings (advanced), 713-714
retrieving media files, 705
sound card compatibility, 711-712
Streaming Media with RealVideo software option, 709
 bandwidth requirements, 712
 proxy server, 711
 transport options, 709-711
Member menu (Microsoft Chat), 727-728
menus
 Internet Explorer, 541-543, 545
 Microsoft chat, 727-728
Microsoft
 32-bit DLC (network protocol), 426
 Batch 98 Automated Setup Resource Kit tool, 40
 Chat
  character information, 718-720
  Chat 2.5 Update, 703
  chatting (talking to others), 722-723
  connecting to, 721-722
  creating personal Chat room, 723-724
  entering, 722
  entering personal Chat room, 724-725
  first time launching, 717-718
  Format menu, 727
  identity profiles, 725
  installing, 701-703
  launching, 717
  Member menu, 727
  Options menu, 727
  quitting, 728
  Room menu, 727
  version numbers, 725
  View options, 726
  Window menu, 728
 Copy Resource Kit tool, 40
 Developer Network (MSDN), 836
 DLC (network protocol), 426
 Family Logon software, 407-410, 412-415
 Internet Locator Server (ILS), 763
 Management Console (MMC), 680-681
 multimedia tools, 701-703
 NetMeeting
  another user's properties, 784
  audio codecs, 778
  audio components, 760-761
  audio options, 777-779
  calling options, 776
  computer systems, 762
  Configuration Wizard, 766-772
  configuring, 766-772, 774
  email, 784
  error message box, 784-786
  hardware requirements, 763
  hosting conference calls, 780-781
  ILS (Microsoft Internet Locator Server), 763
  information, 775-777
  installing, 764-765
  joining calls in progress, 774
  main screen, 772
  protocol options, 779-780
  server connection, 772, 774
  SpeedDial, 783-784
  tools, 781-783
  version 2.1 download Web site, 767
  video components, 761
  video options, 779
  Web site, 760, 786
Network Monitor Agent, 445-446, 448-450
Plus! 98
 components, 803-804
 installing, 804-805
Press Web site, 786
Profile Assistant, 554, 556, 559-560
Remote Procedure Resource Kit tool, 40
Remote Registry Service Resource Kit tool, 40
Security Bulletin MS98-008 Web site, 572
Support Online Web site, 823, 825-826, 828
 Gloassary, 831, 833
 troubleshooting wizards, 828, 830
technical support engineers, 820-821
Update Web site, 486
VRML 2.0 Viewer, 701-703
Wallet, 554, 560-562, 564, 566-568
Web site, 75
Windows 98 Backup utility, 251251-258, 260
Windows 98 Update Web site, 47
Windows NT servers, 400
Windows Update Web site, 703

INDEX

Minitel Emulation Files Resource Kit tool, 40
Miro DC 10, 20, 30 Web site, 762
Miro Web site, 752
MMC (Microsoft Management Console), 680-681
modems
    combining, single Dial-Up Network connection, 389-392
    Dial-Up Networking, 355
    security, 377-379
monitoring
    networking activity, 302-303, 305-306
    performance, 268-269
    system, 272-275
monitors
    colors, 185-186
    configuring, 183-192
    default profile, 190-191
    diagnostic startup settings, 118
    dot pitch, 181
    graphics acceleration speed, 189-190
    multiple, 192-193
    refresh rate, 188
    screen area (resolution), 186
    screen font size, 186-187
    selecting, 181-182
        colors, 181-182
        depth, 182
        glare screen, 183
        video card adapter, 182
    video card, 186
mouse
    configuring, 195-200
    installing, 194-195
    primary button, 67, 197
    secondary button, 67
    selecting, 194
Mouse Properties window, 195
MRU Locations tab (Batch 98 General Setup Options screen), 330
MS-DOS Code Page Changer Resource Kit tool, 41
MSBATCH.INF file, 348
MSDN (Microsoft Developer Network), 836
MSDOS.SYS file, 131-134
Multilink, 389-392

multimedia
    installing tools, 701-703
    Media Player, 704-706, 708-712, 714-715
        configuring, 708-709
        finding video clips, 706
        launching, 704
        media clip properties, 714-715
        playback settings (advanced), 713-714
        retrieving media files, 705
        sound card compatibility, 711-712
        Streaming Media with RealVideo software option, 709-712
    Microsoft Chat, 716
        character information, 718-720
        Chat 2.5 Update, 703
        chatting (talking to others), 722-723
        connecting to, 721-722
        creating personal Chat room, 723-724
        entering, 722
        entering personal Chat room, 724-725
        first time launching, 717-718
        Format menu, 727
        identity profiles, 725
        installing, 701-703
        launching, 717
        Member menu, 727
        Options menu, 727
        quitting, 728
        Room menu, 727
        version numbers, 725
        View options, 726
        Window menu, 728
    WaveTop Data Broadcasting, 750
        configuring, 752, 754-755
        launching, 752
        requirements, 751
        TV tuner card compatibility, 751-752
Multimedia Access Osprey 100 Web site, 762
Multiple Language Boot Resource Kit tool, 41
multiple users, configuring, 415-419
MusicVideos Web site, 706
My Computer icon, 83, 86

N

naming backup jobs, 255
Net Watcher utility, 302-303, 305-306
NetBEUI (network protocol), 427

NetBIOS, 441
NetMeeting, 759-760
    another user's properties, 784
    audio
        codecs, 778
        components, 760-761
        options, 777-779
    calling options, 776
    computer systems, 762
    Configuration Wizard, 766-772
    configuring, 766-772, 774
    email, 784
    error message box, 784-786
    hardware requirements, 763
    hosting conference calls, 780-781
    ILS (Microsoft Internet Locator Server), 763
    information, 775-777
    installing, 764-765
    joining calls in progress, 774
    main screen, 772
    protocol options, 779-780
    server connection, 772, 774
    SpeedDial, 783-784
    tools, 781-783
    version 2.1 download Web site, 767
    video
        components, 761
        options, 779
    Web site, 760, 786
Network dialog box, 423, 434, 451, 463
Network Monitor Agent and Protocol Driver Resource Kit tool, 41
Network window, 407-414
networks
    activity, monitoring, 302-303, 305-306
    adding client software, 407-410, 412-415
    based installation (Windows 98), 321-323
    based printers, 468-470, 472-474
    bridged, 398
    browsing, 453
    components, 420-424
    connecting to others, 397-406
        Artisoft LANtastic server, 401
        AS/400, 402
        DECnet protocol, 401
        DLC (Data Link Control) protocol, 400
        IBM Mainframe systems, 400
        IBM OS/2 LAN and Warp servers, 401
        Microsoft Windows NT servers, 400
        Novell NetWare servers, 400
        Samba servers, 403
        UNIX systems, 400
        VINES server, 401
    connections security, 377-379
    Ethernet, 675
    logging on automatically, 460-461
    managing, 671-672. *See also* ZAIW
    peer-to-peer, 674
        creating and configuring, 674-678
        Ethernet, 675
        thinnet cabling, 676
        token ring, 675
        UTP cabling, 676
    protocols, 425-430
    routed, 398
    sending private transactions. *See* VPN
    services, 444-446, 448-450
    TCP/IP protocol (configuring), 432-434
        address, 434-437
        binding protocols, 443
        default protocol, 442
        DNS server, 439-441
        DNS Server Search Order, 441
        Domain Suffix Search Order, 441
        gateway IP addresses, 439
        NetBIOS, enabling, 441
        subnet masks, 436
        WINS, 437-438
    thinnet cabling, 676
    token ring, 675
    UTP cabling (Unshielded twisted pair), 676
    workgroup names, 462-464
newsgroups. *See also* email
    configuring, 600-606
    contents, 607
    properties, 608
    subscribing to, 606
    unsubscribing, 607
Nogatech ConferenceCard Web site, 762
Novell
    NetWare LAN software, 407-410, 412-415
    NetWare servers, 400
    Web site, 402
Now Resource Kit tool, 41

INDEX

O

octets, 435
Ohio State University RFC documents Web site, 432
OLE/COM Object Viewer Resource Kit tool, 41
Online Help, 813-814
    Contents tab, 814
    Index tab, 815
    Search tab, 815-816
    Web Help button, 816-817
Open dialog box, 448
opening DOS window, 94-97
Optional Components screen (Batch 98), 339
Options menu (Microsoft Chat), 727
Orchid Vidiola Pro/D Web site, 762
ordering
    MSDN (Microsoft Developer Network), 836
    TechNet, 835
Outbox (Outlook Express), 597
Outlook Express
    Accounts area, 611
    Address Book, 617-627
    advanced configuration, 583-585, 587-589
    attachments, 595-596
    compaction and deletion, 609-610
    configuring, 576-579, 581-582
    digital IDs, 628-632
    download options, 609
    Import Wizard, 588-589
    Inbox, 589
    Inbox Assistance, 615, 617
    installing, 574-575
    Internet Connection Wizard, 579-583
    maintenance tasks, 613-617
    messages
        creating, 591, 593, 595
        forwarding, 598-599
        reading, 589
        sending, 596
    multiple users, 611-612
    newsgroups
        configuration, 600-606
        contents, 607
        properties, 608
        subscribing to, 606
        unsubscribing, 607
    Outbox, 597
    Sent Items icon, 597

P - Q

Packard Bell Misc. Audio and Video drivers Web site, 762
partitioning hard drives, 240-242
Password List Editor Resource Kit tool, 41
passwords
    Dial-Up Networking, 359
    file sharing, 459
Pay-per-Incident support (Microsoft technical support), 820-821
peer-to-peer networking, 674
    creating and configuring, 674-678
    Ethernet, 675
    thinnet cabling, 676
    token ring, 675
    UTP cabling, 676
performance changes (system), 293-296
performance monitoring, 268-269
Performance window, 189
performing
    diagnostic startup, 116-118
    selective startup, 118-120
personal Chat room (Microsoft Chat)
    creating, 723-724
    entering, 724-725
personal information, storing, 554, 556, 559-560
Personal Web Server Manager, 659, 661-664, 666-668
Personal Web Server Wizard, 639-644
PGP (Pretty-Good-Privacy) email encryption tool Web site, 806
Philips EasyCam Web site, 762
physical drive devices, toolbar for, 91-92, 94
PIN numbers (calling cards), 369-370
playback settings (Media Player), 713-714
Point-to-Point Tunneling Protocol (PPTP), 379, 388
pointer devices
    configuring, 195-200
    installing, 194-195
    selecting, 194
policies (system), 694

POLICY.POL file (Registry), 148-149
POP3 (Post Office Protocol, version 3.0), 576, 580
ports (printers), 475
Post Office Protocol, version 3.0 (POP3), 576, 580
POTS Dial-Up Networking, 355
Power Toys (TweakUI), 41
PPTP (Point-to-Point Tunneling Protocol), 379
PPTP, Microsoft technical white paper Web site, 388
preparing Windows 98 installation, 26-28
primary mouse button, 67, 197
primary msbatch.inf screen (Batch 98), 339-340, 343
printers
    installing, 468
        Add New Hardware Wizard, 468
        Add Printer Wizard, 468-470, 472-474
    ports, 475
    settings, 475
    sharing, 477-478. See also File and Printer Sharing
Printers folder dialog box, 477-478
Printers tab (Batch 98 General Setup Options screen), 330
Priority Annual support (Microsoft technical support), 821
private transactions, sending over public networks. See VPN
Profile Assistant, 554, 556, 559-560
Profile Manager (Internet Explorer), 546, 549-553. See also ZAIW
    installing, 546-547
    launching, 547
    saving .INS and .CAB files, 552-553
    System Policies and Restrictions section, 551-552
    Wizard Settings section, 549-551
Program Guide (WebTV for Windows), 741, 746
    Program search, 747
    Program Guide Tour, 739, 741
programs. See applications
Programs configuration tab (Internet Explorer), 535-536

properties
    file sharing
        Browse Master, 452-454
        LM Announce, 454
    media clips (Media Player), 714-715
    newsgroups, 608
protocols
    ATM, 427
    binding, 443
    DECnet, 401
    default, 442
    DLC (Data Link Control), 400
    email, 580
    Internet email, 576
    networking, 424-430
    TCP/IP. See TCP/IP
Protocols tab (Batch 98 Network Options screen), 332
Proxy Settings tab (Batch 98 Internet Explorer Options screen), 343
publishing (Internet)
    components, 637-639, 641-644
    FrontPage Express, 646, 648-652
    Personal Web Server Manager, 659, 661-664, 666-668
    Publishing Wizard, 666
    Web Publishing Wizard, 653-654, 656, 658
    Web pages, 653-654, 656, 658
pulse dialing, 361

Quick Launch Express Resource Kit tool, 41
quitting
    Microsoft chat, 728
    WebTV for Windows, 747

R

radio, listening to, 748-749
RAS clients (Dial-Up Networking), 355
reading email messages, 589
RealAudio Player 4.0, 701-703
Recent Documents folder, 88-90
refresh rate (monitors), 188
Regina REXX Scripting Language Resource Kit tool, 42
Regional Settings tab (Batch 98 General Setup Options screen), 329

INDEX

Registration wizard, 47, 50, 52-53
Registry, 149
    backing up, 259
    Checker, 160-161
    defined, 147
    Editor
        disabling encrypted password setting, 403-406
        launching, 153, 162
        launching applications, 153-154, 156-160
        tweaking Dial-Up Networking (more productivity), 374-375
        Windows Update feature, 162-163, 165-167
    encrypted password setting, 403-406
    files, 148-149
    hives (sections), 149-150
    launching applications, 153-154, 156-160
    modifying, tweaking Dial-Up Networking (more productivity), 373-376
    restoring, 151-153
    undo mistakes, 160-161
    Windows 98, Windows 95, compared, 149
    Windows Update feature, 162-163, 165-167
Registry Edit Resource Kit tool, 75
removable hard drive devices, 250-251
removable media drives
    assigning specific drive letters, 245-246
    managing, 244-246
resolution (monitors), 186
Resource Kit, 29
    Adapter Card Help, 44
    Animated Cursor Editor, 35
    Application Performance Optimizer, 36
    Associate, 36
    Automated .INF Installer, 36
    Batch File Wait, 36
    Batch Processing of Files, 36
    Bulk Configuration Utility, 36
    Checklinks, 80-83
    Clip, 37
    Clipboard Buffer Tool, 37
    Clipboard Organizer, 37
    Compound File Layout User Tool, 37
    Daylight Savings Time, 37

    DbSet utility, 347
    Default Printer, 37
    Dependency Walker, 37
    Duplicate File Finder, 38
    Environment Setting Utility, 38
    Error Message Translation, 38
    Expand for Windows, 38
    FAT32 Conversion Information, 38
    File and Directory Comparison, 38
    File Compress, 39
    File Locating, 39
    File Version, 39
    File Wise, 39
    Finding Executable Type, 38
    Free Disk Space, 39
    GRE Protocol Troubleshooting, 39
    Hardware Compatibility List, 44
    Image Editor, 39
    Internet Explorer Administration Kit, 39
    installing, 30-35
    Link Check Wizard, 40
    Log Time, 40
    Long Filename Utility, 40
    Microsoft Batch 98 Automated Setup, 40
    Microsoft Copy, 40
    Microsoft Remote Procedure, 40
    Microsoft Remote Registry Service, 40
    Minitel Emulation Files, 40
    MS-DOS Code Page Changer, 41
    Multiple Language Boot, 41
    Network Monitor Agent and Protocol Driver, 41
    Now, 41
    OLE/COM Object Viewer, 41
    Password List Editor, 41
    Power Toys (TweakUI), 41
    Quick Launch Express, 41
    Regina REXX Scripting Language, 42
    Registry Edit, 75
    ScanReg.Ini Editing, 42
    Server Time Synchronization, 42
    SNMP Service, 44
    String Search, 42
    System File Information, 42
    system management tools, 312-313
    System Policy Editor, 42
    System Stress Testing, 42
    System Tray, 42

System Troubleshooting, 43
Task Killing, 43
Task List Viewer, 43
Text Editor, 43
Text Viewer, 43
Time This, 43
Time Zone Utility, 43
tools, 35, 45
Tweak UI
    displaying DOS prompt at startup, 130-131
    launching, 76
    network log ons (automatically), 460-461
    Recent Documents folder, 88-90
    system icons (desktop), 76-79
USB Device Troubleshooting, 43
User Input for Batch Files, 43
Uudecode and Uuencode Utility, 44
Wait For, 44
Windows
    Boot Editor, 44
    Report Tool Software Development Kit (WINREP SDK), 45
    Scripting Host, 45
Web site, 35
WinAlign, 268, 795-796, 798
Resource Meter, 272-275
restoring Registry, 151-153
retrieving media files, 705
reviewing
    another NetMeeting user's properties, 784
    Dial-Up Networking dialing information, 370
Room menu (Microsoft Chat), 727
routed networks, 398

S

Safe Mode (startup), 140, 142
Samba servers, 403
saving
    .INS and .CAB files, 552-553
    Windows 98 Batch installation, 345-347
ScanDisk, 236
    configuring, 236-239
    launching, 236
    testing (preview mode), 239
ScanReg.Ini Editing Resource Kit tool, 42

Scheduled Task Wizard, 307-310
Scheduled Tasks utility, 306, 306-309, 311
scheduling
    maintenance utilities, 297-301
    tasks, 306-309, 311
screen area (monitors), 186
Seagate Software Web site, 251
Search tab (Online Help), 815-816
secondary mouse button, 67
security
    digital IDs, 628-632
    file sharing access, 455-456
    Internet Explorer, 507
        ActiveX Controls and Plug-ins, 513
        custom settings, 511-514, 516-518
        downloads, 518
        Java permissions and subsection, 514-517
        levels (zones), assigning, 507-511
        miscellaneous, 519-520
        software channel permissions, 520-521
        user authentication, 519
    network connections and modems combinations, 377-379
    resources, 805-806
    sending private transactions over public networks, 379-380
        Adapter, 380-381, 383-384
        connection, 385-388
        Dial-Up Networking session, creating, 385-388
security cracks Web site, 805
Security tab (Batch 98 Internet Explorer Options screen), 341, 343
Select Network Adapters dialog box, 380
selecting
    calling card (Dial-Up Networking)
        sequence, 365-368
        types, 363, 365
    default language (keyboards), 175-179
    hardware requirements, 17-22, 24, 26
    keyboards, 173
    monitors, 181-182
        colors, 181-182
        depth, 182
        glare screen, 183
        video card adapter, 182
    mouse/pointer device, 194
    startup files, 110-115

INDEX

selective startup, 118-120
sending
    confidential data (Internet), 627-632
    email messages, 596
    private transactions over public networks, 379-380
        Adapter, 380-381, 383-384
        connection, 385-388
        Dial-Up Networking session, creating, 385-388
Sent Items icon (Outlook Express), 597
serial oerrun, 389
Server Time Synchronization Resource Kit tool, 42
servers
    Artisoft LANtastic, 401
    DNS, 439-441
    IBM OS/2 LAN and Warp, 401
    Master Browse, 453
    Microsoft Chat, 721-722
    Microsoft Windows NT, 400
    NetMeeting, 772, 774
    Novell Netware, 400
    Personal Web Server Manager, 659, 661-664, 666-668
    Samba, 403
    VINES, 401
Service for NetWare Directory Services, 445-450
services (networks), 444-446, 448-450
Services tab (Batch 98 Network Options screen), 335-336
Setup Prompts tab (Batch 98 General Setup Options screen), 328
share-level access, 338
sharing
    drives, 456-457
    files, 455-460
        Browse Master property, 452-454
        configuring, 451-460
        drive sharing, 456-457
        LM Announce property, 454
        passwords, 459
        security access, 455-456
    printers, 477-478
shortcuts (dead), 80-83
Simple Mail Transfer Protocol (SMTP), 576, 580

Simple Networking Management Protocol (SNMP), 690-692, 694
single-click mode (icons), 101-103
sites (Web). *See* Web sites
SMTP (Simple Mail Transfer Protocol), 576, 580
SNMP (Simple Networking Management Protocol), 690-692, 694
software. *See also* applications ; utilities
    application security Web site, 805
    channel permissions (Internet Explorer security settings), 520-521
    clients, 407-410, 412-415
    Microsoft Family Logon, 407-410, 412-415
    Novell NetWare LAN, 407-410, 412-415
    Systems Management Server, 679-680
    ZAIW, 678-679
        MMC (Microsoft Management Console), 680-681
        Profile Manager utility, 679
        software tools, 678-679
        Systems Management Server software, 679-680
        WBEM (Web-based Enterprise management), 680-681, 683-685, 688
        WMI (Windows Management Instrumentation), 680
Software Environment header (System Information utility), 282-284
sound. *See* audio
sound card compatibility (Media Player), 711-712
Soundblaster SB16, SB32, AWE 32, AWE 64 Web site, 761
SpeedDial (NetMeeting), 783-784
Standard no-charge support (Microsoft technical support), 820
startup
    changing modes, 116-127
    diagnostic
        monitor settings, 118
        performing, 116-118
    disk, 143-144
    files, 110-115
    hardware problems, 137-139
    menu, 131, 140

Safe Mode, 140, 142
selective, 118-120
to DOS prompts, 128, 130-134
STB TV-PCI Web site, 762
STB Web site, 752
storing
    credit card information, 554, 560-562, 564, 566-568
    personal information, 554, 556, 559-560
strategies (troubleshooting), 818-819
Streaming Media with RealVideo software option (Media Player), 709
    bandwidth requirements, 712
    proxy server, 711
    transport options, 709-711
String Search Resource Kit tool, 42
string values, 157
subnet masks, 436
subscribing to newsgroups, 606
surfing, Internet, 484
system
    backing up, 251-258, 260
    Configuration utility
        changing startup modes, 116-127
        DOS prompt at startup, 128-130
        Startup Menu, 140
        launching, 115-117, 140
    File Checker, 277, 288-292
    File Information Resource Kit tool, 42
    files, 134-135
    IBM Mainframe, 400
    icons, 76-79
    identification parameters, 462-464
    Information utility, 276-282, 284
        Components header, 281-282
        Hardware Resources header, 278-281
        launching, 116
        Software Environment header, 282-284
    kernal, 273
    Management tools and utilities, 270-272
    monitoring, 272-275
    Monitor utility, 293-296
    NetMeeting, 762
    performance changes, 293-296
    performance monitoring, 268-269
    policies, 694
    Policies and Restrictions section (Internet Explorer Profile Manager), 551-552
    Policy Editor Resource Kit tool, 42, 694
    Properties window, 185
    resources, 266-267
        finding, 267
        managing, 312-313
    Stress Testing Resource Kit tool, 42
    Tray Resource Kit tool, 42
    Troubleshooting Resource Kit tool, 43
    UNIX, 400
SYSTEM.DAT file (Registry), 148
Systems Management Server software, 679-680

T

tags (HTML), 648
Task Killing Resource Kit tool, 43
Task List Viewer Resource Kit tool, 43
Taskbar Properties window, 96
tasks (maintenance), 306-309, 311
TCO (total cost of ownership), 671
    SNMP, 690-692, 694
    ZAIW (Zero Administration Initiative for Windows), 678-679
        MMC (Microsoft Management Console), 680-681
        Profile Manager utility, 679
        software tools, 678-679
        Systems Management Server software, 679-680
        WBEM (Web-based Enterprise management), 680, 681, 683-685, 688
        WMI (Windows Managment Instrumentation), 680
TCP/IP (Transmission Control Protocol/Internet Protocol), 425, 427, 483
    configuring, 432-434
        address, assigning, 434-437
        binding protocols, 443
        default protocol, 442
        DNS server, 439-441
        DNS Server Search Order, 441
        Domain Suffix Search Order, 441
        gateway IP addresses, 439
        NetBIOS, enabling, 441
        subnet masks, 436
        WINS, 437-438
    Properties dialog box, 434
        Advanced tab, 441-442
        Bindings tab, 443
        DNS Configuration tab, 439-441

INDEX

        Gateway tab, 438-439
        IP Address tab, 434-437
        NetBIOS tab, 441
        WINS Configuration tab, 437-438
TechNet, 834
    CD-ROMs, 834-835
    ordering, 835
    Web site, 835
techniques (troubleshooting), 818-819
telephone numbers (Dial-Up Networking), 357, 370
temporary Internet files, 498-500
Temporary Internet Files Folder (Internet Explorer), 500-502
Temporary Internet Program Files, 502
terminate-and-stay-resident (TSRs), 26, 221
testing ScanDisk, 239
Text Editor Resource Kit tool, 43
Text Viewer Resource Kit tool, 43
thinnet cabling, 676
thunking, 273
Time This Resource Kit tool, 43
Time Zone Utility, 43
timing arrangement (Dial-Up Networking telephone calls), 365-368
token ring, 675
tone dialing, 361
toolbars (physical drive devices), 91-92, 94
tools
    disk drive management, 209, 211
    Resource Kit, 35, 45
        Animated Cursor Editor, 35, 37
        Application Performance Optimizer, 36
        Associate, 36
        Automated .INF Installer, 36
        Batch File Wait, 36
        Batch Processing of Files, 36
        Bulk Configuration Utility, 36
        Checklinks, 80-83
        Clip, 37
        Clipboard Organizer, 37
        Compound File Layout User Tool, 37
        Daylight Savings Time, 37
        DbSet utility, 347
        Default Printer, 37
        Dependency Walker, 37
        Duplicate File Finder, 38
        Environment Setting Utility, 38
        Error Message Translation, 38
        Expand for Windows, 38
        FAT32 Conversion Information, 38
        File and Directory Comparison, 38
        File Compress, 39
        File Locating, 39
        File Version, 39
        File Wise, 39
        Finding Executable Type, 38
        Free Disk Space, 39
        GRE Protocol Troubleshooting, 39
        Image Editor, 39
        Internet Explorer Administration Kit, 39
        Link Check Wizard, 40
        Log Time, 40
        Long Filename Utility, 40
        Microsoft Batch 98 Automated Setup, 40
        Microsoft Copy, 40
        Microsoft Remote Procedure, 40
        Microsoft Remote Registry Service, 40
        Minitel Emulation Files, 40
        MS-DOS Code Page Changer, 41
        Multiple Language Boot, 41
        Network Monitor Agent and Protocol Driver, 41
        Now, 41
        OLE/COM Object Viewer, 41
        Password List Editor, 41
        Power Toys (TweakUI), 41
        Quick Launch Express, 41
        Regina REXX Scripting Language, 42
        ScanReg.Ini Editing, 42
        Server Time Synchronization, 42
        String Search, 42
        System File Information, 42
        System Policy Editor, 42
        System Stress Testing, 42
        System Tray, 42
        System Troubleshooting, 43
        Task Killing, 43
        Task List Viewer, 43
        Text Editor, 43
        Text Viewer, 43
        Time This, 43
        Time Zone Utility, 43
        Tweak UI. See Tweak UI

USB Device Troubleshooting, 43
User Input for Batch Files, 43
Uudecode and Uuencode Utility, 44
Wait For, 44
Windows 98 Adapter Card Help, 44
Windows 98 Hardware Compatibility List, 44
Windows 98 SNMP Service, 44
Windows Boot Editor, 44
Windows Report Tool, 45
Windows Report Tool Softwqare Development Kit (WINREP SDK), 45
Windows Scripting Host, 45
Toshiba Web sites
    JK-VC1, 762
    Misc. Audio and Video drivers, 762
total cost of ownership. *See* TCO
tracking system performance changes, 293-296
Transmission Control Protocol/Internet Protocol. *See* TCP/IP
transporting, 709
troubleshooting. *See also* help
    application faults, 284-285, 287
    calling Microsoft technical support engineers, 820-821
    disk drives, 236-239
    hard drives, not enough space, 212-213
    malfunctioning device drivers, 116-127
    startup hardware problems, 137-139
    techniques and strategies, 818-819
    utilities, 277
    wizards, 828, 830
TSRs (terminate-and-stay-resident), 26, 221
tuner cards (WebTV for Windows), 736
TurtleBeach Tropez, Daytona, PCI, Montego Web site, 761
TV, watching (WebTV for Windows), 733, 737
    configuring, 742-743
    installing, 734-736
    launching, 737, 746
    local program guide listings, 743-744, 746
    Program Guide, 741, 746
        search, 747
        Tour, 739, 741
    quitting, 747
    tuner cards, 736
    Welcome screen, 737

TV tuner card
    radio, listening to, 748-749
    WaveTop Data Broadcasting compatibility, 751-752
Tweak UI (Tweak User Interface), 75, 90
    displaying DOS prompt at startup, 130-131
    launching, 76
    network log ons, 460-461
    Recent Documents folder, 88-90
    system icons, 76-79
tweaking Dial-Up Networking (more productivity), 372
    GUI changes, 372-373
    Registry modifications, 373-376

U

undo Registry mistakes, 160-161
UNIX systems, 400
unsubscribing to newsgroups, 607
Update Device Driver Wizard, 189
Update Device Wizard, 188
upgrading
    information, 46-47, 49-50, 52-55, 57
    Internet Explorer, 485-495
    Microsoft Windows 98 Backup utility, 252
USB Device Troubleshooting Resource Kit tool, 43
user authentication (Internet Explorer security settings), 519
User Input for Batch Files Resource Kit tool, 43
user names (Dial-Up Networking), 359
User Profiles, 415-419
User Profiles tab (Batch 98 General Setup Options screen), 331
user-level access, 338
USER.DAT file (Registry), 148
USRobitics BigPicture Web site, 762
utilities. *See also* applications; software
    Add/Remove Programs, 270-272
    Batch 98, 323
        Advanced Options screen, 344
        Display screen, 340
        General Setup Options screen, 327-331
        installing, 323-324
        installing Windows 98, 324-330, 332-336, 338-341, 343-344, 346-348

INDEX

Internet Explorer Options screen, 341, 343
Internet Explorer screen, 340
Network Options screen, 332, 335-338
Optional Components screen, 339
primary msbatch.inf screen, 339-340, 343
TCP/IP Options screen, 332, 334-335
Checklinks, 80-81
DbSet, 347
Defragmenter, 212
Disk Cleanup, 224
    cleaning up hard drives, 212
    configuring, 224-231
Disk Defragmenter, 223, 232-233
disk drive management, 209, 211
Dr. Watson, 109, 277, 284-285, 287
    determining, files loaded during startup, 110-115
    launching, 110
Drive Converter (FAT32), 220-223
DriveSpace 3
    compressing hard drives, 216-219
    configuring, 216-218
FDisk, 240-242
maintenance, 297-301
Make Compatible, 790-794
Microsoft Windows 98 Backup, 251-258, 260
Net Watcher, 302-303, 305-306
Profile Manager, 546, 549-553. *See also* ZAIW
    installing, 546-547
    launching, 547
    saving .INS and .CAB files, 552-553
    System Policies and Restrictions section, 551-552
    Wizard Settings section, 549-551
Registry Checker, 160-161
Resource Meter, 272-275
ScanDisk, 236
    configuring, 236-239
    launching, 236
    testing, 239
Scheduled Tasks, 306-309, 311
System Configuration
    changing startup modes, 116-127
    DOS prompt at startup, 128-130
    launching, 115-117, 140
    Startup Menu, 140
System File Checker, 277, 288-292
System Information, 276-282, 284
    Components header, 281-282
    Hardware Resources header, 278-281
    Software Environment header, 282-284
System Management, 270-272
System Monitor, 293-296
troubleshooting, 277
Tweak UI, 75
    desktop system icons, 76-79
    DOS prompt at startup, 130-131
    launching, 76
    moving Recent Documents folder, 88-90
WinAlign, 795-796, 798
UTP cabling (Unshielded twisted pair), 676
Uudecode and Uuencode Utility, 44

V

version numbers (Microsoft Chat), 725
video
    capture devices (cameras), 769
    cards, 186
    clips, 706
    conferencing (NetMeeting), 759-760
        another user's properties, 784
        audio codecs, 778
        audio components, 760-761
        audio options, 777-779
        calling options, 776
        computer systems, 762
        Configuration Wizard, 766-772
        configuring, 766-772, 774
        email, 784
        error message box, 784-786
        hardware requirements, 763
        hosting conference calls, 780-781
        ILS (Microsoft Internet Locator Server), 763
        information, 775-777
        installing, 764-765
        joining calls in progress, 774
        main screen, 772
        protocol options, 779-780
        server connection, 772, 774
        SpeedDial, 783-784
        tools, 781-783

version 2.1 download Web site, 767
video components, 761
video options, 779
Web site, 760, 786
VideoLogic
    Captivator Web site, 762
    Sonic Storm Web site, 761
View options (Microsoft Chat), 726
viewing. *See* displaying
VINES server, 401
Virtual Private Networking. *See* VPN
virtual whiteboard (NetMeeting), 782
Vista Imaging ViCam Web site, 762
VPN (Virtual Private Networking), 379-380
    Adapter, 380-381, 383-384
    connection, 385-388
    Dial-Up Networking session, creating, 385-388

W

Wait For Resource Kit tool, 44
Wallet (Microsoft), 554, 560-562, 564, 566-568
watching TV. *See* WebTV for Windows
WaveTop Data Broadcasting, 750
    configuring, 752, 754-755
    installing, 734-736
    launching, 752
    requirements, 751
    TV tuner card compatibility, 751-752
    Web site, 752
WBEM (Web-based Enterprise management), 680-681, 683-685, 688
Web (World Wide Web), 484. *See also* Internet
Web Help button (Online Help), 816-817
Web pages
    creating, 659, 661-664, 666-668
    publishing, 653-654, 656, 658
Web Publishing Wizard, 653-654, 656, 658
Web sites
    ADS, 751
    AIMS Lab, 751
    Aims Lab Video Highway Extreme, 761
    AITech, 751
    Amazon, 30
    Artisoft, 401
    ATI, 751
    ATI All-in-Wonder, ATI-TV, 761

AVerMedia, 751
AVerMedia MPEG Wizard, EZCapture, TVPhone, 761
Aztec Sound Galaxy, 760
Banyan, 401
Barnes and Noble bookstore, 30
Cherry Corp., 174
Cirrus Logic Crystal drivers, 760
Compaq, 401
Compro D-Cam, 761
Connectix QuickCam, 761
Creative VideoBlaster, 761
cryptography software packages catalog, 806
Dell, 762
Diamond
    DVC 1000, 761
    Multimedia, 751
    Sonic Impact and Monster Sound, 760
Digital Vision Computer Eyes, 761
Ensoniq
    Soundscape, 760
    Vivo90, AudioPCI, 760
ESS drivers, 760
Fast Multimedia FPS60, 761
Gateway 2000, 762
Gemstar, 739
GHOST, 349
Guillemot Maxi Sound, 761
hackers, 377
Hauppauge, 752
Hauppauge Wincast, Cinema Pro, Celebrity, 761
IBM, 402, 762
IMAP, 576
Intel Smart Video Recorder, 761
Internet Explorer add-on utilities, 546
Internet PhoneJACK Quicknet drivers, 761
IXMICRO, 752
Kodak, 762
Microsoft, 75
    NetMeeting, 760, 767, 786
    Press, 786
    Security Bulletin MS98-008, 572
    Support Online, 823, 825-826, 828-831, 833
    Update, 486
    Windows Update, 703

INDEX

Miro, 752
Miro DC 10, 20, 30, 762
Multimedia Access Osprey 100, 762
MusicVideos, 706
NetMeeting, 786
NetMeeting version 2.1 download, 767
Nogatech Conferencecard, 762
Novell, 402
Ohio State University RFC documents, 432
Orchid Vidiola Pro/D, 762
Packard Bell Misc. Audio and Video drivers, 762
PGP (Pretty-Good-Privacy) email encryption tool, 806
Philips EasyCam, 762
PPTP, Microsoft technical white paper, 388
Resource Kit, 35
Seagate Software, 251
security cracks, 805
software application security, 805
Soundblaster SB16, SB32, AWE 32, AWE 64, 761
STB, 752
STB TV-PCI, 762
TechNet ordering, 835
Toshiba
    JK-VC1, 762
    Misc. Audio and Video drivers, 762
TurtleBeach Tropez, Daytona, PCI, Montego, 761
USRobitics BigPicture, 762
VideoLogic
    Captivator, 762
    Sonic Storm, 761
Vista Imaging ViCam, 762
WaveTop Data Broadcasting, 752
Windows 98, 822
    Hardware Compatibility, 20
    Windows Update, 47, 572
Windows Logo application information, 34
Windows NT and Novell NetWare network security, 805
Winnov Videum, 762
WinZip, 596

Xitel Storm3D, 761
Yamaha OPL3SA, 761
Zoltrix, 752
Web-based Enterprise management (WBEM), 680-681, 683-685, 688
WebTV for Windows, 733, 737
    configuring, 742-743
    installing, 734-736
    launching, 737, 746
    local program guide listings, 743-744, 746
    Program Guide, 741, 746
        search, 747
        Tour, 739, 741
    quitting, 747
    tuner cards, 736
    Welcome screen, 737
Welcome screen (WebTV for Windows), 737
WinAlign (performance monitoring tool), 268, 795-796, 798
Window menu (Microsoft Chat), 728
windows. *See also* dialog boxes
    Advanced Troubleshooting Settings, 140
    Compression Options, 217
    Create New Compressed Drive, 218
    Create Startup Disk, 218
    Disk Defragmenter, 233
    Display Properties, 71, 98, 183, 193
    DOS
        keyboard shortcut (opening), 95-97
        opening, 94
    Edit String, 158
    FAT32 Conversion, 214
    Keyboard Properties, 175, 179
    Mouse Properties, 195
    Network, 407-414
    Performance, 189
    System Properties, 185
    Taskbar Properties, 96
Windows (OS)
    Boot Editor Resource Kit tool, 44
    Internet Naming Service (WINS), 334, 437-438
    Logo application information Web site, 34
    Managment Instrumentation (WMI), 680
    NT and Novell NetWare network security
    Report Tool Software Development Kit (WINREP SDK), 45
    Scripting Host Resource Kit tool, 45

Web site, 805
Update feature (Registry), 162-163, 165-167
Update tab (Batch 98 Advanced Options screen), 344
Windows 95 Safe Mode, 139
Windows 98
    Adapter Card Help Resource Kit tool, 44
    Hardware Compatibility List Web site, 20
    installing
        Batch 98 utility, 324-330, 332-336, 338-341, 343-344, 346-348
        cloning, 348-349
        hardware systems below standard levels, 28-29
        preparations, 26-28
    network-based installation, 321-323
    Registry. *See* Registry
    Resource Kit. *See* Resource Kit
    Safe Mode, 139
    SNMP Service Resource Kit tool, 44
    Web site, 822
    Windows Update Web site, 572
Winnov Videum Web site, 762
WINREP SDK (Windows Report Tool Software Development Kit, 45
WINS (Windows Internet Naming Service), 334, 437-438
WinZip Web site, 596
Wizard Settings section (Internet Explorer Profile Manager), 549-551
wizards
    Add a New Credit Card Wizard, 564, 566
    Add New Hardware, 192
        installing CD-ROM and DVD-ROM drives, 247-249
        installing printers, 468
    Add New User, 416-419
    Add Printer
        changing printer settings, 475
        installing printers, 468-470, 472-474
    Audio Tuning, 770-771
    Backup, 253-256
    Create Shortcut, 96-97
    Home Page, 661-663
    Internet Connection
        Internet Explorer connection settings, 530
        Outlook Express, 579-583
    Link Check, 81-82
    Maintenance, 297, 297-301
    Make New Connection, 356, 385-387
    NetMeeting Configuration Wizard, 766-772
    Outlook Express Import, 588-589
    Personal Web Server, 639-644
    Publishing, 666
    Registration, 47, 50, 52-53
    Scheduled Task, 307-310
    troubleshooting, 828, 830
    Update Device Driver, 188-189
    Web Publishing, 653-654, 656, 658
WMI (Windows Managment Instrumentation), 680
workgroup names, 462-464
World Wide Web, 484. *See also* Internet

X - Y - Z

Xitel Storm3D Web site, 761

Yamaha OPL3SA Web site, 761

ZAIW (Zero Administration Initiative for Windows), 678-679
    MMC (Microsoft Management Console), 680-681
    Profile Manager utility, 679
    software tools, 678-679
    Systems Management Server software, 679-680
    WBEM (Web-based Enterprise management), 680-681, 683-685, 688
    WMI (Windows Management Instrumentation), 680
Zoltrix Web site, 752

mcp.com
The Authoritative Encyclopedia of Computing

Resource Centers
Books & Software
Personal Bookshelf
WWW Yellow Pages
Online Learning
Special Offers
Site Search
Industry News

▶ Choose the online ebooks that you can view from your personal workspace on our site.

About MCP   Site Map   Product Support

Turn to the *Authoritative* Encyclopedia of Computing

You'll find over 150 full text books online, hundreds of shareware/freeware applications, online computing classes and 10 computing resource centers full of expert advice from the editors and publishers of:

- Adobe Press
- BradyGAMES
- Cisco Press
- Hayden Books
- Lycos Press
- New Riders
- Que
- Que Education & Training
- Sams Publishing
- Waite Group Press
- Ziff-Davis Press

mcp.com
The Authoritative Encyclopedia of Computing

When you're looking for computing information, consult the authority. The Authoritative Encyclopedia of Computing at mcp.com.

Get the best information and learn about latest developments in:

■ Design

■ Graphics and Multimedia

■ Enterprise Computing and DBMS

■ General Internet Information

■ Operating Systems

■ Networking and Hardware

■ PC and Video Gaming

■ Productivity Applications

■ Programming

■ Web Programming and Administration

■ Web Publishing

By opening this package, you are agreeing to be bound by the following agreement:

Some of the software included with this product may be copyrighted, in which case all rights are reserved by the respective copyright holder. You are licensed to use software copyrighted by the Publisher and its licensors on a single computer. You may copy and/or modify the software as needed to facilitate your use of it on a single computer. Making copies of the software for any other purpose is a violation of the United States copyright laws.

This software is sold as is without warranty of any kind, either expressed or implied, including but not limited to the implied warranties of merchantability and fitness for a particular purpose. Neither the publisher nor its dealers or distributors assumes any liability for any alleged or actual damages arising from the use of this program. (Some states do not allow for the exclusion of implied warranties, so the exclusion may not apply to you.)